COOKS & OTHER PEOPLE

PROCEEDINGS OF THE OXFORD SYMPOSIUM ON FOOD AND COOKERY 1995

Mrs Agnes B. Marshall (1855 – 1905)

COOKS
&
OTHER PEOPLE

PROCEEDINGS OF THE OXFORD SYMPOSIUM ON FOOD AND COOKERY 1995

EDITED
BY
HARLAN WALKER

PROSPECT BOOKS
1996

ISBN 0907325726

©1996 as a collection Prospect Books (but ©1995 in individual articles rests with the authors)

Published in 1996 by Prospect Books, Allaleigh House, Blackawton, Totnes, Devon TQ9 7DL, England

Printed by Antony Rowe, Bumper's Farm, Chippenham, Wilts SN14 6QA

Designed and typeset by Wendy Baker and Tom Jaine.

The cover illustation is taken from an advertisement for Mrs A.B. Marshall's cooking school, referred to in the papers of John Deith and Robin Weir, below. Picture supplied by courtesy of Robin Weir, who also supplied the portrait of Mrs Marshall used as the frontispiece.

Contents

CULINARY GUIDELINES OF A THIRTEENTH-CENTURY ASSYRIAN CATHOLICOS, BAR EBRAYA 9
    Michael Abdalla
VELÁZQUEZ' COOKS 15
    Joan P Alcock
EDOUARD DE POMIANE (1875-1964) 25
    Josephine Bacon
A GLANCE AT THE LIFE OF SIR KENELM DIGBY, KNIGHT, AT HIS COOKBOOK CALLED 'THE CLOSET
    OPENED', AND A PEEP INTO A CONTEMPORARY MANUSCRIPT 27
    Priscilla Bain and Maggie Black
AN EXHIBITION OF COOKS, POTS AND CROCKERY 35
    Rosemary Barron and Linda Makris
LOUIS-CAMILLE MAILLARD AND SUBSEQUENT GRAVY MAKERS 36
    A. Blake
THE CEREAL KINGS AND THEIR PRODUCT PRODIGY NOURISH THE WORLD 41
    Fritz Blank
UTILIS COQUINARIO AND ITS UNNAMED AUTHOR 45
    Ruth Carroll
LANARK BLUE CHEESE 52
    Robert Chenciner
OXFORD COLLEGE COOKS, 1400–1800 59
    Helen Clifford
MINEKICHI AKABORI AND HIS ROLE IN THE DEVELOPMENT OF MODERN JAPANESE CUISINE 68
    Katarzyna Cwiertka
ALEXANDER'S CULINARY LEGACY 81
    Andrew Dalby
DUTCH COOKERY AND CALVIN 94
    Janny de Moor
MRS AGNES B. MARSHALL (1855 - 1905) 106
    John S. Deith
THE ART OF APICIUS 111
    Carol A. Déry
ENRIQUETA DAVID PEREZ AND THE CODIFICATION OF PHILIPPINE COOKING 118
    Doreen G. Fernandez
NOUVELLE CUISINE 123
    Henri Gault
COOKING TO SURVIVE 128
    Barbara Haber
CHEZ PANISSE: EVER GREEN 133
    Shelley Handler
A COOK OF 14TH-CENTURY LONDON: CHAUCER'S HOGGE OF WARE 138
    Constance B. Hieatt
MITHAIKOS AND OTHER GREEK COOKS 144
    Shaun Hill & John Wilkins
MANYOKEN, JAPAN'S FIRST FRENCH RESTAURANT 149
    Richard Hosking

COURAGEOUS EATING: MARY MCCARTHY AND AMERICAN FOOD BETWEEN THE WARS 152
   Eve Jochnowitz
GRANDMA ROSE, CHEF EXTRAORDINAIRE 158
   Mary Wallace Kelsey
NIKOLAS TSELEMENTES 162
   Aglaia Kremezi
RUMFORD AND CULINARY SCIENCE 170
   Nicholas Kurti
NILS GUSTAV DALÉN, SWEDISH NOBEL PHYSICIST AND INVENTOR OF THE AGA STOVE 185
   Janet Laurence
MACAUSLAND AND *GOURMET* 194
   Margaret Leibenstein
HANNAH M. YOUNG (1858-1949), CULINARY ENTREPRENEUR 199
   Valerie Mars
MARTHA STEWART 205
   Richard C. Mieli
THE INFLUENCE OF SUPERMARKETS ON CONSUMER CHOICE 210
   Dr. Richard Pugh
PLATINA, MARTINO AND THEIR CIRCLE 214
   Gillian Riley
THE SHEARERS' COOK: A CHARACTER IN AUSTRALIAN FOLKLORE 220
   Barbara Santich
MOHAMMAD 226
   Margaret Shaida
ELIZABETH RAFFALD (1733-1781) 233
   Roy Shipperbottom
LA CUISINE DE M. MOMO 237
   Birgit Siesby
TRYON AND HIS CENTURY 240
   Colin Spencer
VON LIEBEG CONDENSED 247
   Layinka M. Swinburne
OTTO HERMAN: MUCH MORE THAN A CHEF 259
   Dr Louis I. Szathmáry
GREAT PERSONALITIES AND A GREAT CUISINE 266
   Gábor Tasnádi
CAROLINA WELTZIN – COOK OR OTHER? 279
   Renée Valeri
MRS.A.B.MARSHALL, ICE-CREAMMONGER EXTRAORDINARY 283
   Robin Weir
ANTONIN CARÊME: THE GOOD, THE BAD, AND THE USEFUL 290
   Barbara Ketcham Wheaton
THE COOKS (AND OTHERS) AT ERDDIG 296
   Margaret Willes
DOROTHY HARTLEY (1893-1985) 307
   Mary Wondrausch
1995 SYMPOSIASTS 309

Introduction

This volume of papers presented to the Oxford Symposium on Food and Cookery follows the pattern of previous collections. The Symposium was held in September 1995 at Saint Antony's College, Oxford under the joint chairmanship of Alan Davidson and Dr. Theodore Zeldin.

The college staff gave their usual tolerant support to our usual unusual demands. For the last time they had to put up with our miscellaneous strange requests for the Saturday Do-It-Yourself lunch. This event, at which symposiasts brought contributions that we all shared and which gave such great pleasure and interest, is no longer possible with the present rules of hygiene. Pity, it was always great fun for us all!

At the end of this lunch, we were all amazed to watch Dr. Peter Barham make icecream in what seemed like seconds by pouring liquid nitrogen into a bowl of crème anglaise. Clouds of vapour spilled round our feet, but we were soon proving that the icecream was delicious. This was followed by a splendid sorbet provided by Robin Weir. I am not sure whether our pleasure was increased or reduced when we learned that it was made from Château d'Yquem; it probably depended on whether we were by nature puritans or cavaliers.

Dinner on Saturday night was organised for us by Peter Brears and cooked by Mark Walker, the college chef — a Yorkshire Dinner. Here is the menu:

Yorkshire Pudding with Onion Gravy

Yorkshire Cold Platter
Roast York Ham, Pork Pie, Polony, Haslet
Yorkshire Ploughman's Salad

Roast Beef
Potatoes
Seasonal Vegetables
Pickled Red Cabbage & Pickled Cucumber

Baked Custards
Yorkshire Curd Tart
Yorkshire Mint Pasty
Stamford Bridge Spear Pies

Cheeses:
Wensleydale
Blue Wensleydale
Swaledale

The beef was magnificent and the pastries were just as they should be. Peter brought the cold meats and cheeses from Yorkshire; they were excellent. A splendid occasion.

Our lunch on Sunday is referred to elsewhere, but we must again thank Tesco for providing such excellent ingredients and our members, especially Clare Ferguson, who worked so hard to create this magnificent meal.

Finally it is essential that we record another astonishing event created for us by Alicia Rios. To the delight and laughter of all present she demonstrated the contrast of the early 20th century housewife making a COCIDO using natural ingredients and natural experience with the problems of the 21st century young woman having insuperable difficulties in dealing with the tinned product, both in following the instructions and in obeying the detailed rules of hygiene. Where did she get that wonderful 21st century dress?

As always many symposiasts give a big proportion of their time in helping in all kinds of ways to make a success of the weekend from working in the kitchen, running the registration, working slide projectors and going on messages. Without this unstinted help, the symposium could not take place. We are all very grateful to these hardworking people.

Harlan Walker
July 1996

A YORKSHIRE DINNER
St. Antony's College

Cover, drawn by Peter Brears, of the menu for the Yorkshire Dinner

Culinary Guidelines of a Thirteenth-century Assyrian Catholicos, Bar Ebraya

Michael Abdalla

Gregorios Bar Ebraya (Bar Hebraeus), the son of Haroun, was born in 1226 in the city of Malatia (Melitene). When baptised he was named Yohanon (John). He was the fourth, the second-last offspring of his parents. His father was a famous physician and belonged to the city notables. When Gregorios was 17, his family left Malatia due to the persecution by the Tartars and they moved to Antioch which was safer. It was here that at the age of 19 Gregorios was elevated to the rank of bishop. First he served in the city of Gobas and then he moved to Laqabin and finally he settled in Aleppo. On 19 January 1264 in the town of Sis (in Cilicia) he was raised to the rank of catholicos (Mafriono). After that time he supervised the Eastern Church consisting of ten dioceses. He chose to dwell in the ancient monastery of Mor Matay, not far from Mosul, from where he travelled to pay priestly visits to Baghdad (1265, 1277), Takrit (1278) and Tabriz (1279). He died on 30 July 1286 in Maragha and was laid to rest in the Mor Matay monastery.

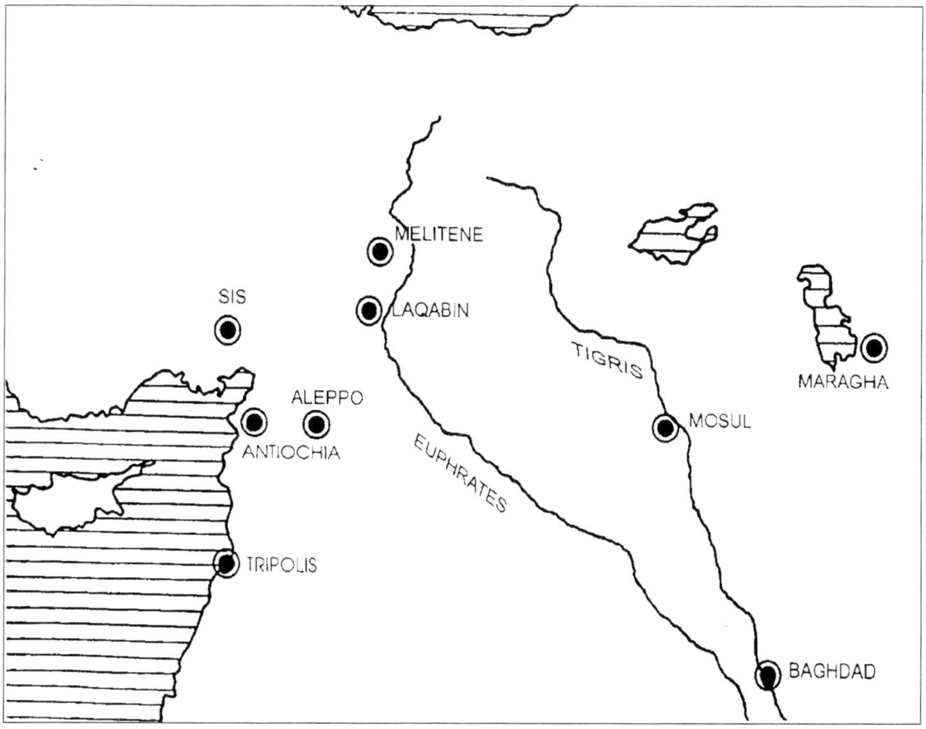

Bar Ebraya can be quoted in many fields of science. Experts on his works referred to him as 'the Encyclopaedia of the 13th century Orient'. His literary output consists of 36 volumes; one can find among them medical, mathematical, astronomical, musical and philosophical treatises. He was an eminent poet. His works in history, philosophy, ethics and canon law are of special value and are still translated into many languages. He wrote in Assyrian, Arabic, Armenian and Persian. He translated from Assyrian into Arabic the astronomy and mathematics books of Ptolemaeus which are called *Almagest*, also some of Euclid's works. His literary output is highly analytical; it is rich in controversial quotations, statements and opinions of authors which he polemizes, seeking the confirmation of his reasoning in the teachings of Christianity and the Fathers of the Church. This fascinating output was created within a relatively short time which spanned the sixty years of his life, during the turbulent times when the whole Middle East was oppressed by the Tartar hordes. He was a revered and respected figure due to the ecumenical activities he was engaged in to the end of his days, a figure appreciated for his vast and widely applicable knowledge. Among mourners there were eminent persons and representatives of many denominations and nationalities.

In one of his works entitled *Ethicon* one may find interesting guidelines concerning eating habits and table manners.[1] This work consists of a dialogue between two cultures: scientific and theological. It comprises four lectures (this number probably corresponds to the number of the seasons in a year), each of which is divided into chapters (52 altogether = the number of weeks in a year) and sub-chapters (365 altogether = the number of days in a year). The titles of the lectures are as follows: 1. Tempering the human body, 2. Shaping the character, 3. Eliminating bad habits, and 4. Perfecting the soul. One of the chapters of the first lecture is wholly devoted to fasting: its benefits, variations, degrees, regulations of canonical and individual fasting as well as to the period of fasting. The second lecture commences with a chapter on food. Information on food can also be found in other chapters and sub-chapters of the book.

How to behave during a meal

Bar Ebraya thinks that each food has some spiritual elements. This makes men use their common-sense when choosing their food and exercise their will so that the food manifests the specific human principles. He stresses that food should be prepared by oneself. He claims that a feast table is brought by angels and therefore people should behave properly when sitting at it. When members of a family commence the meal he teaches them how they should behave and what they should avoid, and therefore he advises the following principles:

- wash your hands before the meal;

- eat only when you feel hungry and leave the table before you feel full;[2]

- the members of a family should eat together, but at their table there should be places for others;[3]

- before starting the meal repeat the words: 'In the name of God, the Provider!', and when you start the first bite – 'Look, how great the Lord is!', when having the second one 'God blesses those who rely on Him!', and at the third – 'Those who ask God will never lack food!'. If the meal and prayers happen at the same time on Wednesdays and Fridays, the prayers can be said after the meal.[4]

- do not eat when lying; you should sit; you might cross your right leg;

- the place at the head of the table should be reserved for the eldest person and that person should commence the meal and remain at the table to the very end. If any of the banqueters finishes earlier than others, he should not get up but stay with the others to the very end;

- do not blow on a hot dish but patiently wait until it cools down itself;

- when all the banqueters sit around a bowl, they should reach out for food in front of them, not towards their neighbour's place;

- put relatively small portions into your mouth and chew them carefully;

- do not take food from the middle of the bowl, but from its sides trying to avoid putting your hand deep into it;

- bread should be broken with your hands and not cut with a knife;

- after biting a piece of bread that has been dipped in food one should not dip it again. A piece of bread should be small enough so that it constitutes one portion;

- the older people at the table should behave in such a way that none of the banqueters should feel discouraged or intimidated;

- when eating fruits with stones, the stones should not be put back on the plate where the fruits are; neither should they be held in the hand or thrown aside; instead, they should be put into a separate plate;

- limit the amount of water you drink during the meal.

How to behave after a meal

After finishing the meal and before leaving the table, Bar Ebraya encourages people not to perform gestures unsuitable for good company as well as to maintain cleanliness. He writes:

- using your left hand you may discreetly remove food leavings which are stuck between your teeth. This gesture should be performed after bowing and turning ones head a little bit and covering the mouth. The rest should be wiped with a towel;

- pick up the crumbs and eat them out of sheer respect for God's grace;

- do not wipe your hands with your lips or your tongue, and do not put them to your mouth to lick them;[5]

- repeat the words: 'God be thanked for His grace!'. And if the food is a gift from someone else and eaten in a new company, then one should say: 'Let God bless my host, give grace to him and his dead and welcome them in His Kingdom!';

- washing the parts of the body which were used during the meal should begin with the palms, teeth and mouth, and finally the whole hand. Dry them with a towel;

- the person offering the finger bowl should stand on the left side of a guest;

- during washing it is not permitted to spit on the floor or in the bowl where the waste water is collected.

Invitation to a banquet

Bar Ebraya mentions that friends and acquaintances should be paid a visit from time to time. It is best when the time of a visit does not overlap with the time of a meal. However, if it is necessary to pay a visit at a meal time, one should not join the meal without being sincerely invited. The host should not ask the guest if he feels like eating something; instead the host should serve everything he has, even if it is only bread and salt. The guest should not demand anything special to eat but with moderation he should consume whatever is served.

Bar Ebraya stresses that the situation is different when someone is officially invited to a party. To meet the Christian requirements the host should not forget the poor, although they can not reciprocate. If the invited person suspects that the invitation is not sincere, he should excuse himself and not participate in the banquet; he should also do the same if he suspects that the banquet is organised with dishonest resources or with those coming from a theft. However, if the invitation is sincere and the invited person does not come to a banquet, then he commits a sin. Neither the distance, nor individual fasting can be an excuse. And if the person participates due to curiosity or other personal inclinations, then the sin is double. The invited person should enjoy the presence of the poor at the banquet.

Where to get seated?

Bar Ebraya claims that the organisers of a banquet should invite as many people as they can treat properly. Guests should be punctual. When arriving at a party they should not choose the best places. It is best if they take a secondary place, somewhere in the back. Knowing the rank of a guest the host himself will give him an adequate place; such a gesture will be perceived with full understanding by others. The guest should not agree to change such a place for a better one, should that be suggested by any other guests. The host's desire should be respected and received with thanks. Before commencing the meal all guests should wash their hands, regardless of whether they are still standing or already seated. The first should be the host himself.

Setting the table

Quoting 'a noble-minded man' whose name is not mentioned, Bar Ebraya stresses that one should not delay setting the table, burying the dead, giving the daughter away in marriage, paying back debts and expiating sins. When the guests are seated at the table, they should not wait long for the food. From Bar Ebraya's description it is clear that there were many opinions at that time about the order of setting the table. Some thought that fresh fruit should be served first, since it gets spoiled easily. Other claimed that first of all the guests should be served the most delicious dishes. But there were also those who did exactly the opposite. Assuming that a hungry person will eagerly eat whatever he is served, they suggested saving the tastiest dishes till the very end. Then all the dishes were consumed with equal appetite. Quoting those examples Bar Ebraya suggests his own way, which he considers the most appropriate, namely serving all dishes at the same time. Then each of the banqueters can choose what suits him most. However, one should remember to put aside some food for those members of the family who do not participate in the banquet. After the meal the host should be the last to wash his hands.

Saying good-bye to guests

Bar Ebraya thinks that when saying good-bye to the guests the host should go out with them outside the house and thank them there for coming and for their company. And the guests should express how happy they were with the banquet, even if some things were missing. Guests should not complain about that to anybody; instead they should find arguments justifying the host. To the out-of-town guests, the host should offer hospitality. If the guest accepts the offer, he should not stay longer than three days.

How much alcohol and where?

Bar Ebraya mentions weddings and birthday parties as those occasions where dishes can be served with *hamro*. Nowadays the word *hamro* is associated with sweet wine only, but it might have signified other drinks, though the home-made wine (from grapes and figs) was and still is the most popular alcoholic drink among the Assyrians. Bar Ebraya adds that *hamro* can be served also during other celebrations, not necessarily related to any of the family feasts.[6]

Secular Christians can drink *hamro*, but with moderation, since everybody has some limits in that respect which should not be disregarded. Small amounts of *hamro* can create a nice atmosphere in a meeting; when exceeded it can cause a disagreement. It is especially important that the company should be properly selected from even-tempered people who respect one another. One should definitely avoid the company of people who are impetuous, hot-tempered and talkative. Discussions should be conducted in a low voice and calm manner, concerning not serious, but light and witty subjects, preferably allowing for the participation of all people present. The youngest should mostly listen, not speak.[7]

If any of the banqueters feels sick, he should stop drinking and not allow others to encourage him to drink any more. And if they insist, he should withdraw and leave the place. If he feels like vomiting, he should go outside and come back only when he feels better, and he should not drink any more. One should eat before and during drinking.

Down with gluttony

In the third chapter of the third lecture Bar Ebraya talks about gluttony and about ways of overcoming this weakness. At the beginning he reports an interesting story exemplifying the hermit's life style and various opinions about gluttony.

– An old man visited Abba Ishaya in his hermitage. He noticed that Abba dips pieces of dry bread in water and then puts them into salt so that he can swallow them through the dry throat. Seeing that the old man cried: 'Look how Abba Ishaya delights himself in soup on the Egyptian desert!' Since then this saying has become known: 'If you want some soup, go to the Egyptian desert.'

– 'A man can be as strong as a lion, but due to gluttony he will get himself into a net.'

– 'If gluttony did not overcome people's will, they would not surrender in their fight with Satan.'

As results of gluttony Bar Ebraya mentions debauchery, greed and desire to dominate others. Thanks to restraint, he claims, one can straighten the mind, broaden the view, smooth thoughts, become more sensitive to spiritual stimuli, be modest and consider the poor, hungry and suffering. Restraint is good for one's health and permits sharing everything with the needy. To those who want to decrease the daily food intake, for example from two loves of bread to one, Bar Ebraya suggests gradual treatment lasting one month. The point is to divide a loaf of bread into thirty parts and he advises to reduce the bread consumption one portion per day. On the first day of the month he advises to consume one loaf of bread and twenty nine portions of the other loaf. In the middle of the month – one loaf and half of the other. Therefore at the end of the month only one loaf is left. Bar Ebraya stresses that imposing such a diet is not harmful to the human body.

Quantity and quality of food and categories of hermits

Depending on the quantity of bread consumed, Bar Ebraya divides hermits into four different categories depending on the daily consumption of bread, which can be one quarter, half, two thirds or three fourths of a loaf of bread. The second division categorises the quality of the bread which could be made of sieved wheat flour, non-sieved wheat flour, sieved or non-sieved barley flour. Additionally Bar Ebraya mentions one more criterion which refers to the frequency of eating.

Since loaves of bread could have various sizes, Bar Ebraya describes them in terms of their volume or coins' weight. He reports that one of the Alexandrine hermits used to break loaves into pieces so small that he could put them into an amphora through its narrow neck. He just took out one piece a day to eat. There were also hermits who did not eat bread at all and consumed only cooked legumes with or without oil. The most surprising were those who did not touch anything except vegetables. Bar Ebraya writes that the sign of permanent fasting is dipping bread into water and salt, and the evidence for that is the fact that flies do not gather above saliva spat on the ground. He informs us that the eating habits of monks in monasteries differed a lot from the model accepted by hermits. Monks ate eggs and fish as well as milk and dairy products.

Conclusions

Bar Ebraya finishes his considerations about food with these words: Health is a gift, the existence of which is due to the complicated mechanisms of the organism. The organism according to its senses known when to demand food and how much. However the decision about that should be made by the will and the mind. Senses are not able to measure God's miracles, but the mind can handle them. The sight notices food, the nose gets the aroma, but the appetite decides about the consumption, and the will decides about the quality of the consumption according to the diet imposed. Does the greedy person lack the will power, which could control his food consumption? Over-eating is harmful for the eater as well as for others.

REFERENCES

[1] Mar Gregorios Bar Hebraeus, *Al-thioqon -alsafat al-aadaab al-khuluqiya* (Ethics – Philosophy of Individual Culture), Qamishli (Syria) 1967, 440. The book was translated from Assyrian into Arabic by Mar Gregorios Paulos Behnam, Archbishop of Baghdad and Basra (1916-1969).

[2] To prove this principle Bar Ebraya quotes (without revealing the sources) doctors who advise that the stomach should be divided into three parts; one part to be filled with dry food, the second to be filled with liquids and the third to be left for good digestion. Definitely not a quotation from the bible.

[3] Although Bar Ebraya acknowledges the superiority of shared meals, he does not see anything wrong with eating alone. He gives here the example of St. John Goldmouth. After being raised to the rank of a bishop, the saint was said to eat alone. This practice of his was used by his opponents, who used to say that he ate alone because he was greedy and his mouth was twisted when he was eating.

[4] Strict fasting was obligatory on Wednesdays and Fridays in Bar Ebraya's times. Considering fasting as a kind of bodily prayer which lasts for these two days of the week from midnight to sunset, Bar Ebraya does not see any need for a double prayer at the expense of a fasting meal. Wednesday and Friday fasting are still observed by the Assyrians and other Christian communities in the East.

[5] Wiping lips with one's sleeve and licking fingers are not, even nowadays, rare sights in the Middle East. It sometimes happens among the Bedouins.

[6] I remember from my childhood that the Assyrian peasants always served wine during Christmas and Easter.

[7] One of the aphorisms among Assyrians reads: 'God gave man one tongue and two ears, so that he should speak less and listen more'.

Velázquez' Cooks and Portrayal of Food in Spanish Still Life Art in the Seventeenth Century

Joan P Alcock

Without the inspiration of cooks, eating would be a matter of routine and not a pleasure nor an opportunity for surprise. Yet it is not just recipes and written descriptions of food which inspire people to try out the creations of cooks. Visual portrayals are often equally inspiring, as witnessed by the lavish care given to illustrations which accompany recipes. Indeed, some people buy cookery books more for admiring the colourful illustrations than with any intention of attempting the recipes. These illustrations can be photographs of food, but more stimulating are paintings showing, in all their rich glory, cooked dishes and the raw material of which they are comprised.

Nowhere did such paintings inspire a longing for food and for the creations of cooks as in the exhibition, 'Spanish Still Life from Velázquez to Goya', held during 1995 at the National Gallery in London. An additional bonus was the physical and psychological portrayal of those persons who cook and serve food, so that the spectator seemed to be party to their innermost thoughts.

Bodegones

Many of these paintings are in the tradition of *bodegones*, popular in Spain between 1620 and 1650 (Harris 1982, 44; Kubler and Soria 1959, 235). These were originally low life tavern scenes or eating places, but terminology soon equated the phrase with still life paintings (Lopéz-Rey 1968, 29) and specifically as a definition of paintings of food and kitchenware (Bermúdez 1819, 26-28). These works are almost certainly influenced by Caravaggesque naturalism with its accent on colour, light and shade giving relief form to the people and objects in the paintings. Texture and shape are emphasised, often lit as if by a spotlight to bring out the colour of natural objects, which gives them a dimension beyond their original meaning.

This is particularly applicable to tableware and victuals, where an atmospheric unity binds the objects together. There is an old proverb that you speak German to your cook, English to your horse, French to your lover and Spanish to your God. Spanish painters, and in particular Velázquez, convey an immediacy and a spiritual depth to still life art which emphasises the almost religious awe in which food is held. They convey in artistic form the fact that food is a gift from God and is part of His benevolence. The shelf or table on which the food is placed becomes the altar, so that, in turn, food becomes an offering returned to God. Every commodity takes on a symbolic role which raises it above its lowly station.

Where a painting depicts both meat and fish, it is suggested (Jordan and Cherry 1995, 20) that the division between them reflects the custom of the division between meat and fish days. Often the background is 'without form and void', black and dense so that nothing detracts the eye from the objects in the foreground. Occasionally the symbolism may possibly be taken too far as with an interpretation of Juan Sánchez Cotán's painting of *Still Life with Game Fowl, Fruit and Vegetables*, where the carrots and long radishes are said to represent four nails from the cross and the cardoon the flail with which Christ was flogged (Denny 1972). The six thrushes, rigidly fixed to the branch are not only a Spanish delicacy, but also recall the legend that a thrush flew down to comfort Christ on the Cross and in so doing brushed against the blood on his chest. But what draws the spectator's eye are the prickly stems of the cardoon and the bright, waxy texture of the lemons, with their promise of the juicy, sharp, tangy taste, hanging temptingly in the right hand corner.

The *bodegón* was a novel type of painting in Spain at the beginning of the seventeenth century (Wind 1987), but it had a long tradition in Netherlandish painting, where kitchen or table scenes often formed a background to, or were incorporated into, biblical and religious scenes. The close connection between Spain and the Netherlands in the sixteenth century, and Spain and Flanders for the next century ensured a familiarity of subject matter. Where, however, the Dutch and Flemish paintings are flamboyant with an almost baroque intensity, the Spanish painters pare their scenes down to the simplest possible elements with a hint of ambiguity which makes the spectator contemplate rather than merely view the objects.

Still life with food

Many paintings are a revelation in their portrayal of food as the raw material used by cooks. Some of the most effective paintings were those illustrating the fewest objects. Thus Juan Sánchez Cotán's depiction of *Still Life with Quince, Cabbage, Melon and Cucumber* (Soria 1945) conveyed with great simplicity these four objects set against a dark, enveloping background, which though intending to represent the interior of a larder or a *contarero* (a cool place for foods) appears to have deeper significance. The quince and the cabbage are suspended ready for the cook to grasp, a common practice in order to keep them fresh or to keep them away from ants; the melon has already been sliced with a sharp cook's knife, and a piece is thrust towards the spectators inviting them to eat its luscious freshness. Not, however, to eat greedily and with passion, but to take humbly in grace.

A similar painting but with four game fowl hanging above has lost the original simplicity. Added on the left is a cucubit (or *chayote*), its representation being one of the first of this vegetable, which was brought from the New World. Given the religious simplicity with which the objects are portrayed, it is no surprise to learn that in 1603, Cotán entered the Carthusian Order as a lay brother, having left all his goods to his family in a detailed will.

A detailed portrayal of vegetables is to be found in Antonio de Pereda's *Still Life with Vegetables*, where what appears to be a jumble of vegetables - leeks, onions, garlic, carrots, artichokes, and a cauliflower - is on second glance carefully arranged with parallel lines and roundels, so that they contrast with the surprise of a huge pork pie, whose rounded form is echoed by the copper bowl placed behind it. Rather curiously a parallel painting, showing fruits does not seem so attractive to cooks, possibly because they feel more creative when dealing with vegetables. In another small painting Peredas has also detailed walnuts, which every cook would wish to use. All aspects are revealed in one small space - the full unbroken nut, a partly cracked and peeled shell, the empty shell and the brown moist wrinkled kernel. These are healthy nuts ready for eating or cooking.

This tradition of painting food with what may be considered an underlying, almost sensual passion continued, so that in the late eighteenth century Luis Meléndez' painting of *Still Life with Fruit, Cheese and Containers* would make any cook wish to seize the plump red fruit, dig deep into the soft, wrinkled creamy-brown cheese, peer into the round wooden container to see if it contains olives and seize the red and white *manises* honey jar. A *Still Life with Oranges and Walnuts* contrasts ripe fruit, backed by a huge watermelon, and the crinkled cracked shells of the nuts with the carefully casually arranged oblong and round wooden boxes containing *dulce de membrillo*, the thick grainy slabs of quince jelly, a wooden olive barrel, and jugs sealed by paper tops hinting at the olives and fruits hidden within them.

His *Sea Bream and Oranges* picks out clearly the two fish, the light playing on their scales; the shiny colour of the oranges is reflected in the orange rim round the glassy eyes of the fish. The combination of baked sea bream (*porgy* or *pargo*) and orange is found as a popular dish along the southern coast of Spain and is a traditional dish for Christmas Eve dating from the time when it was obligatory to fast for Christmas.

Juan Altamiras in his *Nuevo Arte de Cocina Sacado de la Experiencia Económica* gave a recipe for cooking cleaned and de-scaled sea bream by basting it with minced garlic, pepper, salt and the juice of a lemon, lime or orange. In another recipe for marinaded fish he recommends that oranges, vinegar, chopped garlic and herbs should be brought to the boil and cover the fish (Altamiras 1758, 99 and 107).

The spectator can almost smell the tangy scent of the piled oranges and the carefully arranged lemons in Francisco de Zurbarán's *Still Life with a Basket of Oranges* and is tempted beyond endurance by Juan de Espinosa's *Still Life with Grapes, Fruit and a Terracotta Jar*, in which glistening russet, green and purple grapes hang above a split pomegranate, and shiny pears and apples wait for teeth to crunch into them. A bird has succumbed to the temptation of pecking a grape in Juan de Zurbarán's *Plate of Fruit with a Linnet*. A drop of water on the plum indicates that the cook has washed the fruit, but anyone reaching for the fruit must be careful to avoid the wasp greedily gorging itself on the fresh green grapes. These contrast with the red pearly seeds seen in the split pomegranate; they, together with the wrinkly-skinned quinces, will form a fitting end to a meal.

Sweetmeats abound in these paintings to show the skill of the pastry chefs – rolled or flat wafers, *crispells*, *rubiols* with cream or crème patissière, powdery doughnuts, honeyed cakes and *churros*, crisp sticks of fried dough, waiting to be dunked in wine or hot chocolate, the new drink brought from the New World. Pedro de Camprobín's painting of *Still Life with Sweets* arranges his cakes and pastries on a pedestal dish: round sweet breads, sweet biscuits and oblong cakes made with *batata confitada*, candied sweet potato. A modern version of this, used as a filling for pastries and as an ingredient for cakes, is now most conveniently sold in tins under the name *dulce de boniato*.

Cooks and allegory

Some paintings are allegorical. One painting, not in the exhibition, exudes the essential personality of a cook. Juan van der Hamen y León paints *The Cook* (1630), *en face* holding out a bowl of wine directly towards the spectator (Kubler and Soria 1959, 235). To the left fish and a partridge illustrate two products he will use, but on the right is a large leg of beef split open to form a fleshy cornucopia resembling some gigantic succulent mouth. On the table are fish, cheese, game birds, pies, fruits, ringed breads and some coins, the wealth which will buy this wealth of food.

Antonio de Pereda's *Kitchen Scene*, luridly filled with all the contents of a kitchen, crammed on and under the table, reveals both the possessions of a wealthy household and the state the kitchen domain could get into if the cook was not in control of herself and her situation. The cook kneels on the floor, washing dishes, amid an untidy, heaped mass of dirty pots, upturned vessels, a grater and broken crockery. The painting is an allegory of her lost virtue, emphasised in particular by the empty copper vessel lying on its side, the upturned candlestick with the extinguished and crooked candle and the broken plate by which she kneels. The table is loaded with half-eaten food, tasted and cast to one side like the remains of her virtue. Even the lattice fruit tart on the table, so lovingly made by the cook, has not been neatly cut, but is broken and collapsed. The soldier, who has presumably taken advantage of her and is the author of all this ruin, nonchalantly sits on the table pouring himself a beaker of wine.

Christ in the House of Martha and Mary

Amongst the paintings were three by Velázquez, who is more famous for his portrayals of the Spanish royal family in the 17th century, where the stultified world of Philip IV and his court was meticulously recorded, even to the melancholic dwarfs, who acted as playmates to the royal children. Velázquez' earlier career reveals a completely different world for his earliest oeuvre are paintings of *bodegones*, which he executed during his five year apprenticeship (1617-22) to Francisco Pacheco, whose workshop was in Seville.

The two Velázquez paintings, which have cooks as their central characters, are *Kitchen Scene with Christ in the House of Martha and Mary*, painted in 1620 and *An Old Woman Frying Eggs*, now known to have been painted in 1618 (Baxandall 1957). They are very different in concept. In the *Kitchen Scene* a young woman is pounding herbs in a brass mortar, her sullen face displaying a certain resentment. Her expression conveys entirely the feeling that any cook has felt at having to remain in the kitchen to do the work instead of being part of the action, or perhaps some rancour at being instructed by another person, in this case the older woman standing behind her.

On the table are an earthenware jug stained on the outside with oil, two eggs, which soon will be broken open by the resentful cook, garlic, and a pimento, basic ingredients of a Spanish meal, and four fish, their dead eyes paralleling the dead eyes of the cook. It is possible that she may cook the fish with the garlic and pimento, then cover it with a thick *all-i-oli*, one of the most popular of all Spanish sauces composed of eggs, oil and garlic. This sauce requires that the garlic is thoroughly crushed before being blended with the yolks, an action which the cook may be doing in the mortar.

Yet there is also a religious dimension in the choice of the food. Garlic represents life in death, eggs symbolise rebirth and resurrection and the fish is representative of Christ. He sits talking to Mary who reclines listening at his feet. By her side stands a woman, whose posture relates to the older woman standing in the foreground behind the cook.

Velázquez is faithfully representing the scene from the passage in the Bible in St Luke's gospel (10, 38-42) and also hinting at St Mark's gospel (8, 5-9), where Christ feeds the multitude on seven loaves and 'a few small fishes'. But there are some ambiguities in the painting. One interpretation could be that the cook represents the actual person of Martha, who is preparing the food while her sister sits at the feet of Christ in the next room. Another, that the cook does not take the role of Martha; she is merely a servant girl, whom the old woman is reminding of the biblical lesson. The pointing finger draws her attention to this as well as directing the spectator's attention to the cook.

Martha is thus the woman standing behind her sister reclining at the feet of Christ (Müller 1976, 31-32) and she has come to complain about the unfairness of the allotted tasks. Even while accepting Christ's words, there is also the somewhat human feeling that as well as having some person to entertain the guests, another has to prepare a meal, otherwise they will not be fed. Yet the predominance given to the cook seems to somewhat negate the view that she does not represent Martha, and it seems more probable that Velázquez has created the archetype of a woman's role as Martha.

Another ambiguity relates to the group with Christ, painted to the upper right. Is this a mirror reflecting what is taking place in the same room as the cook (Lopéz-Rey 1963, 32), so that her sullen gaze is focused not on the spectator but on an event taking place nearby? Her resentment would be all the more understandable because she is near to the action from which she is so obviously excluded. Or is this a painting within a painting of an event of which the recollection still rankles. It might even be a window through which the spectator views the scene taking place in an inner room. This may have been what was intended because an infra-red photograph has revealed perspective lines indicating that a flat window frame was once painted at the base of this scene (Braham 1965 362; MacLaren 1970,122).

The composition of the relationship of the religious and the profane taking place in the kitchen originated in sixteenth-century Flemish paintings (Mayer 1919; Harris 1982, 45). It is used in particular by Pieter Aertson in the 1550s and Jacob Matham (Craig 1983; eg Muller 1976, fig 12) and is often reproduced in etchings and derivative paintings, some of which may have been known by Velázquez

(Lopéz-Rey 1968, 33). A large number take as their theme Supper at Emmaus or Christ in the House of Martha and Mary.

In Matham's *Kitchen Scene with Supper at Emmaus* (Brown 1986, fig 22), the supper takes place in a back inner room while the foreground is dominated by a female cook pointing to a table loaded with fish, with what seems to be a huge grouper in the foreground and an amberjack and a lobster behind. Two large steaks of salmon have already been placed in a pan. On the right roars a fire, warming the room so much that the cook has rolled up her sleeves. She glances to her right at a young man who is showing her an eel. This miraculous abundance of fish, as well as enhancing its symbolic nature, emphasises the miraculous bounty of Christ's reappearance to his disciples. It removes any lingering doubt that He is present in the inner room, even if the Supper at Emmaus is taking place in a simply furnished Flemish kitchen bursting with food and devoted to earthly pleasures.

Velázquez, in contrast, pares his scene to the bare essentials with the accent on the food ingredients and the powerful emotions of the participants, especially the cook. He uses the device of the half-length figure used by the Flemish painters but Martha exemplifies bodily needs and Mary spiritual needs. Martha, as the biblical text remarks, was 'cumbered about with much serving', while Mary, as Christ commented, 'had chosen that good part which shall not be taken away from her', a contrast emphasising the active and the contemplative life, and the admonishing finger of the old woman behind the cook highlights this.

An Old Woman Cooking Eggs

In the second painting, the old woman bears a similarity to one of the main characters in the *Kitchen Scene*, although as this painting was created three years before the previous one, the woman is looking slightly younger. In fact, in spite of the title, the woman may be old only in the sense of being middle aged or being old before her time, because she had aged due to the hard physical labour, which was the lot of many women. If the *Kitchen Scene* conveys the tediousness of the cook's role, this painting makes the spectator eager to taste the eggs, gently forming in the dish. It is one of the most evocative of all paintings of a cook and the food she is cooking.

Velázquez has arranged his scene so that the cooking process is made explicit. The red earthenware cooking dish is placed on a grill, with the red glow of charcoal in the clay brazier sightly visible beneath it. Two eggs have been put into the oil in a dish and the albumen is just beginning to coalesce so that a slightly browned crispy edge (*puntilla*) is being formed. A tiny glitter of white on the side of the red dish reflects the white of the albumen, which in turn contrasts with the golden egg yolk. The woman holds another egg in her left hand ready to break it with a sharp one-handed gesture and let its liquid contents join the other eggs. This frees the right hand to scoop the oil over the other two eggs with a wooden spoon.

On a table, which, like the one in the other painting, slightly tilts towards the spectator, is the same bronze pestle and mortar as in the *Kitchen Scene*, a white dish across which a knife is laid and a red-skinned onion, so characteristic of those grown in Spain. Two earthenware jugs, one again stained by the oil trickling down its side, the other, white-glazed at the top, stand to the right. Small jugs hang from a post and above the scene is a woven basket from which a dirty grey cloth protrudes. To the left a boy waits holding a glass carafe in his left hand partly filled with rough red wine and with a yellow melon tucked under his right arm.

There are two interpretations of what the woman is cooking. She may be making a garlic or onion soup, a traditional peasant dish, garnished with eggs (Steinberg 1967). But it is more likely that she is preparing a version of *Huevos a la Flamenca*. This simple dish took on a more elaborate appearance at the end of the eighteenth century when Charles VI's approval led to it becoming a classic Spanish dish with the addition of chopped ham, beans and potatoes. In its most simple form it contains a few peas, a sliced tomato and thinly-sliced *chorizo*. In Mallorca *sobrasada*, a soft, paprika (*pimentón mallorguín*) and cayenne flavoured pork sausage is substituted for *chorizo*, and possibly *migas*, stale breadcrumbs fried in olive oil and garlic are sprinkled on the top. The popularity of fried eggs in Spain is such that the dish is often expected to be available as a first course (*aperitivos*) even if it is not advertised on the menu.

Yet there is more to this painting than an invitation to partake of a meal. The eggs represent youth and rejuvenation, which is enhanced by the presence of the boy, as well as being symbolic of resurrection; the old woman represents age, decay and death. There is an unreal quality about the placing of the objects and the participants.

The two people do not look at each other but across each other, the old woman's gaze fixed on something beyond earthly life. They are united by the curved line which outlines the two figures and culminates at the point where the boy's hand hovers over that of the old woman. The boy's carafe and the downward thrust of the woman's fingers ensure that the attention of the spectator is drawn to the central point of the painting, the eggs, both real and symbolic. What appears at first to be a simple comfortable scene of cooking eggs is permeated by a psychological unease, accentuated by the angle of the kitchen implements and the fact that the figures are highlighted against a dark impenetrable background.

This stillness, combined with unease, is reflected in other Velázquez paintings, especially *Three Men at Table* (1620) and *A Girl and Two Men at Table* (1620) (neither of which is in the exhibition), two scenes almost similar in concept, where one figure is detached from the jollity of the others. In the former a loaf of bread is perilously close to the edge of the table and a knife overlaps the edge, its black shadow reminiscent of the one in the *Old Woman* painting. In the latter the girl concentrates on pouring out the wine, so that bread and wine draw attention to the central ingredients of the Mass. Both paintings have a glass of water placed on the left side of the table. This is a common feature in Spanish painting, as indicated by the glittering glass in Luiz Meléndez' *Still Life with Box of Jellied fruits, Bread and Other Objects* (Helston 1983, 72-73)

The Waterseller

Water, a vital element for life, forms the central element in another painting of 1620, *The Waterseller* (also known as *The Water Carrier)*, a painting which also combines stillness and unease. The three figures, which have been interpreted as the three ages of man (Steinberg 1970; Gállego 1974, 132), remain detached: a young boy gazing sideways, the same model as had appeared two years earlier by the side of the old woman cooking eggs, a rigidly frontal-facing figure in the background and the waterseller himself, withdrawn and contemplating. Water unites the three.

The background figure drinks thirstily from a glass of water, the boy and the waterseller hold a glass, filled to the brim with brilliantly-transparent water, three drops trickling down the side, a feature enhanced by the drops of water on the side of the bulbous clay vessel, both evoking the essence and desire for water, which can only be appreciated in a parched hot climate. The object in the bottom of the glass may be a fig, which can freshen the water and impart a faint sweet flavour, or it could be a decorative feature, a bubble moulded into the bottom, as is still created by glassblowers today. Although the glass may have been painted as a showpiece (Moffat 1978), it is part of the stillness of religious contemplation which pervades the scene.

Watersellers were a common sight in Spain until the middle of the twentieth century, when water was finally piped to remote villages. George Borrow in *The Bible in Spain* (1843) describes them as wearing coarse duffel and leathern skull-caps, seated by the fountains, filling water casks, with which they stagger to the topmost stories of the houses. They sold water in the street, though perhaps not in such elegant containers as in the painting.

A *Treatise on Water*, written in Madrid in 1637, says that 'one of the great virtues of Spaniards is that they drink much water and that of all the European nations they are the one least enslaved to wine. The author claims that the Cordoban philosopher, Seneca, drank only water during his life' (*National Gallery News* November 1993). This delight in the different qualities of water is still apparent in Spain in spite of the advent of bottled waters.

Goya

By the 19th century, still life takes on a new meaning. Goya's *Still Life with Golden Bream* represents the glassy-eyed fish at the moment of death, gasping by the sea which faintly looms behind them. His *Still Life with dead Turkey* places the dead bird's head raised beseechingly against the fate which will soon overwhelm it, for in another painting the cook has already plucked the bird, which lies upside down by the pan in which its dismembered body will lie. Cuts of meat in *Still Life with pieces of Rib, Loin and Head of Mutton* relate to the brutality with which a cook attacks meat, and prepares the spectator for the dead meat which men become after death, as Goya was to record in his black and white prints of the *Disasters of War*.

This inhumanity is carried further in his *Still Life with Three Slices of Salmon*, where roughly cut slices, messy with blood and torn skin, contrast with Meléndez' *Still Life with Salmon* in which a neatly cut pink slice rests against the pan in which it will be cooked, the jug of wine with which it will be drunk and the lemon which will flavour it. All is ready for the cook to prepare the meal.

Pottery and earthenware

Much of the pottery can be identified, and many have their counterparts today. In Hamen y León's painting of *Still Life with Sweets and Pottery* are a red stoneware bottle with a hole in it, a product of the Rhineland, and a bottle and a bowl imported from Mexico. His *Still Life with Sweets and Glassware* arranges a glass bowl filled with the cook's pastries and candied figs, a scalloped ceramic dish, a clear glass flask containing *aloja*, an aromatic infusion of honey water, flavoured with spices such as cinnamon and ginger. Regarded as a great delicacy by Madrid society, this would be served in the late afternoon, in a glass similar to that portrayed alongside the flask, accompanying those delicious pastries and the curved *barquillos* (wafers), still served today with dishes of ice cream.

Another drink, often served in red earthenware two-handled bowls was *hipocrás*, a popular drink of wine, sugar and cinnamon, an earlier version of *sangria*. This vessel, as portrayed in Juan Bautista de Espinosa's painting, *Still Life with Silver-Gilt Salvers*, like others portrayed, is still in use today, and cinnamon sticks, portrayed alongside wrapped in a cone, make the spectator hasten to buy them in the spice shops frequented by cooks, herbalists and anyone who wishes to experiment with taste.

Francisco de Zurbarán's *Still Life with Four Vessels* also contains a piece from Mexico, but the white faïence vessel, an *alcarraza*, is typical of those used in Spain for its purpose is to keep water cool through evaporation. In Mallorca, a similar white clay vessel is known as a *botijo* and a glass one as a *porrón*; the former is taken into the fields by workmen to have a cool drink in the middle of the day, the other is placed by the bedside at night.

It remains to say a little about the pottery in the Velázquez' paintings, two examples at least having a modern counterpart. The waterseller rests his hand on a huge jug firmly closed with a bung to which a metal chain is attached. This heavy clay jug has been turned on the wheel and its weight is indicated by the bulk which reflects the bulk of the water carrier himself. On the table is a dimpled pitcher on which a small two-handled drinking vessel rests.

The dish in which the eggs are being cooked is also not without interest. This is the *cazuela*, the shallow red earthenware dish, which cooks food better than any metal ones. In Mallorca this is the *greixonera* and the name is given to a variety of forms. Some have small handles and a rounded bottom; others are low and flat, anything from 3 inches to 15 inches across. These do not have lids; if one is required another *greixonera* is placed upside down on the top. Usually they are covered with deep red glossy slip, but some may be fired black or grey. Some may be used in the oven, some on top of the stove and some used for both purposes.

This distinctive pottery gets its colour from the clay which is used. In Valencia, the pottery produced is a clear orange-red; in Mallorca, it can be that colour or be made from white clay to which a russet brown earth is added, but the final colour depends on the different temperatures at which the glaze is fired. At the pottery of Miguel Serra at Santa Maria, Mallorca, which has been in the hands of the same family for four generations, the local clay is wrapped in huge plastic packs to keep it damp until it is required. Then it is cut into workable pieces, kneaded and puddled to push out the air, before being moulded on the wheel to the required shapes. Señor Serra makes a great variety of cooking pots, jugs and other vessels, and huge jars to hold olives and preserved fruits.

The raw clay *greixoneras* are placed in ovens, which are heated from cold to temperatures between 950 C - 960 C. If a small oven is used, of one cubic metre, the firing takes ten hours, if the large oven is used of ten cubic metres, the firing takes twenty-four hours. In both cases the oven is left at maximum temperature for the last hour. The length of the firing, however, is determined by the amount of moisture in the clay. The oven is then allowed to cool very slowly, while the pottery is still in it.

Next the red slip or glaze is added and a second firing takes place for half the time, at the same temperature. If slip is added to the interior and just round the top of the exterior of the *greixonera*, the dish may be put on the top of the stove. At one time, only a wood burning stove was used so that the smoke flavoured the food. Today gas and electricity provide the main heat.

Before using a dish for the first time each *greixonera* must be soaked in water for two hours; when this is done the water hisses and bubbles as any excess air is driven off. Then the dish is allowed to dry naturally. When used on the wood-burning stove *greixoneras* lasted a lifetime; the fiercer heat of gas and electricity tends to be more destructive.

When shown a coloured reproduction of the Velázquez painting, Miguel's mother, Señora Serra, expressed some astonishment that the method of cooking shown was so similar to the one she used. Her favourite Sunday lunch is cooked in a deep *greixonera*, brushed with a little oil and cradled over a stove, much in the manner with which the old woman was cooking the eggs. Lunch comprises pieces of lamb roasted slowly for about thirty minutes, to which crushed garlic, chopped onions, tomatoes, mushrooms, artichokes and parsley are added together with a little stock, and the meal simmers gently until the meat is almost cooked. Rice is added for the last twenty minutes and the contents must not be stirred. In October and November she sends her son into the mountains to get an alternative to lamb. 'Ah, yes, said Señora Serra, 'lamb is good, but you should wait until the thrushes come.'

PAINTINGS DISCUSSED

Diego Velázquez (1599-1660)
An Old Woman Cooking Eggs 1618 The National Gallery of Scotland, Edinburgh
Three Men at Table 1620 Hermitage Museum, Leningrad (not in the London exhibition)
A Girl and Two Men at Table 1620 Szépmüvézet Múzeum, Budapest (not in the London exhibition)
Christ in the house of Martha and Mary 1620 The National Gallery, London
The Waterseller of Seville 1620 Apsley House, The Wellington Museum, London

Juan Sánchez Cotán (1560-1627)
Still Life with Game Fowl c.1600 The Art Institute of Chicago
Still Life with Quince, Cabbage, Melon and Cucumber c.1600 San Diego Museum of Art
Still Life with Game Fowl, Fruit and Vegetables 1602 Museo del Prado, Madrid

Juan van der Hamen y León (1596-1631)
Still Life with Sweets and Pottery 1627 The National Gallery of Art, Washington
Still Life with Sweets and Glassware 1622 Museo del Prado, Madrid
The Cook 1630 Rijksmuseum, Amsterdam (not in the London exhibition)

Juan Bautista de Espinosa (c.1585-1640)
Still Life with Silver-Gilt Salvers 1624 Masaveu Collection, Spain

Francisco de Zurbarán (1598-1664)
Still Life with Four Vessels c.1658 Museo del Prado, Madrid
Still Life with Basket of Oranges 1633 The Norton Simon Collection, Pasadena, California (not in the London exhibition)

Pedro de Camprobín (1605-1674)
Still Life with Sweets 1663 Private Collection

Antonio de Pereda (1611-1678)
Still Life with Walnuts 1634 Private collection
Kitchen Scene (Allegory of Lost Virtue) c.1650 National Trust, Penrhyn Castle, Douglas-Pennant Collection
Still Life with Vegetables 1651 Museu Nacional de Arte Antiga, Lisbon
Still Life with Fruits 1651 Museu Nacional de Arte Antiga, Lisbon

Juan de Zurbarán (1620-1649)
Plate of Fruit with a Linnet c. 1639-1640 Museu Nacional d'Art de Catalunya, Barcelona

Juan de Espinosa (c. 1628-1659)
Still Life with Grapes, Fruit and a Terracotta Jar 1646 Naseiro Collection, Madrid

Luis Meléndez (1716-1780)
Still Life with Sea Bream and Oranges 1772 Oviedo Masaveu Collection, Madrid
Still Life with Oranges and Walnuts 1772 The National Gallery, London
Still Life with Fruit, Cheese and Containers 1771 Museo del Prado, Madrid
Still Life with Salmon, a Lemon and Three Vessels 1772 Museo del Prado, Madrid (not in the London exhibition)

Francisco de Goya (1746-1828)
Still Life with Golden Bream c.1808-1812 Museum of Fine Arts, Houston Still Life with Dead Turkey c.1808-1812 Museo del Prado, Madrid
Plucked Turkey and Frying Pan c.1808-1812 Alte Pinakothek, Munich
Still Life with Pieces of Rib, Loin and a Head of Mutton c.1808-1812 Musée du Louvre, Paris
Three Slices of Salmon c.1808-1812 Oskar Reinhart Collection Winterthur (not in the London exhibition)

BIBLIOGRAPHY

Altamiras, Juan 1758 *Nuevo Arte de Cocina sacado de la Escuela de la Experiencia Economica,* Barcelona, 99 and 107

Bardi, P.M. 1969 *L'Opera completa a Velázquez.* Milan

Baxandall, David 1957 'A dated Velázquez *bodegón*'. *Burlington Magazine,* 99, 156-157

Bermúdez, Juan Augustín Ceán 1819 *Diálogo Sobre el Arte de la Pintura.* Seville

Borrow, George 1843 *The Bible in Spain* Reprinted 1959 London

Braham, Allan 1965 'A second dated *bodegón* by Velázquez'. *Burlington Magazine,* 107, 362-365

Brown, Jonathan 1986 *Velázquez. Painter and Courtier.* Yale

Craig, Kenneth 1983 'Pars Ergo Marthae Transit: Pieter Aertson's "Inverted" Paintings of Christ in the House of Martha and Mary'. *Oud Holland* 79, 25-39

Denny, D 1972 'Sánchez Cotán "Still Life with Carrots and Cardoon"'. *Pantheon,* 30, 48-53

Gállego, Julián 1974 *Velázquez in Seville.* Seville

Harris, Enriqueta 1982 *Velázquez.* London

Helston, Michael 1989 *Painting in Spain during the Eighteenth Century.* National Gallery Publications, London

Jordan, William B. and Cherry, Peter 1995 *Spanish Still Life from Velázquez to Goya.* National Gallery Publications, London

Kubler, G and Soria, M 1959 *Art and Architecture in Spain and Portugal and the American Dominions 1500-1800.*London

López-Rey, José 1968 *Velázquez' Work and World.* London

MacLaren, Neil 1970 *The Spanish School.* National Gallery Catalogue, revised by Allan Braham. London

Mayer, August 1919 'Velázquez und die Niederlandische Kuchenstücke'. *Kunstchronik und Kunstmarkt,* 30, 236-237

Moffat, John F 1978 'Image and Meaning in Velázquez' "Watercarrier of Seville"'. *Traza y Baza,* 7, 9

Muller, Joseph Emile 1976 *Velázquez.* London

Soria, M 1945 'Sánchez Cotán's "Quince, Cabbage, Melon and Cucumber"' *Art Quarterly,* 225-230

Steinberg, Leo 1965 'Review of José López-Rey's Velázquez. A Catalogue Raisonné of his Oeuvre with an Introductory Study'. *Art Bulletin,* 47, 274-294

Steinberg, Leo 1971 'The Water Carrier of Seville'. *Art News,* 70, Summer, 54-55

Taggart, M N 1990 'Juan Sánchez Cotán and the Depiction of Food in Seventeenth-Century Spanish Still Life Painting'. *Pantheon,* 47, 76-80

Wind, B 1987 *Velázquez' "Bodegones", A Study in Seventeenth-Century Genre Painting.* Virginia, USA.

ACKNOWLEDGEMENTS

I am indebted to Señor Miguel Serra and his mother, Señora Serra, for the information on the pottery produced in their works at Santa Maria, Mallorca, Ballearics, Spain, and for showing me their production lines, and to Pauline Montijano of Palma, Mallorca, for arranging my visits. I am also grateful to her and to my colleague, Maureen Walshe, for discussing interpretations of the paintings and of the food, and for suggesting several ideas which have been incorporated into the text.

Edouard de Pomiane (1875-1964)

Josephine Bacon

'Modern life spoils so much that is pleasant. Let us see that it does not make us spoil our steak or our omelette. Ten minutes are sufficient – one minute more and all would be lost.'

Edouard de Pomiane was the first male 'practical cook', one of the few pioneers of cookery whose work has survived unchanged to this day. It is constantly being revived and relived, as in the recent television series based on his book *La Cuisine en 10 minutes*. His innovations were of many kinds, but most notably he was the first cookery broadcaster (in the 1920s) and the first person to extoll the virtues of the quick and easy preparation of meals. Despite Escoffier's frequently quoted 'Faites simple!' (Do it simply), famous chefs have always extolled simplicity as a virtue while doing everything in their power to avoid putting into practice what they preach. If proof were needed, one only has to consider their favourite creations. De Pomiane practised what he preached, probably because he was not a cookery professional, a chef or a caterer, but a doctor of medicine.

Edouard de Pomiane was born Edouard Pozerski in Cracow, Poland. His father was a Polish aristocrat, his mother was the daughter of a Russian general, but both fought for the independence of Poland. His father was sent to Siberia for his subversive activities but his mother managed to escape with her young son, and settled in Paris. Edouard was brought up in the relative poverty so often experienced by refugees, even aristocratic ones. He took the name 'de Pomiane' subsequently because it is easier to say and it is, in fact, his own, since it is the heraldic family name.

Throughout his life, de Pomiane sided with liberal causes, such as that of Captain Dreyfus, and he displayed a fascination for, and affinity with, Jews. He must have seen people he could identify as Jews in his native Poland but he probably only met them socially in Paris. Nevertheless, he also retained much of the traditional prejudices against them, fed upon by the anti-semitic climate of both his native country and the times in which he lived. This is very clear from what is, to me, his most exciting work, *Cuisine juive: ghettos modernes* (1929) which I translated as *The Jews of Poland: Recollections and Recipes* and published in 1985. It is the only book ever written by a non-Jew about Polish-Jewish cooking and one of the very few books on the subject at all (almost all Jewish cookery books which include Polish-Jewish recipes are post-war and written by descendants of Polish Jews. The only other authentic Polish-Jewish cookery book I have ever managed to trace is a vegetarian cookery book written in Yiddish by a Jewish restaurant in 1938. Only one copy is known to exist.) De Pomiane travelled to Poland especially to collect the recipes and find out something about Polish-Jewish life. He also tries to make his recipes kosher, and indeed this is the only kosher cookery book ever written by a non-Jew, although he does not appear to have fully understood the explanation he received from the rabbi of Dobczyce about koshering meat.

De Pomiane's down-to-earth approach to cooking stemmed from his interest in food chemistry, combined with his eminently practical approach to life and his respect and consideration for women, and – supremely rare in those days – working women. He is the first writer to admit that women are forced to cook, like it or not, and to fit cooking into a busy schedule. He was an immensely practical person, whose clear and concise advice, tips and instructions were perfect for radio listening. His teachings were based on sound commonsense and the principles of physiology. De Pomiane cared not a jot for the fashionable heavy, rich food of the day, and urged his listeners and readers to eat simple, balanced meals. He was the first to point out that eating a fish entrée and a meat main course produced a meal that was far too protein-rich. If only he had been heeded sooner! As recently as the 1940s, hotels still considered it their duty to serve an 'entrée' of fish or cheese before the meat course, however meagre the wartime portions might be. He even dared to flout the orthodoxy of the Escoffier school by eschewing cream in sauces, in favour of a milk-and-flour thickening mixture, for two eminently practical reasons – there was less likelihood of the sauce curdling and, best of all, it was cheaper!

All of this illustrates that De Pomiane was an even greater revolutionary than his parents, though in a completely different way, and he was at least 50 years ahead of his time. All the best food writers, from Elizabeth David to Jéhane Benoît of Canada have expressed their gratitude to Edouard de Pomiane, as their mentor. His work has an enduring quality rarely found in a field which is so heavily prey to fad and fashion.

BIBLIOGRAPHY

I have been able to trace the following titles of books that he wrote between 1922 and 1954, but there may well be more.

Bien Manger pour Bien Vivre, Albin Michel, Paris.
Le Code de la Bonne Chère, Albin Michel, Paris, 1924. Republished in paperback, 1952.
Cuisine Juive, Ghettos Modernes, Albin Michel, Paris, 1929.
La Cuisine en Six Leçons, Editions Paul Martial, Paris.
La Cuisine en Dix Minutes ou l'Adaptation au Rhythme Moderne, Editions Paul Martiale, Paris.
La Cuisine pour la Femme du Monde, Editions Paul Martial.
Radio-Cuisine, Albin Michel, Paris. 2 vol.
Vingt Plats qui donnent la Goutte, Editions Paul Martial pour PIPÉRAZINE MIDY, Paris, 1935.
365 Menus, 365 Recettes, Albin Michel, Paris.
La Cuisine et le Raisonnement, Editions Paul Martial.
La Cuisine en Plein Air, Editions Paul Martial.
Le Carnet d'ANNA, Editions Paul Martial pour les Laboratoires ZIZINE, Paris, 1938.
Hygiène Alimentaire.
La GOUTTE au compte-gouttes, Éditions Paul Martial, Paris, nd, c.1939.
La Cuisine polonaise vue des bords de la Seine, Editions des Bibliophiles.
Cuisine et Restrictions, Corrêa, Paris, 1940.
Recettes Nouvelles pour le Printemps, Corrêa, Paris, 1941. Paginated from p.193; *"La pagination de ce fascicule fait suite á celle du volume* Cuisine et Restrictions.*"*
Manger... quand même. Corrêa, Paris.
La Technique Culinaire Actuelle et les Aliments de Remplacement, Librairie J.B. Baillière & Fils, Paris, 1941.
Des Honnestes Voluptés de Bouche et d'Amour, Editions S.E.G.P.
Conserves Familiales, Microbie Alimentaire, Albin Michel, Paris.
La Cuisine pour les estomacs délicats, Editions de la Couronne.
Réflexes et réflexions devant la nappe, Editions Paul Martial.
La Physique de la Cuisine et son Art, Editions Albin Michel, Paris, 1950.

Translations into English
GOOD FARE: A Code of Cookery, Gerald Howe, 1932.
Cooking in Ten Minutes, tr. Peggy Benton, Bruno Cassirer, 1948.
Cooking with Pomiane, tr. Peggy Benton, Bruno Cassirer, Oxford, 1962. Also paperback, Faber & Faber, with Forward by Elizabeth David, 1976.
The Jews of Poland: Recollections and Recipes, tr. Josephine Bacon, Pholiota Press, Garden Grove, California,1985.

A Glance at the Life of Sir Kenelm Digby, Knight, at his Cookbook Called 'The Closet Opened', and a Peep into a Contemporary Manuscript

Priscilla Bain and Maggie Black

Part 1. A Wasted Life?

According to the author E.W.Bligh, writing in 1932 the best sources for Kenelm Digby's life are his 'autobiography' written when he was 25, and John Aubrey's *Brief Lives* which supplies notes and snippets about his contemporaries and their varied (and often contradictory) views. Aubrey's scraps are the more personal and down to earth as far as they go, because Digby's own tale is deliberately presented as a pseudo-antique allegory justifying the actions and attitudes of his chosen mistress, Venetia Stanley. But both should be read with one eye on the open and sidelong comments of the writers' peers in many other accounts.

Kenelm Digby was indubitably born [he says so himself] at his mother's home Gayhurst in Buckinghamshire on July 11th 1603; and he was raised by her there after his catholic-convert father was hung, drawn and quartered as a traitor following the Gunpowder Plot. It must have been a lonely childhood, with only tutors and an embittered mother to turn to.

However much was in store for the bright if not brilliant youth. His Protestant uncle John was, unlike his idealist father, a career politician, who, when Kenelm was fourteen, was sent (for the fourth time) to Spain, to negotiate a marriage between the heir to the English throne and the eldest Spanish Infanta. Sir John Digby, lacking decision-making power, must have known that the match was doomed from the start because the Spanish side made the unthinkable demand that the English nation should allow full liberty of conscience, or at least that the prince should turn Catholic. Perhaps that was why Sir John took his well-built and pleasing Catholic nephew with him, to beguile the Court ladies while he sought better terms. It would also give the lad a holiday before he went to Oxford.

Young Digby was already too grown-up for English student life when he reached the university.[1] He was a sophisticated young adult while most of his fellows had barely reached puberty. More seriously, he was isolated by his faith. As a Catholic, he was by upbringing conservative. As a Digby, he was forward-looking, modern, intensely interested in all facets of the expanding world around him. However as R.T.Petersson says, he lacked the concentration of a professional or specialist and the ability to deduce new theories from old learning, and in the end his arguments fell back on received teaching and on belief.

This was not yet apparent in his Oxford days because he fell under the spell of two outstanding scholars who were beguiled by his forwardness in their own fields. One was Thomas Allen, a renowned mathematician and astrologer, the other was the erstwhile physician at Gayhurst[2], Richard Napier, a famous mystic and ascetic. Allen in particular developed a strong affection for the young man, and between them the two scholars inculcated in him a lifelong love of books and philosophy and the entwined subjects of pharmacy, alchemy and experimental practical cookery.

Home again, he also fell permanently in love with a beautiful young wanton, Venetia Stanley, who had been lodged for a time near his mother's house. His first literary effusion would be an attempt to present her as the epitome of glorious womanhood, yet with a man's strength of mind, way above such domestic virtues as chastity. But for the moment, he was only one suitor among many of a girl of whom his mother decidedly disapproved. Like parents before and since, Lady Digby decided to send her eldest on a long European tour.

It started well. In France he escaped unharmed when the Queen-Dowager tried to seduce him[3], and in Italy he added to his cook-book collection and recipes, probably acquired among others an alchemical cure for wounds[4] and met both Van Dyck and Galileo. But when, after two years in Florence, he reached Madrid in 1623 he found his uncle (now Earl of Bristol) in the midst of diplomatic turmoil as Prince Charles was there making a last bid for a Spanish bride while some of his entourage behaved like modern football fans.

Digby was knighted by King James[5] on the return to London, and began 'uncertain months of elation and despair'[6] in his relationship with Venetia who by now had dallied with several followers and had a child by the 4th Earl of Dorset. Digby's ardour and persistence won, and culminated in their marriage in 1625. She bore him five children and behaved impeccably until her death in 1633.[7]

But Digby's was a restless soul which needed adventure to make up for the solid concentration which he could not sustain. In January 1628, with Venetia's reluctant agreement, he set sail with two little ships to assert English prestige by harassing foreign ships in the Mediterranean. He sailed first to Algiers, and ransomed some English sailors held captive by Barbary pirates, then to Alexandretta (Scanderoon) where he tried [and failed] to lay hands on the bullion in four French ships guarded by Venetian galleasses – although he fought the great ships and *won*. As a result, the English vice-consul and merchants were fined and imprisoned until he left.

He brought home no gold. But he did feast regally on Turkish partridges, fruit and wine, brought home some antique relics for the King and gave his compatriots a tale to retell and remember with pride. He got a job as a naval Commissioner too,[8] was an active member of King Charles's court circle, and from 1630-35 for divers reasons[9] worshipped as a member of the Anglican communion.

The most crashing disaster of those years was that Venetia, Lady Digby died suddenly in 1633.[10] Even her husband's ebullient spirit could not combat this catastrophe, and Sir Kenelm retired from Court to the seclusion of Gresham's College where he remained for two years, concerned mostly with scientific experiments, philosophical writings and literary reviews. His metropolitan social life seemed over, and as undiluted solitary self-examination was soon unbearable to him, he turned (so Petersson suggests) to analysing and communicating the discoveries of others as well as his own. Out of this melée, he now began to develop his belief that 'a certain airy substance is essential to the life of plants' – an idea which later became possibly his most important contribution to science.[11]

In the summer of 1635, he also reconverted to the Roman Church, and made a firm base for himself in France. He began to socialise again, and thereafter he would shuttle to and fro across the Channel, sometimes trying to claim some of his sequestered property, sometimes under ban, but always active.

He still pursued enthusiastically his studies in physics, botany and philosophy. He corresponded with Hobbes, Descartes (whose theories he introduced to English philosophers) and Mersenne,[12] the French priest-philosopher who like Digby himself was an intellectual 'middle man' connecting the great minds of the age. Under such influence, Digby like many converts, tried to convert in his turn his cousin George and the wild young daughter of the famous judge Sir Edward Coke who was married to the Duke of Buckingham's brother, Lord Purbeck. She was not the only woman who attracted his interest in those days. But he had heavier worries than women. Civil war was approaching at home when he returned in 1639 and Parliament suspected all Catholics of dangerous disaffection from then on. By Midsummer 1641 Digby left again, only to run into serious trouble in France when a French nobleman insulted King Charles at the dinner-table. Digby challenged him, and killed his man in the duel which followed, but (not surprisingly) the French king's valedictory pardon was useless when he reached England, and in November 1642 he was imprisoned until the following July. He spent the time in standardising green glass bottles, and in writing among other pieces a critique of Thomas Browne's *Religio Medici*. Later this would bring him higher repute than his own major work the *Two Treatises*, an attempted analysis of what truth consists of, for both bodies and souls.

Digby himself was always dissatisfied with his great *Opus*, and promised to finish it 'some time'. But the time never came. Instead, he fled back to France, and was waiting there for Henrietta Maria when she arrived as an exile in 1644. She made him her Chancellor then, and he held the post for life, for what it was worth – nothing at all really since King Charles would not go over to Catholicism, and no assistance would be given him without that crucial step.

Henrietta Maria sent Digby to Rome, but he returned with just a draft treaty offering papal help only on impossibly stiff terms. Even his brief backing by the College of Cardinals, who probably disliked the Pope as much as he did, could not prevent Digby having a stand-up row with the Pontiff, and making himself unpopular with all parties.

Still he could not leave well alone. He got caught up with and to some extent inspired an idiotic plot promoted by a priest nicknamed Blacklo to establish a semi-secret chapter of a reformed Roman Church in England with the Pope subordinate to the State. The scheme soon collapsed and part of Digby's cavalier spirit collapsed with it. With the execution of King Charles, and the deaths of his brother and favourite sons, he was both materially and emotionally bankrupted, and now only sought to polish his work, and study his books, medicinal cures and cookery.

However, to do any of these things he needed money, and that need brought him back to England in 1654, following Cromwell's seizure of power and establishment of the Protectorate. Thereafter, although Digby would travel widely in Europe, London would be his real home until he died of 'the stone'[13] on June 11th 1665.

Like any other educated 17th century man, Digby saw good health as quite largely dependant on a wise diet, but the constituents of that diet like much else were still decided by theories and fancies dating back to the 1st century and by the poorly substantiated work of later alchemists and researchers. In Digby's own time, the scientist Robert Boyle was as credulous about Galen's theory of humours as Digby himself was about his own Powder of Sympathy,[14] and neither thought that the 'cures' achieved might be simply cases of mind dominating matter.

Mercifully, most of Digby's medicinal skill consisted of commonsense first aid such as keeping wounds closed, clean and dry until they healed naturally. That he added a little sympathy in the modern sense probably did a bit of good as well.

R.T. Petersson's view of Digby's contribution to medicine and science generally is that he acted as 'translator' between the great minds which emerged in many fields in the 17th century as sceptical, secular thought spread, but that he never fully defined his ideas before flitting off on some new tack. Furthermore like the little French queen he served so faithfully (for he must always have a woman to adore) he was forever fighting last year's battles.

Even after the Restoration in 1660, he had one more to fight because Charles II, although caring little about religion, did whatever his parliament demanded to get money. Digby made one last plea to him for toleration for English Catholics, but without enthusiasm or success.[15] Only he himself had his fortunes bettered a bit. He was repaid, at last, the ransom money for the English prisoners he had freed way back in 1628. It meant, besides more serious things, that he could buy small food luxuries such as honey for the mead in his recipe book, *The Closet of Sir Kenelm Digby Knight Opened*. Today it for this curious collection of recipes that he is chiefly remembered.

When the Royal Society was set up, his name was near the top of the list of those invited to join but he seemed to do little to justify his membership. By the time he died in 1665, he was almost forgotten. Yet there were very few major scientists, mathematicians and philosophers who had not heard of him, and most had corresponded with him, borrowed his books or formulated their own ideas through disagreeing with his. They had dedicated books to him, used his translations and recipes, and eaten his dinners. Then they did not need him any more.

The day of the *virtuoso,* the pioneer amateur, was done. [M.K.B.]

Part 2. *A Closer Look into Digby's Closet – and a peep into another*

Digby liked good food all his life. His mother's house was well known for its good fare, and as a scientist he always enjoyed experimenting with dishes to see what results he would achieve. Unfortunately because his recipes were only gathered together after his death, probably by Hartman, his steward, we cannot tell at which stage of his life they were produced and in what order. Sometimes a reference to a particular person or place will give us a clue, as well as telling us something about the man who collected them, for a very individual voice emerges from the pages.

There are about 330 recipes and comments here, depending on how you count them. Of these, just over a hundred are for mead (meath) or metheglyn, and these can, just plausibly, be considered experimental data for versions of a single scientific product. Indeed I suspect Digby himself may have so viewed them: he was too intelligent to go on churning out drinks recipes just for the 'kick' of trying new ones. The fact that he describes at length the recipe given him by King Charles II's mead maker – 'The first of Septemb. 1663. Mr Webb came to my House to make some [mead] for Me.' – and attaches to it his own various versions may indicate that he intended to round out his material on drinks, like so much else that he left unfinished. Among the recipes is one from Sir John Fortescue who was married to Venetia's sister, Frances, and from whose family the second recipe book discussed in this article comes.

The recipes for foods and preserves which follow the drinks section are distinctly more diverse than the drinks themselves.[16] Digby seems to have collected recipes and cooked just for pleasure and to flatter his friends. As a craft, it did not require long-term or deeply detailed concentration over months or years so it suited his temperament and peripatetic way of life admirably. One is reminded of Sir Harry Luke's *The Tenth Muse* – a twentieth century collection derived from the same sociable and mouvementé way of life. Digby was, we suspect, something of a snob, and certainly a name-dropper. His close connection with the Royal circle and particularly with Queen Henrietta Maria, to whom he became Chancellor, appears throughout the collection. 'The Queen's Hotchpot', 'Portugal Broth as it was made for the Queen' and 'Hydromel as I made it weak for the Queen Mother'. When the Queen was in exile during the Civil War and Comonwealth, Digby was very much one of her inner circle. They were both in extremely straitened circumstances for much of that time, Digby because most of his estates were confiscated and the Queen because she was living on the charity of her nephew Louis XIV's court, not always a very reliable means of support. Possibly the recipe 'To Rost Fine Meat' which goes on to say, 'The Queen useth to baste such meat with yolks of fresh Eggs,' indicates that she did, whether from necessity or interest, actually take a turn in the kitchen herself.

Considering the length of time Digby spent on the Continent it is interesting that there is not more evidence of it in this collection of recipes. True there are a number of recipes with French titles, 'Pressis nourrisant', 'Potage de Blanc de Chapon', 'Cresme Fouettée'. There are also the rather oddly named 'Vuova Lattate' and 'Vuova Spersa' and a recipe which he probably acquired during his prolonged visit to Rome on behalf of the Queen in 1647-8. 'Pan Cotto, as the Cardinals use in Rome…' is a bread-thickened, slowly cooked potage which can then be flavoured with spice or orange juice. It was evidently regarded as part of a wholesome diet – Digby's digestion may well have been in need of that considering the frustrations of his negotiations with the Holy See.

But in two important recipes he does show knowledge of the kind of innovations which La Varenne put into print in 1651.'Concerning potages' begins 'The ground or body of Potages must always be very good broth of Mutton, Veal and Volaille. Now to give good taste, you vary every month of the year according to the herbs and roots that are in season...' Then in 'The Queen's Hotchpot from her Escuyer de Cuisine, Mr. la Montague' the mutton and vegetable stew is thickened thus, 'About a quarter of an hour before you serve it up melt a good lump of Butter (as much as a great Egg) till it grow red; then take it from the fire, and put to it a little fine flower to thicken it (about a couple of spoons)... Stir them very well together; then set them on the fire again, till it grow red, stirring it all the while; then put to it a ladleful of the liquor of the pot and let them stew a while together, stirring it always...' This seems to be an early example of an evolving 'white sauce' but sauces on the whole were still bread-thickened and sharpened with lemon, verjuice or vinegar, or were of the drawn butter variety. Eggs too were used. One curious recipe for eggs is included -'Tea with eggs. The Jesuite that came from China, Ann. 1664, told Mr. Waller that there they use sometimes in this manner...', which is, egg yolks and sugar beaten together with hot tea poured on them. It was evidently regarded as a sort of 'pick-me-up' or egg nog. Coincidentally 1664 was the year from which the East India Company began to ship a small quantity of tea direct to England as regular cargo.

Despite this evidence of modernity there are still more than a few traces of the medieval cuisine in *The Closet*. One of the most curious recipes is 'Pear Pudding' in which minced meat is mixed with currants and nutmeg, egg yolks and cream and is shaped like Bon-Chrétien pears, with pieces of cinnamon for stalks and cloves for heads. Elsewhere the flavouring of meat with sweet substances is evident and there are a number of possets and tansies.

If one reason for Digby's prolonged residence on the Continent was that it was undoubtedly easier – as well as less expensive – to observe the disciplines of Catholicism there, then there are not many signs of the requirements of Catholic Dietary laws in *The Closet*. There are three recipes for stockfish – that old staple of medieval Europe – one of which begins, rather unpromisingly 'Beat the fish very well with a large Woodden-Mallet, so as not to break it but to loosen all the flakes within. It is the best way to have them beaten with hard heavy Ropes...' The red herring also appears in 'Red Herrings Broyled. My Lord d'Aubigny eats Red-herrings thus...' The fish are here soaked in oil and vinegar and cooked on a grid-iron; the process is repeated two or three times after which they are said to be 'very short and crisp and savoury' and are laid on a salad.

A large number of the recipes reflect the tastes of the higher social classes in England at the time, plenty of meat mostly boiled or stewed (roasting presumably didn't normally require a recipe), puddings both savoury and sweet often cooked in pastry or in a bag, for which a cloth as well as animal gut is used. There are too a large number of recipes for preserving and jelly making.
Digby as a 'hands-on' cook appears in 'Preserved Quince with Gelly. When I made Quinces with Gelly, I used the first time these proportions...' which he corrected somewhat at his second attempt. Following the cheese recipes there are eight 'recipes' for feeding and fattening fowl, which might well cause alarm to animal-rights activists today. Some chickens are eaten as young as a fortnight from birth having been kept in a permanent light and supplied with fattening food continuously 'they will be so fat (when they are but of the bigness of a Blackbird) that they will not be able to stand'. They are also cooped in so small a space that they cannot turn round; to do the poultry keepers justice there is also much insistence on regular cleaning of the pens and troughs.

Commentators on *The Closet* always remark on the felicity of Digby's language and rightly so. One is charmed that oatmeal boiling for Water Gruel should 'rise in a great ebullition, in great galloping waves' and that when icing a cake, after the first application the cake is set to dry and 'if there be any unevenness, or cracks or discolouring, lay on a little more of that Mortar.' When making tea 'the water is to remain upon it no longer that whiles you can say the *Miserere* Psalm very leisurely.'

It is impossible to convey the full flavours of *The Closet* in a paper such as this. Despite having been put together after his death it is a very personal document full of the warmth and perhaps rather unfocussed enthusiasm of the man. It also poses a number of questions. How and why did he collect all these recipes? It seems unlikely that someone should collect over a hundred recipes for one drink without having some future purpose in mind. What governed his choice of culinary recipes? Was there an element of snobbery – many of them have personal names attached, often aristocratic? Did he select recipes which he had personally enjoyed or found interesting from a culinary point of view? Certainly they are not copies from the rather sparse collection of printed cookery books which would have been available to him, though many of them are for dishes and types of cookery which seem to have been popular at the time. The answer here may well be that because of the few collections available, it behoved each household to make its own collection and his known interest in culinary matters probably made it easy for him to acquire a recipe in which he was interested. Mutual exchange of recipes must have been a common practice at the time. This may be why he appears as one of the dedicatees in Robert May's *The Accomplisht Cook*, since there is no evidence that he ever employed May, though both men moved in the same Catholic circle.

It was in the same Catholic background that Sir John Fortescue was brought up. His mother was Grace Manners – the child of the romantic elopement of John Manners and Dorothy Vernon – and though her mother's background was Catholic, it was not until she was the wife of Sir Francis Fortescue of Salden in Buckinghamshire that she was truly confirmed in the Catholic faith by the Jesuit Father Gerrard. After she was widowed she, together with one of her sons William and his wife Anne Webb, bought Husbands Bosworth Hall near Market Harborough, Leicestershire, possibly because Anne Webb's family lived there. It is in this house, which has now descended through many marriages within the old Catholic families, to Mr. Robert Constable-Maxwell, that the recipe book is found.

It has in it the name Dorothy Legat and the date 1655, but neither the family nor any subsequent researches so far provide any clue as to who Dorothy Legat was. The book has some 160 pages containing about 260 recipes, culinary and medicinal and is written in at least eight different hands. The family tradition is that it has always been in the house but unfortunately not enough family records of the second half of the 17th century have survived for any of the hands to be positively identified. The view, among those archivists who have seen it, is that it was written over a comparatively short period possibly extending just into the 18th century. Certainly the style and spelling of the later entries seem rather more modern, but the background and education of the writers might well account for this.

Of the recipes the largest number, some 77, are for preserving fruit and vegetables and meat. Hardly surprising since the well-being of the household depended on these products during the winter! They are followed, not literally, since there is no sequence in the book, by 67 recipes for sweetened foods, biscuits, puddings, cakes and pastries, 56 for meat, mostly stews and hashes, and 20 for fish. Medicinal and household recipes amount to some 45, and finally there is what appears to be a draft challenge by a disappointed suitor to his rival in love! This is written in the same hand as several of the recipes.

There is still a lot of work to be done on the book. Comparison with other known collections of the period has only just begun and there are still some words undeciphered, but so far it seems that comparatively few of the recipes are direct copies though many inevitably are for popular dishes of the period such as Calves Head Hash and Quaking Pudding. Of those positively identified as copies, the ubiquitous 'To make Snow with Craime' appears in the exact wording of the recipe in *The Compleat Cook* 1655 and very close to the recently re-printed 1685 edition of Robert May's *The Accomplisht Cook*. The connection with May is interesting: at the time of the publication of the first edition of his book in 1660 he was working for the Catholic Lady Englefield (née Brooksby) of Saxelby also in Leicestershire some 15-20 miles from Husbands Bosworth. There are other recipes in the early part of Dorothy Legat which have a close connection with both *The Compleat Cook* and

Robert May: 'To make the best sausages that ever was eate' where the title and wording are almost exactly as in *The Compleat Cook* and very close to Robert May, and 'To make Allmon Biskett' which is very similar in May and in *A Queen's Delight* (the companion volume to *The Compleat Cook* – both parts of *The Queen's Closet Opened* by W.M.). There are also several which appear in *Martha Washington's Booke of Cookery* and are close enough to suggest that the compiler of that book and 'Dorothy Legat' were drawing on a common source.

Other recipes vary very much in their style and completeness, some being hardly more than lists of ingredients. Others are rather more detailed though not always very well expressed, such as a recipe for a Spreade Eagle early in the book where, while it is possible to understand that a young pullet is to be spatchcocked in a fashion and then apparently reconstituted with its minced flesh, it is almost impossible to follow the whole process through. Certainly none of the instructions has the clarity which Elizabeth David so much admired in Robert May, but he after all was a professional and writing for publication whereas Dorothy Legat's recipes are a collection of domestic recipes which were of interest to the writers and sometimes hardly more than an aide-memoire. Among those perhaps of more note is a butter/flour liaison in a sauce for fish, a recipe for Chocolate Puffs, one for a potato pie, an olive pie, Napill biskies and one 'To make an orior of a Sweet Boun of Porke or a ffillett of veale' in which a spiced pickle is prepared into which the meat is apparently put raw for three days and then dressed – presumably cooked – but the only instruction about this is to baste it with fresh butter. I haven't so far been able to find any other reference to an 'orior'.

Although there was the family connection with Kenelm Digby, none of his recipes as such is to be found except his Aqua Mirabilis which is an exact copy. The two recipes for mead and metheglin are not among his, nor does the *Closet Opened* provide any clue to the curiously named 'The King's Diad Drink'. Perhaps the most surprising recipe of all, sandwiched between 'To make little cakes' and 'A Cordiall Lectuary...' is 'A Better Receipt than the best that ever was made use of to procure Love' which begins 'Take 12 gallons of the best Compliments and all the sweet angredants you can find to these you must add a good bag of money, derive your family from an ancient and honourable Race, you must be the very extract of ...' and here alas it has so far proved indecipherable.

BIBLIOGRAPHY

Aubrey, John. 1. *Brief Lives. A Selection based upon existing contemporary portraits*. Ed. Richard Barber. The Folio Society, 1975.
    2. *The Worlds of John Aubrey. A further selection of Brief Lives together with excerpts from his writings on antiquities, science and folklore*. Ed. Richard Barber. The Folio Society, 1988.
Belloc, Hilaire. *Oliver Cromwell*. (A modern Catholic viewpoint). Ernest Benn Ltd., 1927.
Bligh, E.W. *Sir Kenelm Digby and his Venetia*. Sampson Low, Marston and Co. 1932.
Clark, Sir George. *The Later Stuarts, 1660-1714*. Clarendon Press, 2nd ed. 1955.
Davies, Godfrey. *The Early Stuarts, 1603-1660*. Clarendon Press, 2nd ed. 1959.
Grigson, Geoffrey. *The Englishman's Flora*. Phoenix House, 1958. Paladin, 1985.
Hess, Karen, ed. *Martha Washington's Booke of Cookery*. Columbia University Press, 1981.
Kenyon, J.P. *The Stuarts. A Study in English Kingship*. B.T.Batsford, 1958.
Latham, Robert and William Matthews, eds. *The Diary of Samuel Pepys* G. Bell and Sons, 11 volumes, 1970-1983.
The Recipe Book of Dorothy Legat, 1655. Microfilm of the manuscript book held by the Leicestershire Records Office, Long Street, Wigston Magna, Leicester LE18 2AH.
Macdonell, Anne, ed. *The Closet of Sir Kenelm Knight Opened*. Philip Lee Warner, 1910.
McElwee, William. *England's Precedence*. Hodder & Stoughton, 1956.
May, Robert. *The Accomplisht Cook*. 1660/1685. Facsimile, Prospect Books, 1990.
Mennell, Stephen. *All Manners of Food*. Blackwell, 1985.
Murrell, John. *Two Books of Cookerie and Carving*, 1638. Facsimile, Jacksons of Ilkley, 1985.

Nott, John. *The Cooks and Confectioners Dictionary*, 1723/1726. Facsimile, Lawrence Rivington, with glossary by Elizabeth David, 1980.
Parkinson, John. *Paradisus in Sole*. London, 1629.
Petersson, R.T. *Sir Kenelm Digby*, Jonathan Cape, 1956.
Scott Thompson, Gladys. *Life in a Noble Household, 1641-1700.* Jonathan Cape, 1937.
Wilson, C.Anne. *Food and Drink in Britain*. Constable, 1973.
WM. *The Compleat Cook and A Queens Delight*, 1655/1671. Facsimile, Prospect Books, 1984.

REFERENCES

[1] 'Digby was exceptionally sophisticated for his age (15), mature when most students were hardly out of childhood. Bacon entered the university at twelve, Essex at ten, and Edward de Vere, Earl of Oxford, at only eight. R.T. Petersson. p 35.

[2] Affectionate pen-portraits of both Thomas Allen and Richard Napier are given by John Aubrey in vol 2.

[3] Digby fled to the Queen-Dowager's court from Paris to escape the Plague, but only escaped from her bedroom by blurting out his love for Venetia and bolting past the men-at-arms on guard. Next day he was out of her reach en route for Italy.

[4] Digby's most notorious 'cure' *The Powder of Sympathy,* is described in detail on pp 55-6 of R.T.Petersson's biography.

[5] Prince Charles's return from Spain caused English rejoicing, and Digby was knighted by King James with the help of Buckingham, the King's favourite, who guided the sword. The king was much mocked as a result.

[6] See Petersson p 73 .

[7] Only two of Digby's children outlived their father. They were John, Sir Kenelm's least favoured son, and a daughter whom he never mentioned.

[8] It is interesting to compare Digby's.work as a naval commissioner with Pepys's 30 years later. See (1) Petersson p 85 -87, and Bligh p 166 – 168 and (2) Pepys, ed Latham and Mathews. Vol 1. Introd: p xxxi.

[9] For Digby's period in the Anglican church see Petersson p 93 – 5 and 110.

[10] Venetia's sudden death caused some argument that it might have been caused by her husband trying to 'improve' her complexion with viper wine . But it seems more plausible to.attribute it to a massive stroke. Such a stroke can, I understand, produce a physical loss of brain tissue.

[11] For Digby's lecture, *A Discourse concerning the Vegetation of Plants,* see Petersson p 298-9.

[12] See Petersson p 123-4.

[13] Bladder and kidney 'stones' were one of the chief miseries of the age, and often fatal. They were usually due largely to a high protein diet.

[14] Digby's own alchemical 'Cure.' See note 4 above.

[15] Petersson.p 292.

[16] For English food prices in the mid-17th century see Scott Thomson.

An Exhibition of Cooks, Pots and Crockery
Culinary Utensils in Greek Art, Myth & History
organised by
Rosemary Barron and Linda Makris

> Make ready then: the cooler, the basin, the tripod,
> The cup, the pot, the mortar, casserole and spoon.
>
> Athenaeus, quoting Antiphanis
> *Deipnosophistae* II 86, Epitome.

The exhibition was dedicated to the cooks of the past - the *archimagiroi* of ancient Greece - and their contribution to civilisation. To illustrate the continuity of this time-honoured Greek culinary tradition, photographs of archaeological finds from the Minoan, Classical, Hellenistic and Byzantine periods of Greek history and some references from ancient Greek literature were juxtaposed with traditional utensils still in use in Greece today. Many of these objects are ceramic, because metal has always been expensive while clay is plentiful, cheap and easily moulded into any shape. It is the original plastic material, the root coming from the ancient Greek word *plasso* - to form or create something. Also included were a few items made of reeds and wood.

The organisers wish to thank Ms. Noella Pallagini and Kraft Hellas A.E. of Greece, without whose generous support the exhibition would not have been possible. In addition we would like to thank Mr. George Charalambopoulos, Professor Brian Sparkes of the University of Southampton, Dr. Susan Rotroff and Mrs. Jan Jordan of the Athenian Agora Excavation (American School of Classical Studies), Ms. Virginia Crocker of the American Embassy, Athens, Chris Veneris of Crete and Christos Iliades for their advice and assistance.

BIBLIOGRAPHY

Athenaeus, *Deipnosophistae*, tr. C.D.Yonge, 1895.
Bakirtzis, Ch., *Byzantine Tsouklolagena*, Athens 1989.
Barron, Rosemary, *Flavors of Greece*, NY 1991 and London 1993.
Bozi, Soula, *Politiki Kouzina*, Athens 1994.
Charalambopoulos, Georgios, articles on Greek food history in *Taste*, Athens 1990-93
Homer, *The Odyssey*, tr. Robert Fitzgerald, NY 1961.
Homer, *The Iliad,* tr. Richard Lattimore, NY 1951.
Paradissi, Chryssa, *The Best of Greek Cookery*, Athens 1976.
Perry, Clay, *Vanishing Greece*, London 1991 and NY 1992.
Rhomiopoulou, Katerina, 'An Outline of Macedonian History & Art' in *The Search for Alexander* Exhibition Catalogue 1980.
Sparkes, B.A. & L.Talcott, *Pots and Pans of Classical Athens*, Princeton 1951,1977.
    —, 'Black & Plain Pottery of the 6th, 5th & 4th Centuries BC' in *The Athenian Agora* XII, Princeton 1970.
Sparkes, Brian A., 'The Greek Kitchen' in *Journal of Hellenic Studies* 82 1962.
Thompson, Dorothy B., *An Ancient Shopping Centre - The Athenian Agora*, Princeton   1971.
Wilkins, John & Shaun Hill, *The Life of Luxury: Archestratus*, Prospect Books 1994.

Louis-Camille Maillard and Subsequent Gravy Makers

A. Blake

There are many scientists who do superb science in their lifetime and yet remain largely unknown outside their peer group; there are also those scientists who do very little real science in their field yet become popularly recognised as experts in their subject. There are, however, relatively few scientists who do no work in a particular field of science and yet become so well known that their names are included in its scientific language. Such is the case with Louis-Camille Maillard who never worked on food related problems as such and yet there can be nobody in the food and its related industries who has not heard of his name. In a check on the data base of the Food Research Association at Leatherhead under the word Maillard I found 760 references to articles written in the last 6 years and in the last few years there have been several international conferences devoted exclusively to discussing the Maillard reaction. In this short paper today I would like to talk a little about the man who without trying gained such fame and also the significance of his work; as my title suggests I intend to follow the story through what I call the subsequent Gravy Makers.

A century before the work of Maillard the processes by which cooked food develops its flavour had already fascinated people such as Brillat-Savarin who in 1826 discussed the subject at length in his book *The Physiology of Taste*[1]. In particular the work of Rouelle, Thouvenal and Fourcroy in France on the analysis of meat interested him enormously. In his lifetime the name 'Ozmazome' was introduced by Louis Jacques Thenard and this substance was claimed to be responsible for the savoury taste in cooked meat and bouillons; indeed it was believed for some time that this was caused by a single component produced during the cooking of meat.

Louis-Camille Maillard who was to play such a prominent part in the subsequent understanding of meat flavour was born in 1878 at Pont-à-Mousson in France and had studied at the University of Nancy to receive his medical doctorate at the age of twenty-five with his thesis entitled 'Les recherches sur l'indoxyle urinaire et les couleurs qui en dérivent'. He continued his research but now his attention turned to the subject which was to lead to his fame; he was interested in the way in which amino acids could combine with other constituents found in living cells and initially looked at their reactions with glycerol; this led him into almost eight years of study into the chemistry which takes place between amino acids and sugars, the group of complex chemical changes now grouped under the generic title, the Maillard reaction. He found that when solutions of these materials were heated together they reacted and slowly turned brown. Maillard's initial results published in 1912 mentioned the consequences of these reactions to the physiology of plants and animals[2] but made no mention of food although his second report[3] in the same year did make reference to the occurrence of these reactions in baking and brewing processes and Maillard acknowledged mention of the reactions between amino acids and sugars in a paper[4] given in 1908 by Arthur Robert Ling, lecturer in brewing and malting, at the Sir John Cass Institute. In the next few years there were one or two papers published which discussed the signficance of Maillard's work to the fermentation of sugars and the production of malt but essentially it passed into relative obscurity for the next thirty years and as with many other scientific developments it was the demands of the second world war which were to reopen interest in it.

The supply of food to soldiers in tropical regions of the world was of specific interest to the Americans. It was realised that many of the deteriorative changes in dried and preserved food were associated with browning processes and a problem which had long been recognised as a nuisance now became strategically important. During the war the US government under the sponsorship of the Quartermaster General had set up a co-ordinated study into the underlying chemistry of changes which impaired food quality. A key paper was published in 1947 by two scientists at General Foods research facility at Hoboken N.J.[5] In their introduction, Barnes and Kaufman wrote:

> The authors believe that...there is... sufficient justification for the importance now assigned to the Maillard or browning reaction insofar as the food industry is concerned and its eventual control assumes great importance in our plans for research today.
>
> The present authors now believe that, in addition to being responsible for many deteriorative changes that occur in food products, the Maillard reation may also be the contributing factor in the development of many of our characteristic food flavours. Although no evidence is yet available, there is reason to suspect that the distinctive flavour differences in breakfast foods, the crust of baked bread, roasted coffee etc. may be attributed to chemical combinations brought about during the heat treatment operation.
>
> This area is only now beginning to unfold. Fundamental research on this aspect may provide a means of chemically synthesising some flavours which will nearly approximate the natural flavours.

Their comments were prophetic and within a year the first patent which acknowledges the Maillard reaction was filed for the production of a synthetic maple flavour.

It was not only in America that the war had changed the way governments thought about food related issues. In Britain in the late 40's the nutrition of the nation and the continued need for rationing was still a topic of government concern. In an attempt to eliminate the general shortage of fats and proteins in the diet the 'Groundnuts Scheme' was launched as a project to industrialise on a massive scale the growing of peanuts in Africa and their subsequent processing into edible oil and protein. One of the side effects of this project was the prototype development of industrial processes for texturising vegetable proteins and within the next twenty years there were considerable sums of money spent on the development of meat substitutes from peanuts, soya beans and other vegetable sources. It was realised, of course, that if such products were ever to be accepted by the public then they would also need to taste and smell like meat and the Unilever company with its involvement in many different food industries was heavily committed to these developments. At their research laboratories in the UK and Holland a programme of work was started to examine how to create authentic meat-like flavours synthetically. At this time the skills and equipment of the analytical chemists had been improving dramatically and its was increasingly possible to isolate, identify and synthesise the chemicals which give rise to flavour in many of our foods; the early attempts to analyse the flavour of cooked meat, however, rapidly ran into trouble. Whereas with a fruit such as strawberry the analysis could identify several tens of components responsible for flavour, in the case of cooked meat hundreds of chemical species were found to be present. What made it worse was that none of the more abundant chemicals appeared to possess any identifiable meat flavour as such. In an attempt to get around these difficulties a small group of scientists at Colworth House near Bedford in the UK decided that instead of analysing cooked meat, they would analyse raw meat and try to find the chemicals responsible for generating meat flavour on cooking. The key and now classical experiment they did was to grind up raw beef and to extract this with cold water. The extract was then dialysed or filtered in such a way as to separate the small molecules from the large. The fraction which contained only small molecules was examined by paper chromatography and was found to contain amino acids and sugars. Moreover on heating this solution several of the amino acids and sugars disappeared and recognisably beefy odours were generated. The consequent patents taken out by Unilever in the names of Morton, Ackroyd and May[6] were a major turning point in meat flavour research. Vegetable protein and meat analogues subsequently proved to be at least forty years too early for public acceptance but the growing convenience foods industry assured a need for authentic meat flavours and underlined once again the importance of the Maillard reaction; this was to give it and its discoverer much fame. During the heat processing of many foodstuffs the chemical reactions which create the smell of baking bread, the odour of roasting meat and the flavour of chocolate start primarily by the initial reactions of sugars and amino acids which are present in the uncooked ingredients. The initial steps in a complex cascade of reactions are the thermal breakdown of these two groups of compounds together with the products they form by reacting together. In particular the combination of the reactive amine group of the amino acid and the carbonyl group of the aldose sugar is a key first step. What then happens is far from simple because the initial products of this first stage can rearrange their structure and react in increasingly complex ways (Fig.1). By different reaction routes and depending on the cooking conditions many types of molecular structure can be formed and some of these have remarkably low odour threshold values.

Specific reference to gravy is made in the title because it is in the area of meat flavour that most work has been directed toward unravelling the chemistry of this process. When one tastes a piece of uncooked steak the flavour is mild and slightly salty; put this steak into a hot frying pan or onto the grill of a barbecue for a few minutes and the flavour changes profoundly; in those few minutes literally hundreds of chemical species have been generated and many of them have now been identified. A number of review papers are available for further information on this subject.[7,8] The most important sugar in meat from a flavour point of view is ribose or its phosphate derivative ribose-5'-phosphate; ribose is a sugar from the aldopentose series. Different amino acids play different roles in food flavours but in the case of meat flavour it is known that the amino acid cysteine has a particularly important significance. Cysteine is one of only two naturally occurring amino acids

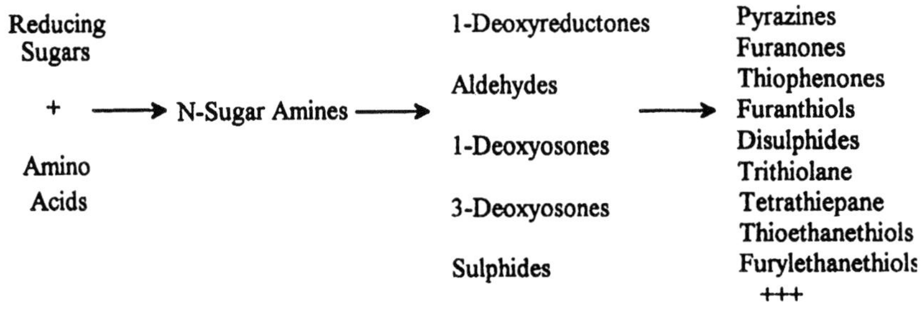

```
Reducing                        1-Deoxyreductones      Pyrazines
Sugars                                                 Furanones
                                Aldehydes              Thiophenones
   +      ⟶  N-Sugar Amines ⟶                     ⟶  Furanthiols
                                1-Deoxyosones          Disulphides
Amino                                                  Trithiolane
Acids                           3-Deoxyosones          Tetrathiepane
                                                       Thioethanethiols
                                Sulphides              Furylethanethiols
                                                       +++
```

Figure 1: Progressive complexity of the Maillard reaction

which contain a sulphur atom and in cysteine the sulphur atom is rather reactive. It is now realised that it is from this source that many sulphur containing molecules are created during cooking (see Fig.2).

It is interesting to digress a little at this point and to consider the evolution of our cooking traditions. Since the time of the Egyptians and perhaps even earlier, garlic, onions and other alliaceous vegetables have been associated with the cooking of meat and it is a feature of all these vegetables that they contain sulphur compounds. It seems more than likely that the cooking of meat with such vegetables leads to chemical reactions which accentuate the meatiness of the final dish by generating specific sulphur containing molecules during the cooking. Such sulphur containing molecules are among the most powerful odorants known and contribute significantly to the flavour of cooked meat. A recently identified compound[9] found in cooked meat is shown in Fig. 3. What is remarkable about this and several similar sulphur containing molecules is that they can be detected in water at levels as low as 2 parts in 10^{14}. To put this fact another way, if you can imagine a lake that is 2 metres deep and some 8 km in diameter, then 2 gms of this chemical would give the water a noticeably beefy taste!

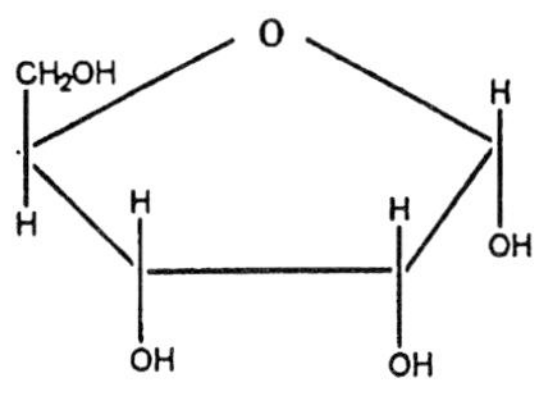

Figure 2.

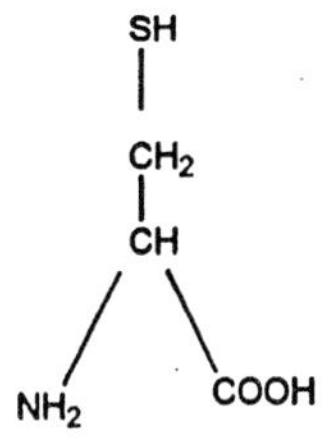

In addition to the sugars and amino acids, we now know that fat can play an important and subtle role in the generation of meat flavour. Fat is particularly important in giving the different flavours from different animals; the flavour of cooked chicken is quite different from duck, and beef from pork. Certain fat soluable components modify the overall flavour during cooking and are largely responsible for these species' specific differences. Not only can the fat add to the overall cocktail of chemicals present in the raw meat but it can fundamentally change the course of the reaction during cooking. Many compounds formed during the cooking process are to different degrees soluble in either water or fat. When meat is cooked in the presence of both fat and water there is a continuous partitioning of the chemicals between these two phases and the subsequent products of the reaction are dependent on the proportions of fat and water which are present. If we add to all the above possibilities the fact that we often cook meat in the presence of herbs, spices and vegetables then we start to realise just how complex cooked meat flavour can actually be. Today there is a major industrial production of meat-like flavourings which are used in soups, gravies and convenience foods. At the last count roughly one thousand chemical compounds have

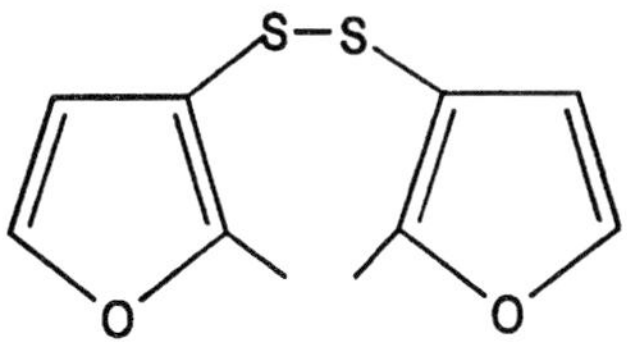

Figure 3: Bis-2-methyl-3-Furyl-Disulphide

been identified in the various cooked meats we eat and there is no sign that research in this area of food flavouring is decreasing.

But this lecture is about Maillard so let us return to the man himself. Louis-Camille Maillard was one of those scientists who bridged the gap between the 19th and 20th century. He was a meticulous and careful researcher who published his first book on his work in 1913. In 1914 he moved to Paris as the head of a biological group in the Chemical Laboratory of the University of Paris but his work was interrupted by the 1914-18 war. In 1919 he became professor of biological and medical chemistry at the University of Algiers where he spent the rest of his life until he died suddenly during a visit to Paris at the age of 58. In his career he had published some hundred or so papers on medical topics ranging from the determination of titanium in the human body to his work on establishing an index for ureological disorders. Nevertheless it is in the vocabulary of the food scientist that the name of Maillard will be most used and remembered.

REFERENCES

[1] Brillat-Savarin, J.A. *The Physiology of Taste* (1826) Tr. M.F.K. Fisher, 1949. Reprint San Francisco: North Point, 1986.

[2] Maillard, L-C. 'Action des Acides Aminés sur les Sucres. *Comptes Rendus Hebdomadaires de Sánces de l'Académie des Sciences* 154, 66-68 (1912)

[3] Maillard, L-C. 'Action des Acides Aminés sur les Sucres. *Comptes Rendus Hebdomadaires de Séances de l'Académie des Sciences* 155 1554-56 (1912)

[4] Ling, A.R. *J. Inst. Malting and Brewing 14*, 494-52 (1908).

[5] Barnes H.M. & Kaufman C.W. 'Industrial Aspects of Browning Reaction', *Ind. & Chem 39* 1167-1170 (1947).

[6] Morton I.D., Akroyd P., May C.G. British Patent 836,694 (1960)

[7] Macleod, G. & Seyyedain-Ardebili, M. (1981) Natural and Simulated Meat Flavours (with particular reference to beef) CRC Critical Reviews in *Food Science and Nutrition*. 14, 309-437 (1981).

[8] Bailey, M.E. 'Maillard Reactions and Meat Flavours Development' Chapter 9 in *Flavour of Meat Products* Ed. F. Shahidi, Blackie 1994.

[9] Farmer, L.J. & Patterson, R.L.S. (1991) 'Compounds Contributing to Meat Flavour', *Food Chem. 40*. 201-205 (1991).

A Lasting Tribute to the Roman Goddess Ceres: The Cereal Kings and Their Product Prodigy Nourish the World

Fritz Blank

No other tetrad of individuals better personifies the subject of this symposium: *Cooks and Others who have influenced what we eat – for better or for worse*, than does the team of Sylvester Graham, John Harvey Kellogg, Will Keith Kellogg and Charles W. Post. The history and ongoing progress of 'healthful' and 'convenient' dried and/or instant cereal breakfast foods as well as their worldwide distribution and enjoyment is a remarkable story. Born from the womb of a Seventh Day Adventist vegetarian health food craze in 1836, nurtured by a 'Sanitarium'[1], and marketed by the genius of a brilliant businessman, breakfast flakes have indeed changed the way the world eats breakfast.

Sylvester Graham (1794-1851), John Harvey Kellogg (1852-1943), Willie Keith Kellogg (1860-1951) and Charles Wilson Post (1854-1914) were the dietary reformers from which today's global billion dollar breakfast food industry was born. Is there a person alive today – save perhaps an undiscovered primitive tribe in some very remote jungle of South America – who has not tasted corn flakes, or some other dried breakfast cereal product?

Sylvester Graham became a Presbyterian minister in 1826, but did very little preaching. Instead he became a zealot for temperance and vegetarianism. To this end, he travelled and lectured extensively on a complete health regimen including hard mattresses, cold showers, and a diet consisting of home-made bread, rough cereals, fruits and vegetables. He promoted the use of unsifted, coarsely ground wheat – so-called 'Graham flour' – and invented the Graham Cracker ©in 1829. He once was attacked by a mob of bakers and butchers during one of his lectures. (Dr. John Kellogg was also physically attacked more than once while proselytizing his cause.)

Chronologically, it was Graham who should be given credit for the origin of the modern breakfast-cereal industry. It was he and his many publications of books, booklets, pamphlets and flyers who first influenced both Kellogg and Post. However, he is rarely given just credit, probably because the real hard-line marketing of these breakfast 'health' foods was accomplished by W.K. Kellogg and C.W. Post.

Thus we remember Graham for his Graham Crackers© and to a lesser extent for the 'Graham' or 'Temperance' boarding houses which sprang up in New York City and Boston. The best known of these was an experimental communal house in Brook Fair, Massachusetts, near Boston. Differing from older classic 'spas' – which emphasised the curing power of water, Graham's new venues emphasised 'total healthful living' – including a vegetarian diet – as a means to achieve godliness. Philadelphia too, served for a time as a popular meeting place for such health-cum-religious groups. This movement would later be epitomised by 'The San' in Battle Creek, Michigan, which was so masterfully operated and promoted by Dr. John Harvey Kellogg and his brother Will.

John Harvey Kellogg was born in 1852, the fifth child of his mother, Ann Jeanette, and the tenth of his father, John Preston Kellogg. As the father and founder of the 'Battle Creek Idea', J.H. Kellogg was brought up with deep religious convictions[2] which were only strengthened by the trials of 'frontier' (Michigan) living. To be sure, life on the American western frontier in the mid-19th century was tough and the lack of competent medical care and doctors[3] took its toll.[4]

With intervention from James ('Elder') and his wife Ellen ('Sister') White – Adventist leaders and founders of *The Western Health Reform Institute* – and after suffering a bout of tuberculosis, John Harvey Kellogg travelled to Florence Heights, New Jersey and attended a course at The Hygieno-Therapeutic College. This was followed by continued studies at State Normal in Ypsilanti, Michigan; The University of Michigan Medical School; and the Bellevue Hospital Medical College in New York City. Financial and spiritual support for this education was provided by the Whites. On October 1, 1876, John Harvey returned home and the health revolution in Battle Creek began.

J.H. Kellogg's younger sibling, Will Keith Kellogg – who would eventually be the single driving-force behind the formation and operation of one of the world's largest and most profitable breakfast cereal manufacturing corporations, The Kellogg Company – in the meantime, was waiting on the sidelines while his brother was becoming a world-respected physician and surgeon. First a worker in his father's broom factory and store and later as a successful travelling broom salesman, W.K. Kellogg graduated from the Adventist sectarian 'select school'[5] in Battle Creek, Michigan and then moved to Texas where he spent some time with another broom manufacturer owned in part by 'Elder' James White. Will hated Texas, and homesickness and lovesickness eventually convinced him to move back to Michigan. Kalamazoo and a course of study at the Parson's Business College earned him a certificate as a 'bookkeeper' and 'accountant'.

Beginning in 1880, the future President and C.E.O. of a one-hundred million dollar business would spend the next 25 years of his life as an 'affiliate' with (and often subservient to) 'The Doctor' – as Will caused his big brother – and The Battle Creek Sanitarium. During this time he was paid $9.00 per week(!) for working a minimum of 120 hours.[6] Among the many responsibilities heaped upon him, Will Kellogg became an astute business manager and was largely, and single-handedly, responsible for the financial success of 'The San'.

Near the close of the century, Will Kellogg began to rebel against 'the Doctor's' autocratic authority. It has been suggested that this was perhaps the result of 'middle-age restlessness'. Over the year, he had manipulated his position at the 'San', and was in a position to mount his revolt against his brother's conservative philosophies – especially regarding advertising and sales. To this end, he already envisioned a national general food business of yet undreamed of proportions. The formation of the Sanitas Company which evolved into The Kellogg Company was the first step in this new direction.

W.K. Kellogg next orchestrated a bold marketing turn from health food products to products which tasted good and which would be appealing to the public at large. He reasoned soundly and correctly that there were more well people than sick people, and sales (and resultant profits) should be so directed.

The elder Dr. Kellogg was not happy about this and, in fact, forbad his name to be used in association with these new general breakfast food products. Thus, W.K. Kellogg surrogated his own name, with the firm belief that the name 'Kellogg' should be a distinguishing trade mark sold by their company although it was still called Sanitas at this time. He also adapted the phrase: 'None genuine without the signature of W.K. Kellogg', which of course has remained a charter hallmark and standard of quality recognised throughout the food manufacturing industry.

1916 found a flood of imitators clamouring for a share of the money being made via these new, quick, delicious, convenient and easily stored breakfast foods. None was so competitive or as close to home as the Postum Cereal company.

Charles Wilson Post was born on 26 October 1854 in Springfield, Illinois. During his early adulthood, he was plagued with general ill-health and suffered variously from such disorders as dyspepsia, nervous exhaustion, and general malaise, to the point of being unable to work for months at a time. An inventor and entrepreneur, Post's mercurial alternations of financial success and total business failure supposedly contributed to his poor health.

It is ironic perhaps that four years before the discovery of any breakfast flake, C.W. Post admitted himself to the care of Dr. Kellogg and his Sanitarium. However, the future cereal mogul and competitor and serious rival of the Kellogg Company, was unaffected by the 'Battle Creek Idea' and in spite of all the biological treatments and dietary regimens – including light baths, diatherapy, enemas, massages, and a patented vibrating chair – he remained 'uncurable'. At one point, Ella Post was told by Dr. Kellogg himself: 'Ella, I think you should know that C.W. has very little time left. He is not going to get well. I have done everything I know how to do.'

Leaving 'The San' in November 1891, Post was put into the care of a cousin-in-law and follower of Mary Baker Edy[7], a Mrs. Elizabeth Gregory, who 'cured' Post, employing the 'natural suggestions' of this new-found religious therapy. Thus began Post's quest for 'the road to welville.'

In addition to a dedication to mental therapeutics and the healing power of faith and prayer, Post also remained convinced that certain foods did affect health, viz. that coffee was deleterious to one's well being. In keeping with his aptitude for inventiveness, he eventually perfected a tasty ersatz coffee which became Postum©. Ever the ambitious entrepreneur, and rejuvenated by his newly regained health, Post soon established in 1892 his own version of Kellogg's health spa, which he dubbed *La Vita Inn*. Almost simultaneously he began to manufacture Postum© in large commercial quantities, and created the Postum Cereal Coffee Ltd., as a subsidiary of La Vita Inn. Recognising caffeine as an addictive substance which he described as 'a poisonous drug', he mounted a mammoth campaign against coffee while advocating its replacement, of course, by his delicious and healthful cereal drink, Postum©. ('It builds red blood.') In 1897 Post sold $262,279 worth of product, but ploughed it right back into yet more aggressive advertising.

In 1898 as an effort to save a failed second *faux* coffee drink, Post converted the product into a cold breakfast cereal which was christened Grape-Nuts.[8] Grape-Nuts© was then marketed with the same aggressive advertising that bolstered the sale of Postum©. Post then became, and is remembered today as, the 'grandfather of advertising'. His success continued when he offered his own rendition of a corn flake product named Elijah's Manna which initially failed to sell, but quickly recovered when renamed Post Toasties©!

Price wars with The Kellogg Company, and competition with other product imitations by 'Me-Too'[9] companies resulted in outrageous statements by Post. A messy legal battle ensued over his often controversial advertising methods and product claims, some of which took decades to settle. Eventually Post's curmudgeon-like cranky personality, his amassed wealth, and some Ross Perot-like political ambitions found him in Washington D.C. where he became less and less interested in the cereal business. Post Cereal Company became General Foods, Inc.

Failing health, fatigue, and a succession of ailments began to plague Post again, and in 1913 he suffered a 'severe physical collapse'.[10] Weakened by disease and coupled with deep mental depression, on May 9 1914, Charles W. Post killed himself with a single 30-30 calibre shot to the head, leaving behind a $70 million estate and a corporate empire built on four products – Postum, Instant Postum, Grape-Nuts and Post Toasties – to his 27 year old daughter, Marjorie Merriweather Post, and instantly she became one of the richest women in the world.

BIBLIOGRAPHY

Powell, Horace B. *The Original Has This Signature – W.K. Kellogg*, 1956.
Bruce, Scott and Bill Crawford. *Cerealizing America: The Unsweetened Story of American Breakfast Cereal*, 1995.
Boyle, T. Coraghessan. *The Road to Wellville*, 1994.
Graham, Sylvester. *Graham on Bread*, 1837 (reprint by Lee Foundation for Nutritional Research)
Fussell, Betty. *The Story of Corn*, 1992.
Woodward, Ann. 'The Road to Battle Creek' *Food Historians of Ann Arbor:* Vol XI, No.2., 1995.

REFERENCES

[1] 'Sanitarium' – originally a misspelling of sanatorium (hospital) by Dr. John Harvey Kellogg – sanitarium is now an accepted cognate and used for various health venues such as spas, including the charter institute: The Battle Creek Medical 'Sanitarium'.

[2] J. Preston Kellogg, with his second wife Ann Jeanette, joined the Adventist movement (later to be called 'the Seventh Day Adventists') with its rather unorthodox religious beliefs, which included also total health reform. Of course, this born-again reformation of the elder Kelloggs included all of their children – John Harvey and Willie Keith as well.

[3] Actually, medical care and practices *anywhere* in the mid-nineteenth century were not especially good under any circumstances, since the level of state-of-the-art scientific knowledge was far behind what we know it to be today.

[4] Indeed, John Preston lost his first wife and a daughter due to atrocious medical practices which, in fact, bordered on witchcraft.

[5] Later to become The Battle Creek College.

[6] J.H.K. did not believe in holidays, although Saturdays were declared the official 'day of rest', as this was the dictum from the Seventh Day Adventist Church.

[7] The founder of the Christian Science movement.

[8] 'Grape' because it contained maltose – an erroneous epithet assigned by Post for 'grape sugar' – and 'nuts' because of its flavour.

[9] In 1911, 107 brands of corn flakes besides Kellogg's were packaged in Battle Creek!

[10] Rumour was that he had 'paresis' or 'Lewes Disease', both euphemisms for syphilis.

Utilis Coquinario and its Unnamed Author

Ruth Carroll

There be of them that have left a name behind them, that their praises might be reported. And some there be which have no memorial, who are perished as though they had never been.

Ecclesiasticus 44:8-9

We are gathered at this Symposium to recognise those individuals who have made substantial culinary contributions to history. Yet often such people have been forgotten or ignored because their names have been lost. I would like to discuss the unnamed individual responsible for a collection of recipes from the late fourteenth century known as *Utilis Coquinario* (I will abbreviate this to *UC*).[1]

It has been said, 'The first recipe books were written where there was both a repertoire of dishes and an eating-culture, and where there was literacy (noble courts and monasteries).'[2] The question of literacy is one to which I will return, but it is worth considering the internal evidence supporting an assessment of the nature of the Middle English recipe collections as aristocratic. A recipe in the *Diuersa Cibaria* collection states explicitly that it is to be served to a lord.[3] A recipe from Bodleian MS Rawlinson D 1222 is entitled 'Sawce sylico', which could mean 'lordly sauce'.[4] The most well-known piece of evidence is the preface to the *Forme of Cury* recipe collection, which states that it was compiled by the master chef to Richard II and contains recipes for *curyous metes for hyȝest astates* (curious foods for the highest estates).[5]

Arguments for the aristocratic nature of other medieval recipes can be based on their unsuitability for common households due to the techniques and ingredients required, or the quantity of food involved. The writer of a French fourteenth-century cookbook makes it clear that an elaborate dish described in it is 'not work for a citizen's cook, nor even for a simple knight's' because 'there is too much to do'.[6] Palatial kitchens such as those at Clarendon and the abbot's kitchen at Glastonbury were large enough for roasting whole oxen, although even the grand recipes of the *Forme of Cury* do not call for whole animals larger than pigs.[7] Within the *UC*, the recipe 'Eles in Counfy' [1][8] is more elaborate than French and Italian parallels, and the recipe for heron [13] is more elaborate even than that of the *Forme of Cury*.[9] The recipe for lamprey [24] involves baking it in an oven, which may indicate that it is intended for use in a castle or manor house since ordinary homes did not have an oven in which to bake.[10]

Expensive ingredients called for by our author include swan [11], which was the most costly of birds, reserved for feasts of the well-to-do,[11] as well as saffron and other spices. Saffron, selling at between fourteen and fifteen shillings per pound,[12] was called for in eleven of *UC*'s thirty-seven recipes. Almond milk, called for even more frequently than saffron in *UC*, was another 'costly imported ingredient' with 'snob appeal'.[13]

Once we accept that the English medieval cooking texts which survive are to do with large and wealthy households, we may discuss *UC*'s author more specifically. It should be borne in mind that to speak of the author of the text is not necessarily to speak of the person who wrote the words on the page, in fact, it is almost certain that our author did not write any of the manuscripts now extant. When we consider all the individuals responsible for a medieval culinary text, we must include those who invented or adapted the different recipes in the collection or translated them from another language (the *Diuersa Cibaria* collection was translated from at least two Anglo-Norman recipe collections),[14] the nobles who may have commissioned the collection, those scribes who made copies of the collection, those who bound the collections into manuscripts, and those who owned and preserved the manuscripts, particularly in our case British Library MS Sloane 468, used as the base manuscript for editing *UC*. The copyists or scribes may be the most important people to remember, since they may have changed the recipes by introducing errors.[15]

This study concerns the person responsible for choosing, perhaps creating or putting personal touches on the contents of this 'distinctive, if brief, collection'[16] It is certain to have been a man. Although it was true during the Middle Ages, as through most of history, that women were responsible for basic domestic cookery, it was men who worked in the kitchens of great houses.[17]

Assuming that our author was the head cook in the kitchen of a large, possibly noble household, what would his early life have been like? Parallels could be drawn from the life of Guillaume Tirel, also called Taillevent, a master chef in fourteenth-centutry France, whose name is associated with a compilation of recipes well known in medieval France, *Le Viandier de Taillevent*.[18] He began his career as kitchen boy (*happelapin*) to Jeannne d'Evreux, wife of Charles le Bel, and rose through the ranks to become master cook (*premier écuyer de cuisine*) to Charles VI. He is said to have been encouraged in his work on *Le Viandier* by Charles V.[19]

As a youth our subject might have been taught other skills necessary for the presentation of a feast, as set out in works such as the *Boke of Keruynge, For to serve a lord, and General rule to teche every man to serve a lorde or mayster*.[20] Working in the kitchens, he would have acquired the skills necessary for the sorts of elaborate recipes mentioned above. His own 'Mortreux of Fish' is divided in two, with each half coloured and spiced separately [26]. If at a royal household, a master chef could have been responsible for supervising the provision of food for nearly ten thousand people on a daily basis.[21] The work required for a feast could have been phenomenal, given that sumptuary laws were passed during the reign of Edward II and again under Edward III attempting to prevent excess in banquets.[22]

According to one historian's list of household help, the cook would have had responsibility for 'several grooms (trained staff) and underlings...waiters, and assistant waiters who brought the food only as far as the hall; assistant cooks, their scullions and spit-boys; pot-boys and bottle-washers', so would have needed to oversee their work and delegate tasks. The chief cook would have had to co-ordinate his own work with that of 'the sewer (head waiter), the pantler or panter (head of the pantry), the butler (in charge of drinks), the ewerer (in charge of hand-washing and linen),...the carver and the lord's cup-bearer'. He himself answered to the marshal (the chief official at dinner) and ultimately to the steward, in charge of the entire household.[23] However, once our subject had attained this high position his life, although filled with responsibility would have been comfortable. The master cook has been described as 'an experienced and influential person who had many lesser cooks beneath his supervision, [who] could earn a salary equivalent to three thousand pounds'.[24]

His talents went beyond even such practical culinary and managerial expertise, encompassing the skills necessary for the creation of a cookbook such as this, a task more impressive than some would have you believe.[25] Although some scholars fail to see order in the way medieval recipes are set out,[26] the *UC* groups together recipes for cooking birds, and for blancmange, ending with recipes involving fruits and flowers [31-37]. Our author may have been familiar with contemporary French texts,[27] revealing at least a reading knowledge of French. His adaptation of the French galantine (in his recipe for lamprey [24][28] is not unique, but the first of his four variations on blancmange [27] differs from English counterparts and is similar to the earliest form given in French cookbooks, in that it is garnished with pomegranate seeds (which were replaced by sugared aniseed comfits in most English recipes), and in not containing (whole grains of) rice.[29]

Our author, as was the case with most cooks of the age, took note of religious restrictions on meat consumption and fasting. His fourth variation on blancmange [30] is one for lent, containing fish rather than poultry. However, that is his only explicit mention of fasting. Recipes like [34] and [35], which allow either almond milk or cow's milk, would have been suitable for any season (dairy products were prohibited during lent), but he does not spell that out.[30] The medieval cook also had to consider the medical theories of the time, balancing ingredients considered hot or cold, and moist or dry to achieve the combinations considered optimum for ingestion. Although the degree to which this influenced the feast menus of the courts can be debated, medical concerns did seem to have a bearing on the willingness of a cook to write down his recipes. Returning to the preface of the *Forme of Cury*, we read that it states explicitly that it was compiled with the assent of physicians dwelling at the court.[31]

So why the interest in Mr X, the master chef responsible for the cookery text? What influence did his work have on cookery, both in his own day and later? The comments with which Hieatt and Butler introduce their edition of his text are a useful starting point for an examination of its legacy: 'While this manuscript group [*UC*] contains some of the inevitable standard fourteenth-century dishes such as 'Viaunde de Cypre' and 'Mawmene'[32] – to the latter eccentrically adding ground figs and raisins – it is interesting in preserving recipes which do not seem to appear elsewhere, such as 'Pyany' (a poultry dish garnished with peonies) and 'Heppee' (rose-hip broth).'[33] Their 'index and glossary' indicates that the *UC* recipes for 'Primerole' (primrose-flavoured pottage) and 'Fawne' (a pottage containing bean leaves and blossoms) are also unique.[34]

The text is also rare in providing recipes for almond cream and butter ('Crem & Botere of Almoundes' [5], and 'Botere of Almand Melk' [7].[35] Culinary historians lament the fact that there is only one extant medieval recipe which is specifically for almond milk,[36] although there do exist recipes for an almond pottage, at least one version of which is basically hot almond milk, 'Cheaut de Almondes' from *A Boke of Kokery* (Harleian MS 4016).[37]

For both the linguist and the historian, it is of interest to note not only the unique recipes contained within *UC*, but also the vocabulary. This collection is a good source of lists of similar items, words from the same semantic field. An excellent example is the list of birds in [15]: *crane, wodekok, botores, curlewes, comoraunz, pluuers, malardis, teeles, larkes, fynches, buntyngges*. These follow the mention of *pekokes & partriches* in [14],[38] and *heyroun* and *swan* in [13]. This is the only mention of woodcocks, *botores* (bittern), *pluuers* (plovers), and teals in the English fourteenth-century collections of culinary recipes, although all are found in fourteenth-century menus.[39] Cormorants and finches are not mentioned elsewhere in the corpus, even in menus. Other semantic fields well represented are flowers, fish, and of course spices.

What audience was meant to be addressed by his text? Historians agree that the level of lay literacy was rising, although the distribution of manuscripts was a 'patchy affair looked at from a modern point of view.'[40] In any case, it would be wrong to immediately assume that the primary task of every cookbook is to educate its readers in the art of cookery, or especially that those who do read cookbooks do so for that purpose. Dena Attar points out that it is difficult at the best of times to learn to cook from a cookbook, and that in many cases the cookbook serves other, sometimes more subtle purposes. She suggests that three functions were fulfilled by the medieval cookbooks: they served as a testimony to the skills of the cooks writing them (documenting the feasts they had prepared), they presented (and influenced) trends, fashions in food, and also secured the status of the master chef as a professional (as distinct from the domestic female cook).[41] The vocabulary of the text may also indicate that the intended audience consisted of other professionals.[42]

This is not to deny the usefulness of such texts as a historical record of diet, a point Attar concedes, although she cautions that theirs is the diet of a 'rich and powerful elite'.[43] They certainly are used by culinary historians, although scholars differ in the generalizations they are willing to draw based on these texts. One says that although the medieval cookbooks in question were 'compiled for and by cooks in royal or noble households, the food described in them was not confined to court circles', citing in evidence the preface of one manuscript of the *Forme of Cury*, which claims that it 'teacheth a man for to make...common meats for household...[and] curious meats... for all manner of states, both high and low'.[44] On the other hand, another manuscript of the same text (already quoted above) says that the *curyous metes* (curious dishes) are *for hyʒest astates* (for the highest estates) rather than *for alle manere of states both hye and lowe.*[45]

Our author's text is not, at any rate, an exceptionally extravagant one, at least in comparison to others which survive. There are calls for 'endoring', the process of gilding food, especially giving food a golden appearance by basting it with egg yolk.[46] Even our author's use of saffron, noted above, need not have implied lavish excess if care was taken in the quantities used. One household's records for 1418-1419 show the use of only three-quarters of a pound of saffron, as compared to five pounds of pepper, two and a half of ginger, three of cinnamon, one and a quarter of cloves and one and a quarter or mace.[47] For this reason, it is judged that 'even the moderately well-to-do' would have used saffron.[48]

Mr X, then, would have been the high-ranking chef of a large kitchen, but not one nearly as extravagant as, for example, that of Richard II. His work leaves us a record of culinary detail to supplement the other cooking manuals which survive (as well as literary and artistic portrayals of medieval dining habits). People still read and use his recipes even today. As recently as 1992, modern adaptations of his recipes were published in Maggie Black's *Medieval Cookbook*. Our anonymous author would be pleased to know that six centuries after the first appearance of his work, connoisseurs of good food continue to enjoy 'Mortreux of fish' [26] ('Departed' Creamed Fish), 'Blawmanger' [28] (Chicken with Rice and Almonds), and 'Syrosye' [33] (Cherry Pottage).[49]

BIBLIOGRAPHY

Attar, Dena. 1987. 'A feminist cookbook?' In Sue O'Sullivan. *Turning the tables*. 7-19.

Austin, Thomas (ed.). 1888. *Two fifteenth-century cookery-books: Harleian MS. 279 (ab. 1430), & Harl. MS. 4016 (ab. 1450): with extracts from Ashmole MS. 1439, Laud MS. 553, & Douce MS. 55*. London.

Bennett, H.S. 1969. *English books & readers: 1475-1557*. 2nd ed. Cambridge.

Berriedale-Johnson, Michelle. 1987. *The British Museum cookbook*. London.

Black, Maggie. 1992. *The Medieval cookbook*. New York.

—. 1993. 'Medieval Britain'. In Peter Brears, Maggie Black et al. *A taste of history: 10,000 years of food in Britain*. London. 94-135.

Braswell, Laurel. 1984. 'Utilitarian and scientific prose'. In A.S.G. Edwards (ed.) *Middle English prose: a critical guide to major authors and genres*. New Brunswick, N.J. 337-387.

Brereton, Georgine E. and Janet M. Ferrier (eds.). 1981. *Le Menagier de Paris*. Oxford.

Bynum, Caroline Walker. 1987. *Holy feast and holy fast: the religous significance of food to medieval women*. Berkeley, California.

Coleman, Janet. 1981. *Medieval readers and writers. 1350-1400*. London.

Harrison, Molly. 1972. *The kitchen in History*. London.

Hieatt, Constance B. 1980. 'The roast, or boiled, beef of Old England: *ore le fraunceis pur un feste araer*'. In *Book Forum* 5. 294-299.

—. 1987. 'Milk: almond vs. cow in Medieval English courtly cookery'. In Tom Jaine (ed.) *Oxford Symposium on food and cookery 1986 - proceedings*. London. 70-73.

—. 1988a. 'Further notes on *The Forme of Cury* et al.: additions and corrections'. In *Bulletin of the John Rylands University Library of Manchester* 70. 45-52.

—. (ed.) 1988b. *An Ordinance of Pottage: an edition of the fifteenth century recipes* in *Yale University's MS Beinecke 163*. London.

Hieatt, Constance B. and Sharon Butler. 1985. *Curye on Inglysch: English culinary Manuscripts of the fourteenth* century (including the Forme of Curie). London.

Hieatt, Constance B. and Robin F. Jones. 1986. Two Anglo-Norman culinary collections edited from British Library manuscripts Additional 32085 and Royal 12.C.xii. In *Speculum* 61. 859-882.

Hörandner, Edith. 1981. 'The recipe book as a cultural and social-historical document: on the value of manuscript recipes as sources'. In Alexander Fenton and Trefer M. Own (eds.) *Food in Perspective: proceedings of the Third International Conference on Ethnological Food Research*. Edinburgh. 119-144.

Matthew, Gervase. 1968. *The court of Richard II*. London.

Napier, Mrs Alexander [Robina] (ed.). 1882. *A noble boke off cookry ffor a prynce houssolde or eny other estately houssolde*. London.

Parkes, M.B. 1973. 'The literacy of the laity'. In D.Daiches and A.K.Thorlby (eds.) *Literature and western civilisation*. London. 555-577. (Reprinted in M.B.Parkes, *Scribes, scripts, and readers*. 1991. 275-297).

Power, Eileen (tr.). 1928. *The goodman of Paris (Le Menagier de Paris): a treatise on moral and domestic economy by a citizen of Paris (c.1393)*. London.

Pullar, Philippa. 1970. *Consuming passions*. London.

Sass, Lorna. 1976. *To the King's taste: Richard II's book of feasts and recipes, adapted for modern cooking*. London.

—. 1981. 'Religion, medicine, politics and spices'. In *Appetite* 1. 7-13.

Scully, Terence (ed.). 1988. *The 'Viandier' of Taillevent: an edition of all extant manuscripts*. Ottawa.

—. 1991. '*Deffaire* and *Destremper* in Early French Cuisine'. In *Petits Propos Culinaires* 38. 14.

—. 1993. 'Medieval cookery and medicine'. In *Petits Propos Culinaires* 44. 11-20.

Serjeantson, M.S. 1938. 'The vocabulary of cookery in the fifteenth century'. In *Essays & Studies of the English Association* 23. 25-37.

Willan, Anne. 1992. *Great cooks and their recipes - from Taillevent to Escoffier*. London.

Wilson, C.Anne. 1973. *Food and drink in Britain: from the Stone Age to recent times*. London.

—. 1979. 'The French connection: part I'. In *Petits Propos Culinaires* 2. 10-17.

—. 1980. 'The French connection: part II'. In *Petits Propos Culinaires* 4. 8-20.

—. 1981a. 'The Saracen connection - Arab cuisine and the Medieval West: part 1'. In *Petits Propos Culinaires* 7. 13-22.

—. 1981b. 'The Saracen connection - Arab cuisine and the Medieval West: part 2'. In *Petits Propos Culinaires* 8. 19-28.

REFERENCES

[1] The name comes from the text itself, which begins *Incipit liber utilis coquinario*. The full text can be found in *Curye on Inglysch* by Constance B. Hieatt and Sharon Butler (83-91), which also contains a discussion of the manuscripts containing the text (19).

[2] Hörandner: 120.

[3] *Comin pou kast in* (add cumin), *& to be lord vorp bringen* (and bring [it] forth to the lord) (Hieatt and Butler 1985:54).

[4] Hieatt 1988b:219,233.

[5] Hieatt 1988a:48. See also below, page 7.

[6] (from *Le Menagier de Paris*)...*maiz il y a trop affaire, et n'est pas ouvrage pour le queux d'un bourgoiz, non mye d'un chevalier simple* (Brereton and Ferrier 281). The translation is from Power (35-36).

[7] See Black 1993: 110, Harrison: 20, and also Matthew: 24.

[8] Throughout this paper I follow Hieatt and Butler's numbering of the *UC* recipes, putting the numbers in square brackets.

[9] Hieatt and Butler: 185, 194.

[10] See Wilson: 236, 240. Lorna Sass also makes the distinction between cooks and bakers (1976: 113).

[11] Wilson 1973: 118,120.

[12] Wilson 1973: 283.

[13] Hieatt 1986: 71.

[14] Hieatt and Butler: 7.

[15] Hieatt says of Yale Beinecke MS 163, '[t]he scribe's errors are remarkably numerous. He frequently misunderstood what he was copying. But that is not unusual for scribes copying this sort of material; few of them could have

[16] Hieatt and Butler: 19.

[17] See Attar (1979: 11-14) for a discussion of the different roles for men and women with regard to cookery in the medieval period. Bynum is also of interest. Maggie Black claims that women did not work even as kitchen maids or scullions at this time (1993: 110-111).

[18] Work by Paul Aebischer has shown that there exists a manuscript of the compilation which predates Tirel. As Brereton and Ferrier put it, this 'makes it evident that Charles VI's cook was no more than the reviser of the work of an earlier master, perhaps another royal cook also nicknamed Taillevent' (liii). In Anne Willan's study of Taillevent, this is mentioned as a 'suspicion' (13).

[19] For information on his life, see Willan's study (9-21) as well as the introduction (in English) to Brereton and Ferrier's edition of *Le Menagier de Paris* (lii-liii). A recent edition of the *Viandier* is by Terence Scully.

[20] See Braswell (342). The titles I have mentioned are later than *UC*, but give an indication of the sort of training which was being committed to writing.

[21] Stow's Annals claim that Richard II's household served this number, and although Black calls this 'fanciful' (1992:99) Hieatt and Butler were able to calculate from the figures in the household ordinances of Edward IV that 'household also could not have been much short of 10,000' (21).

[22] Pullar: 90.

[23] Black 1993: 115-116.

[24] Pullar: 101.

[25] Pullar: 101.

[26] Laurel Braswell, for example, says the recipes 'are rarely consistently organized' (344), although Hieatt points out a deliberate pattern in the recipes of the *Forme of Cury* (1988b: 16-17).

[27] Wilson gives the example of a fifteenth-century English cookery collection containing a recipe lifted 'straight from Taillevent' (1979: 14).

[28] C. Anne Wilson discusses its history in depth (1980: 15-17).

[29] See Hieatt and Butler: 172, and especially Wilson 1980: 17.

[30] See Sass (1981: 8-9) for a discussion of 'religious concerns'. One of many examples of explicit recipe instructions found in other texts is *If...fyssh day, make on the same manere with water and oyle, and if it be not in lent, alye* (mix) *it with ʒolkes of eyren* (egg yolks) (from the *Forme of Cury* [9]).

[31] While Hieatt argues that medical theories had little impact on culinary habits (1986: 71, and see also Hieatt and Butler: 21), Sass presents evidence that 'the medieval physician relied heavily upon the use of spices...with the cooperation of cooks (1981: 9-10). Scully cites the *Forme of Cury* preface and claims that a cook 'had to realize how very much he and [his profession] depended upon the extensive scientific knowledge transmitted by the medical profession' (1993: 12-14).

[32] Both are typical of Anglo-Norman but not French cookery (Hieatt and Butler: 6).

[33] Hieatt and Butler: 19.

[34] Hieatt and Butler: 187, 209.

[35] There is another in the *Forme of Cury* [87].

[36] The text of this recipe (from a manuscript in the Holkham collection, dated c.1467), can be found in Napier and Sass 1976, with modernised versions published in Sass (1976: 117) and Black (1993: 128). Note that Black also quotes the first six lines of the recipe for 'Mete of Cypree' from *Diuersa Cibaria* when discussing recipes for almond milk (Black 1992: 64).

[37] Austin: 96.

[38] A recipe strikingly similar to the one in *Diuersa Servicia* (Hieatt and Butler: 62).

[39] See Austin: 78-80 for a long sequence of fifteenth century poultry and fowl recipes.

[40] Bennett: 1. He does point out that informational works were sure to be circulated due to their 'obvious usefulness' (Bennett: 8), '...while technical manuals concerning the terms and practice of carving, or the placing of company in due order of precedence were plentiful (Bennett: 9).' On the subject of literacy in the period from 1350-1400, Janet Coleman says that even those 'who would never get within miles of the royal court' were being taught to read and write, and that 'the reading of English...appears to have become an assumed skill' (24,26).

[41] Attar: 12,13. Mary Beard similarly argues with reference to the cookbook attributed to Apicius that it was not intended to serve as an instruction manual. Sass affirms that the *Forme of Cury* can be seen to have functioned as propaganda, demonstrating the generosity and high status of Richard II (1981: 11).

[42] Scully notes, with regard to late-medieval France, '[a]s with trades and professions in any age and place, cooks...had a jargon of their own. Certain terms...were more or less universally used within the culinary profession of the time to refer to techniques or procedures that were specific to that profession (Scully, 1991, 14). Serjeantson says of an English fifteenth-century cooking text, '[t]he overwhelming proportion of French technical terms is very noticeable (37).
[43] Attar: 12.
[44] Wilson 1979: 12.
[45] This quote is from Hieatt (1988a: 48), who says that this version is 'probably more accurate' than that cited by Wilson.
[46] See Wilson 1981a: 19-20 for a discussion of this practice.
[47] The records are for the household of Dame Alice de Bryene (Wilson 1973: 283).
[48] Wilson 1973: 280.
[49] Black 1992: 45, 74, 78.

Lanark Blue Cheese –
Humphrey Errington vs Clydesdale District Council

Robert Chenciner

On May 3 1995 a Safeways supermarket truck drove up to Walston Braehead Farm near Lanark in southern Scotland. The truck had been hired by the Clydesdale District Council to seize and take away an allegedly listeria-ridden five tons of Lanark Blue cheese worth £27,000 to be destroyed. It was met by several television crews with cameras a-whirring. The Safeways driver rang his manager worked out that this was an aspect of publicity they would best avoid and the truck left hastily. Soon after, Humphrey Errington, the owner of the cheese, was given an assurance by the Chief Constable that the police would not let the Council remove any cheese from his premises. What was going on?

Errington has now won his case on appeal at the Lanark Sheriff's Court, referred to by Paul Levy as the O.J. Simpson trial of the food world because of its duration. On December 5th the Sheriff delivered his 32-page judgement which vindicated Errington and damned the council and its advisors, including Dr. J. McLauchlin, Director of the Listeria Reference Unit in the Public Health Laboratory Service in London. Errington was awarded about £120,000 to meet legal costs and refunded for the unsaleable cheese.

The story begins eleven years ago. After two years of research and development, Errington began producing cheese in 1985. He produced two blue-vein cheeses made by traditional methods at his dairy near Lanark south of Edinburgh. *Lanark Blue* is made from unpasteurised sheep milk from his 400-strong flock of long-faced glowing-looking Friesland sheep and *Dunsyre Blue* is made from unpasteurised cow's milk from a single outside herd of Ayrshires. Lanark Blue which retails at about £7 a pound is sold by specialist cheese merchants in Britain such as Paxton and Whitfield and is also very popular at the local market in Lanark. It is eaten at well-stocked tables including the Queen's and the House of Lords restaurant and served in good specialist restaurants such as Martin Irons' *Martins* in Edinburgh and Sally Clark's *Clark's* in London. Since February 1995 every cheese wrapping has carried a printed health warning to discourage vulnerable groups of pregnant women, AIDS sufferers and old people from eating the cheese.

Lanark Blue and Dunsyre Blue occupy a small but distinguished place in the UK blue cheese market, estimated at several thousand tons, the major proportion being factory-manufactured Stilton. Current production of Errington's cheeses is about 40 tons a year, and there are seven outside employees at his dairy where he also employs a part-time analyst in his simple laboratory. A sign of Errington's conscientiousness is that he regularly sends samples to independent laboratories when higher than normal bacterial counts are found. In court the veterinary doctor who has looked after his sheep during the last ten years spoke highly of him as a stockman and confirmed that they consulted regularly for signs of listeria. No listeria has been observed since 1991. Listeria organisms are present in both pasteurised and unpasteurised milk. They are not added as part of any process. Listeria organisms can be transferred from silage eaten by the livestock and from their udders which have come into contact with infected dung. Listeriosis affects individual sheep rather than the whole flock. The sheep presents one-sided facial paralysis which spreads to the whole body causing circling movements and death.

In December 1994 Edinburgh Environmental Health Officers carrying out what they called routine sampling of foods in their area took one sample of Lanark Blue cheese in which they claimed that they found listeria monocytogenes (Lm). At the same time a Dunsyre Blue sample tested negative. This appears an inconsistent result as both cheeses were made by the same people using the same equipment and aged on the same shelves. Clydesdale were notified and further sampling was carried out of cheese taken from Errington's farm and also from a retailer in Suffolk. All these samples were claimed to be positive for Lm. As a result Clydesdale, through the Scottish Office, issued a national warning and forced Errington to 'voluntarily' withdraw his product on December 12. They imposed on him a requirement that he demonstrate complete freedom from Lm to obtain release from his 'voluntary' agreement, but when Errington's own sample showed absence of Lm, they refused to accept the independent results. This left Errington in limbo. So, on the advice of his solicitor and Dr. Richard North, a food specialist who has fought on both sides of food banning orders in the past, he withdraw his 'voluntary' agreement. Clydesdale then invoked statutory powers under the 1990 Food Act and seized all the cheese in Errington's stores following the First Hearing before Mrs Elizabeth Wilson, Justice of the Peace for Lanark, on 30 January 1995. ('Seized' is used here with a legal rather than physical meaning). At the Magistrate's Court Errington claimed that the cheese had been illegally seized and that in any event the *serovar* [see the typology described below] of listeria which was found was non-harmful. The JP ordered that the seizure notice be released and substituted with 50 detention notices for each remaining batch in store at the farm. It was agreed to test these batches at an independent laboratory, but Clydesdale soon after withdrew from that agreement and substituted the Scottish Agricultural College (SAC). The 50 batches were sampled and by February 22 SAC reported that all batches were positive for Lm and that 44 were above the (non-statutory) Public Health Laboratory Service (PHLS) guideline limit of 1000 organisms per gram. Errington received only three days' notice of the Second Hearing after he was notified of the results. On February 28 the JP then ordered seizure of the 44 batches and released six batches for sale. The analysis at the SAC claimed up to 5,100,000 organisms per gram of Lm, of which some strains can cause listeriosis. The cheese was withdrawn from sale although 63,000 2oz portions from the same batches had already been consumed by the public with no ill effects. The cheese was labelled and deep-frozen back at the dairy. The SAC analysis was entirely at variance with Humphrey Errington's own laboratory results. By the way, his laboratory does not usually give 100% clear results and he regularly withdraws 5-7% of his cheese because it does not meet quality standards. Subsequent analysis which Errington arranged at independent laboratories also gave lower results than PHLS guideline limit.

Errington decided to continue to fight the Council both on matters of fact and procedure. Errington obtained and won a first Judicial Review before Lord Weir at the Court of Sessions, the Scottish equivalent of the English High Court which sat on 22 March to 29 April 1995. Errington objected that at the Second Hearing Clydesdale had without notice called Dr. Jim McLauchlin, Director of the Listeria Reference Unit in the PHLS in London, to give evidence. Further, Errington's legal representative had not been allowed to cross-examine him and Errington had not been given the opportunity to call witnesses.

And that was the state of affairs when on 3 May the Council unsuccessfully attempted to take away the five tons of frozen condemned cheese to destroy it. On 16 June the appeal by Clydesdale to the Court of Sessions was dismissed, the Second Hearing 'having been conducted in a manner contrary to the principles of natural justice'. There were different courts involved because lower courts hear cases on fact while higher courts hear on principles of law. The Appeal Court recommended that the Third Hearing with cross-examination of witnesses be in front of the Sheriff rather than the JP which Clydesdale were obliged to accept.

Lanark Blue has not been the only cheese under threat. During the past five years more than a dozen small-scale cheese makers have been closed down by Scottish Council Public Health inspectors.

There are about 120 traditional cheese producers in Britain. The outbreak of salmonella in eggs during 1988 led to the stricter 1990 Public Health Act. However, there seems to have been little indication from the government to Local Authorities as to how to enforce the Act, leaving them to make the law on an *ad hoc* basis. Until now no one has had the technical knowledge or financial nerve to resist them. As the costs of the whole series of Errington cases came to £120,000 for each side, it is easy to appreciate why no other small food producers have gone to the court and have had, instead, to accept being closed down. As I will outline below, the questions being considered at this pioneering enquiry and their implications are far wider than would initially appear. Microbiologists, epidemiologists, analysts, veterinary practitioners, legal proceduralists, food producers, restaurateurs, EC and UK public health regulators are all having to concentrate their minds on a hydra of a problem.

There is something rather heroic about Errington and his supporters. If Errington won this enquiry he expected to receive compensation for the eight large freezers-full of his cheese. Although the cheese would have been declared safe to eat, it would taste spoilt after freezing and so be unsaleable. However he thought that he could not then sue Clydesdale District Council or the PHLS for damages or costs. In fact the Sheriff had the power to award costs. On the other hand if he lost, his unlimited company would have gone bankrupt. He was personally liable for costs. A fighting fund had raised £16,000 towards Errington's personal legal costs and his QC Michael Jones had offered to defer his fees which his technical advisor Dr. Richard North had worked without payment for eight months.

Errington was fighting against confiscation and destruction of five tons of cheese in a hearing before Sheriff Allan at the Lanark Sheriff Court. This type of hearing can take as little as five minutes and rarely lasts more than a day. Not so last August when I went to court in Hope Street in Lanark. On Tuesday August 29 the court was hearing its twelfth day's evidence. Each side was represented by a Queen's Counsel.

I was in the public enclosure where various expert witnesses and Council Environmental Health Officers were my only company. It became clear that the cross-examination of Errington's expert witnesses would not be finished by the next day as scheduled so the hearing would be continued on September 27 on the return of the Council's QC from a trip abroad. On Wednesday Dr. North gave two hours of his four hours evidence and two and a half days had been set aside for his cross-examination. The summings up of both sides were to be in written form with oral hearings set for late October 1995. It was the first hearing where witnesses could be cross-examined by the opposing sides. The Council's witnesses had appeared first. Sheriff Allan in his gown and twin-tailed coiled grey wig was a careful man painstakingly writing down reams of scientific argument. As the frozen cheese would not be offered for sale because freezing had impaired its flavour, the Sheriff's prime duty to protect the public from a threatened epidemic was not in question. To his credit he took the trouble to visit the dairy which is more than the Clydesdale Council officials and their advisors had done.

Humphrey Errington was challenging Clydesdale District Council on four grounds:

1. That their analysis was inaccurate.

2. That there is no evidence that the strains of listeria found are infective. And further that by not applying scientific risk analysis (as outlined below), they are condemning Lanark Blue cheese and its makers as guilty established by itself on the basis of incorrect criteria.

Both these arguments are explained in detail below, illustrating the complexity of the case while the following two are self-evident;

3. That even if the cheese is non-infective to healthy persons but capable of harming people in the risk groups, it should not be declared unfit for public consumption.

4. That even if the cheese had been contaminated in February to the levels claimed, it is known that freezing for a long time has a lethal effect on listeria organisms and the levels now will be significantly less than those claimed in February. Therefore the cheese cannot be re-condemned without re-analysis.

To elaborate on the first point, there were two aspects of the analysis which Errington has refuted. Firstly, the results were implausible and there is good evidence that the cheese cannot support the levels of growth reported. Secondly that there are serious anomalies in the results.

Firstly, as pointed out by M. Jean-Jacques Devoyod, former research director of the French national dairy institute (whose evidence the Sheriff especially respected), it was scientifically inconsistent that the Lanark Blue sample tested positive for Lm at the same time as the Dunsyre Blue sample tested negative as both cheeses were made by the same people using the same equipment. The listeria organisms would normally transfer from one cheese to another as they mature on shelves either side by side or with a one-inch gap between the top of one cheese and the bottom of the one above.

The Clydesdale Environmental Health Officer had the tests carried out in February at the SAC where the extremely high levels of up to 5,100,000 organisms per gram were found. Errington was puzzled not to discover listeria on re-testing the same batches of cheese. His results were confirmed by further tests carried out by three independent laboratories in Bellshill, Halifax and the Campden Food Research Association in Gloucestershire again on the same batches (*The Scotsman* August 29, 1995). James Little, aged 47, after a lifetime in cheese production has been Errington's head cheesemaker for the past four years. He gave evidence that the samples had been taken correctly.

Duncan Perry, aged 28, is a microbiologist and until six months ago, when he took a more senior job as a production manager in a food factory, he was an analyst with the highly respected D & M Clark laboratories. He was asked in by Errington as an independent analyst to check the accuracy of the SAC's analysis. In court he confirmed his written report that he had not been present at the tests. He simply confirmed that what he had seen had been Lm cultures but he could not confirm that these had been obtained from Lanark Blue samples. SAC had found 100% pure cultures of Lm organisms. During the past four years Perry and his laboratory have tested in the order of 20,000 food samples for listeria, in regular tests of about 200 samples a week. In the few examples were listeria had been found, the microorganisms had always been a mix of different species, which caused him to be surprised by the SAC results. Perry had access to all 285 sample plates and looked at 50.

During the current hearing, Errington still needed the evidence of an epidemiologist. He found that all the working epidemiologists whom he approached either had been instructed not to assist him or were unwilling to help, even after some helpful first conversations. This was only one manifestation of the unreasonably combative attitude of Clydesdale which was deplored by the Sheriff in his judgement. One reason for Clydesdale's prejudice against Errington might have been an earlier grudge they bore. In the late 1980s Errington was similarly challenged by the Environmental Heath Officer which he evaded by pointing out that the regulations which they were attempting to enforce explicitly applied to cow's milk. Some of the officials involved then are still working for Clydesdale District Council.

It is unclear whether it is the responsibility of the food producer or the public health authority to prove and pay for the proof of clearing a non-pathogenic strain. The public health authority should bear in mind the risk assessment of what is reasonable combined with the resources available, i.e. the council taxpayers' money. The low level of listeriosis would not justify this according to recent government policy. From Hansard's account of the House of Commons debate on February 23, 1995, the government appeared to encourage local environmental health officers to act on the basis of the following three principles taken together: 1. risk assessment; 2. public health factors and 3. testing the product as sold to the public, which is not be relied on alone. Clydesdale did not appear to be following these guidelines.

In Britain, about 50 people die of listeriosis every year. This is a relatively small cause of death compared, say, to heart disease which claims 200,000 to 250,000 a year. According to Dr. Mme Rocourt of the Institut Pasteur there have been no cases of listeriosis in the world which can be linked to blue-vein cheese. In Britain no individual cases have been linked to cheese and furthermore most of the people who have died had low immunity to all diseases caused by AIDS or old age. About 40% of people with full-blown listeriosis die while a far larger number – estimated at three million – of people carry listeria (along with several other potentially noxious bacteria) with no detectable harmful effects. It is also known that listeria can cause foetuses to abort.

The 4b serovar strain of Lm emerged in the UK in 1987 and was later attributed to a Belgian pâté manufacturer selling own-branded products in UK supermarkets. There were over a hundred deaths caused. Dr. Richard North, whose recent thesis investigated the Public Health Laboratory Service which receives £60 millions a year from the Treasury, is convinced that the PHLS should have warned risk groups before it spread.

There are three recent outbreaks of listeriosis which are the first to be directly related to cheese. An outbreak is defined as two or more cases caused by the same strain. In 1985 in California a Mexican-style soft cheese made from pasteurised cows' milk was banned after a number of deaths. In 1987 the Swiss Brie-style cheese Vacherine Mont d'Or made from pasteurised cows' milk was banned following 60 deaths. Both cheeses had serovar 4b of Lm, not the serogroup or strain found in Lanark Blue. In March 1994 listeriosis allegedly caused by the famous French cheese Brie de Meaux resulted in at least 16 deaths in France. The 4b serovar was again identified. Enquiries are still in progress. It was the first unpasteurised cows' milk cheese to be connected with listeria. As a result of these outbreaks, the US and Swiss governments have banned all cheeses with any listeria tested present, which some experts consider to be a knee-jerk overreaction.

Such foreign reactions to outbreaks begged for an interpretation of the UK government policy as set out in the most recent White Paper 'The Health of the Nation' in which food safety, let alone listeria, were not even regarded as a priority. The salmonella outbreaks from 1988-1990 resulted in the government setting up an advisory committee on microbiological safety. While reporting of this type of health hazard has increased, it is not clear that the number of cases has decreased. The government is under widespread pressure to control foodstuffs. The Environmental Health Office has had its budget increased by £30 millions a year and are accordingly under pressure to produce results. Nevertheless central government have decided to make priorities of key areas such as heart disease where they hope to save over 20,000 deaths a year. This results from a scientific form of risk analysis which has been developed for public health since the late 1980s. In contrast the Clydesdale Council are applying the blanket negative policy of 'if there is a risk, then there is a possibility of an outbreak from which we must protect the public.' 'All types of listeria are dangerous, so it is necessary to make distinctions between the various strains.' This is patently not logical. Some people who enjoy varied and special foods consider that the council are abrogating to themselves what is really government policy. Following the EC Directive 92/46 concerning hygiene of milk and milk products of April 1995, the new UK Hygiene Regulations for milk and milk products came into force in Britain. These regulations omitted to set statutory standards for cheese made by traditional methods. Clydesdale are seeking to impose provisional guideline standards promulgated by the PHLS. Professor Verner Wheelock of Nottingham University is a food policy consultant to several large producers. He was involved in the 1988 report on *The incidence of food poisoning in the UK*. He stated that

'PHSL provisional guidelines for microbiology for food examiners providing microbiological advise that more than 1000 listeria organisms per gram is pathogenic goes way beyond government policy.' An EC derogation (or opt-out) is available for cheeses made in the traditional manner and France, Italy, Holland and the UK have opted for it.

To elaborate on Errington's second point, if the SAC analysis is accepted, then the crux of the challenge is the question of the nature of listeria. One of Errington's most impressive witnesses [the Sheriff found his evidence crucial] was Professor T.H. Pennington, Professor of Bacteriology and Head of Department of Medical Microbiology, University of Aberdeen. In brief, he indicated that the method of classification of listeria organisms used by the Environmental Health Officers was not meaningful and had been superseded by recent research.

Even if the historical definition of listeria is accepted, the Clydesdale 'total ban' is flawed. The biological hierarchy nomenclature of listeria is: *genus* listeria; *species* monocytogenes; *serogroups* 1,3,4,6,7; *serovars* 3a, 3b etc.; *strains*. Listeria is a heterogeneous group of organisms comprising several thousand strains which vary widely in characteristics from highly pathogenic to completely harmless. Evidence indicates that the recent crop of outbreaks have been caused by a very limited number of strains within serovar 4b and a few others which have no similarity with the 3a serovar strains which have been recovered from Errington's cheese. This variation in pathogenicity is not unique to listeria.

In a further twist, the Clydesdale Council had commissioned a mouse virulence analysis to a nonstandard protocol. The tests produced equivocal results wrongly interpreted as indicated that the strains found in Lanark Blue are pathogenic. Their logic was flawed as virulence is only one factor of pathogenicity.

This test case may be about cheese, but the result may have a wider effect. There would have been another implication of a judgement against Errington. If provisional guidelines produced by the PHLS are accepted as having the force of law, then the line between processed foods, prepared foods and food preparation in restaurants is increasingly blurred. For example, cheese dishes, ice-creams, crèmes, and pâtés among many other foodstuffs produced in high quality restaurants could all be subject to similar negative assessment and banning, resulting in widespread closures. A further where the 'Clydesdale blanket protection' was spread more widely could result in the survival of only large groups of restaurants such as Trust House Forte, MacDonalds and Pizza Hut. This would obviously eradicate the quality, tradition and creativity of the small restaurant. Supermarkets and large caterers have deep enough purses and sufficient political clout to fight overzealous public health authorities, just as the tobacco lobby has done.

If we value diversity in food as a way to enrich life then we must beware of such control. Humphrey Errington is an articulate individual who has risked his business and more for both survival and principle. Less adventurous small food producers will need to form cooperatives to afford to do the same. Even crosschecking samples can be prohibitively expensive. It costs £50 to analyse one sample in an approved laboratory so that the result would be acceptable as evidence. One such cooperative called 'Euro Toques' has been formed by restaurateurs to organise a united voice in the light of new EC regulations. The first UK meeting was at the Restaurant Show in London in September 1995. (Those who are interested can telephone Martin Irons on 0131 225 3106). As Humphrey Errington realises, the threat of further action by Clydesdale is still present: 'The battle may have been won, but the war is by no means over.'

As the reader knows, the Lanark Blue case had passed before the BSE affair because front page news, so it is hardly surprising that many of the arguments described above also apply to the BSE debate. What is unsettling is how the BSE affair has been distorted by governments, the media and consequent hysterical public reaction.

Three ideas established in the Lanark Blue case would appear to be ignored in the BSE affair:

1. The scientific argument is incomplete. No biological or statistically significant evidence has been produced to link BSE (in cattle) with Kreuzfeld-Jacob disease in humans.

2. No risk assessment has been published giving rise to the following type of question: what other disease which claims 50 deaths a year (mainly unfortunate people with very low immunity) would prompt £2 to £6 billion expenditure with no guarantee of success?

3. Fear of *possible* future deaths, rather than scientific analysis of *actual* deaths, is being used as a reason to determine public health 'policy'.

There can be little confidence in government ability to care for public health based on such a haphazard approach.

Acknowledgements

I thank Dr. Richard North for sight of his forty-page deposition and for verbal advice and reading this report. Humphrey Errington was a contemporary of mine at Cambridge University thirty years ago, though we had not met for fifteen years until the hearing on Tuesday 29 August.

Oxford College Cooks, 1400–1800[1]

Helen Clifford

The Source

The main source of documentation for this study at Oxford college cooks derives from inventories made by Vice-Chancellor's Court of the University. The jurisdiction of the Vice-Chancellor comprehended not only students and graduates of the University, but also a class of privileged persons, composed of servants and tradesmen sworn to the service of the University. These tradesmen were licensed by the University to trade with its members and were therefore exempt from municipal regulations. By the 1520s a fifth of the town's taxable inhabitants were privileged persons. In the early days they were matriculated for which an oath of allegiance to the monarchy and the Established Church was required. Few trades were restricted solely to privileged persons, although the paucity of of printers, booksellers, cooks, apothecaries and surgeons in the Oxford city apprenticeship registers suggests that these were virtually privileged trades.[2] Only fifteen cooks were registered as apprentices in the City of Oxford between 1697-1800. Whereas these apprentices were required to serve seven years before becoming freemen, and thus eligible to trade, the University could admit anybody it chose to its privileges, regardless of apprenticeship or nationality.

If a member of the University, including a privileged person, died without a will, appraisers appointed by the Vice-Chancellor's Court were obliged to make an inventory of the deceased's goods. The practice was introduced in the 1520s in order to protect beneficiaries from inheriting large debts. Thus as well as inventories of privileged apothecaries, appraisers, bakers, barbers, booksellers, locksmiths and stationers, there are also those relating to cooks. Within the University Archives there are twenty boxes of inventories, mainly relating to students and fellows between the 1550s and 1720s. The inventories are a much under-used source. Elizabeth Leedham-Green has extracted book-lists from the Vice-Chancellor's inventories at Cambridge, but little work has been done on those relating to Oxford University.[3] The inventories are usually recorded on separate sheets of paper, or occasionally on vellum. Two appraisers were appointed, and the usual method of recording seems to have been that one appraiser called out the names and values of each item, room by room, while the other wrote them down. A separate group of inventories between 1610-1620 seem to have been recorded in a book.[4]

The Vice-Chancellor's inventories help supplement the information to be found in the matriculation registers, which due to their sporadic survival only give a fragmentary picture of the number and type of privileged persons registered. A list of members of colleges and halls for 1552 includes fourteen cooks. Only one is a 'cookesse', Mawde of Hart Hall.[5] It was customary in college accounts to refer to the cooks, and other servants by their christian names only, thus the cook at Lincoln in the later sixteenth century is simply called Thomas.[6] This anonymity can be overcome by looking at the inventories, which also tell us something about their lives outside of the colleges. Forty-six of the Oxford inventories relate to cooks employed by the colleges, including Alban Hall, All Souls, Balliol, Christ Church, Corpus Christi, Exeter, Gloucester Hall, Jesus, Lincoln, Magdalen, Merton, New, Pembroke, St. John's, Trinity, Queen's, University and Wadham (see Appendix I). Some of the inventories do not specify which college the cook worked for, describing them as 'late cook of the University of Oxford'. While most are called simply cooks, some are distinguished by being 'Master', 'Head', or 'Under' cooks. The earliest Vice-Chancellor's Court inventory relating to a cook is dated 1566, which lists the goods of John Gybson, of St. John's College.[7] The latest, dated 1729, documents the goods and chattels of Mary Faulkner.[8] The value of the goods recorded in the inventories varies enormously, for example Gabriel Cracknell, Master Cook at University College left over £1210, which included the leases on four houses in Oxford.[9] At the other end of the scale is Thomas Downs, a cook at Jesus, who died in 1680, who left only £8 12s 8d.[10]

While no paintings or engravings survive relating to these individuals, it is possible to build up a portrait of them through the inventories of their goods, together with further documentary information within the college archives.[11] The administrative records of the Oxford colleges, in some cases dating back six hundred years, provide a particularly rich source of information. The bursars' accounts reveal annual expenses, including those for the kitchens and payment of wages including those for the cooks. Inventories of college property, often include lists of kitchen equipment, and tradesmens bills tell us what type of food was ordered and when.

The Status of the College Cook

At Lincoln College, the first surviving accounts, prepared by the Bursar, William Kettyll for 1455-6, record the annual pay of its permanent officials. The Rector was paid 40s; the Manciple 26s 8d; the Bursar and the Cook 13s 4d each; the Barber 6s 8d and the Laundress 9s 4d.[12] From the later sixteenth century, a second cook was employed. The bursar at Jesus College made frequent lists of the annual payments made to college servants. Thomas Price, the cook, seems to have retired in 1636, as kitchen expenses included 'To Thomas Price, Cooke, his wages for one halfe year £10' and 'To Robert Davies Cooke, his wages for ye other half £10'. In 1638 the Cook came top of the servant hierarchy, being paid £21 a year while the Butler received £10, the Gardener £4 and the Porter £2.[13] At the same time the College also employed an under-cook at £4 a year. The college cook was at the top of the servant hierarchy. Brigid Allen, the archivist at Jesus College, notes that a new regime began at Jesus in 1650 when the cook's wages were pared down to £2 a year. In 1660, however, the cook was paid £4 13s, the same as the Sub-Steward. The Principal, Mr Ellis was paid £20. This reduction in pay should be set against the 'perks', such as the supply of fuel, salt and mustard, for which the cook at Jesus was paid £40 in 1660.

At Christ Church the cook was paid an additional £4 4s 3d in 1668, listed as an 'extraordinary expenditure', 'for making the pasties of the venison yt my Ld of Arlington gave us for the whole Hall'.[14] The high status of the cook may explain why only one female practising the trade, Mrs Mary Faulkner, appears in the Vice-Chancellor's Court inventories.[15]

At New College it was seen fitting to erect a memorial to the cook, Bartholomew Finch, who died in 1688 aged fifty-nine. The plaque in the north walk of the cloisters reads 'late Master of the Society of the Cooks of the University of Oxon., and Cook of this College', and lies next to Warden Thomas Hayward's memorial of 1768.[16]

Some of the college cooks were obviously, from their inventories, wealthy individuals. Thomas Acton, the cook at Trinity, who died in 1616, possessed £10 worth of silverware, including a 'dubble salt parcel gilte with a cover, a little wine cup gilte, two white little bowles and 9 spoones', much more than the average scholar or fellow.[17] The second cook at Merton College, Robert Griffin lived very comfortably and fashionably. The inventory of his house in St Clements (the lease being for 38 years costing £100) includes 'seaven needlework cushions, one turkey work cushion' and a large cypress chest in his bedroom.[18] Thomas Hall the late cook at Lincoln College had 'three Spanish tables with Red Carpets' and 'twelve lether chayres' in his dining room. He also owned two bullocks and eight horses.[19] John Reeve at Balliol owned in 1708 thirty three pictures in frames which were in his dining room, as well as hangings, twelve turkey work chairs and a looking glass.[20]

Some cooks seem to have run businesses alongside their employment as college cooks. William

Philippe operated a shop as well as working as cook for University College until his death in 1633. His inventory includes the contents of a shop, and a very well stocked kitchen. The other rooms in his house bear intriguing names, as well as the Great Chamber, there is 'a Chamber called the Sonne', another called 'the Moone', a cockloft, 'a Chamber called the Starr', and another 'the Flower de Luce'. Perhaps these titles were just pretentiousness, as the latter room contained only an 'old bedsted, one old cupboard' and an 'old chest'.[21] Thomas Downes, the cook at Jesus, seems to have operated a sizeable brewing business in his house. His inventory dated 1680 includes six barrels of ale and four stillings in the cellar. The pumphouse contained even more barrels of beer.[22] The total valuation of goods at death reflect the wide ranging fortunes of Oxford college cooks (see Appendix II).

The Working Environment

At Lincoln College, the cook, like the manciple, had his own room. In the kitchen the great hearth, on which the cooking was done, mainly burned charcoal, purchased bulk. There were cupboards, a dresser and shelves on which pewter and other kitchen utensils could be stored, baskets to fetch meat and fish, a chafing dish, colanders, a flascobe to fry herring, grid-irons, kettles, knives, a mortar, pails, pots and pans. A section of the college garden was also normally reserved for the cook's use. At New College the Warden had a separate kitchen used for entertaining a constant stream of guests; it was built before 1395.[23]

A detailed picture of the contents of a kitchen can be gained from the Vice-Chancellor's inventories. The list of necessities changes surprisingly little between the sixteenth and eighteenth centuries. The contents of the kitchens in the private homes of the University cooks reveal the standard format: at least one table, and three 'mould' or 'joyned' stools; at least three spits, two grid-irons, a pair of dogs and tongs, pot hooks and hangers; there are always brass pots, two kettles, a skillet and a skimmer, iron frying and dripping pans and chafing dishes, a mincing knife and a cleaver; and pewter trencher plates, pye plates, saucers and porringers. There is also usually a napkin press. The only major change is the introduction of greater quantities of earthenware during the early decades of the eighteenth century. Some cooks had extra specialised equipment, like John Slade of Magdalen who had an apple roaster in 1678. An eighteenth century engraving of the kitchen at Christ Church gives some impression of the size of the average college kitchen. Inventories of college kitchens reveal what type of equipment the institutions provided, compared to that owned by the cooks themselves (see Appendix III).

Responsibilities

The work of the college cook increased over time, as the consumption of meat became more usual and with the rise in the numbers of students and fellows being admitted to the different colleges. At Lincoln College in 1661 it was ordered that the cook should receive an extra allowance of £24 a year to 'provide al manner of fuell...to dresse Commons for the whole Colledge; and also to rost for the fellows' table three or four times a weeke what else they please to have provided to amend theyr Commons'. Major items of regular college expenditure, like bread and meat never appear in the colleges' day to day expenditure, since they were purchased directly by the cook, or sometimes by the manciple. The laundress was often the widow or wife of the cook, and was paid a retaining fee, and separate sums for other jobs she did.[24]

The cook, rather than the Bursar, was also responsible for the college pewter, receiving a quarterly allowance to fulfil this duty, but then any loss was his responsibility. Many colleges made annual audits of their property, including kitchen utensils, nearly always divided according to material: pewter, brass and iron. In 1707 Smith, the undercook at New College, was paid 8s for 'scouring the plate', that is the silver.[25] On great occasions extra had to be hired. At Lincoln the cook was paid 20d 'for the hyre of pewter vessel when my lord of Lyncoln [Bishop Smith] was here' in 1509.[26] One of the jobs that seems to have been the responsibility of the cooks was the location of stray plates. At Lincoln College the cook was paid 1s in 1644 'for the dishes found abroad and gathered up'. At New College, under expenses for the kitchen (Custus Coquina), 1s 3d was laid out 'for finding of stragling plates at ye rate of a penny a plate'.[27] In 1743 2s 7d was paid 'to the Master of ye Cooks Company for finding 31 Plates at 1d each'.[28]

Cooking Equipment

Cooks, like other servants at the top of the college servant hierarchy, provided much of their own equipment, or at least supplemented the basic stock owned by a college. Some of the inventories include estimated sums for goods still at the deceased's college of employment at the time of death. The Vice-Chancellor's inventories offer an excellent opportunity for reviewing the type and number of kitchen utensils used at any given time (see Appendix IV). It is not surprising that in premises occupied by cooks, the kitchen equipment accounts for the greatest number of goods and the greatest cost. For example 'the inventory of the goods and chattels of Mr Roger Acton deceased, late Master of the Company of Cookes, taken and prised the xiiiith of August 1626', includes £13 12s for the kitchen furnishings, while goods in the hall, the major room in the house, accounted for only £5 16s.[29] Acton's kitchen was furnished with a little table, four high stools, two low stools, a cupboard over the chimney, a paire of racks, four pair of hangers, four pair of pothooks, three pair of tongs, a fire shovel, seven spits all valued at £1 16s. The actual kitchen equipment included five brass pots, an iron pot, four kettles, five skillets, two brass skimmers, two brass ladles, two grid-irons, two frying pans, five dripping pans, a safe, a warming pan, two dozen and three pewter dishes, six small plates, six porringers, two saucers, three basons, four pewter candlesticks, three brass candlesticks, a tin candlestick, an iron candlestick, four chamber pots, a quart and pint pot, two flower pots, valued at £5 16s, and two silver chafing dishes, two silver bowls, a double silver salt and six silver spoons valued at £6.

The Food

The number of meals served in college, and their mode of presentation was often included in the founding statutes. At Queen's for example, Robert Eglesfeld, who founded the college in 1340, allowed for two meals a day, each to be heralded by a trumpet call. The Fellows and Chaplain ate two course meals on ordinary days, with an extra course with wine on the five great feast days of the year. The extra expenditure was borne by the College.[30]

At Lincoln College the cook was accustomed to buying a cygnet for St Hugh's Day, 22 December was the account day, celebrated with a banquet. By the late 1530s the wine or good ale, the malmesey and apples had been replaced by 'pyddings' at breakfast followed later by pigs cheeks, feet and sauce washed down by ale; in 1547 the fellows ate mutton with sauce and spiced pottage and at dinner downed a quart of Rhenish wine with their veal and beef; at supper they had a further quart of wine, two couple of fowls and three breasts of mutton 'with puddings in them'. The principle Christmas dish was brawn that is the flesh of the boar made into a colared head; in 1538 for instance the accounts record the purchase of six gallons of small ale to 'sousse the brawne'.

At Exeter College the Bursar drew up 'Rules for the Right Keepinge of the Bursar's Book' in 1636. The notes include references to special food served on feast days. On 'Powder-treason Day...there is rost-beife'. Over Christmas (from 25th-31st December) varying quantities of 'Bread & Cheese', 'Boyld Meat', 'Rost Meat', 'Rabbits' and 'Claret and Wine' were allowed. Only at Christmas Day were all five categories served up.[31]

The Bursar at Lincoln College in the late eighteenth century seems to have been very methodical. In his Day Book for 1783 he recorded the food served on each of these festival days of the year. On Whitsunday the cooks prepared salmon and lobster, quarter of lamb, peas, gravy meat, horseradish, mint sauce and marrow pudding, at a cost of 14s 8d. On All Saints Day the students and fellows were served with fish and oysters, quarter of loinbeef, turkey, sausages, tongue and udder, two fowls, gravy spice, marrow pudding, mince pies and hot apple pie, costing £4 4s 9d. Variations of these staple courses were served on Christmas Day, Candlemas, Easter and Chapter Day (May 6th).

Conclusion

By using a combination of archival sources it is possible to build up a picture of who the Oxford College cooks were and of the environment in which they worked. The purpose of the paper is simply to introduce a fascinating source of information to an expert audience, who will be able to exploit the facts to suit their own research.

Appendix I

List of Oxford College Cooks in the Vice-Chancellors' Court Inventories, University Archives, Bodleian Library.

Name	Title	College	Inventory	MsRef.(HYP/B)
ACTON, Roger	Master Cook	Not specified	1626	10, A-B,f.4
ACTON, Thomas	Cook	Trinity	1616	20, A-Y,f.46-7
AYLE, Roger	Cook	New	1610	20, A-Y,f.1-2.
BERRY, Francis	Cook	Not specified	1720	10, A-B,f.129
BIDGOOD, William	Cook	Not specified	1668	10, A-B,f.145
BLACKMAN, William	Cook	Not specified	1672	10, A-B,f.151
BOLT, John	Cook	Not specified	1669	10, A-B,f.177-8
BRAYDON, Thomas	Cook	Alban Hall	1619	20, A-Y,f.75
BROOKE, William	Cook	Merton	1671	11, Br-C,f.28
BROWNE, Richard	Second Cook	Christ Church	1684	11, Br-C,f.35
CRACKNELL, Gabriel	Master Cook	Univbersity	1620	20, A-Y,f.82-3
CREW, Edward	Head Cook	Christ Church	1630	11, Br-C,f.181
CREWE, George	Cook	Not specified	1644	11, Br-C,f.182-4
CROSSE, Richard	Head Cook	New	1602	11, Br-C,f.193
DAVIES, William	Master Cook	Queen's	17thc.	12, D-F,f.19
DOWNES, Thomas	Cook	Jesus	1680	12, D-F,f.68-9
EVANS, Hugh	Cook	Not specified	1593	12, D-F,f.110
FAULKNER, Mary	Cook	Not specified	1729	12, D-F,f.123
FLYE, Roger	Cook	New	1610	12, D-F,f.149-152
FOWLER, Perry	Cook	Not specified	1714	12, D-F,f.164
GRIFFIN, Robert	Second Cook	Merton	1651	13, G-Hi,f.53-4
GYBSON, John	Cook	St.John's	1566	13, G-Hi,f.10
GYBSON, Thomas	Cook	New	1578	13, G-Hi,f.7-9
HALL, Thomas	Cook	Lincoln	1679	13, G-Hi,f.73-4
HAWSE, Edward	Cook	Magdalen	1671	13, G-Hi,f.93-4
HILL, John	Cook	Queen's	1650	13, G-Hi,f.131-2

HILLHEAD, Robert	Cook	Lincoln	1620	13, G-Hi,f.135
HUNTFIELD, Richard	Under Cook	Corpus Christi	1592	14, H0-J,f.62-3
LANGFORD, William	Cook	St. John's	1711	15, K-L,f.53-4
LEWSEY, James	Cook	Not specified	1623	15, K-L,f.97
LIGHTFOOT, Thomas	Cook	Wadham	1651	15, K-L,f.107-8
LLOYD, Robert	Cook	All Souls	1648	15, K-L,f.118-9
LUCAS, Charles	Cook	Trinity	1707	15, K-L,f.132.
MATHEW, Robert	Cook	Gloucester Hall	1594	16, M-O,f.24-5
MORRIS, Robert	Cook	New	1701	16, M-O, f.61-2
PHILIPPE, William	Cook	Not specified	1633	17, P,f.17
PRICE, John	Cook	Pembroke	1637	17, P,f.92-3
PRICE, Thomas	Cook	Jesus	1638	17, P,f.99-100
REEVE, John	Cook	Balliol	1708	18, R-S,f.23-4
SELWOOD, Edward	Cook	St. John's	1670	18, R-S,f.89-92
SHURLOE, Roger	Cook	Magdalen	1590	18, R-S,f.114
SLADE, John	Cook	Magdalen	1678	18, R-S, f.129-30
SMITH, Samuel	Cook	Balliol	1682	18, R-S, f.149
TURNER, Carl	Cook	Pembroke	1715	19, T-Y, f.84-5
WARLAND, Christopher	Cook	Exeter	1640	19, T-Y,f.102-3
WRIGHT, Samuel	Cook	University	1727	19, T-Y,f.156-7

Appendix II

Select Extract of Total Valuation of Goods in Vice-Chancellor's Inventories to the nearest pound

Name of Cook	College	Date/Inventory	Total Valuation
Acton	Trinity	1616	£21
Brooke	Merton	1671	£10
Browne	Christ Church	1684	£24
Crosse	New	1602	£19
Davies	Queen's	17th century	£80
Downes	Jesus	1680	£89
Flye	New	1610	£34
Griffin	Merton	1651	£164
Hall	Lincoln	1679	£217
Langford	St. John's	1711	£135
Lightfoot	Wadham	1651	£38
Lloyd	All Souls'	1648	£165
Lucas	Trinity	1707	£19
Matthew	Gloucester Hall	1594	£62
Morris	New	1701	£18
Price	Pembroke	1637	£25
Price	Jesus	1638	£27
Reeve	Balliol	1708	£86
Selwood	St. John's	1670	£415
Shurloe	Magdalen	1590	£40
Slade	Magdalen	1678	£95
Smith	Balliol	1682	£23
Warland	Exeter	1640	£45

Appendix IIIa

Queen's College, Bursar's Book, 1692
Queens College. An Acct of Pewter and Other Utensills in the Kitchin taken August the 13th, 1692.

22 large Pewter dishes
29 Somewhat less
33 of a smaller size
54 somewhat less
16 Pottage dishes
4 Plates for cheese
4 Doz and half of Saucers
The weight of the pewter 533 lb of this 49lb useless wch was changed for Plate for the High Table

Appendix IIIb

Exeter College Archives, C.II.4, Liber Implementorum omnia huius Collegii Exoniensis, 1618-1638: Implem[en]ts and utensils belonging to the [Exeter College] kitchen taken Christmas Eve, 1623.

Pewter
Porridg dishes for the fellowes table	on[e] doz & half
Platters for Com[m]ons, for fellowes, soujournors & battlers	2 doz:
Broade porrige platters	on[e] doz:
deepe porrige platters	on[e] doz
Little sawcers	on[e] doz:
Great sawcers	on[e] doz

One Cullender of pewter
one braze[n] ladle
one bread-grater
one slicer
seaven meate spitts, 2 bird spitts
one pair of racks
Three pair dropping panns
Three pound braze potts, parvus, maior, maximus
Three kettles
Two Cauldrons of brasse one bigger then other
One braze skillet
Three pot hangings
One payre of pott hookes
One Iron barre
One Viniger bottle, & mustard pott
Two cole basketts, one flesh basket
One tray, one trugg
Two gridirons, one bigger than other

Appendix IV

Comparison of Kitchen Equipment appearing in the Vice-Chancellor's Inventories

HYP/B/11, Br-C, f.35
Richard Browne, second cook of Christ Church, February 6, 1684

In the Kitchen
7 7lb dishes, 3 5lb dishes, 3 4lb dishes,
12 plates, 6 porringers, 4 sawcers, 1 bason
2 10lb dishes, 1 16lb dish, 2 mazarines,
1 pasty pan   £4 5s 0d

1 Scume, ladle, slice & posnett, 1 skilet,
3 small kettles, 1 pot, 1 warming pan all brass,
1 candlestick, 3 tin covers, 4 spits, 2 grid-irons,
1 jack, 1 iron grate with doggs, fire shovell & tongs,
fender, frying pan   £2 16s 8d

One old flock bed & bolster, pillow & blankett,
& rug, Four wirgen chayres, 1 pair of racks,
2 small cupboard

[Total valuation of allo goods £24 6s 3d]

HYP/B/12, D-F, f.123
Mrs Mary Faulkner, late cook in the Parish of St. Aldates, June 24, 1729

Goods in the Kitchen
Crane & Four hooks, 7 spits, 2 racks
choping knife, toster, dogwheel
3 tables, 7 chairs, 2 pikturs
Dressers & shelves in pantry, saltbox
22 dishes, 36 platts, 3 chamberpots,
1 porenger, 13 spoones, a ladle,
3 Dripping pans, pair of bellows
1 flower box, peeper box,
2 sconces, 2 ragoo spoons,
2 quart mugs
Bed-stead & curtains   £19 10s 6d

In the lillte Roome
1 stewpan, 2 coffeepots, copper cullinder
a bellmettle pot, a brass kettle
[Total valuation of all goods £44 19s 3d]

REFERENCES

[1] The material for this paper was discovered while working on Oxford College silver, a project funded by the Leverhulme Trust and based in the Department of Western Art, Ashmolean Museum. I would like to thank Val Mars for introducing me to the Oxford Food Symposium, and all the Oxford college archivists, especially Mrs Elizabeth Boardman from Brasenose College, Mrs Christine Butler from Corpus Christi College, Mrs Jane Cottis from Magdalen College and Mrs Caroline Dalton from New College. The Vice Chancellor's Court Inventories are part of the University Archives, and I would like to thank the archivist, Mr Simon Bailey for his help and patience in making them available for research. Janna Eggebeen, from the Cooper-Hewitt Master's programme was of invaluable help in transcribing some of the documents.

[2] Malcolm Graham, *Oxford City Apprentices 1697-1800*, Oxford Historical Society, New Series, vol.xxxi, 1986, p.ix.

[3] Elizabeth Leedham-Green, *Book Lists in Cambridge University Inventories*, (Cambridge, 1984). With thanks to Dora Thornton of the British Museum for drawing my attention to this work.

[4] HYP/B/20.

[5] Andrew Clark, *Registers of the University of Oxford*, vol.II, (Oxford, 1887), p.287, from Register I, p.xxxi.

[6] Vivian Green, *The Commonwealth of Lincoln College 1427-1977*, (Oxford, 1979), p.233.

[7] Oxford University Archives, HYP/B/13, G-Hi, f.10, total sum £10.5s.

[8] HYP/B/12. D-F, f.123.

[9] HYP/B/20, A-Y, f.82-3, total sum £1210.11s.

[10] HYP/B/12, D-F, f.68-9.

[11] An impression of a 'cook-at-work' in Oxford survives in the *Oxford Journal* of 25 November 1758, of Ben Tyrell in his kitchen making pies. See Ursula Aylmer, *Oxford Food*, (Oxford, 19950, p.3.

[12] Vivian Green, *op.cit*, p.29. This should be set against the total annual income of the College which was just over £71.

[13] Jesus College Archives, Bursar's Account, 1638, p.76.

[14] Christ Church Archives, Bursar's Account, 1668, venison was a luxury usually provided by the King or some other great man, sent as a gift to the University which the Vice-Chancellor then distributed among the colleges, the venison constituting a welcome change from the regular diet.

[15] HYP/B/12, D-F, f.123, 24 June 1729, total sum £44 19s 3d, living in the parish of St Aldates.

[16] Francis Steer, 'Memorials at New College', in John Buxton and Penry Williams (eds) *New College Oxford 1379-1979*, (Oxford, 1979), p.353. Ursula Aylmer, op.cit. p.169. The Cooks' Guild was established in Oxford in the fifteenth century. Its members were exclusively cooks employed by the University. Its officers were empowered to inspect cooked food sold within the University precincts, and summon those who broke the regulations to the Vice-Chancellor's Court.

[17] HYP/B/20, A-Y, f.46-7, 29 July 1616.

[18] HYP/B/13. G-Hi, f.53-4, 16 February 1651, total sum £164 8s 4d.

[19] HYP/B/13, G-Hi, f.73-4, total sum £216 17s 10d.

[20] HYP/B/18, R-S, f.23, total sum £88 16s 7d.

[21] HYP/B/17, P,f.47, 30 December 1633, total sum £25 2s 10d.

[22] HYP/B/12, f.68/D-F, 29 September 1680, total sum £88 12s 8d.

[23] Gervase Jackson-Stops 'Gains and Losses: the College Buildings, 1404-1750', in Buxton and Williams, p.187.

[24] Green, p.233. Her stipend in the late fifteenth century was 13s 4d, her main duties were to clean the chapel, hall and buttery linen.

[25] New College Archives, 9946 Bursar's Account, 1707.

[26] Green, p.231.

[27] New College Archives, 4241 Bursar's Account, 1702.

[28] New College Archives, 4283 Bursar's Account, 1743, 21 plates were found in 1748 and 16 plates in 1754.

[29] HYP/B/10, A-B, p.4. Total value of goods appraised £285 13s 1d which includes £120 for the lease of the house.

[30] John Richard Macgrath, *The Queen's College*, (Oxford, 1921), p.242.

[31] Exeter College Archives, A.IV.11.

Minekichi Akabori and his Role in the Development of Modern Japanese Cuisine

Katarzyna Cwiertka

Introduction

The late 19th century launched Japan on the path to modernisation and brought it closer to Western civilisation.[1] Transformation from the feudal to modern state started with the opening of Japanese ports in 1954, after more than two hundred years of isolation. Creation of a regular army in 1873, proclamation of the constitution in 1889, and adoption of the Gregorian calendar in 1872 set the basis for this transformation.

Signifcant changes occurred also in the culinary domain. In respect to middle-classes and elite[2], it can be generalised that up to the 20th century there was a great difference in people's attitude towards daily and festive meals. The well-to-do and the middle-classes in Japan valued the taste and aesthetic aspects of haute cuisine, at the same time having very limited expectations towards daily meals. The quality and variety of family meals prepared at home by women or not well-skilled servants was quite poor. For special occasions, catering services were used or banquets took place at restaurants. The gap in the quality of cooking skills between professional chefs, who were mainly men, and amateur cooks, the majority of whom were women, was the result of the refinement of the cooks' profession. It also might have been related to the fact that women had a lower social status than men. The gap between professional and amateur cooking started to narrow in the early 19th century; that is evident in the publication of several cookery books for non-professional cooks.[3] Nevertheless, it is unclear whether these books were indeed used as manuals for cooking, or onlyu as entertaining literature. The similar character of cookery cooks in the late 19th century, and a remarkable switch in the beginning of the 20th century towards more practical and detailed publications, lead us to believe that the growing importance of cooking at home was a direct consequence of Japan's encounter with Western culture. Japanese home cuisine was newly created in the early 20th century, and even the term 'home cookery' (*katei ryôri*) itself emerged in the Japanese language under Western influence. the word 'home' (*katei*) was translated from English in the late 19th century, and was associated with a loving family atmosphere.[4] In the traditional Japanese context, where family members were tied by economical boundaries or feudal relationships, this catholic concept of family love was new. In the modified form of the ideology of 'family happiness' (*ikka danran*), this Western-rooted concept diffused quickly throughout Japanese society. The ideology of 'family happiness' emerged as the new gender ideology promoted by the state and had a great impact on Japanese domestic cookery. Sharing a meal at home started to be regarded as one of the methods to 'bind the family together in a happy circle' and to create family solidarity. Together with the growing importance of eating at home, the quality of meals received more attention, and this directly effected the attitude towards non-professional cooking. The contrast between festive and daily meals gradually became less extreme. The social meaning of the family meal and expectations towards women's cooking skills changed. In such circumstances the first non-professional cooking school for women—Akabori Cooking Class—was established.

Akabori Cooking Class

Akabori Cooking Class (*Akabori Kappô Kyôjô*) was established in the centre of Tokyo in 1882. The founder of this school, Minekichi Akabori[5], was born in 1816 in the central part of Japan (currently Shizuoka prefecture).He devoted himself to women's culinary education after working for several years as a cook in prestigious restaurants in Edo (now Tokyo). His son and grandson followed him using Minekichi's name in their professional activities. Minekichi the 2nd (his real name Kumauemon) was born in 1853 and together with his father developed the activities of the Akabori Cooking Class during the first three decades of its existence. He was also a cooking instructor at the Women's University of Japan (*Nihon joshi daigaku*).

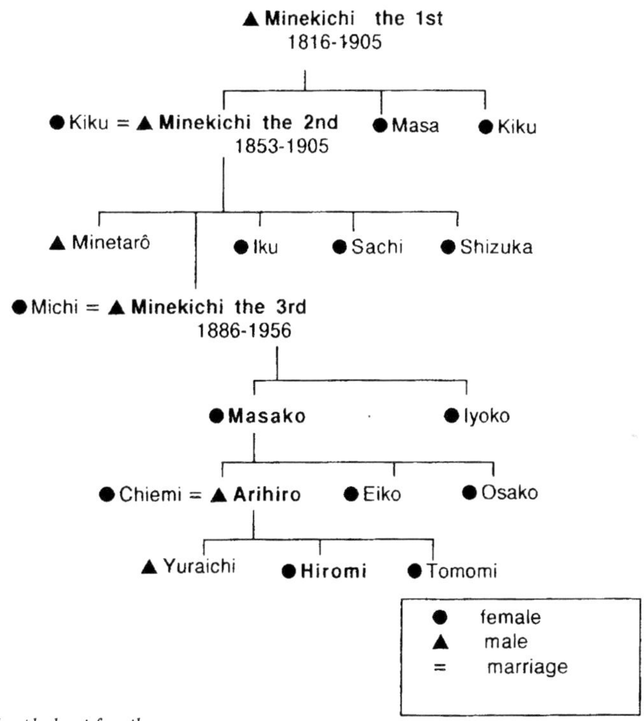

Genealogy of the Akabori family

Minekichi the 3rd[6] (his real name Matsutarô) was a leading figure in Japanese culinary education until his death in 1956. Then, his oldest daughter, Fusae, took over. Under the name Masako, she wrote books and articles for women's magazines, appeared regularly on the radio from 1947 onwards and on television since 1955. Via mass media, she reached the entire country with her cookery advice, educating the middle-aged mothers cooking meals for the majority of Japanese today. In 1960 the school changed its name to the present one—the Akabori School of Cookery (*Akabori Ryôri Gakuen*). As of 1962, the number of graduates exceeded eight hundred thousand and the school employed twenty-three cooking instructors. Since 1972, the school activities have been run by the present director—Ms. Chiemi Akabori, who has recently been accompanied by her oldest daughter Hiromi.

Minechi the 1st, the 2nd and the 3rd—pioneers of women's cooking education, who created the basis for non-professional cookery education in Japan—are discussed in this paper. Against the background of rising social status of the family meal and higher expectations towards women's cooking skills, their activities concentrated on improvement of cooking abilities and menus themselves. These two aspects were essential in the transformation of Japanese domestic cookery. On the one hand, economical and easy dishes had to be invented, and on the other hand, women who cooked family meals needed to be trained in preparation skills.

Creating New Meals

Kunio Yanagida, the father of Japanese folklore studies, defined four significant tendencies with respect to food preferences of the Japanese in the early 20th century. These tendencies were to eat warmer, softer, sweeter and more varied meals.[7] The aspect of sweetness is related to the increase of sugar supplies in Japan, and tenderness might have to do with the gradual replacement of a staple of other grains by rice or by a mixture of these grains with rice, which was softer. The fact that dishes were eaten warm more often was caused mainly by technical innovations such as matches and gas cookers. Replacing a traditionally-used small tray-table for each person (*hakozen*) with a big low table which the diners sat around (*chabudai*) also influenced the temperature of served meals. *Hakozen* was spread with dishes already in the kitchen and had to be transported to the dining room. Use of a *chabudai* involved a smaller interval of time between serving and consumption of dishes, as distribution to individual containers took place in the dining room.

Increasing the variety of Japanese diet was the major area of Akabori's activity. This was achieved by creating new dishes on the basis of already existing festive meals, or by including foreign elements in the traditional menu. Adoption of festive dishes into the everyday diet was possible by making their preparation easier and using ingredients that could be easily replaced by others in relation to family budgets. Concerning foreign elements, it should be noted that up to the 20th century foreign cuisine[8] was a rarity available only for the elite. From the 1850s onwards, Western cuisine (mainly French) became particularly fashionable among the higher classes. However, the greater part of Japanese society became acquainted with Western food culture several decades later, through culinary experiment, such as new dishes created by Minekichi Akabori, combining Japanese and Western elements.

For example, on 17 June 1902, a public meeting took place which was organised by the Kitchen Improvement Society (*Chihôkai*) and advocated the use of pork in Japanese cuisine. Kitchen Improvement Society, established in 1893, was a group of cookery innovators acting for the sake of 'education in cookery and its improvement'. The main attraction of the meeting was a cookery presentation given by the 87 year old Minekichi the 1st.[9] The menu was arranged in the style of a traditional Japanese banquet (*kaiseki*) with the respective courses: clear soup (*suimono*), 'special occasion side dish' (*kuchitori*), raw fish (*sashimi* in such a banquet also called *mukôzuke*), broiled dish (*hachi zakana*), boiled dish (*wan* also called *nimono*), pickles and rice.[10]

Suimono: clear soup with deep-fried pork dumplings
Kuchitori: pork rolls/strawberry jelly/boiled horsebean
Sashimi: slices of boiled pork with scalded leak
Hachi zakana: pork broiled with Japanese pepper/boiled potatoes
Wan: boiled pork/fish cake with carrots/boiled burdock root, *shiitake*[11] soybean curd and chillies.

Pork—a foreign ingredient being the main theme of the banquet—was fitted into the Japanese setting in such a way that the Japanese atmosphere of the meal did not disappear. The revolutionary character of this menu derives from the use of pork. Meat-eating, or at least consuming meat of domesticated animals, had long been taboo in Japan. Although this taboo was officially abolished in 1872, an unconscious resistance towards pork and beef was still present in people's minds. Preparing pork in the Japanese way to a certain extent diminished fear towards the unknown, and until that time forbidden, food. Preparing foreign ingredients according to the Japanese cooking methods was a part of the process of 'Japanising' imported food culture.

In the late 19th and early 20th century, many cookery books containing recipes for Western dishes, often translations from English or French, were published. However, historians agree that they had hardly any impact on the daily nutrition of the Japanese.[12] Despite popularity as a rarity consumed at restaurants, Western dishes were too new to be able to enter Japanese daily diet directly. Moreover, transplantation of Western-style meals to Japanese homes, besides a matter of taste, was impossible because of lack of proper equipment. Using elements from Western cuisines in Japanese home cookery had three advantages. Firstly, it resulted in the improvement of its nutritional value, due to the wide use of foods containing protein and fat. Secondly the variety of home dishes increased. Thirdly, Japanese dishes with Western elements were cheaper and easier to prepare than the entire Western meal. The role of the price of Western ingredients in the process of diffusion of experimental dishes, such as in the example of Minekichi's pork menu, into the middle class kitchen should not be underestimated. The fact that potatoes, cabbage and pork were particularly often used in recipes created by Minekichi might have been determined by a taste preference, but the economical aspect was also important. Potato, cabbage and onions were the first Western ingredients adopted for daily use in the Japanese kitchen. The examples below are taken from the book *Dishes for Daily Use at Home. Part II (Katei Nichiyô ryôri, ge)* published by Minekichi the 3rd in 1911.

Potatoes rolled in *nori*[13] seaweed

5 *gô*[14] potatoes, 2 *gô* 5 *shaku*[15] *dashi*[16], 20 *momme*[17] sugar, 3 *shaku* soy sauce, 3 leaves *nori* seaweed

Cut peeled and washed potatoes in pieces and boil in water until done. Drain the potatoes and bring back to the pan. Add *dashi* and sugar and simmer with the lid closed. Then add soy sauce and stir well so that the potatoes are nearly mashed. Roll in roasted *nori* seaweed.

Crab and soybean curd rolled in cabbage

5 crabs, 2 pieces soybean curd, 5 *gô dashi*, 7 *momme* sugar, 8 *shaku* soy sauce, 1 medium cabbage

Wash and drain crab, and boil it for 20 minutes with a dash of salt. Wash again in water and drain. Shell and carefully take the crab meat out. Then broil the soybean curd as instructed before. Mix curd with crab meat and wrap it in washed, boiled and cooled cabbage leaves with the hard parts removed. Boil in *dashi* with sugar and soy sauce.

Boiled pork

200 *momme* pork, 6 *shaku mirin*[18], 1 *gô* rice wine, 6 *shaku* soy sauce

Boil pork about two hours in water until chopsticks smoothly enter the meat. Cut into pieces and stew in *mirin*, rice wine and soy sauce.

It should be noted at this point that rice wrapped in dried *nori* seaweed, as well as stewing fish and vegetables in soy sauce with addition of rice wine and/or sugar, belong to the traditional repertoire of Japanese cuisine.

Dishes with a 'Western touch' were more attractive than already known Japanese dishes, as they were advocated as healthier, more sophisticated and modern. Minekichi the 3rd's attempts to 'smuggle' Western dishes into Japanese home cuisine went further than the use of Western ingredients. In *Dishes for Daily Use at Home*. Part II he gave, next to the Japanese examples, also models of Western daily menus. He might have intentionally not divided the book into Japanese and Western sections, as was the usual practice, in order to emphasise the possibility of cooking Western meals for daily consumption similarly to Japanese meals. The simplicity of these Western menus, like the two given below, leads us to believe that they were of American origin. Most family dinners and luncheon menus recommended by Fanny Merritt Farmer, the author of *Boston Cooking School Cook Book* published in 1896—one of the most popular cookery books in American history[19]— were quite simple. Minekichi Akabori was said to be in possession of this book.[20]

Menu no.2

Cod fish ball, parsley, tomato sauce
Roast chicken, brown potato
Sponge cake

Menu no.5

Potato soup
Beef steak, mashed potato
Lettuce salad, French dressing
Chocolate ice-cream

Menu no. 24 shows further experimenting with Western and Japanese food. The structure of this meal seems to be eclectical. Japanese names of dishes are used (e.g. *su-no-mono*[21]), but the Western influence is quite clear (soup - main dish - salad - dessert sequence). The styles of dishes are also not consistent: Western (dessert), Western with Japanese elements (salad), or Japanese with Western elements (soup, boiled dish).

Menu no.24

Soup: Japanese style soup with lemon skin
Eclectic boiled dish: a stew of carrot, onions, ham and *shiitake* with the addition of *dashi*, soy sauce, sugar and eggs.
Su-no-mono: salad with mayonnaise dressing (salad ingredients: lettuce, boiled potatoes, boiled eggs; dressing ingredients: egg yolk, olive oil, salt and pepper, mustard and soy sauce)
Dessert: baked apple (in the oven 15 minutes with the core removed and sugar added)

New European and American Seafood (*Ôbei gyokai shin ryôri*) was a cookery book based on the opposite idea. It introduced Western dishes with no 'Japanising' taking place, because the basic ingredients (lobster, oyster, crab, shrimp, snail, clam, anchovy, and several sorts of fish) were very familiar in Japan. Contrary to the introduction of new ingredients such as pork, potato or cabbage taking place via *Dishes for Daily Use at Home,* Part II, this book introduced new cookery techniques. Here again, Western cuisine brought fresh ideas and variety to the Japanese home kitchen.

Lobster croquette (p.45)

Lobster paté (p.93)

Creamed oyster (p.128)

Curried oyster (p.138)

Crab stew (p.179)

Clam chowder (p.219)

Mackerel pie (p.287)

Besides the adoption of Western foodstuffs, seasonings and cookery techniques, economically-conscious and scientifically-minded attitudes towards cooking and eating in Japan were of Western origin. The economically-conscious attitude towards cooking, caused by the so-called 'servant problem' became characteristic for the middle-classes in Europe and the United States from the late 19th century onwards. Domestic service became more expensive and middle class wives had to undertake their own cooking. Many Western cookery books included advice on economical house management, and this aspect was automatically transferred to Japan together with the books. Moreover, an economically-conscious life-style was an important element of the modernization policy of the Japanese Ministry of Education. That policy was again greatly influenced by Western models. The scientifically-minded attitude towards cooking came from the development of nutrition and hygiene related sciences in 19th century Europe. Those ideas were imported to Japan together with other scientific knowledge and very quickly picked up by reformers of the Japanese Armed Forces. Hygienic and nutritional knowledge spread throughout Japan in the beginning of the 20th century. The preface of Minekichi's *Home Cooking for Twelve Months,* Part I demonstrates clearly this economically-conscious and scientifically-minded attitude:

Preparation to cooking:

• Simplicity in your dress should be a rule. Tie up your hair, cut your nails, wash your hands and feet well. You should start after you have rinsed your mouth, put on an apron and a cap made of white cloth.

• Be careful not to use too much water. In order not to waste firewood think beforehand about the menu, not letting the fire burn freely. Before using firewood sprinkle it with water.

• Beforehand wash knives, pans, plates and all other utensils carefully, so that nothing sticks to them.[22]

When it comes to the meaning of the term 'Western cuisine' it is very unclear which Western cuisine is actually represented. Generally speaking, on the ceremonial level, French cuisine dominated. French food was served in the majority of so-called 'Western restaurants', and was adopted by the elite and even at the imperial court. However, it was British cuisine and its American version that overwhelmed Japanese domestic cookery. In most cases, elements from those two kitchens were incorporated into new meals created by Minekichi Akabori. For example, in the November menu compiled by him for *Lady's Magazine (Fujin zasshi)* in 1915, the following names of Western dishes were listed:[23]

Pork cutlet (Friday 5th)

Beef croquette (Monday 8th)

Rolled cabbage, white sauce (Tuesday 16th)

Fried oysters, sauce (Monday 22nd)

Beef cutlet, fried onions (Sunday 28th)

Kaneko Tetsuka, a cookery instructor at the Women's University of Japan, explained in her *Preface to Western Cookery* (*Seiyô ryôrihô: shogen*) why English and American cooking should have been preferred.

> Western cookery lectured on in Japan so far tended to be rather formal, and mainly French cuisine was introduced. In my opinion, however, there is no need for a constant pressure to adopt these labour-consuming and troublesome French dishes in Japanese homes. What about lecturing on things easily applicable in an ordinary family instead? Let's also add French, British and American dishes. I would opt, though, for the latter ones, namely American and British recipes, to be introduced on a wider scale. As democratic as American homes are, and as unsophisticated as English ones are, so extremely simple is their food, and easily adaptable for Japanese homes. Therefore, I find them the most suitable.[24]

Propagating New Meals

New dishes created by Minekichi the 1st, the 2nd and the 3rd, and their culinary knowledge were passed along to Japanese housewives via the Akabori Cooking Class, public lectures, or publications. They emphasised economy, hygiene, nutritional value, as well as the taste and the aesthetic aspect of meals. Minekichi the 1st explained in his diary the importance of cooking education of women as follows:

> The motive of my willingness to establish a cooking school goes back to the proclamation of the educational system 10 years ago. In principle, my ideal of education is close to the spirit of the introduced compulsory education for the whole society, omitting no house in the village and no one in the house. However, I see a problem as far as the education of housewives is concerned. Their interest in learning is disturbed by numerous household responsibilities that diminish their ability to concentrate, and very often they are left like cattle without education. People are born in wealth or poverty, but for pursuit of learning there is absolutely no difference between men and women. Studying does not only mean getting to know difficult characters or deciphering difficult old texts. But in order to study, it is important to know each other's status. We know naturally the status of the woman who is supposed to be a pillar of the family. Food is particularly important among the demanding responsibilities of the housewife. Cooking by the housewife is the sole source of energy for family members' social activities. For this reason, allowing women to get closer to the 'world truth' and enhancing their cultural level through cooking education does not differ from any other study. If all members of Japanese society—young, old, men or women—escape idleness and aim at independence as individuals by perfection in their own field, it will not only result in their achievement of independence as individuals, but it will also lead to independence of our country.[25]

In the early stages of the Akabori Cooking Class, lectures were delivered by Minekichi the 1st, his son Minekichi the 2nd, and his daughter Kiku. In the meantime, Kiku's son Kichimatsu, who worked as a cook at the imperial court, Minekichi the 3rd and his wife Michi joined the school's staff. Instructors from outside of the family were also employed. Initially, the activity of the Akabori Cooking Class focused on Japanese cuisine, but in 1888 a Western cooking course was added.

Ten-day intensive cookery courses were also available in addition to regular courses. They were held twice a year, starting on August 1st or in the second part of December each year. There was also a possibility of taking Sunday courses in Japanese and Western cookery. Classes took place twice a month, on the second and third Sunday, between 9 and 11 a.m. and 1 and 3 p.m. The cost of such a course was 1 yen and 25 *sen*[26] per month: 50 *sen* for the registration fee, monthly tuition fee of 50 *sen*, and 25 *sen* monthly for ingredients and the use of utensils.[27]

The first correspondence cookery course started in November 1910. This yearly course was meant to advocate cookery education on a larger, national scale, and *Akabori Cooking Manual* (*Akabori ryôri kôgiroku*) published on a monthly basis was the textbook for the course. The following lectures were given:

> Lecture on seasonal cookery (*Shiki ryôrihô kôgi*)
>
> Lecture on Japanese and Western side dishes (*Wayô sôzai ryôrihô kôgi*)
>
> Lecture on everyday cookery (*Mainichi ryôrihô kôgi*)
>
> Lecture on Western cookery (*Seiyô ryôrihô kôgi*)
>
> Lecture on Chinese cookery (*Shina ryôrihô kôgi*)
>
> Lecture on preparation of Japanese and Western sweets (*Wayô kashi seihô kôgi*)
>
> Lecture on home nutritional chemistry (*Katei shokumotsu kagaku kôgi*)
>
> Lecture on Japanese and Western etiquette (*Reihô kôgi*)
>
> Lecture on diet for the sick (*Byôsha no shokumotsu*)

In the first edition of this publication, an explanation of the reasons for starting a correspondence cooking course was included:

> It is said that food, clothing and shelter form the basis for human life, but the most important among them are food and drink. Food choice is particularly significant for maintaining health and mental vitality. Both are greatly influenced by the quality of food. Moreover, food and drink expenses make up a substantial part of the family budget. Thus, cooking has a great impact on home economics and a housewife needs to be prepared very carefully for this task. For example, a housewife educated in culinary skills will be able to prepare a nutritious and tasty meal inexpensively. Lack of such education will result in expensive and bland meals. Therefore, every family should be familiar with cookery techniques, and for this reason every one needs to study cookery in order to acquire sufficient knowledge about it. Since women's education and family problems have been greatly discussed recently, cooking education has also become popular. However, regrettably, it retains the traditional formalities and impractical noble cuisine. Nutritional contents of foods are not correct without scientific research. In a world pressured by business, where the importance of physical health and family budget constantly grows, the lack of proper cookery education is most disturbing to us.
>
> For more than ten years, our school has been the pioneer of domestic cooking education. Women, who graduated from our school, are engaged at the main girls'

schools throughout the country, not to mention Tokyo, and have a very good reputation. Therefore people heard about the high quality of our cooking methods. We received from many regions requests to publish our lectures to enable people there to study. It was difficult to refuse these requests, and we decided to publish such a manual. At last, on November 25, the first edition appeared.

A copy of *Akabori Cooking Manual* cost 30 *sen*, subscription for half a year: 1 yen and 70 *sen*, and for a year: 3 yen and 24 *sen*. Besides the monthly published manual, participants of the course could ask questions individually. On request, participants had an opportunity to take a practical examination at the school premises, and would receive a special certificate for cooking proficiency. Such an exam was available for an additional cost of 1 yen plus the ingredients expenses. Moreover, information about Western cookery books, among others *Mrs Beeton's Cookery Book*, or Senn's *Culinary Encyclopaedia* were also provided.[28]

Comparison of the price of courses and publications of the akabori Cookery Class with prices of other products and with an average income of that time proves that in the early 20th century cookery education was affordable only for the upper and middle-classes (see table 1). However, the middle-class family model that emerged in the early 20th century diffused to the lower social strata from the 1960s on. In this respect, the influence of the Akabori Cookery Class on Japanese home cookery in the long term extended further, spreading throughout the whole society after the Second World War.

Table 1[29]

	Price	Year
1 kg sugar	34 sen	1912
10 kg rice	1 yen 78 sen	1912
1,6 km with a taxi	60 sen	1912
a cinema ticket	15 sen	1909
policeman's monthly salary	15 yen	1912
teacher's monthly salary	12-20 yen (10-13 yen)	1918 (1900)
clerk's monthly salary	55 yen	1911
member of parliament's monthly salary	≈250 yen (≈167 yen)	1920 (1899)
a night with the best class prostitute	3 yen	1916

The term 'home cooking' (*katei ryôri*) started to be used in the titles of cookery books not earlier than in 1903[30], but in the following twenty years more than a hundred cookery books with the word 'home' (*katei*) in their titles were published. In 1902 Minekichi the 1st wrote, together with Komako Anzai his first cookery book *Kitchen Improvement Society's Japanese Cookery* (*Chihôkai nippon ryôrihô*). In 1904 his second work *Home Cooking for Twelve Months* (*Katei jûnikagetsu ryôrihô*), written together with his son and daughter, was published. Minekichi the 1st, Minekichi the 2nd, and Minekichi the 3rd published together about 50 cookery books (listed in Appendix I), not to mention articles in women's magazines and other publications.

Akabori family as 'Iemoto System'

Whatever the future of the Akabori family will be, there is no doubt that their contribution to the development of culinary education in Japan has been very significant. The cookery school for women, established by Minekichi the 1st and Minekichi the 2nd, acquired a reputation of being the leading institution for culinary education in Japan under Minekichi the 3rd, and reached the peak of its popularity in the 1960s under Masako Akabori. For half a century, the name Akabori was associated with healthy and economic, high-quality modern cookery. Studying cookery at the Akabori Cooking Class, and later at the Akabori School of Cookery, has become a status-symbol for Japanese housewives. What remains is the question of the reasons that caused this situation to develop. What allowed Minekichi Akabori to have such a great impact on the nation's diet? He would probably not have been able to acquire such an influential position in Japan as an individual. It rather seems that '*iemoto* system' (*iemoto seido*) was responsible for Akabori's success. The so-called '*iemoto* system'—an urban phenomenon characteristic for 18th and 19th century Japan—is defined as follows:

> '*Iemoto*' or 'house heads' were the hereditary masters of lineages or schools of tea, flowers, poetry, kickball, archery, swordsmanship, calligraphy and other arts who dispersed skills to followers for fees.[31]

Although '*iemoto* system' is associated with pre-modern Japan, Isao Kumakura argues that only the emergence of the mass society and modern means of communication in the late 19th and the 20th century created circumstances for its full development.[32] This statement stands in opposition to the theories, like that of Francis Hsu, approaching '*iemoto* system' as a characteristic feature of Japanese society rather than the product of certain historical circumstances. Kumakura stresses that two conditions were crucial for creating '*iemoto* system'.[33]

    1. the character of skills dispersed by *iemoto* is difficult to judge objectively and depends more on the advance in training than on individual talent and creativity;

    2. existence of a large number of non-professional disciples supporting *iemoto* financially.

He claims the lack of '*iemoto* system' structure in modern *kabuki* theatre[34] was caused by insufficient numbers of non-professional pupils, and the flourishing of '*iemoto* system' in modern schools of flower arrangement or tea ceremony by the extreme growth of amateur female disciples. Although schools of martial arts did form '*iemoto* systems' in the 18th and the early 19th century, in modern Japan martial arts came to be regarded as sport disciplines. Their quality could thus be objectively judged on the basis of failure or victory, which does not fulfil Kumakura's first condition. The same holds true for the decline of '*iemoto* systems' in schools of visual arts, which under Western influence came to value individual creativity and talent.

Cooking belongs to the skills learned through experience, and individual creativity plays a crucial role only at a professional level. Moreover, judgement concerning such a subjective sphere as food is hardly ever objective. Concerning the second point, initially women from the elite and urban middle-class formed the majority of Akabori's pupils. However, along with the rise of living standards, a high-speed urbanisation, and popularisation of television, all Japanese housewives became potential disciples of the Akabori Cooking Class. With a growing number of disciples the status of the Akabori '*iemoto* system' gradually rose. The more famous the Akabori Cooking Class became, the more prestige was gained by attending its cooking courses. This again attracted more newcomers, resulting in more power and prestige for the school. It is difficult to say whether the history of Japanese home cookery would have taken a different path without the Akaboris' contribution. However, this contribution would certainly be less significant without the phenomenon of *iemoto*. This authoritarian mechanism was responsible for the Akaboris' success and indirectly also for the transformation of the Japanese diet.

BIBLIOGRAPHY

Ajinomoto Foundation for Dietary culture, 1992 *Bibliography of Dietary Culture*
Akabori Gakuen Shuppan Kyoku, 1963 *Ryôri kyôiku 80 nen no ayumi*
Akabori Minekichi, 1902 *Chihôkai nippon ryôrihô* (Ôkura Shoten)
Akabori Minekichi, 1911 *Katei nichiyô ryôri* (Ôkura Shoten)
Akabori Minekichi, 1912 *Ôbei gyokai shin ryôri* (Hakubunkan)
Akabori Minekichi, 1915 'Jûichigatsu no oryôri' *Fujin zasshi* no. 5.
Akabori Ryôri Kyôjô, 1910-1911 *Akabori ryôri kôgiroku*
Colcutt, M., M. Jansen, I. Kumakura, 1988 *Cultural Atlas of Japan* (Facts on File)
Harada Nobuo, 1989 *Edo no ryôri shi: Ryôrihon to ryôri bunka* (Chûô kôran)
Hsu, Francis L.K., 1975 *Iemoto: the Heart of Japan* (John Wiley & Sons)
Izumo Akira, 1963 *Shinan bôchô* (Akabori Gakuen Shuppan Kyoku)
Kumakura Isao, 1990 'Kaisetsu (2)' in S. Ogi, L. Kumakura and C. Ueno *Nihon kindai shisô taikei 23: Fûzoku, Sei* (Iwanami Shoten)
Kumakura Isao, 1993a 'Enkyô to shite no shokutaku' in N. Ishige (ed.) *Shôwa no sesôshi* (Domesu Shuppan)
Kumakura Isao 1993b 'Kinsei ni okeru geinô no tenkai' in *Nihon no kinsei 11: Dentô geinô no tenkai* (Chûô kôran)
Kumakura Isao, 1995 NHK *Ningen daigaku: Chanoyu bunka shi* (NHK Shuppan)
Levenstein, Harvey A., 1988 *Revolution at the Table: The Transformation of the American Diet* (Oxford UP)
Shûkan Asahi (ed.), 1990 *Nedan no meiji, taishô, shôwa fûzoku shi* (Asahi Bunko)
Tetsuka Kaneko, 1911 'Seiyô ryôrihô: shogen' in *Joshi daigaku kasei kôgi 1* (1) (Nihon joshi daigaku tsûshin kyôku kai)
Ueno Chizuko, 1990 'Kaisetsu (3)' in S. Ogi, I. Kumakura and C. Ueno *Nihon kindai shisô taikei 23: Fûzoku, Sei* (Iwanami shoten)

APPENDIX I

Cookery books published by Minekichi the 1st, Minekichi the 2nd, and Minekichi the 3rd individually or with co-authors.

1902	Kitchen Improvement Society's Japanese Cookery (*Chihôkai nippon ryôrihô*)
1904	Japanese and Western Home Cooking (*Wayô katei ryôrihô*)
1905	Home Cooking for Twelve Months (*Katei jûnikagetsu ryôrihô*)
1905	Japanese Cuisine Textbook (*Nippon ryôri kyôkasho*)
1905	Quick Side Dishes (*Sokuseki sôzai ryôri*)
1905	Japanese and Western Eclectic Recipes (*Wayô setchû katei ryôrihô*)
1906	Five Hundred Side Dishes to Make at Home (*Katei ôyô sôzai gohyaku shu*)
1907	Japanese Cookery (*Nippon ryôrihô*)
1907	Five Hundred Western Meals to Make at Home (*Katei ôyô yôshoku gohyaku shu*)
1908	Side Dishes (*Sôzai ryôri*)
1911	Dishes for Daily Use at Home (*Katei nichiyô ryôri*)
1912	Recipes for Hygienic Food (*Eisei shokuhin chôrihô*)
1912	How to Cook at Home the Entire Year (*Katei nenjû ryôri no shikata*)
1912	New Home-made Drinks (*Katei shin inryô*)
1912	New Practical Japanese, Western and Chinese Cuisine (*Nippon, seiyô, shina jitsuyô shin ryôri*)
1912	New european and American Seafood (*Obei gyokai shin ryôri*)
1912	Latest Recipes for Western Sweets (*Saishin yôkashi no chôsei*)
1913	Easy Japanese and Western Home Cooking (*Wayô katei kan'i ryôri*)
1913	Hundred Unique Recipes for Rice (*Katei ôyô meshi hyakuchin ryôri*)
1913	Japanese and Western Recipes for Hygienic Food (*Eisei shokumotsu wayô ryôrihô*)
1913	Official Cuisine for Auspicious Occasions (*Kasetsu gishiki ryôri*)
1914	Home-made Food Theory (*Katei shokumotsu ron*)
1914	New-style Japanese and Western Home-made Dishes (*Shinshiki wayô katei ryôri*)

1916 How to Cook the Entire Year (*Nenjû ryôri no shikata*)
1917 Japanese Home Cooking (*Katei nippon ryôrihô*)
1917 Seasonal Cuisine (*Shiki no ryôri*)
1917 Side Dishes for Every Day (*Mainichi no sôzai*)
1917 The Cookbook (*Ryôri no maki*)
1918 Practical Side Dishes for Twelve Months (*Jitsuyô sôzai ryôri jûnikagetsu*)
1919 Western Recipes for Practical Use at Home (*Katei jitsuyô seiyô ryôrihô*)
1922 The Newest Japanese and Western Recipes (*Saishin wayô ryôrihô*)
1924 Home-made Egg Dishes (*Katei keiran ryôri*)
1926 Five Hundred Western Home-cooked Meals (*Katei ôyô yôshoku gohyaku shu*)
1927 Banquets at Home for Twelve Months (*Katei kaiseki jûnikagetsu ryôri*)
1928 Akabori's Japanese Cooking (*Akabori nihon ryôrihô*)
1929 Akabori's Western Cooking (*Akabori seiyô ryôrihô*)
1932 The Newest Chinese Recipes (*Saishin shina ryôri*)
1936 Akabori-style Side Dishes (*Akabori shiki sôza ryôri*)
1936 How to Cook Chinese Quick Dishes (*Sokuseki ippin shina ryôri no tsukurikata*)
1941 Chinese Cooking at Home (*Katei muki shina ryôrihô*)
1941 Recipes for Japanese Side Dishes (*Osôzai muki nihon ryôrihô*)
1941 Chinese Cuisine (*Shina ryôri*)
1942 Experimental Dishes for Every Day. Part I and II (*Nichijô jikken ryôri. Jô. Ge.*)
1948 A Complete Book of Akabori Western Dishes (*Akabori seiyô ryôri zensho*)
1949 Akabori Japanese Cuisine (*Akabori nihon ryôri*)
1950 A Complete Book of Chinese Practical Dishes (*Jisshû chûka ryôri zensho*)
1951 Quick *Sake* Snacks (*Sokuseki sake no sakana*)

APPENDIX II

Cookery books published by Masako, individually or with co-authors

1950 A complete Book of Chinese Practical Dishes (*Jisshû chûka ryôri zensho*)
1956 How to Cook Western Food (*Seiyô ryôri no tsukurikata*)
1956 How to Cook Chinese Food (*Chûka ryôri no tsukurikata*)
1956 How to Cook Japanese Food (*Nihon ryôri no tsukurikata*)
1957 Home Cookery for Four Seasons (*Shunkashûtô katei ryôri*)
1959 World's Home Cooking 2: Chinese Cuisine 1 (*Sekai no katei ryôri 2/chûgoku ryôri 1*)
1959 World's Home Cooking 4: Western Cuisine 1 (*Sekai no katei ryôri 4/seiyô ryôri 1*)
1960 World's Home Cooking 1: Japanese Cuisine (*Sekai no katei ryôri 1/nihon ryôri*)
1960 World's Home Cooking 3: Chinese Cuisine 2 (*Sekai no katei ryôri 3/chûgoku ryôri 2*)
1960 World's Home Cooking 5: Western Cuisine 2 (*Sekai no kate ryôri 5/seiyô ryôri 2*)
1961 *Sake* Snacks (*Sake no sakana*)
1961 Twelve Months of Home Cooking (*Katei ryôri jûnikagetsu*)
1962 Ceremonial Dishes, Refreshments, Drinks (*Gyôji ryôri, oyatsu, nomimono*)
1962 Basis for Improvement in Domestic Cookery (*Katei ryôri jôtatsu no kihon*)

REFERENCES

[1] I would like to express my gratitude to Ms. Chiemi Akabori and Ms. Hiromi Akabori for their help in gathering information and sources for this research.
[2] The hand-to-mouth existence of the lower social strata is beyond the scope of our discussion.
[3] Harada: 95.
[4] Ueno: 506.
[5] As an older man he used the name Mineo Akabori (Izumo: 1).
[6] From 1928 on, Minekichi the 3rd used also the name Ôkô Akabori (ibid: 166).
[7] Interpretation of Yanagida's observations after Kumakura 1993a: 29-30.
[8] In the circumstances of the late 19th and early 20th century, 'foreign' meant Chinese or Western cuisines.
[9] After Izumo: 142-148. The same menu was included in *Kitchen Improvement Society's Japanese Cookery*.
[10] All menus, recipes and text are translated from Japanese by the author of this paper.
[11] Flat Japanese mushroom (*Cortinellus shiitake*).
[12] After Kumakura 1990: 497).
[13] Purple laver (*Porphyra tenera*).
[14] Unit of capacity, 1 *gô* = 0.18 litre.
[15] Unit of capacity, 1 shaku = 0.018 litre.
[16] Stock made of fish, *shiitake* mushroom or seaweed *konbu* (*Laminariaceae*).
[17] Unit of weight, 1 *momme* = 3.75 g.
[18] Sweet rice wine used for cooking.
[19] Levenstein: 84.
[20] According to the interview with Chiemi Akabori in October 1995.
[21] Sliced raw or boiled vegetable and/or seafood dressed in vinegar and some other seasonings—salt, sugar, soy sauce, sesame seeds etc.
[22] 2.
[23] 126-127. As the recipes are not given, the authenticity of these dishes cannot be examined.
[24] It should be considered that home economics curriculum at the Women's University of Japan was created on American lines and therefore the above statement might not be entirely objective.
[25] After Izumo: 8.
[26] Monetary unit, 1 *sen* = 0.01 yen.
[27] After the advertisement placed in *Akabori Cooking Manual* No 5.
[28] In *Akabori Cooking Manual* No. 7 and No. 10.
[29] Data after Shûkan.
[30] According to Ajinomoto, the first cookery books with the term 'home' in the title were *Practical Home Cookery* (*Jitsuyô katei ryôribô*) by Kinetarô Hayashi, and *Home Cookery* (*Katei ryôribô*) by Tamako Yokoi, both published in 1903.
[31] Collcutt: 155-156.
[32] Kumakura 1993b: 30.
[33] 1995: 143-144.
[34] For details about *kabuki* theatre see Collcutt: 130-131, 154-155.

Alexander's Culinary Legacy

Andrew Dalby

Some talk of Alexander—how he started from a small kingdom north of Greece, in 335 BC, and in twelve years had conquered almost the whole of the old Persian Empire, and some lands beyond it, and died in Babylon in 323 BC, still planning further conquests. But few, perhaps, talk of his influence on the way we eat.

His conquests stretched from Greece and Egypt in the west to the Indus valley and what is now Tajikistan in the east. And they were long-lasting conquests: that is the most surprising thing. Not that Alexander himself had time to enjoy them, and not that they stayed united as a single empire. They did not. But he had effected a great change in the cultural make-up of a large part of the ancient world. Greek was now the ruling language, Greek culture was the elite culture in Egypt, all of the Near East, Iraq, Iran, Afghanistan and north west India. In Egypt and the Near East this remained the case till the Arab conquests almost a thousand years later; even in Iran and north India Greeks ruled for two hundred years after Alexander, and Greek literature and art exerted strong influence.

And what about food? The results of Alexander's expedition included the bringing of new foods to the west, new foods to the east; the spread of new ideas about cuisine; the mixing of Greek, Macedonian and Persian fashions of dining and entertaining. It will become clear that all these changes had a powerful, permanent effect, distinguishable all through the centuries down to our own times.

First, the new foods that made their way eastwards and westwards in Alexander's time. It would be quite wrong to suggest that east-west exchanges of food ideas had not taken place before Alexander. They go back thousands of years, at least to the time of the Neolithic farmers: between 7000 and 6000 BC Europe first learnt of those highly important foods, wheat, barley and lamb. Even in the few centuries before Alexander we can find one or two food items on their way across the continents.

Westwards had come the domestic hen, domesticated in India long ago: its relative, the jungle fowl, is also a domestic animal in India. When did chicken reach Greece? Reading Greek literature suggests that chickens must have come with the advance of the Persian Empire—which bordered on Greek territories by about 520 BC. The regular name for this species was simply *órnis*, 'bird', or *alektryon*, 'awakener', but if a 5th century BC poet wanted a longer name he said 'Persian awakener' for a cockerel (Cratinus 279 [Athenaeus 374d]) or 'Persian bird' for a hen (Aristophanes, *Birds* 485). Yet that does not seem to be the full story. In even earlier poetry we can read of a 'return home at dawn, at the first call of the awakeners' (*Theognis* 863-4) and from early Greek Sicily we have 'eggs of geese and of awakeners' (Epicharmus 152 [*Epitome* 57d]), both without reference to Persia.

Whenever they reached Europe, they certainly did come from the east, and the 5th century poets were obviously aware that the further east you went towards Persia and India, the more hens you saw. In ancient Europe they were still a bit of a rarity: a luxury item, a centrepiece for supper or symposium, a lover's gift, like hare.[1]

While chicken was on its way westwards, the vine was on its way eastwards. Known for many centuries in Greece and the Levant, grapes and wine had reached Persia itself by the beginning of the Empire, and were known even on the eastern fringes of the Empire in India and Afghanistan. It was from here that the Chinese first learnt of the grape, and brought vines back to the Chinese court, in 128 BC.[2]

New Foods from the East

Alexander studied under Aristotle, and philosopher and monarch perhaps remained in touch throughout Alexander's life. Aristotle sent on Alexander's Asiatic expedition, to represent himself, his pupil Calisthenes. 'Lucky Callisthenes' someone said to the cynic Diogenes. 'Not so lucky', said Diogenes, 'he has to have his lunch and dinner when Alexander's hungry.' Callisthenes came to grief—he is said to have criticised Alexander once too often—but he, and perhaps others in the party, had serious and scientific reasons for their presence. Callisthenes, for example, had been instructed by Aristotle to send home copies of Babylonian astronomical records.[3] And we know of some quite detailed observations that were made of plants, such as fruit trees, in Persia and northern India—we know of these observations because they are recorded, among all his other information, by Aristotle's successor Theophrastus in his great book called *History of Plants* (meaning 'Researches on Plants').

It is as if Aristotle, and Theophrastus after him, were running something in the nature of a research seminar. Aristotle's *History of Animals*, and even more so Theophrastus's *History of Plants*, are 'reviews of progress' up to their dates. Although informants are hardly ever named, one can trace some of the work of Theorphrastus's unnamed helpers by looking at the place names in the book—places from which he had been sent reports, of varying fullness and reliability of course. 'We must find out which of these reports is true,' Theophrastus observes (6.3.6) when faced with a conflict.

If all this had no effect except on science, it wouldn't be important here. If Alexander's troops had tasted and rejected new foods (like the mango, which 'caused stomach ache and diarrhoea, so Alexander ordered that it was not to be eaten' [Theophrastus, *History of Plants* 4.4.5]) that would not have changed our way of eating. But in fact the investigations that were made during Alexander's expedition were the first steps in the bringing of new foods, already known in the Persian Empire, to a wider world. It is time for some examples.

Rice had already a name in Greek, but it was as yet quite unfamiliar to most Greeks. It was reported to Theophrastus from India.

> More than anything else they grow the so-called *óryzon*, which is their boiled cereal. It is similar to emmer, and, when bruised, to hulled emmer grains, and is easy to digest. When growing it looks like darnel, though standing for most of its life in water, but it fruits not into an ear but into a sort of plume, like millet. (Theophrastus, *History of Plants* 4.4.10)

Eventually called *óryza*, rice took a long time to become common in the west. At least one Greek cook had a recipe for rice-cake[4] but for the rich of the Roman Empire (and they would have been the only ones who could afford rice at all) it was prized for medicinal reasons (as spices often were too). Rice pudding for invalids was recommended by Galen as it is by the Byzantine dietician Simeon Seth.[5] Rice as a staple is quite a new thing in Europe, but it was as a result of Alexander's conquests, 2300 years ago, that rice became an item in the European diet.

More exciting than rice were the new fruits of the East. In a dialogue between a cook or grocer and a slave girl, written for the Athenian stage about Alexander's time, we can pick up something of the atmosphere:

> 'It's pointless to talk of good food to those who will eat almost anything, but here, girl, take these apples.'
> 'Oh, lovely!'
> 'Lovely indeed. Their seed has only just now reached Athens from the lands of the King'
> 'I thought they came from the Hesperídes?'

'Artemis! She thinks these are the 'Golden Apples'!'
'There are just three of them, after all.'
'Loveliness is rare, wherever you go, and it is costly.'
'One obol is the top price for me.'
'I'll make a note of it. Now here are pomegranates.'
'What handsome ones!...'

What were these new fruits on the Athenian stage? There are several possibilities. One is citrus fruit, specifically the citron. The first clear sign of what must have been the citron, not yet grown in the Mediterranean basin but soon to reach it, is again in the *History of Plants* of Theophrastus:

> Among other produce, the land of Media and Persia has the so-called 'Persian' or 'Median apple'. This tree has a leaf similar to, and nearly the same size as that of the strawberry tree and walnut; thorns like the wild pear or the pyracantha, smooth and very sharp and strong. The apple is not eaten, but it and the leaves of the tree are powerfully scented. If it is put with clothes it keeps moths off; is useful too if one has drunk poison—because taken in wine it turns the stomach and brings the poison up—and to sweeten the mouth—because the inside of the fruit, cooked in broth etc. and squeezed into the mouth and sucked, makes the breath sweet. The seed is extracted and sown in spring beds carefully prepared, then watered every third or fourth day; when well-grown it is transplanted, in spring again, into soil that is soft and moist but not too thin. It produces fruit all through the season: at any time some is harvesting, some flowering, some ripening. The blossoms that have a sort of distaff protruding from the centre are the ones that will fruit, those that have not are barren. (Theophrastus, *History of Plants* 4.4.2).[6]

The citron, then, a pithy fruit not especially attractive as food, was on its way westwards in the last centuries BC from a native habitat usually considered to be southern China or Indo-China. In Roman Imperial times it reached the western half of the Empire.[7] In Theophrastus's time it had not yet got a distinctive Greek name. The 'Persian apple', one of Theophrastus's terms, meant something different to later Greeks, as we shall see. It was sometimes called 'Median apple', a term Theophrastus also uses.[8] This is in fact why the modern botanical name for the species is Citrus Medica. But there was soon a new Greek name. Here is the medical writer Galen, who notices the status of citron peel as an aromatic:

> There are three parts of the *kítrion*, the acid in the middle, the flesh of the fruit around this, and the skin on the outside. The latter is an aromatic, attractive not only for its scent but also for its taste. (Galen, *On the Properties of Foods* 2.37.2).

The citron, though now as in Galen's time its rind is an aromatic, is otherwise of little value as food. It is, however, good-looking. Once it had become familiar in Greece as an imported exotic fruit, it asked to be identified with the mythical 'apples of the Hesperides', and, whether or not the just-quoted comedy sketch centred on citrons, this particular identification was certainly made. So, strange but true, a fruit of Far Eastern origin was sometimes called in Greek *mêlon hesperikón*, 'western apple'.[9] But its spread to the Mediterranean region is to be traced from that first report to Theophrastus, a report owed to one of the observers on Alexander's expedition.

Let us take something more edible. European summers would be rather less enjoyable without peaches: how did peaches first reach Europe? Once again, the first European author to mention them is Theophrastus, perhaps in some supplementary notes on plants circulated after the main *History of Plants*.[10] Theophrastus' contemporary, the physician Diphilus of Siphnos who possibly served one of Alexander's successors, King Lysimachus of Thrace, also had something to say about peaches: 'the so-called Persian apples, also called Persian plums, are quite juicy and more nourishing than apples.' They were planted in Egypt, too, apparently for the first time, in the early years after Alexander's conquest.[11] Peaches, then, also came from Persia. Greeks called them *mêla persiká*, 'Persian apples', and thus their modern European names, 'peach', 'pêche', and so on, are reminders that Europeans first met them in Persia. Indeed, although a kind of peach was cultivated in China from a very ancient period, the familiar modern type, 'the golden peaches of Samarkand,' came to China too from central Asia at about this time, Samarkand being one of the greatest trading cities of Alexander's central Asian territories. By the first century AD peaches were being planted in Italy;[12] the Pompeiian still life that includes a half-eaten peach is well known. How long would it have taken them to reach Europe without Alexander's expedition, and without the impulses to trade and agriculture given by his successors?

And next to the peach we must place the pistachio, *pistákion*. Closely related trees, terebinth and lentisk, are native to the eastern Mediterranean. The classical Persians were known to themselves and to others as 'terebinth-eaters': it isn't clear to me whether this meant *Pistacia terebinthus* or *P. vera*, the true pistachio. At any rate, the true pistachio, native to central Asia, is first visible in literature when it was reported to Theophrastus as a tree, as yet unnamed, grown in north India, its branches and leaves resembling the terebinth of Greece but with a nut like an almond. Aristobulus, too, a historian who went on Alexander's expedition, described this important tree, naturally enough, as a terebinth: that was the best he could do, for it simply had no Greek name.[13]

But this new nut was to have a Greek name. The poet Nicander, a century after Theophrastus and Aristobulus, refers to the pistachio in language which is pretty close to Theophrastus's but he gives it a name: '...all the pistachios that grow like almonds on their branches beside the Indian flood of the resounding Choaspes' (*Theriaca* 890-891). By that time the pistachio was actually grown in Arabia and Syria as well as further east. According to Pliny the pistachio tree was first brought to Italy by Vitellius, father of the emperor, who served in the Levant between 35 and 39 AD. The pistachio is proagated by grafting. As it spread in Mediterranean lands it may well have been grafted most often on already thriving terebinth trees, as it still is in Turkey.[14]

The Oxford Symposium 1992 heard all about that marvellous Libyan spice, silphium, and about the silphium substitute which came to light in Iran, just in time, for silphium was doomed to extinction![15] Just as the earliest writers called pistachios 'terebinths'—what else could they do?—so the earliest writers called this silphium substitute 'silphium', for there was no other word, and treated the Libyan and Iranian plants as if they were identical. Again the information comes through Aristobulus:

> [Alexander] crossed the mountains to Bactria by ways barren but for a little shrubby terebinth, so short of food that the flesh of beasts was eaten and so short of wood that it was eaten raw; but with the raw meat their digestive was *silphion*, which grew plentifully. (Strabo, *Geography*, 15.2.10).[16]

The silphium of central Asia was, apparently as a result of this discovery, distributed to Mediterranean markets for the first time. It thus became available to finer noses and more discriminating palates than soldiers forced to eat horse-meat to stay alive: and it was soon realised that it was not *quite* the same as Libyan silphium.

> The Libyan, even if one just tastes it, at once arouses a humour throughout the body and has a very healthy aroma, so that it is not noticed on the breath, or only a little, but the Median and Syrian is weaker in power and has a nastier smell. (Dioscorides, *Materia Medica* 3.80.1-2).

Now this silphium was, beyond any doubt, asafoetida,[17] brought to Greece and Rome as it was later brought to China and is now brought to India. In the Indian food trade its name is *hing*. It was 'rather windy' (Galen, *On the Properties of Simples* 8.18.16) and not so powerful as silphium had been, but silphium was extinct—the last stalk, it is said, served up to the Emperor Nero—and the Roman Empire took to asafoetida with enthusiasm. There is a great number of recipes calling for *silfi* and *lasar* (synonyms, essentially) in the Roman recipe book *Apicius*. It was an important ingredient in drugs in Roman, Byzantine and Arabic medicine: indeed, asafoetida is still in the Pharmacopoeia, although not so many chemists stock it these days. Where would Roman cooks and medieval doctors have been if Alexander's troops had not had to look around for something to help them with their horsemeat?

New Foods from the West

And already in Alexander's train experiments were made with naturalising European plants in the Middle East.

> When Harpalus [Alexander's treasurer] took great trouble to plant [ivy] in the gardens of Babylon, over and over again, making a special point of it, he could not do it: unlike the other plants from Greece, it would not take. (Theophrastus, *History of Plants* 4.4.1).

What were these other plants? The Greek cultures that spread through the Near East in the wake of Alexander demanded Greek tastes, including the kind of vegetables and fruits that were known in Greece. The result was experimentation and transplantation of stock in both directions, and this produced both novel varieties and improved methods of growing. Cultivated species now spread not only from east to west but along many paths.[18] Alexander's successors were enlightened in their encouragement of these developments.

Thus Egypt became a place where many European fruits and vegetables were newly naturalised, probably including beet, turnip, asparagus, pear, walnut and winter cherry,[19] while new varieties were developed and new methods of cultivation were tried for others.[20] Babylon and Mesopotamia saw similar developments, begun, as we have seen, under Alexander himself.[21] The geographer Strabo tells us (*Geography* 15.3.11) that the 'Macedonians' were the first to succeed with vines in southern Mesopotamia. Again, we may look at a couple of examples in more detail.

Coriander is the typical Mediterranean herb and spice. A coriander seed (a 'fruit' to be more precise) was found in a level of the Franchthi cave deposits, in southern Greece, deep enough to be dated to about 7000 BC. Whether or not coriander really belonged there, it was in use in Egypt and Greece by 1500 BC without any doubt. We today know coriander as a distinctive flavour not only of Mediterranean food, but also of Indian and south east Asian. It was one of the oldest foreign spices in China.[22] By what stages, and when, did coriander reach these distant kitchens? I can only speculate for the present: but the Chinese evidence would not contradict a theory that it had been planted by the Greeks deposited in Bactria (Afghanistan) by Alexander. From Bactria, by way of the Silk Road, its seeds are likely to have reached China, and had certainly done so by the 6th century AD, probably earlier. India learnt of coriander much earlier still—the word occurs as an example in Panini's Sanskrit grammar, usually dated to the 5th century BC—and perhaps did so by way of Iran, for Sanskrit *kustumburu* is argued by Laufer to be an Iranian word.[23]

The opium poppy,[24] again, is connected by us more with southern China and south east Asia than with Europe. Yet western Europe is its original habitat. What was its route eastwards? Poppy cultivation was certainly one of the branches of horticulture that developed in Egypt in the last centuries BC, encouraged by the Ptolemies, inheritors of Alexander's Egyptian province.[25] Greek physicians were well aware of the soporific and psychedelic properties of poppy latex (though the seeds were also used as a spice and the leaves as a pot-herb) and it is probable that poppies reached Mesopotamia and central Asia, too, with the Greeks who followed Alexander.

The Idea of Eclectic Cuisine

We have said something of the researches initiated by Aristotle, researches aiming to find general principles underlying the dizzying variations to be seen in the natural world and in human behaviour. These researches resulted in such books as Aristotle's *Politics*, the great collection of *Constitutional Histories* compiled under his direction, his own *Study of Animals* and Theophrastus's *Study of Plants*. Gradually, in their pupils and in the Greek intellectual world generally, we begin to see a shift from the general fifth and fourth century ways of thinking, in which someone else's way of life was contrasted with one's own in order to idealise it, as Xenophon and Plato did with Sparta, or to mock it, as was usually the case in the comedies. It begins to be realised that the nature and customs of other places are of interest in their own right, and may be worth adopting and adapting for one's own use.

The reason why this way of thinking spread so widely has less to do with Aristotle and much more to do with Alexander. There were already Greek communities, trading communities mainly, in the territory of the old Persian Empire, but Alexander himself, and all his successors, strongly encouraged Greek settlement and colonisation. Not only Greeks, but a Greek ruling class and a Greek intellectual elite spread all over the Near East, notably in such cities as Alexandria (Alexander's own greatest foundation), Antioch and Pergamum. And one of the impulses of Greek intellectuals of this diaspora was to record, to understand, to systematise the culture they inherited. Like Aristotle, though not for the same reasons, they needed to understand the details of old Athenian, Spartan, Corinthian ways of life—and those of the hundreds of other once-independent Greek cities—so as to make sense of the literature and drama which was their link with their own roots. They edited, commented, made glossaries; they adopted and imitated and conflated.

One can be eclectic also about food. It is so obvious to us that a menu may contain recipes consciously based on several regional and foreign cuisines that it may be hard to see such a development as innovative. Yet in the world of 300 BC it was indeed new. Earlier, certainly, recipes and other aspects of cuisine had in practice been imitated and so gradually spread from one town or region to another; wines and foods able to travel did travel widely in trade; migrant cooks had brought their skills with them. Still, when Archestratus in 350 BC advised his readers to prize the special loaves and cakes of one city or another; he meant that you must go there and buy them. It was only in the Hellenistic period, after Aristotle and Alexander, that one might first find, in a single household, at a single meal, 'cakes of overy kind, Cretan and your own Samian, my dear Lynceus, and Attic, each set out in its individual container' (Hippolochus quoted by Athenaeus 130c).[26]

Cookery books after Alexander

So the cookery books had to change too. Fifth and fourth century Greek cookery books seem not to have included any recipes with regional names. The third century marks the beginning of a revolution.

For example, Athenaeus cites two titles, *Bread-Making* and *On Cakes*, by an author Iatrocles. Iatrocles seems to be later than the fourth century.[27] Only the tiniest fragments of Iatrocles survive, yet an impression of the geographical breadth of his books remains: the few fragments that are known describe cakes from Cos, Thessaly, Syracuse, Athens.[28]

Also from the 3rd century comes a fragment from Baton's comedy *Benefactors*, which gives a further indication that cookery books had taken to distinguishing the origins of recipes, though this time attributing them not to places but to famous cooks. A cook seems to be speaking to a scullery maid:

Right, Sibyne, we don't sleep at nights—we don't even lie down—; with lighted lamp, with book in hand we work out what Sophon has bequeathed to us, or Simonactides or Chios, or Tyndaricus of Sicyon, or Zopyrinus. (Baton 4 quoted by Athenaeus 662c-d).

It is not clear whether these were authors of cookery books: they may have been inventors of recipes which would be written down by others. But they seem to belong to different schools of cookery: Chios and Sicyon recorded elsewhere as such. Sophon (from Acarnania in north west Greece) was independently famous. These days, then, the cook's aim was not defined as devising the ideal combination of flavours but as choosing the best of a varied selection of authorities, from different culinary traditions, for each dish.

Let me mention two more authors of a cookery book. Heracleides of Syracuse and Epaenetus are cited in the *Epitome of Athenaeus* as authorities on quite a significant question:

Epaenetus and Heracleides of Syracuse in *Cookery* say that the best eggs are peahens', next best being those of shelducks. They put hens' eggs third. (*Epitome of Athenaeus*, 58b).

Peafowl had come to the Greek world from the east in the fifth century, following the footprints of the domestic hen. But peafowl were expensive creatures, and the eating of peahens' eggs, which must always be far rarer than those of hens and quail, is a form of conspicuous consumption. Before Alexander's time, so far as the sources tell us, no one in Europe ate a peahen's egg. If they are prized by gourmets, it is for their cost more than their flavour.

The Hellenistic style

This leads me to the single most far-reaching way in which Alexander's conquests changed for ever the way that we eat and entertain. The effect of his empire was to combine aspects of three very different cultures: Macedonian, from which Alexander himself sprang; Greek, because Macedonians traditionally were educated to admire and to participate in Greek civilisation; and Persian, the formerly ruling culture of the empire that Alexander and his successors would now rule.

Greek dining and entertainment had made a special point of equality. Equality in shares of food; equality in the amount of wine drunk and in its mixing with water, so that all would get drunk together. There was little boasting among Greeks, so far as we can see, about the high price of the foods they supplied to their friends at dinner: rather the opposite, Greeks boasted of how they haggled over the price at market and had paid as little as they could. In some cities, like Sparta, dining was a communal affair, regulated by strict codes; where it was not, at Athens for example, it was still the assumption that people would entertain one another. Those who dined out but could not afford to return invitations were stigmatised as *parásitoi*—the word from which we get our term 'parasite'.[29]

Most foods served at Greek dinners were local: those of distant origin, such as the silphium of Libya, the salt tuna of Byzantium, the cheese of Sicily, the wine of various Aegean shores and islands, still came from Greek colonies. Scarcely a single food or flavouring that Greeks used in their food came from outside Greek lands.

Now Greeks of the two centuries before Alexander liked nothing better than to emphasise the differences between themselves and their powerful neighbours, such as the Persians and the Macedonians. These differences were, sometimes at least, a subject for laughter. Here is a stage Persian courtier in a Greek comedy:

> What could leaf-chewing Greeks, with their little tables, manage? Over there you'll get just four bits of meat to the obol. Now as for us, among our forefathers they used to roast whole oxen, pigs, deer, lambs: the latest is that Cook has roasted another whole monster for the King and served him up a hot camel. (Antiphanes [Athenaeus 130e]).

In one of Aristophanes' plays a Greek emissary returns from Persia with tales of how he was treated.

> 'Then he gave dinner, and served up whole oxen out of the clay-oven.'
> 'Who ever saw oven-baked oxen? Of all the tales—' (Aristophanes, *Acharnians*, 85-7).

The reasonable Athenian citizen laughs at the idea, but it's clear that Persians went in for oven-roasting of meat, and for the serving of whole large animals at banquets, an idea that was quite foreign to Greeks at this time.

From the first extract it is clear that Greeks did not think of themselves as typical meat-eaters. A medieval Greek traveller, Nicander Nucius, described the English as 'meat-eaters, insatiable for flesh' (*Travels*, ed. Cramer, p.16). In fact, an ancient Athenian had to look northwards only as far as Thessaly, still within northern Greece, to see the generous beef and porridge and soft furniture, and feel distressed by an un-Greek greediness.[30]

> They pass their days in dicing and drinking and similar licentiousness, and they are more interested in ensuring that the tables served to them are full of all kinds of relishes than that their lives are respectably led. (Theopompus 115F49 [Athenaeus 527a]).

And as you went further north, towards Macedonia, ruled by Alexander's father Philip, table manners seemed only to worsen.

> Knowing that the Thessalians were licentious and unrestrained in their life style, Philip [of Macedon] got up parties for them and tried all kinds of amusements with them, dancing, *kómoi*, every licentious act. He was a vulgar man himself, getting drunk every day and enjoying the sort of pastimes that lead in that direction... He won over most of the Thessalians that came in contact with him by parties rather than by bribes. (Theopompus 115F162 [Athenaeus 260b]).

Philip, of course, was Alexander's father. We can hear what an excellent and lavish host he really was from the description of the celebrations at which his daughter Cleopatra was married—and he himself was murdered, but that wasn't in the timetable—at Aegae in 336 BC.[31]

To Greeks, non-Greek dinners seemed extremely odd. Why, close to Macedonia, King Seuthes of Thrace, at a dinner to which the Greek warrior Xenophon and his companions were invited, threw food to his courtiers!—a custom which Xenophon and the rest politely copied, no doubt creating some confusion.[32] In a similar way a Persian governor, Cyrus the younger, used to send half-finished wine jars to his friends with the message:

> It is some time since Cyrus found a pleasanter wine than this. He sends you some, and asks you to drink it today with your dearest friends. (Xenophon, *Anabasis* 1.9.25).

To a critical outsider, appreciation of food and wine can so easily seem gluttonous; generosity can so easily seem patronising; pleasure in company can so easily seem boorish. Philip of Macedon's entertainments met with all three of these criticisms from the Greeks that he entertained. Yet his entertainment achieved his purposes. Philip, followed by his son Alexander, came to dominate the quarrelsome cities of Greece, and this formed Alexander's springboard for his career of conquest.

The result was a deep and permanent mixing of styles of entertainment.

Luxury foods of the East

The wealth of the Persian court had been spent on fine foods and fine wines, sometimes transported over very long distances. It was said that wherever he was the King always drank the water from a pure cool stream in Persia: the first bottled drinking water? It was said that he drank Chalybonian wine, from vineyards in Syria. It was well known that he had parks and gardens in which selected varieties of fruits and vegetables were developed: King Darius, invader of Greece in 490 BC, spoke of this in a letter which survives as an inscription.[33]

From the Persian Empire, then, I trace the seeking after novelty, distant origin, costliness, which was one of the strands of fashionable dining after Alexander. This is where the evaluation of peahens' eggs comes in. And part of this development was the fashion now begun—and we know that it continued all through Roman and medieval times—to include more and more varied spices in the menu, for spices surprise the diner with unexpected flavours and remind him with every mouthful that the host and cook have spared no expense.

Look at how different things had been, back home in Greece itself, in Alexander's own time. In a scientific study on aromatics Theophrastus wrote:

> One might wonder why exotic and other fragrances improve the taste of wines when, so far from having that effect on foods—whether cooked or uncooked—they invariably ruin them. (Theophrastus, *On Odours* 10).

Greeks had already used exotic aromas in their sacrifices, in their perfumes and in their wines: it seems they did not think of adding them to food. The use of spices in Hellenistic recipes was far more lavish and, some would say, far less discriminating.[34] The trend continued down to the recipes of *Apicius* towards the end of the Roman Empire. Those who dined from *Apicius* experienced complex mixtures of herbs and spices,[35] including several from beyond the imperial frontier; many among them would have been considered by Theophrastus to ruin the flavour of food.

Macedonian cuisine

It is owing to Alexander's successes that Macedonia, recently seen as a barbarous kingdom, destined for gradual Hellenisation, turns into a source of new ideas of the fashionable and the civilised. Macedonia contributed two strands to the Hellenistic style of dining: some fashions in cuisine which had long-lasting effects, and a trend towards generosity in party-giving which was normal in the northern Aegean but new to the wider world.

First, the food. Macedonians enjoyed fertile country, naturally generous in its produce: 'Philip was lucky in *everything*!' said a Greek historian ruefully (Theopompus quoted by Athenaeus 77d). There was hardly any tradition of local gastronomic specialities,[36] as there was in Greece, but Macedonians could afford to be much more lavish than Greeks in their use of meat—which they obtained, traditionally, by hunting. They were also more adventurous with meat in culinary terms. It was at this time, and under Macedonian influence, that Greeks learnt to include meat in the dessert course of their meals. In Menander's *False Heracles*, a play which also obliquely criticised the licentious behaviour of the Macedonian king Demetrius Poliorcetes at Athens,[37] the change was remarked on by a satirically minded host:

> Cook, you seem very tiresome. This is the third time you have asked me how many tables we are going to set out. We are sacrificing one little pig. What does it matter to you whether we set eight tables or one? ... No need to make a stew or to do your usual sweet sauce with honey, bread-wheat flour and eggs. Everything's upside down now: the cook makes pastries,[38] bakes cakes, boils porridge and serves it after the salt fish, along with dolmadhes and grapes; while the pastry-chef, his new rival, roasts bits of

meat and thrushes as dessert. So a man lying down to dinner gets *dessert* to eat [all those fiddly dishes and pastries], and then when he's had some more perfume and a fresh wreath [the usual sign for dessert], he gets his *dinner*, thrushes and honey-cakes! (Menander fragment 451 quoted by Athenaeus 172a, 644c).

To take another example, the costly custom of roasting big animals whole, stuffed with smaller creatures and other delicacies, a custom so famous from descriptions of Roman banquets, can be traced back to Alexander's Macedonia. This is a quotation from a description of a wedding feast in Macedonia about 300 BC:

> Next was served a treasure rather than a dinner! a silver dish (with quite a broad gold rim) big enough to take a whole roast porker, and a very large one, which lay on its back displaying all the good things its carcass was full of. Baked together inside it were thrushes and wombs and an infinite number of beccaficchi, and yolks of egg poured over them. (Hippolochus quoted by Athenaeus 129b).

Finally, there is no earlier evidence than this same Macedonian banquet for the use of a flat loaf of bread as a plate for meat, a function which bread has continued to perform ever since in the *pide* of Turkey, the *pita* of Greece and Bulgaria, the *pizza* of southern Italy, the 'trencher' of medieval Europe.[39]

And then the wine. Macedonians did not trouble to look for new wines and distant vineyards. Wines drunk in Macedonia—archaeology and literature agree closely on this—used to come from the nearest producers, from Mende and Torone on the Chalcidice peninsula, and from the north Aegean island of Thasos.[40] But they drank a lot of it. Alexander's court was infamous for its drinking competitions, which certainly caused deaths and may even have caused Alexander's death. 'You drank more than King Alexander!' said an admiring guest at a comedy dinner party on the Athenian stage (Menander fragment 293). And, unlike Greeks, Macedonians had the taste for *neat* wine. They thought it was better if you did not mix it half-and-half with water; Greeks, for their part, were convinced that drinking neat wine caused insanity.[41] The so-called *Diaries of Alexander's Court*, published soon after his death, were evidently intended to show, to Greeks who were all too ready to believe it, how the regular drinking-parties damaged his health and caused his fatal 'fever'.[42]

> When it comes to the choice between neat wine and half-and-half, it's well known that many modern drinkers are on the side of the Macedonians.

Macedonian style

Finally, the conspicuous consumption that now became fashionable at entertainments of the rich and powerful developed straight from the Macedonian customs with which Philip had won over some Greeks and annoyed others. It owed something too to the riches that the Macedonians had won in the East, and perhaps to the fashions that they themselves adopted as possessors of the Persian Empire.

Athenaeus, incidentally, examines mathematically the question whether the Persian kings had been wasteful in the resources that used to go into the 'King's Dinner' (Athenaeus 145a). He concludes that they had not been: but then his yardstick is how much Alexander used to spend at dinner with his friends. Athenaeus may have proved no more than that Alexander, trained in Macedonia, had learnt to be a Persian king![43]

Alexander was certainly a lavish entertainer. He was said once to have entertained six thousand officers to dinner: though some of them had to sit—on silver stools draped with purple rugs—rather than recline for this occasion. He was said to have sat in a pavilion on a golden throne, surrounded by couches with silver legs, when he and his friends dealt with the business of the empire.[44] With him on his expedition went his famous 'hundred-couch tent'—Greek dining rooms were traditionally measured by the number of dining couches that they could accommodate, and a sixty-couch room was the largest on record till Alexander's tent came along. He had had it made before he left Macedonia, and celebrated in it the commencement of his expedition. A later entertainment in it was described by the Roman historian Quintus Curtius in terms that summarise what I am saying of Alexander's influence on dining:

> Alexander had invited foreign ambassadors and the petty kings to dinner, and organised a party for them. A hundred gold couches were set out, rather close together; around the couches were purple curtains sparkling with gold. At that party, mixing together the vices of two nations, he put on display all that was corrupt in the ancient luxury of the Persians and the new fashions of the Macedonians. (Quintus Curtius *History of Alexander* 9.7.15).

It was in this same tent, no doubt, that the mass wedding was celebrated when ninety-two Macedonians took Persian wives, led by Alexander himself. Was this the tent that was swept away, with everything that it contained, in a flash flood in an Iranian river-bed during Alexander's return from India?[45]

For more evidence of the mixture that Curtius talks of so censoriously, we can look once again to the wedding feast of Caranus. At this stage Greek customs, too, can be seen selectively mixing with Macedonian and Persian. At Caranus's dinner there were numerous courses, all separated by distributions of wreaths and perfumes. There were gifts for all the guests to take home, perfume jars, jewellery, and big gold cups, which you first had to drink dry—'but one of the guests, poor fellow, could not drink up, and sat and cried at not getting his bowl until Caranus made him a present of an empty one!' There was far too much meat, mostly of wild animals and birds, to be eaten by the guests: some of the left-overs were passed outwards to the slaves who waited around the edge of the banquet, and some were taken away by the guests—they were even handed out baskets to take their extra food and presents away in (Hippolochus quoted by Athenaeus 128a-130e).

The Long Term

We have been discussing foods and food ideas which were not new in any one part of Alexander's empire, but, because he made it a single empire (however briefly) and began the process of making it a single civilisation, they were free to spread from end to end of that vast region. Thus they became part of the make-up of Roman and Islamic cultures and of medieval and modern Europe and western Asia. Alexander's contribution was to give the opportunity for a mixture of cultures, the origin of that new 'Hellenistic' civilisation that spread so widely and had such wide influence.

So whenever you eat a pizza, or bite into a peach, or nibble a pistachio, or drink rather too much wine and omit to mix it with water, or give your children's party guests little bags of presents to take home, reflect: if it hadn't been for Alexander, these great ideas might never have reached the world's cultural mainstream!

BIBLIOGRAPHY

Andrews, A.C., 'Acclimatization of citrus fruits in the Mediterranean region' in *Agricultural History* vol.35 no.1 (1961) pp.35-46..
Arndt, A. 'Silphium' in Oxford Symposium papers 1992 (1993) pp.28-35.
Borza, E.N., 'The natural resources of early Macedonia' in *Philip II, Alexander the Great and the Macedonian Heritage* ed. W.L. Adams and E.N. Borza, Lanham, Maryland 1982 pp.1-20.
—, 'the symposium at Alexander's court' in *Ancient Macedonia III*, Thessalonica 1983 pp.45-55.
Bretzl, H., *Botanische Forschungen des Alexanderzuges*, Leipzig 1903.
de Candolle, A., *Origine des plantes cultivées*, Paris 1883.

Food in Chinese culture, ed. K.C. Chang, New Haven 1977.

Crawford, D.J., 'Garlic-growing and agricultural specialization in Graeco-Roman Egypt' in *Chronique d'Egypte* vol.48 no.2 (1973) pp.350-363 [1973a].

—, 'the opium poppy: a study in Ptolemaic agriculture' in *Problèmes de la terre en Grèce ancienne* ed. M.I. Finley, The Hague 1973, pp.223-251 [1973b].

Crawford, D.J., 'Food: tradition and change in Hellenistic Egypt' in *World Archaeology* vol.11 no.2 (1979), pp.136-146.

Dalby, A., 'Silphium and asafoetida: evidence from Greek and Roman writers' in Oxford Symposium papers 1992 (1993).

—, 'Hippolochus: The wedding feast of Caranus the Macedonian' in *Petits propos culinaires* no.29 (1988) pp.37-45.

—, *Siren feasts: a history of food and gastronomy in Greece*, London, 1996.

Darby, W.J. and others, *Food: Gift of Osiris*, London 1977.

Laufer, B., *Sino-Iranica: Chinese contributions to the history of civilization in ancient Iran with special reference to the history of cultivated plants and products (Field Museum of Natural History publication no. 201)*, Chicago 1919.

Lewis, D.M., 'The King's dinner (Polyaenus IV 3.32)' in *Achaemenid history II: the Greek sources* ed. H. Sancisi-Weerdenburg and A. Kuhrt, Leiden 1987, pp.79-87.

Merlin, M.D., *On the trail of the ancient opium poppy*, Rutherford 1984.

Rostovtzeff, *Social and economic history of the Hellenistic world*, Oxford 1941.

Saberi, H., 'Rosewater and asafoetida' in Oxford Symposium papers 1992 (1993), pp.220-235.

Sancisi-Weerdenburg, H., 'Gifts in the Persian Empire' in *Le tribut dans l'Empire Perse* ed. P. Briant and C. Herrenschmidt, Louvain 1989.

Sancisi-Weerdenburg, H., 'Persian food: stereotypes and political identity' in *Food in antiquity* ed. J. Wilkins and others, Exeter, 1995.

Schafer, E.H., *The golden peaches of Samarkand*, Berkeley 1963.

Solomon, J., 'The Apician sauce: ius Apicianum' in *Food in antiquity* ed. J. Wilkins and others, Exeter, 1995.

Thompson, D.J., 'Agriculture' in *The Cambridge ancient history* vol.7 part 1, 2nd ed., Cambridge 1984.

REFERENCES

[1] Aristophanes, *Birds* 705-7; Athenaeus 373a; Aristotle, *Study of Animals* 613b5.

[2] Theophrastus, *History of Plants* 4.4.11; Laufer 1919 pp.220-45.

[3] Diogenes Laertius, *Lives of the Philosophers* 6.45; Simplicius, *Commentary on Aristotle De Caelo* 2.12.

[4] Chrysippus of Tyana [Athenaeus 647e].

[5] Galen, *On the Properties of Foods* 1.17; Simeon Seth, *On the Properties of Foods* 126; cf. Soranus, *Gynaecia* 3.41.9. On rice in India, Megasthenes 715F2 [Athenaeus 153e]; Aristobulus 139F35 and other sources cited by Strabo, *Geography* 15.1.18. Strabo says that rice was grown in 'lower Syria' but there is no other evidence for this. I doubt whether the *oríndes ártos* cited by Athenaeus (110e) from the *Triptolemus* of the fifth century BC tragedian Sophocles (fragment 609) is rice-bread.

[6] Bretzl 1903 pp. 207-217.

[7] Palladius, *Agriculture* 4.10.18. Andrews 1961.

[8] Theophrastus, *Study of Plants* 1.11.4, *Plant Physiology* 1.11.1, 1.18.5; Dioscorides, *Materia Medica* 1.115.5.

[9] Juba, *African Collections*, cited by Athenaeus 83b; Africanus, quoted in *Hippiatrica Cantabrigiensia* 71.15. Andrews 1961 p.38.

[10] Theophrastus quoted by Athenaeus 82e: the quotation is not to be found in the *History of Plants*. Several other citations of Theophrastus *On Plants* by Athenaeus have nothing to do with the text of his surviving botanical works. This citation by Athenaeus, whatever its authenticity, was no doubt the source of Candolle's (1882 p.222) statement, unfairly criticised by Laufer (1919 p.539), that Theophrastus knew of the peach.

[11] Diphilus of Siphnos, *Diets for the Sick and Healthy* quoted by Athenaeus 82f (on Diphilus' date see *Epitome of Athenaeus* 51a). Darby and others 1977 pp.733-5.

[12] Columella, *On Agriculture* 5.10.20, 9.4.3; Gargilius Martialis 2. Schafer 1963.

[13] Theophrastus, *Study of Plants* 4.4.7. Copying the words used by Alexander's contemporaries Aristobulus and Amyntas, two later authors, Strabo, *Geography* 15.2.10, and Arrian, *Anabasis* 3.28 both talk of 'terebinths' in the mountains of Afghanistan, perhaps not realising that what was meant was the nut they themselves knew as

pistákion. Just so, the passage from Theophrastus was copied by Pliny (*Natural History* 12.25), who likewise failed to realise that this unnamed nut was the pistachio, which he had actually named and described elsewhere in his book (13.51).

The typical Persian food is called *términthos* (e.g. Plutarch, *Artaxerxes* 3.2). Sancisi-Weerdenburg (1995) rightly criticises such English translations of this term as B. Perrin's 'turpentine wood' — hardly a palatable food! She also argues that terebinth nuts are in question here, and that pistachios were not known, even in Persia, before Alexander's expedition found them in the Bactrian region.

[14] Poseidonius 87F3 [Athenaeus 649d]; Pliny, *Natural History* 15.83, 15.91.

[15] Arndt 1993; Dalby 1993; Saberi 1993.

[16] Cf. Aristobulus quoted by Arrian, *Anabasis* 3.28. See also Strabo, *Geography*, 11.13.7.

[17] The *sílphion* of Strabo is oddly misunderstood by Jones 1917-32 as a reference not to asafoetida but to terebinth resin; Laufer 1919, p.355 and note 6, is also sceptical about the link between silphium and asafoetida. Laufer often is sceptical, but this time it is without justification.

[18] Rostovtzeff 1941 pp.158-9.

[19] Darby and others 1977. See pp.701-2 for the reference to winter cherry (Chinese lantern, *Physalis* spp.) which these authors misunderstand as a variety of cherry (*Prunus* spp.).

[20] Theophrastus, *History of Plants* 2.2.7 (on pomegranates). Thompson 1984; Crawford 1973a (on garlic), 1979.

[21] Bretzl 1903 pp.234-6.

[22] E.H. Schafer in Chang 1977 p.112.

[23] Laufer 1919 pp.297-9.

[24] Merlin 1984.

[25] Crawford 1973b.

[26] Dalby 1996, pp.157-60. For Samian cakes see also Sopater 4 [Athenaeus 644c]; Cretan cakes, Chrysippus of Tyana [Athenaeus 647f].

[27] The evidence for this comes through one of the major 3rd century standard works that we have just discussed. The poet Callimachus was also librarian of the great library at Alexandria, whose task was the collection of all early Greek literature. Callimachus thus compiled a subject catalogue, the first ever, apparently. It does not survive, but Athenaeus retails its lists of cookery authors and of authors on cake-making (Callimachus fragment 435 [Athenaeus 543e]). Iatrocles is not there. But we have to add that Athenaeus is not quoting verbatim, and might well not have troubled to inclue, with this list of obscure authors, the name of one whose work he had already cited and would shortly cite again.

[28] Athenaeus 646a, b, f, 647b.

[29] Dalby 1996 pp.11, 153-4.

[30] Hermippus 63 [*Epitome of Athenaeus* 27e]; Critias 2 [*Epitome* 28b]; Antiphanes 249 [*Epitome* 47b].

[31] Diodorus Siculus, *Library* 16.91-4.

[32] Xenophon, *Anabasis* 7.3.

[33] *SIG* 22.13.

[34] See for example Epaenetus' recipe for *myma* quoted by Athenaeus 662d.

[35] Solomon, 1995.

[36] Dalby 1996. pp.152,157.

[37] See especially Menander fragment 452.

[38] *Enkhytoi* were deep-fried cheese pastries, coated with honey: Cato, *On Agriculture* 80 gives instructions.

[39] Hippolochus quoted by Athenaeus 128d. For further notes on Hippolochus see Dalby 1988.

[40] Borza 1982 p.16; Hippolochus quoted by Athenaeus 129d.

[41] At least one modern historian, possibly a teetotaller, felt he had to justify the Macedonian view by arguing that Macedonian wine was thinner than Greek.

[42] See especially Aelian, *Miscellanies* 3.23. On Alexander's fateful last party, his illness and death, quotations from these *Diaries* are given by Arrian, *Anabasis* 7.25-6 and Plutarch, *Alexander* 76.

[43] Lewis 1987.

[44] Duris, *History* quoted in the *Epitome of Athenaeus* 17f, Ephippus *On the Deaths of Alexander and Hephaistion* quoted by Athenaeus 537d.

[45] Diodorus Siculus, *Histories* 17.16.4; Chares of Mitylene, *Stories of Alexander* quoted by Athenaeus 538b, cf. Aelian, *Miscellanea* 8.7; Arrian, *Anabasis* 6.25.5. Borza 1983.

Dutch Cookery and Calvin

Janny de Moor

The Dutch and Calvin's legacy[1]

All over the world the Dutch are notorious for their frugal attitude with regard to the joys at table. 'Dutch treats' are meals at which people have to pay for themselves or must bring their own food.[2] Dutch cookery has a bad reputation. After having studied Dutch eating habits for more than a year, Stephen Mennell pronounced Dutch food 'niet ververfijnd of pretentieus... maar gewoonweg goed in zijn soort' (not highly sophisticated or pretentious...but simply good of its kind).[3] Given the British propensity to understatement, this was a devastating judgement.

Do we earn it? Of course I might point out that it is a sport among nations to jest good-naturedly about the food of their neighbours. That one should not believe generalizations of any kind if they come from a foreigner. That I could direct you to countless very good restaurants in the Netherlands. That my aunt was such an excellent cook and taught me so much about Dutch 'haute cuisine'. Etcetera. But I'm afraid there is at least some truth in the statement that the Dutch don't care much for good cooking.

How did this come about? Are there reasons for this manifest disinterest? And is there some consolation and enlightenment to be gained from the circumstance that other countries have to put up with a similar reputation, whether rightly or wrongly?

According to Stephen Mennell the main reason why the Dutch would have such simple cookery is that they never had a court of absolute rulers which set the trend in eating habits.[4] This explanation is totally unsatisfactory. First, the Netherlands have had a *de facto* court since 1572, when the princes of Orange started to act as stadtholders. The argument that they were not *absolute* rulers is too fine a distinction in my opinion. Second, if it is true—I say, *if!*—that the same negligence of cooking can be observed in Britain, in spite of the existence of a court, we must conclude that courts did not have a decisive influence on the development of a nation's eating habits. Third, it has been argued convincingly that the French culinary tradition did not start at the French court, but much earlier, in the cloister of Cluny.[5]

People who are somewhat better informed about Dutch regional cooking often notice a striking difference between the provinces south of the rivers Rhine and Maas, and the northern provinces. The south has more traditional regional dishes, often much more refined, than in the north. Even ordinary people were accustomed to drink wine there. My own grandmother, a farmer's wife just south of the big rivers, used to order a cask of Médoc wine every year. She drank it on birthdays and other special occasions. I still remember her sitting with her friends in the state room of the house, carefully lifting the veil of her large hat to nip from her glass. In rural families in the northern Netherlands such behaviour would have been highly unusual.

Understandably this difference between the north and the south inspired some to attribute the general underdevelopment of Dutch cuisine to the inhabitants of the politically and economically dominant northern provinces. Their more Nordic type of culture would have been uninterested in good food, whereas the more Mediterranean or Burgundian people of the south cherished the good life.[6] At first sight, this seems an attractive theory. In support of it one can point to the undeniable fact that all the oldest Dutch cookbooks come from the southern part of the Low Countries.[7]

Yet this theory too must be rejected. First, as a sign-board along the 'Autoroute du Soleil' near Langres clearly announces, the watershed between the Mediterranean and the North Sea lies much more to the south than the southern Netherlands. Moreover, in the course of history so many people from the south migrated to the north,[8] that an ethno-social explanation alone cannot account for the phenomenon of the general Dutch indifference to dining and wining.

Finally, Simon Schama came forward with an interesting theory in his provocative work *The Embarrassment of Riches*.[9] According to Schama, the rich Dutch merchants of the seventeenth century would have had a bad conscience about their opulent lifestyle and would have used their Calvinistic faith to repent occasionally when they became too uneasy about their eternal salvation or when calamities seemed to indicate some displeasure on high. The Dutch Protestants of the seventeeth century indulged in a kind of ambiguity Schama obviously denounces.

Schama's theory is in accordance with the general feeling of many Dutch intellectuals. They hold John Calvin ultimately responsible[10] for the anti-culinary, anti-hedonistic character of Dutch cookery.[11] A well-known Dutch novelist writes about one of his characters,

> a man who, just like Calvin, mistrusted all pleasure, who wanted to suppress all zest for life...[12]

In view of the fact that up to the present day many Dutch children have to learn the Heidelberg Catechism by heart, his wrath is understandable. In Sunday 50 this catechism states that the Lord's Prayer for our daily bread is solely aimed at the satisfaction of our corporeal needs and should by no means deflect us from focussing our total attention on God as our Provider. This is not likely to save any souls among young people who are ravenous after a good day of trying out their God-given bodies.

Also the officially approved Reformed prayers before and after a meal strongly emphasize strict moderation at table and a total preoccupation with the *spiritual* bread of the Word of God. Up till the present day they are included in many Dutch prayer-books.

The editor-in-chief of a national newspaper recently sketched the modern Dutch Protestant as follows,

> All right, he does celebrate Christian feast days. But he does so more from indulgence than from inner conviction. He celebrates Christmas, but warns against excessive conviviality. He prefers—whether he is secularized or still a churchgoer matters little— to celebrate it soberly, in a way that does not disturb his rhythm.[13]

Of course such denial of the delights of the tongue could not be upheld without strong campaigns to promote it. One of the most influential forces in this respect has been the lawyer-poet Jacob Cats (1577-1660). Up to the first half of this century his works got a place next to the Bible in almost every Dutch Protestant family. I want to quote some of his limping verse to give you an impression of the repressive nature of his influence on Dutch cooking tradition.

> I simply want the wife to cook the gifts of the Lord,
> according to measure; and to serve honourably
> good fare for digestion and to serve this in moderation,
> as is demanded, is permitted to everyone.
> Continuously pay heed to praise the Lord!
> And do not fancy your pots too much!
> He [sic!, JdM] who knows how to lay his table without excess
> will gain pleasure and refreshed limbs from it.
> For he who prepares a pure meal before his God—
> his body will be strengthened and his soul be fed.[14]
> You, woman, buy good food, but not for voracious gluttony!

> You do not need to heed mouth and belly beyond measure!
> Be thrifty as is demanded, but serve when it is expedient
> what will please your guest or other friend.[15]

> Let gorging be enjoyed by those who live for gluttony,
> you, don't be too dainty, not a kitchen-fool!
> It does not befit a pure soul to live in the pot.
> The gullet is a wolf, and what people eat
> slips down in haste and is immediately forgotten.[16]

> He who eats little and drinks less,
> is the one who masters his desires.[17]

And yet, this same wealthy poet celebrated birthdays with extremely lavish parties at his estate 'Zorghvliet', even when he was already quite old,[18] thus vividly illustrating the moral duplicity of the Dutch Golden Age Schama described.

As a matter of fact, such duplicity continues up to this century. Abraham Kuyper, a famous Dutch neo-Calvinist around the turn of the century, approved of festive meals provided they were held in private.[19] A Dutch centre for documentation on the history of Dutch Protestantism preserves menu cards of private dinners held for Neo-Calvinistic leaders. Some of the cards feature no less than fourteen courses and a choice of exquisite wines.[20]

However, one should never confuse practice with ideals. Undeniably the strong bond between the civil political structure of the Republic of the Seven United Netherlands and the Dutch Reformed Church moulded the Dutch moral climate after Calvin's ideals for Geneva.[21] This deeply influenced the spiritual ideals of our country. As a result, the Dutch look with suspicion at good cookery up to our own days. Even people who have nothing to do anymore with Dutch Protestant tradition consider it bad manners to show an open interest in culinary matters.

So I hold that this attitude has everything to do with religion. In support of this thesis, two further arguments may be adduced.

> a. The majority of the population in the southern part of the Netherlands where culinary tradition was not spurned, as indicated above, was not Protestant but Roman Catholic.[22]

> b. The same frugal attitude is found with Calvinists in other parts of the world, for example with the Puritans in Britain, the followers of John Knox in Scotland and the Huguenots in France.[23]

The question now is whether this negative attitude is rightly traced back to John Calvin. Of course some of those who want to keep honouring Calvin for his lasting contribution to the Reformation, and therefore to the history of Western Europe, are anxious to deny he has any responsibility for the rigid attitudes ascribed to him with regard to mundane matters like cookery.[24] Mostly they ascribe these—by now—unpopular ideas to the so-called 'Nadere Reformatie' (Further Reformation) in the Netherlands of the seventeenth century which tried to regulate the life of the pious Protestant in all the minutest details.[25] To some extent this is undoubtedly true. My quotations from Cats whose national impact is illustrated by his common pet name 'Vadertje (Daddy) Cats' would seem to remove all doubt in this respect. In view of the lassitude of the times, especially in cities like Amsterdam, it may be deemed an act of courage that even in the Golden Age some clergymen dared to denounce the excesses taking place at the tables of the rich.[26] They could appeal, however, to ideals shared by the sinners themselves.

The question I want to answer in this paper is whether the roots of the anti-culinary attitude of the Dutch must indeed be sought with Calvin. And if so, is it warranted to say that the latter's statements on eating and drinking may account for the ambiguity in the attitude of the rich Dutch merchants of the 17th century?

Calvin on eating and drinking

Johannes Calvinus (Jean Caulvin) was born in Noyon, France on the 10th July 1509. He lived most of his life in exile in Geneva where he died on the 27th May 1564. There is no need to repeat his biography here because it can be found in any encyclopedia. It may be expedient, however, to note that Calvin's personal life was most difficult. His mother died four or five years after his birth and his father remarried almost instantaneously. Soon after, the young boy was sent away to live with the noble family of the Montmors. Calvin married late with Idelette de Bure, but all their three children died young and eventually Idelette also passed away. According to Bouwsma, Calvin became a driven man only after these tragic experiences.[27] At the same time Calvin had to cope with many corporal ailments.

In view of his unhappy personal circumstances it is admirable that Calvin could write in a positive sense about the pleasures of life. Eating and drinking are gifts of God and are not only there to sustain our bodies, but also for enjoyment. He writes:

> For if we investigate to what end He created food, we will find He did not do this for the sake of necessity only, but also wanted to recommend to us some enjoyment and merriment. Thus his aim with garments was, besides necessity, propriety and decency. In herbs, trees and fruits, besides various uses, their pleasing sight and delicious smell. For if this were not true, the prophet would not mention among God's blessings that wine gladdens the heart of man and oil makes his face shine (Ps. 104:15).[28]

> Since it pleases God that we are in this world we should not at all abstain from drinking and from eating because of our troubles; this would be gratuitously making war on him; God wishes that we should enjoy the good things he gives us for our nourishment.[29]

> If a man can afford to drink a liberal amount of wine, Calvin does not see any reason why he should not do so, provided he does not indulge in unwarranted luxury and immoderation.

Commenting upon the story of the wedding at Cana where Jesus changed water into wine, Calvin remarks,

> But it is wonderful that a large quantity of wine, and of the very best wine, is supplied by Christ, who is a teacher of sobriety. I reply, when God daily gives us a large supply of wine, it is our own fault if his kindness is an excitement to luxury; but on the other hand, it is an undoubted trial of our sobriety, if we are sparing and moderate in the midst of abundance.[30]

One senses a certain uneasiness in this quotation, as if Calvin does not want to deny the rich their good claret, but on the other hand sees it as his duty to emphasize that Jesus was a 'teacher of sobriety', an element which was totally absent from the story itself.

The same wavering we observe in a sermon on Job 1,

> Yet we may note again that Job has observed and known what experience tells us [namely] that in all banquets there is always some disorder if God is not properly honoured. First when people gather, there will sometimes be a surplus of food, and those who will have gathered in companionship will eat and drink more than they ordinarily do. Well, they do not think of all those excesses, and it may take the most holy god-fearing people by surprise. Of course they do not want to be gourmands stuffing

their stomachs, fuddling themselves like pigs, let alone be drunkards dulling their minds. No, but yet they may well exceed the limit. And why? We see that one drifts into these things imperceptibly. That is why there is something bad in these banquets, even if they are held for a good cause and even if the intentions of him who invites his friends and of those who come to keep him company are good. For almost always something wrong will happen, even without they themselves being aware of it.[31]

Obviously Calvin is not in favour of lavish banquets, but at the same time he seems to more or less excuse the god-fearing men who happen to find themselves in the middle of such totally unsuspected orgies. In other places one gets the definite impression that Calvin would be inclined to forgive gourmands if only they perform their religious duties.[32]

For Calvin no food is prohibited, as he writes in his commentary on 1 Corinthians 10:25-25,

> Now, as to the eating of food, he [Paul] makes, in the first place, this general statement—that it is lawful to eat with a safe conscience, any kind of food, because the Lord permits it.[33]

However, luxury can never be excused, as Calvin keeps repeating time and again,

> Isaiah does not absolutely condemn the use of meat or the drinking of wine, but he condemns the luxury and wantonness by which men are hardened in such a manner that they obstinately set aside God's threatenings and treat as fables all that the prophets told them.[34]

> 'They shall not drink wine with a song' (Isa. 24:9). To drink wine is not in itself evil, because God has appointed it for the use of man; but here the Prophet describes the banquets of drunkards, which were full of licentiousness, songs and insolence. Again, because they abused their enjoyment of plenty, he threatens them with want, which men almost bring upon themselves, when by their luxury they turn to a bad use the goodness of God.[35]

However, in far more cases Calvin adds much sterner warnings. Eating and drinking should always be temperate. Luxury inevitably leads to excess. 'When men enjoy abundance they become luxurious and abuse it by intemperance.'[36] 'For we know that if the minds of men are not kept within the bounds of reason and temperance, they become insatiable; and, therefore, a great abundance will not extinguish the fire of a depraved appetite'.[37] In this respect man should learn from the animal world. A beast eats and drinks exactly the amount nature prescribes. Not so man who, if he follows his appetite, will never have enough.

> We are insatiable pits. Instead of taking a normal meal, many seem to deliberately cram themselves up to bursting. To what limit many people drink and eat?...New sweetmeats must be found to stimulate the appetite, even though one is full to bursting. In short, if one observes sharply how it is with human beings one will find they are monsters defying nature.[38]

This rather misanthropic view may have been influenced by what Calvin observed close by in Geneva,

> On the contrary, we see how the world is behaving nowadays in this place. For how many of those heavy drunkards don't we see, of those gourmands who are like pigs at the trough, without any intelligence or reason? They fill their stomachs, but there is no question of lifting their heads to heaven to praise Him who feeds them and supports them so richly. They always have their whole snout deep in the fodder.[39]

Such devastating criticism of excessive eating and drinking prompts the question of what Calvin regarded as the proper God-given norm for moderation. However, in this respect Calvin remains vague. He acknowledges that the Bible does not provide us with a clear norm,

The Lord has not prescribed to us a homer-ration or any other measure for the food we have each day, but he has commended to us frugality and temperance and has forbidden anyone from going to excess because of abundance. Thus those who have riches, whether inherited or won by their own industry and labour, are to keep in mind that what is left over is meant not for intemperance or luxury but for relieving the needs of the brothers... I acknowledge indeed that we are not bound to such equality as would make it wrong for the rich to live more elegantly than the poor; but there must be such equality that nobody is hungry and nobody hoards abundance at another's expense. The poor man's homer-ration will be coarse bread and meagre fare; the rich man's homer-ration will be a somewhat more liberal portion, as his means allow him: but in such a way that they both live temperately and do not neglect others.[40]

The poor on their part do well to carry their burden resignedly.[41]

Christians should 'eat only sparingly and lightly, out of necessity, content simply with black bread and water' to show their willingness to 'bridle themselves'.[42] Calvin was in favour of fasting which he saw as an expression of the moderate lifestyle a true Christian should adopt[43] though it would seem an exaggeration to state that for Calvin, fasting was 'an archetype of Christian behaviour', as Bouwsma puts it.[44] Calvin does not begrudge the poor their pork, cheeses, dairy products, onions and cabbage, nor the rich their dainty dishes, if only they resist the temptation to gorge in excess.[45] That Calvin was not a vegetarian may be clear from these quotations.[46]

So when Calvin occasionally calls eating and drinking 'very despicable'[47] or 'not important'[48] one should not over-interpret such statements. He only wants us to perceive that worries about food are unimportant as compared to the spiritual craving for Christ.[49]

So one cannot maintain that Calvin hated dining and wining. He only called for moderation. Yet it must be conceded that in the practical implementation of his ideals Calvin could be extremely harsh. His power over the magistrates of Geneva enabled him to found a more or less 'theocratic' state in which dissenters risked being excommunicated, incarcerated or even executed.[50] He left little room for joyous feasts. When people celebrated Christmas too enthusiastically on the 25th December 1555, they were imprisoned.[51] Calvin also unsuccessfully tried to replace inns, notorious places of licentious behaviour, by 'abbeys' where it was only permitted to sing Psalms and read the Bible.[52] In other cases the deacons of Calvin's church in Geneva used inns they controlled as places to house poor refugees and drunkards.[53] Conviviality and hospitality were concepts Calvin found difficult to digest. Commenting upon Abraham's typically Near Eastern generosity in receiving unknown guests (Gen.18), he praises such behaviour highly, but then adds sourly,

> It is questionable, however, whether Abraham would always have received all guests as sumptuously as this time, because in that case it might easily have come to excessive crowding... For if he had to slaughter calves for all kinds of travellers, his house would soon have been exhausted by his profuse expenditures.[54]

Small wonder that some unknown follower of Calvin invented Dutch treats!

Looking back, we may say that all ingredients for the stance taken by Cats and other Dutch Reformed leaders of the seventeeth century with regard to eating and drinking were already there in the works of Calvin himself. It is no viable option to exonerate Calvin by accusing his epigones in the Netherlands and elsewhere of undue exaggeration of the master's word in this respect.

With regard to the ambiguity characterizing the Dutch Protestants' attitude to the good life it cannot be denied that it too goes back to Calvin himself. On the one hand he accepted food as a gift of God, on the other he warned not to use this gift without moderation. On the one hand he recognized the right of the rich to lead an elegant life and warned the poor not to begrudge them, on the other his social programme did not go further than admonishing the rich to share their surplusses with their poor brothers. On the one hand he described the human appetite as a natural urge, but on the other he denounced it as unnatural, worse than a beast's voracity. Repeatedly he invokes the limit God has decreed to enjoying food and drink, but nowhere does he specify where in the Bible this limit is defined and what it means in concrete terms.

In an important passage of his major work the *Institutio* he admits that this is rather slippery terrain. Contrary to others who went as far as stating that nothing more than bread and water should suffice the true Christian, Calvin regards this as too stern a limit (even though he himself uses it a few times, as we saw) because the Word of God does not demand it. However, he refuses to leave this matter totally to every man's personal conscience because the Bible has given general guidelines which the Christian must obey.[55] Calvin regarded food as one of the *idiaphora*, indifferent things in which the Christian is free to make his own choice,[56] but this freedom is limited by respect for God as his Provider and by love for his neighbour in need. This is why luxury at table must be avoided.

I am no theologian and will therefore refrain from pronouncing judgement on Calvin in this respect. But in the end I believe Calvin to have been not entirely unambiguous on the matter of moderation with regard to eating and drinking. McGrath ascribes to Calvin 'a sophisticated dialectic between faith and the world.'[57] In my opinion one might just as well say that Calvin left us an unresolved tension between stern Christian principles and acceptance of worldly pleasures. This renders the later confusion in this respect understandable, to say the least. The true Calvinist had to remain a stranger[58] in the same world he had to embrace as a generous gift of God. The best way to cope with this contradiction was to form closely knit self-controlling groups, a kind of social ghetto, and to enjoy the good life in the private atmosphere of one's own group.

Beyond Calvin

In moral issues Calvin was not a real innovator and therefore he cannot be made the sole person responsible for the ethics he preached. It should be remembered that moderation or temperance was one of the four cardinal virtues of Calvin's beloved Greek and Roman antiquity. Calvin found sympathetic supporters of his views in Seneca and Cato.[59] The early church too had preached a life of sobriety and self-denial. The most holy men were monks who starved themselves to death. Augustine declared with obvious satisfaction that the regulations of the church with regard to moderation were harsh enough to discourage any attempt at disobedience. The virtues of modesty and moderation were also praised by Calvin's Humanist contemporary Erasmus. The so-called 'Modern Devotion'[60] and the Anabaptists who preceded the Calvinistic Reformation in the Netherlands had preached exactly the same ideals.[61] So it may be said that in propagating these ideals neither Calvin himself nor the Dutch Calvinists were out of tune with their times.

However, as a Reformer, Calvin wanted to rely on the Bible as the only reliable guide to life. Because the eschatological perspective of most of the New Testament writings left him little to go upon there, he was forced to look for guidance in the Old Testament. As we have seen, many of the passages which he saw as supporting his view with regard to eating and drinking came from the Old Testament.

Now it is interesting that the Jewish philosopher Baruch Spinoza, living in seventeenth century Holland, came to the same conclusion as the Calvinists (who nonetheless bothered him a lot). 'It is the part of a wise man, I say, to restore and refresh himself with moderate and pleasant food and drink.'[62] It is because of the love of God that man is able to restrain his lusts.[63] Without saying so directly, Spinoza seems to take the Hebrew Bible and the traditional Jewish ethics as his point of departure.[64] Being a glutton and drunkard is condemned in the Bible (e.g. Deut. 21:18-21). A famous saying of the Jewish Fathers runs,

This is the way of the Torah: A morsel with salt you shall eat and water by measure you shall drink... you shall live a life of hardship, and labour in the Torah. If you do so, happy be you and may [all] be well with you. Happy in this world, and well in the world to come.[65]

Spinoza firmly denounces gluttony and drunkenness as immoderate lust.[66] Moreover, Jewish cuisine has always been restricted by the voluntary obedience to the dietary laws.

Nowadays it has become clear than many of these old Jewish regulations were formulated in direct opposition to the religious customs of the surrounding Canaanite nations. During their religious festivals the Canaanites ate much larger quantities of meat than the Israelites ever did. And they deliberately drank wine until they were sodden.[67] This explains why moderation is such a prominent part of the Jewish heritage and it is certainly not too far-fetched to assume that Calvin as a faithful biblicist felt that the Bible had something special to say in this respect. Bouwsma discerns a yearning for precise formulation in Calvin's enunciation of the general principles governing Christian behaviour,[68] a precision Calvin was unable to achieve with regard to eating and drinking, possibly for the very reason that he also rejected the strict application of detailed rulings comparable to the Jewish food-laws.

Epilogue

In 1864 a famous Dutch Reformed politician, G. Groen van Prinsterer (1801-1876), profusely praised Calvin's influence on the Netherlands. The Dutch would be such worthy followers of the great Reformer because they nourished themselves on the Bible.[69] Here we see how zeal approaching to fanaticism ends up in reducing the joys at table to a mere metaphor.

This spring I was in Anduze, a small town at the foot of the Cevennes in southern France. On Sunday I visited the Reformed church, remnant of a stronghold of the Huguenots, the staunch French Calvinists. To my surprise a woman entered carrying five French 'baguettes' under her arm which she had apparently just bought at the baker's shop. Immediately I thought, 'Would Calvin have approved of this violation of the Sunday rest in favour of nice crisp bread at dinner?' I'm sure he would have objected—in contrast to the present congregation who apparently thought nothing of it. In matters of practical ethics Calvin was very stern, but in my humble opinion for reasons that were not entirely clear to himself. History has perceived this and has relativized his statements on these matters.

In French, a protestant church is called a 'temple'. Just opposite the 'temple' of Anduze you find a fine inn. It is open on Sunday, of course, and is called *Relais des Templiers* (Resting-Place of the Templars). If food and wine are at stake, the countrymen of Calvin have become masters in seducing you to relativize your stern principles!

REFERENCES

[1] I thank Professor W. Nijenhuis (Groningen) for valuable advice on Calvin's influence on the Netherlands. Thanks are also due to Mr J.F. Seijlhouwer, Secretary of the 'Historisch Documentatiecentrum van het Nederlandse Protestantisme van 1800 tot heden' and to the personnel of the 'Atheneum Bibliotheek' at Deventer as well as the library of the 'Theologische Universiteit' at Kampen.

In this paper the following abbreviations will be used: CR = *Corpus Reformatorum*; CO = *Ioannis Calvini opera quae supersunt omnia*, ed. G. Baum, E. Cunitz, E. Reuss.

[2] On a previous occasion, Ileen Montijn noted the legendary nature of the expression and reviewed a number of real traditional Dutch treats, 'Dutch Treats or Festive Food in an Affluent Society', in *Oxford Symposium on Food and Cookery 1990: Feasting and Fasting*, London 1991, 158-61.

[3] Stephen Mennell, *Smaken verschillen*, Amsterdam 1989, reprinted in: J. van Tol et al (eds.), *Kookboeken door de*

eeuwen heen, Den Haag 1991, 46. Mennell was kind enough not to publish this verdict in English, as far as I know.
[4]Mennell, *ibid*.
[5]Johanna Maria van Winter, *Van soeter cokene*, Haarlem 1976, 13.
[6]See the survey by A. van Otterloo, 'Over de culinaire culturen in Noord en Zuid', *Groniek 95* (1986) 47-54.
[7]W.L. Braekman, *Een Antwerps Kookboek voor 'Leckertonghen'*, Antwerpen 1995, 13-24.
[8]For example, the great number of Flemish refugees who fled from Parma in 1585 and settled permanently in Amsterdam, Leiden and Haarlem. Cf. A. Th. van Deursen, *Mensen van klein vermogen*, 5th printing, Amsterdam 1991, 47.
[9]S. Schama, *The Embarrassment of Riches: An Interpretation of Dutch Culture in the Golden Age*, New York 1987. Dutch translation by E. Dabekaussen, B. de Lange and T. Maters: *Overvloed en onbehagen: de Nederlandse cultuur in de Gouden Eeuw*, Amsterdam 1988.
[10]Of course they were not the first Calvin-antagonists. A beautiful example is Stephan Zweig, *Castellio gegen Calvin, oder Ein Gewissen gegen die Gewalt*, Wien 1936, 67: 'Welch ein lichtloses, freudloses, welch ein einsames und abweisendes Gesicht, das Antlitz Calvins! Unfassbar, dass jemand wünschte, das Bild dieses unerbittlichen Forderers und Mahners an der Wand seines Zimmers zu haben: der Atem würde einem kälter vom Munde fliessen, fühlte man ständig den wachsam spähenden Blick dieses unfreudigsten aller Menschen über seinem täglichen Tun.' And p. 69, 'Von nichts das trunken macht, nicht vom Wein, nicht vom Weibe, nicht von der Kunst, von keiner der Gottesgaben der Erde hat dieser fanatisch Nüchterne jemals Lust gefordert oder empfangen.'
[11]Hugh Jans, in: Saskia Budding (ed.) *De tafel van 8*, 's-Gravenhage 1994, 6; Jobse-Van Putten, *Envoudig maar voedzaam*, Nijmegen 1995, 526.
[12]Maarten 't Hart, *De Ortolaan*, s.l.1984, 82: ';een man, die net als Calvijn alle plezier verdacht vond, alle levenslust de kop in wilde drukken...'.
[13]'Goed, hij viert ook wel kerkelijke feestdagen. Maar dat is eigenlijk meer uit toegeeflijkheid dan uit innerlijke overtuiging. Hij viert wel kerstfeest, maar waarschuwt tegen excessen van gezelligheid. Hij viert het (of hij nu geseculariseerd of nog kerkelijk is, dat maakt weinig uit) het liefst sober, op een wijze di zijn ritme niet doorbreekt.' Jan Greven, 'Carnaval', *Trouw* 16th February 1991.
[14]Ick wil maer, dat het wijf de gaven van den Heer
Sal koken opte maet, en rechten metter eer
Te nutten goede kost, en dat in rechter maten,
Te schaffen na den eysch, is ieder toegelaten;
Hebt maer geduerigh acht te loven uwen God,
En hanght niet al te seer de sinnen aen de pot.
Die sonder overdaet sijn tafel weet to decken,
Het sal hem tot vermaek en frische leden strecken;
Want die voor sijnen God een reijne maeltijd doet,
Wort aen het lijf gesterckt, en in de siel gevoet.
Jacob Cats, *Alle de wercken*, ed. J. van Vloten, dl.1, Zwolle 1862, 482.
[15]Ghy vrou koopt goede spijs, maar niet tot gulsigh brassen,
Ghij dient niet buiten maet op mont en buyck te passen;
Weest suynig naar den eysch, maar schaft wanneer het dient,
Wat best bevallen sal uw gast of ander vrient.
Cats, dl. 2., 828.
[16]Laet vraten lecker sijn, die level om te brassen;
En weest niet al te kies, niet al te keucken-sot.
't En voeght geen reyne ziel te wonen in de pot.
Het keelgat is een wolf, en wat de menschen eten
Glijdt in der haesten deur, en is terstont vergeten.
Cats, dl.1, 485.
[17]Die weynigh eet en minder drinckt,
Die is'et die de lusten dwinght.
Cats, dl.2, 825.
[18]Such parties are attested for his 78th and 82nd birthdays. See Johanna Breevoort, *Vader Cats en de vrouw*, Kampen 1915, 39-40.

[19] Abraham Kuyper, voorwoord in: Johanna Breevoort, *Vader Cats en de vrouw*, Kampen 1915, x.
[20] Information generously provided by Mr J.F. Seijlhouwer.
[21] Van Deursen, *Mensen van klein vermogen*, 289.
[22] For a fine illustration of this point see the following (translated) fragment from the novelist Cees Nooteboom: '"This is a Brabantine lunch", Taads said with satisfaction and sat down. "Disgusting late-Burgundian affectation. Those rich flax-farmers still cherish the idea they are the inheritors of the Burgundian court. This is the Bavaria of the Netherlands, my boy! A Calvinist does not belong here."
"I thought you too were a Roman-Catholic?" Inni said. "Above the big rivers all Dutch are Calvinists. We do not like too much, too long, too expensive. If the people here have it their way you are going to sit at table until three."' (Cees Noteboom, 'Een Brabantse Koffietafel', in: J. Müller (ed.), *Het litterair eetboek*, Amsterdam 1985, 71).
[23] D.F. Kelly, *The Emergence of Liberty in the Modern World: The Influence of Calvin on Five Governments from the 16th through 18th Centuries*, Philipsburg 1992.
[24] This was the line of argument chosen by one of my spokesmen, Professor C. Augustijn of the Free University, Amsterdam. He flatly denied any influence of Calvin on Dutch attitudes towards good cooking and stated I would find nothing of substance on this theme in Calvin's works.
[25] This is the line of argument chosen by W. Nijenhuis, *Hoe calvinistisch zijn wij Nederlanders?*, Amsterdam 1993, esp. 15. See also Jan Greven, *Trouw*, 31st December 1994, 10.
[26] R. Evenhuis, in *Ook dat was Amsterdam: De kerk der Hervorming in de Gouden Eeuw*, dl.2, Amsterdam 1965-78, 117-43.
[27] J. Bousma, *John Calvin: A Sixteenth Century Portrait*, Oxford 1988, 29.
[28] Iam si reputemus quem in finem alimenta creaverit, reperiemus non necessitati modi, sed oblectamento quoque ac hilaritati voluisse consulere. Sic in vestibus, praeter necessitatem, finis ei fuit decorum et honestas. In herbis, arboribus et frugibus, praeter usus varios, aspectus gratia et iucunditas odoris. Nisi enim id verum esset, non recenseret propheta inter beneficia Dei, quod vinum laetificat cor hominis quod oleum splendidam ejus faciem reddit. (Ps. 104,15). (Inst. III.x.2, CR30=CO2, Brunsvigae 1864, col. 529-30).
[29] Puis qu'il luy plaist que nou soyons en ce monde, que ce nest pas pour nous abstenir de boire et de manger du tout par noz fasheries; car ce seroit luy faire guerre de nostre bon gré;... Dieu veut que nous iouyssions des biens qu'il nous donne pour nostre nourriture.' (Sermon No.39 on II Samuel, cf. J. Calvin, *Predigten über das 2. Buch Samuelis*, ed. H. Rückert (Supplementa Calviniana: Sermons inédits), Neukirchen 1961, 346-7.
[30] Sed mirum est quod Christus, frugalitatis magister, vini et quidem praestantissimi magnam copiam largitur. Respondeo, quum nobis quotidie Deus largum vini proventum suppeditat, nostro vitio fieri si eius benignitas irritamentum est luxuriae: quin potius haec temperantiae nostrae vera est probatio, si in media affluentia, parci tamen ac moderati sumus. (Comm. on John 2:8, CR 75 = CO 47, Brunsvigae 1892, col.41).
[31] Mais cependant encores nous avon à noter, que Iob a bien regardé, et cognu ce que l'experience nous monstre, qu'en tous banquets il y a tousiours quelque desordre, là où Dieu ne sera point honoré comme il doit. Premierement, si on s'assemble, il y aura de la superfluité quelques fois aux viandes, et ceux qui seront assemblez par compagnie mangeront et boiront outre leur portion ordinaire. Et bien, on ne pense point à tous ces excès-là, et les plus saincts gens craignans Dieu y sont surprins. Vray est qu'ils ne seront point gourmans pour se farcir le ventre, et pour se saouler comme des pourceaux, tans moins encores seront-ils yvronges pour avoir leur esprit abruti: non, mais tant y a qu'ils peuvent bien exceder mesure. Et pourquoy? Nous voyons que sans y penser on s'escoule en cela. Ainsi donc voila desia un mal qui se fait en ces banquets, encores qu'ils soyent instituez pour bonne cause, et que l'intention de celui qui convie ses amis, et de ceux qui y viennent pour lui tenir compagnie, soit bonne: car à grand peine se passera-on qu'il n'y ait quelque faute, de laquelle mesmes on ne s'apperçoit point. (Sermon No.2 on Job, CR 61 = CO 33, Brunsvigae 1887, col.40).
The same comparison of gourmands with pigs occurs in Sermon 123 on Deut. 21:18-21 (CR 55 = CO 27, Brunsvigae 1884, col.683) and Sermon No.180 on Deut. 32:14 (see below).
[32] E.g. Inst.III x 3 (CR 30 - CO 2, Brunsvighae 1864, col.530)
[33] Nunc quod ad esum ciborum pertinet, initio ponit generalem sententiam, sana conscientia licere vesci quibuslibet, quia Dominus permittit. (Comm. on John 2:8, CR 57 = CO 49, Brunsvigae 1892, col.469).
Slaughtering cattle is not a sinful act, Comm. on Isa. 22:12-13 (CR 64 = CO 36, Brunsvigae 1888, col. 375).
[34] Nec enim usum carnis aut potum simpliciter damnat Isaias, sed luxum atque etiam proterviam, qua sic

indurantur homines, ut animo pervicaci minas Dei reiiciant et habeant pro fabula quidquid a prophetis nunciatur. (Comm. On Isa. 22:12-13, CR 64 = CO 36, Brunsvigae 1888, col.375).

[35]Bibere vinum per se malum non est, quantenus hominum usui divinitus fuit destinatum: sed hic propheta ebriosorum convivia, lasciviae, cantilenarum, petulantiae plena describit. Deind quia abusi fuerant sua saturitate, penuriam illis minatur, quam sibi fere accersunt homines dum liberalitem Dei luxuria sua corrumpunt. (Comm. on Isa. 24:9, CR 64 = CO 36, Brunsvigae 1888, col. 403).

[36]Comm. Isa. 5:11 (CR 64 = CO 36, col.110). See also Comm. Dan. 1:8 (CR 68 = CO 40, Brunsvigae 1889, col.543-44.

[37]Scimus enim, nisi intra fines rationis et temperantiae se contineant hominum animi, esse inexplebiles, ideoque saturitate non restingui pravi appetitus ardorem. (Comm. on Ps. 78:30, CR 59 = CO 31, Brunsvigae 1887, col 731).

[38]'...nous sommes gouffres insatiables, au lieu de prendre refection, il semble que beaucoup s'y veulent crever à leur escient. En quelle mesure est-ce que beaucoup de gens boyvent et mangent?...il faudra trouver de nouvelles friandises pour aiguiser l'appetit, quand on sera tant soul qu'on creve. Brief, si on regarde bien que c'est des hommes, on trouvera que ce sont monstres comme en despit de nature.' (Serm.No.2 on 1 Cor., CR 77 = CO 49, Brunsvigae 1892, col.603). See also Sermon No.180 on Deut. 32:14 (CR 56 = CO 28, Brunsvigae 1885, col.705); Comm. on Ps. 128:2 (CR 60 = CO32, Brunsvigae 1887, col.327). In other places Calvin compares man to a horse which becomes restive and obstinate if one feeds it too well, Sermon No.47 on Deut. 6:11-12 (CR 54 = CO 26, Brunsvigae 1883, col.448); Sermon 180 on Deut. 32:14 (CR 56 = CO 28, Brunsvigae 1885, col.704).

[39]'Or nous voyons au contraire comme le monde se conduit auiourd'huy en cest endroict: car combien en voit-on de ces gros yvrongnes, de ces gourmands qui sont là comme des pourceaux à l'auge, sans aucune intelligence ne raison? Ils se rempliront bien le ventre, mais il n'est point question de lever la teste au ciel, pour faire hommage à celuy qui les nourrit et entretient si grassement, ils ont tousiours le groin et le museau fiché en bas apres la pasture.' (Sermon No.180 on Deut. 32:14, CR 56 = CO 28, Brunsvigae 1885, col.706). See also Sermon No.3 on 2 Sam. 2:28, J. Calvin, *Predigten über das 2. Buch Samuelis*, ed. H. Rückert, 25.

[40]'Neque homer, neque alia mensura nobis ordinata est a Domino, ad quam uniuscuiusque diei victus exigatur: sed nobis commendata est frugalitas et temperantia: et prohibitum ne quis abundantia fretus lasciviat. Ergo quibus sunt divitiae, sive ex patrimonio relictae, sive industria partae et laboribus, illi cogitent excessum non intemperantiae aut luxuriae destinatum esse, sed tolerandae fratrum egestati... Fateor quidem non praecipi nobis illam aequalitatem, ut nihilo nitidius fas sit divitibus vesci quam pauperibus: sed eatenus servanda aequalitas, ut nemo esuriat, nemo abundantiam suam supprimat, alios fraudando. Pauperum homer panis erit cibarius, victusque parcior: divitum homer liberalior quidem portio, prout tulerit facultas: sic tamen ut temperanter vivant, neque desint aliis.' (Comm.2 Cor. 8:13-17, CR 78 = CO 50. Brunsvigae 1893, col.102). See also Inst.II. viii.45.

[41]Inst. IIIx5 (CR 30 = CO 2, col.531).

[42]'Nam hoc est vere ieiunare, ubi homines sibi fraenum iniiiciunt, ne comedant nisi parce et tenuiter, idque ad necessiatatem, et contenti sunt atro pane et aqua.' (Comm. Dan 10:3, CR 69 = CO 41, Brunsvigae 1889, col.196). See also Comm. on Matth. 14:16 (CR 73 = CO 45, Brunsvigae 1891, col.438).

[43]Inst. III.iii.17 (CR 30 = CO 2, Brunsvigae 1864, col.447-8); IV.xii.16, 18 (Ibid, col.915-6).

[44]Bouwsma, *John Calvin*, 89.

[45]Comm. Num. 11:6 (CR 53 = CO 25, Brunsvigae 1882, col.167).

[46]See also Comm. Num. 11:4 (CR 53 = CO 25, Brunsvigae 1882, col.166); Comm. Rom 14:2 (CR 77 = CO 49, Brunsvigae 1892, col.258).

[47]Comm. on Rom. 14:15, 'causam tam levem'—'for such a light reason', 'turpiter'—'disgracefully', 'cibum, rem vilissimam'—'food, a most despicable matter' (CR 27 = CO 49, Brunsvigae 1892, col. 265). See also Comm. on Rom 14:17, 'Quibus in summa vult ostendere cibum et potum res esse viliores quam ut earum causa debeat cursus evangelii impedire'—'By which, to sum up, he Paul wants to show that food and drink are too despicable matters to hold that because of them the course of the gospel should be impeded'—a significant restriction!

[48]Comm. on 1 Cor. 10:31 'in re tantula'—'in a minor matter', 'actionem tam minutam'—'such a little act' (CR 77 = CO 49, Brunsvigae 1892, col.471). See also his disdain for normal food and drink as non-spiritual matters, Sermon No.2 on 1 Cor. 10:3-6 (CR 77 = CO 49, Brunsvigae 1892, col. 594).

[49] See also Inst. III..4 (CR 30 = CO 2, Brunsvigae 1864, col.531).
[50] See e.g. E. Choisy, *La Théocratie à Genève au temps de Calvin*, Genève n.d.
[51] R. Guerdan, *La vie quotidienne à Genève au temps de Calvin*, Paris 1973, 99.
[52] Guerdan, *La vie quotidienne à Genève*, 99, 155.
[53] J.E. Olsen, *Calvin and Social Welfare: Deacons and the Bourse fra**nçaise*, London 1989, 103-4, 233-4.
[54] 'Quaeritur tamen an ita promiscue solitus fuerit quoslibet excipere Abraham. Maior enim futurus erat concursus quamut turbae satisfecisset... Nam si obviis quibusque mactasset vitulos, statim immensis sumptibus exhausat eius domus fuisset.', Comm. on Gen. 18:2-3 (CR 51 = CO 23, Brunsvigae 1882, col.251).
[55] 'sed quum scriptura generales legitimi usus tradat regulas, secundum illas certe limitandus nobis est.'—'but about which Scripture hands down general rules regarding their legitimate use by which we certainly must set limits to ourselves.' (Inst. III.x.1, CR 30 = CO 2, Brunsvigae 1864, col.529).
[56] J.D. Douglass, *Women, Freedom, and Calvin: The 1983 Annie Kinkead Warfield Lectures*, Philadelphia, 1985, 14-6.
[57] A.E. McGrath, *A Life of John Calvin: A Study in the Shaping of Western Culture*, Oxford 1990, 221.
[58] The Geneva Catechism (1545), Question 107, implementing Rom. 12:2, 1 John 2:15. Cf. E.F.K. Müller, *Die Bekenntnisschriften der reformierten Kirche*, Leipzig 1903, 106, lines 38-40.
[59] See e.g. F.L. Battles, 'Against Luxury and License in Geneva: A Forgotten Fragment of Calvin', in: R.C. Gamble (ed.), *Articles on Calvin and Calvinism*, New York 1992, 198-202.
[60] Calvin underwent the influence of the Brethren of the Common Life when he studied at the Collège de Montaigu in Paris. Cf. McGrath, *A Life of John Calvin*, 27.
[61] Nijenhuis, *Hoe Calvinistisch zijn wij Nederlanders?*, 18. I also thank Professor A. Jelsma (Kampen) for bringing this circumstance to my attention.
[62] 'Vir, inquam, sapientis est, moderato, et suavi cibo, et potu se reficere, et recreare', Ethics IV, P45, cf. Spinoza, *Opera—Werke lateinisch und deutsch*, ed. K. Blumenstock, Bd. 2, Darmstadt 1967, 450-1.
[63] Ethices V, P42, Spinoza, *Opera* 556-7.
[64] See J. Freudenthal, *Spinoza: Leben und Lehre*, Teil 1, Heidelberg 1927, 29.
[65] Pirque Aboth 6:4.
[66] Ethices II, P56, Spinoza, *Opera*, 344-5. See also Ethices IV, P48.
[67] See M.C.A. Korpel, *A Rift in the Clouds: Ugaritic and Hebrew Descriptions of the Divine*, Münster 1990, 399-424.
[68] Bouwsma, *John Calvin*, 50.
[69] G. Groen van Prinsterer, *La Hollande et l'influence de Calvin*, Amsterdam 1864, 14.

Mrs Agnes B. Marshall (1855 - 1905)

John S. Deith

One hundred years ago the name of Mrs Marshall was as well known as Delia Smith or Keith Floyd, to name but two, are now. Today, Mrs Marshall is completely forgotten except by a few collectors of old cookery books. It may be inevitable that people who were once household names should be forgotten. Inevitable, but highly regrettable. Especially when their success was gained through the exercise of extraordinary talent bordering on genius and against all the odds.

Why is it that Mrs Beeton, who died twenty years before Mrs Marshall published her first cookery book, and Auguste Escoffier, who published his nearly twenty years after Mrs Marshall, are so well remembered while she is forgotten? I shall address that question later on but first a few words about Mrs Marshall herself and her books.

Frustratingly little is known about Mrs Marshall and almost nothing about her early life. She was born, Agnes Bertha Smith in Walthamstow, Essex on 24 August 1855. Her parents remain shadowy figures. Her father described himself as John Smith of Walthamstow and on her marriage certificate Agnes says that he was a clerk. That is the only firm information we have about Agnes' early years. Although from later evidence we can deduce that she had at least one brother and that her father died at a relatively early age. Her mother, Susan, remarried a Charles Wells. He was the father of four children, Eliza, Thomas, John, who later became the manager of Marshall's School of Cookery, and Ada, who later became Agnes' housekeeper.

As to where she learned to cook so well and gained those extraordinary presentation skills which were to serve her so well, we can only guess. Agnes herself gives us one small, tantalising clue in the preface of her first cookery book where she wrote:

> Neither have any of the recipes herein been learnt or gathered from any books, but they are the result of practical training and lessons, through several years, from leading English and Continental authorities, as well as a home experience earlier than I can well recall;...

Her husband, Alfred is equally tantalising. In an interview with the *Pall Mall Gazette* in October 1886 he said:

> 'I should tell you that Mrs Marshall has made a thorough study of cookery since she was a child, and has practised at Paris and Vienna under celebrated chefs.'

Agnes married Alfred William Marshall at St. George's, Hanover Square on 17 August 1878 and from here on the outlines of her life are easier to trace. The couple set up home in St. John's Wood and had four children. Ethel, born in 1879, Agnes, known as Aggie in the family, also in 1879, Alfred in 1880 and William born in 1882.

In January, 1883 Marshall's School of Cookery opened its doors for the first time at 31 Mortimer Street, London. Unfortunately all the records relating to the school and later developments have been destroyed so the details of the original transaction, and much else, will never be known. From the article already quoted and the early publicity for Marshall's School of Cookery we can be certain that the school was bought from Mary Ann Lavenue who ran a school of cookery at 57 Mortimer Street. From later evidence it seems probable that Agnes bought the school with her own money. The Married Women's Property Act had just come into force so Agnes would have been able to buy, and keep, the school in her own right. Certainly, and unusually for the time, it was made quite clear from the outset that Mrs Marshall was the owner and the main driving force.

From the outset Marshall's School of Cookery was more than just a school. There was a cook's registry on which, according to Alfred, they lost £200 a year 'Because the ladies do not pay their fees'. (He went on to infer that there was no such problem with the cooks). Very soon the school had its own warehouses and a shop where all manner of kitchen equipment could be bought. Above all, Agnes pioneered the sale of her 'Own Brand' equipment and food, especially Marshall's Patent Freezers, which she claimed as her own invention, ice caves and, later, refrigerators.

According to Alfred, there were no pupils on the day the school opened. But, through careful advertising, hard work and Agnes' undoubted ability and flair, the numbers slowly built up and by the end of 1885 there were between twenty and forty pupils a day. In the same year Agnes published her first book, *The Book of Ices*. As was to be the case with all her books, initially at least, it was published by Marshall's School of Cookery.

Well over a hundred years later the book is a model of its kind. Clearly and well written, well printed and produced with good illustrations. In this case, in addition to four superb chromolithographs of some of her ices in many marvellous shapes including swans and baskets of fruits, there are also line drawings of Marshall's Freezer and Marshall's Ice Cave. The recipes are admirably clear and easy to follow. *The Book of Ices* can lay claim to being the definitive book on the subject.

A year later, in 1886, Agnes started her own weekly paper. *The Table*, which was described as 'A weekly paper of Cookery, Gastronomy, Food amusements etc....' Throughout the rest of her life Agnes contributed a weekly recipe page to the paper. In addition, for the first six months, she contributed a weekly article on just about anything which took her fancy. Her articles were written in a chatty, witty and ironic, Jane Austenesque style. She promoted her recipes and rode some of her favourite hobby horses. These included tennis (she agreed with the man who asked 'Why don't they pay someone to do it for them?'), horsey types, keen gardeners and 'Baby babblers'. She also contrasted the treatment of cooks and horses in aristocratic households and went on to suggest that if they treated their staff as well as they did their horses there would be no 'Servant Problem'. There were spirited attacks on the catering trade and, whenever the opportunity arose, her main competitor and *bête noir*, the National School of Cookery. In later years, when she again contributed weekly articles to the paper, Agnes would return to the 'Servant Problem' and the need for proper training of both employers and employees, the deplorable state of English catering and many other matters. Other sections of the paper were equally outspoken. A financial venture launched by Horatio Bottomley was heavily criticized. Bottomley was furious. He questioned their right to make any judgement about financial matters, threatened a libel action, which never materialised, and, as the printer of *The Table*, said he would refuse to print any future unfavourable or critical remarks. The Marshall's reply was swift and unequivocal: 'Impudent' and promptly changed their printers. Had other journals been as forthright as *The Table*, Bottomley would have been exposed as the fraud he was long before the law finally caught up with him.

In 1887 Agnes decided to publish her second book with a publication date set for the following February. *The Book of Ices* had received favourable notices but mainly in the provincial press. To reach a wider audience and increase sales it would be necessary to get more coverage. To publicise her forthcoming book Agnes decided on a nationwide lecture/demonstration tour. The lecture was to be called *A Pretty Luncheon*. As she was busy at the school from Monday to Friday, many of the lectures could only be held on Saturdays. The first part of the tour took place in August, when the school was closed, and took in Midland and Northern towns including Birmingham, Manchester, Leeds, Newcastle and Glasgow. The tour was successful and well reported in all the local papers. Agnes was encouraged to set off on the second leg of her tour during the autumn and winter. The second stage took in Bath, Brighton, Bristol, Cheltenham, Colchester, Leicester, Liverpool,

Nottingham, Plymouth, Shrewsbury, Southampton and Worcester. Before that however she held two demonstrations in London on successive Saturdays in October. The dates chosen were the 15 and 22 October. The Banqueting Hall at Willis' Rooms, St. James was booked and Agnes prepared herself for the events which would make her the best known cook since Soyer.

For over two hours Agnes held her audience spellbound. She took London by storm. All the national dailies reported the lectures and were unanimous in their acclaim. *The Times* reporter was swept off his feet and wrote: 'Talk of transformation scenes, or legerdemain, they were nothing compared to the astounding changes Mrs Marshall made.'

Agnes' strategy worked well. By the time the tours were over she was the most talked about cook in England. Unfortunately, there was a delay in the publication of the book and it was not until 12 May 1888 that Agnes was able to announce with obvious frustration that after 'avoidable delays' her book was available.

Mrs A.B. Marshall's Book of Cookery was everything a good cookery book should be. Practical, well planned and arranged, it was also lucid, accurate and comprehensive with a good and extensive index. Perhaps, above all, it was also well written. Foreshadowing her more famous contemporary, Auguste Escoffier, Agnes codified all the main processes in cookery and presented her public with many wonderful recipes. There is nothing that Escoffier wrote later that is not covered by Mrs Marshall's admirable book. With the publication of *Mrs A.B. Marshall's Book of Cookery* her position in the first rank of cookery writers was assured.

The success of Marshall's School of Cookery was equally assured. It went from strength to strength. Her lessons were more popular than ever and sales increased. Agnes did not take a back seat but her energies were no longer devoted solely to the school. Some of her time was devoted to charity work. Being Agnes, her contributions were characteristically practical. She provided Xmas dinners for the 'Hungry Poor' of Poplar and Stepney and made sure that soup was sent down throughout the winter. In 1890 she took time out to have her portrait painted by George Sheridan Knowles and the following year saw the publication of her third book *Mrs A.B. Marshall's Larger Cookery Book of Extra Recipes* dedicated 'By permission' to Princess Christian. As the dedication implies this is as much of a prestige publication as a practical cookery book. But like all Agnes' books it is well written and well produced with delightful illustrations. The recipes are aimed more at the Haute Cuisine end of the market but, as ever, many of them are very good and written in Agnes' clear, crisp prose.

In the same year Agnes started negotiations to buy a property in Pinner. *The Towers* was an estate of some seven and a half acres in extent with the river Pinn running through the North Eastern part of the estate. Agnes had the original buildings totally refurbished and the gardens were landscaped.

1894 saw the publication of Agnes' last book, *Fancy Ices*. A follow-up to *the Book of Ices* published nine years before. It is the scarcest of Agnes' books and in many ways the most attractive. The cover, in blue on a silver background, depicts a polar bear standing on an ice floe holding a tray of ices. There is the familiar clear prose and superb illustrations. In particular, a lovely drawing of a woman standing on a chair spinning sugar. The recipes are as ever clear, crisp and accurate.

In the 1890's Agnes began her weekly contributions to *The Table* again. Once again she wrote about anything and everything that aroused her eclectic and omnivorous interest, from the frivolous to the serious. Food: she decries the spread of tinned food and agrees with a medical contemporary who suggested that tinned food would be shown to be the cause of an increase in cancer; the poor food at railway stations and in dining cars (which seems to have been as bad then as it is now). 'But,' wrote Agnes 'one despairs of reform in this direction. We are a foolishly patient nation.' The unavailability of good tomatoes where she lives and, of course, that hardy perennial of Victorian and Edwardian times, the 'servant problem'. It is, however, in her reflections on the society around her and her speculations on the future, that Agnes really comes into her own. Reading her remarks at the remove of close on one hundred years, it is amazing how many of the subjects she tackled still resonate today.

On the rights of women: Agnes commented on a paper read by Mrs Farquharson at The International Congress for Women held in London during the summer of 1889, '...If energy can accomplish that for which, if justice were done, there would be no need to fight, then Mrs Farquharson may be sure of realising her hopes.'

An early and enthusiastic motorist, Agnes predicted that it would not be long before the motor car would '...revolutionise trade and facilitate the travelling of the future.' and went on to suggest that the railways '...better wake up to it before it is too late.' At another time, she speculated on the probability of refrigerated lorries delivering fresh food throughout the country.

Speculating on the future generally, Agnes correctly predicted the growth of the larger stores and 'small provision shops will be entirely swallowed up...' Easier to predict, but nonetheless perceptive she opined that the day would come when 'Drinking water will be supplied chemically pure to all dwelling places as a matter of course,' with tongue in cheek she goes on to say 'and with bacilli kept at bay everyone will live to a patriarchal age.'

On another occasion she discourses on the gullibility of people at the beginning of the 20th century with their beliefs in 'palmists, crystal gazing, clairvoyance...never was there a time when superstition held greater sway...'.

On diet, 'In this age of eating the dietist has become a kind of fetish...Anything new in this direction is sure of a hearing...'

The examples could be almost endless but one more will have to suffice. On the then incipient 'internationalisation process' Agnes commented: 'Very soon there will be no change of life anywhere...Kabul and Helsingfors...will be in no way distinguishable from London, Paris or New York.'

The interest in everything did not stop there. In 1902 *The Table* was advertising dishwashing machines and an early version of the Teasmaid. While at *The Table* offices, the front door was being operated by what they called a 'Sesame Door': a door that opened automatically as people approached it.

In 1900 Agnes carried off her last big deal. Marshall's bought out Cowan's Baking Powder: 'lock, stock and barrel.'

By the early nineteen hundreds Agnes was a far from well woman and had frequent bouts of ill health. She carried on gamely until, early in 1904 she was thrown from a horse. In May she went to Brighton to convalesce. She remained there for most of the next year, returning to her home in Pinner to compose herself for dealth which occurred in the early hours of the morning of 29 July 1905. She was three weeks short of her fiftieth birthday.

And then?

And then, within the year Alfred had remarried, to a woman who had once been Agnes' personal secretary. That there had been an affair between the two before Agnes' death is almost certain. There had been a fearful row between Agnes and her secretary, Gertrude Walsh, who left the Marshall's employ.

In 1907 Alfred junior died and his ashes were placed next to those of his mother. Alfred senior died, in Nice, in 1917. His ashes were brought home after the 14-18 war and, at his request, were also laid next to those of Agnes, in 1920.

Marshall's became a limited company in 1921 and increasingly diversified into multiple stores in many parts of the country and, later, property. It became a very successful company which throughout the following years earned good dividends for the company shareholders.

Marshall's School of Cookery went on until the outbreak of World War II when it closed its doors for the last time. *The Table* ceased publication at the same time (16 September 1939). Marshall's Ltd was finally, voluntarily, wound up in 1954 and all the records destroyed.

Some time in 1927 or 1928 the copyright of Agnes' books was acquired by Ward Lock Ltd. They published *The Cookery Book* and *The Book of Ices* but not, it seems, the *Larger Book* or *Fancy Ices*.

Thus far, the certainties. Now the speculation. In 1928 Mrs Beeton's portrait was donated to the National Gallery. Mrs Beeton became front page news in every paper in the land and the sales of *Household Management* boomed. The publishers of *Household Management* were of course Ward Lock. Coincidence or strategy? At this remove of time I suppose none of us will ever know. But, if the Marshall family had donated her portrait to the National Gallery, could it be that Mrs Marshall would now be the best known cookery writer of the last century? She certainly deserves to be.

[See also the paper by Robin Weir, 'Mrs A.B. Marshall, Ice-creammonger Extraordinary', below, for illustrations of Mrs Marshall's works, and the frontispiece and cover, above, for further illustrations.]

The Art of Apicius

Carol A. Déry

The name of Marcus Gavius Apicius is well known in connection with the Roman cookery book, the *De Re Coquinaria*, which is traditionally ascribed to him, but we know relatively little of the man himself, aside from the few anecdotes which tell of his extravagance and profligacy in food, and indeed, the luxurious nature of his ultimate demise. The ancient authorities actually speak of three figures bearing the name Apicius, each of whom was celebrated in antiquity for luxury and gourmandry.[1] The earliest of these Apicii lived at the turn of the first century BC, and is mentioned by Posidonius in his *Histories* as a man who transcended all in prodigality (Athenaeus, *The Dinner of the Sophists*, 4.168d). The second was Marcus Gavius Apicius to whom the present study is devoted, whilst the third lived at the time of the Emperor Trajan in the second century AD, and is best remembered for his invention of special packaging to preserve the freshness of oysters during their transportation over long distances:

> When the Emperor Trajan was in Parthia, at a distance of many days' journey from the sea, Apicius caused fresh oysters to be sent to him in packing skilfully devised by himself.
>
> Athenaeus, 1.7d

Marcus Gavius Apicius flourished during the reign of the Emperor Tiberius in the first century AD. Renowned for his inventive genius in haute cuisine, he came to be regarded as the archetypal *bon viveur*, to such an extent that his name became proverbial for wealth and gourmandry.[2] Luxurious in life, he was even luxurious in death as an epigram of Martial demonstrates:

> Apicius, you had spent 60 million [sesterces] on your stomach, and as yet a full 10 million remained to you. You refused to endure this, as also hunger and thirst, and took poison in your final drink. Nothing more gluttonous was ever done by you, Apicius.
>
> Martial, *Epigrams*, 3.22[3]

Cassius Dio also found the extravagance of his suicide worthy of note in his annals of Roman history:

> Apicius so far surpassed mankind in prodigality that when he wished to know how much he had already spent and how much he still had left, on learning that 10 million [sesterces] still remained to him, he became grief-stricken, and feeling that he was destined to die of hunger, he took his own life.
>
> Cassius Dio, *Roman History*, 57.19.5

What of Apicius' culinary exploits? The grammarian Apion, a contemporary of Marcus Gavius, wrote a treatise *On the Luxury of Apicius*, which, had it survived, would doubtless have provided considerably more information about the man and his gastronomic adventures that we actually have, but unfortunately nothing remains of it other than its tantalizing title (Athenaeus, 7.294f). Nevertheless Pliny the Elder, who compiled the encyclopaedic *Natural History* during the first century AD, preserves the following details of three of Apicius' gastronomic prescriptions:

> i) Apicius, the most gluttonous gorger of all spendthrifts, taught that flamingo's tongue has a particularly fine flavour.
>
> Pliny, *Natural History*, 10.68.133

The flamingo was originally brought over from Africa as a delicacy to grace the tables of wealthy epicures. By Imperial times they were actually being reared on Italian farms in response to the gastronomic demand for their flesh. They were to be found alongside other exotic birds at Faustinus' farm at Baiae for example (Martial, *Epigrams*, 3.58.14). The *De Re Coquinaria* contains a recipe for boiled flamingo in a spicy date sauce (6.6.1.), but does not mention flamingo tongues. Nevertheless the success of Apicius' precept amongst contemporary and later gastrophiles is apparent from the several references made to them by authors such as Seneca and Martial.[4] Flamingo's tongues constituted one of the many bizarre ingredients gathered from all around the empire for the gastronomic monstrosity of a dish, the notorious *Shield of Minerva, Protector of the City*, created in AD 69 by the emperor Vitellius.[5] The third century emperor Elegabalus, renowned for his eccentric dining habits, usurped the trend begun by Apicius by serving the tongues of peacocks and nightingales at his imperial banquets.

> ii) There is also the art of treating the liver of sows like that of geese, the discovery of Marcus Apicius. The pigs are stuffed with dried figs, and when full, they are killed after having been given a drink of *mulsum*.[6]

Pliny, *Natural History*, 8.77.209

Roman epicures greatly appreciated foie-gras;[7] indeed Pliny cites Scipio Metellus or Marcus Seius as its probable discoverers, so that this dish is not a French invention as its name implies, but was originally Italian. It was usual for the liver of the goose, which had been enlarged firstly by cramming the bird, to be made larger still by soaking it in milk sweetened with honey after removal (Pliny, *Natural History*, 10.27.52). Apicius' innovation was to create a similar sort of dish from an entirely different animal, with the figs and *mulsum* on which the pig was fed being intended to impart an unusual and delicate flavour to the meat. The *De Re Coquinaria* preserves two recipes for *ficatum* (the liver of a pig fed on figs) in which the liver is served marinated in different combinations of the following condiments: pepper, thyme, lovage, *liquamen*,[8] wine, oil and laurel berries (7.3.1-2).

> iii) Marcus Apicius, a man born for every device of luxury, thought mullets excellent when killed in a sauce of their companions (*garum sociorum*), and also *allec* (fish-paste) made out of their livers.

Pliny, *Natural History*, 9.30.66

Garum was a type of fish sauce made from fermented fish, similar to the modern Vietnamese *nuoc mam* or Thai *nam pla*, which was highly esteemed by wealthy Romans. *Garum sociorum* was a particularly high-grade *garum* imported into Italy from New Carthage in Spain,[9] but the phrase *garum sociorum* in Pliny's text may be considered humorously ambiguous; 'socius' in Latin means 'friend' or 'ally', so that in one sense it means that the mullets are served in a sauce made by the federation of garum manufacturers in this particular district of Spain,[10] but in another sense that the mullets are served in a sauce of their 'fishy friends' (as in the translation above). *Allec* was originally the sediment that remained at the bottom of the jar after the production of *garum*, but later it came to be regarded as a luxury item in its own right. *Allec* made from mullet's liver, oysters, sea urchins and sea nettles was particularly esteemed, according to Pliny (*Natural History*, 31.44.95).

Red mullets were greatly favoured by Roman epicures, and the following extract from Seneca reveals the highly competitive world of the gourmets who were prepared to pay enormous sums for the prestige of obtaining the finest specimens:

> Tiberius Caesar ordered a mullet of enormous size that had been sent to him to be sent to the market and put up for sale. Why should I not mention its weight and excite the palates of epicures—they say it weighed four and a half pounds.[11] Caesar said, 'Friends,

I shall not be surprised if either Apicius or Publius Octavius[12] buys that mullet.' His conjecture exceeded expectation. The two gourmands bid, Octavius was victorious and he gained a great reputation amongst his peers, since he had purchased for 5,000 sesterces a fish which Caesar had sold and which not even Apicius had succeeded in buying.

Seneca, Epistles, 95.42

Apicius' taste for another type of seafood and the lengths and expense to which he was prepared to go in order to have the best are demonstrated in the next passage.

There lived in the days of Tiberius a man named Apicius, an exceedingly rich luxuriant from whom many kinds of cake are called *Apician*.[13] He had spent countless sums on his belly at Minturnae, a city of Campania, and lived there eating mostly expensive shrimps, which grow bigger there than the largest shrimps of Smyrna or the lobsters of Alexandria. Now when he heard that they also grew to excessive size in Libya, he said forth at once, encountering very bad weather on the voyage. As he approached those regions, fishermen sailed to meet him even before he left his ship (for report of his coming had spread far and wide among the Libyans), and brought him their best shrimps. On seeing the shrimps, he enquired whether they had any that were larger, and when they replied that none grew larger than those they had brought, he thought again of those shrimps at Minturnae and ordered the helmsman to sail back to Italy by the same route, without his even having approached the Libyan shore.

Athenaeus, 1.7a-c

Apicius thus appears as a wealthy Roman with a passion for fine food, often with a taste for the unusual and exotic. Indeed the following extract from Seneca suggests that there was nothing that Apicius and other gourmands would not sample for the sake of the culinary art:

Behold Nomentanus[14] and Apicius, digesting, as they say, the blessings of land and sea, and reviewing the creatures of every nation upon their table.

Seneca, On the Happy Life, 11.4

Marcus Gavius Apicius was the author of two works on cookery: a general cookbook and a more specialized treatise on sauces.[15] There is no conclusive evidence to support the view that he was a professional chef however, as some have maintained. Perhaps he should be considered primarily a food writer, and, at any rate, a man with the leisure and means to pursue an interest in gastronomy. Tacitus refers to him as a rich man and a prodigal (*Annals*, 4.1). His creative culinary precepts were much admired and imitated by many with a similar penchant for gourmandry, but Apicius was also reviled as the archetypal epicure by the moralists who were concerned about the effects such luxuroisness in food might engender in contemporary society. Seneca for example says of Apicius 'learned in the science of the cook-shop' that he 'defiled the age with his teaching' (Seneca, *To Helvia, On Consolation*, 10.8).

Apicius remains one of the most enduring and enigmatic figures in the history of cookery, but the cookery book which has come down to us in association with his name is not the original work of Apicius however, but rather a collection of more than 500 recipes made by an unknown editor during the fourth century AD. By associating his compilation with the name of Apicius the editor endowed it with a certain credibility which no doubt helped to ensure its survival to the present day. A second collection of 32 additional recipes made by Vidinarius in the fifth century AD is also extant, of which a modern adaptation is readily accessible in Edwards' book listed in the bibliography.

The *De Re Coquinaria* has the unique quality of being the most complete cookery book to survive from the ancient world. The titles of more than thirty Greek works on cookery are known, but their contents survive only in fragmentary form, if indeed they survive at all. Written in a style of Latin which confirms that it was compiled at a later date than Apicius' own lifetime,[16] the *De Re Coquinaria* comprises ten books under the following headings, curiously given in Greek[17]: 'The Careful Housekeeper' (*Epimeles*), 'The Meat-Mincer' (*Sarcoptes*), 'The Gardener' (*Cepuros*), 'Many Ingredients' (*Pandecter*), 'Pulse' (*Ospreon*), 'Birds' (*Aeropetes*), 'The Gourmet' (*Polyteles*), 'The Quadruped' (*Tetrapus*), 'The Sea' (*Thalassa*), and 'The Fisherman' (*Halieus*). The recipes are drawn from a number of sources including Apicius' original textbooks, agricultural manuals, medical writings and works on dietetics, both Greek and Latin. The result is a fascinating combination of the exotic and the ordinary, from peacock rissoles to dressings for wild herbs, from stuffed dormice to aromatic salts to aid the digestion. Book 10 of the *De Re Coquinaria*, which is concerned exclusively with sauces and dressings for different types of fish, is often considered to be genuinely Apician, deriving from his treatise on sauces, although recipes for sauces are also to be found elsewhere in the book. There are in addition seven recipes which expressly bear the name of Apicius, which are given below, and it is highly probable that these dishes were invented by Marcus Gavius. Certainly they show a certain consistency in their use of seasonings. Two recipes are for hot meats served with cold sauces, in which the contrasting temperatures would have appealed to novel tastes. It is uncertain precisely which of the other recipes in the De Re Coquinaria derive from Apicius' original texts, but many are clearly gourmet dishes of the type that Apicius himself would have favoured, incorporating exotic meats and expensive spices, with which to titillate the palate.

Ethnic fashions and flavours are also represented in the *De Re Coquiinaria* by such dishes as Parthian style lamb or kid (8.6.10), Alexandrian sauce for fish (10.1.6-7), Numidian chicken (6.9.4), and Indian style peas (5.3.3), which demonstrate the enormous variety of influences available to the ancient cook empire-wide. The vast range of flavourings, herbs and spices used in the book is often taken as evidence of the necessity to disguise the taste of meats and fish that are going off because of a lack of proper refrigeration, but this attitude does an injustice to Roman culinary inspiration and adventure. The *De Re Coquinaria* mentions about sixty different condiments, a sixth of which grew outside the empire, the majority of which are familiar to the modern cook. The demand for spices at Rome for sophisticated cookery cost the state millions annually. For a long time the Arabs held the monopoly over eastern spices, but the discovery of the Monsoons in the first century AD enabled a direct sea route to be opened up to Southern India, primarily to obtain pepper, the Roman seasoning *par excellence*, which is widely used in the *De Re Coquinaria*, even in the few recipes for desserts which the book contains.[18] Apicius appears to have made a significant contribution towards the fashion for highly spiced foods during this period, and indeed he is mentioned in such a connection by the Christian writer Tertullian.[19]

Apicius' influence was considerable. He became a model for gastronomers everywhere to emulate,[20] and he is cited as the inspiration for the culinary digressions and outlandish banquets of the emperor Elegabalus, at which he would serve such extraordinary dishes as camel heels, cocks combs and the tongues of peacocks and nightingales in imitation of Apicius. Indeed Elegabalus claimed to have even surpassed the banquets of Apicius in extravagence and novelty (*Augustan Histories, Elegabalus*, 18.4; 20.5; 24.3).

Schools of cookery hailed Apicius as their patron; indeed Tertullian describes him as the patron saint of cooks (*Apology*, 3.6), whilst St. Jerome noted in his *Epistles* that a good cook was often called 'an Apicius'. Apicius' culinary digest is said to have furnished bedside reading material for the second century emperor Aelius Verus, who was also noted for his excessive dining habits (*Augustan Histories, Verus*, 5.9). The book appears to have had continued usage amongst the upper classes in the Medieval period, who drew inspiration from Roman cuisine, and it is known to have been in circulation at the court of the Frankish emperor Charlmagne.[21] Renaissance physicians may have found it worthy of interest from a dietetic point of view, but other scholars probably found it stimulating for the insights it afforded into the lives of the Ancient Romans. Apicius' influence does not end there however. Many modern students of ancient cookery find it both useful and exciting to put theory into practice and try to recreate the tastes of antiquity by following the guidelines offered by the *De Re Coquinaria*.[22] Some of the dishes may not be to our taste, but there can be no denying the variety and complexity of ancient Roman cookery, even if the multitude of ingredients may sometimes seem to us to lack a certain subtlety.

Recipes from the De Re Coquinaria *which are associated with the name of Apicius.*

Sala Cattabia Apiciana. Put celery seed, dried pennyroyal, dried mint, ginger, fresh coriander, stoned raisins, honey, vinegar, oil and wine in a mortar and pound. Place pieces of Picentine bread[23] in a dish, and arrange in alternate layers with chicken pieces, goat's sweetbreads, Vestine cheese,[24] pine kernels, cucumbers, and finely chopped dried onions. Pour over the dressing. Chill in snow and serve. (*De Re Coquinaria*, 4.1.2).

Patina Apiciana[25] You shall make it thus: take pieces of cooked sow's udder,[26] fillets of fish, chicken pieces, fig-peckers[27] or cooked breast of turtle-dove, and whatever other goodies you might have. Chop all these carefully, except for the fig-peckers. Then beat raw eggs with oil. Pound pepper and lovage, moisten with *liquamen*, wine and *passum*,[28] put in a pan, heat, and thicken with wheat-starch. However add all the chopped meats first, and let them cook in the sauce. When cooked, add whole peppercorns and pine kernels, and then transfer the meats into a dish with the sauce, using a ladle, and arrange in layers as follows, with a *laganum* [a type of thin, flat pancake][29] between each layer to act as a base; however many *lagana* you have put in, place a ladleful of the meat-mixture on top of each one. Then pierce one *laganum* with a reed, and place it on top. Sprinkle with pepper. However you should bind the meat-pieces with beaten eggs before putting them into the pan with the sauce. You ought to have a bronze pan like the one shown below. [Evidently there was an illustration of a pan following this recipe which is now lost]. (*De Re Coquinaria*, 4.2.14).

Minutal Apiciana. Let oil, *liquamen*, wine, leeks, mint, small fish, tiny rissoles, testicles of capon, and sweetbreads of sucking-pig all cook together. Pound pepper, lovage, and fresh coriander or coriander seed, and moisten with *liquamen*. Add a little honey and some of the cooking liquor, blend with wine and honey and bring to the boil. When it boils, crumble in *tracta*[30] to bind. Stir well. Sprinkle with pepper and serve. (*De Re Coquinaria*, 4.3.3).

Conchiclam Apicianum.[31] Take a clean pan in which you cook peas, and put into it chopped Lucanian sausage, small pork rissoles, meat pieces and pork shoulder. Pound pepper, lovage, oregano, dill, dried onion and fresh coriander. Pour on *liquamen*, and blend with wine and *liquamen*. Place in the pan, and add a little oil. Prick the items so that the oil is absorbed. Simmer over a low flame, then serve. (*De Re Coquinaria*, 5.4.2).

Anserem Elixum Calidum ex iure Frigido Apiciano [Boil the goose]. Pound pepper, lovage, corinader seed, mint and rue, and moisten with *liquamen* and a little oil. Dry the hot boiled goose with a clean cloth. Pour over the sauce and serve. (*De Re Coquinaria*, 6.8).

Ofellas Apicianas. Bone the meat pieces, roll them up, bind together and put in the oven. After they are crisped, brown them, take them out and dry them on a grill with a low flame, so that they yield up their juice but do not let them burn. Pound pepper, lovage, *cyperus*,[32] and cumin, and moisten with *liquamen* and *passum*. Put the meat pieces in a dish with this dressing. When cooked, remove and dry. Serve without sauce and sprinkled with pepper. If the meat is fatty, remove the skin when preparing the pieces. You can make this dish with pork belly also. (*De Re Coquinaria*, 7.4.2).

Porcellum lacte pastum elixum caldum iure frigido crudo Apiciano. [Boil the sucking-pig]. Pound pepper, lovage, coriander seed, mint and rue in a mortar. Moisten with *liquamen*, then add honey and wine, and blend with more *liquamen*. Dry the hot boiled piglet with a clean cloth, pour over the dressing and serve. (*De Re Coquinaria*, 8.7.6).

A Modern Bibliography of Apicius

Edwards, J., (1984) *The Roman Cookery of Apicius: translated and adapted for the modern kitchen* (London). The recipes are given in English (no Latin text is provided), and many have been adapted for the modern kitchen with recommended weights and measures, and suggested modern equivalents for Roman ingredients. The introduction discusses typical Roman ingredients and menus. The book concludes most usefully with the 32 recipes from the collection of Vidinarius, which most other editions omit.

Flower, B., and E. Rosenbaum, (1958) *Apicius: The Roman Cookery Book* (London). This is the established edition of Apicius, comprising Latin text with accompanying English translation, and an introduction to the Latin terminology of the principal Roman ingredients and types of cooking equipment. There is also a detailed account of the manuscript tradition. The recipes have not been adapted for the modern cook, excepting the occasional comment in the notes, and the book is therefore mainly of scholarly, rather than practical, interest.

Giacosa, I.G., (1992) *A Taste of Ancient Rome*, (Chicago).A particularly fine edition of selected recipes of Apicius supplemented by a small number of additional recipes taken from the agricultural manuals of Cato and Columella. It gives not only the Latin text with direct English translation, but also a convenient adaptation of the recipes for the modern cook. The book is supplemented by useful discussions of Roman dining practices and foodstuffs, and beautifully illustrated with colour photographs and numerous line drawings throughout.

Solomon, J. & J., (1977) *Ancient Roman Feasts: and recipes adapted for modern cookery*, (Miami). An easy-to-follow book with useful introduction to Roman food, containing a wide selection of recipes from Apicius adapted for the modern cook, along with recipes derived unusually from accounts of foodstuffs in Varro, Pliny and Petronius, and a single contribution from the Greek cookery writer, Chryssipus of Tyana.

Vehling, J.D., (1936) *Cookery and Dining in Imperial Rome*, (Chicago), (reprinted 1977, New York). This was the first translation of Apicius into English, but since Vehling was a professional cook rather than a scholar, the translation is sometimes inaccurate and therefore misleading (no Latin text is provided). Vehling claims to have tested many of the recipes and found them, 'practical, good, even delightful', but unlike the most recent modern editors, he offers little assistance to the reader inspired to try them for themselves. The text is often difficult to follow because of the jumble created by parentheses and interpolations, but the commentary occasionally has some points of interest.

REFERENCES

[1] Sidonius Apollinaris speaks of the 'gourmandizing Apicii' in his *Epistles*, 4.7.2.

[2] Juvenal, *Satires*, 4.23; 11.3.

[3] Cf. Seneca, *To Helvia on Consolation*, 10.10: 'How great was his luxury for whom 10 million sesterces were as poverty!'

[4] Seneca, *Epistles*, 110.12; Martial, *Epigrams*, 13.71.

[5] Suetonius, *Life of Vitellius*, 13.2.

[6] *Mulsum* is honeyed-wine, usually drunk as an aperitif, but here used as flavouring. For its preparation see Columella, *On Agriculture*, 12.41.

[7] For foie-gras, see for example Martial, *Epigrams*, 13.58; Juvenal, *Satires*, 5.114; Horace, *Satires*, 2.8.88; Athenaeus, 9.384c.

[8] *Liquamen* is the generic term for fish sauce in the *De Re Coquinaria*.

[9] Pliny, *Natural History*, 31.43.94; Martial, *Epigrams*, 13.102.

[10] See Étienne, R. (1970) 'A propos du Garum Sociorum', *Latomus*, 29, 279-313.

[11] Red mullets rarely exceeded two pounds in weight, so that larger specimens frequently commanded high prices (Pliny, *Natural History*, 9.30.64).

[12] Evidently a contemporary gourmand.

[13] Cakes named after Apicius are also mentioned by Chrysippus of Tyana who wrote a treatise *On Breadmaking* in the first century AD (Athenaeus, 14.647c). There is also a type of grape called Apician mentioned in the agricultural manuals of Varro and Cato, but since these works date from the first and second centuries BC respectively, the grape must have been named from an earlier Apicius than Marcus Gavius.

[14] Nomentanus, who is mentioned by Horace (*Satires*, 1.1.102; 2.1.22), is depicted here as a gluttonous character.

[15] Scholion on Juvenal, *Satires*, 4.23.

[16] Other clues which point towards the fact that the *De Re Coquinaria* is a late compilation include a number of recipes associated with the names of emperors who reigned long after Apicius' own lifetime; for example, 'Sucking pig à la Trajan' (emperor, second century AD) (8.7.16); 'Conchicla à la Commodus' (emperor, second century AD) (5.4.4); 'Julian pottage' (emperor, fourth century AD) (5.1.1).

[17] The Romans increasingly adopted a Greek culinary vocabulary, just as the English utilize numerous terms from French cuisine.

[18] Pepper: Pliny, *Natural History*, 12.14.29. For spices in general see Miller, J.I., (1969) *The Spice Trade of the Roman Empire, 29 BC to AD 641*, (Oxford).

[19] Tertullian, *On the Soul*, 33.

[20] Seneca, *Epistles*, 120.19.

[21] Mennell, S. (1985) *All Manners of Food*, (Oxford).

[22] Very few recipes in the *De Re Coquinaria* contain weights and measures, so that educated guesswork and a little common sense, particularly with regard to quantities of herbs, spices and other flavourings, are required. This suggests that Apicius' cookbook was originally intended for the experienced cook rather than the complete novice.

[23] A type of bread made with raisin juice; see Pliny *Natural History*, 18.26.106.

[24] A cheese made in a neighbouring region of Rome.

[25] Modern recipes are usually given as a series of step-by-step instructions, but this is not always the case with ancient recipes, as shown here.

[26] A favourite Roman delicacy. See for example Martial, *Epigrams*, 13.44. Sow's womb was similarly esteemed: Martial, *Epigrams*, 13.56.

[27] A small bird, eaten whole as a delicacy; the beccafico.

[28] *Passum* is raisin wine, often drunk by women, but also used for cooking. For its preparation see Columella, *On Agriculture*, 12.39.

[29] The name, nature and function of the *laganum* all suggests that it was probably the forerunner of modern lasagne.

[30] *Tracta* was a type of pastry, but here pieces of *tracta* dough are used to thicken a sauce. For a thorough discussion of the nature and various uses of *tracta* (and *laganum*) see: Solomon, J., (1978) 'Tracta: A Versatile Roman Pastry', *Hermes*, 106, 539-556.

[31] Flower and Rosenbaum suggest that the name of this dish may derive from the shell-shaped vessel in which it might have been served as part of the first course of dinner; ie. conchicla from conch.

[32] Probably galingale.

Enriqueta David Perez and the Codification of Philippine Cooking

Doreen G. Fernandez

Where does a country cuisine begin? Surely at the fireside, perhaps in the field, on the hunt, in the village clearing, and then surely in the homes. Its codification probably begins in courts, where the demands of kings and their banquets cause records to be written, and chefs and their assistants to develop. The hunter, the ploughman, the village cooks, the housewife and mother, give way to the person to whom cooking is a profession rather than just a daily task.

In the Philippines, where there were no kings, and the nearest to a court would be the *datu*'s (chieftain's) home, the earlier stages of cooking are still represented. The *Aetas* still live generally nomadic lives, cooking over open fires, sometimes in bamboo tubes, food gathered in field and forest. Fishermen may take with them tomatoes, salt and rice, with which to cook part of the catch—sometimes right in the boat, sometimes on a spit of land. Men ploughing or planting or harvesting may take with them food cooked at home, or have food brought to them in the field, or cook their noonday meal over a fire built in a corner of the field or under a tree. *Datus* may host feasts, at which the cooking is done by women of the family and their friends and helpers. For a home celebration, or a village/town fiesta, the cooking may be done by housewives and/or the best cooks of the town, as a co-operative venture.

In all these cases, the food is basically home cooking, the recipes part of tradition, not written down, but preserved in memory and handed down through apprenticeship or informal teaching. Perhaps a grandmother or great aunt may write down her or the family's recipes, but not for circulation, only to act as reminders, in order to keep them better in memory, or possibly to teach a daughter, especially one no longer in the home.

Formal cookbooks, or collections of recipes, began to be written in the Philippines towards the end of the nineteenth century. A historian has found one among the papers of an Augustinian convent—a collection, mainly Spanish. In the 20th century, one of the earliest cookbooks was *Condimentas Indigenas* (1918), a thin booklet written by Pura Villanueva Kalaw, writer, suffragist, and wife of scholar/writer/editor Teodoro M. Kalaw, who was director of the National Library. She wrote it in order to earn money to buy her husband a billiard table, because he'd had a leg amputated and needed some exercise. She did it by collecting recipes from her friends, and writing them down in Spanish—and yes, she got the billiard table.

One dated 1919 is titled *Pastelería at Repostería Francesa at Española*, a translation by Crispulo Trinidad, *Profesor sa Latinidad*, from a Spanish cookbook. It has illustrations showing *pièces montées*, which I would guess were admired but seldom executed by cooks and housewives. There are cookbooks in Cebuano and in Ilonggo, obviously for circulation only in the regions in which those languages are spoken.

Quite popular was *Everyday Cookery for the Home* (1930) by Sofia Reyes de Veyra, dean of the Domestic Science Department of the Centro Escolar University, and Maria Paz Zamora Mascuñana, associate editor of the *Woman's Home Journal*. Half the book is in English and half in Spanish, and reflects the new 'scientific' consciousness brought about by American education. It speaks of health and nutrition, cooking methods and materials, waste and advantage, and of 'culinary science'.

Many cookbooks that followed were written by home economics graduates and teachers, or by personnel of such government institutions as the Food and Nutrition Research Center or the Philippine Coconut Administration. Sometimes they were compiled by the editors of the women's pages in newspapers and magazines. Only decades later were they gathered, tested and published by food manufacturers (Del Monte, Magnolia, Maya) and their nutritionists, dietitians, home economists, and test kitchens.

Unique in this landscape is Enriqueta David Perez's *Recipes of the Philippines* (1953). First of all, the author was not a professional cook or home economist; she was a journalist and a housewife. Secondly, she had no training in cooking, only informal learning from the women members of her family, and the experience gained cooking for her husband and children. Thirdly, she was motivated not by goals of health and nutrition, not even by a wish to share her recipes. She wanted a cookbook that housewives could follow, one which listed the basic Filipino recipes for everyday and for special occasions, and one so simple that even kitchen help and minimally educated readers could use it. Behind the book was her belief: 'If you can read, you can cook.'

The result is the most popular and most long-lasting cookbook in Philippine annals. From 1953 to the present, it has sold about 200,000 copies, and still continues to sell at the rate of about 7,000 a year.

Enriqueta David Perez, known as Etang, was born on 15 July 1909, the feast of St. Henry (Enrique in Spanish), hence her name. She was born in Bacolor, Pampanga, to Juan Batac David and Epifanio Valencia, and was the eldest of five daughters and three sons.

Her father was from San Fernando, Pampanga, and had been sent to school in Manila, where he earned a *bachillerato* from the Colegio de San Juan de Letran. He wrote poetry in Spanish and Pampango, and had translated Jose Rizal's last poem, 'Mi Ultimo Adios' into Pampango. He was known to be a bon vivant and a good provider though of unsteady income, and to hire himself out sometimes to serenade young ladies, because he could sing, play the guitar, and improvise verses.

These accomplishments did not add up to a secure life for his family, and on the day he was buried, a rich lady came in a car and revealed that the house the family had lived in was mortgaged, with no payments made. The family had to leave the house right after the funeral, and the children were sent to stay with relatives.

Enriqueta, his eldest daughter, had learned to recite poetry as a young girl, and used to perform in such places as Fort Stotsenburg in Angeles, Pampanga (later known as the American Clark Air Base). In the late 1920s she was sent to Manila to study at the Philippine School of Commerce, and would go home every Friday to see the family.

After her father's death, she went to work as a clerk in a drugstore, then found work with the *Graphic* magazine, where the editor was Agustin G. Fabian, who is remembered for having encouraged many young writers of fiction and poetry. Enriqueta, who had finished what one would now call 'commercial high school', was immediately assigned to do interviews. Among those she met and wrote about were Mary Pickford, Florence Vidor (Mrs Jascha Heifetz), Aimee Semple Macpherson (who was unwilling to be interviewed), Mrs Henry Hawes, and Maria Kalaw Katigbak, writer and Barbour scholar, who became Miss Philippines and much later Senator. An American senator's wife offered her a scholarship, but she could not accept because she was supporting her family with her writer's salary.

She met Rodrigo Perez, her husband, on November 30 1929, at the gate of the University of the Philippines. The date is significant because it was the celebration of National Heroes' Day, and he, a law student, went up to her when she was about to leave because she could not afford the admission price to the University Fair. They were secretly married in 1931 (13 December), but were unable to set up house together because she was still supporting her family.

In 1932, A.G. Fabian, suspicious of the young man's frequent appearances at the office, asked her to leave the *Graphic*, and so the young Perezes were jobless when she was expecting their first child. She often told of finding a ten-centavo coin on Ayala Bridge, and how bright it made a very dark day. It brought them a late breakfast of *bicho-bicho* (Chinese crullers) and coffee.

Eventually she found a job at the Bureau of Science, working with Maria Crosa and editing a publication. In the mid 30s she worked for the *Monday Mail*, a weekly newspaper, then for the home page of *The Philippines Herald*, then for the *Tribune*, and later again for the *Herald*. In 1940 she managed a publication of the Plant Utilization Division of the Department of Agriculture, called *For Better Homes*. The four issues included articles on hog-raising, vegetables, substitutes for imported foods, and the famous Maria Crosa *palayok* oven (an oven modelled on the native clay cooking pot).

Her husband, in the meantime, who had been a clerk in the Land Registration Office at the age of 18, became the private secretary of Senator Elpidio Quirino, then went to work at the Department of the Interior in the division in charge of elections. When the Commission on Elections was created in 1940, he became its first secretary. When Quirino became President, Rodrigo Perez was appointed one of the COMELEC commissioners, a post he held till 1956, when he retired.

When Pearl Harbor was bombed in 1941 and war declared, the newspapers closed soon after (the *Herald* was bombed because of Carlos P. Romulo's articles on Japan), and with them Etang David Perez's livelihood. As many housewives did at that time, she bought and sold goods and real estate; and as even more did, she cooked food to sell to friends and neighbours.

Her elder son Bobby (Fr. Bernardo Perez, O.S.B.) remembers that yes, she could cook and indeed cooked all their meals, but she was no expert. And so she was always cooking and experimenting, and would sometimes name her successes after her family, for example the Rodrigo Roast (pork).

Bobby recalls that he and his brother Spanky (Enrique) would watch her as she mixed and baked cakes every afternoon during the Japanese occupation. Mornings were for her buy-and-sell and real estate businesses. One day, when she hadn't come home before the usual mixing-baking time, the two worried boys, knowing that the cakes were due for delivery, carefully sifted flour, broke eggs, and mixed batter as they had seen her do. They poured the mixture into pans, put them in the oven, and went to the bedroom to pray before a crucifix.

When their mother returned, she was pleased to find that the boys had taken over and the cakes were a success. She therefore turned the enterprise over to them. Bobby remembers that these cakes included sponge cakes made with ducks' eggs and cassava flour (wheat flour not being available during the war). She also made cassava *bibingka*, peanut butter, cinnamon rolls, *pinipig* ice cream, *katuray* salad (there was a tree in the garden), and, at Christmas time, *jamon en dulce*.

Their father was then working in the Manila City Hall, in the radio reconditioning office. He brought home every evening an unreconditioned radio, and the family was able to listen to shortwave broadcasts from the U.S., including that of MacArthur's landing in Leyte—a strictly forbidden activity which could have brought them death, had they been caught.

After the war Mrs Perez went to work for the Red Cross, and for a women's magazine called *Yours*, then for the *Evening News* for a couple of years, and finally for the *Herald*, which had been revived about 1950. She edited the women's page, did some work for advertising, and edited the annual supplement called *June Bride*.

It was at this point that her cookbook came to be.

The idea of writing a cookbook was proposed to her by friends at a meeting of the Philippine Association of Women Writers. Why not, they thought, prepare a Philippine cookbook in anticipation of the 1953 International Exposition?

Etang had of course been compiling recipes for her work and for her own home cooking. She herself owned cookbooks by Escoffier and by Ida Bailey Allen, and others released by such companies as Nestle, Gold Medal, and Purico.

She embarked on the cookbook as her own project, kitchen-testing every recipe and trying them out on her family. She took her completed manuscript to the Capitol Publishing House printing press, and had 5000 copies printed at her own expense. This was in 1953, when that might be called a rash decision, since the largest print runs for books then were usually under 1000.

With the books bound and bundled and stored in her home, she called the Philippine Education Company (PECO), the city's largest book distributor, and inquired whether they sold cookbooks. They did. 'How many did they sell each month, on the average?' she asked. 'About ten or twelve', was the answer. Although her heart sank, she asked if she could give them some of her books to sell, and they suggested that she send 30. Since her books were packed in bundles of 50, she asked to be allowed to deliver one bundle, which she did the next day on her way to work, disheartened that it would take decades to sell her first print run.

By the time she reached her newspaper office, the phone was ringing, and PECO was asking her to deliver more books, because the first 50 had been sold. The next year she had to print about 3000 more, and since she found herself reprinting yearly, she decided in the 1960s to sell the book to Socorro Ramos of the National Bookstore. The book has been reprinted regularly since then, and a yearly check (in 1994, P16,000 after taxes) sent to the family.

Bobby recounts the family's first and only trip together to the United States and Europe—by boat, car and train. At a Filipino home in New York, they were invited to dinner by a friend staying with a Filipino family. The lady of the house boasted that she could serve them real Filipino food because she had a Filipino cookbook, *Recipes of the Philippines*. She was astonished to learn that the visitor introduced as 'Etang' was the author.

The present cookbook is exactly like the first one in content. The pictures and cover were changed once or twice, but since her death in 1971, her only daughter Veronica has refused to consider a new edition, because she wants her mother's work kept as it was in her lifetime. There used to be a special edition for brides, bound in white with gold printing on the cover. That is no longer being printed, but the book goes on, a favourite present for daughters, brides, bridal showers, foreigners, Filipinos abroad, and the like. Although no reliable figures were available, the family calculates that in the book's 42 years of existence, some 200,000 have been printed. The price has risen from P2.50 in 1953 to P110 (book-paper edition) and P65 (newsprint). It continues to be the uncontested favourite Philippine cookbook on the market.

Etang David Perez's accomplishment goes beyond the writing of a book, the value of which has been proven by its longevity and popular success. More importantly, she codified the home cooking she had learned from family, personal experience, and work as a woman's page editor. The recipes are thus rooted in tradition, but reflect the 'new' thinking of the '50s on health, efficiency and nutrition, and are 'scientific' in that they have been kitchen-tested, standardized, and, yes, codified.

Recipes of the Philippines features 264 recipes classified into: Fiesta Fare, 21; Everyday dishes, 135; Sweets and Desserts, 35; Breakfast and Merienda, 58; Pickles and Relishes, 5; Refreshments, 10. In a very brief and modest introduction, Ms Perez acknowledges the multi-cultural roots of Philippine cooking:

> Part of Philippine history is a record of the inhabitant foreigners—the Indonesian adventurer, the Chinese trader, the Spanish governor, the American schoolmaster...who have influenced not only Filipino thinking, art and fashion, but also food tastes and practices.

It is however, despite 'betraying foreign marks,' 'still highly characteristic and national,' she points out. It has 'submitted to revisions imposed by contemporary speed and accepted practicability,' gradually discarding some traditional methods, acceding to pressure-cooking and the use of canned food, and thus finding cooking methods that are less labor- and time-intensive. Hospitality and neighbourly assistance, she reminds us, made the hours spent in kitchens light and enjoyable, but since the contemporary housewife has less time and help, Ms Perez compiled this book with her in mind.

She translated 'yesterday's guesswork into definite amounts measurable by cups and spoons,' and compiled recipes 'reconstructed from now illegible handwritten notes from another age...from careful instructions of grandmothers and friends' contributions.' She acknowledges her live sources, among them her mother Epifania V. David, her mother-in-law Sabina Mejia Perez, her sister Emiliana Capati, and the rightly renowned Maria Y. Orosa; and also the Institute of Nutrition, the Home Extension Service Bureau, the Philippine Manufacturing Co., the National Teacher's College, and the Philippine Women's University.

The collection is not complete, she confesses; the recipes were chosen for having 'a more or less general appeal' and for giving 'a good glimpse of the Filipino heart.'

Despite the modesty, the recipe range is amazing, when one considers that Ms Perez was from one region (Pampanga) among many, and lived most of her life in Manila, without ever having been employed professionally in the food business, except for her brief term as writer in the Bureau of Science.

Fiesta fare, for example, includes the *Lechon de Leche*, the suckling pig that is the traditional centrepiece for the festive table. In her recipe, however, it can be spit- or oven-roasted, and two recipes for its liver sauce are provided, one starting with the pig's liver (roast, pound, grind it) and the other with canned liver pâté.

The rest of the fiesta fare are Spanish dishes because colonial dishes were expensive and considered élite, and thus became festive food. Among them are *Paella, Lengua, Morcon, Callos con Garbanzos, Relleno, Caldereta* and *Jamon en Dulce* (sugar-glazed ham traditional to Christmas). The one non-Spanish dish on the fiesta list is *Pancit Molo*, a somewhat luxurious soup of pork-stuffed wontons, chicken and shrimps, from the Chinese heritage.

Dishes for everyday range through the whole of Filipino culinary history: indigenous dishes from different (ethno-linguistic) regions and provinces (e.g. *Pinais, Bachoy, Bulanglang, Pinacbet, Dinengdeng, Sinigang, Tinagoctoc, Tinutungan, Kinunot, Laksa*); dishes indigenized from foreign cuisines, such as Spanish (*Bacalao a la Vizcaina, Calamares Rellenados*), Mexican (*Tamales, Champorado*) and Chinese (*Lumpia, Arroz Caldo, Pancit*); and even a few of American extraction (fried chicken, pork chops).

Names in Spanish, English and the local languages identify these, as well as snacks (*bibingka, palitao, broas*) and sweets (*leche flan, bukayo, nata de pina*), breakfast dishes (*puto maya; churros*), refreshers (*ube* ice cream, *duhat* juice) and relishes (papaya and *singkamas* pickles). Almost all of them are still being cooked in homes, markets, cafeterias and restaurants, and in some cases in the streets.

The recipes are simply-worded, with occasional, minimal explanations. Ms Perez does not explain origins historical or regional, nor does she explore the cultural context. The table of contents lists a glossary, but in the 1966 edition (11th printing) it was omitted. It is back in the 1973 edition.

I can attest from experience both as a young bride and an older researcher/food writer that all the recipes are eminently reliable. They work. I dip into the book when writing a column, describing a dish, discussing a cooking process, considering dietary patterns and partnerships, tracing culinary history, and am always rewarded with solid information. My first copy of the cookbook I had when I got married in 1958; it stayed in my kitchen till it fell apart and was given to a kitchen helper who was getting married herself. It was speedily replaced with more copies through the years, some eventually given away to friends who pleaded need of them, one still residing in the kitchen, and one on my bookshelf.

I believe Enriqueta David Perez's cookbook has had more influence on the cooking of housewives, cooks, and home-trained chefs than have government bureaus, schools of Home Economics, cooking shows, test kitchens and other cookbooks. It ranges through Philippine culture, regions and history, and is a guide, a lexicon, and an artifact of Philippine culinary culture that has succeeded, as she wished, in giving generations of cooks 'a good glimpse of the Filipino heart.'

Nouvelle Cuisine

Henri Gault

During the summer of 1973 some extremely virulent articles about French cuisine appeared in the English and American press, in particular in *Time* magazine, accusing it of having completely degenerated. If one believed these criticisms, one ate badly in France and the reputations of the most famous establishments (Tour d'Argent, Maxim's, la Marée, le Grand Véfour, Taillevent, Prunier, Lucas-Carton, Lasserre in Paris, Point at Vienne, la Mère Brazier at Lyon, Bise at Annecy, Thuillier at les Baux, Pic at Valence, Hure at Avallon, etc.) had become fraudulent - as well as those of bistros and fashionable restaurants. Putting aside the claims in these articles that one ate as well in England and the United States - which is ridiculous - the reproaches that came to us from abroad were not that far from the truth: the Haute Cuisine Française was now no more than the sum of its parts. It was pompous, archaic, heavy, without the least imagination, dishonest, and based on hundred year old recipes which were not in any way relevant to contemporary needs. As for the repetitive cuisine of the old-fashioned bistros, it was running out of steam for the same reasons of irrelevance to today's way of life and undermined by the fashion for salads, grills, 'herbes de Provence' and the developing 'fast food'.

Four years earlier, with Christian Millau, I had founded the magazine *Le Nouveau Guide Gault-Millau* and, in 1972, our first *Guide de la France* appeared as a competitor to the old impersonal *Guide Michelin*. I was therefore in a good position to judge the gastronomic situation in France. Whatever I felt about it, I had to recognise that it was not brilliant and even that its reign was coming to an end. (At the time, as of course today, French cuisine was regarded everywhere in the western world as the highest point of the art, and there was not a restaurant from Berlin to San Francisco, from London to Melbourne which did not honour it by copying it). I saw its faults and its limitations but nevertheless I was not seriously concerned because I felt secret tremors and the promise of renewal.

In fact the beginning of the '70s saw the appearance of a new class of cooks: enterprising young men, filled with curiosity and above all much more free than their predecessors. They were free in their minds, with the memory of the spirit of revolt and even anarchy that had overtaken France in 1968 and even more they were free in their work. As opposed to the previous generation, when cooks were employed in brigades in palaces or grand restaurants, they had set up on their own account, learning to manage their businesses, to direct their own staff, and above all to escape from the routines, constraints and immutable rules of the old cuisine. They were called Bocuse, Troisgros, Barrier, Chapel, Haeberlin and Vergé in the provinces and Denis (died in 1982), Delaveyne, Manière (died in 1990), Peyrot and Minchelli in Paris.

They were already known and appreciated in the guides and by amateurs, but they had not found their place in the elite of 'great cooks'. Behind them the next group was pushing forward and already showing much promise: Loiseau, Senderens, Guérard, Robuchon, Savoy (Paris), Outhier,(La Napoule), Boyer (Reims), the Swiss Girardet and the Belgian Wynants. But however free they were, and of course because of that freedom, they felt themselves lost in a kind of fog and thrust defenceless into the everlasting war between the Ancients and the Moderns. They even felt unable to consolidate technically and commercially the ideas that were boiling away in their skulls, even more than in their casseroles.

For my part while I was sure that something was happening, I was far from imagining that it would all suddenly swing into place. And that it would be 'my fault'!

Fed up by the attacks of my British and American colleagues, even though I knew they were well founded, and excited by the famous 'tremors', I decided to write an article which would be both attacking and full of hope. In writing it I unleashed a great movement starting its march forward, and in all innocence produced a veritable manifesto. Here it is

1. COOKING TIME REDUCED for most fish, for all shellfish, for poultry with brown meat and game, for roasts, veal, some green vegetables, pasta. Roast lobster and carré de veau by Denis, haricots verts by Bocuse, fish by Le Duc, frogs by Haeberlin, duck by Guérard, crayfish by Troisgros, woodcock by Minot, among others, are convincing examples.

2. NEW UTILISATION OF PRODUCTS. It is undeniable that our epoch of overproduction and bastardised technology is poisoning, even eliminating, many products. Gastronomically speaking, there are practically no more chickens, veal, fruit, potatoes, beef, game, trout, cheese, etc... Nevertheless the old style of cooking, even 'haute', continues to use, without flinching, these asepticised and rigorously insipid products. The new chefs are giving up such products rather than masking their poverty by aggressive sauces. For them there are two solutions:

a) to make what we call the cuisine du marché, made with products chosen and bought that very morning (these new chefs get up early) or very specifically ordered. They seek out from the good quality merchants rare, precious (and expensive) good chickens, veal, crayfish, partridges, frogs, tomatoes, eggs, truffles, etc...

b) They use what the modern world has not yet destroyed or what it has made more accessible, more fresh: products of the sea (oysters are better than ever), butter, generally very honourable, vegetables in spite of pesticides, foie gras from Israel, asparagus from California, etc...

3. These methods lead the modern cooks to REDUCE THE CHOICE ON THEIR MENUS. This practice has already been applied for a long time in the provinces where there is a bigger turnover of customers. In Paris one is beginning to see less of those gigantic menus with a ridiculously varied choice, which necessitate huge stocks and a regrettable amount of cold storage. (God knows what must have been the state of 'fresh' products in restaurants that had five hundred dishes a la carte in the time of our grandparents). These new arrangements have produced lower storage costs, a more immediate cuisine, more inventive, fresher, less routine - which is always cooked against orders. And a happy elimination of those fonds de sauce languishing in bain-maries, the glory of pre-war days.

4. The new cooks are NOT SYSTEMATICALLY MODERNIST. They know in particular the danger facing many products, especially fish and shellfish, when they are refrigerated, whether cooked or raw.

In contrast to the old school, which would serve you a jellied buisson d'écrevisses, dried up soles Duglèré on a block of ice, the new cooks use the refrigerator with discrimination.

5. On the other hand they do not let out cries like violated virgins at the sight of all the processes and machinery of cooking, conservation, cleaning and comfort that are offered

by ADVANCED TECHNOLOGY. Their new and clean stoves are supplied with accurate and simple temperature controls. They have hot plates for their dishes and crockery, they work in an atmosphere that is not scorchingly hot and is free from unsupportable smells and in rooms that are bright and spacious. They use mixers, icecream makers, automatic rotisseries, potato peelers, and waste disposal units. They work carefully with the deep-freeze, about which they know, at least in the case of certain products, that the commercial problems are due more to the basic quality of the product than to the process itself. Raymond Oliver gives constant demonstrations of this. In fact they use methods of cooking and heating up that make the old toques shudder. The latter would do well however to go and taste the red mullet cooked in its juice in the micro-wave oven by Paul Bocuse. And this does not stop the Troisgros brothers cutting their marvellous haricots verts one by one, longways and by hand.

6. They have banned from almost all their preparations those so-called culinary principles, (but in reality boring relics) which insist that game (or certain butcher meats that it is hoped can be passed off as such) be marinated in oil, brandy, wine or spices for days on end, let alone the awful question of 'high' game (the contemporaries of Curnonski regaled themselves with putrified woodcock). The new chefs serve GAME HUNG BUT FRESH and the spices that covered up the shameful fermentations have disappeared from their arsenal.

7. Bit by bit the new school recognises the pretension, the inanity, the mediocrity of those rich and heavy sauces. THESE TERRIBLE BROWN SAUCES AND WHITE SAUCES, these espagnoles, périgueux, financières, grand-veneur, béchamel, mornay that have assassinated so many livers and have covered up so many insipid pieces of meat. Meat glaze, veal stock, red wine, Madeira, blood, roux, gelatine, flour, cheese, corn flour, these are not inscribed on the tablets of the law. The chefs retain of course fumets, cream, butter, pure jus, eggs, truffles, lemons, fresh herbs, fine peppers, and they honour clear sauces, sauces that blend, that exalt and sing and leave the spirit clear and the stomach light.

8. From this point of view, one can say that they KNOW ABOUT DIETETICS. Without bowing to the inconsistencies of men in a hurry and women on a diet, they are discovering the pleasures of light dishes, of well made salads, of fresh vegetables simply cooked, of rare meat. The entrecote of the Troisgros is less fattening that the broth of the macrobiotic... And one does not peel tomatoes only for the pleasures of taste and teeth, but also for those of the stomach.

9. They have also understood, in the same kind of way, the DANGER OF DECEITFUL PRESENTATIONS, of which the redoubtable Carème launched the fashion 150 years ago. They like to adorn, to embellish, but they understand the limits which must not be passed and the aesthetics of simplicity - as well as the vanity of sonorous nomenclature. A 'langouste à la parisienne, escalopée sous sa gelée, parmi ses barquettes et ses oeufs durs' is less good than 'en vinaigrette' (well, with a bit of truffle, as done by Minot) and nothing is more naturally beautiful than a roast partridge, simple but exquisite.

10. Finally, THESE PEOPLE INVENT. It has been said that for thousands of years and in particular during the 19th century, everything had been tried and established: all the equipment, the cooking methods, the successful combinations. Well, this is false. It is already sixty years since Jules Maincave, farsighted creator of genius, had the idea of

replacing vinaigrette with a mixture of pork jus and rum, of marrying chicken with lily of the valley, of veal à l'absinthe... There are millions of dishes that can be created and certainly hundreds of them that will survive.

Further these new cooks have turned away from routine accompaniments. They do not consider it sacrilege not to serve mutton with beans, lobster with rice, sole with steamed potatoes, veal with spinach, steak with chips, fowl à la creme aux morilles, nor white wine with fish or foie gras with truffles. Everything is permitted, and if carrot purée doesn't suit andouillette, one can use lentils or broccoli. They are not afraid of offering raw fish (Minchelli, Manière, even Bocuse), they introduce new or little known ingredients (green pepper, basil, dill, passion fruit, etc...), they reintroduce forgotten dishes, adjust them and make them popular (quenelles of hare, mutton ham by Senderens), they discover (or rediscover) new forms of cooking and of presentation, like the gilt-head bream that Guérard cooked in the oven in seaweed, or the profiteroles (without chocolate) that Denis stuffed with sweetbreads. They do not scorn exotic products, spices and recipes, they get their saffron from Iran for soupe aux moules (Bocuse), lacquer their ducks (Oliver), mix crab and grape fruit (Girard). And they rehabilitate simple things like salt cod (Girard), goose (Guérard), tunny (Denis), boiled eggs (with caviar, it is true - Manière), vegetables à la grecque (Peyrot), le pot-au-feu (à la jambe de 'boa' by Bocuse, au canard by Guérard), sorrel (Troisgros), soups (Haeberlin) and many others. Likewise they give rare products which were being spoiled by too many sauces, feuilletages and fancy rubbish, every chance (sautéed truffles by Chapel, lobster in a vegetable soup by Delaveyne). And everyday they work, they invent, they create, they succeed.

And if you will allow me, as today we are playing deus-ex-machina of the new French cooking, we will add an eleventh commandment which these chefs did not expect to see codified: friendship. They are people who love one another. Speak about Bocuse to the Troisgros, about the Troisgros to Haeberlin, about Haeberlin to Guérard, about Guérard to Delaveyne, about Delaveyne to Manière, about Manière to Senderens, about Senderens to Peyrot, etc... lengthen the chain if you like, the links will not break. They like one another; they are not jealous; they give one another recipes, ideas, addresses, even customers. And it is because of this that these people have so much talent, so much freshness, and that one can shout from the housetops: 'VIVE LA NOUVELLE CUISINE FRANÇAISE.'

This 'manifesto' dating from October 1973 and published in the magazine *Gault-Millau*, of which it was the cover, was entitled 'Vive la nouvelle cuisine française'.The formula, which would conquer the world, was launched, and, even more, the theoretical basis (or alibi) of modern cooking was offered to unknown young cooks. They poured in through the open door.

On reflection this manifesto contained three errors:

1. It is in the form of 'ten commandments', an arbitrary number and a tyrannical pretension replacing an earlier one (without mentioning the 'eleventh commandment' on friendship, which I set out very naïvely...).

2. It says nothing of the need to preserve the achievements of the past and to keep alive traditional country cuisine. As a result the new chefs totally abandoned the latter, forgot it and made it forgotten, which is a great loss. Contrary to what they say in the journals, there is no going back, other than in the names of dishes of peasant cooking: 'ragouts',

'daube', 'sautés', 'à l'ancienne', etc.; as for the bistro cooks, they don't know how to do it any more.

3. This nouvelle cuisine, wishing to be without roots and open to every influence, was the band wagon on to which jumped, along with the authentic cooks, a crowd of mountebanks, antiquarians, society women, fantasists and tricksters who did not give the developing movement a good reputation. Furthermore fashions, mannerisms and trickery attached themselves to this new culinary philosophy: minuscule portions, systematic under-cooking, abuses of techniques in themselves interesting (mousses, turned vegetables, coulis), inopportune marriages of sugar, salt and exotic spices, excessive homage paid to the decoration of dishes and 'painting on the plate', ridiculous or dishonest names of dishes...

So much so that, after the initial surprise and sympathy, Nouvelle Cuisine was subject to innumerable detractors and an avalanche of criticism, both with the public and with the press.

Only the restaurateurs - and this is what matters - and all the best of them, were converted to the cause. After more than twenty years, sometimes hiding it, sometimes dressing it up as a 'return to the past', the good French chefs, followed by most foreign ones, make modern cuisine in accordance with the essentials of my 'ten commandments' - and sometimes without even knowing it. In this way in 1973 and for long thereafter, French gastronomy recovered its prestige, its pre-eminence (and its tyranny).

There was a unique exception: Paul Bocuse. After proudly carrying till towards the end of the 70s, the title of 'Pope of Nouvelle Cuisine', rather rapidly bestowed on him by the gastronomic press, the Maitre from Lyon, the incomparable leader of French cuisine, became uncomfortable to see flourishing around him numerous chefs so brilliant that he asked himself whether he would be able to stay at the top of the class for ever. So he made a 180 degree U-turn and declared that Nouvelle Cuisine didn't exist, that everything had been invented centuries ago, notably by his grandmother (!). From then on he presented himself as the defender of tradition and, being the only 'great one' in this situation, did not risk being no longer the first. Poor Paul!

Nevertheless it is interesting to note that the volte-face of such a great lord in no way changed the current of the revolution which was the birth of Nouvelle Cuisine. Having on the whole got rid of most of its tricksters and of its mannerisms, having rightly abandoned its epithet of 'Nouvelle', the cuisine of today is free, inventive, controlled, even erudite, good looking, well balanced, healthy, infinite. And exquisite. Permit the one who was its sorcerer's apprentice to be proud of his incomplete and unplanned Manifesto.

(Translated by Harlan Walker.)

Cooking to Survive

Barbara Haber

One of the many illuminating insights Theodore Zeldin makes in *An Intimate History of Humanity* is his comment that 'women seem...to be looking at life with fresh eyes, and their autobiographies, in various forms, are the most original part of contemporary literature.' Part of the appeal in reading what women have to say about themselves is the fluidity with which they move from the private to the public aspects of their lives and then back again as they struggle to provide a narrative of their histories. These stories often reveal the tensions beneath the surface of everyday life, the struggles of authors to construct meaning and drama to their existence. In this paper, I will contrast two American women who cooked for a living: Alice Foote MacDougall, an upper-class white woman from New York, and Cleora Butler, a working-class African-American who grew up in Oklahoma. Although MacDougall was born in 1867 and Butler in 1901, they both lived through many of the tempestuous events of the first part of the 20th century and their histories invite comparison, showing us that race and class are as important as gender in defining women's lives.

Alice Foote MacDougall, who might have stepped out of a novel by Edith Wharton, began life as the privileged oldest child of an upper-class New York family. She preferred her father to her mother, and in her autobiography she speaks lovingly of his sophistication and hospitality, especially on matters of food and drink. She says:

> Papa took great pride in his wine cellar. He was accustomed to having wine at dinner always, not so much for himself as for the many English and French gentlemen who were constant dinner guests. After our drive, Commodore Vanderbilt...or some other gentlemen would return with Papa to our home on 11th St. Then Papa would set out his choicest wines for their delectation—brandy, fifty years old, filling the room the moment it was uncorked with a delicious, indescribable aroma, whiskey, sherry, port, all choice and very old. Conversation sparkled and the open fire glowed, but not more warmly than did my father as he thus entertained his friends.

About her mother, MacDougall says:

> In my mother's home, good housekeeping stood out predominant. You could tell the time of day by what the maid was doing. If Jenny was brushing the fourth step of the front stairs, you could lay your last dollar that it was ten-thirty, and as sure as it was Thursday night so did we feast on chicken. Order and method carried to its nth degree—a little of a strain to irregular Papa and me, but excellent for the smooth running of the house. Mama was a religious woman, but her real God was good housekeeping...

Thus normal life for MacDougall consisted of a well-managed home filled with the trappings of wealth, and the companionship of a loving father who included her when he went on his gentlemanly rounds. He was her 'first and perhaps, only great love'. When the wolf came to their highly respectable door, in the form of doomed financial investments, it destroyed her father's existing fortune and any hope his family had for a return to their affluent lifestyle. MacDougall in language full of passion and terror, describes her reactions to her father's futile attempts to regain his economic and social status: 'Night after night I lay awake, weeping and worrying, unable fully to understand, magnifying the danger, powerless to help, impotent to avert the approaching catastrophe.' This event was to be the central drama of her life, for it colored everything that followed.

She tried to restore her life to normal by marrying a man fourteen years her senior who, from all appearances, should have been able to keep her in the style to which she had been accustomed. He was a successful businessman, perceived to be a coming leader of Wall Street, but he disappointed her profoundly, and disappeared from her life, leaving her with three young children to support. In her autobiography, MacDougall does not tell us what happened to him. We do not know if he died, or went mad, or ran off with another woman. Characteristically, she tells us her reactions to events, without ever explaining what exactly happened.

About this period in her life she says: 'I taught myself new economies...and reduced life to its lowest terms of the most meagre necessities.' Brushing her teeth in the morning with only plain water and no tooth powder became to her a hated symbol of her reduced circumstances. By paying close attention to economies, she scraped along until she was forty when her children were almost grown and she went into business. Because her husband had been in the wholesale coffee-bean business, she fell into the same work, and got her start with the help of loans from people she had known in her former life.

At first she peddled coffe beans in and around New York, delivering them to the back doors of homes she had visited as a guest. Eventually she opened a coffee shop which she developed into a successful chain of stylish restaurants. She gave them romantic names—Cortile, Piazzetta, Firenze and Sevillia—and decorated them with such details as whitewashed walls, Moorish arches and Italian and Spanish pottery. Her ideas were drawn from long-ago trips to Europe. At this point in her now successful life, her autobiography is similar to other accounts—generally in fiction and film—of gentlewomen falling on hard times who manage to pick themselves up by their bootstraps by commercializing on their domestic skills. The British television series, *The House of Eliott* comes to mind (especially since it is being recycled continually on American cable television), the story of sisters who discover unexpectedly after the death of their profligate father that they must earn their own living and succeed brilliantly by establishing a fashion house, as does the book, *Gentle Breadwinners* by Catherine Owen, a fictional account of an indigent gentlewoman who overcomes poverty by selling baked goods on consignment through a women's exchange. The latter especially is a cautionary tale meant to encourage enterprise from women whose futures have suddenly gone awry. The moral of these tales is that female pluck and enterprise within certain acceptable public arenas will allow women to overcome personal adversities. Having been conditioned to expect these sorts of messages, I was more than a little surprised to discover that Alice Foote MacDougall did not hold herself up as an example for other women to emulate, but instead cautions her female readers to stay at home and consider themselves lucky if they can do so. She espoused anti-suffrage and anti-feminist positions all of her days. Despite the great success she characterizes as developing from 'A bowl of [waffle] batter in a place 12 feet by 16 feet in February, 1921 [to] six large Restaurants and a business amounting to about $2,000,000 in February, 1927', she seemed to remain in continual mourning for the vanished entitlements of her lost Eden, the upper-class life of privilege her 'darling Papa' had provided.

MacDougall's approach to food is a reflection of her life, a blend of opulence and parsimony, tensions which show up in her cookbook. In a chapter entitled, 'Reflections on Waste but not Wasted Reflections', she gives some prosaic tips for using up leftovers—breadcrumbs from stale bread, chowder from fish heads and tails. But when we get to her chapter on canapes, she insists that delectable tidbits can be made from almost any scrap found in the ice box as long as it makes its appearance on bread cut into fancy shapes; however, the first three recipes she offers call for caviar, pate de foie gras and Roquefort cheese, hardly the typical leftovers of middle-class families. At the same time, she makes such parsimonious suggestions as saving paper by slitting envelopes in order to use their insides as note paper, and even gives directions for using cereal cartons to make soles for children's worn-out shoes.

MacDougall is offering herself as a moral guide as well as an advisor who can inspire women along the path to gracious living. But most of all, she is a product of her time and of her circumstances. Forced to earn her own living, she more than rose to the occasion, but never interpreted her success as an appropriate role for herself or for women in general. She would have preferred not to have been disturbed from the privileges of a life in which her father continuously stuffed her purse with money and arranged for her to charge things at all of her favourite stores. Her attitude, which is unambiguous about her preference for her original life, flies in the face of feminist ideology which has as its basis the need for female autonomy. What seems clear is that some people are more in need of autonomy than others.

Cleora Butler, born in 1901, the daughter of working-class African-Americans, grew up in a large family with the expectation that she would have to earn her own living. Her great-grandmother had been a housecook on a large plantation outside of Waco, Texas. Butler and her family moved to Oklahoma when she was a young child, as part of a convoy of African-Americans who sought free land and independence with the opening of the Oklahoma territory. They formed all-black townships, or at least strong communities within white towns and cities.

Her grandparents had a farm which she and her three brothers used to visit every summer. Some of the earliest food pleasures she describes in her book: *Cleora's Kitchen: The Memoir of a Cook & Eight Decades of Great American Food* occur at the farm where the children were given gunny sacks filled with nuts and ribbons of sugar cane candy. The latter came from her grandfather's last crop of the season, the sale of which contributed much to the household income. Butler's mother, the oldest of eleven children, also cooked and baked for a living, and taught her daughter many of her skills. She tells us how her mother magically mixed ingredients together into marvellous dishes that seemed deceptively easy to produce.

Butler's impulse to cook showed up early. She describes her first attempt as occurring when she was only ten, but 'determined to strike out on [her] own'. She was alone in her house, and with the aid of a twenty-five cent cookbook published by the Calumet Baking Powder Co., she made a double recipe of excellent baking powder biscuits dramatically produced just in time for the family's supper. However, this early success was not always followed by others. Subsequent attempts at baking cakes and cookies sometimes failed, and she began to bury their remains in the backyard in what she came to call her 'dough patch'. This graveyard of baked mistakes was ultimately discovered by Cleora's mother who tried to seem stern, but was overcome by hilarity, eventually getting her daughter to stop her secret burials in exchange for lessons in baking.

And those lessons must have been excellent, for Cleora Butler's mother had been baking and selling loaves of bread to neighbors for twenty-five cents a loaf at a time when bread was available in stores for five cents. Working on a wood-burning stove, she also turned out popovers, cream puffs and all kinds of cakes. In later years, while standing in her modern kitchen, Butler often thought about her mother who, she knew, would have been thrilled by the Cuisinart and many of the other conveniences.

After finishing high school, Butler had a year at Oberlin College, but then returned home to start earning a living. She took on well-paying jobs with Oklahoma oil barons, but lost them now and then when an oil well went dry, or during the 1929 stock market crash. But Butler makes clear that even during hard times, friends gathered to eat together. 'Everyone loved parties and a good time as much as they ever did, even though few could afford to throw a bash for even four or six friends. Our way around this was for everyone to bring something. We'd get together and brew our own beer. Then each would bring his or her share of ingredients for the planned menu. It always turned out to be an exciting evening. After the bottom dropped out, the well-to-do…followed our example…their parties were perhaps more grandiose than those we had, but I know they were never more fun.'

At one point in her life, Butler took up a career as a hatmaker, the result of an unfortunate shopping experience she had in the 1940s. While African-Americans were allowed to shop in some white establishments, they were usually not permitted to try on clothing, especially hats and shoes. Cleora Butler had been insulted in this way, and resolved never again to buy another hat. She brings up another example of the racism of the period when she describes how black musicians survived in those pre-Civil Rights years when most hotels were closed to them. All over the country, people like Cleora Butler and her mother welcomed these travellers by housing and feeding them as a matter of course. In 1937, during one of these visits, the World Heavyweight Championship fight between Joe Louis and Max Schmeling took place. Members of the band along with friends and neighbors gathered in Butler's yard to enjoy fried chicken, potato salad and homemade ice cream as they listened to the radio. When Louis knocked the German out in the first round, Butler tells us that 'the blacks of North Tulsa literally danced in the streets...We didn't often get a chance to cheer about anything, let alone a hero of our very own.'

When Butler decided to open up her own business, she turned to catering, for it required much less overhead than a restaurant. She came into her own with her pastry shop and catering service which became a popular landmark in Tulsa from the 1960s through the 80s.

Butler's relation to food could hardly be more different than MacDougall's, though both women enjoyed success in their chosen fields. In describing her food memories, Butler speaks about how dishes tasted and smelled as well as how they looked. She could remember the look of yams eaten in her childhood which oozed syrup as they come from the oven. And in later years in the pastry shop, she described a neighbor who 'would come into the shop every Thursday evening just as our bread for the next day's sale was coming out of the oven, to purchase a loaf of our sourdough bread for the family for whom she worked. Each week she would also buy a second loaf for herself, but before she would let us wrap it, she'd break open the top of her loaf with her fingers. Reaching into her purse, she would withdraw a stick of butter, push it down into the still-warm loaf, and hand the bread back to us for wrapping. This, she allowed, was her weekly treat to herself.'

These kinds of descriptions are typical of the joy Butler finds in the preparation of food and in its eating. The feelings and attitudes she voices throughout her book of memoirs reveal a person who experiences life on its own terms and is resourceful about dealing with whatever comes along. Her color and class place Cleora Butler within a particular context of American life in which she could not have hoped to have what Alice Foote MacDougall had and lost. Some might think that she lived a less significant life than her aristocratic counterpart whose losses carry tragic overtones in the classical sense of the term. This is certainly arguable, for who is to say whose life story is the more important? One of the most important conclusions we can draw from reading womens' autobiographies is the importance of the diversity in the lives of women and that their lives must be understood on their own terms.

Cleora Butler is not only writing about herself but about her community and culture. She may begin by writing about food, but her comments usually lead directly to her regard for family and friends, and these revelations tell us about how other African-American women think and feel. In her famous essay, 'In Search of Our Mothers' Gardens', Alice Walker describes how inventive gardens and beautiful quilts are the expression of black women's art. In a better world, these women would have been educated and given opportunities that might have led to their becoming famous writers and artists. Walker could just as well have included cooking as a positive creative expression for these women. Who can deny Cleora Butler's creativity?

In contrast, Alice Foote MacDougall's story does not connect to a larger community of people. She constructs a narrative with only one heroine, and she seldom even refers to world events outside of the drama of her own particular life. Her remarkable achievements reveal the intelligence and acumen of a talented businesswoman, yet her central identity remained in the past as the loving though disappointed daughter of a doting father.

Postscript *(My very own Proustian experience)*

I recalled this incident when I came across Cleora Butler's reference to her 'dough patch'. I too had been a child of ten when I at last found myself alone in the house giving in to an overwhelming urge to bake an orange layer cake. It is important to know that my mother was a famously fastidious housekeeper, and that for me to mess around in her kitchen was a daring idea. Being a good reader, I understood the recipe, executed all of the essential steps in preparing the cake batter, and only fell down when it came to technology by putting the tins into a 500 degree oven. At first, the aroma of oranges was exquisite, but everything changed when a burning odor began to permeate the kitchen and I smelled disaster. Opening the oven, I saw two pulsating tins of batter with blackened tops which I quickly removed and rushed into the basement where I hid them behind the furnace. Of course, I forgot all about them. But within a week or two, I was confronted by a bemused and horrified mother who held in her hands the remains of my crime, and scolded me for creating a situation which might have attracted rats. I can remember my responses—never stated, but firmly believed—amazement by how thoroughly my mother patrolled her house, and disbelief that any rat would ever dare to enter her domain.

BIBLIOGRAPHY

Butler, Cleora, *Cleora's Kitchen: The Memoirs of a Cook & Eight Decades of Great American Food*, Tulsa, Oklahoma, Council Oak Books, 1985.
MacDougall, Alice Foote. *Alice Foote MacDougall's Cook Book.*, Boston, Lothrop, Lee and Shepard, 1935.
MacDougall, Alice Foote. *The Autobiography of a Business Woman*. Boston, Little Brown, 1928.
MacDougall, Alice Foote, *Coffee and Waffles*, Garden City, N.Y., Doubleday, 1926.
Walker, Alice. *In Search of Our Mothers' Gardens: Womanist Prose*. New York, Harcourt Brace, Jovanovich, 1983.
Zeldin, Theodore. *An Intimate History of Humanity*. New York, Harper Collins, 1994.

Chez Panisse: Ever Green

Shelley Handler

Chez Panisse did not grow out of some grand design. The simple notion of a place where good friends could meet over good food to discuss life and politics inspired its birth. Travel in France during her college years awakened Alice Waters to the joys of gourmandise and the two ideas were joined to form the iconoclastic restaurant. Berkeley, with its seventies' mix of activism and hedonism, welcomed Chez Panisse. But Alice and her partners were totally unschooled, innocents in the rough-and-tumble world of restaurants. Due, perhaps, to the anti-establishment air of the time, they had no business plans, no set menus, no purveyors, no trained chefs to lead them through the treacherous shoals of a new restaurant. The cooks shopped in local supermarkets, unaware that restaurants bought through wholesalers. They hired friends, equally untrained, who brought their enthusiasms and their problems into the Chez Panisse kitchen. Wine consumed by the staff at the end of the night was not considered part of inventory. Chez Panisse faced bankruptcy many times in the early years, but loyal benefactors kept it from harm. This kind support allowed Alice and the staff to learn as they went along, and slowly the restaurant of Alice's imagining took shape.

The core of Chez Panisse, the heart of Alice's vision, is simplicity and quality – food so good that it needs no fanfare, no dressing up. This forthright style, though French-inspired, found a perfect home in casual North California. At Chez Panisse there is no interest in culinary pyrotechnics. Those traveling far to eat at the restaurant are often surprised at the plainness of it all. Much of what is prepared there is quite traditional; novelty comes in the quality of the ingredients and the little touches that put a new frame around a familiar picture. Classic onion soup is lightened with a bit of chicken stock and relieved of its smothering blanket of cheese, replaced by a crisp crouton of *pain levain* and parmesan. Delicately smoked local salmon is dressed, not with the ancient rhyme of eggs and capers and onions, but with a spry relish of thinly sliced onions and lemons still in their skins. One is struck, not with the brilliant invention of the dishes, but with the pristine flavor and quality of the food. Chez Panisse intends less to startle with newness than to stun with the recognition of something familiar made right.

Alice sets the taste of the restaurant and the four chefs plan the menus, but nothing is done without the creative input of the kitchen staff. The basic form of the menu comes from the chef; the little twists, the variations come from the interchange between the chef and staff, arising naturally during the course of cooking. The cooks are commonly left to produce their own version of a dish, but with this unusual amount of creative freedom comes the responsibility of maintaining the restaurant's high standards and its implied style. 'Alice doesn't like it too (garlicky, spicy, beefy, etc.)' is as harsh as directives get at Chez Panisse, but this simple phrase carries as much gravity as a brandished ladle. 'It's your dish' is another common phrase in the Chez Panisse kitchen, a statement both ominous and liberating. This open approach leaves plenty of room for the muse to step in, keeping both the cooks and the customers interested.

The consensus in the kitchen is not a happy accident. An unusual interviewing style has created a well-integrated team. Prospective cooks are questioned more vigorously about their tastes in movies and literature than their taste in food; the chefs appear to be selecting roommates rather than cooks. Food is certainly part of the interview, but the bigger question is whether personalities will mesh. The hopeful is then invited to work in the kitchen for a day or two, to further assess compatibility. The final nerve-wracking step is to prepare a meal for Alice and the chefs. This careful process ensures that those hired can be trusted to work independently, yet remain part of a subtly functioning organism. Alice's eye for nascent talent is excellent – the Chez Panisse family tree now comprises a veritable Who's Who of the American culinary world.

Peggy Smith, café chef, describes her fifteen years with Alice as 'unpredictable. I never know what her vision of the dishes will be. It's never dull around here. Her ideas are always changing.' 'She's a perfectionist,' states Peggy 'Oh, she can be pleased, but it's not easy. She's constantly pushing us to get the best results. For Alice, satisfaction is momentary. If a dish is successful, she won't rest; she'll push us to improve it or move on to the next idea.'

To follow Alice through any part of her daily rounds is to see her perfectionism and artist's eye at work. Alice was once observed standing over the decorative bowls of ingredients at the entrance, clearly, if silently, displeased. She stared at length at the bright combination of citrus fruits, and then swiftly plucked an orange from the bowl, split it crosswise and set it back down with a decisive 'There!' The change, though slight, was a definite improvement. She is constantly nipping at the heels of the restaurant, picking off wilted lettuce or a shriveled bloom to keep the food and room crisp. Attention to detail this minute may seem obsessive, but it is just this restless attention that keeps Chez Panisse on the cutting edge of quality.

For twenty-four years Alice's energy and vision have led the way, but without the dedicated troops behind her the battle for the palates of America would not have been won. In the early days, Chez Panisse was staffed solely with friends, for better or worse, drawn by Alice's good food and the congenial atmosphere. Today, that small handful of comrades has grown to a staff of over 100. Some chefs have worked with Alice for as many as fifteen years, an unheard of number in the volatile world of restaurants. Partner and pastry chef Lindsey Shere has baked there for the full twenty-four. Though the food and the atmosphere are the primary draw, this longevity is due in no small part to Alice. She may not admit it, but Ms Waters possesses all the skills of a good revolutionary. She has a gift for making others understand her vision of flavorful, wholesome food, and she is equally good at convincing them to take up the cause. She is unafraid to enlist compatriots with skills beyond her own to maintain and advance her dream.

Simple rhetoric, however, would not have drawn such a fiercely loyal crew. Instead, Alice uses her own stunning palate and painterly eye to cajole others into her delicious scheme. Far more than a revolutionary, Alice is a seductress. And like every good seductress, Alice has created surroundings that both warm and delight. The cooks, as well as the diners, are treated to the sensual pleasures of Chez Panisse. Along with food of exquisite quality, the kitchen itself is a source of pleasure. Warm copper lights, a brick hearth and Japanese wooden cabinets make the uncommonly large kitchen a delight to work in. The space over the utilitarian vegetable sink is set with hand-painted Spanish tiles, giving even the dreariest tasks a lovely view. This beguiling atmosphere is yet another part of Alice's plan. Happy cooks will remain, and inspired surroundings often give rise to inspired food.

For the diner, the seduction of Chez Panisse begins at the gate, where wisteria bends watchfully over the menu box that shows the daily offerings. On entering the first floor of this 1915 Craftsman house, one is greeted by a small table that holds the best of the season – bowls of perfect artichokes or fava beans or tomatoes, serving as art and enticement, a prelude to what lies ahead.

Twin sirens of scent and visual beauty lure one further into the restaurant. Huge floral displays, as alluring as the smells emanating from the kitchen, draw the eye further into the separate dining rooms of the café and restaurant. Always striking, often eccentric, the flowers are the work of Carrie Wright, a local florist and longstanding member of the Chez Panisse family. Her arrangements are as expressive of the Chez Panisse aesthetic as anything on the plate. Lush red peonies and wild garnet plums still on the branch, cuttings of gnarled, pocked willow and bruise-coloured orchids (for a dinner inspired by the dark themes of Baudelaire); all are breath-taking. More than simple ornament, they turn the eye towards nature and the mind towards the season, and serve, along with the food, as a quiet plea to care for the earth. They also stand as a symbol of Alice's extravagance.

Said to 'spend money like Waters,' Alice has never been able to deny the restaurant luxuries, especially the flowers, even when it would be prudent to hold back. For Alice, money is seldom an object and profit is secondary. Indulgence reigns supreme throughout the restaurant, whether for hand-made copper lamps for the restrooms or the best quality olive oil for the kitchen. The search for quality is an all-consuming task at Chez Panisse. Alan Tangren, the restaurant's full-time forager, spends his days 'phoning or visiting producers throughout Northern California, maintaining existing sources and developing new ones. Once the goods arrive, they are subject to Alan's expert scrutiny; any that do not measure up to the restaurant's exacting standards are returned. This sort of vigilance has been practiced since the opening of Chez Panisse. Faced with the task of reproducing the vibrant food Alice found in France, the neophyte cooks were forced to adapt recipes to local ingredients and find sources for the quality ingredients they sought. From this evolved the media-dubbed 'California Cuisine', and what was then strange or unavailable has now become vernacular. Over the years the restaurant has established a large network of farmers and purveyors who share the Chez Panisse vision of good, healthful food. The growth of this network, like everything else at the restaurant, has been organic – pun intended. In fact, nearly 90 percent of the ingredients now used in the restaurant are organic. Alice's increased awareness of the endangered environment and the need for sustainable agriculture has caused Alan and the foragers before him to seek producers who respect these principles.

Alice's quest for flavorful, environmentally-sensitive ingredients has led other restaurateurs, both locally and nationally, to follow suit. San Francisco now has a fully organic farmer's market, developed and run by a former Chez Panisse cooks. Bay Area cooks now have easy access to mesclun, fresh herbs, heirloom varieties of produce and locally made goat cheese due to the demands of the Chez Panisse kitchen. That Midwesterners now know radicchio and that goat cheese is produced in Texas can be traced back to the little restaurant in Berkeley. 'In the last five years we've seen a huge increase in farmer's markets in the Minneapolis area,' says Sue Zelickson, writer and food reporter for CBS Radio in Minneapolis. 'On Thursdays and Saturdays there's a market right downtown in front of Neiman-Marcus and Saks [department stores]. Office workers and shoppers carry home huge bags of local, seasonal produce, and gorgeous bunches of flowers. I'm sure the market idea trickled up here from the West Coast, along with restaurant gardens and grilling every vegetable in sight. Even if these ideas didn't come directly from Chez Panisse, we 'foodies' instantly think of the restaurant as the attributable source.'

The path from Alice's dream to national trend was a meandering one. In the early days of Chez Panisse, the search for good lettuce led to a regular customer's offer of whatever she could grow in her garden. When the café added considerable clientele, Wendy's arugula was no longer enough. Chez Panisse soon had several vegetable gardens in the Berkeley hills, tended by Chez Panisse staffers Andrea Crawford and Sibella Kraus. Eventually Sibella elected to become the restaurant's first full-time forager. A wish to expand local sources led her to establish the Farm-Restaurant Project, polling Bay Area restaurants for the goods they most desired and finding the growers best suited to produce them. Sibella went on to head Greenleaf Produce, a quality organic produce wholesaler, and eventually to mastermind the San Francisco Ferry Plaza Farmer's Market, where she presides today. Her experiences have led her to become a nationally respected voice in sustainable agriculture, and in turn have influenced many choices at Chez Panisse.

The search for good bread gave rise to an in-house baker. Steve Sullivan, son of Chez Panisse patrons, made a reputation for himself at college baking bread made from a starter that he kept under his bed. Those early experiments showed a talent for flour and yeast that caught Alice's eye, and Steve was recruited to bake for the café and restaurant. The local demand for well-made bread became so great that Steve left in 1983 to begin the benchmark bakery Acme Bread. What began as a small concern has grown to serve restaurants and grocery stores throughout the Bay Area. At least ten speciality bakeries have since followed suit to fill the demands of a rapidly growing market. That it is now possible to walk to the corner convenience store and buy an Acme *pain levain*, good enough to hold its own against Poilâne's, is directly due to Chez Panisse. In the past five years this phenomenon has spread across the United States. Minneapolis has several new bakeries turning out a wide variety of European-quality breads. Portland, Oregon has gone from zero to seven artisan bakeries in less than four years. Seattle and New York bulge with them. Sightings of bakeries, farmer's markets, community gardens and 'designer' pizzerias have been reported in a large portion of the fifty states. Which leads us, sadly, to the downside of this far-reaching transformation.

The evolution of the modern pizza offers the perfect case in point. This staple of the contemporary Californian menu, though not invented at Chez Panisse, experienced its metamorphosis there. Jeremiah Tower (an early Chez Panisse chef and now a figure in the American culinary pantheon) was improvising *pizzette* in the Chez Panisse kitchen as early as 1975. When in 1980, the upstairs Café included a wood-burning oven in its arsenal, pizza became a regular menu item. And Wolfgang Puck, on numerous forays from Los Angeles, became a regular customer. This unchallenged emperor of 'designer' pizzas openly acknowledges Alice and the Chez Panisse Café as inspiration for his upmarket (read non-traditional) pizzas. Puck later hired Mark Peel, a Chez Panisse cook, to run the kitchen at Spago, Puck's star-studded Hollywood eatery.

Both the Spago and Chez Panisse pizzas were light years away from the enormous soggy-crusted, oil-dripping wheels of cheese and tomato that pass for pizza in America. Fashioned after the Italian model, the new pizzas were spare and crisp, eschewing tomato sauce and mozzarella for original combinations of wild mushrooms and fresh herbs or leeks and local goat cheese. In Wolfgang's hands the pizzas went even further, sporting duck sausage or smoked gouda and occasionally crème fraîche and caviar. This was a far cry from both the rubbery early American pizzas and the sparse pizza margheritas and pizza biancas of Italian design. Though Puck's creations were more adventurous than those at Chez Panisse, their flavors were well-balanced and the combinations restrained. And then the inevitable happened. Through the common mytosis of chef borrowing from chef, American pizzas spun out of control, sprouting everything from snails to swordfish. Crossover calzones reuniting Marco Polo with China held stir-fried chicken, bean sprouts, cheese and sesame oil. It did not help that Wolfgang's pricey pizzas were frozen and available everywhere from suburban supermarkets to in-flight meal service. His well-crafted models had unleashed a flood of recombinant spin-offs made by less talented hands.

When an Alice Waters or a Wolfgang Puck chooses to reinterpret Mediterranean or Chinese cuisine, using informed palates and hand-selected ingredients, it is often a felicitous adventure. But when untutored cooks attempt to sail the same uncharted waters, the results are often a tragic wreck. The countless sorry versions of limp greens and tepid goat cheese, the aberrant pairing of lentils and bananas, pork and blueberries, monkfish and Lord-knows-what are enough to send any good cook scurrying back to Escoffier. However, for every terrifying twist and kink in contemporary cuisine there are also edifying results. Gifted chefs, in such disparate places as Boston, Hawaii, Australia and London are using indigenous ingredients to create sprightly versions of contemporary cuisine. Lydia Shire of Boston's Pignoli restaurant has created a sumptuous fusion of Italian and American cookery in such dishes as Chilled Maine Crab Zupetta. Roy Yamaguchi and other Hawaiian chefs have tapped the tropical bounty of the islands to prepare Coconut-crusted Hawaiian Goat Cheese Tartlets and Coconut-Chilli Beef with Taro Crêpes. These dishes are intelligent offspring of educated palates and careful execution. Nothing less is needed to produce the next stage in the evolution of modern cuisine.

The sons and daughters of Chez Panisse have done their share to further this evolution. Through their books and restaurants they have spread the word widely and well. Mark Miller, with his Coyote Cafés and Red Sage restaurants, has carried lessons learned at Chez Panisse to the far-flung cities of

Santa Fe, Las Vegas and Washington D.C. Deborah Madison combined her Chez Panisse training with her devotion to Zen Buddhism and began a landmark vegetarian restaurant known as Greens. Cookbook readers nation- and world-wide are acquainted with her deft touch through her *Greens* and *The Savory Way* books. Mark Peel and his wife, Nancy Silverton (a former Spago pastry chef), have charmed Los Angeles with Campanile, their rustic Italian restaurant, and the accompanying La Brea Bakery, cited as L.A.'s premiere bread shop. The Chez Panisse family tree, too large to fully enumerate, has branches in all aspects of the American food world.

The open kitchen at Chez Panisse has had the same far-reaching effect as the food. Though Chez Panisse was not the first restaurant to open the kitchen to the diners, the earlier open kitchens were stages for flamboyant displays of kitchen acrobatics, rather than a view onto a serious work-in-progress. After a fire in 1982, the downstairs kitchen at Chez Panisse was rebuilt precisely to that end. The wall dividing the kitchen from the diners was torn down, and watching the cooks became part of the meal. Removing the wall between cooks and diners also removed any sense of secrecy. The customers are encouraged to make a tour of the kitchen, to meet the cooks, to watch the meal take shape. Though many (if not most) kitchens in the free and easy air of California are visible to the public, it is quite unusual to let the public wander through. Before the fire, the prime seat in the house was a table in the kitchen, between the stoves and the pastry section. This warm place of honour was commonly reserved for friends of the restaurant, but on very busy nights occasional lucky strangers would find themselves dining in the inner sanctum. By removing the wall, all of the guests now dine in the kitchen.

Athough Alice's dream of simple, vibrant cuisine is fulfilled daily at Chez Panisse, her quest has not ended. If she had her way, the world would file through her dining room, not just so she could be certain that all have eaten well, but also to unite and inspire people to save our ailing earth. Alice's restoring fare, so dependent on a healthy planet, might help convince the multitudes that the world bears saving. Her greatest hope, however, lies with the next generation. She would like to teach children to feed themselves well and acquaint them with the sustaining power of the garden. Her latest plans draw on striking examples that have arisen in the Bay Area. Catherine Sneed, a counselor at the San Francisco County jail, has begun a garden with young inmates, some deemed incorrigible. Their produce goes to local soup kitchens and restaurants; since the garden's inception recidivism and drug use rates have dropped notably. Ruth Brinker of Fresh Start Farms employs homeless people to grow produce for restaurants such as Chez Panisse. In turn they are given a paycheck and an opportunity to leave the streets. In a similar vein, Alice recently began the Edible Schoolyard project. To offer children an alternative to the violence around them and give them a taste of garden fresh food, the local middle school has planted a garden where the children will grow a portion of their daily lunch. Set up in response to the franchising of school lunches to Pizza Hut and McDonald's, and inspired by French programs that teach children the nuances of taste, the project will eventually include cooking classes. It is considerably easier to get children to eat their peas if they grow them themselves, and by being a part of this cycle of life they may understand the need to protect their environment and slow its destruction. Through instilling a love for the earth and the pleasures of good food, Alice may ensure that the lessons of Chez Panisse are carried forward.

From neighbourhood bistro to standard of excellence for a generation of chefs, Chez Panisse has evolved in its own instinctive way. It has given rise to numerous stellar careers and countless culinary ventures. Whether by direct experience or association, it has acquainted many of us with the joys of the seasonal table, and alerted us in a very tangible way to the need to keep the planet alive. It touches us at our daily meals, from the bread we eat to the vast array of produce we now choose from. Chez Panisse has awakened the American palate and, above all, taught us to eat simply and well.

And I should know because I worked there.

A Cook of 14th-Century London: Chaucer's Hogge of Ware

Constance B. Hieatt

Members of the Symposium may wonder why I proposed to talk about a fictional cook: fictional he may (or may not) be, but Chaucer's Canterbury pilgrim is the only medieval English cook about whom we can know a good deal. An examination of what Chaucer tells us about his Cook in the light of other information about cooking and the food trades in late medieval England shows him to be a truly worthy example of his trade—that is, worthy of note from our point-of-view: his 'worthiness' is dubious in the usual Chaucerian sense of 'respectable, of good standing'.

The Cook makes three appearances in the course of the 'Canterbury Tales': in the General Prologue, the Cook's Prologue and Tale, and the Manciple's Prologue. The first of these passages is the shortest. It follows the description of five prosperous London guildsmen, traveling as a group:

> A COOK they hadde with hem for the nones
> To boille the chiknes with the marybones,
> And poudre-marchant tart and galyngale.
> Wel koude he knowe a draughte of Londoun ale.
> He koude rooste, and sethe, and broille, and frye,
> Maken mortreux, and wel bake a pye.
> But greet harm was it, as it thoughte me,
> That on his shin a mormal hadde he.
> For blankmanger, that made he with the beste.
>
> [They had a cook with them for the occasion,
> To boil the chickens with the marrowbones
> And sharp spice powder and galingale.
> He could easily recognize a draft of London ale.
> He could roast and boil and broil and fry,
> Make 'Mortreux' and bake a pie well.
> But it was a shame, it seemed to me,
> That he had an ulcer on his shin.
> He was among the best at making 'Blankmanger'.]

This tells us almost as much about the guildsmen as about the Cook himself: hiring a private cook to ensure the gourmet quality of their meals on such a trip would have cost them a pretty penny. And this is a cook who is a master of his trade. Not only was he expert at all the basic techniques of cooking (roasting, boiling, broiling, and frying); his repertoire also included the expensive, elaborate dishes characteristic of medieval 'haute cuisine'. The spices with which he seasoned his special chicken dish, which gets two whole lines here, and the rice and almonds which were the base of his notable 'blankmanger' were imported from the east and quite beyond the means of humbler households.

But we have also been informed that he was very familiar with London ale, a predilection which may strike us as familiar. Many of my colleagues fondly remember the excellent cook under whose regime the culinary standards of our faculty club reached unheard-of heights. Alas, he turned up drunk once too often; the president of the university had to fire him. Also familiar are the implications of that unattractive skin eruption on the Cook's leg: whatever else it may mean, this surely suggests a lack of personal hygiene which is unpleasantly juxtaposed with his skill in making a delicate dish. We would all prefer to think that our favorite foods were prepared in immaculate kitchens by well-washed hands; today, as then, this may not always be the case.

When we meet the Cook for the second time in the Prologue to his tale, we find out first that he greatly enjoys a truly dirty joke. His immediate reaction to the Reeve's Tale is loud laughter and approbation of this second indecent story in a row. But Hogge (as he here identifies himself) thinks one or two hot ones isn't enough, and offers to continue the series. The Host agrees, telling him to make it good, but adds a few stinging professional insults:

> For many a pastee hastow laten blood,
> And many a Jakke of Dovere hastow soold
> That hath been twies hoot and twies coold.
> Of many a pilgrym hastow Cristes curs,
> For of thy percely yet they fare the wors,
> That they han eten with thy stubbel goos,
> For in thy shoppe is many a flye loos.

> [You have let blood for many a pasty,
> And have sold many a Jack of Dover
> That has been twice hot and twice cold.
> You are cursed by many a pilgrim
> Who is worse off because of your parsley,
> Which they have eaten with your stubble goose,
> For there is many a fly loose in your shop.]

This casts a new light on the Cook's professional activities. We now know that he is the proprietor of a cookshop, the medieval equivalent of a caterer and fast-food and take-out restaurant. The Host has suggested that the premises are unsanitary, with flies buzzing around—and probably falling into—the food, and that the Cook has engaged in at least one dangerous and fraudulent practice: reheating cooked food, so that yesterday's stale (or possibly spoiled) food could be passed off as freshly cooked. In a world without refrigeration, this was clearly dangerous, and a 15th-century city ordinance insisted that cooks must not 'bake rost nor seeth Flessh nor Fisshe two times to sell'.

It is also possible that the Host is accusing the Cook of making unsavory or illegal 'pastees'. In 1379, the city ruled,

> Because the pastelers [pasty makers] of the city of London have heretofore baked in pasties rabbits, geese, and garbage [giblets and other odds and ends of poultry], not befitting and sometimes stinking, in deceit of the people, and have also baked beef in pasties and sold the same for venison, in deceit of the people; therefore, by assent of the four master pastelers and at their prayer, it is ordered and assented to:
>
> In the first place—that no one of the said trade shall bake rabbits in pasties for sale, on pain of paying, the first time, if found guilty thereof, 6s. 8d. to the use of the Chamber and of going bodily to prison, at the will of the mayor; the second time, 13s. 4d. to the use of the Chamber and of going etc.
>
> Also, that no one of the same trade shall buy of any cook of Bread Street or at the hostels of the great lords, of the cooks of such lords, any garbage from capons, hens or geese to bake in a pasty and sell, under the same penalty.

The regulation specifies the same penalties for baking beef pasties and selling them for venison, and for baking and selling a whole goose or part of a goose in a pasty. Clearly passing off beef as venison was a fraud, and we can see that chicken livers and giblets might have been sitting around too long, but I do not know exactly why rabbits and geese were especially liable to go bad. Other pasties were not forbidden; another regulation of 1378 lists the prices to be charged for capons and hens baked in pasties, and the price for baking in a pasty a capon or a goose provided by the customer—no doubt safer than trusting the 'pasteler' (or cook) to provide a fresh bird.

But Roger (for which Hogge is a nickname) was not a 'pasteler' or pie-man: since he ran a cook shop, he would have belonged to a separate guild, and may have been one of those cooks of Bread Street referred to in the regulation, although cook shops also clustered in other locations—notably Eastcheap and Thames Street. A cook shop sold a great variety of roast poultry (among other things), and it must have been a temptation to make use in pasties of the 'garbages' removed from these roasted birds. Or to sell them to the members of the guild which specialized in such pasties.

Some may wonder why a cook would 'let blood' in order to make pasties. Medieval cooks were expected to kill, pluck, and eviscerate their own poultry. A typical recipe for a roast bird tells us, 'Cut a swan in the rofe of the mouth touward the brayn of the hed, & let hym blede to deth; & kepe the blod to colour the chaudon [a sort of giblet gravy] with, or cut the necke and let hym dye. Then skale [pluck] hym, draw [eviscerate] hym, rost hym, & serve hym forth'. Another 15th-century ordinance spoke of cooks 'with their hands dirtied and fouled' who, in attempting to sell their wares, offended passers-by by plucking at their clothing, and a group of cooks in Coventry were fined for throwing poultry entrails into the street.

Thus almost everything in the Host's words cited above contains unpleasant insinuations, or is potentially libelous. However, the Host is not, as some readers have thought, accusing the Cook's geese of being old and tough: a 'stubble goose' is a mature goose fattened up at harvest time. While younger ('green') geese have sometimes been said to be preferable, a well-fattened stubble goose has always been the traditional treat for Martinmas (November 11). And the Host goes on to urge the Cook not to be angry at words he has spoken in 'game': although it doesn't amount to much of an apology when he ends, 'A man may seye ful sooth in game and pleye', which suggests he meant every insulting word of it.

And so Roger evidently understands the Host when he threatens to retaliate with a story about an innkeeper. Here we are viewing a hostile confrontation between members of rival professions. Tavern-keepers were the third group (along with cooks and pie-men) of the guilds known as victuallers, and there was considerable overlap in the wares they offered to the public. Nor is this the only fellow pilgrim with whom a cook may have reason for conflict, as we see in the Manciple's Prologue, the third and last passage in which the Cook is a central character.

This begins with the Host remarking that the Cook seems to be napping on horseback and is likely to fall off his horse; he asks the Cook why he is so sleepy at this time of the morning, suggesting he may have been troubled with fleas all night, or had too much to drink, or spent an active night with a prostitute. But while this may sound insulting, the Cook doesn't take offense, and simply replies that he would rather sleep than have the best gallon of ale in Cheapside. The real insults come from the Manciple, who describes his drunkenness, concluding,

> Thy cursed breeth infect wole us alle.
> Fy, stynkyng swyn! Fy, foule moote thee falle!
>
> [Your cursed breath will taint all of us.
> Fie, stinking swine! Fie, bad luck to you!]

Fighting words indeed, but the Cook evidently deserves them because his anger at the Manciple causes him to fall off his horse. The Host, however, reminds the Manciple that it may not be in his best interests to make an enemy of the Cook; the Manciple agrees, and makes his peace by offering the Cook some wine. (Strangely, the Cook is able to thank him for this obviously superfluous drink.)

The Manciple's job was to buy the provisions for one of the Inns of Court; naturally, his professional success depended on his getting the most for his money. He would no doubt have had to buy food from a cook shop, at least from time to time, and thus his financial interests and those of the Cook would have been in direct opposition. And since this particular manciple is clearly likely to cook his books for his own profit, it would be unwise of him to provoke the Cook into exposing him by pointing out what he had 'really' paid, as against what he asked his employers to reimburse him for.

The Cook's extreme drunkenness here confirms the hint in the General Prologue that he was entirely too familiar with London ale. It has been proposed that the Cook is modeled on an actual Roger of Ware, a cook of London who was found guilty of being a 'common nightwalker', which means someone who was habitually in the streets after curfew and was suspected of keeping company with thieves and prostitutes. It is interesting that Harry Bailly, the only Canterbury pilgrim (aside from Geoffrey Chaucer) whose full name is given, also has the name of an actual 14th-century counterpart, an innkeeper in Southwark. We learn both names in the same passage—the Prologue to the Cook's Tale—and Harry Bailly's remarks assume a prior acquaintance between the two.

But whether or not the Cook is modeled on a real, not-so-model citizen, the tale Chaucer assigns to him—what we have of it—is exactly what we would expect of him. The central character is an apprentice working in a cook shop. As the proprietor of such a shop, the Cook would have considered Perkyn Revelour's behaviour intolerable for an apprentice. The master cook's business would certainly be impeded by an apprentice who took every excuse to rush out of the shop in pursuit of fun and games. Hogge's attitude toward his central character is, thus, not one of approval, and presumably if the tale were complete, we would find that Perkyn got his comeuppance, one way or another. Readers of this tale may well suspect that a fragment which breaks off just after introducing a woman who earned her living as a prostitute would have been even more indecent than the two tales which proceed it, and this is quite in keeping with the Cook's ribald admiration of the Reeve's Tale; but that does not necessarily mean that the Cook himself was given to gambling, the company of prostitutes, and other low forms of 'revelry'. He was, after all, very successful in his profession, and, indeed, a cut above most of the cooks associated with cook shops of the period.

The average London cook shop was a very small place of business, occupying a frontage on the street of from six to twelve feet. To judge by the price regulations laid down in 1378, such a shop's normal offerings were fairly limited. This ordinance set prices for various roast meats and poultry, ranging from 1 d. for ten roast finches to 20 d. for roast bittern, and including roast pig and roast lamb for 8 d. and 7 d., respectively; the ordinance includes pasties (8 d. for 'the best capon baked in a pasty') and eggs (boiled?), which were to be sold at ten for 1 d.

All of these were 'basic' foods for medieval Londoners, and just the kind of thing people were likely to patronize a cook shop for, although some – like the bittern and finches – may sound pretty exotic to us today. Most Londoners did not have kitchens properly equipped to do roasting and baking, and even those who did evidently found such items useful additions to a basic meal when unexpected guests had to be fed. But there is little evidence that cook shops usually sold other prepared foods. No doubt they sold sauces to go with the roasts; medieval diners expected a sauce with their meat, and the cook shop's goose evidently came with a sauce or stuffing containing parsley.

It is highly doubtful, though, that cook shops ever sold the elaborate 'pottages' characteristic of court and upper class cooking, or indeed much of anything beyond the sort of items listed in that 1378 ordinance. To be sure, the unfortunate country bumpkin of the 15th-century poem 'London Lickpenny' says

>   Cokes to me they toke good intent
>   called me nere for to dyne
>   and proferyd me good brede ale and wyne

> a fayre clothe they began to sprede
> rybbes of beef bothe fat and fyne
> but for lack of money I might not spede.
>
> [Cooks tried to get my attention,
> called me to come near and dine
> and offered me good bread, ale, and wine;
> they began to spread a handsome cloth
> with fine, fat ribs of beef,
> but, lacking money, I couldn't have what I wished.]

Later he is offered hot peasecods (fresh green peas cooked in the pod, to be eaten more-or-less as we eat artichoke leaves) and hot sheep's feet (I have no idea how these were cooked), among other things. But the cooks offering ribs of beef are likely to have been tavern keepers: pie-men and cook shops were not allowed to sell ale or wine. And the peasecods and sheep's feet may have been offered by hucksters specializing in these goodies—perhaps vendors with carts, and almost certainly vendors who had no connection with a cook shop.

Yet we are told that Hogge of Ware, a cook of London, is well-known for two of the sophisticated dishes found on aristocratic menus and in the cookery books which claim to come from the highest social circles: 'mortreux' and 'blankmanger'. Both dishes appear in many versions, made with ground chicken or other poultry—or, in the case of 'mortreux', pork—on 'flesh-days', and with fish on days when 'flesh' was not permitted. 'Mortreux' differed from 'blankmanger' in that it was usually thickened with bread and eggs, and never contained the whole rice which was basic to 'blankmanger'. They can both be found in the menus for notable feasts printed in Austin's *Two Fifteenth-Century Cookery-Books*: 'blamanger' is in the menu for the funeral feast of Nicolas Bubwith, Bishop of Bath and Wells, and 'mortrewys' in the menu of the induction feast of his successor, John Stafford.

The Cook's other major specialty is probably also represented in Austin's feast menus: 'Brewys' and 'Chykonys y-boylid' appear on the supper menu of a Trinity Sunday feast for Henry IV, and 'Browes' and 'Chekenos boiled' on the one for the installation of John Stafford as Archbishop of Canterbury. Neither menu mentions marrow bones; nor does the title of a contemporary recipe. Instead, the writers emphasize the accompanying 'brewis' (i.e., toast used as a 'sop'). What King Henry and the Archbishop were served was the recipe in MS Harleian 279, 'Schyconys with þe Bruesse', which is printed in Austin's edition. Comparing this recipe with a contemporary French one for 'Trumel de Beuf au Jaunet' (beef shank in saffron sauce) makes it evident that the beef to be used is the leg, and that the Harleian 279 recipe is, thus, chicken cooked with marrowbones. However, it is impossible to say exactly what went into the 'poudre-marchant tart' with which the cook seasoned his chickens. The name means that this is a ready-made spice mixture, available at the spice merchants' shops, but there is no record at all of what the basic ingredients were. My best guess is that it was probably something like a modern French 'quatre épices' powder, containing pepper and other sharp spices such as cloves and ginger.

It is equally impossible to say what sort of 'pye' the Cook was likely to have baked, although that re-warmed 'Jakke of Dovere' may have been a pie. Pies of all sorts turn up in medieval recipes and on medieval menus. Some are actually 'pasties', i.e., meat, poultry or fish, with or without various seasonings, wrapped in a sheet of pastry and baked. Others are open tarts of various sorts, including 'crustards', which contained egg-based fillings (plus meat or fish) and closely resembled a modern quiche; this type turns up most frequently in the records of aristocratic feasts. But there were also closed pies, usually with a filling of more than one type of meat, which could be quite a production: one recipe calls for a filling of beef, pork, veal, or venison, plus capons or pheasants, dried fruits, a vast assortment of spices, and boiled egg yolks.

A final culinary problem here is: what, exactly, was the parsley the Cook's customers ate with their roast goose? Virtually all the sauces recommended to accompany goose in England and France called for garlic; the sauce supplied by Roger's cook shop may, then, have been a simple 'green sauce' of the kind which was a usual accompaniment to fish. *The Forme of Cury's* version of this sauce is typical, calling for parsley, mint, garlic, thyme, sage, cinnamon, ginger, pepper, wine, bread, vinegar, and salt, to be ground with saffron. But a versatile cook like the highly reputed Hogge of Ware may have been capable of producing a far more sophisticated treatment, which starts out as a stuffing: 'Sawse Madame' calls for fruits (quinces, pears, and grapes) as well as herbs, garlic, wine, and spices. This might not have been suitable for the clientele of a London cook shop. But we know that this cook also cooked for private parties: that is how he happens to be among the Canterbury pilgrims, in the company of, among others, Geoffrey Chaucer.

Some references

Austin, Thomas, ed., *Two Fifteenth-Century Cookery-Books: Harleian MS. 279 (ab. 1430), & Harl MS. 4016 (ab. 1450), with Extracts from Ashmole MS. 1439, Laud MS. 553, & Douce MS. 55*. EETS 91; London: Oxford University Press, 1888; repr. 1964.
Benson, Larry D., General ed., *The Riverside Chaucer*, 3rd ed. Boston: Houghton Mifflin, 1987.
Hammond, P. W., *Food and Feast in Medieval England*. Stroud, Gloucestershire: Alan Sutton, 1993.
Hieatt, Constance B., and Sharon Butler, eds.,*Curye on Inglysch: English Culinary Manuscripts of the Fourteenth Century (Including the 'Forme of Cury')*. EETS ss. 8; London: Oxford University Press, 1985.
'London Lickpenny', in Eleanor Prescott Hammond, ed., *English Verse Between Chaucer and Surrey*'. Durham, N.C.: Duke University Press, 1927.
Riley, Henry Thomas, ed. and trans., *Memorials of London and London Life in the 13th, 14th, and 15th Centuries*. London: Longmans, Green, 1868.

Mithaikos and Other Greek Cooks

Shaun Hill & John Wilkins

The gastronomy of the Greeks has been studied recently by Andrew Dalby (1994: chapters 5 and 6) in his work on eating in Greek society. On this topic he looks at the quality of wine, quality in food, and 'influences from the periphery', the Lydians of Asia Minor and the Greek cities of Sicily. Moving to literature, he cites the cookbooks of Mithaikos and Glaukos of Lokri, and then the gastronomic poetry of the fourth century BC, which appeared in the form of lyric, comic iambic and the epic verse of Archestratus. In this paper we consider this material from different perspectives, with particular reference to the cookbook of Mithaikos which was written around 400 BC. His influence in antiquity appears to have been extensive, but what we know about him is minimal. General issues arising from the gap between these two statements are instructive. In case we may be thought perverse in our choice of cook, we hasten to point out that no more is known about any other ancient chef. We thus propose a way of recovering the famous cooks of antiquity.

'Gastronomy' can be an imprecise term. Dalby covers a time span of several centuries and a large number of independent states. He understands gastronomy as eating at a level well above basic subsistence, at a level of luxury where both choice and quality production are available, and where foreign influence is felt. People are not 'just eating', they are eating thoughtfully and probably with an element of social competition. But these conditions obtained in aristocratic city states for some centuries before the cookbook of Mithaikos appeared. Aristocratic men reinforced their social position by eating and drinking with their friends, presumably using the best materials for foods and tableware and furniture that they could afford. Named wines are cited in poetry of the seventh century BC, the luxury of the Lydians in the sixth. Is all this gastronomy? Or is it the standard behaviour of a social élite which marks out its superiority with social ritual and displays? Can the case be sufficiently demonstrated? If the evidence did exist, would it actually add up to 'gastronomy'? We are told, for example, of the fine wines and the fine cuisine of Chios. Prima facie a good case. But how to demonstrate it, particularly in the badly documented period before Mithaikos? Certain conditions must be met before it will be possible for a 'cuisine' or an influential cook to emerge. One set of such conditions is set out by Goody (1982). In Chapter 4[1] of his book on food and eating in West Africa, he looks at why cuisine and elaborate foods emerge in some cultures and not others. Comparing the 'simple cuisine' of Gonja in Ghana with Egypt, China and Europe, Goody argues that essential elements for the development of a 'high' culinary culture are (1) availability of a number of ingredients, some imported, together with a wide variety of recipes, (2) demand from critical eaters, (3) the association of pleasure with eating, (4) developments in agriculture and commerce. He also stresses the importance of intensive agriculture, writing, and especially a hierarchical structure of society in which cooking for the rulers and the rich is transferred from the hands of women to men.

Of these criteria, Dalby's picture for the early period before Mithaikos meets 1 (but without the recipes) and perhaps 4, but 2 and 3 would be harder to show. Only some of the conditions for 'gastronomy' or 'cuisine' are met. We believe that Sicily and southern Italy from the late fifth century BC probably meet all these criteria. Concentration on this region will also allow us to narrow the geographical area under consideration. Sicily and southern Italy fit Goody's criteria well. Here was some of the most fertile agricultural land known to the Greeks; the fishing grounds were good too.[2] There were large and flourishing cities, some of them of fabulous wealth—Taranto, Agrigento, Syracuse, Gela—and they traded with the Greek mainland and the eastern Mediterranean.[3] Recipe-writing could be brought to a region whose wealth had been legendary over several centuries, in particular in the case of the city of Sybaris which was sacked in 511 BC. One wealthy citizen, Smindyrides, son of Hippocrates, who, according to Herodotus 6.127, took luxury to unparalleled lengths, is reported[4] to have e3ntered the race for the hand of an aristocratic bride on the Greek mainland and to have taken with him to impress the family 1000 cooks, wild-fowlers and fishermen. Wealth, luxury, aristocratic competition and display: but this does not constitute cuisine or gastronomy.[5] There are (unreliable) reports of the patenting of recipes in Sybaris—indicating a competitive approach to cooking—and the piping of wines.[6] It is in this rich region, a century later, that the earliest-known recipes in Europe were written, in Syracuse. For some 150 years before Mithaikos, Sicilian poets had written about food[7]—the interest was there—but not in the form of recipes. The book of Mithaikos appeared precisely at the moment when prose treatises on various sciences and crafts were beginning to evolve, in medicine, science, botany, biology, horsemanship and many other areas. This is crucial. With the development of the treatise, the recipe could be invented, on the pattern of medical recipes for various disorders in Hippocrates or veterinary recipes for dealing with horses. The form of the writing makes a huge difference.

On other criteria in Goody, pleasure[8] and luxury were already associated with dining by this date,[9] and philosophers were preparing moral attacks against it.[10] By the time of the presumed date of Mithaikos' book (400 BC), the preparation of prestigious food was entirely in the hands of men.[11]

It might be objected that there are better criteria to be used that those proposed by Goody. But Goody is valuable for our purposes because his scheme can be applied across cultures without value judgements of what is better and what is worse.[12] He enables us to define our terms and draw lines between what is 'high cuisine' and what is not. We therefore exclude all those good cooks of antiquity, male and female, who influenced those around them and passed on recipes by word of mouth, perhaps from mother to daughter. These cooks may have developed new techniuques, but they are excluded because their names have not entered the historical record, and in this sense their recipes have not been influential on haute cuisine. If Mathaikos had lived a hundred years earlier, when there was no demand or format for the writing of a recipe book, then he too could in theory have cooked the same dishes but not have been heard beyond his circle of employment and acquaintance, and not qualified for Goody's criteria.

What we know of Mithaikos

Plato, in his dialogue *Gorgias* writes [518b], 'if I asked who were good at caring for the body [as opposed to the mind and spirit] you would say in all seriousness Thearion the baker and Mithaikos who wrote the Sicilian cookery book and Sarambos the merchant have become fabulous carers of the body, the one preparing fabulous loaves, the second delicate dishes, the third wine.'[13] This passage describes a culture of food provision in which bread can be brought from a baker (obviating the need for home baking), wine from a merchant instead of direct from the farm, and recipes can be read. Plato does not approve. This disapproval is echoed in his *Republic*, whre he dismisses the 'Syracusan table' and the 'Sicilian elaboration of delicate dishes' (404d). At 373c, 'cooks and makers of delicacies' are in the category of the luxurious.

The sage of Athens does not approve. Instead of the simple old-fashioned preparation of food at home, there are now enterprises set up to market bread and wine. Worse, there is this Sicilian cookery book. How does he know about it? If it is circulating in Athens, then it is influential indeed. If Plato came across it on a visit to Sicily, as Aelius Aristeides surmises, then he has been drawn to the luxurious world of the Western Greek tyrants which gave birth to the work.[14]

Perhaps we should not take Plato too seriously, perhaps he has just flipped with puritanical horror at this outrage to the ascetic life of the philosopher.[15] Let us examine Mithaikos in the context of Goody's categories.

All that remains of the cookery book is three notes in Athenaeus.[16]

Fragment 1 (7.282a): 'Mithaikos mentions the *alphestes* (wrasse?)[17] in his cookery book'.

Fragment 2 (7.325a): 'Mithaikos in his cookery book says 'gut the ribbon-fish, cut the head off, wash it and cut it into slices and pour on cheese and oil'.'

Fragment 3 (12.516c): 'The Lydians were the first to invent *karuke*, on the preparation of which the composers of cookery books have pronounced, Glaukos of Lokri, Mithaikos, Dionysios, the two Herakleides of Syracusan descent, Agis, Epainetos, Dionysios, Hegesippos, Erasistratos, Euthydemos and Krito, and in addition Stephanos, Archtas, Akestios, Akesias, Diokles, Philistion'.[18]

On these fragments we note:

(1) Fine fish were the main component of haute cuisine at this time. They were plentiful off the coasts of Sicily.[19] Meat was classified as festive but often not suitable for haute cuisine.

(2) Clear, practical instructions resemble those of Archestratus,[20] but the Sicilian taste for cheese with fish was rejected by the later author.

(3) *Karuke* was a famous sauce, originally from Lydia in western Asia Minor.[21] The book of Mithaikos clearly extended to more traditions than the Sicilian, and even to a tradition with a meat-based speciality. Some on this list—Diokles certainly—were doctors advising on diet. Sauces were often associated with luxury, as in other cultures. The cooking of Mithaikos could thus be described as 'luxurious' on two counts, the use of whole fish (the wrasse) and sauces.

Of the form of the book, we should note that it is in prose (and therefore closer to a practical treatise than the poem of Archestratus mentioned below) and (to judge from fragment 2) in the Doric dialect spoken in Sicily and the Peloponnese. It was not in the influential Attic dialect.[22] There are clear and practical instructions, with no ornamentation, not indeed any boastful claims.

The influence of Mithaikos—beyond Plato.

The next Sicilian writer was Archestratus. We have less reason to call him a chef, for he wrote in epic verse rather than prose and seems to give a gourmet guide for the discerning palate based on product and place more than recipe. When he does give recipes they are simple and elegant treatments of the best products. He censures his predecessors for using cheese sauces (Archestratus fr. 45). From the second fragment, it is plain that he has Mithaikos in mind. Mithaikos is the earliest of many Sicilian and south Italian cooks. Among his successors were (from fragment 3 above) Glaukos of Lokri, the two Herakleides from Syracuse, Hegesippos of Tarentum.

After Mithaikos, the gourmet chef, particularly the Sicilian chef, became a stock figure in Athenian comedy.[23] This implies, unless comedy existed in a purely literary world divorced from reality (this we deny), that Mithaikos contributed to a large social development, the hiring of speciality chefs for private dinner parties. If he made no contribution whatsoever (the minimalist position), he nevertheless wrote his cookery book at precisely the time that such chefs are first mentioned. Plato implies that he was of note on the Greek mainland, in towns, Athens in particular, who were receptive to outside influence.

The demand for hired chefs at private parties reflects a social development in the fourth century BC as important for our argument as the appearance of the treatise-format. The rich élite in Athens (in particular) and other towns over several decades moved towards greater privacy, towards the concerns of their friends and families rather than the concerns of the community. This change of emphasis was probably felt in dining, as home entertainment was undertaken on a scale not seen before. People still ate at civic and religious functions, but we hear much more of private meals than in the fifth century BC. To reflect this new emphasis and new style, the chef was hired to lay on something special. This increased the demand for novelty and new recipes, and was the motor behind the popularity of the newly-discovered form of the recipe book.

Goody had something to say of Greco-Roman culture in his chapter but confines himself to Athenaeus and Apicius, familiar names at these meetings, but neither of them a cook. The book that carries the name of Apicius was not written by him,[24] nor did he cook any of the recipes, in all probability. The collection is named after one, two or three gourmets of that name who travelled the world in search of expensive and rare treats. Apicius and his/their compiler attest a cuisine based on spices and exotic products such as flamingos. Athenaeus, in his turn, attests a society in Greece and Rome in which the luxurious banquet provided the demand for the inventive chef and his recipes.[25] In a literary way, he gives ample evidence for the importance of the chef as cook and performer in the banquets of Greece and Rome. His interest extends to cookery books, but rarely to the extent that he preserves much of them. It is possible that when he does quote from them, it is only at second hand. We would class Athenaeus and Apicius/the Apicii/the compiler(s) of 'Apicius' as consumers rather than preparers or producers of food, whereas Mithaikos we consider a more suitable subject for the present enquiry. Archestratus seems to belong somewhere in between.

If Mithaikos was so important, why does so little of his book survive—three fragments in the text of Athenaeus? Cookbooks can be influential in what they inspire, and ephemeral in themselves. They are a form of treatise that the author thinks worth writing, but that people do not keep in the long term. In the second century AD, Aelius Aristeides was wondering how Plato came to see a copy—was it in Athens or was it during his first trip to Sicily? We should note that nearly all the cookery books cited by Athenaeus do not survive and had probably not survived to his day (they were perhaps not thought worthy to have a place in the great library collections). Recipes in verse fared better, and that is why Athenaeus saw a copy of Archestratus and Matro's *Attic Dinner*, but even the latter is cited as a rarity.

Another rhetorical author of late antiquity, Maximus of Tyre, mentions Mithaikos[26] as the Syracusan master chef[27] who went to Sparta and was told to leave for cities elsewhere in Greece. The story may well be apocryphal, but reflects broad knowledge of the name as a cook of influence.

We believe he is important, both in the ways we have set out, and also because he is at the head of the Sicilian/southern Italian tradition which formed the backbone of ancient haute cuisine as far as we can tell, at least in the two metropoleis in which it was first mocked, Athens and Rome. There were other influences, but this is *the* influence.

We live in a time when the printed and electronic media exert enormous influence on cooking of every kind. What of a period (and this covers most of human history in most cultures) without such media? Influence depends on royal or other patronage: a cook could never have the power to be an independent agent. Quality of work could rarely carry the day. Ancient Greece is a little different. There was the written word to a limited extent. But who does the writing? And who does the cooking? And who influences what is on the plate?

BIBLIOGRAPHY

F. Bilabel, 'Kochbücher' in G. Wissowa (ed.) *Paulys Real Ecyclopädie der classischen Altertumswissenschaft* (Stuttgart 1922) 11.934-5.
Dalby A. 1994, *Unequal Feasts: Food and its Social Context in Early Greece* (thesis, Birkbeck College, London).
Goody J, 1982, *Cooking, Cuisine and Class* (Cambridge).
Lombardo M. 1995, 'Food and Frontier in the Greek Colonies of South Italy' in Wilkins, Harvey & Dobson.
Thompson D'Arcy W. 1947, *A Glossary of Greek Fishes* (Oxford).
Wilkins J. 1996a, forthcoming 'Concept of luxurious eating in ancient Greece' in Dalby A. and Riley G. *Food, Culture and History* vol.2 (London)
Wilkins J. 1996b forthcoming 'Food preparation in ancient Greece—the literary evidence' in Donald M. and Hurcombe L. (eds) *Gender and Material Culture* (London).
Wilkins J., Harvey D. and Dobson M (eds) 1995 *Food in Antiquity* (Exeter).

Wilkins J. and Hill S. 1994 *Archestratus: The Life of Luxury* (Totnes)
Wilkins J. and Hill S. 1995 'The sources and sauces of Athenaeus' in Wilkins, Harvey and Dobson.

REFERENCES

[1] 'The high and the low: culinary culture in Asia and Europe'.

[2] Fertile agriculture: Lombardo (1995) 267, Diodorus Siculus 12.9, Strabo 6.2.7, Varro 1.44.2; good fishing: Athenaeus *Deipnosophistae* 12.518c (quoting Clearchus of Soli) 'famous for luxury were the tables of the Sicilians also. They claim that the sea off their shores is sweet, such pleasure do they take in the foods produced from it'. See note 19.

[3] There was also political instability—the overthrow of Sybaris in the sixth century BC, warring tyrants, a democratic interlude in Syracuse, wars with the Carthaginians.

[4] By Chamaileon of Pontos in Athenaeus 6.273b-c; cf, Lombardo (1995) 267.

[5] The Persian king brought many bakers and special chefs with him on his invasion of Greece in 480BC, but this was royal provisioning, not gastronomy: Herodotus 9.82.

[6] A year's patent on a recipe and tax exemption for eel sellers, Athenaeus 12.521d; wine pipelines Athenaeus 12.519d. See Lombardo (1995) 267-9.

[7] Dalby (1994) 108-10, Wilkins and Hill (1995) 430-1.

[8] We discuss pleasure in our edition of Archestratus (1994) 25-8.

[9] In his description of the luxurious city, Plato (*Republic* 373b-c) lists among many other things dining couches, dining tables, delicate dishes, myrrh, incense, party girls, cakes, chefs, cooks and swineherds.

[10] Wilkins has argued (1996a forthcoming) that the concept of luxury in ancient dining (and more widely) was seen as a threat to a well-ordered male society built on restraint and traditional values. This conformed with ancient notions of restraining appetites, particularly of people seen as a threat, women, slaves and men who were insufficiently masculine. Athenaeus in Book 12 has examples of cities brought low by men who lived too softly and had too little body hair.

[11] See Wilkins (1996b forthcoming).

[12] Athenians did not produce cookery books at c. 400 BC and freely judged adversely those who did.

[13] Dalby points out (1994 111) that Plato mentions the Greek triad of cereal, protein and wine. This may imply that Mithaikos' book was principally concerned with fish, the most favoured protein-delicacy; but it may simply reflect Plato's elegant composition.

[14] Athens, with her democracy and comparatively simple cuisine, was a fine producer of philosophers and tragic poets, but they showed much interest in the courts of the tyrants in Syracuse (Aeschylus and Plato) and Macedonia (Euripides and Aristotle).

[15] Plato, incidentally, shows few signs of living such an ascetic life.

[16] Their context in Athenaeus is discussed in Wilkins and Hill (1995).

[17] Neither the *alphestes* nor the *tainia* (ribbon fish) is securely identified: see D'Arcy Thompson (1947) 10-11 and 258.

[18] Some of these names appear only here. Pollux gives a rather different list of ancient chefs—he is not picking out *karuke* recipes—at *Onomastikon* 6.71.

[19] See Epicharmus' comedy *The Marriage of Hebe* which celebrates dozens of fish in a glorious wedding banquet (early fifth century BC), and Archestratus, fragments 8, 11, 16, 19, 24, 34, 38, 40, 51.

[20] Whom we cite because there are far more fragments extant.

[21] Ingredients, according to Hegesippus of Tarentum: meat, breadcrumbs, cheese, anise and fat meat stock.

[22] We can probably discount forgery, a problem considered seriously by Dalby (1994) 112. If fragment 2 were a forgery, we might disbelieve also Athenaeus' citation of Mithaikos in fragment 3. If these were to prove two forgeries, then Mithaikos' reputation remains strong (he is worth forging) but what little remains of his work is misleading.

[23] Mithaikos himself is mentioned only once in Athenian comedy, in a fragment of unknown date and author (Adespota 374 Kock).

[24] The Apicii we know of date from the first century BC and the first AD. The book we have is a compilation probably of the fourth century AD.

[25] He writes in the early third century AD.

[26] *Dissertationes* 17.1.

[27] Maximus describes Mithaikos as a great sophist or philosopher. The same term is used of a chef from comedy adduced by a chef in Athenaeus at 9.376e-380c, especially 377f. Maximus also compares Mithaikos, famous in Greece for his cooking, with Pheidias, famous in Greece for his sculpture (eg. Athena in the Parthenon).

Manyoken, Japan's First French Restaurant

Richard Hosking

In one of the best locations in the main street of Kyoto, there is a French restaurant with a long and interesting history.

Kyoto was the seat of the imperial court for over a millenium until 1868 and to this day it is the traditional centre of Japan. The best shops and businesses, as well as the kabuki theatre, are located in a street called Shijo Dori, and in the heart of Shijo Dori is an impressive façade with the name of Manyoken. Manyoken is a French restaurant, the oldest one in Japan.

It has a fascinating history that takes us back to the early years of this century. The court had already moved to Tokyo, but the old palace, *Gosho*, was not shut down, nor did its functions as an imperial palace cease. Kyoto Gosho is to this day a functioning palace of the Emperor and his court and indeed many of the imperial suppliers are still located in Kyoto. This also applies to Manyoken's French food in a curious way that will become clear in the course of this paper.

The story centres on the Itani family, a socially prominent family that, at the turn of the century, were the oldest and largest textile wholesalers in Kyoto. In the 33rd year of the Emperor Meiji, AD1900, there was a severe economic recession in the textile industry and the Itani business went bankrupt. This meant that a few years later, when Achirobe IXth, son and heir of the Itanis, returned from service in the Russo-Japanese war at an age when he should enter the family business, there was no family business for him to enter.

A family conference decided that what was greatly needed in Kyoto was a high-class French restaurant and that young Ichirobe should go abroad to gain knowledge and experience of the restaurant trade. He first went to America, but it became obvious to him that France would be much better, so to France he went. Instead of working for money as in America, he had to pay to be taken on for training in France and soon funds began to get low. Enterprising young man that he was, he took himself off to Monte Carlo, where he won so much money that after three days he was advised to leave for his own safety.

He took himself and his newly won riches off to London, and realizing that he now had enough capital to open a restaurant, he marched into Mappin and Webb and bought sufficient silverware for the restaurant he was planning to open. This silver turned out to be a very sound investment, since it is still in use! It was used in the restaurant for 75 years and is now kept for the exclusive use of the Imperial family, for whom Manyoken has become a French restaurant by appointment. In 1985 Manyoken approached Mappin and Webb to make them replacement cutlery of the same design by special order, but Mappins were not interested in such a small order, so the restaurant changed to Christofle, still smarting under what they perceive to be the slight of a snooty English company.

Ichirobe returned to Kyoto and at first was steward of the Kyoto Hotel. Then in 1910 (Meiji 43), the first Manyoken opened in the Itani's house in Fuya-cho at Nishiki-koji. *Man* means 'many, ten thousand', *yo* means 'to feed' and *ken* means 'house, building', so the name literally means 'a house to feed many people'. At this time, *man* was pronounced *ban*, a phonetic variation also found in the expression of goodwill *banzai*, 'may you live ten thousand years'.

Instead of a floor of floorboards, Japanese houses have what is called *tatami*, which consists of very thick straw matting covered in finely woven rush made from a plant called *igusa*. The Itanis covered their tatami with carpets, on which they set tables and chairs. the tables, of course, were laid with the Mappin and Webb silver, and waiters, known as 'boys' (*boy-san* in Japanese) led the distinguished guests (in Japanese there is no distinction between 'customer' and 'guest') to their tables. Because it was western and expensive, all high society came to Manyoken. Indeed the Empress Dowager (*Shoken kotaigo*) was a frequent visitor. Unfortunately, the boys were really not up to the task of waiting at table in anything so exotic as a French restaurant, and geisha had to be called in from Gion, the high-class entertainment district. The famous novelist Jun'ichiro Tanizaki thought the whole set-up quite extraordinary.

Perhaps even more extraordinary was the amusing incongruity that when the French dinner was finished, the customers didn't feel satisfied until they had really completed the evening with *o-chazuke*. Japanese *o-chazuke* is a bowl of rice with bits of fish and seaweed on top, liberally doused in green tea and drunk rather than eaten as a final snack of the day. I understand this very well in reverse, since I never feel satisfied with a Japanese meal and need to eat something sweet to finish, even if it means popping into a coffee shop or Mr Donut on the way home from an evening in a Japanese restaurant.

Manyoken's first chef was Tokuzo Akiyama, who came to the restaurant from the Kyoto palace (*Gosho*) having studied French cooking in France. He was followed as head chef of the Imperial Household (*Daizen no kami*) by Nakajima, then Shinohara and currently Wakabayashi, all of whom have had a close association with Manyoken, where Akiyama remained until 1930, thus spanning three reigns during which he maintained close contact with the *Gosho*, helping the palace whenever French food was required.

As a result of this Manyoken has become responsible to the Imperial Household for western food not only at *Gosho*, but whenever any such food is needed by them in Western Japan. On such occasions Manyoken's cooks and waiters set off with all the ingredients, equipment and table settings required and go to wherever the food is needed. Since the Imperial family eat a western-style breakfast and dinner, Manyoken still provides these meals wherever the Emperor or his guests, such as the Queen or Prince Charles and Princess Diana, stay at the *Gosho*.

In 1913, a rich businessman who was a great friend of the Itanis, Tokutaro Osawa, sold them an excellent site in Shijo Dori very cheaply, and Manyoken moved there. Shijo Dori can be considered the main street of Kyoto, and the restaurant is still on this prime site. The first building was built of brick with a weatherboard front, designed by the architect Goichi Tokeda, who also chose *Rendez-vous* as the name of the main public room of the restaurant, seating 40 people. There are three other rooms for private functions, seating 30, 40 and 50 people respectively, and a banqueting room for 120.

In 1968 the weatherboard front of the restaurant was removed and the present concrete façade built instead. The brick is still visible at the back of the restaurant.

When Ichirobe died, his son Shu took over, and now Hiroshi, Shu's younger son is in charge. Akiyama retired as chef in 1930, though he continued his connection with the Imperial Household and was still alive when the Queen came to *Gosho* in 1975. He was succeeded as chef of Manyoken by Suzuki, in turn succeeded by Atsumi in 1962. The present chef, his successor, took over in 1981.

Manyoken is proud of its association with the Imperial Household and *Gosho*, in particular preparing breakfast and other meals for visiting royal guests and catering for garden parties at the palace. Some royal guests they have found difficult to cope with. In particular, Prince Charles. His requirements for organic foods are not easily met in Japan, for instance the need for wholemeal bread, which until the last two or three years was simply unobtainable in Japan unless you did what I used to do when I could get some wheat, and that is grind the flour myself. His Royal Highness's request for cucumber soup caused great consternation, mainly because it was unheard of and a recipe was only found with difficulty. On the other hand, the Queen is liked because she takes a 'proper' English breakfast, and the Duke of Edinburgh even more so, with the addition of cereals and fruit juice.

From the street, Manyoken looks quite forbidding, almost grim. Reception faces the door and is flanked on both sides by stairs curving up to the first floor, opening into *Rendez-vous*, the dining room. This is a rather sombre room, and the heavy elegance is only relieved by the attentions of the handsome waiters, no longer referred to as 'boys' and much more adequate to the task than their earlier counterparts, as well as by curiosity about other diners.

Not surprisingly, the menu is quite uninfluenced by such recent fads as *nouvelle cuisine*, despite its Japanese roots. The main influence seems to be very much Escoffier, and certainly the standard of cooking comes up to that set by the great man.

The menu is in Japanese-style restaurant French, English and Japanese and is headed by *Table D'Hôte*, of which there are five, (S), (A), (B), (C) and *Bifteks*. (S) is top of the range and for ¥20,000 (£150) [per head] you got the following (12 May 1995):

Plat d'Oreille de Mer et Jeune Pousse de Bambou
Escalope de Fois-gras Grillé au Epinard
Parissoise (Cold Cream Soup on top Cold Consommé)
Crevette et Poisson Phocéenne
Medaillon de Bœuf Fines herbes
Salad d'Asperges Vertes
Crêpes au Chocolat
Fruits, Café

The night I dined there with a friend in March 1995, we both had (A) *Table D'Hôte*

Hors-d'œuvre variés [excellent]
Potage Saint Germain
Homard à la Bordelaise
Filet Mignon Grillé Jus de Raifort
Asperges Verts sauce Chantilly
Biscuit Glacé Délices
Fruits, Café

With two glasses of sherry and two excellent bottles of wine, the meal for the two of us came to ¥50,000 (£350). It was a first-rate meal and not expensive by Japanese standards.

Manyoken's original menus also began with Table d'Hote but the dishes were not specified. Top of the range, in the traditional Japanese manner, was *Sho* (pine), next was *Chiku* (bamboo) and last was *Bai* (Japanese apricot). A la Carte contained Caviar among the Hors d'Oeuvres and a number of interesting dishes among them Poisson, Oeufs, Entrees such as Chateau Briand, Fride Fish, Hambarg BeefSteak, Cabbage Boll and Tongue Cutlets. Among the Legummes, along with Asparagus and Salad we find Ceroly. The Desserts include Glass; and Coffee, Tea or Chocolate (very expensive) to conclude the meal. By reproducing the original spelling I am not intending to mock. These were the early days of using foreign languages in Japan, and even today, the Japanese are not nearly so careful over the spelling of foreign languages as they are of their own. Writing in a foreign language is perceived as graphic decoration rather than something substantial, which will always be written in Japanese.

Manyoken is a well-established Kyoto institution, important socially because of its relationship with the Imperial Household and as a place for top people to eat and be seen. The food and wines it offers are of the highest standard. It is still very much a family establishment, now run by Mr Hiroshi Itani, president of the company and grandson of the founder.[1]

---

[1] I sincerely wish to thank both Mr Hiroshi Itani and his elder brother Mr Shunichi Itani for all their help and kindness. Mr Hiroshi Itani in particular gave up much valuable time in recounting to me the history of Manyoken and answering all my questions.

Courageous Eating: Mary McCarthy and American Food Between the Wars

Eve Jochnowitz

First Course: Olympia Salad
Food and A Jewish Cookbook

Olympia Salad

On a bed of shredded lettuce, put a slice of tomato, heart of artichoke; put on crab legs, shrimps, or lobster. Over all pour thousand island dressing. Garnish with riced egg.

Mrs S. Aronson (*Temple de Hirsch*, p.129)

Olympia Salad is a typical recipe from *The Ladies Auxiliary to Temple de Hirsch Famous Cook Book*. It is a very fancy dish. Each serving much be constructed separately, the ingredients are expensive, and the instructions do not include the preparation of the artichoke heart and the Thousand Island dressing, which would have been taken care of, it is assumed, by household help. It also unkosher, as are many of the recipes submitted to this synagogue community cookbook of 1925. I first saw a copy of the *Famous Cook Book* only this year, but I first read about, and was astonished by, this salad nearly twenty years ago, in a remarkable book by Mary McCarthy called *Memories of a Catholic Girlhood*.

Mrs S. Aronson, in fact, is Mary's Aunt Eva, the stately and imperturbable older sister of her Jewish grandmother, Augusta Preston, one of the countless outlandish relatives presented in *Memories*. This small book is a diamond. McCarthy tells the story of her childhood with recipes, a long digression about the Gallic wars and vivid portraits of the grownups who acted as her guardians after the premature deaths of her parents.

McCarthy's grandparents fall into three very clear groups based on religion and ethnic origin: the mean and petty Catholic McCarthys, who are not merely indifferent to beauty, but actively hate anything beautiful, their gorgeous daughter-in-law, McCarthy's mother, included; the upright, dignified and correct Presbyterian Harold Preston, whose name was a byword for honesty, McCarthy tells us three times, among all who knew him; and the lavish and sensuous Jewish Augusta Morgenstern Preston, the most beautiful woman in Seattle, the real star of the book and the most extraordinary character in all of American letters. The grandparents fall into stereotypical categories, but they are by no means stereotypical characters. Each portrait is very real and distinct; so much so that the characters are almost incredible. McCarthy herself comments that if her book were a work of fiction rather than a memoir, she would have had to explain her McCarthy Grandmother to make her believable. Other grownups who play a role in the McCarthy's upbringing are the Ladies of the Sacred Heart, who 'like all truly intellectual women, were romantic desperadoes.' and a great aunt and uncle on the McCarthy side, the Schreibers, whose cruelty and stupidity are nearly bottomless.

The descriptions of food are what makes the differences between the McCarthy and Schreiber homes and the Preston home not just the work of a memorist but of a genius. Here is the second on mealtime chez Schreiber.

> We had prunes everyday for breakfast, and corn-meal mush, Wheatena, or farina, which I had to eat plain, since by some medical whim it had been decided that milk was bad for me. The rest of our day's menu consisted of parsnips, turnips, rutabegas, carrots, boiled potatoes, boiled cabbage, onions, swiss chard, kale and so on; most green vegetables, apparently, were too dear to be appropriate for us, though I think that, beyond this, the family had a sort of moral affinity for the root vegetable, stemming perhaps from everything fibrous, tenacious, watery, and knobby in the Irish peasant stock. Our desserts were rice pudding, farina pudding, overcooked custard with little air holes in it, prunes, stewed red plums, rhubarb, stewed pears, stewed dried peaches. We must have had meat, but I have only the most indistinct recollection of pale lamb stews in which the carrots outnumbered the pieces of white, fatty meat and bone and gristle; certainly we did not have steak or roasts or turkey or fried chicken, but perhaps an occasional boiled fowl was served to us with its vegetables (for I do remember the neck, shrunken in its collar of puckered skin coming to me as my portion, and the fact that if you sucked on it, you could draw out an edible white cord), and doubtless there was meatloaf and beef stew. There was no ice cream, cake, pie or butter, but on rare mornings we had johnnycake or large wooly pancakes with Karo syrup. (*Memories*, p.66)

The house had no 'dustcatchers', that is, no toys and no kind of art or decoration. It should be noted here that the McCarthys were not poor. They were one of the richest families in town. The home of the McCarthy grandparents was less barren. Catholic art and Italian scenes (which were Catholic by 'regional infusion from the Pope') were tolerated and the food was not so wretched:

> For all her harsh views, my grandmother was a practical woman and would not have thought it worthwhile to unsettle her whole schedule, teach her cook to make lumpy mush and watery boiled potatoes... in order to approximate the conditions she thought suitable for our characters. Humble pie could be costly, especially when cooked to order. (*Memories*, p.42)

When she was eleven, McCarthy was rescued by her maternal grandparents and taken back to her hometown of Seattle. In Seattle Mary attended Catholic boarding school, and on the weekend tagged along with her grandmother, and sometimes one or both of her aunts, the queenly but dim Aunt Eve Aronson and the bohemian intellectual Aunt Rosie Gottstein. The Three Morgenstern sisters probably provide a good cross section of the Reform German Jewish community of Seattle in the teens and twenties. One of the revelations of the book is that what must have still been the frontier town of Seattle had a real and very sophisticated high society, and that it was Jewish. Aunt Rosie was middle class, 'poor, compared to her sisters.' The living room of her small apartment was 'lined with signed photographs of opera stars,' but the room needed painting. Aunt Eva, on the other hand, was part of the 'hard, smart set' in Jewish high society that travelled and gambled for high stakes. Augusta Preston herself, of course, had married into the upper crust, but took part in neither Jewish nor Protestant social events. Her amusements, shopping, dressing, gardening and eating, were solitary pleasures. One of the most brilliant points in this sparkling gem of a memoir is that McCarthy uses her aunts' recipes to illustrate the gap in their social standing.

> The cookbook of the Ladies' Auxiliary of the Temple de Hirsch...has many recipes contributed by Mrs M.A. Gottstein. Her chicken stewed with noodles, hamburger in tomatoes, and rhubarb pie are quite unlike the recipes contributed by Mrs S. Aronson, ... which begin with directions like this: 'Take a nice pair of sweetbreads, add a cup of butter, a glass of good cream, sherry, and some *foie gras*.' Or her recipe for baked oysters: 'Pour over each caviar and cream and dot with bits of butter. Serve hot.' (*Memories*, p.206)

The *Famous Cook Book*, alas, has no recipes contributed by Mrs H. Preston, but we are given a good idea of what meals were like in her home:

> 'Take a spring chicken,' many of her recipes began, and the phrase often salted her conversation. 'She's no spring chicken,' she would say of another woman. Baby beets, new potatoes, young asparagus, embryonic string beans, tiny olympia oysters, tiny curling shrimps, lactary ears of corn...our food was almost too choice, unseemly for daily use. The specialities of our table were like those of a very good hotel or club: Olympia oyster cocktail and devilled Dungeness crabs; a salad, served as a first course, that started with a thick slice of tomato, on which was balanced an artichoke heart containing crabmeat, which in turn was covered with Thousand Island dressing and sprinkled with riced egg yolk; a young salmon served in a sherry sauce with oysters and little shrimps; eggs stuffed with chicken livers. We ate this company food every day; every meal was a surprise, aimed to please some member of the family, as though we were invalids who had to be 'tempted'. On Sundays, ice cream, turned by the gardener in the freezer on the back porch, was chosen to suit me; we had strawberry (our own strawberries), peach, peppermint (made from crushed candy canes), and the one I was always begging for—bisque. (p.224). (*Memories*, p.224)

The *Famous Cook Book* offers no clue as to what bisque ice cream is, but it is an inestimable source of information about the Jewish community of Seattle in the twenties. Unlike other *treyf* cookbooks of the era, such as *Aunt Babette's Cook Book*, the *Famous Cook Book* does not make any distinction between recipes that are kosher and those that are *treyf*, nor does it offer any possible substitutes for cooks who might wish to adapt the recipes for a kosher kitchen. It does, on the other hand, include a note (p.8) that 'Where liquor is mentioned in recipes, substitutes may be used.'

The cookbook must have looked very beautiful when new. With its white leatherette cover and gold gothic lettering on the front, it looks almost like a bride's bible, and it must have been given, along with or instead of a white bible as a wedding or confirmation gift to many Seattle maidens. In addition to 400 pages of recipes, the cookbook includes a section on care for the sick (recipes for flaxseed tea and raw beef are in this section, and a recipe for sweetened boiled milk with wine) (pp. 432-434) and a section of household hints, which include care instructions for ermine (rub with cornmeal, renewing meal as it becomes soiled), white silk stockings (put a teaspoon of turpentine in the rinsing water), and ivory handled knives (keep away from hot water) (p.440). Augusta Preston had an ivory handled revolver.

The recipes in the *Famous Cook Book*, like those in any community cookbook, are of inconsistent style and quality. Nonetheless, they can be said to constitute a cuisine. For one thing, the bountiful produce of the Northwest is used to good advantage by many contributors. There are recipes which call for fresh figs, artichokes, asparagus, eggplants and chestnuts. Second, while about half of the recipes call for some kind of seafood (another regional speciality), and there are a handful of recipes for ham, there are no recipes that call for pork or lard, which remained repellent to Jews who had shaken free of the other restrictions of kashrut (*Kirshenblatt Gimblett*, p.78) There are two very good recipes for 'fish balls' (*gefilte fish*), one of which is made with halibut and salmon, and sweetened, the other is made with halibut and cod and onions, and is served with a broth that has been enriched with cream and egg yolks. Both recipes are examples of traditional recipes adapted to take advantage of the freshest local fish. In one of the few concessions to kashrut in the book, fish and shellfish are in separate chapters. There are two recipes for *matzo kloese*, one plain, and one with fried onions, ginger and pepper, and also a recipe for 'cracker balls', clearly an attempt to make a non-sectarian version of a Jewish favourite. A very rich flourless carrot cake (p.274) calls for six yolks, half a pound of sugar, half a pound of grated almonds and half a pound of raw carrots. The recipe would be ideal for Passover, but is not identified as a Passover recipe, no more is any other recipe in the book, not even the *matzo* balls.

The ladies of the Temple de Hirsch loved strong vivid flavours, but one also comes away with an overwhelming sense of whiteness. All that cream and mayonnaise; all that ermine, silk and ivory. They loved their legacy of traditional German Jewish foods, but wanted to have them separate from the Jewish rituals with which they were associated. They combine the best of the produce of the Wild West and civilization of the Old World. The utter sensuality of many of these recipes is in marked contrast to the fad of 'Food Science' that gripped the east in the early decades of this century.

Second course: Canned beans and Campbell's Soup
Food and Fashion

Even while the Sisterhood of the Temple de Hirsh and other small pockets of resistance continued to prepare good food through the 20s and 30s, the fashionable young people hilariously sent up in *The Group* are sure they have found a better way. In one episode that is grotesque but very funny, Kay and Harald tell their Boston friend Dotty about the future, when Harald hopes that architects will eliminate foyers and dining rooms, as well as the foods of the past.

> Harald was teaching her to cook. His specialities were Italian Spaghetti…and those minced sea clams,…terribly good—that they had had the other night, and meatballs cooked in salt in a hot skillet (no fat), and a quick and easy meatloaf his mother had taught him: one part beef, one part pork, one part veal; add sliced onions, pour over it a can of Campbell's tomato soup and bake in the oven. Then there was his chile con carne, made with canned kidney beans and tomato soup again and onions and half a pound of hamburger; you served it over rice, and it stretched for six people…Kay had found a new cookbook that had a whole section on casserole dishes and another on foreign recipes—so much more adventurous than Fannie Farmer and that Old Boston Cooking School… The trouble with American cooking, Harald said, was the dearth of imagination in it and the terrible fear of innards and garlic. He put garlic in everything and was accounted quite a cook… 'You ought to get your cook to try the new way of fixing canned beans. You just add catsup and mustard and worcerstershire sauce, and sprinkle them with plenty of brown sugar, cover them with bacon, and put them in the oven in a pyrex dish.'
>
> 'Have you tasted the new Corn Niblets?' asked Kay. Dottie shook her head. 'You ought to tell you mother about them. It's the whole kernel corn. Delicious. Almost like corn on the cob. Harald discovered them.' She considered. 'Does your mother know about iceberg lettuce? It's a new variety, very crisp, with wonderful keeping powers. After you've tried it, you'll never want to see the old Boston lettuce again.' Dottie sighed. Did Kay realise, she wondered, that she had just passed the death sentence on Boston lettuce, Boston baked beans and the Boston School Cookbook? (*Group*, p.65)

The new cookbook Kay had found may well have been a current issue of the *Settlement Cookbook* which would have had the chapters described. There is certainly nothing in particular wrong with that cookbook, or with the concept of having a chapter on casseroles. And Harald's recipe for the meatballs cooked in salt sounds just wonderful, but the overriding force in the food theories of the 30's is a disdain for anything seen to be outdated or old-fashioned, like corn on the cob. An editorial that appeared in the *New York Times* in 1938 predicted an entirely synthetic food supply in the near future. It is hard to understand that at the time, this was an unambiguously *optimistic* prediction.

Like the futurists in Italy, middle-class Americans of the thirties really did believe that up until their own time, humans had fed themselves like animals and only a radically new way of eating would propel mankind to a higher level of evolution.

The breakfast served at Kay's wedding, eggs benedict and baked Alaska, is a perfect example of the kind of food valued by the group. It is such a very good idea and yet so very terrible. The baked Alaska is part burnt and part raw, and the cake is stale and soggy, but the girls in the group are delighted with it.

> The Baked Alaska was the *kind* of thing that in Kay's place the group hoped *they* would have thought of—terribly original for a wedding and yet just right when you considered it. They were all tremendously interested in cooking and quite out of patience with the unimaginative roasts and chops followed by molds from the caterer that Mother served; they were going to try new combinations and foreign recipes and puffy omelets and soufflés and interesting aspics and just one hot dish in a pyrex; no soup, and a fresh green salad. (*Group*, p.25)

On the side: Butter or Margarine?
Food and Politics

Much has been made of Mary McCarthy's youthful political career and her controversial break with Stalinism. From her own memoirs one might guess that McCarthy found more fault with the wretched food habitually served by the members of the New York Stalinist crowd than with their politics, about which she is always very vague. They served 'Horrible drinks in paper cups' (*Intellectual Memoirs*, p.18) and sometimes even charged for them. Phoniness, of ingredients and of ideology, was what marked the Stalinists in the McCarthy's fiction as well as autobiography. In *The Group*, the unsympathetic Norine is 'surrounded by articles of belief, down to the last can of evaporated milk.' (p.128) but most hateful is the heroine's husband Harald.

> Only the other night they had had quite a debate, ending in tears on her part, about margarine vs. butter—margarine, Harald maintained, was just as tasty and nourishing, but the butter interests had conspired to keep the margarine people from coloring their product; he was right, yet she could not bear to have that oily white stuff on her table, even if her reaction to the whiteness was a conditioned reflex based on class prejudice. (*Group* p.85)

It is interesting to note that Lillian Hellman, McCarthy's Stalinist arch rival, wrote a cookbook of her own. McCarthy might have been able to predict that *Eating Together*, Hellman's memoir of her life with Dashiel Hammet, had recipes that called for such ingredients as canned cream of mushroom soup, onion soup mix and 'Kitchen Bouquet'.

To Drink: Applejack Rabbit
Elegant Alcohol

During the years of prohibition, social drinking rituals for the younger set inevitably involved moonshine, some of it poisonous. In *Memories*, McCarthy recalls having felt she had to drink more than she wanted to fit in with her friends, all of whom were accustomed to hard liquor.

> At length I discovered that I could take a gulp and hold it in my mouth, and work it down gradually, while no one was looking. This prevented me from talking for long periods. [My date] sang, and I rode along tight lipped beside him, with a mouth full of

unswallowed moonshine, which washed around my teeth as the car bumped along the rutted road.(*Memories*, p.181)

Once prohibition was repealed, popular drinks swung to the opposite extreme, becoming very sweet and precious. The cocktail and the punch, both loaded with class issues, became the drinks necessary and sufficient for any occasion.

> A punch was being served, over which guests were exclaiming 'what *is* it?' 'Perfectly *delicious*' 'How did you ever think of it?' and so on. To each one, Kay gave the recipe. The base was one-third Jersey applejack, one-third maple syrup, and one-third lemon juice, to which White Rock had been added... The recipe was an ice-breaker, just as Kay had hoped... Everyone tasted it and said that it was the maple syrup that made all the difference... There was a discussion about applejack and how it made people quarrelsome, to which the girls listened with fascination... They were very much interested, just at this time, in receipts for drinks; they all adored brandy Alexanders and White Ladies and wanted to hear about a cocktail called the Clover Club that was one-third gin, one-third lemon juice, one-third grenadine and the white of an egg. (*Group* p.18)

The applejack rabbit punch is loaded with cultural markers. The rustic and hard-to-find applejack, and the rustic and expensive maple syrup make the drink special and unusual. The mass market ginger-ale stretches it for a crowd and makes it drinkable. The Clover Club does not look like it should have been drinkable at all. The playful use of thirds shows up in nearly every recipe in *The Group*. A three part recipe is simple enough to transmit verbally and complicated enough to make it seem worthy of transmission.

The passionate love of beauty that McCarthy calls 'almost a kind of violence' (*Memories*, p.17) included passionate love of beautiful food and a fierce contempt for food that was phony. Mary McCarthy is not widely considered to be a food writer, but she was a writer who took food, and its preparation and consumption, very seriously. She gave exquisite attention to details of food habits, food beliefs and food fads thirty years before it became fashionable, and in doing so, she had a hand in bringing us all here for this symposium.

BIBLIOGRAPHY

Brightman, Carol, ed. 1995. *Between Friends; The correspondence of Hannah Arendt and Mary McCarthy 1949-1975*, New York, San Diego, London: Harcourt Brace and Co.

1992. *Writing Dangerously: Mary McCarthy and her world*. New York and London: Harcourt Brace and Co.

Gelderman, Carol, 1988. *Mary McCarthy: A life*. London: Sidgwick and Jackson.

Jochnowitz, Eve, 1996. 'Cooking up the future: Women, food, and building the typical American at the New York World's Fair' in *Through the kitchen window* forthcoming from New York: The City University Feminist Press.

Kirshenblatt-Gimblett, Barbara, 1990. 'Kitchen Judaism' in *Getting comfortable in New York*, Joselit and Braunstein, eds. The Jewish Museum, New York.

The Ladies' Auxiliary to Temple de Hirsh Famous Cook Book., 1925, Seattle, Washington.

McCarthy, Mary, 1942. *The company she keeps*. San Diego, New York, London: Harcourt Brace and Co.

1963. *The Group*. New York: Harcourt, Brace and World.

1987. *How I grew*. San Diego, New York, London: Harcourt Brace Jovanovich.

1992. *Intellectual memoirs: New York 1936-1938*. San Diego, New York, London: Harcourt Brace and Co.

1953. *Memories of a Catholic girlhood*. New York and London: Harcourt Brace Jovanovich.

Grandma Rose, Chef Extraordinaire

Mary Wallace Kelsey

Such a tiny woman she is to have done as much hard work as she did in running her two restaurants. Rose Naftalin, known to lovers of her cookbooks as Grandma Rose, was born in Russia at the end of the last century. (Rose doesn't talk about age; from piecing tidbits together, I've concluded that she must be in her late nineties.)(3)

Her family immigrated to the United States when Rose was five years old. According to her, she was brought up in Chicago by a mother who couldn't cook. Rose was married at eighteen to a man who loved good food but Rose had never made so much as a bowl of soup before the marriage. Because she took her responsibilities as a wife seriously, Rose set about learning to cook. She asked people, she bought books, she wrote for correspondence courses, she went to a cooking school in Chicago, and she practiced. She says some of the food had to be discarded without being eaten, which was hard on the budget for the newlyweds. (1,2,3)

At the cooking school, Rose met a Viennese woman who taught her all the secrets of baking. Rose also used to go to a shop in Chicago known for its excellent food, Henrici's, and she'd examine everything by looking and smelling. She was afraid the staff would think she was trying to steal the food, when she was really stealing the knowledge of what made good quality baked goods. Then she'd go home and try to reproduce what she had seen. (3)

During the time she was learning, Rose picked up the idea that if the food was to taste wonderful, the best ingredients must be used. There were no substitutes for butter, cream or pure vanilla in any of Rose's food. That's why it became so famous - that and the fact that she followed directions. As to the use of high-quality ingredients, Rose often says, 'You take out what you put in'.

With the fall of the stock market and resulting depression in the United States after 1929, Rose's husband lost his job. Having heard about a similar one in Toledo, Ohio, he moved his family there. By then, Rose had developed enough skill in baking to win prizes at fairs. One first prize she won was a dining room table with matching chairs - quite a prize in those hard times. (3)

Her husband's job didn't work out; in desperation, they bought a neighborhood delicatessen that had only a one-burner stove in its kitchen. Much of the preparation was done at home, and the results carried to the shop. Rose describes it this way:'.. .we used to boil corned beef on the delicatessen's one burner, and [prepare] other food back at our apartment. I would bake all the pastries at home and we would carry them to the delicatessen as they were finished. We worked in shifts until one in the morning when I would go home, set the yeast dough, and while it was rising, make cupcakes, ice a sheet cake, bake a batch of cookies and then roll the schnecken to let them rise again. I would stick another batch of cookies in the oven, and by that time the yeast dough would be ready to bake. So each day went in a terrible struggle to survive.' (1, 2)

With the upturn in the American economy, the shop did well. Rose began to take a day off each week (the family says now that was from the wartime directive that stores remain closed at least one day a week) . She liked to shop, and would sometimes take the train to Chicago. She was always looking for good baking ideas, and when customers said they'd had something good at a place in another city, Rose would ask them to bring her a piece. Food was brought from Reuben's and Lindy's in New York. One time, when a customer had raved about a particularly delicious cake from Rumplemeyer's, Rose traveled to New York to try it so she could duplicate it. (No one remembers now which of her famous cakes that one was.) 'Nothing stopped me', says Rose. 'I wasn't rich and everything was expensive, but I went to seek in every little corner.'' (3)

Her children were nine and four when Rose's husband died, leaving her with Rose's Food Shoppe to support the family. She only had one goal, she said, that both of her children would be college graduates – and they are. Daughter Davida became a dietitian and worked in a very well-known hospital in Chicago. Bud is an engineer. (3)

Davida (Dee) began to work in the delicatessen after school and on weekends by the time she was 10 or 11, but she was so busy at the front of the shop that she never learned to bake until she moved to Oregon after her marriage. She didn't need to do this for long, though, because Rose soon followed her children west. After her arrival, Dee didn't have to bake again. (3)

When Rose sold the Ohio Food Shoppe she retired to Portland, Oregon where she baked for her children and grandchildren. That didn't keep her busy enough, though. Also, she was astounded that there were no delicatessens in Portland, and it was impossible to find a hot corned beef sandwich or a cheese blintz or gefilte fish. 'That's what she'd been feeding her Toledo customers for 30 years', Dee commented. Just over a year after moving to the Pacific Northwest, Rose opened her delicatessen, called 'Rose's', in 1956. (3)

It wasn't long before the restaurant was so popular with customers from all over the United States that baked goods were mailed as far as the east coast in boxes especially designed for shipping the goodies. This was not unusual for Rose to do; while running the Ohio store, she regularly shipped some brown sugar pecan cookies to comedian Joe E. Brown, a native of Toledo, at his California home. Eventually she received permission to name the cookies Joe E. Browns. (1)

Not only were customers delighted with the quality of Rose's food, they were also pleased with the serving sizes. Portions were gargantuan, and clients often took leftovers home in paper bags at a time when it was not usual to do so. Hostess Emma Swann remembers taking bags to most tables during her shift at the restaurant. (6) (Americans now call these bags of leftovers 'doggy bags', implying that the food is for the dog at home to eat. A few restaurants realistically call the containers 'people bags'.)

When she first began the Portland restaurant, Rose had two chefs hired to cook the main course food while she did the baking. The standards of the chefs were not equal to Rose's standards, so she soon fired both chefs and took charge herself. She did use helpers, but performed the most important tasks on her own. 'I wanted things done right, and the help was so poor that I had to do it myself', says Rose. 'I liked to feed people good…not just give 'em scraps, but the best, the best.'(3) Rose's family members say that she worked 20 hours a day; she was 'setting dough' three or four times daily. She didn't trust anyone else to do it correctly.

Because of her involvement in the kitchen, Rose needed to have someone she could count on at the front of the house. She found that person in Emma Swann, who had run her own restaurant in Wisconsin before moving to Oregon. Emma's husband was usually away as a sea captain, so she could and did devote long hours to the restaurant. Emma says that Rose rarely was seen by her customers, because she was so busy behind the scenes. In addition to serving sit-down meals, the restaurant also had a take-out department, so Rose baked and cooked for that part of the business as well. (3,6)

There were a few clients who did see Rose. Two of them were Oregon's current senior senator Mark Hatfield and his wife-to-be Antoinette, who courted at the restaurant. Rose always remembered them, they said, and sent cinnamon rolls home with Mark, who became Oregon's governor soon after the marriage.

Emma says it was unbelievable how good the food was, and after Rose had sold the place, people who'd see Emma on the street would complain that Rose's wasn't the same without Rose and her high-quality ingredients. People had said that eating at Rose's was 'like coming home'. There were many steady customers Emma remembers, and pleasing them was more important to Rose than making money. She never became wealthy from her restaurant or Food Shoppe. (6) Her daughter explains that because her mother wouldn't compromise on quality, she made very little profit. 'She wasn't looking for the almighty dollar,' says Dee. 'She was looking for happy people.' (3)

Although she didn't trust her staff to take charge of baking, Rose did think a lot of her staff. Dee tells that if one of the staff needed a warm coat or some shoes Rose would have them charged to her. One former employee tells that Rose used to give her extra money 'for gas'. Hostess Emma still keeps in touch with Rose regularly. 'She's one in a million', according to Emma. (3,6)

She was generous not only to her employees and her customers, but also to others. One Portland woman tells about Rose asking the staff of a business that received confections in tins to save the tins for her. She filled them with treats to send to servicemen.

After operating Rose's Restaurant for 10 years, Rose was told by her doctor son-in-law that she was knocking herself out and needed to get out of the restaurant business. She sold it 'with tears in her eyes', but stayed on to train the people who took over. After that, she never went to the restaurant again. (1,3)

Instead, Rose began using the apartment kitchen that she hadn't used during the 10 years at the restaurant. She had not seen her apartment in daylight for those 10 years say her family. She began cutting recipes down to family sizes, and supplied her children and grandchildren with home-made baked goods. Rose tells about the time one of her grandsons was asked to take her garbage outside to be disposed of, and he said, 'Grandma, even your garbage smells delicious'. (1,3)

Because so many people had asked for Rose's recipes over the years (she hadn't shared because they were her livelihood), and because the family needed a project on which to concentrate after the death of a grandson, Rose, her daughter, and daughter-in-law began to write the recipes in cookbook form. They sent recipes, and some copies of publicity Rose had received while in business and for serving pastries at an event for a local politician, to Random House publishers. An alert secretary insisted that her editor look at the very rough manuscript before preparing a special dinner for guests. Some of Rose's recipes were made, pronounced delicious, and the book was launched. (3)

The publishers began with a modest number of books, but *Grandma Rose's Book of Sinfully Delicious Cakes, Cookies, Pies, Cheese Cakes, Cake Rolls & Pastries* had 10 or 12 printings. In its second year of publication, the book was third in popularity among cookbooks published in the US. Books one and two were by Julia Child and James Beard, respectively.

Three years later, the second book, *Grandma Rose's Book of Sinfully Delicious Snacks, Nibbles, Noshes & other Delights* followed. This book was runner-up to *Julia Child and Company* for the Tastemaker Award in 1978. As a result of her books' popularity, Rose was featured in an edition of *Family Circle* magazine.

Dietitian daughter Dee says that these books were done just at the right time – before the American public became conscious of cholesterol and saturated fats and began to avoid butter, eggs and cream. (3) There is one recipe in the dessert book called 'Low Calorie Frosty Lemon Torte'. It calls for only two tablespoons of butter and for nonfat milk, along with cookie crumbs, sugar and two eggs in addition to the lemon. The recipe is headed with this statement: 'This recipe is as low calorie as this book gets'. (1) The snack book has a recipe for 'Relatively Low-fat Chocolate Meringues' which are called '....only a little fattening, compared to other things'. (2)

Before a large Portland bookseller was to host an autograph party for Rose, she attended one for Jackie Kennedy's former chef to see what an autograph party was like. The chef had prepared some samples for clients to taste. The bookstore personnel told Rose to bring a couple of cakes for display, but Rose said she couldn't have cakes for folks to look at without tasting. Instead, Rose brought enough samples to cover an eight-foot table, and so her autograph parties were started. She was invited to bookstores all over the Northwest, and as far south as San Francisco. For every one she took boxes of samples. Dee tells about spreading sheets on the floor of Rose's six-by-six foot kitchen so platters could be set out for cookies. Emma Swann, the former restaurant hostess, came to help and traveled with the women on the bookstore trips. (3,5,6)

When the now-defunct San Francisco store Liberty House asked Rose to an autograph party, they sent a limousine to meet her – and her boxes of pastries – at the airport. She made such a hit at Liberty House that rival Macy's insisted she have an autograph-tasting session at their store on a return trip to San Francisco. (5)

Rose was asked to be one of the judges in a James Beard cooking contest held in Oregon, Beard's home state. Since she'd retired from the restaurant and had finished baking for numerous autograph-tasting parties, she had time to take on some honorary assignments. Her accomplishments as a baker had earned her respect among her fellow food experts. (4)

Still baking for her family and guests, Rose had made buttery sesame seed cookies and cinnamon rolls to serve with tea during our interview. I was thankful that the rolls were reasonably sized, compared with huge ones which could feed a family when Rose made them at the restaurant. The flavours and other qualities of our teatime treats were unbeatable.

The most astounding part of this success story is that for most of her baking days, Rose DIDN'T TASTE THE FOOD. She could tell by smelling, looking and feeling that foods were good – and, of course, by following directions and using the best ingredients she could find. This shoots a hole in my theory that in order to produce good food, a cook must learn to taste. On a recent television show in the United States, Julia Child's guest, well-known New Orleans area chef Warren LeRuth said that he didn't taste everything either, but that he 'knows the numbers'; that is, he knows what proportions of ingredients to use to make things taste right. I have to believe that these chefs, in order to make the high quality food they are known for, must have tasted at the beginning.

And so it was that Rose Naftalin, a very small woman who was 'oh, so strong' according to Emma – it was necessary for her to lift so many heavy kettles and pans of food – became a legend among those of us who patronized her delicatessens and baked from her excellent recipes. Rose Naftalin, chef extraordinaire.

Acknowledgement

Special thanks to Barbara Durbin, food writer for *The Oregonian*, and to the newspaper for sharing information for this biography, as well as a photograph for display at the conference.

BIBLIOGRAPHY

1. Naftalin, Rose: *Grandma Rose's Book of Sinfully Delicious Cakes, Cookies, Pies, Cheese Cakes, Cake Rolls & Pastries*. New York: Random House, Inc. 1975.
2. Naftalin, Rose: *Grandma Rose's Sinfully Delicious Snacks, Nibbles, Noshes & Other Delights*. New York: Random House, Inc. 1978.
3. Naftalin, Rose and Davida Naftalin Rosenbaum: personal interview, February, 1995.
4. Rothert, Yvonne: 'Desserts face skilled cook's culling.' *The Oregonian*, April 14, 1976.
5. Rothert, Yvonne: 'Rose's cookbook autograph parties invariably end up as pastry tastings.' *The Oregonian*, March 30, 1977.
6. Swann, Emma, telephone interview, July, 1995.

Nikolas Tselementes

Aglaia Kremezi

For Greeks his name is synonymous with the word 'cookbook'. The man who put béchamel sauce on top of moussaka, hated garlic and thought the look of food was more important than its taste...

ΟΔΗΓΟΣ ΜΑΓΕΙΡΙΚΗΣ

ὑπό

ΝΙΚ. Κ. ΤΣΕΛΕΜΕΝΤΕ

ΕΚΔΟΣΙΣ ΤΕΤΑΡΤΗ
ΕΠΗΥΞΗΜΕΝΗ ΚΑΙ ΒΕΛΤΙΩΜΕΝΗ

ΕΚΔΟΣΙΣ
Β. ΠΑΠΑΧΡΥΣΑΝΘΟΥ
ΟΔΟΣ ΠΡΑΞΙΤΕΛΟΥΣ 12
ΑΘΗΝΑΙ, 1929

'...It is difficult to calculate the vast number of newly weds' households which were spared the large expense of hiring cooks, but foremost, saved from divorce. The bed and the dining table keep couples together, while at the same time they may drive them apart. The young husband and wife have made the table safe today, because of Tselementes. The only thing the new little wife needs to do, in order to get everybody's congratulations, is to lean over Tselementes' book for five minutes every day...' wrote Spyro Melas – one of the outstanding Greek authors and journalists – in his column in an Athens daily.[1]

'...Thousands of Greek couples owe to him the secret of their happiness. Tens of thousands of women kept their men at home following his advice... Most of today's chefs in hotels, boats, mansions and big restaurants owe their success to him,' wrote a well-known journalist in a half-page obituary in another Athenian daily.[2]

'... He [Tselementes] is the man who refined the Greek palate. He has taken the arbitrary elements of Greek cooking and brought them to order. He gave us our food constitution in a° culinary tradition that was neither eastern nor European...' wrote Pavlos Paleologos – one of the most well-known columnists of all times – in post mortem praise.[3]

'...Tselementes, with his book, gave happiness to the Greek family and made men enjoy the table while women found peace,' wrote Grigorios Ksenopoulos, a very well-known author of novels and plays. What he means by 'the peace women found' is better explained in the obituary published in the newspaper of the wealthy Egyptian Greek community[4]: 'Many Greek women were saved by Tselementes. It was enough to say to their complaining husbands 'It is written by Tselementes' and all the complaints stopped. What could the men do. Contradict Tselementes? It was like contradicting the God of the kitchen. He was the one who had managed to get inside the Greek cooking pot deciphering its mysteries and thus conquering and saving millions of hungry stomachs...' And the obituary ends with the following paragraph: 'Unfortunately in our modern times women no longer follow his advice. Cooking is considered an anachronistic chore. Contemporary wives spend their day playing cards and when the husband returns home from work he no longer finds the steaming pot on the stove...'

Even if we manage to overlook the strong male chauvinistic tone of the articles, the impression one is most likely to get from the statements of such well-known men of letters and esteemed journalists, is that before Tselementes there was chaos in the Greek kitchen. Idle, ignorant women who very little about cooking forced their poor husbands to live on one bad meal after another, a situation that often resulted in divorce...

Nothing, of course, could be further from the truth. The unanimous adoration for the author of the first complete cookbook written in modern Greek, and based on French cooking, was the result of a sweeping trend that started at the turn of the century. This trend was created by the rich and travelled upper classes – especially those wealthy Greeks living in the Egyptian cities of Cairo and Alexandria – who, imitating their English and French neighbours, were eager to leave their Eastern past behind and become Europeans.

Tselementes' book, *Odigos Mageirikes (Guide to Cooking)*[5], published in 1910, sold more than 100,000 copies and had come out in ten editions by the time the author died in 1958. After some revisions, the book made another eight editions, selling about 600,000 copies. Recently an illustrated edition was available in exchange for coupons provided by a popular TV magazine, helping increase its circulation quite sharply. Taking into account that the country had less than nine million inhabitants in the thirties – a large percentage of them illiterate – the success of the book was phenomenal, even when compared with today's best sellers. And we must also take into account that for about 10 years – between 1940-1950 – Greeks were in no condition to think about stylish foods or lifestyle, as they endured terrible suffering during the Greek-Italian war, the Nazi German occupation and the civil war that followed.

Tselementes was much more than a cookbook writer. He preached the new, modern way of life of which the rising Greek upper and middle class dreamed. He was the right person at the right time, and his large format 500 page cookbook – which resembled the bibles used in church ceremonies – made an enormous impression and fundamentally changed the taste of modern Greek food. Athenian *nouveau riche* society felt that this book was all a household needed to leave the miserable provincial past behind, and step into the glorious 20th century.

Cook, author and teacher

Nikolas Tselementes was born in 1878, in Athens, to a family that had recently left the small Aegean island of Sifnos, in search of a better life in the capital. When he graduated from high school, he started working as a public notary's clerk and his father wanted him to study law. His uncle – his father's brother – was the owner of Aktaion, an hotel and restaurant in Neo Faliro, Athen's seaside suburb. Neo Faliro – about 5 km. south of the city centre – was the most fashionable summer location. People went there in their carriages or by horse drawn buses, to bathe in the segregated men's and women's cabins. In the hot summer evenings, one could attend the opera, comedies or musical reviews performed at the open air theatre. Dinner was taken in one of the many simple seaside taverns or in more elaborate restaurants, such as the one owned by Tselementes' uncle. The young Tselementes spent all his free time in the kitchen of Aktaion, tasting various foods or helping the cooks and learning their secrets.

Finally, his family became convinced that studying law or working in an office – although at the time both considered most prestigious professions – were not what Nikolas wished to do. So he was sent to Vienna to study cooking. This is the official version of the story, published in various newspapers. Unfortunately, I haven't been able to find any details of his 'cooking studies'. Nobody knowns if he actually went to a cooking school or if such a school existed in the Austrian capital at the turn of the century.

One of his obituaries mentions that he studied Food Conservation, but he might simply have worked in the kitchen of some restaurant or hotel in Vienna, where he picked up the basic techniques of French cooking and a lot of ideas. In the first pages of the later editions of his book, together with much rapturous praise given to the book by many famous people, we read that he served as executive chef at the Sacher Hotel. As this piece of information is missing from all newspaper articles and obituaries, we may conclude that he probably worked in the kitchen of this famous hotel during his training in Vienna.

He came back to Athens after 2 1/2 years and – according to the published stories about him – he already had a shining talent. Upon his return, Mrs Falkenheim, the wife of the Austrian ambassador, employed him as the embassy's cook. At that time, the Austro-Hungarian empire was one of the most important world forces and its embassies must have been centres of social life in capitals all over the world. 'Tselementes knew precisely what pleased a French, an English, an Italian, a Swedish or an Oriental guest. He could cook fantastic dishes for a South American gourmet or for a hermit...'[6]

He must have been one of the most sought after cooks in Athens, but there are very few details regarding his professional employments during the years preceding the publication of his book. An article published eight years before his death – to coincide with the 10th edition of his book – mentions that he served as cook in the German and other embassies, as well as in wealthy Greek homes in Cairo, Istanbul, and other European capitals, following his employers in their moves, because they didn't want to lose him.' At the time, all wealthy Athenian homes had cooks, since society ladies were not supposed to go near the kitchen. In most cases the cooks were women who came from the poorer islands: Syros, Andros and Naxos were the most likely places. From a tender age these women had been in the kitchen, helping the cooks – usually their mothers or other relations, since this well-paid profession was normally kept strictly within the family.

There were also women who had had the chance of working close to an Egyptian cook, who were considered the best but very difficult to find in Athens. Cooks in the Athenian homes usually prepared traditional Greek foods, often adding local variations from their native places to the basic recipes. But they were also able to prepare some French dishes, especially sweets and a couple of dinner menus, which they had learned in the homes of wealthy and travelled employers.

During the first years that Tselementes worked in various homes, he must have started to take notes and collect recipes for his book. He had also studied the Greek cookbooks that had been published earlier, especially a very interesting one that came out in Istanbul and was reprinted in Athens in 1886.[7] Contrary to most cooks – who even if they were extremely talented and creative, were semi or completely illiterate – Tselementes could read more than one language, was very articulate, ambitious and possessed an inquisitive mind. Judging that the time was right, he made it his life's goal to introduce European society customs, manners and taste to every Greek home.

In his book he doesn't confine himself to cooking and manners. He goes much further, including the 'Ten commandments to the ladies' written by the 'learned royal' Carmen Silva – pen name of the princess Von und Zu Wied, who later became queen of Romania. 'Never start an argument and if you happen to be in the middle of an unexpected one, stay silent. Be sure that your constraint will make you the winner' is the first of the commandments. Another, urges the wife" 'From time to time say to your husband that he is an ideal spouse. It is a compliment that will give him pleasure. You should also confess that you have faults to.' The husband's faults are, somehow, taken for granted.

The book has an extensive introduction about the history of food and includes some of Brillat-Savarin's aphorisms and parts of his scientific explanations about taste and food. Table manners and *Savoir vivre* are covered at length, together with all kinds of housekeeping instructions, even descriptions and illustrations about the way servants should be dressed. The Greek *nouveaux riches* could certainly use all the advice they could get, absorbing the directives and rules Tselementes had collected from his readings or picked up in the embassies and the grand homes where he had served. Following the success of his book he started to teach 'the art of housekeeping...to Athenian ladies and girls, especially those belonging to high society.'[8]

'Without accepting that a woman's total activity must be included in the K.K.K. as Mr Hitler preaches – in German: *Kirche* (Church), *Kinder* (Children) and *Kuche* (Kitchen) – one must confess that good housekeeping, tidiness and especially good cooking, are qualities that especially decorate each women...' so starts a newspaper article, and continues with the cliché about the love of a man that passes from his stomach and the ability of good cooks '...to keep their husbands at bay, easier than if they tried different methods...' It is a key paragraph included in all articles about Tselementes, so it must have been often repeated by him.

The school gave three different courses – for beginners, intermediate and advanced – each completed in 20 lessons. It was lodged in a spacious patisserie workshop and take-out, entitled *Despotikon*, in Merlin street, in the upmarket Kolonaki area.[9]

Around the mid thirties, electric stoves appeared in Athens for the first time. AEG, the German manufacturer, hired Tselementes to give demonstrations and introduce the modern appliances to Athenians, who, until then, had cooked on big stoves fired by wood or charcoal. Tselementes didn't confine his activities to Athens. He also taught courses in Piraeus. Pipina Panagiotou, one of my mother's friends now in her mid eighties, has fond memories of those classes. 'He was so well organized and neat while preparing the various dishes, that we could hardly believe our eyes watching him work with such dexterity,' Mrs Panagiotou told me. She remembers that the classes were packed with enthusiastic young and older ladies frantically taking notes.

It is interesting to note here that the cooking part of Tselementes' classes of the 1930s, must have been very similar to the modern cooking schools that flourish all over the US and Europe. After him, though, there was nobody to revise and continue similar courses. To this day there is not a single cooking school for amateurs in Greece. Only the professional training for men wanting to become restaurant cooks, which Tselementes also founded, still exists and, as far as I know, has changed very little, although more than 60 years have passed.

But he didnt't stop there. He had suffered much when obliged to eat horrible food while serving in the army, so when he became famous, he spoke to the head generals insisting that a school for army cooks was needed. They not only agreed, but promoted him to the rank of major, so that he could start to train enlisted men. His students became the cooks of the infantry and navy, while the more talented ones were employed in the various officers' clubs, where more refined menus were prepared.

His book was translated into English to be sold in the wealthy Greek-American community.[10] One of his most important professional employments was in the Continental Room, one of the restaurants in New York's Saint Moritz Hotel. He first went to New York around the late 20s and again later, probably spending some of the war years there.

In his middle years he married a widow with two sons, who was of Italian origin but lived in Istanbul. She was called Ersilia and in her honour he gave her name to a couple of recipes he had created. 'Ersilia was an extremely sweet and lovely lady', I was told by Mr Fytrakis, who published Tselementes' book from the time of the author's death until recently. In an interview for one of the obituaries[11] Ersilia was asked what kind of person her husband was. She replied that he was: 'A very calm person. All he cared about was how he could help men gain happiness. He spent fifty five years pursuing this goal.' 'He must have made quite a fortune?' the journalist said, and Mrs Tselementes answered: 'Not at all. He offered his help without asking for compensation. We just lived a comfortable life, nothing more. Our life was always simple and calm.'

In one of his rare newspaper interviews – parts of which were repeated in his obituary[12] – when asked what he loved most, Tselementes replied: 'My wife, cooking and music.' When asked to explain the connection between cooking and music, he gave the poetic answer: 'The smell of a dish, is what the sound of music is for the ears.'

Very few details of his personal life are known. John Tselementes – his nephew and godchild, the only surviving relative – was very young when his uncle was around. When Ersilia died, he inherited a couple of albums with pictures and a few press clippings, but the rest of Tselementes' papers and personal belongings were just thrown away when his home was demolished to make room for an apartment building.[13]

He published many articles in magazines and newspapers, dealing with the history of food and with nutrition. He was convinced that French cooking had its roots in ancient Greece. Nutrition was one of the subjects that occupied him greatly. While he was working in New York, he attended lectures on nutrition at Columbia University. At one point he had asked the head of a large Athenian hospital to assign him five of its patients. He wanted to experiment with a diet he had invented which he was convinced would immediately improve the patients' condition.[14] Unfortunately we have no other record about this. He even intended to translate Athaenaeus' *Deipnosophist* sinto modern Greek.

A magazine article he published in October 1939[15] reveals some very interesting details about life in Greece just before the war, while the country was ruled by a fascist and hated dictator. Tselementes writes that he wants to instruct people how best to follow, '…the wise recommendations regarding foods, issued by our esteemed government.' He speaks about sugar shortage, and insists that this shouldn't be a problem, since one can use honey and dried grape juice, instead. He also points out that Greeks should learn to eat potatoes because '…with the government's orders there will be plenty.' He ends his piece with the recipe for *Boiled potatoes with chicken liver sauce*.

He often visited Sifnos, his place of origin, and helped the people of the island as best as he could. In one of the local newspapers[16] we read that he had given financial assistance to local authors to publish their books, especially the ones dealing with the stories and customs of the island.

No garlic and lots of béchamel sauce.

But let's get to the taste of Tselementes' food.

'He ate very simply, preferred spaghetti with tomato sauce and parmesan, rice pilaf, fried eggs sunny side up and burger with French fries' said his wife, when asked to name her husband's preferred foods, and continued: 'He hated garlic and cucumber. Even their smell bothered him.' Why then did he suggest the use of garlic in some dishes, the journalist asked, and she replied, 'he suggests its use to others. He never tasted it. He also hated sour tastes and pickles. In his recipes he uses lemon with great moderation. You should make a non-sour egg and lemon sauce. Whoever wants more lemon he can add it to his plate he often told his students.'[17]

In his cookbook, garlic does not appear until the recipe for *garlic sauce*[18] and is mentioned only a couple more times. 'People who like foods with intense and bad smelling taste...may try the following recipe' he writes in the introduction to a delicious *arni skordostumbi* from Zakynthos (Lamb with garlic)[19] one of the very rare regional recipes in the book. I'm sure that very few of his delicate readers would even read further than that introductory sentence.

In the beginning of the book, in a piece about the history of Greek cooking[20], he writes that the various traditional foods need to regain the 'Greekiness' they lost during the long Turkish occupation. So they should, '...be revised by learned cooks who will rid those dishes from the influence and contamination they suffered trying to conform to the taste of the Eastern peoples, so that they don't appear too greasy, over spiced and unappealing.' It is the key point around which he built his recipes.

The greasiness that bothered him was the olive oil, which he almost totally banned from his book. Before him almost all traditional foods were cooked with olive oil, since that was the Greek fat from antiquity. Butter was introduced to the country by the Ottomans but was still scarcely used by ordinary people, because cattle raising was very limited and the traditional sheep and goat farmers produced very little butter. In the north, where olive oil was not produced, pork fat was the grease used in cooking. Tselementes' idea of making the dishes less greasy was to bind masses of butter with flour in his thick, creamy sauces.

His exclusion of spices and even herbs from the spicy and fragrant traditional Greek foods resulted in totally insipid dishes. Furthermore, he created the notion that spicy foods are for provincial people and bad for the health, which you will hear repeated by most Athenians to this day. I wonder how, having read even parts of Athenaeus' *Deipnosophists*, he managed to miss the extensive use of spices and herbs by the ancient Greek cooks, whom he so much admired. He goes as far as to omit thyme and bay leaves from the *sauce Espagnole*, when he writes his version which is clearly based on Escoffier's recipe.

We can safely conclude that Tselementes favoured sweet and very mild tastes and this partly explains his adoration for béchamel sauce. He uses it all the time, mostly as a substitute for fresh cream, an ingredient that was missing from the Greek market until the late 60s. Béchamel is even present in his recipes for cold *mousse*. His most important creations, based on béchamel sauce, were his versions of *moussaka*, *pasticcio* and *kotopoulo milaneza* (Milanese chicken), a dish that he seems to have invented.

When I first started to research the origins of the various traditional Greek dishes, I was convinced that the very popular *moussaka* was invented in Istanbul, by a creative French educated cook. But my new investigation revealed that before Tselementes there was no *moussaka*, as we know it today. Just layers of fried aubergines, topped with meat and tomato sauce with, maybe, some cheese at the top. More or less the dish called *moussaka* in the Middle East. This was the version my grandmother used to cook. Although it is very difficult to prove it, the new *moussaka* that is topped with a thick layer of béchamel sauce, seems to have become part of the Greek kitchen after Tselementes' book came out. In the book, in a separate chapter entitled *Moussakas*, he gives six recipes, basically substituting zucchini or potatoes, for the aubergines. He even has one very interesting version with alternate layers of zucchini and tomato slices, both dredged in flour and fried.

Pasticcio evolved in much the same way. Before him, thick spaghetti mixed with chopped liver, meat, eggs and cheese, was the filling of a pie wrapped in *phylo* pastro. This version was nearer to the original Italian recipe that uses a pastry crust. But he completely changed the dish and made it a kind of *au gratin*. His *pasticcio* – the one served at all Greek restaurants today – has the pasta mixed with béchamel sauce together with ground meat, then placed in a greased pan, topped with a thick layer of béchamel and baked. My mother remembers an argument about which pasticcio was better, between her mother and her older sister, who had received Tselementes' book as a wedding present, and was eager to use it. Finally there was a compromise and an intermediate version of *pasticcio* was cooked in her home for some time: it had *phylo* pastry at the bottom but was topped with béchamel sauce.

Tselementes also invented army versions of *moussaka* and *pasticcio*, substituting tinned corned beef – imported by the English during the war – for fresh meat.

Milanese chicken was a molded chicken pilaf, where the rice was cooked in rich chicken stock. Boned chicken pieces were scattered over it and a rich béchamel sauce with Parmesan cheese sprinkled on the top, covering the dish. It is the perfect comfort food, lush, creamy and sweet, so it is easy to understand why it was an instant success and became the traditional Sunday food of the upper classes. Although out of fashion now, if you ask older Athenians about their favoured food, 'Milanese chicken' is the likely answer.

He believed that it was extremely important for the food to be beautifully served so he includes lengthy descriptions of how to make the nearly forty different *canapés* he included in his appetizers. Following the appetizers there is the *meze* section which includes various tartlets, bouches, turnovers and even Welsh rarebit. Less than a third of the recipes in that section are Greek. *Taramosalata* isn't part of the *meze* but is included in a section with no title[21] which contains a compilation of all sorts of dishes with potatoes, rice, homemade pastas, stuffed vine-leaves and some other Lenten foods. Following *taramosalata* is caviar salad, which, he explains, is made in much the same way, substituting caviar for the *tarama*. Caviar couldn't have been so expensive in those days, because it was served in large quantities during dinner parties.

Roughly one third of the book is devoted to baking and patisserie. All kinds of cakes, tarts, puddings and creams are included. There is even a section with the subtitle *Anglo-American sweets with baking powder* which includes shortcakes and even a wedding cake, which only became part of Greek wedding parties in the late 80s.

It is interesting to note that the very few pure tasting traditional dishes, with neither béchamel nor lots of butter, that he included in the book originate in his native island of Sifnos – Chick peas, *melopita* (honey pie), *skaltsounia* (small sweet cheese pies with honey).

Hero or villain?

There is no doubt that Tselementes was a remarkable man who felt that he had a mission to bring civilization and refinement to the Greek traditional kitchen which he considered almost barbarian. He was an honest, hard working man, probably an excellent cook by the standards of his time, who spent a lot of time reading and researching. His book is well written and documented but quite difficult to follow for the inexperienced cook. The problem is that its phenomenal success resulted in the abandonment of the simple honest peasant cooking of Greece.

Considered the Bible of cooking to this day, Tselementes' book is the source of the vast majority of the foods served in Athenian restaurants. This, in turn, greatly influenced home cooking, even though in most cases the book itself was used by home cooks mainly for party menus and sweets. Tselementes' ideas made Greek women who were good cooks – and probably personally disliked his creamy dishes – feel that they were not modern. So they felt ashamed of the foods they learned from their mothers. It is no wonder that those marvellous simple peasant dishes of the poor have almost disappeared as people became wealthier and moved to the big cities.

I have the feeling that if, instead of imposing French cooking and techniques on us, Tselementes had recorded some interesting regional recipes in his book, Greek cooking in general wouldn't be too different from that of southern Italy. To find the original dishes today, one has to search very hard. 'How can Athenians eat those hospital foods which are served in the restaurants?' an elderly woman from Crete asked me recently. But she was a rare exception. Usually village women are not that outspoken. They are convinced that they are wrong and city people are right, even if they have no taste.

Acknowledgements

I express my warm thanks to Yannis Tselementes, the son of Nikolas' cousin and his godchild, for his generous help. Also my gratitude to Manos Haritatos of ELIA (Hellenic Literary and Historical Society) for his much needed assistance.

REFERENCES

[1] *Eleftheria*, April 5, 1958.
[2] *Acropolis*, April 4, 1958.
[3] *To Vima*, April 5, 1958.
[4] *Tachydromos*, April 5, 1958. Column by Dinos Koutsoumis.
[5] The earliest edition I have seen is the 4th, published by B. Papachrsanthou in 1929.
[6] *Acropolis*, April 4, 1958. Written by Th. Drakos.
[7] *Sygramma Mageirikis*, by the cook Nikolas Sarantis. Published in Istanbul in 1863 and in Athens by N. Mihalopoulos, in 1886.
[8] *Athinaika Nea*, January 21, 1934.
[9] By a strange coincidence, the same space remained in the memory of Greeks as *Merlin*, a place of horror, because it became the headquarters of the Gestapo during the Nazi occupation. Thousands of Greek freedom fighters were tortured and died there.
[10] *Greek Cookery* by Nicholas Tselementes, D.C. Divry Inc., New York, 1950.
[11] *Acropolis*, March 4, 1958. Written by Th. Drakos.
[12] *Athinaiki*, April 3, 1958.
[13] Ersilia's sons lived abroad, and Yannis Tselementes told me that he knows neither their names nor their whereabouts.
[14] *Sifnos News*, March 1958. Article by Theodoros Sperantasas.
[15] *Bouketo*, weekly magazine, October 12, 1939, page 13.
[16] *Signos*, monthly newspaper, April 1958.
[17] *Athinaiki*, March 3, 1958. Obituary by Veta My.
[18] Page 163 of the 10th edition, the last one revised by the author.
[19] Page 229 of the 10th edition.
[20] Page 19 of the 10th edition.
[21] From page 101 of the 10th edition.

Rumford and Culinary Science

Nicholas Kurti

Biographical Note and General Information

Benjamin Thompson was born in 1753 in the Commonwealth of Massachusetts. He came from farming stock but, with an eye on higher things, he studied experimental philosophy, chemistry and medicine as well as French, became a schoolmaster at the age of 19 and soon after married a rich widow fourteen years his senior. Two years later he abandoned his wife and their baby daughter. He never saw his wife again and his daughter not until she was 22 years old.

During the American war of Independence Thompson was a loyalist and spy working for the Governor of Massachusetts. Later he raised and commanded the 'King's American Dragoons', a regiment known and hated for its atrocities on Long Island: his first 'British' career, spent partly in America and partly in England, during which he was knighted, elected a Fellow of the Royal Society and became a full colonel, ended in 1784 when, at the age of 31 he left for Munich and entered the service of Carl Theodor, the Elector of Bavaria, first as Aide-de-Camp, then Minister of Police and Grand Chamberlain. The fifteen years in Munich were very productive. In addition to his seminal contributions to the theory of heat he also designed the 'English Garden', a lasting memorial. He was created a Count of the Holy Roman Empire and chose for his title Rumford, the original name of the town of Concord (New Hampshire).

In 1798 he returned to England and founded in 1799 the Royal Institution of Great Britain. He settled in Paris in 1803, married the widow of Lavoisier (they separated after five years) and died in 1814.

Anyone interested in the colourful life of this remarkable man should read the biography of the late Sanborn C. Brown, for many years Professor at Dartmouth College, New Hampshire (The MIT Press, Cambridge, Mass. 1979).[1] The opening paragraph of W.H. Brock's review (*New Scientist*, 27 March 1980) gives the flavour of the book:

> Of what other man of science could it be said that he was a loyalist, traitor, spy, cryptographer, opportunist, womanizer, philanthropist, egotistical bore, soldier of fortune, military and technical adviser, inventor, plagiarist, expert on heat (especially on fireplaces and ovens) and founder of the world's greatest showplace for the popularization of science, the Royal Institution? Devoted, like Baron Munchausen, to self-aggrandisement and the ruthless suppression of opponents in the quest for patronage and power, Count Rumford is a biographer's dream subject. The physicist, Professor Sanborn Brown who has spent some 40 years working on his subject rises to the occasion with a warts-and-all narrative which is at once informative, definitive and extremely readable.

There are two editions of Rumford's published work. One dates from 1870, the other, which is used for this essay, was edited by S.C. Brown and published in 1970 by the Harvard University Press. The five volumes, about one million words, cover such varied subjects as methods of heating dwellings, the causes and cures of smoking chimneys, the physical properties of silk, the force of fired gunpowder, the design of frigates and of travelling carriages, army regulations, work-houses, the source of heat excited by friction etc. but less than one tenth of it is relevant to food and nutrition. In reporting on these aspects of Rumford's work I quote verbatim rather than summarize or paraphrase so as to show the leisurely way in which scientific research was carried out and the informal way it was reported two centuries ago. What present day editor of a scientific journal would tolerate in a learned paper a passage like:

> These minute investigations may perhaps be tiresome to some readers, but those who feel the importance and perceive the infinite advantages to the human species that might be derived from a more intimate knowledge of the science of preparing food, will be disposed to engage with cheerfulness in these truly interesting and entertaining researches?[2]

Apple pie and the transfer of heat by convection.

(Based on 'The propagation of heat in fluids, Part I, Chapter I' in *Collected Works*, Vol. I, 119-284)

It is often said and seldom contradicted that Rumford discovered convection by observing that hot stewed apples or apple-sauce cooled more slowly than clear soup. This is cited sometimes as an example of observations in everyday life leading to discoveries in basic science. Rumford did indeed try to find the reason for the vastly different behaviour of a clear broth and a viscous pureé but it was a chance observation in an entirely different field that gave him the clue:

> When dining I had often observed that some particular dishes retained their Heat much longer than others, and that apple-pies, and apples and almonds mixed (a dish in great repute in England), remained hot a surprising length of time.
>
> Much struck with this extraordinary quality of retaining Heat which apples appeared to possess, it frequently occurred to my recollection; and I never burnt my mouth with them, or saw others meet with the same misfortune, without endeavouring but in vain, to find out some way of accounting in a satisfactory manner for this surprising phenomenon.
>
> About four years ago, a similar accident awakened my attention, and excited my curiosity still more: being engaged in an experiment which I could not leave, in a room heated by an iron stove, my dinner, which consisted of a bowl of thick rice-soup, was brought into the room, and as I happened to be too much engaged at the time to eat it, in order that it might not grow cold, I ordered it to be set down on the top of the stove; about an hour afterwards, as near as I can remember, beginning to grow hungry, and seeing my dinner standing on the stove, I went up to it and took a spoonful of the soup which I found almost cold and quite thick. Going, by accident, deeper with the spoon the second time, this second spoonful burnt my mouth. This accident recalled very forcibly to my mind the recollection of the hot apples and almonds with which I had so often burned my mouth a dozen years before in England; but even this, though it surprised me very much, was not sufficient to open my eyes, and to remove my prejudices respecting the conducting power of water.[3]

It was months, or perhaps years later that, while on the sea shore at the hot baths of Baia, near Naples 'where the hot steam was issuing from every crevasse and even rising up out of the ground' he noticed that although the surface of the sand on which the waves broke was cold, at the depth of two inches the sand, still wet, was so hot that he had to remove his hand.

> I then, for the first time, began to doubt of the conducting power of water, and resolved to set about making experiments to ascertain the fact. I did not, however, put this resolution into execution till about a month ago, and should perhaps never have done it, had not another unexpected appearance again called my attention to it, and excited afresh all my curiosity.
>
> In the course of a set of experiments on the communication of Heat, in which I had occasion to use thermometers of an uncommon size (their globular bulbs being above four inches in diameter) filled with various kinds of liquids, having exposed one of them, which was filled with spirits of wine, in as great a heat as it was capable of supporting, I placed it in

a window, where the sun happened to be shining, to cool; when, casting my eye on its tube, which was quite naked (the divisions of its scale being marked in the glass with a diamond), I observed an appearance which surprised me, and at the same time interested me very much indeed. I saw the whole mass of the liquid in the tube in a most rapid motion, running swiftly in two opposite directions, *up* and *down* at the same time. The bulb of the thermometer which is of copper, had been made two years before I found leisure to begin my experiments, and having been left unfilled, without being closed with a stopple, some fine particles of dust had found their way into it, and these particles, which were intimately mixed with the spirits of wine, on their being illuminated by the sun's beams, became perfectly visible (as the dust in the air of a darkened room is illuminated and rendered visible by the sunbeams which come in through a hole in the window-shutter), and by their motion discovered the violent motions by which the spirits of wine in the tube of the thermometer was agitated.[4]

This is how Rumford discovered the transport of heat by convection: currents of the warm liquid passing on the heat either to the cold walls of the tube or to the colder parts of the liquid. The difference in the behaviour of broth and of apple sauce becomes clear. In the apple sauce the circulation of the water is hindered by the fibrous material suspended in it. In a series of experiments he measured the heat transfer through water, through apple sauce, through a mixture of eiderdown and water and through a viscous starch solution (to increase the viscosity) and proved the correctness of his explanation.

The Choice of Cooking Temperature

(Based on the essay 'On the Construction of Kitchen Fireplaces and Kitchen Utensils, together with remarks and observations relating to the various processes of cookery and proposals for improving that most useful art'. *Collected Works*, Vol. III, 57-384).

This 300 page long essay has for its *leit-motiv* Rumford's zeal for saving fuel by the proper design of the equipment it is used in and by advocating cooking methods which are economical in the use of fuel – especially if the resulting dishes are superior in taste and more nutricious.

The 15-page Introduction to the essay makes two important points. The first is that there is nothing magical about 212°F (100°C), the temperature at which water boils at sea level, for instance in London. But if meat can be boiled satisfactorily in Munich where the boiling point is 209°F, why raise the temperature to 212°F in London, except for convenience, and he advises cooks to experiment with various cooking temperatures. He explains that violent boiling is unnecessary, it just wastes fuel and similarly 'boiling' should be done with the lid on rather than with the lid off. The final pages of the introduction provide a good summary of Rumford's aims and ideas about 'scientific' cooking and are given here:

My principal design in publishing these computations is to *awaken the curiosity of my readers*, and fix their attention on a subject which, however low and vulgar it has hitherto generally been thought to be, is in fact highly interesting, and deserving of the most serious consideration. I wish they may serve to inspire cooks with a just idea of the importance of their art, and of the intimate connection there is between the various processes in which they are daily concerned, and many of the most beautiful discoveries that have been made by experimental philosophers in the present age.

The advantage that would result from an application of the late brilliant discoveries in philosophical chemistry, and other branches of natural philosophy and mechanics, to the improvement of the art of cookery, are so evident and so very important that I cannot help flattering myself that we shall soon see some enlightened and liberal-minded person of the profession take up the matter in earnest and give it a thoroughly *scientific* investigation.

In what art or science could improvements be made that would more powerfully contribute to increase the comforts and enjoyments of mankind?

And it must not be imagined that the saving of fuel is the only or even the most important advantage that would result from these inquiries: others of still greater magnitude, respecting the *manner* of preparing food for the table, would probably be derived from them.

The heat of boiling water, continued for a shorter or longer time, having been found by experience to be sufficient for cooking all those kinds of animal and vegetable substances that are commonly used as food; and *that degree* of heat being easily procured, and easily kept up, in all places and in all seasons; and as all the utensils used in cookery are contrived for that kind of heat, few experiments have been made to determine the effects of using *other degrees of heat*, and *other mediums* for conveying it to the substance to be acted upon in culinary processes. The effects of different degrees of heat in the same body are, however, sometimes very striking; and the taste of the same kind of food is often so much altered by a trifling difference in the manner of cooking it, that it would no longer be taken for the same thing. What a surprising difference, for instance, does the manner of performing that most simple of all culinary processes, *boiling in water*, make on potatoes! Those who have never tasted potatoes *boiled in Ireland*, or cooked according to the Irish method, can have no idea what delicious food these roots afford when they are properly prepared. But it is not merely the *taste* of food that depends on the manner of cooking it: its nutritiousness also, and its wholesomeness, – qualities still more essential if possible than taste, –are, no doubt, very nearly connected with it.

Many kinds of food are known to be most delicate and savoury when cooked in a degree of heat considerably below that of boiling water; and it is more than probable that there are others which would be improved by being exposed in a heat greater than that of boiling water.

In the seaport towns of the New England States in North America, it has been a custom, time immemorial, among people of fashion, to dine one day in the week (Saturday) on *salt fish*; and a long habit of preparing the same dish has, as might have been expected, led to very considerable improvements in the art of cooking it. I have often heard foreigners, who have assisted at these dinners, declare that they never tasted salt-fish dressed in such perfection; and I well remember that the secret of cooking it is to keep it a great many hours in water that is *just scalding-hot*, but which is never made actually to boil.

I had long suspected that it could hardly be possible that *precisely* the temperature of 212 degrees of Fahrenheit's thermometer (that of boiling water) should be that which is best adapted for cooking *all sorts of food*; but it was the unexpected result of an experiment that I made with another view which made me particularly attentive to this subject. Desirous of finding out whether it would be possible to roast meat in a machine I had contrived for drying potatoes, and fitted up in the kitchen of the House of Industry at Munich, I put a shoulder of mutton into it, and after attending to the experiment three hours, and finding it showed no signs of being done, I concluded that the heat was not sufficiently intense; and despairing of success, I went home rather out of humour at my ill-success, and abandoned my should of mutton to the cook-maids.

It being late in the evening, and the cook-maids thinking, perhaps, that the meat would be as safe in the drying-machine as anywhere else, left it there all night. When they came in the morning to take it away, intending to cook it for their dinner, they were much surprised to find it *already cooked*, and not merely eatable, but perfectly done, and most singularly well-tasted. This appeared to them the more miraculous, as the fire under the machine was gone quite out before they left the kitchen in the evening to go to bed, and as they had locked up the kitchen when they left it and taken away the key.

> This wonderful shoulder of mutton was immediately brought to me in triumph, and though I was at no great loss to account for what had happened, yet it certainly was quite unexpected; and when I tasted the meat I was very much surprised indeed to find it very different both in taste and flavour, from any I had ever tasted. It was perfectly tender; but though it was so much done, it did not appear to be in the least sodden or insipid, – on the contrary, it was uncommonly savoury and high flavoured. It was neither boiled nor roasted nor baked. Its taste seemed to indicate the manner in which it had been prepared; that the gentle heat, to which it had for so long a time been exposed, had by degrees loosened the cohesion of its fibres, and concocted its juices, without driving off their fine and more volatile parts, and without washing away or burning and rendering rancid and empyreumatic its oils.
>
> Those who are most likely to give their attention to this little history will perceive what a wide field it opens for speculation and curious experiment. The circumstances I have related, however trifling and uninteresting they may appear to many, struck me forcibly, and recalled to my mind several things of a similar nature which had almost escaped my memory. They recalled to my recollection the manner just described in which salt-fish is cooked in America; and also the manner in which *samp* is prepared in the same country. (See my Essay on Food). This substance, which is exceedingly palatable and nourishing food when properly cooked, *is not eatable* when simply boiled. How many cheap articles may there be of which the most delicate and wholesome food might be prepared, were the art and the *science* of cooking them better understood. But I beg my reader's pardon for detaining him so long with speculations which he may perhaps consider as foreign to the subject I promised to treat in this Essay. To proceed, therefore, to those investigations which are more immediately connected with the construction of kitchen fire-places.[5]

Writing on the imperfections of Kitchen Fireplaces 'now in common use' he says:

> The great fault in the construction of kitchens in private families, particularly in Great Britain, is... that the fireplaces are not *closed*. The fuel is burned in a long open grate called a *Kitchen range* over which the pots and kettles are freely suspended or placed on stands... The loss of heat and waste of fuel in these kitchens is altogether incredible; but there are other evils attending them... All the various processes in which fire is used in preparing food... are extremely unpleasant.[6]

Rumford summarises the inefficiency of the kitchen range by remarking that 'more fuel is consumed in it to boil a tea-kettle than, with proper management, would be sufficient to cook a dinner for fifty men.'[7]

Rumford's remedy sounds obvious to our ears but the underlying ideas were novel 200 years ago:

> Each boiler, kettle, stewpan should have its separate *closed* fireplace. Each fireplace should have its grate for the fuel and its separate ashpit closed by a well-fitting door and furnished with a register for regulating the air intake. It should also have its separate canal furnished with a damper for carrying off the smoke into the chimney.[8]

Rumford's roasting oven must have seemed even more revolutionary to some. To avoid the wastefulness and uneven heating which characterises roasting on the spit, Rumford conceived the closed oven – a hollow sheet iron cylinder, 18 inches in diameter, 24 inches long with a door at one end, closed at the other, set horizontally in brickwork and heated from underneath by a small fire whose intensity could be controlled in the same way as the kitchen fireplace previously described. A 'steam-tube' provided with a damper is attached to the top of the oven to carry off steam which escapes in roasting and a set of 'blow-pipes' which, together with the steam pipe, permit the regulation of the dryness as well as the temperature of the oven. These 'blow-pipes', iron tubes 2 1/2 inches in diameter, 23 inches long, lie immediately under the roaster, are exposed to the fire and lead into the far end of the oven. If the dampers at the front ends of the blow pipes and on the steam tube are opened, a blast of burning hot air rushes into the oven and the joint is browned without its being exposed to a fire.

Rumford arranged a blind tasting of two roast legs of mutton from the same carcass, one being roasted on a spit before a fire, the other in his roaster. The latter was unanimously preferred. Moreover its weight loss was several percent less than that of the one cooked on the spit.[9]

In his eagerness to prove the versatility of his roasting oven Rumford placed a three pound piece of beef into an earthenware pot, filled it up with boiling water, put the lid on and placed it in the oven which had a small fire under it. After three hours the meat was found to be perfectly cooked and judged by the company of nine persons as 'uncommonly savoury'.[10] The water, on the other hand, was clear and practically tasteless. In a second experiment using the same quantities the water was allowed to boil continuously and the result was a tasty beef broth but boiled beef of inferior quality. The following quotation is a suitable ending for this chapter.

> The result of this experiment recalled very forcibly to my recollection a dispute I had had several years before, in Germany, with the cook of a friend of mine, who at my recommendation had altered his kitchen fire-place; in which dispute I now saw I was in the wrong, and, seeing it, felt a desire more easy to be conceived than to be described to make an apology to an innocent person whom I had unjustly suspected of wilful misrepresentation. This woman (for its was a female cook), on being repeatedly reprimanded for sending to table a kind of soup of inferior quality, which, before the kitchen was altered, she had always been famous for making in the highest perfection, persisted in declaring that she could not make the same good rich soup in the new-fashioned boilers (fitted up in closed fire-places, and heated by small fires) as she used to make in the old boilers, set down upon the hearth before a great roaring wood fire.
>
> The woman was perfectly in the right. To make a rich meat soup, the juices must be washed out of the meat, and intimately mixed with the water; and this washing out in boiling must be greatly facilitated and expedited by the continual and rapid motion into which the contents of a boiler are necessarily thrown when heat is applied to one side of it only, especially when the heat is sufficiently intense to keep the liquid continually boiling with vehemence. I ought, no doubt, to have foreseen this; but how difficult is it to foresee anything! It is much easier to explain than to predict.[11]

How to Feed the Poor

> (Based on: 'An Account of the Establishment for the Poor of Munich' *Collected Works* Vol.V, 1-98; 'Of Food; and particularly of feeding the Poor', Vol V, 169-262.)

The subject of the first of the two essays on which this chapter is based would seem strange source material for a Food Symposium. However it was the plight of the poor and of the beggars of Munich which led Rumford to the creation of the 'Rumfordsche Suppe' (Rumford's Soup) which is a slightly less lasting memorial to him than 'Der Englische Garten' in Munich – and certainly less cherished.

When Rumford arrived in Munich in 1784 he found the city swarming with beggars of both sexes and all ages. There were about 2000 of them in a city of 60,000 people and they made life very unpleasant for the inhabitants.

> By far the greater number of the poor people to be taken care of were not only common beggars, but had been bred up from their very infancy in that profession, and were so attached to their indolent and dissolute way of living as to prefer it to all other situations. They were not only unacquainted with all kinds of work, but had the most insuperable aversion to

honest labour, and had been so long familiarized with every crime that they had become perfectly callous to all sense of shame and remorse.

With persons of this description, it is easy to be conceived that precepts, admonitions, and punishments would be of little or no avail. But, where precepts fail, *habits* may sometimes be successful.

To make vicious and abandoned people happy, it has generally been supposed necessary, *first*, to make them virtuous. But why not reverse this order! Why not make them first *happy*, and then virtuous! If happiness and virtue by *inseparable*, the end will be as certainly obtained by the one method as by the other; and it is most undoubtedly much easier to contribute to the happiness and comfort of persons in a state of poverty and misery than by admonitions and punishments to reform their morals.[12]

The last paragraph earned Rumford, with some justification, the epithet of a visionary reformer and his idea was later taken up by others. Thus the German philosopher Ludwig Feuerbach (1804-1872) wrote in his prospectus for J. Moleschott's *Treatise on Food for People* (1850): 'Do you want to improve people? Then, instead of preaching against sin give them better food.' The same idea was revived by Brecht in the *Threepenny Opera* with '*Erst kommt das Fressen, dann kommt die Moral*' (Fodder first, morals follow). Feuerbach summed up this view in the punning aphorism '*Der Mensch ist was er isst*' (One is what one eats), which recalls Brillat Savarin's often quoted aphorism '*Dis moi ce que tu manges, je te dirai ce que tu es*' (Tell me what you eat, I'll tell you what you are).

Having established the ethical basis of his plan to reform the beggars of Munich, Rumford set about putting it into action. To make people happy you must give them something useful to do and something nourishing to eat. He commandeered a large disused factory in a suburb of Munch, restored it, fitted it out with a large kitchen, a large eating room and large halls where the beggars could work. Several hundred spinning wheels were bought for hemp, also for flax, for cotton, for wool as the spinners' skills improved. And when everything was ready, on the 1st January 1790, Rumford went into action and here is a description of how, in literally a few hours, the beggars of Munich were no more.

An Account of the taking up of the Beggars at Munich. – The Inhabitants are called upon for their Assistance. – General Subscription for the Relief and Support of the Poor. – All other public and private Collections for the Poor abolished.

New-Year's Day having from time immemorial been considered in Bavaria as a day peculiarly set apart for giving alms, and the beggars never failing to be all out upon that occasion, I chose that moment as being the most favourable for beginning my operations. Early in the morning of the 1st of January, 1790, the officers and non-commissioned officers of the three regiments of infantry in garrison were stationed in the different streets, where they were directed to wait for further orders.

Having, in the mean time, assembled at my lodgings the field-officers and all the chief magistrates of the town, I made them acquainted with my intention to proceed that very morning to the execution of a plan I had formed for taking up the beggars and providing for the poor, and asked their immediate assistance.

To show the public that it was not my wish to carry this measure into execution by military force alone (which might have rendered the measure odious), but that I was disposed to show all becoming deference to the civil authority, I begged the magistrates to accompany me and the field-officers of the garrison in the execution of the first and most difficult part of the undertaking, that of arresting the beggars. This they most readily consented to; and we immediately sallied out into the street, myself accompanied by the chief magistrate of the town, and each of the field-officers by an inferior magistrate.

We were hardly got into the street when we were accosted by a beggar who asked us for alms. I went up to him, and laying my hand gently upon his shoulder told him that from thenceforwards begging would not be permitted in Munich; that if he really stood in need of assistance (which would immediately be inquired into) the necessary assistance would certainly be given him, but that begging was forbidden; and, if he was detected in it again, he would be severely punished. I then delivered him over to an orderly sergeant who was following me, with directions to conduct him to the town-hall, and deliver him into the hands of those he should find there to receive him; and then, turning to the officers and magistrates who accompanied me, I begged they would take notice that I had myself, *with my own hands*, arrested the first beggar we had met; and I requested them not only to follow my example themselves, by arresting all the beggars they should meet with, but that they would also endeavour to persuade others, and particularly the officers, non-commissioned officers, and soldiers of the garrison, that it was by no means derogatory to their character as soldiers, or in any wise disgraceful to them, to assist in so *useful* and *laudable* an undertaking. These gentlemen, having cheerfully and unanimously promised to do their utmost to second me in this business, dispersed into the different parts of the town, and with the assistance of the military, which they found everywhere waiting for orders, the town was so thoroughly cleared of beggars *in less than an hour* that not one was to be found in the streets.

Those who were arrested were conducted to the town-hall, where their names were inscribed in printed lists provided for that purpose, and they were then dismissed to their own lodgings, with directions to repair the next day to the newly erected *Military Workhouse* in the Au, where they would find comfortable warm rooms, a good warm dinner every day; and work for all those who were in a condition to labour. They were likewise told that a commission should immediately be appointed to inquire into their circumstances, and to grant them such regular weekly allowances of money, in alms, as they should stand need of; which was accordingly done.

Orders were then issued to all the military guards in the different parts of the town to send out patrols frequently into the streets in their neighbourhood, to arrest all the beggars they should meet with: and a reward was offered for each beggar they should arrest and deliver over to the civil magistrate. The guard of the police was likewise directed to be vigilant; and the inhabitants at large, of all ranks and denominations, were earnestly called upon to assist in completing a work of so much public utility, and which had been so happily begun.[13]

While the working arrangements in the establishment for the beggars, called either the Military Workhouse – since its output was used for clothing the army – or the House of Industry, was exemplary by 18th century standards (10-12 hours working day for men, women and children over 5) the same cannot be said about their food. This was mainly due to Rumford's strange ideas about nutrition, which is surprising since by the end of the 18th century, thanks to Priestly, Cavendish, Lavoisier etc., enough was known of basic chemistry to make some of Rumford's views astounding.

> *Great Importance of the Subject under Consideration. – Probability that Water acts a much more important Part in Nutrition than has hitherto been generally imagined. – Surprisingly small Quantity of solid Food necessary, when properly prepared, for all the Purposes of Nutrition. – Great Importance of the Art of Cookery. – Barley remarkably nutritive when properly prepared. – The Importance of culinary Processes for preparing Food shown from the known Utility of a Practice common in some Parts of Germany of cooking for Cattle. – Difficulty of introducing a Change of Cookery into common Use. – Means that may be employed for that Purpose*

There is, perhaps, no operation of nature which falls under the cognizance of our senses more surprising or more curious than the nourishment and growth of plants and animals; and there is certainly no subject of investigation more interesting to mankind. As providing subsistence is, and ever must be, an object of the first concern in all countries, any discovery or improvement by which the procuring of good and wholesome food can be facilitated must contribute very powerfully to increase the comforts and promote the happiness of society.

That our knowledge in regard to the science of nutrition is still very imperfect, is certain; but I think there is reason to believe that we are upon the eve of some very important discoveries relative to that mysterious operation.

Since it has been known that water is not a simple element, but a *compound*, and capable of being decomposed, much light has been thrown upon many operations of nature which formerly were wrapped in obscurity. In vegetation, for instance, it has been rendered extremely probable that water acts a much more important part than was formerly assigned to it by philosophers; that it serves not merely as a *vehicle* of nourishment, but constitutes at least one part, and probably an essential part, of the *food* of plants, that it is decomposed by them, and contributes *materially* to their growth; and that manures serve rather to prepare the water for decomposition than to form of themselves, substantially and directly, the nourishment of the vegetables.

Now a very clear analogy may be traced between the vegetation and growth of plants and the digestion and nourishment of animals; and as water is indispensably necessary in both processes, and as in one of them (vegetation) it appears evidently to serve as *food*, why should we not suppose it may serve as food in the other? There is, in my opinion, abundant reason to suspect that this is really the case; and I shall now briefly state the grounds upon which this opinion is founded. Having been engaged for a considerable length of time in providing food for the poor at Munich, I was naturally led, as well by curiosity as motives of economy, to make a great variety of experiments upon that subject; and I had not proceeded far in my operations before I began to perceive that they were very important, even much more so than I had imagined.

The difference in the apparent goodness, or the palatableness and apparent nutritiousness, of the same kinds of food, when prepared or cooked in different ways, struck me very forcibly; and I constantly found that the richness or *quality* of a soup depended more upon the proper choice of ingredients, and a proper management of the fire in the combination of those ingredients, than upon the quantity of solid nutritious matter employed, – much more upon the art and skill of the cook than upon the amount of the sums laid out in the market.

I found likewise that the nutritiousness of a soup, or its power of satisfying hunger and affording nourishment, appeared always to be in proportion to its apparent richness or palatableness.

But what surprised me not a little was the discovery of the very small quantity of *solid food* which, when properly prepared, will suffice to satisfy hunger and support life and health, and the very trifling expense at which the stoutest and most laborious man may, in any country be fed.

After an experience of more than five years in feeding the poor at Munich, – during which time every experiment was made that could be devised, not only with regard to the choice of the articles used as food, but also in respect to their different combinations and proportions, and to the various ways in which they could be prepared or cooked, – it was found that the *cheapest*, most *savoury*, and most *nourishing* food that could be provided was a soup composed of pearl barley, pease, potatoes, cuttings of fine wheaten bread, vinegar, salt, and water, in certain proportions.[14]

The following quantities of the above ingredients are needed to feed 1200 people:

	Quantity (lb)	Price in 1800		
		£	s.	d.
Pearl Barley			71	
Peas	66	0	11	3
Potatoes	230			
Bread (Croutons)	70	0	10	2
Salt	20	0	1	2
Vinegar	47	0	1	5
Water	983			
	1487	1	4	0
Add fuel (88 lb Wood or 50 lb Coal)		0	0	2
Total		1	4	2^{15}

[At 1995 prices about £80, or 7p per person]

The method of preparing this soup is as follows: The water and the pearl barley are first put together into the boiler and made to boil, the pease are then added, and the boiling is continued over a gentle fire about two hours. The potatoes are then added (having been previously peeled with a knife, or having been boiled, in order to their being more easily deprived of their skins), and the boiling is continued for about one hour more, during which time the contents of the boiler are frequently stirred about with a large wooden spoon or ladle, in order to destroy the texture of the potatoes, and to reduce the soup to one uniform mass. When this is done, the vinegar and salt are added; and last of all, at the moment it is to be served up, the cuttings of bread.

The soup should never be suffered to boil, or even stand long before it is served up after the cuttings of bread are put to it. It will, indeed, for reasons which will hereafter be explained, be best never to put the cuttings of bread into the boiler at all, but (as is always done at Munich) to put them into the tubs in which the soup is carried from the kitchen into the dining hall; pouring the soup hot from the boiler upon them, and stirring the whole well together with the iron ladles used for measuring out the soup to the poor in the hall.

It is of more importance than can well be imagined that this bread which is mixed with the soup should not be boiled. It is likewise of use that it should be cut as fine or thin as possible; and, if it be dry and hard, it will be some much the better.

The bread we use in Munich is what is called *semmel* bread, being small loaves weighing from two to three ounces; and as we receive this bread in donations from the bakers, it is commonly dry and hard, being that which not being sold in time remains on hand, and becomes stale and unsalable. And we have found by experience that this hard and stale bread answers for our purpose much better than any other; for it renders mastication necessary, and mastication seems very powerfully to assist in promoting digestion. It likewise *prolongs the duration of the enjoyment of eating*, a matter of very great importance indeed, and which has not hitherto been sufficiently attended to.

The quantity of this soup furnished to each person at each meal, or one portion of it (the cuttings of bread included – , is just *one Bavarian pound* in weight; and, as the Bavarian pound is to the pound avoirdupois as 1.123842 to 1, it is equal to about nineteen ounces and nine tenths avoirdupois. Now to those who know that a full pint of soup weighs no more than about sixteen ounces avoirdupois, it will not perhaps, at the first view, appear very extraordinary that a portion weighing near twenty ounces, and consequently making near *one pint and a quarter* of this rich, strong, savoury soup, should be found sufficient to satisfy the hunger of a grown person; but when the matter is examined narrowly and properly analyzed, and it is found that the whole quantity of solid food which enters into the composition of one of these portions of soup does not amount to quite six ounces, it will then appear to be almost impossible that this allowance should be sufficient.

That it is quite sufficient, however, to make a good meal for a strong healthy person, has been abundantly proved by long experience. I have even found that a soup composed of nearly the same ingredients, except the potatoes, but in different proportions, was sufficiently nutritive and very palatable, in which only about *four ounces and three quarters* of solid food entered into the composition of a portion weighing twenty ounces.

But this will not appear incredible to those who know that one single spoonful of *salop*, weighing less than one quarter of an ounce, put into a pint of boiling water, forms the thickest and most nourishing soup that can be taken; and that the quantity of solid matter which enters into the composition of another very nutritive food, *hartshorn jelly* is not much more considerable.

The *barley* in my soup seems to act much the same part as the *salop* in this famous restorative; and no substitute that I could ever find for it, among all the variety of corn and pulse of the growth of Europe, ever produced half the effect, – that is to say, half the nourishment at the same expense. Barley may therefore be considered as the rice of Great Britain.

It requires, it is true, a great deal of boiling; but when it is properly managed it thickens a vast quantity of water, and, as I suppose, *prepares it for decomposition*. It also gives the soup into which it enters as an ingredient a degree of richness which nothing else can give. It has little or no taste itself, but when mixed with other ingredients which are savoury it renders them peculiarly grateful to the palate.

It is a maxim as ancient I believe as the time of Hippocrates, that '*whatever pleases the palate nourishes;*' and I have often had reason to think it perfectly just. Could it be clearly ascertained and demonstrated, it would tend to place *cookery* in a much more respectable situation among the arts than it now holds.

That the manner in which food is prepared is a matter of real importance, and that the water used in that process acts a much more important part than has hitherto been generally imagined, is, I think, quite evident; for it seems to me to be impossible upon any other supposition to account for the appearances. If the very small quantity of solid food which enters into the composition of a portion of some very nutritive soup were to be prepared differently and taken under some other form, – that of bread, for instance, – so far from being sufficient to satisfy hunger and afford a comfortable and nutritive meal, a person would absolutely starve upon such a slender allowance; and no great relief would be derived from drinking *crude* water to fill up the void in the stomach.[16]

Rumford believed that 20 fl.oz., say 560 ml of his nutritious soup could be the main, perhaps sole, daily diet of the inmates of the Workhouse. A.F. Dufton presented a paper at the 1936 meeting of the British Association (*The Lancet*, December 16, 1936, 1535) and gave 960 calories as its calorific value, which is far below the then recommended standard between 3000 and 3600 calories. So, unless the 'ex-beggars' could supplement their dinner at the House of Industry, theirs was a starvation diet.

Nevertheless Rumford's essay should not be brushed aside as unscientific and useless and dangerously misleading stuff. These 200 pages contain a lot of interesting views and culinary tips – though mainly for the mass caterer rather than the gourmet. Thus he suggests that 'these cheap soups may be made exceedingly palatable and savoury by mixing with them a very small quantity of *red herrings* (smoked herrings), minced very fine or pounded in mortar. There is no kind of cheap food, I believe, that has so much taste as red herrings or that communicates its flavour with so much liberality to other eatables...'[17] He also advocates sprinkling some grated strong cheese over the soup after it is dished out. More generally he bemoans the fact that although 'our extensive commerce enables us to procure and we do actually import most of the valuable commodities which are the produce either of the soil, of the ocean or of the industry of man, in all the various regions of the habitable globe: *but the result of the EXPERIENCE OF AGES respecting the use that can be made of these commodities* has seldom been thought worth importing.'[18]

Rumford devotes a whole chapter to Indian Corn (maize)[19] which he regards as even more nourishing than rice. 'In those countries where rice and Indian corn are both produced in the greatest abundance, the negroes have frequently had their option between these two kinds of food and have invariably preferred the latter. The reason they give for their preference they express in strong though not very delicate terms. They say that 'rice turns to water in their bellies and runs off' but *'Indian corn stays with them and makes strong to work'*.[20] He gives several recipes for 'hasty pudding' (identical with Italian polenta) and 'bag pudding' made of Indian meal, both savoury and sweet. He ends the chapter with the exhortation that Indian corn might at least be used in this country as fodder and remarks that 'hogs and poultry ought never to be fed with any other grain. Those who have tasted the pork and the poultry fatted on Indian corn will readily give their assent to this opinion.'[21]

Rumford the Epicure

(Based on the Essay 'Of Excellent Qualities of Coffee and the Art of Making it in the Highest Perfection' *Collected Works*, Vol. V, 205-315.)

The use of science is so to explain the operations which take place in the practice of the arts, and to discover the means of improving them; and there is no process, however simple it may appear to be, that does not afford an ample field for curious and interesting investigation.

Among the numerous luxuries of the table unknown to our forefathers, which have been imported into Europe in modern times, *coffee* may be considered as one of the most valuable.

Its taste is very agreeable and its flavour uncommonly so; but its principal excellence depends on its salubrity and on its exhilarating quality.

It excites cheerfulness without intoxication and the pleasing flow of spirits which it occasions last many hours, and is never followed by sadness, languor or debility.

It diffuses over the whole frame a glow of health, and a sense of ease and well-being which is exceedingly delightful. Existence is felt to be a positive enjoyment, and the mental powers are awakened and rendered uncommonly active.

It has been facetiously observed that there is more wit in Europe since the use of coffee has become general among us; and I do not hesitate to confess that I am seriously of that opinion.

Some of the ablest, most brilliant, and most indefatigable men I have been acquainted with have been remarkable for their fondness for coffee; and I am so persuaded of its powerful effects in clearing up the mind and invigorating its faculties that on very interesting occasions I have several times taken an additional dose of it for that very purpose.

That coffee has greatly contributed to our innocent enjoyments cannot be doubted; and experience has abundantly proved that so far from being unwholesome it is really very salubrious.

This delicious beverage has so often been celebrated, both in prose and verse, that it does not stand in need of my praises to recommend it. I shall therefore confine myself to the humble office of showing how it can be prepared in the greatest perfection.[22]

Rumford first enumerates the conditions which must be satisfied in order to get good coffee.

1. The beans must be freshly roasted. In this connection he carried out some experiments to discover the nature of the substance which is responsible for the all-pervading fragrance of coffee being roasted. In this way he 'condensed this aromatic substance which did not originally exist in the grain. The liquor which resulted from this condensation had an acid taste, was very highly flavoured and as colourless as pure water; but it stained the skin a deep yellow colour which could not be removed by washing with soap and water; and this stain retained a strong smell of coffee for several days. I have made several unsuccessful attempts to preserve this fragrant aromatic matter by transferring it to other substances. Perhaps others may be more fortunate.'[23]

2. Use boiling water to extract the soluble ingredients from the freshly ground beans. Water at lower temperatures gave unsatisfactory results. It is surprising that Rumford did not experiment with water above 100°C by using a 'Papin-digester' (the fore-runner of our pressure cooker) and thus missed being feted as the inventor of espresso.

3. The coffee, while being made and afterwards, should be boiling hot but without actually boiling. Any violent agitation is deleterious.

He designed, presumably after 1805 in Paris, a steam-jacketed filter coffee maker which satisfies the above conditions. The figure, drawn to scale, shows this coffee pot. Many of these coffee pots or coffee urns were manufactured and sold in Paris and Rumford remarked 'I cannot help flattering

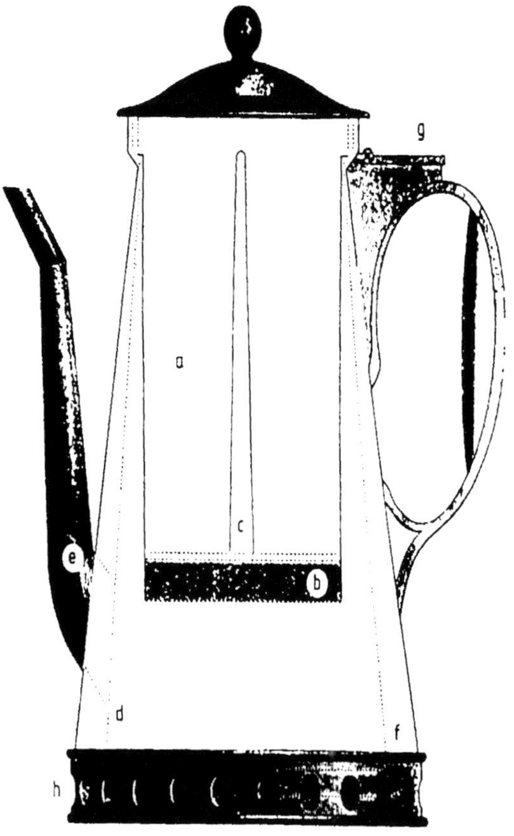

a is the cylindrical strainer, into which the ground coffee is put, in order that boiling-hot water may be poured on it: when this strainer is filled with boiling water (after an ounce of ground coffee has been properly pressed down on its bottom), the quantity of liquid is just sufficient for making four cups of coffee.

b is the ground coffee in its place.

c is the handle of the rammer which is represented in its place.

d is the reservoir for receiving the coffee which descends into it from the strainer; and

e is the spout through which the coffee is poured out.

f is the boiler, into which a small quantity of water is put, for the sole purpose of generating steam for keeping the reservoir hot.

g is the opening by which the water is poured into the boiler or out of it: this opening has a flat cover, which moves on a hinge that is represented in the figure.

myself that they will find their way to England and there meet with approval. I shall never cease to be particularly desirous that my labours to improve the domestic arts may be found useful in that country.'[24]

Rumford also makes the point that coffee is a relatively cheap beverage and should become part of the English diet.

He prescribes 1/4 oz (7 g) of coffee to 4 fl.oz. (113 ml) of water. He also points out that:

> As common brown sugar is quite as nourishing as the best refined loaf sugar, and as a great many persons prefer it for coffee, it appears to me to be extremely probable that coffee may be found to be one of the cheapest kinds of food that can be procured, and more especially in Great Britain.
>
> Half a pint of the best coffee or two full cups may be made with half an ounce of ground coffee, which, if one pound avoirdupois weight of raw coffee can be bought in the shops for twelvepence sterling, will cost only *six sevenths* of a farthing; and, if a pound of brown sugar can be bought for one shilling, one ounce of sugar, which would be a large allowance for two cups of coffee, would cost only three farthings; consequently the materials for making half a pint of coffee would cost less than one penny.
>
> As coffee has a great deal of taste, which it imparts very liberally to the bread which is eaten with it, and as the taste of coffee is very agreeable to all palates, and the use of bread greatly prolongs the duration of the pleasure which this taste excites, a very delicious repast may be made merely with coffee and bread, without either butter or milk.
>
> The taste of coffee predominates in such a manner that the butter would hardly be perceived, and might be omitted without any sensible loss. But I acknowledge that in my opinion the addition of a certain quantity of good cream or milk to coffee improves it very much. Milk, however, is not a very expensive article in Great Britain; and if the butter be omitted, which is by no means necessary (and is even unwholesome), a good breakfast of milk coffee might be provided for a very small sum.
>
> What a difference between such a breakfast and that miserable and unwholesome wash which the poor people in England drink under the name of *tea*!
>
> All the coffee that can be wanted may be had in the British colonies, and paid for in British manufactures; but tea must be purchased in China, and paid for in hard money.[25]

But I must hasten to put an end to this Essay, which has already exceeded the limits to which I had hopes of being able to confine it. Being anxious that it might be read by many persons (as I thought that it would be very useful), I felt the necessity of making it as short as possible. I shall conclude with a few observations on the means that may be employed for rendering the use of coffee more general among the lower classes of society.

In the first place, the method of making *good coffee* must be known; and the utensils necessary in that process must be so contrived as to be cheap and durable, and easy to be managed.

It will be in vain that the laws are repealed which laid restrictions on the free use of coffee, as long as the great mass of the people remain ignorant of its excellent qualities; they will be little disposed to substitute it in the place of another beverage, to which long habit has given them an attachment.

As long as coffee shall continue to be made according to the method generally practiced in England, I shall have no hope of its being preferred to tea; for its qualities are so inferior when prepared in that way that it is hardly possible that it should be much liked.[26]

Conclusion

When possible titles for the 1995 Food Symposium were discussed one suggestion was 'Heroes and Villains'. Where should one place Rumford between these extremes? He certainly was not a villain. Even the 1000 calorie 'nourishing' soup, though inadequate, at least removed the fear of death by starvation. Also, while one may laugh today about Rumford's theory of the nutritious value of water, many of his remarks about the diverse roles of water in cooking stand up to scrutiny.

On the other hand, neither was he one of gastronomy's heroes. But he should be remembered as probably the first notable scientist to use the knowledge, the techniques, the methods of the day to understand the culinary processes and to improve them and he has thus, to use his own words 'powerfully contributed to increase the comforts and enjoyments of mankind.'[27]

REFERENCES

[1] Peter Day's excellent biographical sketch, '...the European Odyssey of Count Rumford', *European Review*, Vol. 3, No.2, 103-111, 1995 is also recommended.
[2] *Collected Works*, I, 227.
[3] C.W. I
[4] C.W. I
[5] C.W. III, 74-78
[6] C.W. III, 80
[7] C.W. III, 85
[8] C.W. III, 81
[9] C.W. III, 160
[10] C.W. III, 222
[11] C.W. III, 223
[12] C.W. V, 29
[13] C.W. V, 36-39
[14] C.W. V, 171-173
[15] C.W. V, 187
[16] C.W. V, 173-177
[17] C.W. V, 215
[18] C.W. V, 217
[19] C.W. V, 217-273
[20] C.W. V, 219
[21] C.W. V, 243
[22] C.W. V, 265-266 (selection)
[23] C.W. V, 269
[24] C.W. V, 290-292
[25] C.W. V, 302
[26] C.W. V, 306-307
[27] C.W. V, 308-309

Nils Gustav Dalén, Swedish Nobel Physicist and Inventor of the Aga Stove

Janet Laurence

Nils Gustav Dalén was the third of five children born to a farmer in Stenstorp, south-west Sweden on November 30th 1869. Their mother was apparently determined to give her children a good education. Of Gustaf's three brothers, Gottfrid became a priest, Albin a doctor and Sweden's foremost eye specialist, and Hjalmar a lawyer. Their sister, Hildur, became a teacher.

After Gustav completed his preliminary education, he studied agriculture, horticulture and dairy farming and displayed a remarkable mechanical talent. It seems that it was decided that Gustaf's career would lie in farming, where he could make practical use of his mechanical abilities. According to the Swedish Cultural Department in London, who consulted their reference books for me, he became a gardener and dairyman.

Dalén, though, had more than mechanical aptitude. He had an enquiring mind that could produce original solutions to engineering problems. While still at school he designed and constructed several improved versions of farm equipment. And he had a strong sense of initiative. This led him to offer his device for measuring butterfat in milk to Gustav de Laval, the great Swedish engineer who invented the cream separator and built up the international Laval company. In the way that so often happens with original research and development, de Laval had just patented a similar system. However, he encouraged Dalén to continue inventing and suggested he should study engineering. And around this time Dalén was attracted to a young lady who firmly stated she could never see herself as a farmer's wife.

In 1892, at the age of twenty-two, Dalén enrolled at the Chalmers Institute in Gothenburg, graduating four years later with a degree in mechanical engineering. He then studied post graduate work for a year at the Federal Institute of Technology in Zurich, Switzerland. Back home again in 1897, Dalén settled in Stockholm, established himself as a consulting engineer and began conducting research into hot air turbines, compressors and air pumps. In 1900 he and a colleague founded an engineering company, Dalén and Alsing. At the same time as they were trying to exploit their inventions (which included a successful milking machine), Dalén also joined Swedish Carbide and Acetylene Company as technical manager.

Throughout his life Dalén had only to be presented with a problem for him immediately to start trying to solve it. The Swedish Carbide and Acetylene Company in the same year that Dalén joined them acquired the Scandinavian patent rights to a French invention called Acétylène Dissous, known as a gas accumulator. Acetylene with its intense light, far brighter than that produced by any other medium, was considered ideal for lighting buoys and beacons, except that even with the French Acétylène Dissous process the gas was too volatile to be used with any safety.

Dalén first designed an improved gas accumulator which enabled the gas to be safely transported. Then he invented a valve that delivered the gas to a pilot flame in short bursts. This produced a series of bright flashes and reduced gas consumption to a tenth of its previous rate. The invention transformed shipping. It meant a single cylinder of acetylene could light a buoy for six months or more, meaning it could be left unattended for that time. So light buoys and beacons could be installed in places where manned light stations had not been viable, making night time traffic possible in a wide range of shipping channels and around the coast, increasing safety and reducing journey times. It also meant that many manned beacons could now be left unattended and servicing could be organised at favourable weather times. At one and the same time the safety of ships was enormously increased and navigation costs were greatly reduced.

Dalén then went even further and invented a sun valve that cut off the flash during daylight times, thereby again greatly reducing gas consumption. It was a device of singular simplicity, beautiful in its efficiency. Dalén used the difference in the expansion properties of dark and shiny metals when exposed to light to stop the supply of gas to the beacon during daylight hours. Dalén's sunvalve consisted of four vertical metallic rods enclosed in a transparent glass tube and fixed at their upper ends. Three highly polished rods surround a fourth blackened one. When heated by sunlight reflected onto it by the polished rods, the blackened rod expanded in length and depressed a lever that closed the gas vent, thus extinguishing the light. At nightfall, cut off from sunlight, the blackened rod cooled and contracted, which permitted the spring activated lever to rise and open the vent, allowing the passage of gas that was then ignited by a bypass jet. The apparatus could be adjusted to light up at any degree of darkness.'[1]

When Thomas Edison first heard of the sunvalve he is reported to have said, 'It won't work.' Even after he'd been told that sunvalves were in use, turning gas beacons on and off automatically at sunset and sunrise, he apparently refused to believe it. He wasn't the only one to doubt the efficiency of the device. The German Patent Office in Berlin at first flatly refused Dalén's patent application. He had to go to Berlin and demonstrate the fact that the sunvalve worked. Dalén's simple but ingenious lighthouse inventions provided a system that is still in use today.

In 1909 the Swedish Carbide and Acetylene Company changed its name to the Swedish Gas Accumulator Company, later the Amalgamated Gas Accumulator Company, and appointed Dalén as Managing Director. By 1912 Dalén's name and the AGA lighting system were internationally famous in lighthouse and shipping circles. The company had grown rapidly and won, against keen competition, the order for the Panama Canal lighting system. A new plant was being built at Lidingö, design work on gas mantles to provide even stronger light was in the final stages, and experiments and tests to improve the system and its safety were being constantly carried out.

In September 1912 one of the safety tests being carried out in a deserted quarry near Stockholm went wrong and Dalén was badly burned. His eye specialist brother fought to save his sight but failed. The system that had brought light and safety to so many sailors had now condemned its inventor to darkness. The news that Gustav Dalén had been awarded the Nobel prize in physics 'for his invention of self-regulating mechanisms which in combination with gas accumulators are used for illumination in beacons and buoys came a few weeks after the accident. Dalén was not able to attend the ceremony, one of his brothers accepted the award on his behalf, and so did not deliver a Nobel lecture.

At first Dalén thought he would have to resign his position as Managing Director. Friends and colleagues apparently encouraged him to remain, pointing out that he could have reports read to him and drawings made to his instructions by other engineers. He allowed himself to be persuaded and remained as head of AGA until his death in 1937. Dalén developed the ability to memorize enormous amounts of information and figures and continued to invent new technical ideas.

The girl who had stated she could never become a farmer's wife had married Dalén the engineer. Convalescing at home after the accident, Dalén became struck by how tied his wife appeared to be to her stove. It must have been a wood burning range, very popular in Sweden at the time with its vast quantities of woodland, because apparently she spent a lot of time tending to it, carrying in the wood, storing it and feeding it to the range, then more time looking after the food while it was cooking, checking that the process was proceeding satisfactorily, no doubt also complaining about the inefficiency of the oven and the fluctuating nature of the heat.

So here was this inventive mind for the moment deprived of mental stimulus and its life work, with no books, no reports to monitor, no drawing board to work on; an inventive mind that had always grappled with practical problems, seeking solutions that had eluded others. And here was a practical problem that was making his wife's housekeeping difficult. Dalén decided to improve his wife's cooking facilities by inventing a stove that cooked efficiently, operated economically and required the minimum of attention. The very parameters that had transformed the safe navigation of shipping and earned him the thanks of sailors the world over, were now applied to designing a stove that would earn him the gratitude of cooks.

Over a period of seven years, Gustav Dalén designed one of the most efficient of all stoves. As might have been expected from the inventor of the sunvalve, it was magnificently simple in the way it utilised scientific principles (see description in the Appendix). It was economical in its use of fuel, it cooked superbly with utmost reliability and, equally important in Swedish winters, it provided a background radiant heat which kept the kitchen warm. In those days not every Swedish home had central heating; many relied on a series of large, efficient stoves throughout the house to keep their homes warm. These stoves, many highly decorative, dispersed their heat through enamelled tiles and its was probably these that inspired the finish of the AGA.

Food has always been important to the Swedes. The average Swedish family cook of the time produced what might be called country fare. Many housewives were, in fact, farmers' wives. Hearty casseroles, roasts, boiled meats, a wide variety of meat farces, including the famous Swedish meatballs, and patés, were produced in large quantities. Most housewives also did a great deal of baking, making their own bread as well as a wide range of cakes and biscuits. All food that was ideal for the AGA.

The patent for the new stove was taken out in 1922. Dalén's Aktiebolaget (Amalgamated) Gas Accumulator Company then arranged to put it into production. The prototype AGA was very similar to the popular two oven version that is sold today. It had two ovens, the first with a temperature of about 250°C, the lower oven with one of about 95°C. It had two top plates, the left-hand plate with a temperature of about 400°C, the right of about 250°C. The fire-box, which was designed to use coke, reckoned to be the most economic of all fuels then available, held sufficient fuel to keep the stove going for twenty-four hours, during which time only one riddling of the grate was needed. A hot-water tank holding about 40 litres was built into the cookers. Its sole purpose was the supply of hot water for the kitchen. Later boilers to heat radiators and water for the bathrooms became available.

The first AGA cooker was put on the market in June 1929, called after the initials of the company that made it, the Amalgamated Gas Accumulator Company. The company had branches in various parts of the world and the stove sold well. According to the *AGA Journal*, of January 1932, 'At first a good many people were sceptical of the various advantages claimed for it in the advertisements, but when these advantages were confirmed by personal experience and by testimonials as to its efficiency, sales mounted with increasing rapidity. True, many thought the price high, but it was soon realized that thanks to its amazing economy the cooker was in many instances capable of paying for itself in three or four years. It is indeed a striking fact that those who have had experience with the AGA cooker for any length of time have frequently told us that they consider they made an extremely good bargain when they bought an AGA.

The original AGA had been designed for private households but soon a number of different models were produced that were more suitable for commercial establishments. In the early thirties, four large and two smaller cookers and six hot cupboards were installed in the Hotel Bondeheimen in Oslo, which prepared food daily for 400 guests, 100 of whom (according to the *AGA Journal*) took breakfast and 300 dinner. 'A pretty good idea is gained of what this installation means financially to the concern in question when one realises that the cost of fuel before the AGA Cookers were installed amounted to about 3,800 kronor (close on £200) a year whereas now the corresponding expenditure will be limited to about 700 kronor (about £35).

In the same issue, the *AGA Journal* reported that the previous November the thousandth AGA Cooker was sold in Switzerland and the five thousandth AGA Cooker in Sweden. 'Moreover, we were able to claim just then that the total number of cookers sold throughout the world had reached 20,000. No less than over 12,000 of these had been sold by our English friends Messrs Aga Heat Ltd., to whom we take this opportunity of expressing our sincere compliments on the keen and successful manner in which they have promoted the sale of the Cooker.' In 1929 the AGA was imported into the UK by Bell's Asbestos & Heat Engineering Supplies Limited. In 1932 Bell's associated company, Bell's Heat Appliances Ltd of Slough, started manufacturing the AGA under licence at Smethwick.

According to my Swedish mother, after the Second World War, with the advent of reliable gas and electric stoves, Swedish housewives ripped out their faithful AGA stoves and installed the more modern versions. It became unfashionable, she says, to have an AGA. Also I suspect that by then central heating had become almost standard and the background heat supplied by the AGA was no longer needed. Also the drawbacks of an AGA had no doubt been noted.

Superb stove that it is, there are certain cooking functions that are difficult on an AGA. Any baking that requires an accuracy of temperature, such as choux pastry, even puff pastry, can be hit and miss. Using the top plates for any length of time, for making delicate sauces, for instance, lowers the overall heat available drastically. If your AGA provides the household hot water and you have a bath before your dinner party, expect the meat to take much longer to cook. AGA claim that frying can be done in the roasting oven, but bacon won't crisp, sautés aren't successful. If you are the sort of cook who is adventurous, likes haute cuisine, the AGA has serious drawbacks. Also the fact that you can't smell food cooking in the oven isn't all good news. Many charred chunks of forgotten food have been found by forgetful AGA owners. And unless you get into the habit of using long gauntlet oven gloves, you are branded an AGA owner by the burn stripes bestowed as you try to get food out from the back of the oven. Some AGAs, particularly oil fired, have an annoying trick of going out when the wind blows down the flue from a particular direction and can be extremely difficult to relight.

To be completely happy with an AGA, it is necessary to suit your cooking to what it does best. Either forget the rest or install a conventional stove as well.

There was no drop off in demand from Great Britain for the AGA after the Second World War. Here few houses were centrally heated and fewer and fewer servants meant landed wives had to turn to doing the cooking themselves. In the depths of the country, in large, draughty houses, the AGA was a life saver. The AGA, with its constantly available heat, its ability to more or less look after itself, its superb cooking qualities for the roasts and casseroles that suited country life styles, was the perfect stove. Owners quickly mastered the art of doing the baking after a roast had reduced the heat of the main oven; the porridge cooked overnight in the slow oven, as did first the stockpot and then the thick vegetable soups that provided lunches, suppers and starters. Farmers' wives found that the slow oven could keep food hot until the fading light at last drove their harvesting husbands home for their meals. The dogs, damp Barbours and wet shoes were dried off in front of it, kitchen cloths and socks hung on the handy rail. The door of the warming oven on the four oven model was left open as newborn chicks, cold and wet lambs and sickly puppies were popped inside to revive in the gentle heat.

Such was the demand for the AGA in Great Britain that in 1947 the manufacturing unit opened at Ketley, Telford to increase the production capacity and the De Luxe models were introduced, featuring chrome lids instead of the original polished black, a styled top plate and raised splash back. In 1941 all existing cooker models, both domestic and heavy duty, had been withdrawn and replaced by a range of units with standardised parts. This 'AGA standard' was in production until 1972. In 1964, the oil fired AGA was introduced, in 1968 the gas fired AGA and 1975 the Electric AGA. Originally produced in non-cast iron styling, in 1985 a cast iron electric model was introduced.

As for colours, the original AGA had had a black top and cream body. In 1956 pale blue, pale green, grey and white were also offered, either the same colour all over or with a black top. In 1961 the coloured tops were abandoned in favour of all black tops. In 1968 red, dark blue, dark green, yellow and black body colours were added to the range, indicating the increasing popularity and fashionableness of the stove. In 1971 yellow and pale green were withdrawn, in 1975 grey, pale blue and black were withdrawn. 1991 saw the addition of jade and 1992 of claret and emerald; brown was withdrawn.

Today the AGA is only produced in Great Britain. The Midlands-based AGA-Rayburn company manufacture both types of stove at the same foundry, the oldest in the world, to be sent round the world. Rayburns are assembled at the factory but AGAs have always been assembled at their point of use, so that the idiosyncracies of individual houses can be taken into account.

Two models are available, one almost identical to the original, two oven model, and a rather larger, four oven version. This has a baking oven and a warming oven in addition to the roasting and simmering ovens, and a wide, uncovered, warming plate beside the boiling plate.

Nils Gustav Dalén died on December 9th, 1937. He had built up one of Sweden's most diversified enterprises. Of the some two hundred and fifty patents the company took out during Dalén's lifetime, he is credited with the invention, alone or in part, of roughly half. He and his managers established the AGA Company internationally, setting up subsidiary companies in some thirty different countries. Dalén also served on the boards of many organizations and committees. He was a highly respected figure in both the scientific and business worlds. In 1937 he was diagnosed as suffering from inoperable cancer. His indomitable willpower and determination kept him at work until just before his death. For several days afterwards, ships entering Stockholm harbour lowered their flags to half mast as they passed the waterfront AGA plant in a final tribute to the man who had increased the safety of their lives.

The AGA company went from strength to strength. By the sixties, a hundred years after Dalén's birth, the company no longer made stoves but it had grown into one of Sweden's most diversified enterprises specialising in gas and electronics. Today, in 1995, the electronics operations have been discontinued and AGA is one of the world's largest gas companies; its key products oxygen, nitrogen and argon. The group produces and sells industrial and medical gases in some thirty countries in Europe, the US and Latin America and employs over 10,000 people.

Dalén could never have foreseen the way his perfect stove would become an eighties status symbol. The young and upwardly mobile of that era embraced the idea of country living, epitomised for them by polished chintz, swagged curtains and live-in kitchens whose state-of-the-art technology was humanised by the favourite stove of the landed gentry, the AGA. Serious cooks overcame its drawbacks by installing a conventional stove as well. There were even urban flat dwellers who had their floors specially strengthened to take the weight of an AGA.

By the mid eighties some 5,000 AGAs a year were being sold in Australia, New Zealand and France as well as the UK. In 1986 dealerships were established in the US, with John Updike being quoted as the owner of an aged, cream-coloured model which had come with his Massachusetts house, 'The previous owner loved her AGA and used to talk about it to us as if she had passed on a great treasure. Her eyes would get moist at the thought of not having it anymore.'[2] Americans were told that Princess Diana and Prince Charles had installed a blue model at Highgrove and that Paul McCartney had a red one.[3]

Cookery writers specialising in the AGA appeared, Mary Berry began giving lessons on using it. Cheaper versions enjoyed almost equal popularity—and others appeared that were equally expensive. By the mid-eighties, cooking instructions for AGA users were given in addition to gas marks and Fahrenheit and centigrade temperatures on that popular cookery television show *Food and Drink*.

AGA-Rayburn are coy about divulging sales figures these days. However, they have recently taken on a new overseas development manager and claim that the market is still expanding. The AGA sells throughout Europe, there are dealerships in New Zealand, Australia and the Far East and recently a model was sent to Siberia. The US dealerships are continuing though the number sold annually is not great and as far as the general American public are concerned, the AGA is unknown. I have had several letters from American readers asking exactly what is the AGA that I mention in my novels.

The price of an AGA has always been high. Servicing is carried out once or twice yearly by specially trained technicians, which is also expensive. When the stove was launched on the Swedish market in 1929, it cost 950 Swedish Crowns, as against 260 Crowns for a wood range, 400 Crowns for a gas stove and 650 Crowns for an electric stove, but the AGA company was able to demonstrate that their stove was dramatically cheaper to run. Prices today for an AGA range from £3,575 for a two oven gas fired AGA with a conventional flue to £5,850 for an electric fired model. Four oven AGAs range from £4,600 for a gas fired stove with conventional flue to £6,000 for an electric model. But what is money when you are buying life style?

Acknowledgements

I am indebted to the AGA-Rayburn company of the UK and the AGA company of Sweden for much information on the AGA stove and its history. The AGA company of Sweden have also provided the background information on Gustav Dalén. Other sources used:

Nobel Prize Winners (as above)

Larousse Dictionary of Scientists, Ed. Hazel Muir, 1994

Biographical Encyclopaedia of Scientists, second edition, published by Institute of Physics Publishing, Bristol and Philadelphia, 1981, 1983, 1994.

Appendix

Technical description of the AGA as contained in AGA Journal, June 1930[4]

> The AGA cooker is simultaneously an accumulating and a direct-acting stove. How this has been made possible will be seen from the technical description given below. By this means the cooker possesses the merits of both the above-mentioned stoves, while at the same time it lacks their disadvantages. In order to ensure the highest economy, the heat must be created by a technical process, which, by using the cheapest raw material obtainable, will develop a maximum of thermal units. After a careful study of this problem, it became evident that the combustion of coke was the process sought for. The AGA cooker is therefore based on fuel of this kind. Anthracite may also be used, the only disadvantage being the increase of about 50% in the cost of fuel.
>
> Economy further required that the losses involved in the smoke carrying away a certain amount of heat should be reduced to a minimum. This, on the other hand, asked for a combustion brought as near perfection as possible, but neither with air in excess nor with lack of air. To render this possible the firebox must be well insulated in order to be able to maintain the ignition temperature of the fuel even when accidental interruptions occur in the normal combustion. All inner heat-conducting parts of the AGA cooker are therefore insulated from the outer casing, partly by means of silicious earth and partly by asbestos rings and frames. The consumption of fuel is hereby brought down to 3-3 1/2 kilos of coke per 24 hours, requiring 1/3 litre of air per second for

combustion. Owing to the small quantity of combustion gas per unit of time a low velocity of the escaping fumes is obtained, which allows nearly all the carbon monoxide to be converted into carbon dioxide, and also a maximum heat capacity to be delivered to the various parts of the cooker instead of being lost up the chimney.

Lengthy researches have shown that the smoke from an AGA cooker rarely contains more than 0.6% of carbon monoxide; the combustion as a rule taking place with almost theoretical completeness. The average amount of carbon dioxide is about 16%. In using 3.5 kilos of coke per 24 hours with 9% of ashes and 4% of moisture, about 23,000 calories per 24 hours are thus obtained. The total losses due to preheating the air, the super-heating of the moisture, the super-heating and gasifying of the moisture in the coke and the losses due to the escaping carbon monoxide, carbon dioxide and nitrogen gases, amount to about 3,800 calories. Thus about 19,200 calories remain for the heating of the kitchen, the cooking and supply of hot water, and the efficiency of the cookery may therefore be said to be about 84%. As a matter of fact the above 19,000 calories are all radiated into the room in which the cooker is erected and in consequence the kitchen will be adequately heated during the winter. Notwithstanding this fact, the cooker can also be used in the summer, the radiation of its heat not causing the slightest inconvenience on account of the constant and continual combustion and the comparatively low temperature thereby obtained.

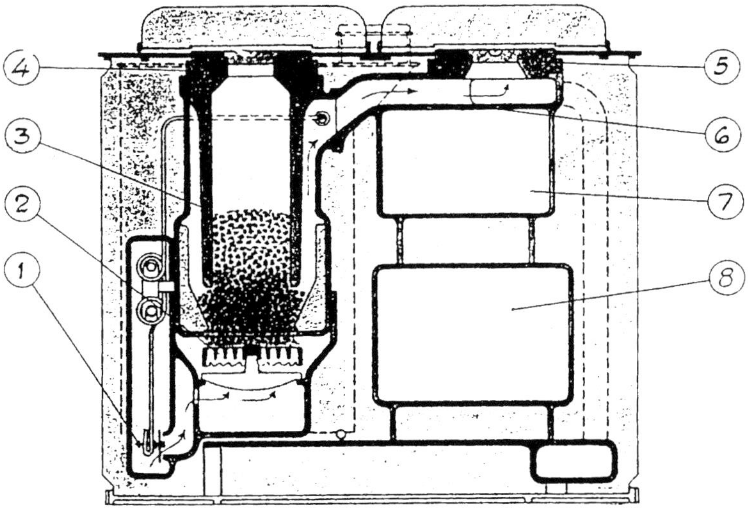

Cross section of the AGA-cooker.

The grate (2, on the above illustration), where the combustion takes place, is situated inside the ash-room door, which is visible from the outside and should always be kept closed. The grate is of a special rotating type and is very easy to keep free from refuse and ashes simply by riddling. The necessary air for the combustion is regulated by means of a thermostatic valve (1) which automatically closes when the cooker becomes too hot, and which opens when the temperature tends to drop. The cooker automatically maintains a constant temperature by means of this device. The regulating device can to a certain degree be adjusted as required by turning an indicator, and this also forms a valuable contribution to the applicability of the cooker.

The combustion gases when passing to the chimney transmit their heat to the accumulating iron masses (3 and 6) which connect the two hot plates (4 and 5) and the ovens. The left-hand plate has a temperature of about 400°C and the right about 250°C, which is the same as that of the baking oven (7), and finally the lower oven (8), about 95°C. The fire-box, situated above the ash grate, is adapted to accommodate the amount of fuel required for 24 hours. When, therefore, the fire-box has been filled and the grate riddled, the combustion of the fuel will automatically be maintained, the only further attention necessary during a period of 24 hours being one more riddling of the grate.

The hot-water tank is built into the cooker and holds about 40 litres of water. A tap cock is placed on the front panel of the cooker, and a drain cock for complete emptying and cleaning of the tank is also provided. The replenishing with cold water may be done either by hand or by connecting the tank to the water supply pipe, as desired. The roasting and baking oven of the AGA cooker has been highly appreciated for its even heat and good baking qualities. The temperature of the oven may be easily ascertained from the thermometer on the door. The steam and the smell of baking are carried off by means of a pipe connected to the flue.

The lower oven is roomy and can be provided with a sliding plate in order to enable the convenient removal of pot and kettles, even if they have been placed at the very back of the oven. The cooking is as a rule simplified to a great extent by using the lower oven. All that is necessary is to bring the pot to the boil on one of the hot plates and then to remove it to the lower oven, where the cooking is completed without any trouble or any further attention. By its well-adapted temperature, which is somewhat below boiling point, the danger of over-cooking is eliminated. In the opinion of experts the cooking of the food should preferably be completed at a temperature of somewhat below 100°C, as the vital juices and vitamins so valuable to the organism are thereby preserved as far as possible. In ordinary cooking nothing is gained by violent boiling; on the contrary the heat is only wasted in producing steam which makes the kitchen unpleasant and also tends to increase the cleaning work.

Ordinary flat irons can be heated quickly and effectively on the hot plates.

There then follows a detailed examination of the comparative costs of running an AGA compared with other stoves. The findings are summarized as follows:

SUMMARY OF COMPARISONS.

	Wood range	AGA cooker	Gas stove	AGA cooker	Electric stove	AGA cooker
Cost of fuel per year . Sw. Cr.	260—390	55—65	105—315	55—65	175—330	55—65
Deduction for heating abt. »	20	40	15	40	15	40
Balance............ »	240—370	15—25	90—300	15—25	160—315	15—25
Initial cost .... »	250	950	400	950	650	950
Difference in price between AGA cooker & other ranges .... »	—	700	—	550	—	300
10 % interest & amortization thereon ..... »	—	70	—	55	—	30
Comparable cost per year »	240—370	85—95	90—300	70—80	160—315	45—55
Cost per year in comparison with that of the AGA cooker	282—390%	—	128—375%	—	355—570%	—

...In the construction of the AGA cooker aesthetic and hygienic requirements have been most carefully studied. The top has been finished in black and the front panel in white enamel, which renders it easy to keep clean and smart in appearance. The covers for the plates are polished and all fittings are nickle-plated. From an economical, aesthetic and hygienic point of view the AGA cooker may be said to fulfil all the reasonable requirements that may be expected from a modern kitchen range.

E. Palm

REFERENCES

[1] *Nobel Prize Winners*, ed. Tyler Wasson, H.W. Wilson Company, New York 1987, see entry of Nils Dalén.
[2] *Star Tribune* of May 7th, 1989.
[3] *USA Today*, 1986-01-02.
[4] This house organ was published in English for the international market.

MacAusland
and
Gourmet: The Magazine of Good Living
1941 to 1980

Margaret Leibenstein

It was January 1941 and World War II raged in Europe, Africa and the Pacific. In America, four years after saying he saw 'one third of a nation ill-housed, ill-clad and ill-nourished,'[1] Franklin D. Roosevelt's words still resonated. Yet it was in this international climate of terror and domestic privation that *Gourmet: The Magazine of Good Living* was launched.

Some might have thought it a less than propitious time to initiate a journal dedicated to developing 'a finer appreciation of food in this country...', a magazine whose publisher believed that 'more thought should be given both to the preparation of foods and to the manner of eating them,' and whose stated aim was 'to eliminate the attitude ... of eating merely to satisfy one's hunger.'[2] This was, after all, an era where many Americans felt that the primary purpose of eating was in fact the satisfaction of hunger; a time when too many of them couldn't even get enough food to do that.

A Gallup poll conducted at the time found that '...approximately four families in every ten thought they were going without food that [made] for better health chiefly because they [didn't] have the money.'[3] The poll found that 40% of Americans (approximately 13,000,000 families) claimed '...they would be more healthy if they had more money each week to buy food.'[4] Of those polled, 37% reported they would spend additional money on meat, beef being preferred; 31% specified vegetables, potatoes leading the list; 27% said fruit—'including fresh and stewed fruits'[5]; almost three-quarters of the 21% answering that dairy products were what they would buy, specified milk as their choice, 16% (frequently persons on *relief*, the term then in use for welfare, or the dole) simply wished for 'good solid food'; 7% would spend the additional monies on bread and cereals, including flour and cornmeal; eggs 7%; 5% on foods with a large sugar content; 2% on 'food with more vitamins'; and all other answers comprised 14%.[6]

How then could anyone have believed that this was the time to begin a glossy, upscale magazine containing reminiscences of drives through Burgundy in a 'hired Hispano' visiting the vineyards of Gevrey, Morey, Chambolle, Vougeot, Meursault, and Pommard; one that contained recipes for Crabmeat en Gelée, Hot Madrilène, or French Creamed Oysters that began with 'Put one cup of butter into the top of a lighted chafing dish;...'?[7] Earle R. MacAusland believed it. He was determined that if there was no interest in fine food, he would forge it and, as history proved, starting *Gourmet* when, unbeknownst to most, the country was being forced out of its provincial isolationism and dragged into economic recovery by the fast approaching war, proved to be either remarkable prescience or the greatest good luck.

Earle R. MacAusland was born in Taunton, Massachusetts, in 1892, one of three sons and a daughter born to Scottish immigrant parents. His father was an accomplished silversmith who worked for the venerable firm of Reed & Barton Silvermasters. When the elder MacAusland became the general manager of that firm, he moved the family from Taunton to Beacon Hill in Boston.

Although the MacAuslands were not wealthy there was always sterling silver on the table and Earle grew up believing that one needn't be rich to appreciate the finer things in life.

He was expected to follow in the footsteps of his older brothers and become an orthopaedic surgeon. But, as he later explained, he couldn't bear the sight of blood and, having flunked Latin, he couldn't get into Harvard. Instead, he enrolled in the Massachusetts Institute of Technology to study engineering. This proved a poor move. After only one year he left college.

While a student, he shared an apartment in Boston with his brothers, struggling young doctors. Earle was designated the cook and often visited the old Fanueil Marketplace to 'squeeze the melons' (his term for shopping for fresh ingredients). There he learned it wasn't necessary to be able to afford expensive food in order to eat well; that the simplest dishes, if they were properly prepared using fresh, wholesome ingredients, could be delicious. His cook-from-scratch philosophy later became one of the elements that differentiated *Gourmet* from its competitors.

His career as a cook, however, ended with the end of his student days. On the advice of his father he left Massachusetts and went to New York to look for work more to his liking.

MacAusland was hired by a publishing group to sell advertising space in their national 'ladies' magazines and he soon found himself in Chicago as their Mid-West Advertising Manager. He later became Vice President and Advertising Manager of *Parent Magazine* whose financial success, with characteristic modesty, he ascribed to his own efforts.

Working for someone else, though, didn't prove satisfying. He quit his job and began his own magazine. It was a disastrous decision. The venture ultimately left him bankrupt. With no prospects at age 40, he returned to New York.

Times were extremely difficult. The Great Depression was in full swing and he was penniless. MacAusland knew he could not go on that way for long, so he was particularly primed for any idea that might result in success. The idea did, indeed, present itself.

When asked how *Gourmet* was born, he often said 'I was sitting in my Packard convertible with my poodle by my side, driving out to the suburbs to see a lady friend and I was thinking about the S.S. Pierce Catalogue.' In other words, why not a *magazine* devoted to fine food.

With the skill and self-confidence bordering on arrogance, of an experienced advertising man, he convinced his father and brother to lend him the money to produce the first issue of *Gourmet*. It was started on a shoe string. The first year he had to sell advertisements during the day and edit copy at night in order to bring it out. By the time the second issue was on the stands he had however acquired two wealthy backers; Gladys Guggenheim Straus, of the publishing house of Farrar, Straus and Giroux, and Ralph Reinhold.

The first headquarters were in the old art deco building at 330 W. 42nd St. in Manhattan which had been the headquarters of McGraw Hill Publishing. Within the year they had moved to a fourteen room penthouse duplex in the Plaza Hotel which had once been Conrad Hilton's. The new headquarters were elegant, as befitted a magazine devoted to fine living, and was a monument to Mr MacAusland's belief that 'if you can't go first class, better not go at all.'

It was said of Mr Mac (as his employees sometimes called him), that he always looked the part. He was a living example of the epicure and gentleman. When he appeared in the lobby of the Plaza, wearing an English handmade suit and homburg hat, with his poodle on a leash, if someone asked who he was and was told 'the publisher of *Gourmet*' they would have said, 'of course'. But he had an irascible temperament and was known to fly into a rage at the slightest provocation.

One day MacAusland was seen hauling the magazine's distinguished restaurant critic along the red carpet which led from the penthouse's private elevator to the rotunda where the receptionist sat, shouting 'Out! Out!. How could you? Absolutely no bribery will be tolerated.' Apparently someone had sent the reviewer a case of champagne in gratitude for a good review. It was entirely unsolicited, but that was not sufficient excuse for MacAusland. The Champagne was returned immediately. Accepting gratuities by reviewers was strictly forbidden.

Another time, a couple of subscribers had just stepped off the elevator intending to visit the headquarters of their favorite magazine when they were confronted by a very angry Mr MacAusland shouting and dragging some poor hapless employee through the rotunda to his office. When they were out of sight a quick-witted receptionist smiled at the visitors and said: 'It's a rehearsal for our Christmas play.'

His was a noisy, quick to ignite, anger, but it was also quickly dissipated and since he forgot quickly he was surprised that others did not. Opposition often triggered his tirades and perhaps it was his anger that prompted Samuel Chamberlain and James Beard to leave the magazine after many years of association.

From the beginning MacAusland, whose opinions were never clouded by doubt, conceived *Gourmet* not as a 'woman's service' magazine but very much a man's magazine that would also appeal to women. To this end he hired writers whose professional interests were not necessarily food but who were accomplished and recognised story tellers. Recipes, on the other hand, were supplied by professional food writers and hotel chefs like Louis de Gouy and the *chef de cuisine* of the Ritz-Carlton Hotel, Louis Diat, who was credited with 'inventing' *vichyssoise*.

While the circulation was slowly climbing it was advertising that was the magazine's life's blood and for years revenue depended heavily on the liquor industry.

The '4 to 1' dry martini was the ultimate in chic and the men who were sole importers of Beefeaters gin introduced it to the American public in *Gourmet*. Beefeaters soon became the major selling label. In addition, ads for expensive wines, whiskies, liquors and, of course, Champagnes aimed at male readers, bordered almost every page. Food ads were conspicuously small in number.

It must be remembered that such items as olive oils, aromatic vinegars, prosciutto di Parma, Vidalia onions, even the mail order *filet mignon* that grace the pages of today's magazines were simply not available, and MacAusland was determined to keep ads for canned foods out. *Gourmet* was to remain a cook-from-scratch journal.

Articles and columns appearing in the early issues were about food and wine, but it was the quality of the writing that set them apart from the content of 'women's' magazines. Often the authors were men, but women writers such as M.F.K. Fisher and Clementine Paddleford, whose column 'food flashes' appeared monthly, more than matched their male colleagues in wit and literary quality. It was, after all, in the pages of *Gourmet* that M.F.K. Fisher serialized her now famous *Alphabet for Gourmets*.

During the war (1941-1945), Samuel Chamberlain was a regular contributor, vividly describing his experiences in pre-war France. Then from its liberation well into the 1950s, he reported on his epicurean tours through the French provinces. This series later became the core of his book *Bouquet de France*.[8]

During this period James Beard wrote the restaurant column. One such, entitled 'A Few Paris Restaurants' is amusing to read today in light of present day travel experiences. He begins by pointing out his problem in choosing a restaurant to review, there being so many good ones, then goes on to tell of his trip to Paris. 'The first thrill of this trip—and I am certain that anyone who travels Air France feels the same—is feeling that you are in France the moment the plane door is closed.'[9] He then goes on to extol the meal that followed. We can but pine for those long lost days. Beard's experience was clearly a far cry from what Calvin Trilling refers to as today's 'affliction of an airline meal.'[10]

Lucius Beebe wrote 'Along the Boulevard', a monthly column whose subject was the activities of New York, San Francisco and occasionally, when business or personal commitments brought him back to his home town, Boston's society. It was written in a style that had the sardonic flavor of the 'Algonquin round table'. Not surprising, since Beebe frequented the Algonquin Hotel restaurant where he hobnobbed with writers like Dorothy Parker, Bennet Cerf, Robert Benchly, Robert Sherwood, Ogden Nash and others, many of whom later shared the pages of *Gourmet* with him.

Though he was always amusing, his column smacked of the snob he probably was. He reported on the celebrities he'd seen at parties, the theater, or restaurants, and he rarely pulled his punches. In one issue he described the food at a very prominent restaurant as being so bad that 'the screams of the dead and dying could be heard outside.' It was a miracle that no one sued for libel.

In subsequent years authors such as Joseph Wechsberg, Leslie Charteris, Alvin Kerr, Frederick S. Wildman, Jr., Roy Andries de Groot, and many others filled the magazine with well written, witty, always informative, articles. Readers were treated to historical pieces on gastronomes such as Escoffier and Alexandre Dumas, and the eating experiences of such notables as Bret Hart, Robert Louis Stevenson, and Lola Montez in the San Francisco of the 1850s. It was a journal that made the discussion of food, its consumption and preparation both intellectually stimulating and fun. It told its readers that food was something intelligent people, both men and women, could think, read and talk about.

In the mid 1960s Jane Montant, who for some years had been responsible for reading and answering every letter written to the magazine, became Executive Editor. She knew, better than anyone, what the readers wanted and slowly, patiently, she convinced Mr MacAusland to add travel articles, more women writers, to put more emphasis on cuisines other than French, and finally, to test and retest every recipe before it appeared in print. Shockingly, I learned that prior to Mrs Montant's stewardship, recipes were not tested.

Gourmet made excellent reading but did it influence America's eating and drinking habits? I contend that it did. I believe that the magazine made a profound contribution simply by being there; it was the only one solely devoted to fine food and drink at a time when American GIs were returning from a war that brought them into intimate contact with new gastronomic experiences, a time when Americans could afford to, and did, travel. These new Americans wanted to reproduce the foods they had tasted on their travels. Food had become inextricably tied to their memories and experiences. *Gourmet* gave them the tools (the recipes and techniques) to produce those dishes, incentives to aspire to higher levels of gastronomic expertise, and the encouragement to expand their experiences by experimenting further.

Through its pages readers were painlessly educated in the art and language of French cuisine. *Sauce Béchamel* substituted for the ubiquitous white sauce of their childhood, and *Bavaroise au Fraise* elbowed strawberry Jello off dessert tables. From an amusing tale by Stephen Longstreet readers learned that their knives and kitchen tools were, in fact, *poignées*, their wire whisks were *fouets*, and, years before Julia Child's wonderful TV series, that one could pick dropped food off the floor and with a smile and great élan call it *coup du ballet Parisien*.

By the 1960s and for a long time after, the dollar was strong and Americans travelled in unprecedented numbers. The cry of Coca Cola imperialism was heard all over the world but, unlike the imperialists of old, Americans were quick to adopt and accept the foods of the countries they visited. While they may preferred their hamburgers, they readily accepted *keftethe* as substitutes. *Gourmet* reflected their changing tastes and from its pages readers learned new gastronomic languages. They learned to make such dishes as *Cappelletti Romagna* from scratch, *Vasilopitta*, Greek New Years Cake, and *Driekoningenbrood*, Dutch Christmas bread. Travel articles by writers like Samuel Chamberlain, Naomi Barry, and Lillian Langseth-Christianson were so precise and enticing that readers used them as travel and restaurant guides. In addition, *Gourmet* had become the favorite sources of recipes for home entertaining.

While one might not have prepared an entire meal for the family from its pages, such meals were often prepared for colleagues or the boss. Many a promotion hinged on how much the boss enjoyed his meal. It is not surprising, therefore, that for many years the largest number of subscribers came from the Washington DC area where elegant entertaining was, and still is, a professional imperative.

In 1950 Mr MacAusland published the first *Gourmet Cookbook* which he financed through pre-publication sales to his subscribers. The book contained nearly 2,400 recipes 'the majority ... French and American,'[11] and a section entitled 'Memo to the Cook' with suggestions on seasonings, substitutions, oven temperatures, use of the index, and explanations of the language used. The impression was that it was written for friends with like tastes.

The magazine, and all the cookbooks published by *Gourmet*, were designed to give the reader a feeling of belonging to a special group, a kind of club. It has been accused of being elitist and perhaps it was, but it was aimed at a gastronomic elite. It was a kind of club, never restrictive, but rather always open to all who possessed, or aspired to possess, epicurean tastes. Today this 'elite club' is made up of approximately 900,000 subscribers.

ACKNOWLEDGEMENTS

I would like to express my gratitude to Mr MacAusland's nephew, Dr. William MacAusland, his grand nephew, Russell MacAusland, who was the magazine's Vice President for advertising for 25 years, Mrs Jane Montant, Executive Editor of *Gourmet* for over 20 years and senior editor for many years before, Phoebe Vreeland, writer and editor at *Gourmet* during the early years of its existence, and to The Schlesinger Library of Radcliffe College and Samuel Chamberlain's collection. They are not in any way responsible for any errors that may have crept into this paper. However, they are all responsible for having made this project enlightening and pleasant.

REFERENCES

[1] Franklin Delano Roosevelt, Speech in Chicago, Illinois, October 5, 1937.
[2] MacAusland, Earle R., *Gourmet*, April 1941, letter in 'Sugar and Spice' feature, p.2.
[3] *New York Times*, Sunday, December 22, 1940, p.1.
[4] ibid
[5] ibid
[6] ibid
[7] *Gourmet*, January 1941.
[8] Chamberlain, Samuel, *Bouquet de France*, Gourmet Distributing Co.Inc., 1952.
[9] Beard, James, 'Spécialities de la Maison', *Gourmet*, November, 1949, p.4.
[10] Trilling, Calvin, *Alice Let's Eat*, Random House, 1979, p.51.
[11] *The Gourmet Cookbook*, Volume I, Gourmet Distributing Corp, New York, December 1950, p.8.

'Much Pleasure and Profit':[1]
Hannah M. Young (1858-1949), Culinary Entrepreneur

Valerie Mars

A new style of women cookery writers appeared in the last quarter of the nineteenth century. What distinguished some of these later writers from their predecessors was their activity in overt commercial promotion of branded foods and their involvement in the formal teaching of cookery. With the growth in branded food products and a greater diversity in mass manufactured kitchen wares, manufacturers needed to promote their goods. At the same time there was both a revival in cooking as a genteel accomplishment while it was being incorporated on a large scale into girls' schools curricula.

The most well-known of these new women cookery writers was the energetic Mrs Agnes B. Marshall (1855-1905) who took over the school of cookery at 30 Mortimer Street, London, in 1883. She published her first cookery book, *The Book of Ices*,[2] in 1885. She sold branded foods and kitchen equipment, published a journal[3] and also ran an employment agency.[4]

Mrs Young has for the most part vanished into obscurity, whereas she could be considered a northern counterpart to Mrs Marshall's London style, for Mrs Young wrote for a wider public than Mrs Marshall's exclusively *recherché* constituency. Her recipes included both local traditional dishes, such as 'Rook Pie'[5] and a more fashionable repertoire. Like Mrs Marshall she also sold cooking equipment and some branded foods as well as teaching cookery. It is apparent that she too was a woman of some energy and entrepreneuriality. Her books, like Mrs Marshall's, included advertisements for her lectures, kitchen equipment, and grocery products. She claimed a First class diplomée as demonstrator of cookery and a medal from Berkhamsted Mechanics Industrial and Fine Arts Exhibition, 1886, awarded for 'special merit'. It is shown on the cover of *Domestic Cookery*[6] and *The Housewife's Manual of Domestic Cookery*.[7] edited by Mrs Young. This is from the note that precedes the entry in Elizabeth Driver's *Bibliography of Cookery Books 1875-1914*.[8]

'The daughter of the author's sister-in-law informs me that Hannah Young was born in Birmingham on 24 June 1858. Mrs Young's father, Cornelius Young, made and sold gas cookers in Warrington, Lancashire and she demonstrated the cookers for his company. Her husband was William Riding of Ormskirk, Lancashire. Since Hannah Young was well known professionally by her maiden name, he changed his name on marriage to Dr William Young. The author is buried in Harston, Cambridge.'

Books: Both 'Choice' and 'Domestic'

Why choose Mrs Young as a subject when there are so many inspired cooks to choose from? It is that Mrs Young is a reminder of the poor state of much of English middle class cookery at the end of the last century and that is still with us. Over-cooked and inappropriately elaborately arranged dishes were for many a daily expectation. But it is such an unattractive subject to investigate that it can easily be forgotten. Mrs Young took what was described as 'plain cookery' as a standard which she then embellished, as an added refinement. Plain cookery in the nineteenth century and early this century had a limited basic repertoire. It was often a euphemism for cookery employing cooks with limited skills allied to the employers' parsimonious expenditure on food, fuel and equipment.

Mrs Young's recipe books can be seen as strange acultural collections. Perhaps her readers selected what was appropriate to their repertoire? Or were these books simply culinary rag-bags? It is possible to see several tendencies: traditional recipes, bits of French cookery, novelty variations and product driven recipes.

Mrs Young's first cookery book published in 1886 was called *Domestic Cookery, with Special Reference to Cooking by Gas*. It was, she says in the preface, written at the request of 'many ladies who have attended my lectures on cookery'. She goes on to say the recipes 'will not be found to be high class' but 'domestic and economical'. When mentioning the use of the gas range, she says it is not 'absolutely necessary to the success of the dishes' but, she rather disingenuously remarks, 'my personal experience has taught me its extreme utility and convenience'.[9] Her father was the manager of the Thynne Street Works, Warrington of Fletcher Russell & Co, stove manufacturers, until 1898 when he retired. His son Cornelius was also an employee of the company. Her book was published four years before Marie Jenny Sugg's more comprehensive book of gas cookery.[10] Mrs Sugg was the daughter of a French restaurateur and the wife of a manufacturer of gas appliances.

By the 1897 edition of Mrs Young's *Domestic Cookery*, she included some new recipes from her demonstrations: 'some are the fruits of a closer acquaintance with foreign cookery and are in for giving information on well-known dishes by name.' Fashion was infiltrating local 'domestic' cookery. The Liebig Company employed Hannah M. Young to write their cookery book,[11] and some of the recipes in the appendix of *Domestic Cookery*, which were added after she had written the Liebig book, use Liebig's Extract of Beef, but none in the main body do so. The Liebig book was published in 1893.[12] Those recipes using Liebig's Extract include Polish Stew[13], Spanish Stew[14] and also, on the same page, Stuffed Onions, Pork Cutlets, and Fillets of Beef with Tomatoes[15]. The section on the gas stove is clear, concise and comprehensive. At the back of the book there are advertisements for two gas cookers: 'The New Kensington – the cheapest ever made' and 'No.140 – the quickest heating oven in existence'. The firm Fletcher Russell & Co Ltd, also advertises water heaters, a broiler griller, an iron and two coal-effect gas fires. Under the title: 'Revised Price List of H.M. Young's Specialities' there are five pages of advertisements for kitchenware, including a special steamer (Hutchings Patent) with four layers and with a device for shutting off the steam from any one tier when its dish is done. These items could all be obtained from H.M. Young, The Waverley Hotel, Chester, A Temperance hotel at 31 City Road. Her partner in this business was a Miss Fanny Beck. 1892 is given as the date for the start of their venture.[16]

In Mrs Young's next book, *Choice Cookery*, 1886,[17] the preface describes it as a 'practical guide to those ladies desirous of becoming acquainted with the art of cooking in its choicest and most economical form'. It was more fashion-conscious and genteel than her first book. There are more entrées: Boeuf à la Rosine[18] is sautéed fillets of beef on a browned potato platform and pyramid, garnished with mushrooms on a hatalette skewer. If this was too recherché for her readers, she suggests a garnish of heather or berries, which owes more to seventeenth-century festive food than nineteenth-century recherché dinners. It in fact suggests that the old styles of food decoration had not entirely vanished by the end of the century. This book, unlike the earlier one, has no recipes for mutton. Mutton was not for 'choice' cooking. The soups include that Victorian dinner party favourite, Julienne (consommé with shredded vegetables). It is a book unlike typical London-based cookery books of the period, and contains recipes for home-made wines and one for 'mock preserved ginger' made with carrots. It also has pomegranate jelly and maraschino jelly which uses a quarter pint of maraschino. The overall impression is of a strange mixture of innovation and tradition.

This book, again, has advertisements for goods supplied by H.M. Young – 'Fine Leaf Gelatine and Superior Baking Powder manufactured by H.M. Young, 27 Arpley Street, Warrington'. In the census of 1891, 27 Arpley Street is the home of Cornelius (head) and Hannah (wife), two sons,

Cornelius and Alfred, and a boarder. The gelatine is advertised where appropriate recipes require it, and the baking powder has many unique qualities ascribed to it. Also advertised is Flor-Ador Food, designed to take the place of cornflour, arrowroot and tapioca. Opposite this advertisement is a page of recipes by Mrs Young using Flor-Ador food. They include Flor-Ador cake, which of course requires H.M. Young's baking powder, as do Flor-Ador biscuits. Other recipes are for ice cream, a chocolate blancmange, and basket-shaped fancy cakes. There are also advertisements for moulds and forcing bags, again supplied by H.M. Young and an advertisement for Practical Lessons and Demonstrations by Mrs Young.

From these ventures it is not hard to see why Mrs Young should have been chosen by Liebig and Co to write their recipe book, for she must have been one of the earliest recipe-writers for the new manufactured foodstuffs. Most recipe books of the period did not use any manufactured products in their repertoires. There were exceptions, such as Major L[19] who recommends a soup made from Liebig's Extract and vegetable stock as a more economical alternative to home-made beef stock.[20] An 'Old Bohemian' in *Philosophy in the Kitchen*, published in the same year, 1885,[21] used Liebig Extract in a curry,[22] and in a tomato dish.[23] Maybe an instant, long life ingredient, like Liebig Extract, was particularly useful for bachelors or colonial army officers.

Mrs Young also wrote one other cookery book, *Home Made Cakes and Sweets*.[24] By this time (1904), she had moved to Harston, Cambridge. She describes the book as 'a useful aid and reliable guide for those who make cakes for afternoon tea'. This seems to suggest that making fancy cakes was a genteel branch of cookery for 'ladies'. After the foundation of *The National Training School of Cookery* in 1873 and the subsequent introduction of cookery into girls' education, there were many more books and articles encouraging 'ladies' to cook or at least understand cookery. Mrs Marshall taught both professional cooks and 'ladies'.

There are photographs of some of the cakes in this last cook book which look decorative but not too complicated for a competent amateur. They are displayed on cotton or paper doilies on a silver salver or an entrée dish. To give a more spectacular finish to some cakes or puddings, there are instructions for making spun sugar and at the back of the book there are, once again, several pages of 'H.M. Young's Specialities' including items of kitchenware for baking: a patent flour sifter, and again, Hutchings Patent Steamer. These were supplied from her Harston address.

Mrs Young and the Liebig Cookery Books

Liebig's beef extract was the result of work by the German chemist Justus von Liebig, published in 1847. In 1865 a factory, which employed about a thousand workers, was built at Fray Bentos, in Uruguay where cattle were raised on the surrounding grassland. They were then slaughtered and 'reduced' to meat extract for export.[25] This was before the introduction of refrigerated ships and was a way of turning meat into a transportable commodity. Liebig's Extract was sold in white jars with Justus von Liebig's autograph in blue on a black and white label. It was widely advertised and as well as cook books there was other promotional material which included sets of themed menu cards, such as European queens and regimental uniforms.

The book Mrs Young wrote for Liebig and Company was her third cookery book. It came out in 1893 priced one shilling. In the preface she describes cookery as 'the culinary art' and says its study 'affords much pleasure and profit' and notes the spread of education in the field during the previous decade. Teachers who had trained at the National School, founded in 1873, were beginning to pass on their knowledge as cookery was moving into school curricula. She notes that there are new products to 'reduce labour and drudgery', and that 'the Liebig Company's Extract of Meat holds foremost place in the field.' The last part of her preface sets out with the new voice of what would now be described as a home economist: 'The true object of cookery – to maintain and enhance the nutritive value of the food cooked and secure its digestibility ... to render it as palatable as possible and to please the senses of sight and smell.' She adds, that 'variety and economy' are both assisted by Liebig's Extract.

Her recipes in the Liebig book cover the range and style of her two previous cookery books; *Domestic Cookery* and *Choice Cookery*. Every savoury dish uses some Liebig Extract including the fish recipes. Her range of recipes can be shown by two of her game recipes. One for Pheasant à la Madrid[26] – a nice kitchen Franglais title – includes two or three truffles or mushrooms, and Rook Pie[27] which may be rustic but is not entirely plain, uses puff pastry but 'not too rich', and beefsteak.

Liebig's Extract is added to all of these dishes in very small amounts. Unfortunately it has so far not been possible to ascertain the strength of the original Extract. Onion Soup[28] used three large onions, parsley, a bay leaf, salt and pepper to two quarts of water. Apart from a thickening of roux and two egg yolks, there is no other flavouring. Yet the amount of Liebig Extract advised is only two small teaspoons. Unless the flavour was very strong, the effect must have been minimal. About half a pint of soup is allowed per diner.

This book is unusual for a Victorian cookery book that was written for the British market in that it is full of decorative rather than functional illustrations – one at least on every other page and frequently more. This is explained by the book having been printed in Germany. Its illustrations are typically German and these mostly do not quite match the text. Some are rather kitsch. One for Lobster Soup[29] shows two 'water babies' brandishing saucepans, one standing on a giant lobster, the other ready to assist. A recipe for 'Cutlets en Surprise' has a substantial cook, frying on a very German-style stove with a kitchen maid wiping a dish. There are puns: Liebig Stimulant or Nightcap,[30] has a man wearing a nightcap and scarf and the title page for 'Miscellaneous' recipes has the portrait busts of five very different men, fat and thin, in various styles of dress and fashions in facial hair. In German, this is a feeble pun. The translation of 'miscellaneous' or 'many-sided' is *die Mannigfaltigkeit*, and of man is *der Mann*.[31] There are also illustrations for dishes grander than the recipes below them. 'Cabinet Pudding' for instance, has a bird rising, phoenix-like, from a grand moulded and decorated *pièce de resistance*. Although Cabinet Pudding is also a moulded pudding, the instructions in no way match the illustration.

This book is in fact peopled by a motley cast that includes a clown making fish jump through a hoop for Dressed Skate[32] and a pig contemplating a ham for Ham Omelette. For Sauce Robert, we are shown a monocled 'man-about-town' flanked by a pair of sauce boats, and so it continues. This edition is in maroon cloth with fine lettering and is priced at 1/-.

The most elaborate illustration is to be found on the card cover of the 1894/5 edition, that was issued 'with the compliments of Liebig's Extract of Meat Co.' It is in colour and shows a rather grandly-dressed young woman lifting the lid from a steaming copper pan while a young maid takes a jar of Liebig's Extract from a shelf. The kitchen illustrated is full of furnishing details in German Rococo style. Its walls and the stove are tiled and on the walls hangs a pendulum clock. Other furnishings include decorative shelves with blue-and-white storage jars and a pretty set of spice drawers hung next to a wrought- or cast-iron bracket with a glass lamp. There is a rococo water fountain and basin in the corner. Beside the stove stands a towel-rail with typical red-bordered German towels. Beside this, on the floor, is a soup tureen and a marmite with a pile of generously displayed assorted vegetables. These overflow into the gold rococo border at the bottom of the page with a jar of Liebig's Extract enclosed in its own shell-shaped frame! Above the window which looks onto the view of a lake, mountains and trees, is the scrolled title 'Liebig and Company's Practical Cookery Book'. Its general effect is of bourgeoise luxury. The book's back cover has two jars of Liebig Extract surrounded by plentiful vegetables, game and a lobster. At the base of this arrangement are three scrolled texts giving uses for the Extract and the whole is framed with a fine rococo border.

This luxury contrasts with the plain and simple illustration on the cover of the American Liebig cookery book,[33] which was printed in America. It was produced in 1893 and is of the same size and quality, but has fewer recipes than the English book. It was written by Miss Maria Parloa, described as the founder of two schools of cookery and author of *The Kitchen Companion*, *Miss Parloa's New Cookbook*, *Miss Parloa's Young Housekeeper*, *The Appledore Cookbook*, etc.

The coloured card cover of the American book sets a very different tone to its European companion. Shown using the recipe book is a young housewife in a flower-sprigged print dress and white apron. In the picture is a plain kitchen table with two jars of 'Liebig', a saucepan and gravy boat. There is a china cupboard with leaded glass doors and a stove with meat plates above. There is neither servant nor rococo decor. Its back cover has a scene showing long-horn cattle, two gauchos, rolling plains, distant mountains, and of course, two jars of the Extract.

Recipes in the American book are for the most part not very different in style and content from those in Mrs Young's book. There is Julienne Soup[34] and similar entrées and sauces. A few of the dishes can be said to be truly American, such as Creole Soup,[35] some of the shell fish recipes, such as Oysters à la Baltimore,[36] and a Clam Soup.[37] There are also recipes, unlike those in the English book, that use tinned foods: Walled Salmon[38] uses tinned salmon – the 'wall' is a potato border. There are no sweet dishes and every dish uses the Extract.

In the American book the Introduction and Preface are subsumed into one piece and the language is much more informal that of the English book. It is written rather like a story book, and begins: 'Have you ever thought of the history of the little cream colored jars so common in American households...?' It goes on to say how the Extract is, 'a boon to thousands of families', was turned into an enterprise which grew. It describes then the care with which it is examined at various stages, its uses in the kitchen and as a reviver of exhausted travellers and fainting invalids.

Both books are addressed to a middle range of consumers and their dishes are from the conventional repertoire – there is nothing extreme. This production of appropriate books is very much in the same style as modern commercial recipes directed at a known and well-understood middle-of-the-road public. Neither book, as with their modern equivalents, catered to the most recherché taste.

'Nature's Great Remedy'[39]

Mrs Young's only publication on another subject is a very slim volume, *Health without Medicine*, 1893 It is a polemic advocating a douche, for which there is an illustrated advertisement at the end of the book. The device is used as an enema that can be self-administered. Douches were at the time frequently also used as a contraceptive aid. She ascribes the need for this device as an enema to the lack of effective medicines for all illnesses and to the nineteenth-century 'mode of life'. It is put forward as a 'cure-all' and only uses water, 'Nature's great remedy'.[40] Its appeal was to avoid what was often called 'feeling seedy' and worse. Its great advantages were summed up in the direction 'Used at night the douche is a splendid appetiser for breakfast the next morning'! There speaks the busy cook and entrepreneur: keeping fit to keep eating, who, maybe should not be relegated to such obscurity.

REFERENCES

[1] Mrs H.M. Young *Liebig Company's Practical Cookery Book*, Liebig's Extract of Meat Co.Ltd., London, 1895, VIII.
[2] Mrs Agnes Bertha Marshall, *The Book of Ices*, Marshall's School of Cookery, London, 1885.
[3] *The Table*, a weekly publication published at 32, Mortimer Street, London.
[4] Elizabeth Driver, *A Bibliography of Cookery Books, published in Britain in 1875-1914*, Prospect Books, London. p.420 The information on Mrs Marshall is derived from Barbara Ketcham Wheaton's 1976 facsimile edition of *The Book of Ices*.
[5] Young, 1895, 47.
[6] Mrs H.M. Young, *Domestic Cookery with Special Reference to Cooking by Gas*, Mackie and Co Ltd., Warrington and London with H.M. Young, Chester, c.1886.
[7] Mrs H.M. Young, editor, *The Housewife's Manual of Domestic Cookery*, Fletcher Russell & Co Ltd., Warrington, 18—?
[8] Driver, 1989, 667-671. This bibliography includes a range of editions of Mrs Young's works, but she has not been able to date them all. Several publishers are used, including the author.
[9] Young, c.1886, Preface.
[10] Marie Jenny Sugg, *The Art of Cooking by Gas*, Cassell & Co.Ltd., London, 1890.
[11] Young, 1895, VIII.
[12] Mrs H.M. Young, *Domestic Cookery with Special Reference to Cooking by Gas. 500 Tried Recipes*, John Heywood, Manchester and London, H.M. Young, Chester, 1897.
[13] Young, 1897, No.423, 167.
[14] Young, 1897, No.410, p.163.
[15] Young, 1897, No.410, p.163.
[16] Information from David Roger, the area librarian at Warrington Library.
[17] Mrs H.M. Young, *Choice Cookery*, H.M. Young, Warrington, John Heywood, Manchester and London, 1889, first published 1888.
[18] Young, 1897, No.38, 22.
[19] Major L (Major James Henry Landon?), *The Pytchley Cookery Book*, Chapman and Hall Ltd., London 1885.
[20] *Major L, 1885*, No.2, 105.
[21] An Old Bohemian, *Philosophy in the Kitchen*, Ward & Downey, London, 1885.
[22] Young, *Choice Cookery*, 1888, 63-64.
[23] Young, *Choice Cookery*, 1888, 160.
[24] Mrs H.M. Young, *Home Made Cakes and Sweets*, W. Heffer & Sons, Cambridge, Simpkin Marshall & Co, London, 1904.
[25] Young, 1895, VI.
[26] Young, 1895, No.73, 45
[27] Young, 1895, No.77, 47.
[28] Young, 1895, No.18, 10.
[29] Young, 1895, No.14, 8.
[30] Young, 1895, No.142, 82.
[31] Young, 1895, 81.
[32] Young, 1895, No.44, 26.
[33] Maria Parloa, *One Hundred Ways to Use Liebig Company's Extract of Beef: a guide for American Housewives*, Liebig's Extract of Meat Co Ltd., London, 1893 (printed in America).
[34] Parloa, 1893, No.6, 17.
[35] Parloa, 1893, No.9, 19.
[36] Parloa, 1893, No.21, 28.
[37] Parloa, 1893, No.16, 24.
[38] Parloa, 1893, No.31, 36.
[39] Mrs H.M. Young, *Health without Medicine*, John Heywood, Manchester, 1893.
[40] Young, 1893, 41.

Martha Stewart

Richard C. Mieli

The mention of Martha Stewart's name throughout the U.S.A. almost always brings an immediate reaction. Many responses are very positive while many are very negative.

She is known for her numerous cookbooks that have had an influence on how people eat and primarily how people entertain in the U.S.A. From the smallest intimate dinner party to the grandest wedding reception she has become the authority figure. The themes that are associated with her are *Class, Elegance, Perfection, Fantasy* and *Femininity*. This paper will trace her success from her initial cookbook *Entertaining* to her present status as head of a multi media empire.

Martha Stewart was born Martha Kostyra in Nutley, New Jersey, August 3, 1941, the oldest of six children of Martha and Edward Kostyra. Martha's mother was a teacher and her father a pharmaceutical salesman.

She attributes three kitchens as the sources for her introduction to cooking. Her parent's kitchen, her maternal grandmother's kitchen and her neighbours, Mr and Mrs Maus's kitchen. Her maternal grandmother had emigrated from Poland and adapted the cuisine of Poland to America. In both her mother's and grandmother's kitchens she was taught preserving, canning and making dishes such as *pierogi* and stuffed cabbage. With such a large family she also learned quantity cooking which was helpful as she entered the catering business. Mr and Mrs Maus, her next-door-neighbours, were retired German bakers. 'From the time I was four until I reached ten, when Mr Maus died, I found excuses to visit them: I was welcomed as an apprentice and as a taster.'[1]

She states that 'recipes are like folktales, small parcels of culture.' She was influenced by many of the classics such as the banquet scenes from Sir Walter Scott, the Roman punch dinners in Edith Wharton's novels, and the country weekends in Tolstoy's *Anna Karenina*[2].

Martha's first career was modelling which she began at the age of twelve. The modelling continued through her last year at Barnard College. At Barnard she received a degree in European and Architectural History.

She married Andrew Stewart in 1961 (divorced in 1987) and gave birth to her daughter Alexis in 1965. After the birth of her daughter she returned to work at Monness, Williams and Sidel, a Wall Street firm and worked as a stockbroker. She left in the early 1970s. After moving to Connecticut she eventually went into a catering business with Norma Collier. This partnership lasted less than one year.

Martha created her own company called Martha Stewart Inc., which in less than ten years grew into a one million dollar plus business, with corporate accounts all over the East Coast. Her first cookbook was published in 1982 and was titled *Entertaining* and became an immediate success and now has more than 500,000 copies in print. *Entertaining* has become a reference for many caterers throughout the U.S.A.

Since her initial cookbook was published, her success as a cookbook writer has rocketed. The following are the cookbooks that have been written by Martha Stewart and published by Clarkson N. Potter, an imprint of the Crown Publishing Group, which is owned by Random House.

Entertaining [1982] over 500,000 copies in print

Martha Stewart's Quick Cook [1983] 465,000 copies in print

Martha Stewart's Hors d'Oeuvres [1984] 457,000 copies in print

Martha Stewart's Pies and Tarts [1985] 237,000 copies in print

Weddings [1986] 180,000 copies in print

Martha Stewart's Quick Cook Menus [1988] 350,000 copies in print

Martha Stewart's Christmas [1989] 630,000 copies in print

Martha Stewart's Menus for Entertaining [1994] 256,000 copies in print

Other books written by Martha Stewart are as follows:

The Wedding Planner [1988] 133,000 copies in print

Martha Stewart's Gardening Month-by-Month [1991] 250,000 copies in print

Martha Stewart's New Old House [1992] 125,000 copies in print

Martha Stewart Living Enterprises that is jointly owned by Time Inc. Ventures, a division of Time Warner, Inc. and Martha Stewart encompasses the *Martha Stewart Living* magazine and the *Martha Stewart Living* TV Program.

The magazine was first published in 1990 and deals with recipes, crafts, entertaining ideas, antiques, etc. Initially it was published bi-annually, then bi-monthly. It is now published ten times per year with two special issues. Four years after its initial publication, *Martha Stewart Living* is selling 1.2 million copies per year. *Martha Stewart Living* is also a syndicated television program and is distributed to 138 stations.

All of her books are in hard cover. Currently, it is estimated that she has nearly four million books in print. Her book tour appearances led to the lecture circuit. Her lectures are priced at $15,000 per lecture. She gives approximately a dozen lectures a year.

Along with the positive reception of her first book, came much criticism that was focused on it by the food critics. Many food critics accused her of stealing recipes from other cookbooks without giving credits to the original sources. From her first book she was viewed with a mixture of envy and undisguised contempt.

Over the years I have been amazed to observe how these vitriolic attacks have been continued by the press. Diane White, a syndicated columnist, called her the 'Hostess from Hell'. In a May 1, 1995 article in the *Boston Globe*, Diane White ends a dream she is having about O.J. Simpson and Martha Stewart this way 'Your Honor, I say, if I can't get out of this dream, can I petition for a change of venue? To some dream where they have never heard of O.J. Simpson or Martha Stewart.' 'There is no such place', says Judge Ito, 'even in your dreams, petition denied.'[3]

In an article that appeared in *Working Woman*, September 1991, titled 'heart-shaped wreaths, perfumed sprayed notepaper and ribbon wrapped linens — is this what women want?' by Meryl Gordon, the following is stated, 'Wasn't feminism supposed to free us from the unnecessary, labor-intensive women's work?' By its very popularity, the Martha Stewartisation of every shopping mall in America appears to be a repudiation of the two-career couple phenomenon, the 'Why should I be the one to cook?' ultimatums – and every other cause that once marched under the banner 'Sisterhood is Powerful'.[4]

Almost four years later what appears to be an answer to the article 'Is this what women want?' is seen in *Working Woman*; only this time it is a feature story. On the cover of the June 1995 issue of *Working Woman* is a picture of Martha Stewart which reads 'Martha Inc – How the Diva of Domesticity built a multi-media Empire'. The article is by Jeanie Russell Kasindorf and covers five and a half pages. The article traces her success with particular emphasis on the creation of Martha Stewart Living Enterprises, a new corporation that she will head as Chair and CEO. The new company will be a partnership between Martha Stewart and Time, Inc.

One response in the article, by a Time, Inc. executive, was 'Everyone around here is talking about how funny it is to see the largest company in the world being dragged around by the nose by a former caterer.'[5]

Another article, this time in the *New York Magazine* with Martha on the cover, by Barbara Lippert, titled 'Our Martha, Ourselves', in its introduction states 'It's no longer sufficient to dismiss Martha Stewart as a control-freakish, middle-browed tastemaker. She's bigger, much bigger. Coming to terms with an emblematic figure of our times.'[6]

The author makes a very important observation that can probably explain the immense popularity of Martha Stewart in America presently. 'The attempts to explain Martha proliferate but one thing is clear: she taps into a very obvious longing for lost ritual and tradition in this country. One can make fun of the increasingly competitive mood at flea markets, Williams Sonoma outlets and Smith & Harken garden accessories stores. But the people who have turned these pursuits into contact sports are seeking to replace a sense of lost familial order. Martha is the ritual healer. Her poultices are crisp linens, delicious tarts, and a beautiful mosaic of turkey and infused oils.'[7]

This is the third time in this century that self-help books have been embraced. In the 1920s, immigrants pursued etiquette books for advice on how to assimilate into American society. Transitions from one social class to another was the final goal.

In the 1950s the next domestic movement occurred which was the movement of young couples from the cities to the suburbs. This was the era of the progressive dinners, where various courses were consumed at different couples' homes often within the same neighbourhood. Cooking at this point took on a competitive role that needed self-help cooking and entertaining books to provide the much needed instruction manual of what was 'right and proper'.

Some observers of the 1990s feel that this latest trend is due partly to the frustration many working women feel with their careers. Today's working women do not define their identities by their cooking or decorating skills as their mothers often did, they seek out experts such as Martha Stewart, who is also a working, highly successful woman.

An interesting comment by a French liberated woman in Theodore Zeldin's book *An Intimate History of Humanity* provides support for Martha Stewart's popularity. It reads 'the feminists went too far, she says, making demands, nothing but demands. It was a mistake. But on the other hand, "We wanted to show that we were the equals of men." Now she says women must go back to femininity.'[8]

In *Vanity Fair*, October 1993, in an article by Christopher Hitchens, he notes, 'she is a possible answer to the question "what do women want?"' 'She is an artist of the deal, she is a balm to all those who fret themselves about the unsayable word CLASS.' He continues, 'There is a great deal of status insecurity out there and it vibrates powerfully to the influence of someone who can assure you that you are doing the right, the tasteful, the elegant thing to do.'[9]

I have noticed an interesting fact: when men write about Martha Stewart, what appears in most of the articles is her Polish heritage. In *Outlaw Cook* by John Thorne, with his wife, Matt Lewis Thorne, he states, 'Martha Stewart herself, although she radiates WASPy self-assurance, (the federalist colonial home in Westport, Connecticut, the Barnard College degree, the long blond hair, and the casual haute-preppy outfitting), was actually born in Jersey City of second-generation Polish parents.'[10]

A parody on Martha appeared this spring and has become very popular. It is a duplicate of Martha's magazine and is called *Is Martha Stuart living?*. Subsequent to the appearance of the parody, Martha appeared in a television advertisement for American Express where she cuts up other credit cards and tiles her pool as a portrait of Venus. This appears to be a parody on parody where she laughs at herself.

The following are excerpts from Lyn Povich, editor of *Working Woman* magazine 'Letter from the Editor', June 1995, and sums up many women's responses to Martha:

> Hearth and Home – Martha Stewart is a woman people love to hate. It is not just her looks, her success and her fame, it's a feeling among her detractors, that she is creating a fantasy which is unattainable in our time-pressed convenience-driven world. On the other hand, many of the busiest, most successful women are among her loyal and growing leadership. They devour the twenty-seven step instructions for pruning dwarf rosebushes and making spun-sugar angels even if –or perhaps because – they will never have the time for these projects themselves. They want to know who does her hair and how she does it all. Yes, that's it: amid the chaos, Martha Stewart has figured it all out, and if we just do what she says, our lives (and maybe our looks) will be like hers. But if Stewart has been pilloried and parodied, she has also been recognised – finally – as a genuine business phenomena. This is a woman who has built a multi-million dollar, multi-media empire in sixteen years.[11]

The following are excerpts from 'A letter from Martha', in her November 1994, issue of *Martha Stewart Living* which projects Martha's reaction to the negative responses to her magazine:

> I [Martha] recently received a letter from the sister of one of my subscribers. It was critical of many things, but especially my calendar. 'Get real.' she wrote. 'Come down to earth and smell the roses. With you it is all job and no living. Living is having to struggle from day to day for rent, food, bills, health. Leave your fantasy world and live in today's world. I am enclosing my calendar for September for you – that's living.'

> This reader, who described herself as 'artist, wife, mother, friend, employee' did not list a single thing that she did for pleasure or self-fulfilment. The only possible entry was 'quality time' with her husband and children, which was limited to after school hours since her children are of school age. My magazine calendar is intended to gently remind and inform. Windows do have to be washed, gardens must be tended and pleasures should be experienced. Indeed I do have a personal life – one that is full of friendships and family. I doubt if my readers want to know that I take Rollerblading lessons or that my daughter and I eat Japanese food and go to the movies and to a book store together once a week. I know that the calendar is full but it is full to coax all of us into balancing our lives so that there will be time to plant daffodils, cook a special meal, or collect old-fashioned Christmas tree ornaments. For me, 'living' is filling my day with activity that is meaningful, productive and interesting.[12]

I hope I have presented an objective view of one of the most controversial women in today's American cooking scene. The most interesting phenomenon that I can identify is that with all the negative press she receives she continues to grow in popularity. The final questions, for me, are 'Will Martha Stewart achieve continued success?' and 'Is the acceptance of Martha Stewart a response to the change in the women's movement and the family structure in the United States?'

In my opinion, YES, Martha Stewart will continue to be a positive influence to define social entertaining in the U.S.A. If anything this paper has taught me a lot about survival techniques in the highly competitive world of culinary education. Martha Stewart has identified and filled a need. The second question regarding the women's movement and family structure will be answered from an historical view many years from now. However, even now it is apparent that Martha Stewart has achieved a wide and varied following among today's American women.

Bibliography

Boston Globe, May 1, 1995 'Only in my dreams: O.J. and Martha' by Diana White.
Connor, Tom and Jim Downy, *is Martha Stewart Living?*, parody. Southport Beach Productions 1995.
Forbes FYI, September 26 1994, S84 (5).
Martha Stewart Living, November 1995.
New York Magazine, May 15 1995,'She's Martha Stewart and You're Not' by Barbara Lippert, 28.
Peoples Weekly, February 21 1994.'The Cult of Martha', 15.
Publishers Weekly, December 12 1994, 19.
Publishers Weekly, January 2 1995, 29.
Stewart, Martha, *Entertaining*, Clarkson N. Potter, 1982.
Thorne, John with Matt Lewis Thorne, *Outlaw Cook*. Farrar, Strauss Giroux, 1992.
Vanity Fair, October 1993.'Martha, Inc.' by Christopher Hitchens, 80.
Vanity Fair, October 1994.'The Martha Chronicles', 180.
Working Woman, September 1991.'Is this what women want?' by Meryl Gordon, 74.
Working Woman, June 1995, 26.
Zeldin, Theodore, *An Intimate History of Humanity*. Harper Crown 1994.

REFERENCES

[1] *Entertaining*, 2.
[2] *Entertaining*, 365.
[3] *Boston Globe*, May 1, 1995, by Diane White.
[4] *Working Woman*, 1991, 76.
[5] *Working Woman*, June 1995, 29.
[6] *New York Magazine*, May 15, 1995, 27.
[7] Ibid, 35.
[8] Zeldin, 110.
[9] *Vanity Fair*, October 1993, 80.
[10] Thorne, 268.
[11] *Working Woman*, June 1995, 'Letter from the Editor', Lynn Povich, 8.
[12] *Martha Stewart Living*, November 1994, 'Letter from Martha', 6.

The Influence of Supermarkets on Consumer Choice

Dr. Richard Pugh

[Tesco, who had recently launched fresh fish counters in several of their stores, generously supplied the symposium with the ingredients of a lunch on Sunday, which well demonstrated the excellence and range of their products. Everything that was needed came from Tesco, from butter and olive oil to salmon and sea bass. From these ingredients Clare Ferguson aided by other symposiasts created a splendid fish lunch. We are very grateful to Tesco for all that was needed for an impressive and delicious meal.

Before lunch Dr. Richard Pugh, technical director of Tesco, gave the following paper.]

Supermarkets are sometimes accused of influencing, even manipulating, the eating habits of their customers. The charge is that we tempt people away from healthy, natural ingredients, stuff them full of convenience and processed food and deprive them of the pleasure of preparing food for themselves.

So do we influence? I say we do, by making products Available, Accessible and Affordable.

Do we manipulate? Emphatically no, for the simple reason that we can't dictate what our customers buy. All we can do is understand their preferences and do our best to satisfy them. If we don't, they won't shop with us. Tesco will fold and I'll be out of a job.

We therefore take great care to ascertain what our customers want. A great deal of time, money and effort is devoted to market research, customer panels, tasting sessions and encouraging feedback from our shoppers. In particular, we are concerned to understand the trends that will influence choice in the future. For example,

- more people going abroad for their holidays – and not just to Spain but to Florida, Phuket or Fiji.
- The changing profile of the family; more working mothers; more single-person households.
- Changing demographics. By the year 2000 there'll be two million fewer 16 to 24 year olds in the UK than there were in 1990.
- Fewer people with time to cook – indeed fewer people who know how to cook.
- The decline of the family meal as people increasingly graze on the move.
- The influence of pressure groups such as animal rights campaigners.
- The kind of things food writers are encouraging people to try.

Our findings under all these headings closely influence the products we decide to sell.

So are we influencing or are we following the tastes and preferences of our customers? In a sense, both. We are trying to anticipate tomorrow's needs, and in doing so to make the shopping experience as exciting as possible. But we are guided by the trends of the past and present; far from manipulating, what we are attempting to do is understand…and then respond.

The best way to illustrate our approach is to take an imaginary walk round one of our stores and to look at what's on offer. As we do so, you will find that practically everything we do is guided by four principles:

- *Choice.* Everybody wants variety and we aim to provide it. In the last 20 years, the number of Tesco lines has expanded from about 600 to about 20,000.
- *A recognition that people have different lifestyles.* Ours is not an homogeneous market. We cover the spectrum from the leisured and dedicated cook, to the busy housewife, to the bedsit student.
- *Value for money.* Increasingly important in these cost-conscious times.
- *Service.* People don't just want food, they want it offered in a helpful and convenient way.

With those principles in mind, let me take you round one of our stores for a look at what's on offer. Before we go in, let's pause and look at the whole concept of the superstore.

I (just) remember as a child going down to the high street with my mother and calling at the butchers, the greengrocers, the bakers and so on. The positive side was meeting the shopkeepers and discussing what you wanted. As for the drawbacks – well the bags weren't half heavy to bring back on the bus, especially when so much more was in cans and jars. And, because you could only carry so much and it didn't keep anyway, you had to go back again practically every day. Now we have cars and freezers, both of which incline people to shop at stores like ours. Whether superstores have encouraged freezers and cars, or freezers and cars have opened the way to superstores, is debatable and probably unanswerable. The fact is, this is the way people now shop, so we aim to make the experience as easy as possible.

Incidentally, we're not wedded to the out-of-town superstore. Many people still want to do their shopping in town centres, we're opening a series of high street Metro stores to give them what they want. What we're *not* doing is forcing a particular format on our market. As in everything, we aim to respond to the known needs of our customers.

The process of creating an enjoyable shopping trip begins in the car park. It's well-lit; it's safe; it's smoothly surfaced, so people can push their trolleys without hitting bumps; there's plenty of space and we keep reserved places near the door for disabled shoppers and parents with young children.

Moving inside, we try to offer wide and welcoming aisles with clear information and staff on hand if you can't find what you're looking for. With 12 types of trolley, we can cater for everybody's needs from mothers with babies to elderly people who can't bend down. Most importantly, we make sure our trolleys steer straight!

Baby changing facilities make life easier for parents. At the checkouts, our one-in-front rule means that if any queue is longer than two, we open another until they're all in operation.

All this has to do with service and convenience. Does it therefore mean we're influencing people's tastes? Yes, if it allows the disabled, or the elderly, or harrassed mothers, or the very busy to benefit from all that a Tesco store can offer. On the other hand, it's also a response to what our customers plainly want.

So let's move on to the food itself.

First stop is the sandwich display. It's near the door so people can dash in and grab one quickly in their lunch hour. And just look at the variety that's now available. A far cry from the standard cheese and pickle that many of us used to take to work. This is a case where we define our business *not* by the products we sell, but by the needs we meet or the lifestyle we serve. It is an important distinction. If you think of this part of the store not as 'the sandwich section' but as 'that bit which serves people who want a snack at lunchtime', you're immediately into a different game. That's why, alongside the sandwiches, you'll find salad snacks with a fork in the lid for eating at your desk. And alongside that, an individual slice of chocolate pecan pie with a pot of whisky sauce. Not far away, fresh sliced pineapple in a plastic container that doubles as a dish. The office snack has rarely been as varied, as healthy, or as convenient.

Much of this has only become possible the development of the chill chain the last ten years. By that I mean the ability to make the product, chill it at source, transport it in refrigerated vehicles and put it straight onto the shelves without holding it in storage. That couldn"t have happened without such things as computerised ordering and just-in-time delivery. The chill chain not only makes possible a vast new range of products, it also means that the goods on the shelves are fresher and will last longer when customers get them home. It's easy to forget that it's only very recently that we have been able to sell fresh milk or freshly squeezed fruit juice. The chilled section now makes up a good quarter of most of our stores. Among other things, it has opened the way to a vast range of prepared meals. On just a few feet of shelf we find chicken tikka breast fillets, tandoori chicken breast fillets, chicken dhansak, chicken koorma, chicken Madras, chicken masala, orange and yogurt marinated chicken, Lousiana style chicken, black bean chicken stir fry, oriental chicken, teriyaki marinated chicken, chicken parisienne, lemon and pepper chicken, chicken breasts in tomato and garlic and chicken breasts in country herb marinade. And that's without even looking at the pork and beef.

We want people to be excited about food, to branch out from the conventional and enjoy their food more. We think that offering this amount of choice, with this degree of convenience, is one way of achieving this end.

Moving along to the fresh fruit and produce sections, you would notice new products like watermelons, pawpaw and star fruit and the growing number of varieties of traditional items like tomatoes with real flavour; we'll pause at the salad section.

Recent years have seen rapid growth in part-prepared salads. That's partly a response to people's busy-ness: it saves them one more job in the kitchen if they don't have to chop and wash their lettuces. By the same token, it also introduces variety. If you put the lettuce in bags, you can have several sorts together. From there, it's a short step to selling complete salads. Look at some of these: gourmet salad, four seasons salad, continental style salad, summer picnic salad, Italian style herb salad, crisp mixed salad. Any of these would be fiddly to make from scratch – but we've made them available by doing the work instead. It then makes sense to put different kinds of dressing on the same shelf – all part of allowing people to experiment.

Our next stop is at one of our sub-brands that brings together a range of products from Italy. 'Flavours of Italy' comprises high-quality, authentic ingredients for Italian cooking – things like the proper rice for making risotto, chianti wine vinegar, real egg pastas, mushrooms in olive oil, artichoke hearts and much, much more. If you've been to Italy, enjoyed the cooking and now want to try it yourself, here are most, if not all, of the things you'll need, conveniently labelled and displayed. Variety, lifestyle, service and value – 'Flavours of Italy' meets all four of those criteria.

Now I'd like to take you to the meat section. As I'm sure you know, meat sales are declining, partly for cultural reasons and partly because people don't know how to prepare it any more. It would be a great shame if people's ignorance of meat put them off, so we believe it's very important to display it well. An interesting feature here is the RSPCA Freedom Food label which tells customers that the animal has been humanely reared. It's a genuine concern on the part of many of our shoppers, so we've tried to respond in a helpful, intelligent way. Of course, we still have a lot of customers who know about meat and want to be able to select their cuts in the old-fashioned way. That's why many of our stores now have a specialised meat counter. Here you can choose at leisure and discuss what you want with someone who knows the subject. Should it be braising steak or mince? How much do you need for eight people? Our staff are only too happy to advise.

In the same spirit, increasing numbers of stores also have a specialised fish counter staffed by experienced fishmongers. Tesco, in fact, is far and away the country's biggest purveyor of fish. I'm sure you'll agree, a bountiful display like this with everything from fresh tuna to calamares can only encourage people to be more experimental.

Much of what you would see here has come about through our own innovation. There is even tilapia or St. Peter's fish. As you know, this is a warm-water, Caribbean fish, but since last year we've been getting ours from Derbyshire. The Courtaulds factory in Spondon produces warm water as a by-product of its paper manufacture. It's a perfect environment for St Peter's fish and they grow very quickly. When we place an order, they're harvested at once and in our stores in less than 36 hours. Is this a case of creating demand or responding to it? I can't say there was a groundswell of opinion saying 'Give us St Peter's fish', because most people had never heard of it. On the other hand, people increasingly come to Tesco expecting to be surprised; expecting their horizons to be broadened; wanting ideas for new things to try. So in that sense we *have* responded to a need and St Peter's fish is selling very well.

One more point before we leave the fish counter. The lunch menu at the symposium includes Tesco's wild Icelandic salmon. You probably think of wild salmon as costing £12.99 a pound in Harrods. The fact is, we now offer it at £3.99 a pound, which puts it in reach of most shoppers. How have we done it? Again through innovation. Our Icelandic salmon are bred for a year as farmed fish and then released into the wild. Nature takes its course and eventually they return to the same spot where we catch them – or at least about 30 per cent of them, which is enough to keep the price this low. Also for lunch there is striped sea bass – Californian, grown in water from geo-thermal springs, flown in weekly and available Thursday to Sunday.

In our industry, we've moved from the high street shop of our parents' and grandparents' era, to the pile 'em high, sell 'em cheap supermarket; to the interesting situation today where we seem to be coming full circle.

Choice is back. So is fresh, healthy produce. So is the personal interaction with the shop-keeper. So is service, to the extent that we're even starting to look at home delivery. It may not be the traditional boy on a bicycle, but the concept is one our grandparents would have recognised. The difference is, it all comes with the value and convenience of the supermarket. Customers have never been more discerning than they are today. They want better, fresher, more varied food and they want it cheaper. To some extent, we and our competitors are to blame – or can take the credit, depending on your point of view – because we've educated shoppers in this direction. The result is, we're now having to be far more versatile in what we offer.

- For the bedsit student, we still need to provide the 16p yogurt or the 25p loaf of bread, which we do, mainly through our Value Line.

- For the office worker at lunchtime, we need to provide fresh, tasty snacks in ready-to-eat form.

- For the busy working mother – or anybody else who can't or doesn't want to cook – our vast range of recipe meals means they can still enjoy quality food at affordable prices.

- For the person who loves cooking, either every day or just now and then, we try to make the process pleasurable and the options as varied as possible.

- For all those who want freshness and quality, we offer the reassurance of the Tesco guarantee. Anything at all that isn't up to standard can be instantly changed.

In all these cases we are clearly influenced by the needs of our customers. Our business is to understand the choices people want and to make them available. If you enjoy preparing food, we'll give you what you need. If it's a drudge, we'll remove that drudge – so there's choice on that level too.

At the same time our customers increasingly look to us to make life interesting. People frequently come to Tesco not knowing what to eat and expecting us to help. And what a dull world it would be if we didn't try to titivate their tastes and extend their eating experience. So do we influence? I say the answer is yes – in directions that people are already heading and in ways that anyone who loves good food would be willing to endorse.

Platina, Martino and their Circle

Gillian Riley

Quem coquum, dii imortales, Martino meo Comensi conferes?
A quo haec quae scribo magna ex parte sunt habita

What cook can compare with my friend Martino of Como?
The greater part of what I write is his.

Taken out of context this seems a less than gracious acknowledgement of the source of the recipes in Bartolomeo Platina's *De honesta voluptate et valitudine*[1], tucked away as it is in the middle of a recipe for *Biancomangiare*. The recipes are indeed based on those by the professional cook Martino of Como,[2] whose work circulated in manuscript during the last half of the fifteenth century.[3] Platina speaks of him as someone very much alive in 1467, and we know that until 1461 Martino had been cook to the fortunate Patriarch of Aquileia.

The implication that Platina, the cultivated humanist, put his friend's rough vernacular handbook into elegant literary Latin, becoming a best-seller on the back of a semi-literate craftsman has a familiar ring. But it is perhaps unfair to read too much into this act of amicable co-operation. Martino's manuscript was copied and passed around in his lifetime. As a state-of-the-art cookery book it had its virtues, and these were appreciated by his contemporaries.

Platina's book was somewhat different. It extols the ideals of moderation and restraint, in life as in gastronomy, (a concept which, coming from him, his friends would have regarded with some astonishment), and is in part a health handbook, with deft quotations from classical literature and medical works, and a smattering of quite shameless name-dropping. As well as Martino's recipes Platina includes sections describing the qualities and medical properties of different ingredients and a section on fish which very nearly defeated him.

A closer look at the recipe for *biancomangiare*[4] puts Platina's praise of Martino in a happier perspective. It is precisely this well-known and much loved medieval and renaissance dish that inspires the key passage in the work. It is worth quoting in full because it sums up the aspirations of the early renaissance humanists rather well. *Biancomangiare*, says Platina, can be served as a main dish or a sauce or condiment.

> I have always preferred this to the sauces in Apicius. There is really no reason why the tastes of our forebears should be esteemed above our own, for although they may have been superior to us in most of the academic disciplines in matters of taste we are unbeatable. There is not a single luxury in the world that has not been served up in our taverns, those grammar schools of gastronomy, where the finer points of seasoning are fiercely disputed. What cook, oh ye immortal gods, could compare with my Martino, from whom I have learned most of what I write. You would think he was another Carneade, to hear him improvise on the themes tossed at him.

No 'dwarves on the shoulders of giants' here; Anselm's diffident way of implying, in the twelfth century, that he and his fellow scholastics, perched on the shoulders of the great writers of classical times, could, with the benefit of Christianity, perceive broader horizons than those pagan philosophers.

Instead we are in a mid fifteenth-century Roman tavern, where a brash, self-confident, iconoclastic, irreverent, prickly, combative and penniless man of letters is asserting that gastronomically and culturally we are superior. And the leader of the pack is Martino, cook and orator.

This apparently throw-away praise of his friend tells us a lot about Platina and the early humanists, about their intellectual and gastronomic inclinations. Along with their tireless pursuit of classical literature, art and architecture, was a self-confidence, a pride in being 'modern', a disrespect for authority, a sense of being pioneers.

Platina was born in 1421 into a poor and undistinguished family in Piàdena, a small town near Mantua. Mantua is a place of some importance in this story. The Duke Ludovico Gonzaga was an enlightened patron of the new learning, employing Alberti, persuading Mantegna to accept the post of court painter and bringing up his children according to the progressive new educational principles of the humanists. Platina eventually became their tutor and always remained on good terms with the family, even when he left to study in Florence and later find work in Rome, where he died in 1481.

Platina wrote *De honesta voluptate et valitudine* while recovering from a spell of imprisonment and torture in Castel Sant'Angelo. Totally dependent on his patron, the young cardinal Francesco Gonzaga, once his pupil, Platina was his guest at the estate near Albano, one of the present day Castelli Romani.

Martino wrote his cookery book in the vernacular; Platina's version was in Latin. This had always been the language of the church, of educated men, and was a universal diplomatic currency, as well as a means of communciation between those who may have been baffled by each other's local dialects. But Platina and the Roman humanists, members of the Roman Academy, took a delight in conversing in the language of Horace and Virgil, of Cicero and Martial for its own sake; Latin tripped pleasurably and effortlessly off their tongues and pens, celebrating pagan themes and pagan activities. Dressed in togas, crowned with laurel wreaths, they re-enacted ancient ceremonies, of which feasting was one. A procession to the catacombs, where they reverently added their pseudonyms, in elegant roman letters, to the names of early Christian martyrs, votive offerings rather than graffiti, was an innocent activity, not the orgies or conspiracies they were later to be accused of.

Pomponio Leto, the gifted and much-loved teacher of literature at the Sapienza in Rome, and head of the Roman Academy, lived at one time in a house in what is now Trastevere, the other side of the Tiber, with a garden and orchard stretching down to the river. A much more appropriate place for orgies than the catacombs.

He took his students on guided tours, in Latin, of the vast acres of ruins that were all that remained of the splendours of ancient Rome. One student copied these succinct notes, on a ramble some time after 1484, and they survive today.[5]

Pomponio's was perforce a frugal existence. He and his companions in the Roman Academy made a virtue of necessity, enjoying a simple life and simple food, mainly vegetarian, like the heroic founders of the Roman Republic. Later Pomponio moved to a house on the Quirinale, where he had a renowned collection of antiquities and a vineyard and a garden in which he put into practice the theories of ancient writers.

Platina adds comments to Martino's recipes, reminding us of the frugal and sometimes eccentric tastes of his friends. He ends a bitter outburst with the defiant statement that he and Pomponio and their companions dine on onions and garlic.[6]

In his section on fish[7] Platina becomes eloquent over the *spigola*, sea bass,[8] that Pomponio fished from the Tiber, *nel tratto fra i due ponti*, between the Ponte Milvio and today's Ponte Sant'Angelo. He would invite Platina over to enjoy them when they were in season, in March, April and May. They cooked them in various ways, innards removed through the gills and grilled or roasted, served with a nice *salsa verde*, or boiled and eaten covered with **biancomangiare**.

The chapter on eggs is revealing; among the simple and delicious recipes for eggs, fried, boiled, scrambled, poached and made into various kinds of omelettes or *frittate*, Platina tells us how Pomponio would never cook his eggs in hot ashes, the cheapest and simplest way, because there was always the risk of cracking the shell and losing them altogether, something he was too poor to risk.[9]

Two simple chicken recipes[10] are particularly interesting: *Pollo in agresto* and *Pollo arosto*. In the first the chicken pieces are fried with chopped bacon and when half done simmered in unripe green grapes with their pips removed and seasoned at the end with chopped parsley and mint and ground pepper and saffron.

The second is plain roast chicken, served hot with a squeeze of bitter orange juice, a splash of rosewater and a sprinkling of sugar and cinnamon.

Both recipes use simple seasonings, not the complex spice mixtures of earlier cookery. They are quick and easy to prepare, nourishing, wholesome; family food, not banqueting stuff. 'Nothing could be more healthy,' said Platina of the chicken in *agresto*, 'Poggio often served it at his dinners, to which I too was invited.'

Here we have a direct link with the greatest of the Florentine humanists, Poggio Bracciolini, witty, womanizing and something of a gourmet; Poggio was scribe and secretary to cardinals and archbishops. His job took him all over Italy and Europe, including some rather miserable years in England, although he did get to see some of our great monastic libraries. He had better luck in Switzerland and France, where he 'liberated' some important copies of hitherto unknown classical literature from the unappreciative monks of St Gall and Cluny.

The script in which they were written concerns us, for Poggio and his contemporary Niccolò Niccoli were hard at work rediscovering the literature of classical antiquity, and were impressed by the caligraphy, even though they realized it was not the script of the Latin authors themselves. (It was probably 9th or 12th century). They aimed to write like that too, and this eventually became the accepted script of the cultured intellectual elite. To them it was 'old' writing, *lettera antica*; the various gothic scripts in which people normally wrote was *lettera moderna*. Poggio and his friends relished this old writing because it was *castigata et clara*, clear and simple.[11]

This gets us very close to the phrase used by Cristoforo Landino, Latin scholar and art critic, when describing the paintings of another famous Florentine, Masaccio – puro senza *ornato*, plain and clear.[12]

Landino was comparing the sculptural, powerful, monumental painting of Masaccio with the complex, elegant, decorative work of Filippo Lippi and others. We can see how the simple letterforms on the tombs in Santa Croce in Florence, sans serif capitals, with very pure, geometric, Roman proportions, were completely different in spirit from the decorative gothic inscriptions on earlier tombs. Alberti used a version of these letters across the facade of Santa Maria Novella; Masaccio used them on his painting of Saints Jerome and John the Baptist.

Was there a gastronomic equivalent of the *castigata et clara*? An edible version of the *puro senza ornato*? Was there a New Cuisine developing hand in hand with the New Learning? Might the complex, rich and heavily-spiced dishes of the past have been superseded by a lighter, plainer style of cooking? The recipes discussed above seem to indicate that there was. Martino would certainly have been able to contribute energetically to the argument. He cooked for rich patrons as well as poor scholars, catering for formal banquets, where the menu would have had old-fashioned, spicy, elaborate dishes as well as fresh, modern ones. This mixture of styles can be seen a century later in the monumental work of Bartolomeo Scappi, cook to popes and cardinals.[13] He prints the menus of scores of fine banquets where grand aristocratic dishes are brought to table along with fresh simple ones, like a dish of tiny raw baby artichokes in early spring, or crisp slices of fennel to clear the palate after six or seven lavish courses.

Poggio had always enjoyed his search for antique lettering, and the encounters on the way, chatting up girls in Tivoli, having little meals in out of the way places. When he lived in Rome he went on enthusiastic expeditions, drawing the remains of buildings and copying inscriptions, sharing his finds with friends. Many inscriptions now lost are known only through these notes. Poggio also wrote a chapter on the architectural ruins of Rome, *De varietate Fortunae*, part of a treatise on the vagaries of fortune.[14]

His zest for life brings us a taste of the first edible woman. If this paper has a heroine, as well as all these charismatic, roistering humanists, it must be Vaggia, Poggio's young bride, only seventeen years old when, at the ripe age of fifty he decided to negotiate a wife and dowry and settle down. She must have been a person of considerable charm and character. Poggio wrote enthusiastically to a friend not long after his marriage that she was like a perfect meal, nothing could be added to or subtracted from the exquisite balance of ingredients.

Later, in 1452, established and honoured as the Rector of Florence, he wrote on behalf of his wife and six children thanking his friend Bartolomeo Roverella for the gift of some salt fish. The same Roverella to whom Platina would later dedicate his book. Perhaps they were all guests together at the meal Platina remembers with such smug satisfaction.

Poggio was not alone in his enthusiastic expeditions in search of classical antiquities. *Jubilatio* was Felice Feliciano's description of a manic trip to Lake Garda on a fine autumn day in 1464.[15] 'A Rejoicing' as it were. It was one of those occasions when everything was perfect, the weather, the company, little incidental things along the way, and the successful conclusion of the enterprise: a harvest of eighteen beautiful classical inscriptions, for which the company offered up prayers of gratitude, in a distinctly pagan spirit, in the little church of San Pietro in Sirmione.

Felice Feliciano was an antiquary, calligrapher, scholar and eccentric. His own brother described him as 'unstable, a vagabond here today and there tomorrow; fantastic, prodigal, an imitator of difficult things; an alchemist, a time-waster and a spendthrift on every vain and foolish enterprise.'[16]

He, too, wrote a recipe book, recipes for constructing the Roman alphabet, based on a sensitive geometrical analysis of the inscriptions he collected and recorded on his ramblings.[17]

He was not alone in his enthusiasms. Among the frolicsome companions on the trip to Lake Garda was the painter Andrea Mantegna, not a person normally associated with any kind of fun. Most of Mantegna's financial problems were due to his zeal as a collector of classical antiquities, and inscriptions were one of the things he took a keen interest in. He used his own sophisticated interpretation of Roman inscriptional letters in his paintings, as did his in-laws, the Bellinis, Carpaccio, and even the Venetian Carlo Crivelli, somewhat isolated in the little hill towns of the Marche, where he spent most of his working life, but embellishing his paintings with these majestic letterforms.

The link between all these creative artists is the city of Padua, where Mantegna was born and studied under Squarcione, as did Crivelli and many others. As well as accurate renderings of Roman letters, these artists painted fruit and vegetables as decorative and symbolic elements in their paintings, both Christian and secular. Swags of fruit, trompe l'oeil apples and cucumbers, vases of flowers, hang improbably in intricate perspectives, or ask to be picked up in the hands and eaten. The oranges and lemons glimmering in those autumnal groves around Benaco, frequented as Felice and his companions knew, by Ovid and Virgil, appear often in Mantegna's work, using voluptuous pagan delights to embellish orthodox Christian subjects.

Padua had a renowned and ancient university which was a focus for humanist activities in the north of Italy. Galileo would teach there early in his career, running up an astronomical butcher's bill. Giovanni Marcanova, last seen disporting himself on Lake Garda, was a Paduan. One of the foremost calligraphers of the time, Bartolomeo Sanvito, lived and worked there. He used Roman inscriptional letters to superb effect in the manuscripts he copied for his wealthy and important clients. He also spent some time in Rome, and knew Platina and his friends in the Roman Academy.

A diary once survived covering a period of years at the end of his life. This is a painful thing to have to explain to food historians: a selection from it was published in 1907 by Silvio de Kunert[18] who deliberately omitted all references to domestic affairs... *'senza interesse per lo studioso'*. The diary disappeared after De Kunert's death, so we shall never know if there was a gastronomic link with his friends in Rome. Padua was famous for its poultry, though, so perhaps Bartolomeo cooked and enjoyed Poggio Bracciolini's favourite chicken recipe.

Martino had worked for another Paduan, the Patriarch of Aquileia, the warrior priest who fought the Turks in Dalmatia and was an enthusiastic patron of the humanists. Platina dedicated *De Honesta Voluptate* to Cardinal Bartolomeo Roverella, another powerful cleric, diplomat and scholar. Both were rich patrons of the arts, happy to demand, and pay for, the choicest of luxuries. Not so our author, Platina, who momentarily loses his cool when describing that over-rated dish, roast peacock, and lashes out in bitterness at those who, not through merit or their own achievements, clamber up from the basest position to more than mere riches, which would be tolerable, but to the highest ranks, *alle più alte dignità*, which can only mean the papal court and the pope himself. The luxuries these upstart opportunists can enjoy are denied by a capricious fate to those who like Platina and his circle, chose poverty and a simple diet.

If a new cuisine was emerging it was not only to suit the tastes of rich patrons of the arts. The frugal aspirations of the men of letters they employed, deliberately cultivating the austere *mores* of the founders of the Roman Republic, lead to unsettling concepts like vegetarianism and democracy or rather civil autonomy. No wonder the Pope felt threatened.

Paul II was a cultivated humanist, from the noble Venetian family, Barbo. When elected to the papacy, however, he pursued a ruthless persecution of any deviations from strict Catholic orthodoxy. Pomponio Leto and his Roman Academy seemed to the bigoted Barbo to be a bunch of immoral pagans; their innocent gatherings in the catacombs were conspiracies against his authority, a convenient excuse to dismiss all the humanists from their posts in the papal chancery. Platina's response to this had been to write an intemperate letter threatening to call a council and excommunicate the Pope if he did not reinstate them, and personally harangue the pontiff for not replying. Inevitably he and his companions were thrown into the dungeons of the Castel Sant'Angelo and tortured.

This is when the Mantua connection was helpful. Platina's old pupil, the young cardinal Francesco Gonzaga, got him out of prison and took him to recuperate on his estates in Albano. It was there that Platina wrote *De honesta voluptate et valitudine*. After another spell in prison, from which he was rescued again by the Gonzagas, Platina faced a bleak prospect. Barbo was a vigorous and active man in the prime of life and his papacy looked set to go on for some time.

At this point it is pleasing to recall the prophetic remarks about melons in the early sections of *De honesta voluptate*. Eaten on an empty stomach they are all right, but Platina warns that taken in excessive quantities after a meal they can do a lot of harm, being both cold and humid, impeding the digestive process and causing all kinds of intestinal mayhem.[19] Spurred on perhaps by the example of the emperor Clodio Decimo Albino, who ate in one evening a hundred peaches from Campania and ten melons from Ostia, Paul II, one hot summer night on the twenty-eighth of July, 1471, retired to the Vatican gardens to quench his thirst on too many melons, and expired of apoplexy.

Within a few years Platina had made friends with the new pope, Sixtus IV, della Rovere, and on the completion of his highly successful *Lives of the Popes* in 1475, was appointed to the post of Vatican Librarian. At last he found himself with a secure job, a decent salary, a nice house on the Quirinal, a horse to get himself to work on (the equivalent of a company car), and a housekeeper.

The painting by Melozzo da Forlì, commissioned by Platina, shows our hero in the centre of a distinguished group to inaugurate the opening of the new Vatican Library, pointing with proud dignity to the dedicatory inscription. Vindicated at last, Platina claimed his place, earned by merit alone, among the rich and powerful he had once so vehemently despised.

Nothing is known about the fate of Martino. It is unlikely that his friend Platina would have given up his wild ways entirely; there must have been noisy nights in the *bottigliere* of Trastevere as well as sumptuous banquets down the hill in the Vatican. Martino's recipes seem to have covered his entire gastronomic spectrum, reflecting changes of taste, innovation and continuity, in Italian cooking. Platina may have pioneered the idea of a cookery book as literature, but he was also swimming with the tide, adding his own elegant contribution to the impressive number of neat, beautifully written cookery manuscripts which survive today. They are a reminder of all the grease-stained, dog-eared, much-loved technical manuals, in all crafts, which were used to death and thrown away. The unknown cook, Martino, and the distinguished man of letters, Platina, personify the polarities of any investigation into an activity which can be described only up to a certain point, the absorbing, sensuous, creative business of cooking and eating, *de honesta voluptate et valitudine*.

REFERENCES

[1] Bartolomeo Platina, *Il piacere onesto e la buona salute*, translated and edited by Emilio Faccioli. Turin, 1985.
[2] Emilio Faccioli (ed.) *Arte della Cucina in Italia*. Turin, 1992, 127-218.
[3] Bruno Laurioux, *Liste des Manuscrits contenant des Recettes de Cuisine*. Private circulation, Paris, c. 1990.
[4] Faccioli 140-141.
[5] Biblioteca Marciana n. 3453 (MS Lat. cl.X, n. 195); reproduced with a translation by Cesare D'Onofrio in *Visitiamo Roma nel Quatrocento, la Città degli Umanisti*. Rome, 1989.
[6] Faccioli, 105.
[7] Faccioli, 226-228.
[8] Alan Davidson, *Mediterranean Seafood*, London, 1972, 77.
[9] Faccioli, 209.
[10] Faccioli, 130.
[11] James Wardrop. *The Script of Humanism*. Oxford, 1963, 5.
[12] Michael Baxandall. *Painting and Experience in fifteenth-century Italy*. Oxford, 1972, 118.
[13] Bartolomeo Scappi. *Opera*.... Venice, 1570, 168-327.
[14] Cesare D'Onofrio, 67-100.
[15] E. Ziebarth, 'Cyriacus von Ancona als Begründer der Inschriftenforschung', *Neue Jahrbücher für das klassische Altertum*, ix, Leipzig, 1902, 214-26.
[16] Wardrop, 17.
[17] Felice Feliciano. *Alphabetum romanum*, edited by Giovanni Mardersteig. Verona, 1960.
[18] 'Un padovano ignoto ed un suo memoriale de'primi anni del cinquecento (1505-1511)', in *Bolletino del Museo Civico di Padova*, x, Padua, 1907, 1 and 64.
[19] Faccioli, 26.

The Shearers' Cook: a Character in Australian Folklore

Barbara Santich

The shearers' cook is a recognisable character in Australian literature and folklore. In slang, he's the baitlayer. Henry Lawson tells the story of the shearing of the cook's dog and Alan Marshall one about the cook stewing the shearer's dog. There are tales of cooks getting the better of shearers and shearers getting the better of cooks. And there's the irreverent dialogue which has been absorbed into colloquial language:

'Who called the cook a bastard?'
'Who called the bastard a cook?'

He – and he is typically a man; which is not to say there are no female cooks, but the archetypal shearer's cook is a man – can be rough and ready, flabby and paunchy, or wizened and wiry like a well-used jockey, and always with a wispy cigarette stuck to his bottom lip. Some cooks are so thin and bent and stooped it seems they could barely lift a tea urn on to the back of the ute[1], others are tough enough to take on all comers. Myth would have it that all shearers' cooks are more or less mad – why else would they live and work in such conditions – or at least roaring drunk on lemon essence. As one ex-shearer recalled:

> I've seen them all. There was Benny the Dutchman who went through nine bottles of beer a day, and 'Tasteless George', who could take the taste out of bacon. 'Frying Murphy' hit the boss over the head with a frying pan full of fried eggs. The 'Busted Oven', he'd thrown a bucket of cold water into an old brick oven to bust it – there were some dreadful old ovens and no one blamed him.[2]

It's possible that similar stories could have been told about any kind of worker in the outback, but the shearers' cook has earned a place in local folklore through the importance of wool, sheep and shearers in Australian cultural history. In the late nineteenth century, Australia's wealth was in wool, though while it was still on the sheep's back it was virtually worthless. In order to realise their assets pastoralists depended on shearers, but they also exploited them, often providing the barest essentials and primitive facilities, and refusing to pay for sheep they considered badly shorn. In a move to secure better working conditions, shearers' unions were formed in the 1880s – a move strongly resisted by the pastoralists, who preferred free, non-unionised workers. A strike by the shearers' union in 1891 saw property owners and workers pitted against one another, though the graziers, as a ruling class, had the forces of law and tradition on their side. In protest shearing sheds were burnt down and troops brought in to maintain peace at a defiant camp of around 1,000 shearers, set up near Barcaldine. Out of this, however, was developed the Australian Workers' Union, which in turn spawned the Australian Labor Party. This helps to explain the symbolic significance of the shearer, and in turn of the shearers' cook – for shearers were also dependent on their cook, who could make difficult living conditions better – or worse. The cook of a large shearing shed 'is a highly paid and totally irresponsible official' remarked Rolf Boldrewood in 1865. Writing of the early twentieth century, Alan Marshall described the shearers' cook as:

> ...a man to be reckoned with and a power in any shed, many of them attained a fame that spread far beyond the station boundaries within which they operated. If a shearers'

cook was a good cook he had the backing, against an odd complainer, of those who enjoyed his dishes. If he were a bad cook, however, then he only retained his position by force of arms, as it were. All bad cooks who held on to their jobs could fight like threshing machines.[3]

The working conditions and rates of pay for shearers – and cooks – were eventually established in the Pastoral Industry Award and in the Rural Workers Accommodation Act and Regulations. The New South Wales Act, which came into effect in the 1920s, was modified over the next 40 years or so and a new act and regulations passed in 1969. This Act sets out the specifications for accommodation buildings, from their site to their construction, ventilation and heating; it also details accommodation for meals, and for bathing and washing and the water supply. According to the Act, meals are never to be served in the kitchen but in a room adjoining the kitchen and connected with the kitchen by means of a door and a servery at least four feet wide. The rooms used for cooking and eating are not to be used for sleeping. The kitchen, meat room, dining room and storehouse are to be completely flyproof, and all doors are to be at least six feet six inches high and two feet six inches wide.

The Regulations which accompany this Act go into even greater detail, specifying the amount of refrigeration space to be provided, according to the number of workers, and the dimensions of tables and seating benches. They also list the equipment and utensils required in the kitchen and the eating utensils to be supplied to each rural worker.

Each kitchen shall contain:

(a) a stove with a double oven or a cooking range with a double oven;

(b) a grating for heating plates;

(c) means of supplying hot water by tap or other approved device; and

(d) a sink of galvanised iron, enamelled iron, stainless steel, plastic, or other approved material, and having drainage boards. Where the kitchen is used for the cooking of meals for thirty or more persons, the sink shall have two bowls.

Each kitchen shall contain:

(a) tables or benches of sufficient number and size for the preparation of meals...

(b) cooking utensils suited to their purpose and (where more than one of any kind is to be provided) in sufficient number, including a tea pot or coffee pot or (in lieu of a tea pot or coffee pot) an urn with a close-fitting lid and a spout or tap, a meat mincer, a meat axe or cleaver, a wood axe, a butcher's knife and steel, a carving knife and fork, a soup ladle, a potato masher, large mixing spoons, an egg beater, a flour sifter, a rolling pin, a colander, a tin opener, an alarm clock, large and medium-sized saucepans of cast iron or aluminium, buckets, cooking meat dishes, serving meat dishes, a large meat fork, mixing bowls, baking dishes for sweets, baking dishes for cakes, small cake moulds, pie dishes, salt cellars, butter basins and sugar basins having close-fitting lids, frying pans, scrubbing brushes, common soap, sand soap, washing soda, pudding cloths, dish-washing cloths, tea towels, a broom, a shovel and a water dipper. Butter basins, sugar basins and salt cellars shall be of glass, china or other approved material;

The eating utensils with which each rural worker is to be provided pursuant to clause (24) of the Schedule shall be one knife, one fork, two spoons, one cup (or, in lieu of a cup, a one pint enamel or delf mug) and two plates. Such utensils shall when so provided be in good condition, thoroughly clean, and free from cracks, chips and rust.[4]

The Rural Workers Accommodation Act applies to farm workers in general, but particularly to shearers; and shearers, because of the size of the team and the nature of the work, were probably the only group to have their own cook. Shearers are either 'found' or 'not found', as agreed with the employer. When shearers are 'found' the employer or property owner is required to provide them with – in the words of the Pastoral Industry Award 1986 – 'good and sufficient rations cooked by a competent cook'. In such instances a fixed amount (currently $10.31) is deducted from the daily rate paid to shearers to cover the cost of meals, including a contribution towards the cook's wage. The minimum pay for a cook (in 1992) was $8.85 per day 'found' for every man for whom he cooks, not counting himself; if this comes to less than $115.02 per day the employer is required to make up the deficit. When shearers are 'not found' they are responsible for their own rations and cooking, though they may purchase food from the property owner, whose charge is not to exceed cost price plus freight – save for meat, for which he is allowed to charge 12 cents per point, if killed on the property.

What conistutes 'good and sufficient rations' is illustrated by the list of opening or base stores, such as the one supplied by a firm of stock and station agents which also acts as a shearing contractor. (Appendix I) Roger McDonald gives another example.

> He looked at his opening stores list. It lay on a table in front of him, an inky fax. It said black sauce, parisian essence, cream of tartar, gravy powder, custard powder, lemon essence, mixed herbs, flavoured jellies, saltpetre. It ran to three closely typed columns. It was like something from another century.[5]

These provide an indication of the kind of food shearers typically eat, and shearer's cooks prepare – the plain, no-frills food of the Anglo-Australian in the first half of the century, with hearty, bacon-and-egg breakfasts and plenty of tea. (The scale of rations for a pastoral employee (Appendix II) is even more antiquated). Inexplicably, the list of base stores omits bread – presumably bread would be bought in the town and delivered to the shearing shed every day or so. Nor does it include meat, which would be killed on the property and supplied to the kitchen. Depending on the number of shearers, a sheep – usually an ordinary wether, more or less aged – would be slaughtered every day or every couple of days. The cook is not required to kill and dress the sheep, but has to butcher it (a meat axe or cleaver and butcher's knife and steel are included in the list of kitchen equipment).

> Davo and Barbara had given him their pointers. Breakfast: plenty of chops. Morning smoko: heaps of sandwiches, some of them toasted. Lunch: a choice of two dishes, one of them hot. Tea: the roast.[6]

The cook's duties are listed as section 41 of the Pastoral Industry Award. First, he is required to 'perform his duties with reasonable dispatch and in a good and workmanlike manner' – nothing fancy, as long as it is on time and there is enough for everyone. If he wants an assistant he will, at his own expense, arrange for 'such suitable assistant or assistants of good behaviour as may be necessary for proper cooking and serving the food'.

The shearers' cook not only has to provide sufficient quantities of 'appropriate' food (food the shearers know and like) but also has to be a good manager, especially when 'not found' rates apply. He has to supply three meals – breakfast, dinner, tea – and two smokos, for shearers work an eight-hour day, with four two-hour shifts: 7.30-9.30, 10-12, 1-3, 3.30-5.30. Shearers stop work on the bell, and the food must be ready at the same time – hence the importance of the alarm clock amongst the kitchen essentials.

> Shearers must have meals on time, and right on time, because time is money, and rest is gathering strength to shear more and so earn enough to make the hard work worthwhile. If a shearer is in the habit of a small rest after lunch, he needs his meal on the table as he walks in. ...But then, a shearers' cook must be a good caterer. He is

miles from stores. He should not waste food, but he must never be short. If it rains and the shearers sit around for a week eating their heads off, he must have food for them and God help him if he hasn't.[7]

Shearers work hard and most of them have hearty appetites. One shearer's wife, who was a cook in the 1960s, wrote:

> I've never seen anyone eat like they do, near enough to a sheep a day for meat. ...At least three different sweets and same in vegetables, one of those big black pots of soup, the same size pot of stew or curry, legs of meat and the biggest pie dish of savoury things, plus two shoulders cold meat, spuds, tomatoes, lettuce, hard-boiled eggs, puddings, plus bread and toast. It doesn't matter how much extras they have they still eat a lot of bread. At smoko it's a loaf and a quarter cut into sandwiches, cakes and hot scones. Damned lucky they can't chew china or there'd be no plates left. ...They have second and third helpings of everything that can be chewed. Nothing is left on their plates, and leftover stew or curry etc., is cleaned up at breakfast along with two or three chops; same of eggs plus bacon and leftover vegetables.[8]

Shearers used to be renowned for their meat consumption. Dr J.W. Springthorpe calculated that shearers in the 1880s ate, on average, 2lb 10 1/3 oz meat per day (this included bone, and made no allowance for waste). Even today they still tend to be big meat eaters; many eat mutton five times a day – mutton chops for breakfast, cold mutton doorstop sandwiches at smoko, with perhaps some slices of buttered brownies[9], for dinner roast mutton, mutton stew and mutton casserole.

But even the most stoic shearer could tire of mutton, as Henry Lawson so eloquently described in his poem, 'The Green-Hand Rouseabout' (written towards the end of the nineteenth century):

> Call this hot? I beg your pardon. Hot! – you don't know what it means.
> (What's that waiter? Lamb or mutton! Thank you – mine is beef and greens.
> Bread and butter while I'm waiting. Milk? Oh, yes – a bucketful.)
> I'm just in from west the Darling, 'picking-up' and rolling wool.
> Mutton stewed or chops for breakfast, dry and tasteless, boiled in fat;
> Bread or brownie, tea or coffee – two hours graft in front of that;
> Legs of mutton boiled for dinner – mutton, greasy-warm for tea –
> Mutton curried (gave my order, beef and plenty greens for me).
> Breakfast, curried rice and mutton till your innards sacrifice,
> And you sicken at the colour and the smell of curried rice.
> All day long with living mutton – bits and belly wool and fleece;
> Blinding by the yoke of wool, and shirt and trousers stiff with grease,
> Till you long for sight of verdure, cabbage plots and water clear,
> And you crave for beef and butter as a boozer craves for beer.
> ...
> What's that? waiter? me? stuffed mutton! Look here, waiter, to be brief,
> I said beef! you blood-stained villain! Beef – moo-cow – Roast bullock – Beef![10]

Yet, despite the monotony of the provisions, the cook must be versatile. Good cooks build their reputation on their ability to adapt and improvise and to provide a variety of appetising foods from a familiar repertoire.

> Jules Innocence with two young sons cooked with a brick oven for eighty men in an open-walled building with a bricked oven at the end and little fires around it for warming in the morning. You could stoke a brick oven with coals overnight. In the morning this cook would put the red coals into warmers around the mess room and in pots to keep sausages warm. In the hot oven he'd cook in various stages of temperature throughout

the day – bread, then meat, etc. For breakfast he had rissoles, chops, steaks. When you're out there cooking with mutton there's not much variety, fatty too, but he managed.[11]

However, the ultimate example of ingenuity on the part of the shearers' cook would have to be shortbread biscuits made with mutton fat (plus flour, sugar and custard powder) recorded by Roger McDonald, a writer who took on the job of cooking for a team of New Zealand shearers and wrote about his experiences in *Shearers' Motel*.

Appendix I

Base/opening stores for about 20 people expected to last about 7-8 days. Supplied by Grazcos (shearing contractors), Burra, SA.

10 kg margarine
12 kg sugar
10 kg bacon
12 kg SR flour
8 kg sausages
4 kg plain flour
2 pkts puff pastry
1 baking soda
15 doz eggs
1 bag cooking salt
1 large coffee
1 pkt sultanas
1 x 600 ml cream
2 pkts brown sugar
4 kg cheese 3 kg rice
2 x 24 sliced cheese
8 x 825 g baked beans
3 kg sliced ham
8 x 825 g spaghetti
8 litres ice cream
8 x 825 tins tomatoes
6 pkts tea
4 x 825 g corn kernels
200 tea bags
4 x 825 g mushrooms
750 g Milo
2 pkts icing sugar
2 x apricot jam
2 pkts coconut

2 x raspberry jam
3 large coleslaw dressing
1 marmalade
1 white vinegar
1 plum jam
2 condensed milk
3 small Vegemite
3 pkts macaroni
4 large table salt
3 pkts spaghetti
4 x 100 g pepper
3 pkts lasagne sheets
1 x 250 g cocoa
10 x 2 litre cordial
3 tins Carnation milk
4 mustard pickles
10 pkts instant milk
parsley flakes
3 capsicums
2 celery
4 bunches spring onions
6 lemons
2 kg bananas
1/2 kg broccoli, zucchini or brussel sprouts
50 kg potatoes
3 large pumpkins
2 cauliflowers
3 large cabbages

8 kg carrots
4 lettuce
1 case tomatoes
10 kg onions
6 kg apples
1 case oranges
3 peanut paste
4 chutney
3 x 2 litres tomato sauce
4 x 500 ml worcestershire sauce
3 tins (catering size) each of: peaches, pineapple, fruit salad/two fruits, pears
2 honey
2 large Weet-Bix
1 pkt rolled oats
4 tins pie apples
2 large Corn Flakes
1 pkt Chux
1 mint sauce
1 disinfectant
1 pkt soup mix
16 toilet paper
12 x 750 g frozen peas
12 x 750 g frozen beans
2 pkts scourers
1 flyspray
1 paper towels

Appendix II

Schedule – Scale of Rations (for a pastoral employee provided with 'keep')[12]

Bread or flour	Meat

Vegetables, potatoes, onions, beans, peas (split and blue), green vegetables when reasonably procurable

Oatmeal	Fish
Rice	Cornflour
Tapioca or sago	Macaroni
Barley	Jam
Fruits—currants or raisins, dried apples, apricots, prunes	Tinned fruits
Sugar	Syrup
Honey	Tea, coffee or cocoa
Milk (fresh, condensed or powdered)	Curry
Salt (fine)	Mustard
Spices, herbs, pepper	Essence
Pickles	Vinegar
Sauce	Soap/washing soda (for cleaning
Carbonate of soda	cooking utensils)
Cheese	Butter (when reasonably procurable)
Suet	Cream of tartar
Eggs	Dripping
Jelly crystals	Custard powder

BIBLIOGRAPHY

Pastoral Industry Award 1968. Australian Government.
Rural Workers Accommodation Act 1969. New South Wales Government
Adam-Smith, Patsy. *The Shearers*. Nelson, Melbourne, 1982.
Boldrewood, Rolf. *Shearing in the Riverina, 1865*. Halstead Press, Sydney, 1983.
Harney, Bill. *Bill Harney's Cookbook*. Rigby, Adelaide, 1977. First pub. Landsdowne Press, 1960.
Lawson, Henry. *Collected Verse, Vol.I*: 1885-1900. Ed. Colin Roderick. Angus & Robertson, Sydney, 1967.
McDonald, Roger. *Shearer's Motel*. Pan MacMillan, Sydney, 1992.
Marshall, Alan. *The Complete Stories of Alan Marshall*. Nelson, Melbourne, 1977.
Springthorpe, J.W. *Hygienic Conditions in Victoria*. Stillwell, Melbourne, 1889.

REFERENCES

[1] Utility, pick-up truck
[2] Adam-Smith, 268.
[3] Marshall, 197.
[4] Rural Workers Accommodation Act 1969.
[5] McDonald, 11.
[6] McDonald, 34.
[7] Adam-Smith, 270.
[8] Adam-Smith, 272.
[9] There are several versions of brownie, some like a boiled fruit cake and others more like a sophisticated damper. This version is made with a scone-like dough. Bill Harney's *Brownie (Bush Plum Cake)*:

To 2lb of flour, to which rising has been added, put two or three good spoonfuls of fat, which should be rubbed thoroughly into the flour. Add sugar to taste, and plenty of currants and raisins. Add sufficient water to make a nice soft dough. Grease the inside of the camp oven thoroughly, scrape in the dough and cook like a Damper. Harney, 22.

[10] Lawson
[11] Adam-Smith
[12] Pastoral Industry Award, Section 66.

Mohammad:
the Man who Changed the Diet of a Billion People

Margaret Shaida

Introduction

There is a turning point in the history of nations, when an event occurs that alters the destiny – and, sometimes, the eating habits – of those countries for ever. For many, this turning point was the Arab invasion in the seventh century. From that time, the diet of people in Iran, the Middle East and North Africa was irrevocably changed by their Moslem conquerors.

One man – Mohammad – had ignited the Arabs and founded the religion of Islam. He prohibited pork and alcohol to all Moslems, and these prohibitions, along with the Moslem doctrine, were carried under the banner of Islam in the great Moslem conquests of the seventh and eighth centuries. He was thus responsible for exerting a deep influence on the eating habits of not only the people of Arabia, but also of Iran, the Middle East and North Africa, and of many other countries in Asia from the seventh century to the present time. Indeed, today, the diet of almost a billion people (a fifth of the population of the world) is determined by the strictures of Mohammad. It is for this reason that I have chosen him as the subject of my paper this year.

Background

For more than a thousand years (at least from the time of Herodotus in circa 500 BC to 500 AD), the Arabian peninsula had been inhabited by the nomadic bedouins in the central desert and the Arab traders in the city ports. They played a pivotal role in the trade between the Middle East, Africa and the Indian sub-continent.

The harsh life and shifting sands of the great Arabian desert had produced a hardy people who lived within a primitive, tribal and egalitarian society. They were polytheists and Mecca was their focal point. Mecca was believed to be the wilderness where Abraham, at Sarah's instigation, had abandoned Hajar and their son, Ishmael nearly 2,000 BC. They were saved from certain death by Gabriel who created a well of water – known to this day as the Zamzam spring. Mecca became a monotheist shrine. However, by the fifth century Ishmael's descendants had dissolved into a number of local tribes and warring factions, and Mecca had long since become a centre of local idolatry.

The tribes converged annually at Mecca and worshipped many gods in an atmosphere of temporary peace, equality and tolerance. They constructed no great buildings to house their gods, nor any complex hierarchy within which to practice their religion.

This was in complete contrast to the monotheist Jews and Christians of the Fertile Crescent to the far north of the Arabian peninsular. However, there had been a centuries-old Jewish presence both in the Hejaz region of Arabia and further south in the Yemen, as well as a number of Christian sects which had spread throughout the Middle East, notably the Monophysites in Syria and the Nestorians in Persia. Both Judaism and Christianity had found some modest support among the Arabs.

The two great powers ruling what is now known as the middle east were in the sixth century Rome (or New Rome, the eastern empire based on Constantinople) and Persia, both of them somewhat weakened by their continuing battle for supremacy. Persia was monotheist, following its thousand-year-old state religion of Zoroastrianism, which had also extended its influence to the borders of India and Greece and which was known to the Jewish exiles in Babylon. New Rome was

The Life of Mohammad

Mohammad was born in the southern Hejaz in about AD 570. His father died before he was born, and his mother when he was only five or six years old. Thereafter he was brought up by the poorest of his wealthy uncles, Abu Taleb. He became a shepherd when young, but on reaching the age of maturity, he became the commercial agent of a wealthy widow, Khadija. He and Khadija married and continued their activities in commerce.

It wasn't until the age of forty that Mohammad had his first numinous experience. Over the next fifteen years or so, he continued to receive messages from God, and these eventually formed the Moslem scripture, the Qor'an. After some time, and upon instructions from God, Mohammad began to spread the word.

In Mecca, his young movement was initially viewed with amused tolerance by his pagan countrymen, but as the monotheist Mohammad began to disparage their idols, relations became increasingly strained. In a world where tribal skirmishes settled most disputes, Mohammad and his small band of followers sought protection among the tribes. To this end, he left Mecca for Medina in the Christian year 622. This 'emigration' is called the *hijra* and the Moslem calendars are dated from from this event.

Mohammad continued to receive more revelations. At the same time, he devoted himself to consolidating his position. He intercepted rich Meccan caravans in order to enhance his finances, carried out successful attacks in the southern Hejaz, and finally returned in triumph to Mecca. His military successes were matched by the growth of his religious influence, as the Arab tribes were either defeated or voluntarily submitted to Mohammad's authority. In the last two years of his life, Mohammad began to move northward beyond the largely unified Hejaz to the edges of the Roman and Persian empires.

Throughout the Qor'an, the Jews and the Christians are referred to as 'followers of the Book'. Mohammad 'saw himself as the last in a line of prophets... from Moses down to Jesus'.[1] There seems little doubt that his message was well received by many Arabs who saw it as a re-affirmation of their direct descendancy from Abraham through Ishmael.

When Mohammad died in 632 AD, Islam was the leading monotheist religion in Arabia. The messages he had received directly from God had been gathered together in *ayat* (verses) and *sura* (chapters) to form the Qor'an; and the basic rituals and duties had been established. His sayings and explanations *(hadiths)* had also been gathered together as an aide to understanding and interpreting the Qor'an. His followers had developed into a morally responsible and disciplined fighting unit that looked far beyond the boundaries of Arabia to carry the message.

The Moslem Conquest

Within ten years of the death of Mohammad, the Moslem army had already made deep inroads into the Persian empire, and in 651, King Yazdegerd was killed, signalling the total collapse of Persia. Islam, however, was less speedily accepted. Eventually, the dwindling Zoroastrian communities withdrew, settling deep in the great deserts in central Iran (around Yazd), or fleeing to India where they established themselves in the Bombay area. Here, they are still known as the Parsees.

The Moslem conquest of the high Iranian plateau took less than twenty years and their conquest of the fertile crescent and the North African coast was equally rapid. By 711, they had invaded Spain and overwhelmed the ruling Visigoths. They reached up into northern Spain and as far north as

Poitiers in France, though in these northern regions their dominion remained weak. They ruled southern Spain for seven hundred years.

The desert tribes of pagan Arabia had exploded onto the world. United by Islam, they overran the sophisticated Persian empire, the ancient civilisations of the Near East (Syria, Egypt, Palestine and so on), the commercial centres of the southern and western Mediterranean, and a great part of the Iberian peninsula. Along the way, they picked up ideas on culture and the arts, administration, horticulture, astrology, philosophy, engineering, – and culinary skills – from their subject nations.

By the eighth century, the Caliphate of Baghdad, the heart of the Moslem empire, had become a centre of gastronomic and cultural excellence. Within the Islamic prohibitions, the Arabs had adopted the finest foods of its subject nations, and they went on to influence the food of Europe – through Spain and southern France, and later, via the Crusaders. As Reay Tannahill noted, while most of Europe was sunk in a barely literate daze, 'the banquets at the caliphs' court were renowned for the extravagance of the food, the poetry and the gastronomic erudition of the conversation.'[2]

The Dietary Code

Many of the rituals and duties (including the dietary regulations) had their origins in Judaic law or in pre-Islamic Arab custom. As Ali Dashti says in his book *Twenty-three Years,* 'the civilisation of every community or nation is coloured by elements from the civilisations of others.'[3] He went on to say, however, that irrespective of the Jewish or pagan origins of these rules, their purpose in Islam was undoubtedly the establishment of order and cohesion within the new, small and frequently embattled community.

This statement particularly relates to the ban on intoxicants – a prohibition that was new in both the Judaic-Christian and pagan Arab traditions, and also one that has resulted in much controversy. Mohammad actually conceded that wine (and gambling) had some good points, but he emphasised that 'their evil is greater than their utility' *(Sura* 2). Alcohol and gambling had often caused strife among the Arab tribes, and abstention would certainly have given the young, vulnerable community a reliable and sober superiority in battle. On three occasions, and with increasing fervour, Mohammad decried strong drink and called on his followers to abstain.

This would explain the anomaly of the Moslem promise of wine in the next world. Paradise is described as having 'rivers of wine, pleasant unto those who drink.' *(Sura* 47). There would, presumably, be no need for sobriety and battle fitness in heaven, and the warriors could look forward to a freer and easier life. Today, of course, many Moslems, accustomed to looking upon alcohol as unclean, recoil at the suggestion that heaven may be running with rivers of wine.

However, there are also many faithful Moslems who do drink alcohol, though not to the point of intoxication – and who argue their right to do so with force and imagination. Of course, Moslems have also been known to drink only for the escape that intoxication brings 'for the joy of losing pesonal identity and achieving union with God',[4] or, more prosaically, simply to get drunk. Chardin noted that 'if the Brandy is not as strong as Spirits or Wine, it does not please in Persia, and the Wine that is most esteem'd there, is that which is most Intoxicating.'[5] However, the fact remains that nowhere in the Qor'an is alcohol expressly forbidden *(harâm).*

The Qor'an's rules concerning diet are simple. Only three items are forbidden: carrion, blood and swine's flesh. According to the Qor'an, food is classified into two groups: *harâm* (unwholesome and forbidden); and *halâl* (wholesome and allowed). However, both groups may be consumed in times of dire emergency. It is better, in the sight of God, to eat carrion than to die. Throughout the Qor'an, fruit and herbs are highly commended.

Halâl animals may become forbidden if the method of slaughter does not shed blood – blood being *harâm.* Animals consecrated to other gods are also prohibited, which means that the name of God must be invoked at the moment of slaughter. By extension, therefore, any animal slaughtered by a non-believer is forbidden. This was clearly an attempt to deter Moslems who might have been tempted by pagan sacrifices. It is a problem that scarely arises in a country where Islam is the state religion, but one which has created difficulties in the modern world of international trade.

I should like to think that the three principal prohibitions (carrion, blood and pork) were declared because, in the days before refrigeration, they were considered to be potentially dangerous. However, I suspect that the origins may also be rooted in the long-held belief by peoples in many parts of the world that 'you are what you eat'.

As late as the 17th century, Iranian physicians were 'unanimously of the Opinion, that the Man becomes the same with the Animals upon which he feeds'.[6] The filth of swine, and the diseased quality of carrion are clearly undesirable attributes. Blood is the life force of a living creature and had long been sacred in sacrifice. Speculation as to why and how such food prohibitions came to be enforced has long engaged students and thinkers. It is a question that was discussed (inconclusively, it must be said) by Sami Zubaida at the Oxford Symposium ten years ago.[7]

According to Zubaida, in ancient times, 'swine avoidance was widespread in the Near East', and he goes on to suggest that the ancient Israelites may well have adopted some of their rituals from the Canaanites. The prohibitions that were adopted by Islam from the monotheist Jewish and pagan Arab rituals have their roots in prerecorded history. With the exception of the ban on alcohol, the restrictions probably did not come as a novel prohibition or severe hardship to the desert Arabs.

The simple prohibitions quickly became complicated by the *hadiths*. Once Mohammad had established himself in Medina, he was frequently consulted on all manner of points of Islamic law. His pronouncements were gathered together to form the *hadiths*. It is within these *hadiths* that we find a third classification – *makrooh* (unwholesome but allowed). Here we find that the meat of animals with fangs, claws and talons (i.e. predators) is *makrooh,* as are fish with teeth or without scales, and round creatures (i.e. snakes and eels).

There are many other recommendations concerning the quality of various foods and the correct way to eat them. He advised his followers on matters of health and manners – never eat while standing up; never pray on a full stomach; always leave the table hungry; always keep your food covered; ensure that food is well cooked and cooled before eating; and so on. He recommended the consumption of a date a day; and that grapes should be eaten one at a time to prevent flatulence. He said that an excess of cheese was inadvisable; and that forty paces should be taken after every meal. Many of these sayings were judgements, others recommendations, others explanations, most in response to requests and questions from his followers.

Over the centuries, the *uluma* (Islamic judges) have made a variety of pronouncements on the true meaning of these sayings (which relate to every aspect of life). For many Moslems, the *hadiths* have come to carry the same force as the Qor'an.

The Effects of the Dietary Code

There is limited information on the eating habits of the peoples of the Middle East before the Islamic conquest. Much can be gleaned from the pre-Islamic Judaic scriptures and the post-Islamic Arabic books of the Caliphate of Baghdad. But, by the very nature of these books, it follows that there are no recipes for pork or for dishes made with wine.

Nevertheless, there is little doubt that the Persians, at least, consumed both pork and alcohol before the Moslem conquest. There are frequent references to wild boar hunting by the ancient kings and aristocrats in Persian poetry and mythology; and the master masons at Persepolis are said to have been paid in wine.

A contemporary tale of the Sassanian King Khosrow (AD 535-579) refers to pig meat and its preparation. This is the story of a young aristocratic orphan who applied to the court of King Khosrow for a position in his entourage. In determining his aristocratic credentials, the king questioned him closely on the skills required of a young courtier. He asked him about riding, archery, music, hunting, and about food – and not just about the best-tasting or best-looking of foods but also about the methods of food preparation. In his responses, the lad refers to the meat of the boar and of the domesticated pig as being 'the finest', as well as 'ragout of hare'.[8]

The restrictions on certain types of fish would have had little effect on the majority of the Iranians on the high plateau, many of whom, even in this century, had never tasted fish. There might have been some problems in the Caspian region where fish is an important food item, but the Iranians were ever resourceful when it came to the *makroob* definition.

I suspect that the prohibition on wine had a far more cataclysmic effect, because the art of wine-making and beer-brewing goes back a long way in Iran. According to the bible, the first act of Noah after his ark had landed on Mount Ararat[9] (2,348 BC) was to plant a vineyard and then get drunk (Genesis IX, 20-21).

The presence of wine and beer in the north-western regions of Iran from a very early time has since been backed up by a report by Martin Bailey in *The Observer* of London last year. He wrote that 'wine and beer residues' found in a large room overlooking a courtyard at Godin Tepe (an archaeological dig in western Iran) were found to be 'more than five thousand years old.' Bailey goes on to quote Patrick McGovern, the Pennsylvanian chemist who analysed the residues, who said, 'There must have been some serious drinking going on in that room.'[10]

Herodotus, the Greek historian who travelled to Persia in about 450 BC, also commented on the serious drinking habits of the Persians and their propensity to get drunk. The Persians, he wrote, 'are very fond of wine, and drink it in large quantities.'[11] These comments should come as no surprise to anyone who has tasted the grapes from Shiraz, or, indeed, the wine that was made in Iran prior to the Revolution.

The transition to abstinence must have been very hard, and may explain why Iran was conquered in twenty years, but not converted to Islam for a further hundred years. And three hundred years after that, Omar Kihayyam was still exhorting his countrymen to:

> Drink! for you know not whence you came, nor why;
> Drink! for you know not why you go, nor where.[12]

Marco Polo noted that the Persians quieted their conscience by boiling wine so that 'they are free to drink it without breach of any commandment or law'.[13] And as recently as two hundred years ago, Sir John Chardin wrote that the Iranians made 'excellent wine everywhere.'[14]

Resistance to the alcohol ban appeared all over the Moslem world. Glubb Pasha wrote of the 'wine drinking parties among some of the heroes of the first muslim conquests only a few years after the death of the Prophet.' He went on to say that 'in Damascus, wine was regularly consumed at the court of the Umaiyad Khalifs.'[15]

It seems that the Moors also consumed alcohol in Spain. (Incidentally, I was interested to learn that, despite the centuries of Moslem occupation, pork and ham are very popular in Spain. I have been told that this was a result of the expulsion of the Moslems and the Jews: the one certain way to flush out any loiterers was to serve pork or ham. Today, Spain is reportedly the largest consumer of dried ham in the world – an indirect and unintended effect of Islamic and Judaic dietary prohibitions.)

In the past, I have speculated that the Iranians were accustomed to using wine in their cooking before the Moslem prohibition,[16] and that this was gradually replaced by the addition of vinegar, verjuice, sumac or other sour fruits. It seems a good way under difficult circumstances to maintain a piquant flavour. Raisins, currants and other dried grapes are used in many dishes – although today, good Moslem women will sauté the raisins in hot oil, three times, to ensure they don't ferment in the meal.

The Qor'anic reference to 'intoxicants' created problems for Moslems when coffee first made an appearance in Arabia in the fifteenth century. The question was eventually resolved, along with that of opium and tobacco, all being vegetable products and therefore *halâl* – although each is still subject to questioning and interpretation by the *uluma*.

Personal Experience in Twentieth-century Iran

When I went to Tehran in the mid-fifties, I was completely unaware of any restrictions on food, although I felt the absence of ham and pork. I also wondered why it was impossible to find a 'medium' steak in a restaurant, let alone a 'rare' one – and was told that meat running with blood is not considered appealing to Moslems. I wondered why my mother-in-law soaked meat in fresh water for at least five minutes before cooking it (to wash out the blood); and once I found her pouring away a bottle of vinegar – which, she explained, had turned to wine.

It was during the Revolution that I became more conscious of Moslem prohibitions. Many people recall the scenes on television of Moslems enthusiastically pouring away bottles of wine and spirits. The Armenian pork butcher in the centre of Tehran discreetly closed down, and foreign restaurants took to serving wine in teapots.

Clarification was required on many of the finer points of the dietary code that had for so long been ignored. In response to a question about frozen lamb, Ayatollah Khomeini declared it *harâm* – and he was probably right, since none of the imported frozen meat was slaughtered ritually. The import of meat had been allowed during the Shah's reign according to the Qor'an statement that 'the food of those to whom the scriptures were given is also allowed as lawful unto you.' [*Sura* 5]. This was taken to mean 'meat slain or dressed by Jews or Christians'.[17]

When asked for his views on this matter after the Revolution, Ayatollah Khomeini stated that imported meat was forbidden because it had not been ritually slaughtered. Once arrangements were made to correctly slaughter the animals before freezing, he agreed that such frozen meat would be *halâl* and could be imported into Iran. (Moslem slaughtermen were employed by New Zealand abbatoirs, and a mollah was sent to New Zealand to certify the correctness of the slaughter.)

The Ayatollah then proceeded to send shivers of horror through the managers of the caviar processing plant in the Caspian region when he responded that caviar was *harâm* – because it came from a scale-less fish. They hurried to explain to him that sturgeon had scales, which could be seen only under a miscroscope; he listened carefully and conceded that since they were the experts, he would take their word. Caviar was then pronounced *halâl*. Since sturgeon kebab had always been a great delicacy in the beach restaurants along the Caspian, we all sighed with relief to discover that we could go on enjoying it.

Conclusion

Throughout the centuries, religions have sought to ban alcohol and certain foods to their followers. These bans have been imposed for a variety (and a combination) of reasons ranging from a need for social identity, self control, social order, health and defence.

The egalitarian nature of Islam, its lack of hierarchy and nominated authority, has resulted in a continual re-definition and interpretation of the precepts of the Qor'an and the *hadiths*. Mollahs amass a following according to their personality, their character, and their judgements and interpretations of the scriptures. They may rise to become an ayatollah because of their knowledge and wisdom, but they are never formally elected. Ayatollah Khomeini rose to the top because he was perceived by many Moslems to be wise, honest, courageous and scrupulously fair in his judgements concerning Islam. His following extended far beyond the borders of his country because beliefs cannot be confined by borders on God's earth. This approach has led to a remarkably cohesive religion.

Despite the schism between Sunnis and Shi'as, and the numerous and diverse countries where Islam is the state religion, or where Islam is a thriving (or struggling) minority, the three basic dietary prohibitions of the Qor'an are adhered to by the great majority of Moslems. The differences in the interpretations of the *hadiths* have resulted in numerous variations in the observation of minor dietary rules in different regions, in different countries and in different centuries. But the basic prohibitions remain, and continue to exert an influence on the eating habits of a billion people in the world today.

Bibliography

Bailey, Martin. 'Drinking habit distilled form lees of a record vintage' in *The Observer*, 25 July 1993.
Cook, Michael. *Muhammad*, Oxford University Press 1983.
Chardin, John. *Travels in Persia 1673-1677*, reprinted Dover Publications 1988.
Dashti, 'Ali. *Twenty-three Years*, George Allen & Unwin 1985.
Fischer, Michael M. *Iran: from Religious Dispute to Revolution*, Harvard University Press 1980.
Glubb, John Bagot. *The Life and Times of Muhammad*, Hodder & Stoughton 1970.
Heron-Allen tr., *The Rubaiyat of Omar Khayyam*, Nicholas 1898.
Humphreys, Eileen. *The Royal Road*, Scorpion Publishing Ltd. 1991.
Latham, R.E. tr., *The Travels of Marco Polo*, Penguin 1958.
Montgomery Watt, W. *Muhammed, Prophet and Statesman*, Oxford University Press 1961.
Rawlinson, George tr., *The Histories of Herodotus*, Everyman's Library 1910.
Rodinson, Maxime, *Mohammed*, Penguin 1971 (in English).
Sale, George tr., *The Koran*, Frederick Warne & Co. 1891.
Shaida, Margaret. ' The Sometimes Sweet but Mostly Sour Flavour of Persian Food Today', *Oxford Symposium 1992*, Prospect Books 1993.
Smart, Ninian. *The Religious Experience of Mankind*, Charles Scribner's Sons 1969.
Tha'alibi, Abou Mansour Al. *Histoire des Rois des Perses*, H. Zotenberg 1900. I am indebted to Charles Perry for sending me a copy of a translation of the relevant section of this book.
Tannahill, Reay. *Food in History*, Penguin 1988.
Tapper, Richard. 'Blood, Wine and Water: social and symbolic aspects of drinks and drinking in the Islamic Middle East', *Culinary Cultures of the Middle East*, ed. Zubaida and Tapper, I.B.Tauris 1994.
Zubaida, Sami. 'Explanations of Biblical Food Prohibitions', *Oxford Symposium 1984 & 1985*, Prospect Books 1986.

REFERENCES

[1] Smart, 487
[2] Tannahill, 143
[3] Ali Dashti.
[4] Tapper, 225.
[5] Chardin, 106.
[6] Chardin, 232.
[7] Zubaida, 180-183.
[8] Tha'alibi.
[9] Mount Ararat was in Iran until this century when Reza Shah gave it to Turkey.
[10] Bailey.
[11] *The Histories of Herodotus*, tr. Rawlinson, 75.
[12] *The Rubaiyat of Omar Khayyam*, tr. Heron-Allen.
[13] *The Travels of Marco Polo*, tr. Latham, 31.
[14] Chardin, 242.
[15] Glubb, 82.
[16] Shaida, 243-246.
[17] *The Koran*, tr. Sale.

Elizabeth Raffald (1733-1781)

Roy Shipperbottom

In 1769, in Manchester, Elizabeth Raffald, a woman of prodigious energy and unflagging industry published her cookery book, *The Experienced English Housekeeper*; it was an immediate success. She described herself as a confectioner, a convenient but inadequate title that described just one of her many activities involved with food and cookery.

She was born in Doncaster, in 1733 and baptised Elizabeth Whitaker and she was given a reasonable education including a little French. Her sisters became confectioners or entered domestic service for there was ample work in the great houses of Yorkshire and with the growing middle and merchant class.

Servants were then one of the largest occupational groups with a distinct hierarchy and a division between the upper and lower domestics that was not only marked by duties and wages but also dress, food, access to the master and mistress and to some perquisites. Additionally, as Jean Hecht has pointed out, they were able to observe and imitate their dress, customs and manners.

Elizabeth began working in the homes of what she described as 'great and worthy families' when she was about fifteen years old and it is likely that she had some experience as a confectioner before this; some of the Yorkshire outlets she used to sell her book were confectioners and grocers. Certainly she knew York, the centre of social, ecclesiastical and military life in the North of England with its Assembly Rooms, theatre, racecourse and the town houses of the landed gentry where, particularly in the season, splendid dinners were given with elaborate table decorations and architectural dessert courses with sugar temples, fruit pyramids, sugar paste plates and wet and dry sweetmeats, supplied by confectioners and, as the invoices show, sometimes hired for the occasion. Elizabeth included in her book a chapter headed 'Decorations for a Table': the spinning of gold and silver webs to cover sweetmeats, the making of jelly, sweet and savoury, fish ponds and gilded fish, playing cards in flummery, hen's nests, floating and rocky islands and a Solomon's Temple. These elaborate confections were also regularly made, advertised and sold by Elizabeth Raffald in her shops in Fennel Street and, later, the Market Place, Manchester.

One early December day in 1760 she left Yorkshire to travel to Cheshire and become housekeeper to Sir Peter and Lady Elizabeth Warburton whose residence, Arley Hall, was undergoing substantial improvements; the black and white structure given a brick facade and additions and fashionable sash windows. The pleasure gardens were improved by the head gardener, John Raffald, a tall man of prepossessing appearance and an able botanist. It is likely that he suggested that Elizabeth Whitaker would make an admirable housekeeper; personal recommendation was a more certain method of recruitment than advertisements or the register offices and he too had worked in, and travelled from, the same part of Yorkshire to work for the Warburtons.

Lady Elizabeth Warburton, affectionately known as Lady Betty, was the eldest daughter of the Earl of Derby, her sisters included Lady Charlotte, who eloped with John Burgoyne, dramatist and soldier who was successful in becoming Member of Parliament for Preston, Lancashire but is usually remembered as the general who was defeated at Saratoga. He used to visit Sir Watts and Lady Horton of Chadderton Hall near Manchester; Lady Horton was another member of the Derby family.

The new housekeeper had among her many duties the business of making preserves and pickles, potting and collaring meats, the making of savoury jelly and cakes and country wines. She bought from those who came to the kitchen with oysters, lobsters, codfish and herrings, tripe, eggs and butter and kept a small imprest account to reclaim the money from Peter Harper the House Steward. She was familiar with making cakes and biscuits and elaborate party food and the correct way of dressing the peas, beans, asparagus and cucumbers brought in by the head gardener, John Raffald. Their acquaintance grew into love and Elizabeth Whitaker and John Raffald were married at Great Budworth on 3rd March 1763 and soon left Arley Hall for Manchester, a market town, not yet a boom town, but famous for fustians and linens and now turning to cotton. It was free from guild restrictions and was the home of many merchants who gave employment to the cottage industries. Defoe wrote it was 'the greatest mere village in England'. John Raffald's brother had a nursery within half a mile of the Market Place and a stall on the market so there was work for John, and, of particular interest to Elizabeth there was no shop that offered anything which could possibly rival what she was about to offer; fine food and confectionery, table decorations and a supply of servants to fill the needs of men of thrusting ambition, new wealth, and unencumbered money. The capital the Raffalds had is not known; twenty pounds, nineteen shillings and eleven pence was the amount Mrs Raffald received when she left Arley on the 23rd April 1763, for she had not drawn her sixteen pounds wages for 1762; John Raffald's wages were twenty pounds a year. Legally he had complete dominance and control over her money, but in fact Elizabeth with her strong personality was able to exercise considerable influence; among the factors she controlled were her skill, experience and enterprise. She may have known Defoe's contempt for those who fitted up with mirrors and silver and glass a pastry-cook's for two or three hundred pounds when twenty pounds might suffice for all that was necessary; she wasted neither time nor money in setting up shop.

They rented property in Fennell Street, near the collegiate church, grammar school and Chetham's Hospital and library; out of the main stream of trade but a reasonable beginning and she made the street burst into life. She advertised her spare rooms for use as storage, she sold her brawn, salmon and cakes for wedding and christenings and started a Register Office, a simple way of bringing together, for a fee, employer and servant. This system, reputed to have been devised by Henry Fielding, the novelist, was sometimes interpreted as a means of procuring women and was the subject of a farce in two acts by Joseph Reed. During what was a simple Manchester season, a race meeting, dinners and assemblies, there came a theatrical company who performed extracts from plays and included scenes from 'The Register Office'. The farce consists of a number of stereotypes, with pronounced accents and the scene they chose involved a Yorkshirewoman, Margery Moorpout, who was given the position of Housekeeper and charged accordingly 'Our Fee is only a shilling for a common place but for a Housekeeper's...half a crown'. She had left her previous employer Madam Shrillpipe in 'St Poles Kirk-Garth' because the squire 'ad not let me be... he was after me Mworn, Noon, an Neeght... if I wad but ha consented to his wicked ways'. Later enters Mrs Snarewell, a Procuress, the reputation of whose house 'would be utterly blasted for want of fresh faces'. She is told that fifty damsels have replied to an advertisement and 'you might have cull'd half a dozen at least,... such fresh blooming damsels'. An ingenious institution was now apparently perverted and a disguise for pimping.

Elizabeth Raffald, a Yorkshirewoman with a Yorkshire accent, a former Housekeeper running the only Register Office in Manchester, was offended and inserted the following tailpiece to her advertisement in *The Mercury*. 'As several of Mrs Raffald's friends in the country have mistook the Terms and Designs of her Register Office she begs leave to inform them that she supplies Families with Servants...'.

Mrs Raffald kept in contact with Lady Elizabeth Warburton; the Arley accounts show that on one visit on July 12 1766 the horses for Mrs Raffald's post chaise were fed. She would go the expensive journey on business and take the opportunity to make deliveries, suggest a servant, or ask permission to dedicate her new venture, a book, to one to whom she 'had the happiness of giving satisfaction', and 'it would be a still greater encouragement should my endeavours for the service of the sex be honoured with the favourable opinion of so good a judge of propriety and elegance as your Ladyship'; perhaps she went to show off her baby. The number of babies she had has always fascinated those who have written about Elizabeth Raffald—they usually settle on sixteen, which is what the *Dictionary of National Biography* says. This entry was written by the Manchester City Librarian, Charles Sutton, who picked up the information from an interview, full of errors, in 1852, with a granddaughter of Mrs Raffald whom she had never met. The same interview mentions nine entries in the missing family Bible but the parish registers show six, all girls; and they were named Sarah, Emma (1766), Grace (1767), Betty (1769), Anne (1770) and Harriot (1772).

She made regular use of the advertising columns of the *Manchester Mercury* and, later, the rival *Prescott's Journal* and often, taking advantage of the special terms, repeated advertisements week after week. Business flourished, she added cookery classes to her activities, expanded her stock and in 1767 moved to the Market Place near the Exchange. She now superintended public dinners and also supplied the food.

In 1768, among the goods for sale at Raffald's Shop Near the Exchange, were 'Canterbury, Shrewbury and Derbyshire Brawn, Newcastle Salmon, Yorkshire Hams, Tongues and Chaps, Potted Woodcocks, Char and Potted Meats, Portable Soups for Travellers… fresh Mushroom Catchup, Walnut Catchup, Lemon Pickle and Browning for made Dishes, Pickled Mushrooms, Barberrys, Mangos, and other sorts of Pickles; dry and wet sweetmeats, Plumb cakes for Weddings and Christenings, and all sorts of Cakes, Mackroons and Biskets, Jellies, Creams, Flummery, Gold and Silver Webs for covering sweetmeats, and all other decorations for cold Entertainments…' the list continues with what are clearly bought-in spices, imported foods and fruit and goods for gardeners.

This and other advertisements reveal that when she was writing her book she was indeed writing from experience and could justly claim to be writing 'from Practice'.

In 1769 she advertised her book:

> an entire new Work, Wrote for the Use and Ease of Ladies, House-keepers, Cooks, &c. entitled The EXPERIENCED ENGLISH House-keeper by ELIZABETH RAFFALD. Wrote purely from Practice, and Dedicated to the Hon. Lady Elizabeth Warburton, Whom The Author lately Served as House-keeper. Consisting of near 800 Original Receipts, most of which never appeared in Print.
>
> First Part, Lemon Pickle, Browning for all Sorts of made Dishes, Soups, Fish, plain Meat, Game, made dishes both hot and cold, Pyes, Puddings, &c.
>
> Second Part, All kinds of Confectionery, particularly the Gold and Silver Web for covering of Sweetmeats, and a desert of Spun Sugar, with directions to set out a Table in the most elegant Manner, and in the most modern Taste, Floating Islands, Fish Ponds, Transparent Puddings, Trifles, Whips, &c.
>
> Third Part, Pickling, Potting and Collaring, Wines, Vinegars, Catchups, Distilling, with two most valuable Receipts, one for refining Malt Liquors, the other for curing Acid Wines, and a correct List of every Thing in Season in every Month of the Year.

The book was subscribed in North West England, Yorkshire and London, Five Shillings to subscribers, Six Shillings to those who waited until after publication. The book 'to be signed by the Author's own Hand-writing'. The work, she complained, affected her health.

She was encouraged by receiving over eight hundred subscriptions. In her preface she assured readers that the recipes were 'not borrowed from other authors, nor glossed over with hard names or words of high style but wrote in my own plain language and every sheet carefully perused as it came from the Press, having an opportunity of having it printed by a neighbour, whom I can rely on doing it the strictest justice, without the least alteration'. The neighbour was Joseph Harrop who also printed and published, weekly, *Harrop's Manchester Mercury*.

The book sold swiftly, a second edition soon appeared and included about a hundred additional receipts and she immediately revealed that some originated from the collections of 'a noble generous-minded lady' and other 'worthy ladies'. She wrote 'Those I have tried, I found really valuable and those which I have not yet had such an opportunity of proving the goodness of, I have weighed them the best I could, and carefully examined their probable goodness, before I ventured to publish them. These are given genuine as they were purchased at a considerable expence from the inventers.'

There were seven editions of the book published in her lifetime and she entered one of the various methods of selling the copyright to R. Baldwin of Paternoster Row for the reputed sum of £1400. He asked that some northern words be changed but she refused; one of these words must have been 'garth'. The wooden garth or hoop in which she advised cakes to be baked is still a word used, nostalgically, in Manchester to describe a child's toy hoop. The book continued in print well into the nineteenth century; there were thirteen genuine and at least twenty three spurious editions.

In 1772 she compiled and published her *Manchester Directory*, the town's first Directory, a necessary guide to the rapidly developing commercial and manufacturing centre, by which time the Market Place shop was sold and the Raffalds had moved a short distance across the river to the King's Head, Salford, a 'commodious coaching inn'. She produced a second Directory in 1773. They established Florists Feasts, re-started the Card Assemblies, and hired out chaises and funeral coaches but adverse trade, and pressing creditors compelled them to leave. Elizabeth's problems were exacerbated by John's drinking. Once coming down from bed at midday with a heavy hangover he said he was tired of life and threatened to drown himself. This met with the retort from Elizabeth, 'Well, I'll tell you what John Raffald I do think that it might be the best step you could take for then you would be relieved of all your troubles and anxieties and you really do harass me very much'.

To maintain the family Elizabeth started a refreshment business 'during the strawberry season' at the Racecourse on Kersal Moor selling coffee, tea, chocolate, strawberries and cream.

John Raffald, now an improvident spendthrift, became the Master of the Exchange Coffee House, Manchester and Elizabeth took over the catering, mainly soups, and with unremitting industry compiled and issued a third *Manchester Directory* and continued to sell her cookery book; the eighth edition was in preparation when Elizabeth Raffald died, 'of a spasm' on the 19th April 1781 at 5.27 p.m. 'lamented by a numerous acquaintance'. She was buried at Stockport fashionably early in the morning, mourned by her husband and three surviving daughters.

SOURCES

The Warburton muniments
The Raffald papers
Harrops Manchester Mercury 1758-1785
Prescott's: every available issue
York Courant 1759-1771
The Experienced English Housekeeper, 1st edition, Manchester 1769 and 2nd edition R. Baldwin, London.
Lancashire Memories by Louisa Potter, published MacMillan, 1850.
The *Manchester Directories* 1771, 1772 and 1781 compiled by Elizabeth Raffald and printed by J. Harrop
The Domestic Servant in Eighteenth-Century England by J. Jean Hecht, published Routledge and Kegan Paul, 1956 and reprinted 1980.

La Cuisine de M. Momo

Birgit Siesby

M. Momo is no other than the painter Henri de Toulouse-Lautrec. He was born in 1864 into a wealthy noble family. As a child he was crippled after a fall and his legs stopped growing. It may have been caused by being a child of two first cousins. He usually claimed that if his legs had grown normally, he would never have become a painter.

Being French he had a vital interest in food. He loved to talk about food, to eat, and not least to cook. He cooked for himself, for a few friends and he even went out cooking for friends. Momo never invited more than 8-9 guests of whom no more than one or two might be women. They should behave like men and should not use the charms of their sex to distract attention from the meal. 'Philandering impedes, as everyone knows, the ability to concentrate.'

He made up menus and illustrated them and some of these have been kept. He did culinary field studies, often together with his childhood friend, Maurice Joyant. They spied on the skills and the recipes of good chefs and family recipe collections and took elaborate notes. Momo died in 1901 and Maurice Joyant published in 1930 a commemorative book, *La Cuisine de Monsieur Momo*, containing his collection of recipes, menus and *formules* – suggestions for two main courses around which the menu should be composed. The menus mostly consist of an hors-d'oeuvre, vegetables, salads, pies, (entremets), cheese, fruit and dessert, in addition to the two main courses, usually a fish and a meat course. 'The harmony of the luncheon is achieved by a combination of the two main courses which are the focus of the menu.'

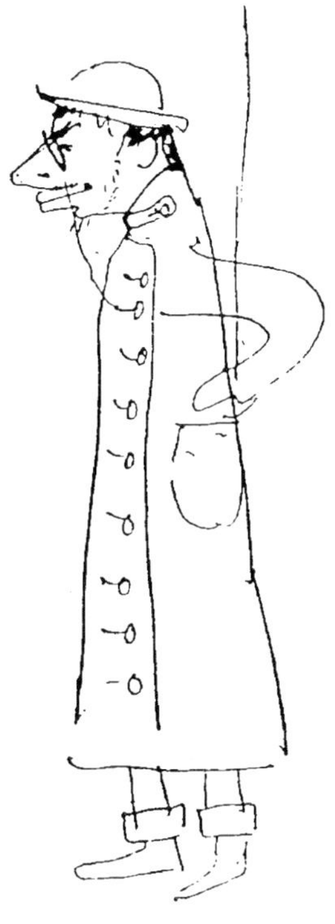

The book was published in only 250 numbered copies. In 1966 a second edition was published, but it did not contain all the information of the original book. There are only, of course, a handful of copies left of the first edition. I knew one was to be found at the Bibliothèque National in Paris and I tried through our Royal Danish Library to get a photocopy or a microfilm – but in vain. So I decided to go to Paris. I was lucky to be able, through librarian friends, to get admission to the rare book collection at BN.

After several formalities – they took hours – I was admitted to the holy rare book department and the book was ready on the desk for me. The whole atmosphere in the reading room was solemn. Well, I had done my homework in order to get the most out of the book and I started to take out my pen and paper. Immediately the librarian came tiptoeing in and without a word handed me a pencil – how did I dare use a pen. I looked through the book and again he turned up, this time with a heavy kind of textile-sausage to put over the pages so that I did not soil the leaves by touching.

The book was wonderful. I would call it a genuine pearl. And as genuine pearls gain in beauty by being used regularly I

H. de Toulouse-Lautrec par lui-même

decided that these recipes should certainly be used by today's consumer. So I went home starting to write my little book. I read all I could get hold of about Toulouse-Lautrec and I found in one of the last books an innocent footnote that THE book was to be found in one of our Danish art collections. So do come to Copenhagen to see it for yourself. I shall gladly guide you to the pearl. So far you do not have to apply for admission and you may even touch the book, though they do not allow you to take photocopies or microfilms.

In the 1966 edition all the illustrations, and there are many, over two hundred – are printed over the text in a very disorderly manner. The illustrations disturb the text and the text blurs the illustrations. The original book contains simple drawings printed on separate pages, 24 altogether. The recipes in the two books, apart from a few omitted in the 1966 edition, are just about identical, but the original book also mentions the source of each recipe, which gives an idea of the life of the artist. Many of the recipes are from chefs and people he met on his journeys. He often went on the small freighters going between Le Havre and Dakar in Senegal asking the captain to stop at a port in Brittany so that he could inspect the fishing boats' cargo of fresh fish. He then used the ship's boiler-room as a kitchen and made wonderful dishes. I am especially fond of his fish recipes.

But most of the recipes he got from family and relatives, though he claims that the dessert *pets de nonnes* (nuns' farts) originates from the Notre-Dame Nunnery at Verdelais, Gironde. I wonder if he is pulling our legs.

Together with the recipes Momo often tells little anecdotes, like when carving poultry the grandmothers insisted on giving the breast to the sons, sons-in-law and the grandsons. They were to continue the family and the breast was considered the very best part of the poultry. The daughters and daughters-in-law got the drumsticks and shoulders and the granddaughters got the rest – and it was extremely difficult to swop the pieces, you had to be very shrewd.

It is not enough to have a good recipe, the dish must be prepared and tasted in the right atmosphere. Momo was going to prepare *Homard à l'Americaine* in the flat of a good friend, the antiquarian bookseller, Georges Henri-Manuel, whose walls were covered by his invaluable book collection, and who had many other precious objects in his bachelor's flat. Momo insisted on cooking in one of the living rooms – which had the right atmosphere – so the slightly irritated host had to cover up with sheets. The dish was magnificent and the host forgave him.

The one hundred year old recipes generally do not have too many ingredients and are simple to prepare. It is not what you would call elegant food – food arranged on the plate with more or less every ingredient served beautifully with appropriate distance. It is food where most of the ingredients are cooked together to give the dish a full-bodied, satisfactory flavour. It is not food of today. Do not misunderstand me if I say, it is food of yesterday. Our young people have probably never tasted anything like it. I dedicated my book to my son, who was almost euphoric during the period we were testing the recipes and he declared he had never eaten such delicious food.

Quoting Momo again, he says that the quality of the foodstuff is crucial, the careful preparation and the long simmering are some of the secrets of a good meal. The correct use of herbs and spices is also invaluable. A good cook uses his herbs like a musician his notes and a painter his colours. Herbs makes the dish sing. Momo always carried a nutmeg and a small grater, mostly using it for his port but also to give taste to a dish. How important good food was for TL can be illustrated by the dish *Ramereaux aux Olives*, Wood Pigeons in Olive Sauce. He invented the recipe together with good friends and whenever he spoke about amateur painters or people with dubious taste, he remarked that they would not appreciate the wood pigeons in olive sauce.

Whether the meal should finish with cheese or sweets is debatable. Cheese and wine is a perfect ending. But a single biscuit, dipped in wine is not bad either, not to mention roasted almonds or nuts, which tempt one to drink some more.

Toulouse-Lautrec never had any doubts about what to drink with a meal: wine enriches the sense of taste during a meal, water degrades it. 'Never be tempted by water. The water tap should be sealed at lunchtime; if for example a sauce goes wrong, adding water doesn't help at all, one only achieves a taste of dishwater.' Momo demonstratively put a carafe of water on the table with a goldfish in it, to discourage anyone. The wine should be of the best quality. That was easy enough for Toulouse-Lautrec; he regularly received wine sent from his mother's estate and the estates of other family members. It is he who said: 'this Burgundy unfolds on the palate like a peacock's tail'. One thing is certain, the coffee ending the meal must be impeccable. Just as a mediocre coffee can ruin a good meal, a first rate coffee enhances it.

All the recipes in the book are wonderful, but I chose for my book the recipes of the dishes he mentions in his menus and *formules* as I assume those are the ones he used when he was cooking for friends. Care, effort and humility are some of the secrets of being successful in art as well as in preparing a culinary meal. You have to take the time to choose the best foodstuffs, to prepare and to cook them. Some of the recipes demand very long cooking. But that does not mean that you have to sit and stare at the dish cooking for hours. It does mean that the ingredients are allowed time to blend and give the right aroma and flavour to the dish.

One of my favourite dishes is red cabbage stuffed with chestnuts and meat and cooked in red wine – for 8-10 hours. Once I served my husband this dish; his first remark was that 'you know I am not fond of cabbage'. Well, there was very little left over at the end of the meal when he declared that this dish we must serve for friends.

Momo despised intricate cooking – good raw material should speak for itself. The dishes should be genuine and honest and should not be drowned in a multitude of accompaniments. The dishes are genuine and many of them rather solid, maybe best suited for weekend cooking when there is time to enjoy both the preparation and the consuming of the meal.

I shall end by quoting my absolute favourite recipe of Momo's. It is *Poissons de mer bouillis avec des pommes de terre*, a fish casserole with potatoes. It contains all that characterizes Momo's recipes: it unites the good raw material in a simple, refined, easily prepared and a delicious dish. It is meant to be cooked on the beach, where you catch the fish and put it in the pot directly. But even without a beach the dish is exquisite: Boil some potatoes, cut in pieces, half-covered by salted water (Momo used sea water) for 15 minutes, chop some shallots coarsely and put them on top of the potatoes together with fresh herbs, continue boiling for 3 minutes and on top of this you arrange the cleaned fish, without stirring, put the lid on and continue to cook for about 10 minutes. Then you pour over melted butter mixed with a little grated shallot and white wine vinegar and sprinkle with chopped parsley. Serve the dish in the pot and eat from deep dishes with a spoon and a fork. It is food with a soul.

'Nos contemporains chez eux', Le Docteur G.T. de C. composant une sauce

Tryon and his Century

Colin Spencer

Thomas Tryon's life straddles a curiously vital part of British history, and much of what occurred within his life-span is pertinent to the way our society works today. He was born in 1634, a few years after Charles I dissolved Parliament. The dissolution sprang out of the monarch's belief in his Divine Right. Tryon died in 1703, one year after Queen Anne had ascended the throne and fifteen years after the 1688 Glorious Revolution, which allowed a Parliament to be formed independent of the monarch. So Tryon's formative adolescent years were spent in a republic ruled by rigorous ascetic beliefs, while he was twenty-six when the Restoration occurred, a period notorious for its amorality and licentiousness.

The seventeenth century is crucial to the understanding of our own century, and Thomas Tryon seems to me important because he is not only a product of it, but also a severe critic of much of the emerging characteristics which identify that century. Tryon remains the only voluble ascetic, celebrating the foods of asceticism, in a long tradition which links the ancient world with our own contemporary concerns. Yet Tryon is also very much a product of Cromwell's Republic; he is self-educated, rising from the rural working class to become an author of fifteen books, many of them going into second and third editions in his lifetime. These works influenced luminaries of succeeding centuries like Benjamin Franklin, Joseph Ritson and Shelley. Indeed, he influenced his own contemporaries too, like Aphra Behn, the playwright and her circle. Because the English seventeenth century created so many of the systems and concepts that are part of our social structure today, I have set Tryon firmly within its context, trying to suggest what were the main trends, often disturbingly new to society, which Tryon either rebuffed or immersed himself in.

He was born in the small village of Bilbury, near Cirencester. His father, William, was a tiler and he was sent to the village school, but he barely learnt to read when his father, in 1643, put him to work spinning and carding. As this was the time of the Civil War and the Puritans were at that time losing the struggle, it must have seemed a time of great uncertainty. No doubt his father found the boy the first job he could get which earned him two shillings a week. The war ended in 1646 with the Puritans victorious. Thomas was eleven and he became a shepherd tending a small flock of sheep. But he longed to travel, so in 1652, having sold his three sheep for the sum of three pounds, he trudged to London and became apprenticed to a hatter in Bridewell Dock, Fleet Street. Soon after, following his master's example, he became an Anabaptist, working overtime in order to buy books. Through endless reading he educated himself, studying in particular astrology and medicine. In 1657, influenced by the mystical works of Behmen he broke with the Anabaptists and became a Pythagorean – he was twenty-three.

The German mystic, Jacob Behmen (1575-1624) managed to combine Biblical doctrine with Renaissance nature mysticism, incorporating elements of the Hermetic tradition, re-discovering both Pythagoras and Plutarch with their central compassion for animals and refusal to eat flesh. Between 1644 and 1662 all of his writings were translated into English. Behmen regarded astrology as a partial road towards the truth. He taught that the fundamental human kinship with the universe was the basis for mystical union with God. This is the heart of Behmen's non-violence. To kill is to break and sunder the mystical union. To slaughter animals for food is to build barriers between the soul and God.

Behmen's works much influenced the Ranters who travelled and preached about the land. One of them, Jacob Bottomley, wrote, 'I see God is in all creatures, man and beast, fish and fowl and every green thing from the highest cedar to the ivy on the wall; and that God is the life and being of them all.'[1] It is a sentiment which permeates the books which Tryon will write later. In becoming a Behmen at 23 he was joining a lively, radical but intensely pious tradition which in its unorthodoxy shocked and frightened the majority. But Tryon joined this faith just a few years before the Restoration; such faiths were not only already unpopular, they were now heartily detested.

The seventeenth century saw the change from a largely agricultural society, where both men and women were labourers, to a mercantile society where feudalism finally died and the petit-bourgeoisie grew in its stead. Tryon starts off as a shepherd and ends up as a member of the bourgeoisie. He has become part of this brave new world where the market ruled, for it 'depended on the spread of a new personality type, one able to control animal urges and to delay the satisfaction of present wants for future gains, one governed by internal constraints...'.[2] It was a society where the *parvenu* first appeared in any appreciable number[3] and made a huge splash; where fortunes were made by speculation on the soaring markets of the East Indian trade – like Sir Josiah Child who rose from a merchant's apprentice to the management of the East India Company's Stock and was worth, according to John Evelyn, £20,000. Evelyn wrote of visiting his gardens constructed in a barren spot in Epping Forest where planting walnut trees and making fishponds many miles in circuit had cost a prodigious amount.[4]

But the less successful members of society knew now that there was also a faint possibility of them becoming rich beyond their wildest dreams. This new society of middle-class people redefined the gender roles (see below) and that of the family itself. They put a high premium upon self-discipline, hard work and frugality, ('I betook myself to water only for drink, and forebore eating any kind of flesh, confining myself to an abstemious self-denying life. My drink was only water, and food only bread and some fruit.'[5]) for class, for the first time, was now fluid and by these means a person could rise in the world, as Tryon was doing, to positions of power, wealth and authority. And if not quite that, at least to owning a handsome new house and being able to commission a portrait of the family to adorn it.

Men went out into the world to trade and make their fortunes, while the women stayed at home and became the living symbol of the husband's wealth and position. The end of the seventeenth century saw the first stirrings of the birth of capitalism which turned the male into a competitive animal. Also, a copulating one within the confines of marriage.[6] The burgeoning population tended to be crowded into urban centres which grew into a seething morass of human hunger and desire, in Defoe's phrase, 'the miserable that really pinch and suffer want.'[7] It is a century of extremes, of science, reasoning and new discoveries, the beginning of agricultural technology and the growth of cities and the first official fire engines; an age where the first English settlement in India began and the new Cathedral of St Paul's was built; an age which saw the Societies for the Reformation of Manners, which wanted to banish prostitutes from the streets and make it illegal for a man to eat a mutton pie on the Sabbath; where Congreve's *Double Dealer* and Farquhar's *Beaux Stratagem* were staged and Jeremy Collier's *Short View of the Immorality and Profaneness of the English Stage* was eagerly read. It is an age which created the Bank of England and the coffee house, where tea and chocolate were also first drunk, where Hawkesmoor built elegant churches and Queen Mary collected blue and white Delft china. In the year of the Restoration one of the first Ice Houses was built in St. James' Park where summer drinks were kept and sold from a stall.

There was a new emphasis on sexuality within the marriage, which Puritanism spawned. It came particularly from Calvin who said that sexual expression between man and wife need not only be for procreation, it could also be part of the love which bound the marriage. This was revolutionary. Earlier, sex for pleasure had tended to occur outside the marriage. But the age of marriage was still late, around 28 for men and 26 for women between the years 1600 and 1850. Tryon married Susannah, 'a sober young woman' whom he did not succeed in converting to his 'innocent way of living'[8] in 1661 when he was twenty-seven. The celibacy rate declined from 25% in 1641 to 10% in 1690. The beginnings of the industrial revolution meant a little more money for the lower classes, which meant savings could be put aside and commitment to marriage made.

The end of the seventeenth century also marks the beginnings of a new social obsession which would become a great driving force in the commerce of the new industrial age about to dawn in the following century – that of social emulation. With the onset of the new petit-bourgeoisie eager to rise we have a social structure which is all eyes upon everybody else, ever watchful for new styles and modes, for the details of public display. By the eighteenth century everyone had a money income and were prepared to spend it on the details of social emulation. 'Social imitation and emulating spending penetrating deeper than ever before through the closely packed ranks of eighteenth century society.'[9] A huge increase in small rural factories which produced non-essential goods occurred at this time: toys, pins, lace, glasses, cards, puppets, toothpicks. The class that bought were neither poor nor rich, they were the middle-income market, the artisans, tradesmen, the engineers and clerks. Exactly Tryon's social strata when an apprentice and newly married. The textile industries began to flourish, turning out cottons, woollens, linens and silks. Crockery in new designs poured out of Staffordshire potteries. Birmingham factories produced buckles, buttons and brooches. All this to bedeck the female who was in search of a partner and the resulting family. This fusion between sexual needs and the beginnings of capitalism marks the age in a most striking manner. But what placed an idealistic gloss upon the biological need was also completely new. Publishers were booming, women's journals, stories and novels were being read and they had one theme – romantic love.

It had now become fashionable to marry for love. Before, marriages had been planned by parents and the suitability of partners was worked out strategically: for land, property and class. And though these issues still had great power to persuade and occupy the concerns of parents, the younger generations themselves were obsessed with the concept of 'falling in love'. So we myst accept that Tom Tryon and Susannah married for love and settled down in the London of the Restoration. Charles II had returned the year before and almost at once the Republic that had moulded the young shepherd vanished into the shadows of society and became a butt for jokes and caricatures in the new drama. How this new society must have dazzled Tryon where lewdness was flouted as flagrantly as the new money that stemmed from trade. One can well understand his vision of a hard-working, restrained and dedicated society, fueled by self-sacrifice, becoming strengthened by the excesses of the Restoration.

Yet undoubtedly, Tyron was caught up into it too, for the relationship between sex and capitalism had a spin-off, and it was the connection between consumerism and the family.[10] All the new goods and clothes were bought, worn and used, firstly to beguile and attract sexually; the end result being marriage and a family. And secondly, society placed enormous significance upon the family as an effective system which consumed. Hume wrote that in order to govern men they must be fueled and animated 'with the spirit of avarice'. Later, 'people work harder to consume more.'[11] More clothes and objects were used to raise the status of the family, to emphasize its attraction and place in society. Consumerism was the new machine which activated the whole of society; Bernard de Mandeville (1670-1733) in his *The Fable of the Bees* argued that if pride and luxury were banished, goodly numbers of artisans would starve within half a year. 'The idea of man as a consuming animal with boundless appetites, capable of driving the economy to new levels of prosperity, arrived with the economic literature of the 1690s.'[12] How Mrs Thatcher would have revelled in this new age.

But what of food and man's appetite for that? Was this boundless too? If we look at a writer like Gervase Markham, who, though he died in 1637, his book *The English Housewife* went on being published after his death, one gets a picture of what was thought to be a suitable meal for the dawn of the middle classes, who were furiously emulating their gentry. Markham refers to a 'humble feast' of thirty-two dishes which 'is as much as can conveniently stand on one table.' There are sixteen items of meat, a brawn with mustard, three boiled capons, boiled beef, a chine of roasted beef, a neat's[13] tongue, a roast pig, goose, swan and turkey, a haunch of venison, a venison pasty and a kid with a pudding in its belly. There were also side dishes, an olive pie, a custard, salads and fricassees. A simple fricassee contained fried eggs, collops of bacon, ling[14], beef and young pork. While a compound fricassee described as 'Things of Request and Estimation in France, Spain, Italy and the most Curious Nations,' contained all that as well as tansies, scrambled egg made with cream and the juice of blades of wheat, violet and strawberry leaves, spinach and walnut tree buds, with grated bread, cinnamon, nutmeg and salt, sprinkled with sugar. The meal finished with a marrowbone pie, made by alternating layers of jerusalem artichokes, currants, dates, sliced sweet potato, candied eringo roots and marrow, spiced with sugar.

Young Tryon could never have eaten such a meal, it was far out of his class, but he must have read the book (Markham was a well-known and famous author) for he was soon to write cookery books himself. What would have struck him most forcefully, I believe, was a sense of staggering waste. Though all of the uneaten food left at table was eaten by servants and any over would then have been given to the beggars waiting around the kitchens outside. For in the one hundred years up to Tryon's birth the price of food rose by 120% without any corresponding increase in wages. As an infant and growing lad, food must have been scarce and, because of the Civil War, possibly infrequent, for the only meat usually eaten by farm labourers – poultry – became expensive and sought after as a luxury food. Pepys writes in 1661 that, 'At night my wife and I had a good supper by ourselves of a pullet which pleased me much to see my condition come to allow a dish like that.' His condition then was £600 a year. In 1665 Pepys gave a dinner for nine friends to celebrate the anniversary of 'being cut for the stone'[15] in which he served a fricassee of rabbits and chickens, a leg of boiled mutton, three carps in a dish, a side of lamb, a dish of roasted pigeons, four lobsters, three tarts and a lamphrey pie.

London was a frenetic centre of trade and commerce, with animals being driven through the streets to supply the carcasses for such feasts. Every time Tryon walked out of his door he would have passed the butchers and the slaughtering premises at the back of the shops, heard the cries of frightened animals and smelt the spilt blood. He would also have passed the Cook Shops where 'four spits, one over another, carry round each five or six pieces of Butcher's Meat, Beef, Mutton, Veal, Pork and Lamb; you have what quantity you please cut off, fat, lean, much or little done; with this, a little Salt and Mustard upon the Side of a plate, a bottle of beer and a Roll; and there is your whole feast.' So reported a French visitor.[16]

Tryon could not but be aware of the great events of the day or not hear the details of such things as royal banquets. In 1679 the corporation of Edinburgh welcomed the King's brother, James, the Duke of York with a feast which among the usual amounts of beef, mutton, ducks, hens and rabbits, included large decorated pies, a large gilded turkey pie the colour of rubies, a lambs pie 'a la mode' also gilded with a gold fringe, a shrimp pie in vermilion colour and three gilded trotter pies. It is not surprising, considering the amount people ate, that in most cookery books there were recipes for Surfeit water, concocted especially for the digestion. One contained aniseed water, poppy flowers, 'lickorices', saffron, figs, raisins and a handful of marigold flowers.

Vegetables were not much liked, certainly they did not appear in the royal banquets, except as an ingredient in a meat dish or as a flavouring in a soup or sauce, for they were thought to be working class food as country people grew them. Yet as towns grew so did market gardens sited just outside; every large town had its belt of gardens which supplied the markets with vegetables and fruit. Tryon would have seen and noted with satisfaction that the towns now had a supply of vegetables, which, when he was a boy, would only have been available in the country. London had market gardens at Lewisham, Blackheath, Wanstead and Ilford.[17] But the standard of cooking vegetables was no better than when Castelvetro had written about the subject some eighty years before. The same French visitor complained that when they boiled beef they 'besieged it with five or six heaps of cabbage, carrots, turnips or some herbs or roots well salted and swimming in butter.' The English he thought were not 'delicately served'.[18]

Given all this one is not surprised to find Tryon rather gloomily having to accept that society cannot be converted to a vegetable diet. Yet constantly in all his books he recommends it as the only healthy manner of eating. He was born in the country, he knew the farm labouring poor intimately for they were his family which he had left behind him. So what did they eat? Certainly not the prodigious amounts of meat consumed by the rich. It was only at the end of the century that farmers began to experiment with feeding their cattle throughout the winter with root vegetables and cakes made out of rape seed after the oil had been pressed for domestic lighting. In the winter the wealthy ate game, including much venison. The poor made do with powdered beef, meat preserved by powdering with dry salt, which was described as 'tough, hard, heavy and of ill nourishment, requiring rather the stomach of another Hercules (who is said to have fed chiefly of Bulls flesh) than of any ordinary and common ploughman.'[19] The poor ate bread, fish, beans, cheese, a little bacon and what they could trap or snare. 'Husbandmen and such as labour can eat fat bacon, salt gross meat, hard cheese…coarse bread at all times, go to bed and labour upon a full stomach, which to some idle persons would be present death.'[20]

Tryon knew that the cottage gardens were a source of a supply of vegetables to these hungry people. He had learnt as a boy to value them as good food, seeing his mother prepare and cook them. But he also knew that once people moved away from the soil they immediately affected a snobbism. English maids when they went to France stuck their noses up at eating the vegetables which all the French maids loved. So Sir Ralph Verney writes in his Memoirs.[21] Tryon must also have been aware that once those self-same farm labourers enlisted in the army or navy their diet would be notable for a complete absence of vegetables. Though they would be fed with beef, bacon, fish, butter, cheese, vinegar, bread and beer and have pepper, sugar, nutmeg and ginger to flavour their food, their diet would be totally deficient, we now know, in Vitamin C.

Hardly surprising then that Gideon Harvey, physician to Charles II, called scurvy the Disease of London.[22] Gerard had graphically described the symptoms some fifty years before. The gums are loose, swollen and ulcerous, the mouth stinking, thighs and legs full of blue spots, the feet swollen and the face pale. Gerard recommended garden cresses as being good against the disease. William Cockburn, physician to the Fleet at the end of the century, believed scurvy was caused by an overindulgence in salt foods. There is a terrible story of some ships in 1695 being moored in Torbay for a month, during which time the men had not been allowed to land. Cockburn urged the Commander, Lord Berkeley, to put the sick men ashore, but Berkeley claimed that if he did they would all desert. But the men became so ill that they were finally numbering a hundred gaunt skeletons, scarcely able to move. These men were rowed to land where they were able to get carrots and turnips and 'other Green Trade'. Within a week they were crawling about and soon all but two or three were fit to return to duty.[23]

Scurvy was almost unknown in France, an outbreak in Paris in 1699 caused much concern, which shows the protection the French maids were acquiring in eating up their green salads. It was not that the antidote to scurvy was not known, for when a person succumbed they were given either oranges, lemons, scurvy grass[24], parsley, chervil, lettuce, rocket or strawberries. They were simply not thought of as part of a necessary preventative diet, though all were thought to cure loose teeth and heal spongy foul gums. There were infusions of barley and lemon ring or scurvy grass ale. This last was made up of one pint of juice of scurvy grass, watercress and succory (chicory) mixed with one gallon of ale. It was mostly drunk in the early spring when the symptoms of scurvy would have been at their worst.

So when Tryon first started to write in his 48th year his books were full of advice for healthy eating. He recommended a vegetable diet and abstinence from tobacco and alcohol. He also wrote on the benefits of clean sweet beds, the cure of bed bugs, and toothache, on the excellency of herbs, how to make all people rich. He pleaded for the humane treatment of black slaves and a new method of how to educate children. Even a tract upon the evils of war, and in particular, religious war, a dialogue which one writer thought was 'worthy of the most trenchant of the humanitarian writers of the next century.'[25] All this was interspersed with much mystical philosophy. He described his objects in writing as 'to recommend to the world temperance, cleanness and innocency of living...to give his reader's Wisdom's Bill of Fare...and at the same time to write down several mysteries concerning God and his government.'[26]

Though a Pythagorean from the age of twenty-three, his wife, as we have seen, refused to be converted and so meals at home must still have had meat in them for the rest of the family. There is often something definitely testy in his remarks, an asperity that creeps in not unlike George Bernard Shaw. 'Though I have before shown the inconveniences of the feeding upon flesh (so commonly and in such excess as nowadays practiced) and rather recommended the lovers of wisdom and health to more innocent use of grains, fruits and herbs, yet since there is no stemming the tide of popular opinion and custom, and people will still gorge themselves with the flesh of their fellow animals, I have thought fit here to give a particular account of each sort of flesh, that at least you may choose that which is most proper for your constitution and least prejudicial to your health.'[27] He goes on to give advice on various meats and the best way of cooking them. For example: 'There are various sorts of fowls, most of which men eat, some wild, others tame, of the two the wild are the more wholesome for food, their nature is more airy and cleaner and of a dryer substance, affording a better and firmer nourishment.'[28]

Much of his advice has a contemporary ring to it. 'All kind of melted butter and fried food, be they what they will, are hurtful to the health of all people.' Butter was only eaten by the poor, but the rich cooked in great amounts of it. 'Fatness is very comely in Men and Women when it doth not exceed the medium, nor proceed from Idleness and intemperance in Meats and Drinks...'[29] It would be another thirty years before obesity reached a zenith in society.

Tryon is against sugary foods and thinks they are especially bad for children. Though advocating temperance he also writes a book on the *New Art of Brewing Beer, Ale and other sorts of Liquors* which went into three editions in the same year – 1691. The Wine Act of 1688 had imposed a heavy tax on wines from France giving a stimulus to home brewing. A crop of books and pamphlets appeared at that time with instructions on how to make wine from vinegar, clary juice, pippin cider and blackberry water. Tryon's more reliable work must have seemed a blessing.

Tryon in advocating asceticism and self-discipline in diet and life was only in fact reflecting the hard work ethic which had imbued the new mercantile middle-class, but he took it one or two steps further into forms of dietary self-abstinence which they would find it hard to countenance. What is also interesting is that Tryon was not in the least hide-bound by the zealous forms of Christianity which he must have been immersed in as a child. He would eulogise the milder manners of the followers of Pythagoras or of the Hindus[30] and condemn the violence of Christians, '...far greater advantages would come to pass amongst Christians, if they would cease from contention, oppression, and (what tends and disposes them thereunto) the killing of other animals, and eating their flesh and blood...'

Tryon's main contribution to the history of food was to revive the metaphysical concepts of the pre-Socratics, that all living matter contains the divine spirit. Then to apply it to daily life, though ironically his own business contradicted such a personal belief. An inconsistency which endears itself to me. Yet his proselytising for the vegetable diet was an astonishingly brave commitment to make within his age. He made his mark and was to influence not only those writers mentioned above but also Lewis Gompertz, the founder of the RSPCA. What Tryon did was to keep the Pythagorean ethic alive in a society alienated by it, so that his views in our century not only seem familiar, but also reflect the discoveries of contemporary nutritional research.

REFERENCES

[1] Quoted in Cohn, Norman. *The Pursuit of the Millenium*, Paladin, 1957.
[2] Lacqueur, Thomas W. *Sexual Desire and the Market Economy during the Industrial Revolution. Discourses of Sexuality from Aristotle to Aids*. Ed. Domna C. Stanton, University of Michegan Press, 1992.
[3] Continuing to appear in even greater numbers throughout the next three centuries until they became commonplace.
[4] *Diary of John Evelyn*, August 27th 1685, ed. William Bray, 1859.
[5] Tryon, Thomas, *The Way to Health and Long Life*, 1683.
[6] There is an astonishing rise in the population of England from 4.9 million in 1680 to 11.5 million in 1820. Between 1791 and 1831 (the core years of the Industrial Revolution) it grew 72% from 7.7 million to 13.28 million, the fastest rate of increase anywhere in Western Europe. Life expectancy at birth increased by 6 years from about 32 in the 1670s to 39 in the 1810s. Fertility rose 2.5 times more than mortality.
[7] Earle, Peter. *The World of Defoe*, 1976.
[8] Tryon, Thomas. *A Memoir*.
[9] Mcendrick, Brewer and Plumb, *The Birth of a Consumer Society*. London, Europe Publications, 1982.
[10] He was a Hatter, after all, and dealt in beaver skins. In his mind he must have known that he made a living out of the slaughter of that animal.
[11] Hume, David. 'On Commerce'. *Essays, Moral, Political and Literary*. T.H. Green and T.H. Grose, New York, 1898.
[12] Mcendrick, Brewer and Plumb.
[13] A cow, ox or calf.
[14] *Molva molva*, a long fish rarely distinguished from cod, and like cod generally salted.
[15] Pepys was operated on to extract a gallstone on March 26th 1658 and he kept the day as a festival each year where his stone was passed around at dinner. Stones were a common affliction, possibly caused by a high incidence of calcium and a deficiency of Vitamin A in the diet.
[16] Misson, Henry: *Memoirs and Observations in his Travels*, trans. and ed. by Ozell.
[17] A vegetable market at Liverpool grew up because of an influx of French Canadians who wanted cheap vegetables for their soups.
[18] Misson.
[19] Muffet, Thomas. *Healths Improvement*. 1655.
[20] Burton, Richard. *The Anatomy of Melancholy*. 1621.
[21] Verney, Francis P. ed. *Memoirs of the Verney Family*. 1892.
[22] Harvey, Gideon, *The Disease of London, a new discovery of the Scurvey*. 1675.
[23] Cockburn, William. *Sea Diseases*. 3rd Edition. 1736. Quoted in *The Englishman's Food*. Drummond and Wilbraham. Cape 1957.
[24] *Cochlearia officinalis*, part of the Cruciferae family, abundant on the shores of Scotland. A small, low-growing plant with thick, fleshy, glabrous, egg-shaped leaves. (Hence other name – spoonwort.)
[25] Williams, Howard, *The Ethics of Diet*. John Heywood, 1883.
[26] Tryon, Thomas. *Way of Long Life, Health and Happiness*. 3rd Edition, 1763.
[27] Ibid.
[28] Ibid.
[29] Ibid.
[30] They were rapidly becoming a popular example among philosophers. Voltaire was to praise them in the following century both in essays and novels.

Von Liebeg Condensed

Layinka M. Swinburne

> If extract of meat
> Is all you can eat,
> You'll never grow strong.
>
> Isn't it grivi'g
> That Justus von Liebig
> Who went on believi'g
> So long, was WRONG!

When the great German scientist Justus von Liebig died in 1873, three colleagues were asked to give commemorative addresses as it was felt that no single tribute could cover all his contributions to science.[1] Even today, there are frequent passing references to him in books on cookery, nutrition, the history of medicine, occupational health, chemistry, agriculture, gardening, biology, and the history and philosophy of science. The effects of his work on cookery were both direct and indirect, for he devised theories about cooking methods as well as applying his new scientific techniques to the systematic analysis of foods, the principles of nutrition, and the improvement of agriculture. In later years he became involved in the production of several novel foods and their promotion.

The first edition of Eliza Acton's *Modern Cookery in all its Branches* appeared in 1845.[2] At this time some of Liebig's popular writings such as *Familiar Letters on Chemistry*,[3] were being published in England. These had first appeared as supplements to the *Augsburger Allgemeine Zeitung* and covered topics such as the history of science but were also a vehicle for many of Liebig's theories and comments on food and cooking. They caused such enthusiasm and interest that Eliza Acton revised her work and published the sixth edition in 1855[4] with the added explanation 'in which the principles of Baron Liebig and other eminent writers have been as much as possible applied and explained.' She admitted that she 'had gladly taken advantage of such of their instructions (those of Baron Liebig especially) as have seemed to me adapted to its character and likely to increase their real utility.'

The principles which she incorporated included his instructions for the preparation of Extract of Beef or very strong plain beef gravy soup, referring to it 'as this admirable preparation which could be used to convert cold meat which often abounds so inconveniently in an English larger ... into good nourishing dishes which the hashes and minces of our common cookery *are not*'. The method depended on soaking fresh meat in very cold or iced water to extract what von Liebig believed to be 'all the nutriment that the meat will yield'. His observations on the composition of foods had shown that they were made up of albuminous or flesh-forming principle [protein in modern terminology] containing nitrogen, and heat forming materials [carbohydrates and fats]. He also referred to the two components as plastic and respiratory materials. He had shown that the proteins derived from plants and animals were similar in composition and hence believed that they were equivalent in nutritional power. Proteins coagulate when heated, and he used this fact to conclude that to make a good extract you needed cold water to allow the contents of the meat fibres to diffuse out, whilst to conserve the nutriment in a piece of meat you should start with a high heat so as to coagulate the outer layer of albumen as quickly as possible to 'seal the outside

LIEBIG COMPANY'S
EXTRACT OF MEAT,
Manufactured by Liebig's Extract of Meat Company, Limited,
43, MARK LANE, LONDON,
AT THEIR MANUFACTORIES IN SOUTH AMERICA.

This extract is supplied to the British, French, Prussian, Russian, Dutch, Italian, and other Governments, in preference to all other Extracts.

ANALYSED AND CERTIFIED GENUINE BY BARON LIEBIG,

One Pound of this Extract contains the soluble parts of 34lbs. of FINE BEEF, free from fat and gelatine, corresponding with about 45lbs. of English butchers' meat, inclusive of the usual quantity of fat and bones.

It is not only used for medical, but much more extensively for household purposes, and is the cheapest and finest flavoured stock for soups, entrees, sauces, etc. At the present retail price of 11s. per lb. Extract, a pint of delicious beef tea costs two-pence farthing, whilst made from fresh meat it would cost about one shilling.

CAUTION!

This is the ORIGINAL EXTRACT, manufactured under Baron Liebig, the Inventor's control and guarantee; every GENUINE Jar bears HIS SIGNATURE thus, and THAT of his DELEGATE, Professor Max von Pettenkofer.

The name of "*Liebig's Extract of Meat,*" being applied, contrary to Baron Liebig's expressed will, and without his guarantee or genuineness, to all sorts of Extract of Meat, the Public are cautioned not to allow the substitution of any other sort for this Company's genuine article, which should distinctly be asked for by the name of

LIEBIG COMPANY'S EXTRACT,

Require BARON LIEBIG'S SIGNATURE upon every jar.

Sold by all Chemists, Grocers, Italian Warehousemen, Provision Merchants, and Ship Chandlers.

and keep the juice in.'

Eliza Acton tried hard to reconcile this teaching with her practical experience as a cook. She described in full the Liebig method for making meat extract and referred to it whenever appropriate to a dish. However the residual meat is useless and has to be discarded whilst in the traditional French method of making *bouilli* according to Carême, which she also included, the meat becomes succulent and tasty, as well as flavouring a splendid soup. When it came to roasting beef she gave the Liebig method of exposure to high heat before a brisk fire, but commented that whilst it would do for beef, to prevent certain other meats such as mutton from drying out, they should thereafter be cooked at twice the usual distance from the fire. She added her own receipt and said proudly that it gave excellent results and would prove more economical in fuel.

In her comment on boiling she described the Liebig method of scientific boiling but common sense won in the receipt for 'Boiled Leg of Mutton with Tongue and Turnips'. 'We have left this receipt unaltered instead of applying to it Baron Liebig's directions for his improved method of boiling meat, because his objections to the immersion of the meat in cold water are partially obviated by its being placed immediately over a sound fire and heated quickly; and the mutton is very good thus dressed.' When it came to fish she was even more doubtful, but bravely commented that the Liebig method was 'worth a try', especially with a large turbot being cooked in nine gallons of water. She added the observation: 'This is the best practical application that we can give of Baron Liebig's instructions'. In the sections on pork and game she kept Liebig firmly out of the kitchen.

Eliza Acton complained bitterly that much of her work was copied by other authors without acknowledgement and this included her extracts from von Liebig. Mrs Beeton's *Book of Household Management*[5] certainly took advantage of her work in her pompous remarks on the history of cooking. She quoted the Liebig experiments and philosophy on the cooking of meat with the comment, 'these interesting facts discovered in the laboratory, throw a flood of light upon the mysteries of the kitchen.'

She followed with what 'the great chemist' said about plunging meat into boiling water to coagulate the albumen on the surface, and repeats the comments in the sections on roasting and the memorandum on the same subject. According to Liebig, beef or mutton cannot be said to be sufficiently roasted until it has acquired throughout the whole mass a temperature of 158°. She was less critical than Eliza Acton and the methods have been perpetuated ever since and the logic remained almost unchallenged until recently.

'A gentleman in every way entitled to speak with authority' who wrote the preface to Cassell's *Dictionary of Cookery* (c.1880)[6], was clearly a Liebig disciple. He posed the questions '*Why* ought you to put a leg of mutton into boiling water? *Why* ought you to peat meat for soup into cold water?

One to keep the flavour *in* another to get the flavour *out*!' Its introductory section on the principles of cookery contained a seven page account of gravy, and the text included Baron Liebig's recipe for Beef Tea from Fresh Meat, and several detailed discussions of the roasting of meat. 'As to the position of the meat before the fire "doctors disagree". According to Baron Liebig, who is decidedly an oracle, '...the surface should be hardened at once by placing the meat before the fire'. After describing a gentler method the author pointed out that 'greater judgement is necessary, if Liebig's directions are observed, or the meat will be either sodden or burnt.' Experiments done in Edinburgh on boiling, roasting and boiling showed that the loss of weight was less in boiling but did not go into the question of heat sealing.

Harold McGee has traced the history of this practice and describes experiments done in the 1930s in the University of Missouri which showed that the weight loss is far greater and the result less tasty if the meat to be roasted is 'sealed first'.[7] This is different from the development of flavoursome by-products through the Maillard reaction in browning, but this is a complex process and not traceable to a single product as in the old osmazome theory. He points out the shift in emphasis from a comparison of the supposed nutritional value in the taste of the meat. Now that economy is again dictating culinary practice, flavour is again being displaced in importance: one may be served pallid, grey, *steaming* 'roast' beef in the previously famous carvery at Simpson's in the Strand.

The recipe for beef juice which found its way into so many cookery books arose from a personal experience like so many of Liebig's inspirations. Whilst the father of Sheridan Muspratt, a former pupil and professor of Chemistry at Liverpool, was staying with him in Giessen, he devised a meat extract for Muspratt's sick daughter. She was described as suffering from Cholera (although in the *Familiar Letters* Typhus is blamed).[8] She recovered and he published his method, as 'A new Soup for invalids', as he claimed, for the benefit of mankind. The extract became a popular treatment for convalescence and intestinal complaints and was incorporated in the Bavarian pharmacopoeia as *Extractum Carnis* and used (according to Liebig) by several successful doctors in private practice in Munich.

Doctors were enthusiastic about this successor to the laboriously prepared beef tea but doubts had crept in and Florence Nightingale in her *Notes on Nursing* of 1859[9] was scornful of the nutritional value of beef tea, but conceded that there might be 'a certain reparative value in it – but we do not know what'. This did not prevent the success of the Liebig version or the commercially prepared beef extract which was developed from it and was sold for the first time in 1862, promoted for its medicinal value.

Florence Nightingale wrote to the Liebig Company in 1866 thanking them for a sample and acknowledging that she had used it herself and it was excellent.[10]

Correspondence in the Giessen archives shows that Liebig was approached by many businessmen wishing to exploit his discoveries over the years but it was not until 1862 that he met Georg Christian Giebert, a road engineer, and they formed a company in Fray Bentos, Uruguay, to produce the extract on a large scale as Liebig's extract of meat.[11] The massive production of cattle in the New World was aimed at producing valuable hides for leather. The carcasses were left to rot or rendered down to yield fat as there was no way of preserving or exporting meat. The new extract may seem wasteful in that the advertisements claimed that 34lbs of beef were reduced to one lb of extract but the meat had previously been virtually a waste product. Von Liebig believed that the extract contained all the useful components of meat and that the discarded fat and fibre were unimportant. In fact they contain most of the protein. He hoped that the extract could be used to feed the 'craving multitudes', workers whom he referred to as 'the potato-eaters of Europe' who could not afford meat. He had changed his view that all vegetable and animal proteins were identical and now believed (wrongly) that muscle was consumed during physical work and could only be replaced by eating meat. The new product was heavily advertised as a concentrated food and praised by doctors as much simpler than the traditional beef tea. At first it was only available on prescription. It followed in the wake of Osmazome, the essence of meat devised by Magendie, in which French cooks such as Soyer fervently believed and had exhibited in the food section of the Great Exhibition of 1851.[12] The idea of the 'goodness' of meat being concentrated in a small jar for travellers, cooks and invalids was highly attractive even though the facts were soon challenged by those capable of doing a little arithmetic. Florence Nightingale wrote in her *Notes on Nursing* that the solid matter obtained by evaporating down beef tea amounted to no more than a few grams. In the course of preparation, the protein was largely thrown away and one can calculate that from the annual production of thousands of tons of beef, 95 per cent was wasted. Criticism of the nutritional claims grew and eventually the advertisements were withdrawn from medical and pharmaceutical journals. At the height of the controversy Liebig's partner, von Pettenkofer, who was responsible for quality control of the extract, withdrew as he disagreed with the claims and feared that the Prussian Army might substitute the product for more nutritious elements. There were different responses to the needs of armies. During the Crimean War Queen Victoria offered to send eau-de-Cologne, whilst Alexis Soyer had used his skills free to organise kitchens and make nourishing soups from army rations and imported or local vegetables.[13] During the Franco-Prussian war Liebig negotiated contracts for meat extract with the Generals, and there were many who maintained that it was useful for soldiers on the march. Liebig continued to insist that there must be some stimulating property even though in terms of a sheer body-building principle the content was insignificant.[14] Dr Stanley famously carried a jar of the Liebig extract with him to Africa in 1865 and later explorers like Nansen, Amundsen, Shackleton and Scott included one or other of these products in their supplies. In fact the extract contains the B vitamins riboflavin and nicotinic acid together with mineral salts, especially phosphates, all of which have considerable value in convalescence and debilitated states. The extractives also stimulate the flow of saliva and gastric juice which helps appetite and digestion. In spite of all the criticism it remained popular with some doctors and Hutchinson's dietetic manual (1909) has a whole chapter of detailed comparison of soup, beef extracts, beef juices, beef-tea and beef powders.[15] Other experts were incensed by the continued popularity of a product which a Professor complained 'instead of an ox in a tea cup, the ox's urine in a tea cup would be much nearer the fact, for the meat extract consists largely of products on their way to urea.'

The Liebig company were pioneers in imaginative promotion of their product. To advertise the domestic uses from about 1870 they offered sets of colourful chromolithograph cards in return for tokens. These were so successful that they are now collectors' items. They promoted not only beef extract but presented a heroic and idealised version of scenes from Liebig's life. Many other series portrayed adults advertising the extract, production of the extract, German army uniforms, cooks in the kitchen, production of the cards themselves, and every imaginable subject, entertaining or educative followed. The demand was so great that sets of cards and special albums could be had on application. They were distributed in 14 countries and no less than 7,000 cards in 1,100 series were sent out in Germany alone. They were the forerunners of many similar cards and the later developments of the company's products such as Lemco, Oxo, Bovril and the Brooke Bond Company which later became the parent company of Liebig, continued the tradition.[16]

It is hard now to appreciate the adulation and reverence which von Liebig attracted. The development of the near-cult and personal myths have been traced by Munday[17] and the fact that Liebig did little to discourage them. He visited England many times and addressed the Agricultural Society of Great Britain in 1840 to expound the principles of the application of Chemistry to Agriculture and toured England and Scotland to learn more about methods of farming and production of cheese and butter. He visited York in 1844 and Glasgow in 1847. His followers naturally included many former pupils at Giessen but his audiences at the meetings of the Pharmaceutical Society and followers amongst the medical profession were kept informed of his nutritional work supplemented by regular reports and comments in the *Lancet*, the *Medical Times* and other journals. In 1859 the latest in the series of *Familiar Letters* displayed an advertisement for the fans who could purchase 'A small bust of von Liebig in artificial ivory' for ten shillings and sixpence. He was usually referred to as the great chemist and there were few who could challenge his ideas or criticise the failures which occurred when they were put into practice. Those who did were subjected to ridicule and powerful attack which silenced them for a considerable time.

Justus von Liebig was born in Marburg in 1803, the second of ten children.[18] His father was a dealer in dyes, drugs and associated chemicals and from an early age Justus showed an interest in chemistry. He was apprenticed to an apothecary but was sent home in disgrace after one of his experiments ended in an explosion which blew out the attic windows. He persuaded the Grand Duke of Hesse-Darmstadt to fund wider studies and after periods in Bonn and elsewhere, he went to Paris to work in Joseph Gay-Lussac's private laboratory.

From there he was appointed Professor of Chemistry at Giessen, Hesse, at the age of 21. In 1825 he founded the first school for the training of chemists in a converted military barracks. It attracted pupils from all over the world. Many of his pupils made outstanding contributions to science in their turn. W. Hofman for instance, was invited by Prince Albert to found the college of chemistry in Oxford Street which was later incorporated in the Imperial College of Science. Liebig's laboratory is still preserved in Giessen in the University named after him. He was a superb teacher and a prolific writer and after twenty years in Giessen, moved to Mannheim as Professor in 1843. Having worked hard in developing the science of organic chemistry, he decided in the late 1830s to turn to the application of the new science, first as it applied to agriculture and later to food and nutrition.

He was made a baron by the Grand Duke of Hesse in 1843 in the old order of Freiherr but claimed that the title had brought nothing but envy and ill-feeling. His own autobiographical notes, somewhat bowdlerised, were the basis of early biographies. Recently a more critical view of his social progress and relationships have been put forward.[19] He was impulsive and hot-tempered and used both fair and foul means to counteract criticism or encroachment on his commercial territory but this does not lessen the record of his remarkable achievements.

He worked and corresponded with the famous chemist Wöhler, and spent time working in Berzelius' laboratory in Sweden. They devised new methods which he and his pupils used to analyse the chemical constituents of foods and biological materials. He found that proteins from whatever source contained the same proportions of nitrogen to other constituents. It was against the background of the belief that animals used a mysterious vital principle that the new discoveries of the universal chemical basis of these processes astonished the world and aroused discussion and further experiment. His views were summarised in the book *Animal chemistry*, written in 1840[20] and translated into English very soon after. *Researches on the Chemistry of Foods* was published in USA in 1848.[21] He produced the first coordinated theory of nutrition and the idea that the main three components of food had different functions in the animal body. His Law of the Minimum is still important in nutrition of infants.[22] He stated that the best result you can obtain from any particular dietary is limited by the degree of its greatest fault. In other words, if in an otherwise perfect diet there is one fault only, such as a deficiency of iron, the net result will be bad for the infant who subsists on it, because he will soon become anaemic.

Liebig was always interested in making the best use of available foods for the benefit of mankind and wrote extensively on the evils of adulteration of flour, and described ways of improving bread as well as a way of making bread from sprouted grain in times of scarcity. His work was quoted frequently by Christopher Hassall who used his methods of analysis of foods.[23] Eliza Acton included 'Professor Libig's Bavarian Brown Bread' in the 1855 edition of her book. It was baked from flour prepared from the whole grain. 'Baron Liebig pronounces this to be very superior to that which is made with fine flour solely, both in consequence of the greater amount of nutriment which it contains and from its slight medicinal effect which renders it valuable to many persons accustomed to have frequent recourse to drugs, of which it supersedes the necessity. It is made from wheat exactly as it is prepared, no part being subtracted nor any additional flour mingled with it.'

The same recipe is included in her *English Bread Book* of 1857[24] but this time without direct acknowledgement to Baron Liebig. There is a coy reference to some of the first scientists of the present day and 'a very superior writer' whom we can identify with Liebig. Liebig's original note was more earthy: he claimed that the boundaries between the Lower Rhine and Westphalia may be traced by the very remarkable size of the remains of the preceding meals left by passengers behind the hedges; and possibly it is from observing these excellent evidences of the digestive capacity of the Westphalians that English physicians have been induced to recommend brown bread '...which in many rich families adorns the breakfast table.'[25] The promotion of wholemeal bread had indeed recently been taken up by doctors and other nutritionists such as Sylvester Graham and the lesson was pointed out all over again by Dr Burkitt a century later.

Liebig believed that fermentation was a type of combustion and argued fiercely against the idea that yeast could be a plant in a bitter correspondence with Louis Pasteur. He later devoted several years to the study of yeast, wine and other fermentations, such as the production of vinegar and cheese and butter and pursued several ideas for the improvement of bread. He set up a factory with Fanny Höhler to produce bread on chemical principles and was so impressed by the work of Eben Horsford, an American pupil who had successfully made baking powder in the United States, that he set up a factory to market it in Germany, an ironic sequel to his acrimonious dispute with Pasteur over the action of yeast in earlier years. However, there were technical problems and difficulty in obtaining the right quality of ingredients. The bottles sometimes exploded during storage. There were many rivals in the field and the product was not commercially successful, which he attributed to the prejudice of German bakers. The history of this venture is described by Paul R. Jones.[26] In other experiments on yeast Liebig showed that it not only had a high protein content but could be subjected to autodigestion to yield an extract very similar in taste to meat. This was at first used as a cheap adulterant of meat extract but later was taken up by a company looking for a use for surplus yeast from the brewing industry and sold at the beginning of the century as a food in its own right, 'Marmite'.

Liebig's interest in bread arose from its importance as a staple food. He equated nutritional power, i.e. the flesh-forming principle, with its nitrogen content and this error gave rise to many misconceptions about the relative value of foods. At first he thought that all proteins were equal in value but was puzzled by experiments set up by Magendie for the gelatine Commission in Paris which showed that dogs fed exclusively on gelatine rapidly died. He went so far as to say in his *Letters on Chemistry*, quoted by Kettner[27], 'it has now been shown by the most convincing experiments that gelatine which by itself is nauseous possesses no nutritive value. Its use has been shown to be hurtful rather than beneficial'. 'People without any sufficient reason adopted the opinion that the substance (gelatine) was the most important, indeed, the chief constituent of good soup' and went on to rail at those selling jelly tablets who from 'ignorance and the love of gain exchanged the valuable constituents of flesh for gelatine which was only to be distinguished from common joiner's glue by its high price.'

Liebig's doubts as to whether gelatine was a true protein and had any nutritional value can be followed in Mrs Beeton and various cookery writers. However in the 1840s several patents were taken out for the preparation of refined gelatine, a by-product of the meat industry. Brand's company was set up to exploit New Zealand lamb. Swinborne, Nelson and Young produced their versions. The new products were supported by heavy advertising about which there was some suspicion because of the association of public advertising with quack medicine in the past. Recipe books and leaflets were to be had on application for many of the new foods, from Arrowroot to Sea mais (cornflour), and set an interesting new trend in popular education. Many advertisements boasted medical approval. Beef suet was highly prized and the Hugon meat company was another early starter using British Beef. In an age when starvation and malnutrition were widespread, doctors were happy to prescribe suet and dairy products for convalescence and for patients suffering from consumption and rickets, without being aware of the true causes of these diseases. The setting of standards by the Great Exhibition was followed by other international exhibitions which awarded gold medals for purity. The Liebig extract was only launched after the Great Exhibition of 1851. At the Paris Exhibition of 1867 von Liebig was one of the Presidents. The meat extract won two gold medals and was equally successful in later exhibitions, being awarded the Grand Diploma of Honour 'Superior to the Gold Medal' in Amsterdam in 1869. Advertisements and labels of foods and patent medicines used quotations or citations from Hassall's articles in the *Lancet* and the books which followed, and that of his mentor Jonathan Pereira, endorsing freedom from adulteration. The 'by appointment' system added a little glamour. The Liebig company took advantage of all these until the name became a household word. Von Liebig's signature in blue ink adorned many an advertisement and every jar of the product. Unfortunately the practice rebounded when von Liebig himself lent his signature to endorse a product which turned out to be worthless. He in turn vigorously sued other manufacturers who sold products as Liebig extracts or Liebig baby foods. It became impossible to protect the name 'Liebig' in England as a result of an unsuccessful legal action prior to the Trade Marks Registration Act 1875. Thereafter the Liebig products were sold throughout the British Empire under the brand name LEMCO, although the original name survived in Germany.

The Liebig Company was continued by Justus's son after his death. Their *Practical Cookery Book*[28] was written by the industrious Mrs H.M. Young, the Delia Smith of the late nineteenth century. She wrote books promoting the products of her husband's company Young's Gelatine and they also made or sold kitchen ware and patent devices from their shop in Warrington, much as other famous cooks such as Soyer and Escoffier had marketed their sauces and bright ideas. She was awarded a gold medal by the Berkhamsted mechanics 1886 and offered practical lessons and demonstration from the base in Warrington with special emphasis on cooking by gas. The Liebig company published little recipe books in many countries. The English version was printed in Germany and includes whimsical illustrations of buxom Mädchen and a typical German kitchen alongside recipes for Yorkshire Pudding with Liebig, Liebig on toast and rook pie. In Germany the extract was promoted in the book written by Henrietta Davidis (1870) and an American version was written by Maria Parloa.[29] At the same time recipes using the essence and advertisements appeared in other cookery books such as later editions of Mrs Beeton's *Household Management* and Cassell's Dictionary where one can find Liebig sandwiches, Liebig soup. The LEMCO book written by Eva Tuite about 1905 had moved up the social scale.[30] Quails replaced the rooks.

In 1899 the name Oxo appeared and was later applied to the solid cubes which followed the liquid extracts. The previous sales of the extract as a nutritional aid helped cooks to accept this and other convenience foods without guilt as healthful short-cuts. In spite of the old criticisms no book on nutrition was complete without a mention of the material both for infant and invalid feeding. Rivals appeared such as Brand's essence and Boots liquid Beef but Liebig products remained top of the heap.

Liebig was keenly interested in local industries and wrote on the prevention of souring of German wine in the Pharmaceutical Journal. Hassall quoted his views on the healthful properties of wine which were so marked that 'In no part of Germany do the apothecaries establishments bring so low a price as in the rich cities on the Rhine; for their wine is the universal medicine for the healthy as well as for the sick; it is considered milk for the aged.' He was so taken with his chemical principles that he could not believe that fermentation of alcohol was anything but a chemical degradation and a form of combustion. The demonstration of fermentative activity of the yeast plant brought his scorn and ridicule on the proponents which for a time won the day.[31] Once again he was wrong though modern knowledge of enzymatic fermentation could be said to combine both views.

It has been said that he applied the same ideas of the three principal components of biological materials needed as essential nutrients equally to manure and to baby food. Two of his daughters were unable to bread-feed their babies. He therefore devised as a substitute *Suppe für Saüglinge* in which he calculated the constitutents were identical to the proportions present in human milk. Under his supervision the babies thrived and a simple version is printed in Cassell's *Dictionary*. He then manufactured and sold a commercial version, a 'perfect' infant food, composed of wheat flour, malt flour, cow's milk and potassium bicarbonate. It was troublesome to sell with a short shelf life and was not a success. He later devised a dried milk with less cow's milk and added pea flour to provide more nitrogen. He was annoyed when doctors still found that it gave babies indigestion which he claimed could not be as the formula was identical to human milk. As quoted by Drummond and Wilbraham, 'These findings suggest that there is still substance in the view attributed to Oliver Wendell Holmes that "A Pair of substantial mammary glands has the advantage over the two hemispheres of the most learned professor's brain in the art of compounding a nutritious food for infants"'.[32] Liebig's work on vacuum drying was emulated by the Horlick brothers and many others. The ups and downs of the Liebig product, its promotion and the rivals and imposters which took advantage of the Liebig name are entertainingly described by Rima D. Apple.[33] It is interesting that his response to criticism of his product was personal and emotional. His idealism and trust in the uses of science was his driving force. It was his dedication to the improvement of the lot of mankind through applied science which enthused his followers and remarkably, did not blind them to his errors even when it clouded his own logic. He claimed to have received no benefit from his discoveries but in fact the profits of the meat extract alone made him a rich man. However he published his discoveries at an early stage so that all could benefit from them and in several cases others had tried to exploit them many years before he developed his own products commercially. Gardiner's baby food was advertised in 1850, as being concocted according to the principles of von Liebig. It was found by Hassall to consist of plain rice flour. This was one of a number of fraudulent manufacturers taking advantage of his name.

What was insufficient for invalids was fine for bacteria. The discoveries of Louis Pasteur led to the establishment of microbiological laboratories where the newly discovered organisms could be isolated, grown on and identified. Bacteria can be grown in liquid broth or solidified jellies and the Liebig company marketed Lemco, advertised in Mrs Beeton 1907 along with a recipe for Liebig soup. Similar products were sold as 'Lab Lemco' the standard material for making up microbiological media. These are equally important in the study of human disease, animal health and for monitoring food hygiene and the safety of water, drugs and other products.

Unlike those of many innovators, his ideas so forcefully put and publicised, were soon accepted. He suggested that plants might feed on chemical compounds and the world-wide application of factory-made chemical plant foods to farm and garden soils has resulted from this hypothesis. He led the way in trying out his theories on his own garden and then purchased a ten acre farm, applying his new artificial fertilisers to the growing of turnips. The disappointing results did not dissuade him from his theories and disastrous ventures in the production of artificial fertiliser ensued. His friend Sheridan Muspratt of Liverpool lost a large amount of money through the enterprise. In America there were similar problems. Because of soil exhaustion in Europe and America farmers were desperate for a solution. In England, a former pupil, Henry Gilbert, was engaged by a wealthy landowner John Bennett Lawes to test the theories systematically at his own vast estate at

Rothamsted.[34] The belief was current that to obtain maximum yields it was necessary but to lime, where lime was needed, and to fertilise the soil with appropriate quantities each season of suitable chemicals containing nitrogen (N), phosphorus (P) and potassium (K). The problem was that the form of phosphate chosen by von Liebig was largely insoluble and could not be taken up by plants. Gilbert and Lawes found a way of making soluble phosphates and supplying nitrogen in the form of nitrates. The first laboratory was an old barn and the trial grounds of wheat grown with various additives led to the development of a massive industry in artificial fertiliser which increased the yield of each acre at a time of rapid population increase and shift to towns and industry. This was the foundation of the Rothamsted agricultural research station and for many years the use of chemical fertilisers became an almost unquestioned garden practice.[35] Eventually Rudolph Steiner (1861-1925) questioned the wisdom of the NPK theory and use of 'artificials' even though they produced excellent results. He brought into consideration the effect on the total environment and produced new lines of enquiry, the beginnings of the bio-dynamic method of organic gardening. Enthusiasts for artificial fertilisers had ignored von Liebig's own insistence on the importance of returning to soil everything that has been removed from it by cultivated crops. This is made clear repeatedly in his early writings and later work on manure.[36] He was himself one of the first of the 'greens'.

Von Liebig travelled widely to give lectures and advice and was a member of many organisations. He hated waste and observed the loss of gluten in the bolting of flour and even more in process of making starch for the cotton industry from good wheat. He commented on the loss of the whey proteins in cheese-making. He was invited to London to advise on the problem of disposal of London sewage by pushing it out to sea. He was appalled at the waste of good organic material which might have been used as manure and even calculated that the amount of urine produced by two men in a year would be sufficient to fertilise an acre of ground[37] and would moreover produce a fair crop of turnips.

Was he a mad professor or a noble scientist? Magnus Pyke has used him as an example of the dangers of basing nutritional practices on too little knowledge.[38] With our swings from one dietary crusade to another, animal fat and poly-unsaturates swapping places in a Shepherd's Hay as goodies and baddies for example, we are guilty of exactly the same faults: the belief that what is known and can be measured is all there is to know. The radical thoughts and discoveries of von Liebig should be seen against the background of deep ignorance and the tail-end of superstitious and irrational beliefs about the basis of life. His discoveries were the foundation of the whole science of organic chemistry, that is the chemistry of life, and his influence on cooking was as much through the development of agriculture and the science of nutrition as through his views of the function of foods. When crudely applied as to the feeding of the inmates of institutions or babies against all common sense or experience, the results were harmful and his huge reputation made it difficult to refute the more erroneous claims.

The strength of his standing had an adverse effect on the elucidation of the cure and causes of scurvy, which we now know to be due to lack of vitamin C. Liebig's arguments delayed proper interpretation of the known facts.[39] He maintained wrongly that all food was antiscorbutic and whilst his views prevailed confusion over the effectiveness of treatment with fresh meat, vegetables and fruit or their juices remained.

Too often he was bewitched by his own hypotheses and regarded them as fact in spite of contradictory or conflicting evidence. These deficiencies are more than outweighed by the stimulating effect of the basic ideas since the failures reinforced the need for more research by others. At the same time we can be grateful for the introduction of a number of convenient short cuts to a whole generation of cooks and which we can use in the kitchen without guilt. Claude Bernard said that great men teach us by their errors as much as by their discoveries. Liebig's early views on the similarity of animal and vegetable proteins stimulated the early founders of the

Vegetarian movement. His revised views on the need for meat as being necessary for the replenishment of muscle were equally seized upon by those opposed to it.[40] Some of his views on digestion were equally erroneous: he announced 'all riddles have been solved by chemistry' but denied the existence of two important enzymes – diastase and pepsine, believing that digestion of food in the stomach was a function of degeneration of the mucous membrane![41]

The French scientist Magendie wrote scathingly 'let us leave the theories to the Germans. We will try experiment.' The Royal Society of Arts recognised his practical achievements by awarding Liebig the Albert medal in 1863 for distinguished merit in advancing Arts, Manufactures and Science. His followers and rivals at Rothamsted were jointly honoured by the award of the same medal in 1879 by which time they were Sir Bennett Lawes and Sir Henry Gilbert. Queen Victoria herself was one of other recipients of the medal instituted in memory of her dear husband who had been president of the society from 1843 to 1861. Many other famous names are in the list of recipients including Bunsen, Pasteur, and most recently Sir Ernest Hall, who has rejuvenated Halifax, my home town, by developing small businesses and promoting artistic ventures in the huge old carpet mill Dean Clough.

The combination of an eye for questioning the unusual and diving straight to practical applications was in the spirit of the age. A chance observation that silver nitrate left a silver coating on the test tube led to a new method of silvering mirrors which rapidly replaced the dangerous old method of using mercury amalgam which ruined the health of the Italian craftsmen and caused premature death. Mercury poisoning from this cause soon disappeared. He was aware of the dangers of cyanide poisoning which had caused the deaths of famous chemists in the previous century and having found a safe way of analysing this material, applied it to the popular cherry laurel water, bitter almonds, both of which were in the pharmacopoeia or in home use and had been known to cause an occasional death as mentioned in von Rumohr's note in his *Essence of Cookery* on a lady who died from eating marzipan.[42] The Royal Society lists 315 papers by von Liebig and the voluminous archives at Giessen will no doubt reveal many more examples of the range of his interests and relevance to our current preoccupation with diet, nutrition and food.

The verdict of one professor on Liebig was that there may have been better chemists but none have been more influential.[43] In acknowledging his influence on cooks and nutritionists it is wise to remember Eliza Acton and not to be too eager to discard experience, taste, enjoyment and satisfaction at the table in favour of scientific theories, however persuasive.

Beef teas and extracts

Soyer noted several versions of making beef-tea in his Modern Housewife or Menagère (1850). Both Eliza Acton and Isabella Beeton quoted his recipes, given below.

Brillat-Savarin said that 'Professors never eat boiled beef, out of respect for their principles and because they know the incontestable truth that *boiled beef is flesh without its juice.*

Soyer's New Way of Making Beef Tea

Cut a pound of solid beef into very small dice, which put into a stewpan, with a small pat of butter, a clove, two button onions, and a salt-spoonful of salt, stir the meat round over the fire for a few minutes, until it produces a thin gravy, then add a quart of water and let it simmer at the corner of the fire for half an hour, skimming off every particle of fat, when done pass through a sieve. I have always had a great objection to passing broth through a cloth, as it frequently spoils the flavour.

The same if wanted plain, is done by merely omitting the vegetables, salt and clove: the butter cannot be objectionable, as it is taken out in the skimming; pearl-barley, vermicelli, rice &c., may be served in it if required.

Pure osmazome, or essence of meat

Take two pounds of the flesh of any animal or bird, the older the better for obtaining the true flavour, as free from sinew as possible, and mince it well; place it in a Florence oil-flask, and cork it; put this in a saucepan filled with cold water, leaving the neck uncovered; place it on the side of the fire until the water arrives at 160° Fahr., at which temperature it must remain for twenty minutes; then remove it and strain the contents through a tammie, pressing the meat gently with a spoon; should it require to be kept for some time, put the liquor in a basin or cup, which place in the saucepan; subject it to boiling heat until it is reduced to the consistency of treacle, removing the scum; this, when cold, will become solid, and will keep for any number of years. Osmazome is known under various names in different cookery books, as 'fumet', 'essence', &c., and is obtained in a different way, which causes the gelatine to be produced with the osmazome; but by the above plan the gelatine is left in the meat, and the osmazome and albumen are extracted; the albumen is afterwards removed as scum.

A new soup for invalids (Von Liebig *Familiar Letters on Chemistry*)

Take half a pound of newly killed beef or fowl, chop it fine; add 1 1/8 lb, distilled water with four drops of pure muriatic acid, and 34 to 67 grains of common salt, and stir well together. After an hour the whole is to be thrown on a conical hair sieve and the fluid allowed to flow through without any pressure. The first thick portions which will pass through are to be returned to the sieve, until the fluid runs off quite clear. Half a pound of distilled water is to be poured in small portions at a time on the flesh residue in the sieve. There will be obtained in this way about a pound of fluid (cold extract of flesh), of a red colour and having a pleasant taste of soup. The invalid is to be allowed to take it cold a cupful at a time at pleasure. It must not be heated, as it becomes muddy by heat and deposits a thick coagulum of albumen and colouring matter of blood.

In hot weather the extract was to be made with iced water and external cooling.

REFERENCES

The University of Reading library holds the collection of Justus von Liebig's writings assembled by Professor Cyril Tyler, a delegate at the Oxford Symposium who sadly died in February 1996.

[1] Shenstone, C.W. *Justus von Liebig, his life and work*, 1895, Justus von Liebig, *Encyclopaedia Britannica*, 1968 edition.
[2] Acton, Eliza, *Modern Cookery for Private Families*, First edition, 1845.
[3] Liebig, Justus von, *Familiar Letters on Chemistry*, 1st edition, 1843.
[4] Acton, Eliza, *Modern Cookery, newly revised and much enlarged edition*, 1855.
[5] Beeton, Isabella, *Book of Household Management*, 1861, facsimile edition, 1961.
[6] Cassell, *Dictionary of Cookery*, c.1890.
[7] Harold McGee, *On Food and Cooking*, 1986.
[8] Heilenz, Siegfried, *The Liebig-Museum in Giessen*, Giessen, 1988.
[9] Nightingale, Florence, *Notes on Nursing*, 1859-6.
[10] Vincenzi, Penny, *Taking Stock* (1985) written to commemorate the Diamond Jubilee of the Oxo cube.
[11] Brock, W.H, 'Liebigiana: Old and New perspectives', *History of Science*, 1981, 19:201.
[12] Illustrated Catalogue of the Great Exhibition, 1851.

[13] Calkins, Beverly M,' Florence Nightingale: on Feeding an Army', *American Journal of Clinical Nutrition* 1989 50:1260-5 gives Soyer's recipe for soup.
[14] Liebig, Justus von, *Pharmaceutical Journal* 3rd series iii, 283.
[15] Hutchinson, Robert, *Food and the Principles of Dietetics* 1900.
[16] Finlay, Martin R., 'Quackery and Cookery', *Bulletin of the History of Medicine*, 1992, 66:404.
[17] Munday, Pat, 'Social Climbing through Chemistry', *Ambix*, 1990, 37,1.
[18] Rossiter, Margaret W, *The Emergence of Agricultural Science: Justus von Liebig and the Americans, 1840-1880*, 1975.
[19] Hornix, W.J., 'The tales of Hofmann'. *Annals of Science*, 1987, 44:519.
[20] Liebig, Justus von, *Animal Chemistry*.
[21] Liebig, Justus von, *Researches on the Chemistry of Foods*, 1848.
[22] Cuthbertson, W.F.J., 'Infant foods in the United Kingdom from Victorian times to the present', *Infant Nutrition*, ed. A.F. Walker, 1994.
[23] Hassall, Christopher, *Adulterations Detected*, 1857.
[24] Acton, Eliza, *The English Bread Book*, 1857. Ed. Elizabeth Ray, 1990.
[25] Liebig, Justus von, *Familiar Letters in Chemistry*, 4th Edition, 1859.
[26] Jones, Paul R., 'Justus Liebig, Eben Horsford and the development of the baking powder industry'. *Ambix*, 1993, 40:2.
[27] *Kettner's Book of the Table* (1877) edited by Derek Hudson (1968).
[28] Young, Hannah M., *Liebig Company's Practical Cookery Book* (1893)
Young, Hannah M., *Choice Cookery* (1888).
[29] Davies, Jennifer,*The Victoria Kitchen*, BBC Publications (1989).
[30] Tuite, Eva, *Lemco Dishes for All Seasons* 1905.
[31] David, Elizabeth, *English Bread and Yeast Cookery* (1968).
[32] Drummond, J.C. and Wilbraham, A., *The Englishman's Food* revised edition (1957).
[33] Apple, Rima D., '"Advertised by our loving friends" The Infant Formula Industry and the Creation of New Pharmaceutical Markets, 1870-1910', *Journal of the History of Medicine and Allied Sciences* (1986) 41:3.
[34] Spargo, Demelza, editor, *This Land is our Land*, Catalogue of the Exhibition organised for the Royal Agricultural Society of England (1989).
[35] Marshall Cavendish, *Encylopaedia of Gardening* (1968), page 1386.
[36] Muspratt, Sheridan, *Manure Chemistry: Theoretical, Practical and Analytical as applied to Arts and Manufactures* (1860).
[37] Campbell, Susan, *A Calendar of Garden Lore* (1983).
[38] Magnus Pyke, *Food for the millions* (1963).
Mackarness, Richard, *Eat Fat and Grow Slim* (1958).
[39] Carpenter, Kenneth J., *A History of Scurvy and vitamin C* (1986).
[40] Spencer, Colin, *The Heretic's Feast* (1995).
[41] Liebig, Justus von, *Pharmaceutical Journal* (1851).
[42] Von Rumohr, Baron, *The Essence of Cookery*, 1806, trans. Barbara Yeomans (1993).
[43] Osler, Sir William, *Silliman Lectures on the history of Medicine*, (1913).

Otto Herman: Much More Than a Chef

Dr Louis I. Szathmáry

Chefs and others begins the first sentence describing this year's papers for the Oxford Food Symposium at St. Antony College. My intention is to write about one who belongs among the *others*.

Professor Otto Herman, the hero of my paper, was as far from being a 'chef' as possible, but he was indeed that 'other' who, in my opinion, did more to describe and promote the preparation, and serving of the 'results' of agriculture, animal husbandry and the utilization of flora and fauna as food than anyone else in his generation.

Knowing his scientific achievements (appendix) will help the reader to measure the scope of his work and his influence. Otto Carl Herman was the son of a country doctor who moved in the early 19th century from the north-eastern border region of Hungary to the middle of the country, seeking better opportunities for himself and his family. Otto Herman was born in June 1835 in Alsóhámor, a small mining and industry town, in the county of Borsod. During a difficult childhood, his education was interrupted at the age of 14 by the uprising of the Hungarian nation under the leadership of Louis Kossuth against the rule of the Habsburg dynasty. He had to abandon his studies and start a new life as an apprentice in a small blacksmith shop, working not only with iron and steel but other metals such as copper and bronze.

He was forced by law to enter the army and his career led him, after several miserable years as an infantryman, to a metal workshop in Vienna. There he became a freelance assistance in the world-renowned botany collection of the then well-known naturalist, Karl Brunner von Wattenwyll, whose herbarium was housed at the Naturalkabinett, a 'Museum of Nature', in Vienna. Otto Herman excelled so greatly as a draftsman, graphic artist and preparator, first of plants and then of animals, that he became a much appreciated member of the growing group of natural scientists working at that time in Vienna, the capital of the Austro-Hungarian monarchy.

In 1864 he was invited by the scientist Sámuel Brassai to the capital of Transylvania, Kolozsvár, First he worked as an assistant to Professor Brassai in the Museum of Transylvania (Erdélyi

Self-portrait by O. Herman

Múzeum), which was founded in the late 1600s by the rulers of Transylvania. Later he became an assistant curator at the Transylvanian Museum Society, and created the still-existing animal collection of all known Transylvanian fauna from the smallest insects to the largest European buffalo and brown bear. From there he was invited to join the Hungarian National Museum in Budapest, where he started as the organizer of the Museum's animal collection. He worked there until 1875 and founded one of the most important Hungarian periodicals (*Természeterajzi Füzetek*). This still-existing periodical tried to link Hungarian literature on natural history to similar publications in western Europe – from Holland to Spain, from France to Middle Europe, and later to the entire scientific world.

Working in the Hungarian National Museum, Otto Herman entered the political life of the country and became a member of Parliament in 1875 as a member of the National Independent Party. He served as an MP for 11 years. In 1891 he organized the Second National Ornithological Congress, and as a result founded the Hungarian Ornithological Centre in 1894. The same year he started an ornithological periodical, *Aquila*, and continued his scientific writings. After this skyrocketing career, he kept publishing great and diverse works on many areas of science.

From childhood a keen observer of spiders, he published a scientific work in this field, *The Spider Fauna of Hungary*, in three volumes, 1876-1879. This resulted in personal correspondence with Louis Kossuth, who lived as an immigrant in Turin, northern Italy. Kossuth, himself an amateur naturalist, was fascinated by spiders and wrote a very approving, but keenly critical study of Otto Herman's book. This made them lifetime friends and strongly influenced the political ideas of Otto Herman.

He was a scientist who, throughout his life, worked on several subjects at once. His scientific books were published by the foremost publishing houses of Hungary, but also the Austro-Hungarian Monarchy and several European publishers. We are now most interested, among his books, in the ones relating to the oldest occupations of the Hungarian nation: animal husbandry, herding and fishery. Today, in 1995, it is hard to imagine that Hungary in the 1870s and 1880s was still known as a country in which one of the most important foods was fish, and that fishing was a strong and viable industry with a 1,000-year old history. During the active scientific working years of Otto Herman, the Carpathian basin was one of the most prominent fish-producers of the world. The lakes, swamplands, rivers and brooks of Hungary were the habitat of several hundred species of fish.

It is no surprise that Otto Herman and several other Hungarian scientists and agriculturalists were interested in fish-merchandising and consumption. But Otto Herman was the first scientist who included in his works, besides the management of fresh water fishing, the history of fishing and fishermen, actual fish recipes and descriptions of meals. He carried the topic of fishing all the way through to the description of contemporary fish drying methods, and also the cooking and consumption of dried fish. This is the reason I felt that this year's symposium should pay tribute to Otto Herman when we are discussing chefs *and others*.

Among the works by Professor Herman listed in the appendix, the most important for us is a two-volume work, *Halászat és Pásztorélet*, 1898, and the *Magyarok Nagy Ősfoglalkozása*. These are the works in which he elaborated most on the actual gastronomical and culinary aspects of fish after it is caught and brought via the kitchen to the table. To the best of our knowledge, Herman was the first among 19th century natural scientists to base the age of the different tools, gadgets, nets, etc. used by 19th century Hungarian fishermen on a comparison with descriptions of the same items mentioned in the Bible. (See, for instance, Luke 5, 2-7; Matthew chapter 4, 18-21.)

If the method of fishing and the fishing gear were identical with those used in 19th century middle Europe, then it was simple to assume that the tools and equipment, as well as the various metals used, could be the very same ones which the forebears of the Hungarians brought along from their earlier existence before they entered the Carpathian Basin during the sixth to ninth centuries.

For nomads such as the forebears of the Hungarians (just like the forebears of the Germans, the Saxons, and the Basques, to name a few groups which entered Europe from the East), fish was one of their most important foods. They didn't have to sow, till, or harvest it, and its availability was not determined by the quality of the soil, the temperature of the air, or the amount of precipitation. The fish were simply there in abundance, and the skill and tools of the fishermen ensured a well-fed, well-nourished population regardless of its location. Fish always were and still are today one of the easiest raw materials to prepare for the table. The only spice really needed is salt, There is no doubt that the addition of spices, herbs or other forms of vegetation add to the enjoyment of fish but it was easy to turn raw fish into edible nourishment. This was accomplished chiefly by the simple method of cooking above a small fire, generated from a small amount of reeds, canes, or other heating fuel available in abundance around rivers and lakes. The mere fact of the presence of fish presumed the presence of water; after all, most of the edible fish from sweet water dwell in drinkable water.

Professor Herman describes an old-fashioned, simple meal he attended on a very cold winter day, not far south-west of the north-eastern Carpathian mountains, around the slopes of the Tokaj mountains, the most famous wine-producing region of Hungary. A group of fishermen went out on the ice to a swampland which contained several fishing posts built above the water on stilts (just like houses are still built on stilts along the Mississippi River). When the fishermen succeeded in catching as many fish as they wished through holes cut in the ice around the fishing post, a group of them gathered under a several centuries old oak tree in a makeshift resting place quickly assembled from willow branches, reeds and cane, chiefly to protect them from the wind. After very carefully cleaning an area three or four feet in diameter, they built a small fire in its centre. They quickly cut open the belly of the fish, removed and discarded the guts, then pierced the whole fish as close to the vertebrae as possible with a young willow branch strong enough to hold the weight of the small fish. They rubbed the fish with a mixture of salt, a little pepper, and some paprika, and held the fish on a willow branch close to the fire – close enough to bake, but not to burn. In ten to fifteen minutes, depending on the size of the catch, the meal was ready – the fish remained juicy and cooked through while the skin became a highly crunchy, tasty protective layer.

Getting that far, they 'fished' out for everyone a piece of bread from their shoulder bags. The bread was packed in a towel which represented the table and substituted for a plate. The only tool used was a pocketknife. If it was on hand, they sliced a snow-white, crispy, tangy slice from a fist-sized onion, and had a royal feast, killing the thirst after the meal with some of the light, not too sweet young wine of the Tokaj region. A similar type of Tokaj wine called *Szamorodni* is still available today in England as well as in the United States. If you are fortunate enough to live in a place which has a distributor of this delightful wine, you can still copy the meal of the 19th century Hungarian fishermen, who invited Professor Herman to a similar meal.

Of course, most people who love to eat freshly caught and grilled fish want to enjoy some type of fish in the wintertime. The larger part of the population must rely on fish caught during the late spring or early summer, and processed by sun-drying during summer and fall. Also, certain religious groups which consume nothing but fish during Lent, which in Hungary are mainly the Greek Catholics and Eastern Catholics (Orthodox), started to preserve fish when it was in abundance. The oldest and best (and pre-Biblical) method of preservation was the filleting, salting and sun-drying or air-drying of fish. In Hungary this was usually done along Lake Balaton, the largest body of freshwater on the European continent, and along the 'lower Danube' – the part of this huge river which turns toward the east before Vienna and goes east until north of Budapest, turning south until arriving at the southern part of Hungary where, after it is joined by the largest, longest Hungarian river, the

Tisza, it turns from west to east again and continues to the Black Sea. The population of southern Hungary used to invest tremendous and successful efforts in the drying of salted (sometimes smoked and salted) fillets of fish in the 19th century. This product was very popular throughout Poland, Rumania, Greece and even Turkey.

In Hungary this type of fish was consumed mostly with boiled cabbage. The cabbage was the firm, snow-white type. It was cut into eight wedges and placed in a pot. Depending on the time of the year, dried or fresh dill, tarragon (or in Transylvania, dried or fresh *csombor*, savory) was used in this dish besides salt as the principal flavouring along with some sliced onion, sliced (not chopped) garlic, whole black and white peppercorns, and juniper berries. The cabbage was simmered for approximately 20 minutes, then the dried fish, first washed, soaked for two to three hours, then washed again was laid on the cabbage, covered with water, and simmered for another 20-30 minutes. Sometimes the same dried fish was cooked with sauerkraut instead of fresh cabbage, and in old times the smoked, salted fish was made into another, very special Eastern Catholic Lenten dish. It was simmered together with dried apples, dried pears, or prunes. Towards the end of the 19th century, people started to cook this fish with peeled raw potatoes.

The daily life and daily food of the fishermen were in many ways similar to and yet extremely different from the part of the Hungarian population occupied with the other great original occupation: animal husbandry, or rather herding.

Some nations which migrated two to three thousands years ago to Europe from Asia like most of the Indo-Germans, the Aryans – forebears of the people who settled in northern and western Europe, the Scandinavian countries, the Netherlands, Belgium, the Anglo-Saxons, were already

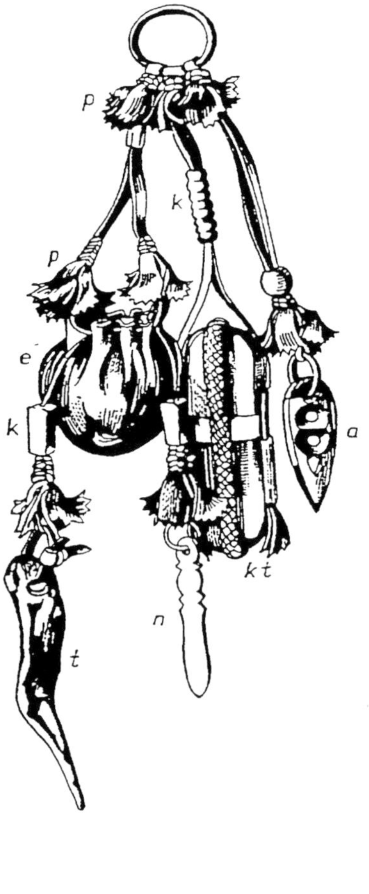

The Hungarian shepherd's 'Cakkumpakk', after an original drawing by O. Herman.

The word has a military origin. According to Otto Herman, it comes from 'sack' (a bag) and 'paket' (a package). It is used to describe the small items one would carry on one's person as part of one's most imprtant, frequently used tools and implements.

a) steel
kt) flint and tinder
t) special needle to sew skin and leather and a bone tool to smooth leather (scraper)
p) butterfly ornamentation
k) carved bone decoration
e) tobacco pouch

agricultural tribes and nations when they moved to Europe. The Uralic-Altaic nations were nomads, with much less interest in agriculture than in animal husbandry. To many scientists the main reason why Hungarians (starting with the Avars) settled between the sixth to ninth centuries in the Carpathian basin was that the geographical and geological conditions of the Carpathian basin, with the Danube and its tributaries coming through the regions, were ideal for settlement by people whose main occupation was herding. The land of origin of the nation which later came to be called Hungary we still don't know, but it is certain that as these tribes travelled through centuries, they always travelled with their considerable sized herds of cattle, horses and pigs, as well as a type of prairie-hen or chicken. According to the very recent and still ongoing research by Professor Gyula László, University of Budapest, the forebears of the Hungarians and their not-too-distant relatives, the Avars, moved through the Asiatic continent very slowly, staying for at least one and sometimes two to three generations in the same area. When they arrived in the Carpathian basin, they already had very large herds of the animals mentioned above, and they continued herding as their main occupation.

The herding methods of the Hungarians were very similar to those of other herders throughout history. Professor Herman was among the first who wanted to prove his theory that, beside fishing, herding was the first and most important occupation of Hungarians. He went into detailed investigation of the usage of the language among herdsmen tending horses, cowboys, shepherds and swineherds (*kanász* or *kondás*) who tended and herded the pigs. These occupations differed from each other for a thousand years or more. Professor Herman went through tens of thousands of documents, mostly in Latin, relating to agreements among shepherds, herdsmen, cowboys, and between state and local governments, owners of herds and their employees. He extracted Hungarian words from these documents relating to daily life, occupation, duties, and methods of herding, as well as the words relating to the food and drink, clothing and housing, etc., of the herdsmen and shepherds. He wrote one of his most significant books on the language of the herdsmen. In this book he included the approximately 300 food-related words under the heading of 'kitchen'. Approximately one third of the words are the names of dishes, foods, and ingredients, the rest are cooking methods and utensils supplying a tremendous amount of information on how and what the Hungarian herdsmen ate, how they obtained it and how they cooked it from approximately the 13th century until the end of the 19th century, when the book was published. This work is mainly an 'encyclopedic dictionary' in which all relating to the occupation of tending domestic animals is contained. It is not a cookbook, but in our estimation it is a scientific work written by a natural scientist published by the Royal Hungarian Society of Natural Sciences.

As we know, the entire food picture of Europe was dramatically and forever changed by the discovery of the western hemisphere by Columbus and his forerunners, contemporaries and followers. The appearance of potatoes, corn, tomatoes, capsicum, fruits and nuts (such as pineapple and pecans), vegetables such as the entire squash family, spices such as cocoa beans and vanilla, and animals such as turkey and Maine lobster, to mention just the most well-known, changed the concept of food and the concept of cooking in the entire Old World. This affected especially the food customs and food ways of Europe from north-eastern European Russia to south-western Spain and from the islands of Albion to the islands of Greece. As Hungarian food changed dramatically, so did the food of Hungarian shepherds and herdsmen, and this dramatic 'change within a change' was wonderfully documented by Professor Herman. Whatever subject he wrote about, he always paid more attention to food, food preparation, and eating than any other contemporary scientists working in the field of the natural sciences devoted to the subject.

It is not the task of this short paper to compare Otto Herman's work with that of his contemporaries, but it is significant that German, French, British, Italian and Spanish books on agriculture and animal husbandry and herding of the second half of the 19th and the first half of the

20th centuries do not have a comparable amount of information regarding food that Dr. Herman's do. It is not our task to elaborate on the descriptions of food from his book, but we would like to mention a few, and even describe a few samples of dishes which originated in Hungary through the centuries as food for shepherds on the great Hungarian plain, and which are still prepared by contemporary Hungarians. His book mentions the dishes in alphabetical order, and in many instances even gives a date when it was first recorded. Of course, this does not mean that was the time of the origin of the dish. It is very interesting how the dishes were named. For instance, a dish which was very popular with herdsmen was called 'orphan's soup' already in the 1700s. It was a soup without meat made from various vegetables.

Many of the dishes are made from the oldest grain in the Hungarian agriculture, millet. It is also interesting to note that Hungarian shepherds carried along from central China the custom of germinating (sprouting) different seeds such as millet, beans, lentils, wheat and rye, as well as preparing, with the addition of dried fruits and wild honey, boiled or baked sweet dishes, as well as savory or vegetable dishes made from sprouts. We do not know of any other group in Europe which ate sprouts, both raw and cooked or both sweet and savoury, through the ages. These dishes were not known by other parts of the Hungarian population, or, rather, they were forgotten after agriculture developed. To me it is significant that herdsmen and shepherds lived year-round with their herds in the open spaces of the Hungarian plains in very simple one-room abodes seldom 'built' from conventional materials, but mostly assembled like tents and multipurpose single rooms from reed, cane, willow or even from dry weeds, or at other times stuck together with clay or mud to withstand the winds.

During his long life, almost every year, Professor Herman spent months and months roaming the countryside, living with the shepherds and herdsmen before tape recording was in use.

Dr. Otto Herman died in 1914, but his notebooks containing thousands and thousands of pages are still consulted by contemporary scientists following in his footsteps, developing new sub-territories of anthropology and other natural sciences.

Thanks and Acknowledgements

First and foremost, I have to thank the 'sources' of my research, the University of Chicago Regenstein Library (Alice Schreyer, Curator of Special Collections), Johnson & Wales University's Culinary Archives and Museum (Barbara Kuck, Curator), the Library of the University of Iowa (David Schoonover, Curator of Rare Books), and in Hungary, Dr Istvan Gedai, Director General of the National Museum of Hungary, Budapest, and Dr Rezsö Szij, President of the Otto Herman Society, Budapest, who all permitted me to search and research my difficult subject.

To Mrs Cheryl Soderholm, for technical assistance, design and layout, Mrs Gabi Doyle for typesetting, Miss Ida Takach, Mrs Maria Szilagyi and Mr Steven Sevics, for Hungarian language assistance, and last, but not least, my wife Sada, who helped me through this project in any and every way possible.

Appendix

1. Biographical Notes

Herman, Carl Otto. Born in Breznóbánya, Hungary on June 26, 1835; died in Budapest, Hungary on December 27, 1914. Natural scientist, ethnographer, polyhistorian, politician. Studied at Miskolc. Graduated from the Polytechnicum of Vienna, Austria in 1853. His first mentor and professor in Vienna was Karl Brunner von Wattenwyll.

In 1863 he was invited to join Professor Sámuel Brassai as preparator and conservator at the museum in Kolozsvár. He made the foundations of the (later very famous) collection of 'Animals of Transylvania'; became involved in politics and was elected a member of the Hungarian Parliament.

Although he considered himself first and foremost a zoologist, he worked on a high scientific level in ethnography and anthropology, as well as in publishing and scientific writing. He was a member of the Board of the Royal Hungarian Society of Natural History, a member of the Hungarian Linguistic Society, a member of the Hungarian Society of Ethnography, and a member of several learned societies in England, France, Germany, Italy, etc. He was one of the founders of the Cave Exploring Committee of the Geological Society, a member of the Transylvanian Museum Society, and a member of many European ornithological associations.

His lifetime work was recognized with the Kálmán Szily Gold Medal and prize and the Andrassy Medal of the Hungarian School Society, among many other Hungarian, Austro-Hungarian and European honors and medals. His wife, Camilla Borosnyai was a writer and novelist. She also wrote short stories and poems. She assisted her husband's political career by writing political pamphlets and articles.

2. Otto Herman – a select bibliography

Magyarország pókfaunája, I-III, Bp., 1876-79, The Spiders of Hungary
A magyar halászat könyve, I-II, Bp., 1887-88, Book of Icthyology in Hungary
A halgazdaság rövid foglaltja, Bp., 1888, A Short History of Fishery in Hungary
A miskolci palaeolith lelet, Bp., 1893, The Discovery of Paleolithic Remains in Miskolc
A madárvonulás elemei Magyarországon, Bp., 1895, Bird Migration in Hungary
Az osfoglalkozások: Halászat és pásztorélet, Bp., 1898, The Oldest Main Occupations: Fishing and Herding
A magyar osfoglalkozások köréből, Bp., 1899, Studies Relating to Fishing and Herding, the Oldest Hungarian Occupations
A madarak hasznáról és káráról Bp., 1901, Birds as Useful Helpers and Birds as Pests, *A magyar pásztorak nyelvkincse*, Bp., 1914, Language of the Hungarian Herdsmen
Term észeti képek, Bp., 1959, Nature Scenes: A Book of Short Stories

3. Books on Otto Herman

Lambrecht Kálmán: *Herman Otto élete és kora* (Bp., 1920)
Székely Sándor: *Herman Otto* (Bp., 1955)
Banner János: *A magyar oskokorkutatás történetéhez* (Miskolc, Herman Otto Múz. Évk. 1958)
Sáfrán Györgyi: *Herman Otto és Kossuth Lajos* (Magy. Tud. 1960)
Ortutay Gyula: 'Otto Herman' (*New Hung. Quart.*, 1964)
Allodiatoris Irma: *Herman Otto* (Élövilág, 1964. 3.sz.)
Komáromy József: *Herman Otto levelei a miskolci múzeumban* (Herman Otto Múz.Évk. 1964-65)
Varga Domokos: *Herman Otto: A Kalandos és Küdzelmes Sorsú Nagy Magyar Tudós Élete* (Móra Ferenc Könyvkiadó, Budapest, 1976)

Great Personalities and a Great Cuisine

Gábor Tasnádi

'Transylvania, after France and China, produced one of the world's three greatest cuisines.'

Egon Ronay, 1989

'Hungarian Transylvanians are the most colorful and gastronomically interesting group in the area.'

George Lang, 1971

I. HISTORY AND BACKGROUND

Transylvania is a particular area on the eastern plateau of the Carpathian Basin, a geographically and historically special region with great traditions and a varied fate. It is bordered by the Great Hungarian Plain on the west and by the mountain chain of the Carpathians, shaped like a half ring from all other directions.

In Transylvania Hungarians, Rumanians, Saxons and, to a lesser extent, Armenians and Jews have been living together for many centuries, and as a consequence of their living together the area, in terms of language, religion and culture, has a particular place in Europe (Kós, 1934). The Seklers, the biggest group of the Transylvanian Hungarians, about 1 million people, live in the eastern part of Transylvania called Székelyföld (Seklerland).

Transylvania was an integral part of medieval Hungary as her east bulwark for centuries; later it became a principality, relatively independent first of the Turkish power and later of the House of Habsburg (by right of the Hungarian crown). For a short time in 1848 and for more than half a century from 1867, Transylvania was reunited with Hungary. Since the end of World War I Transylvania has belonged to Rumania, except for four years during World War II when the northern part of the country belonged again to Hungary (Köpeczi and Barta, 1994).

One can read in Paul Kovi's unique book entitled *Transylvanian Cuisine* that in Transylvania Hungarians, Rumanians, Saxons, Armenians and Jews coexisted for centuries enriching one another, yet each of these cultures retained its own distinctive characteristics. The ethnographer will be astonished while wandering in this small area from valley to valley, from plateau to plateau. He will find wooden structures and men blowing mountain horns like in Tibet, towers and belfries such as

Calvinistic belfry from 1570 (Mezőcsávás, Mezőség region)

those seen in the Caucasus, carved gateways reminiscent of China, ancient Roman triumphal arches, gravestones shaped like headboards as seen in the Basque region, and embroidery recalling Siberian and Macedonian influences. Similarities to Transylvanian Hungarian pentatonic music and song can be found in the area of the Urals and of northern Tibet, and the Transylvanian folk ballads rival the most beautiful Scottish ones (Bartók and Kodály, 1921).

II. THE CUISINE

Despite these borrowed influences, one senses the true Transylvanian spirit so indigenous to this region and to its cuisine. Transylvanian people have tasted the meals of their neighbours near and far, evaluated and respected them, even learned how to prepare them, but have always retained their own dishes. This holds true, for example, among the Hungarians in Transylvania, whose methods of preparation for one delicacy can vary from town to town: a marinade is used for the bacon at Szatmár different from that at Marosvásárhely. It is difficult to decide which is better, but it is not important; nobody wants to unite the two into one representative Transylvanian bacon. One is pleased that a single food can taste equally good when prepared in so many different ways.

In Paul Kovi's book one of his co-authors, the cultural historian, writer and critic, István Szőcs (born 1928) living in the capital of Transylvania, Kolozsvár, summarizes the main characteristics of Transylvanian Hungarian cuisine as follows.

In the basic Hungarian cuisine, a roux is the most important thickener of soups and sauces; onions and flour (but usually just the latter) are browned in fat, thinned with a liquid, then added to the soup. Another thickener is made from just flour, sour cream and eggs. The Seklers of Transylvania and Rumanians are not fond of a roux, hence many of their soups are of a different type. They also use a lot of vegetables and meat cooked in a great deal of water, without any prior browning. The central source of calories in Hungarian cuisine is pork fat, while the Rumanians use oil, chiefly from sunflower or pumpkin seeds. The Hungarians, at least in the past, used cooking oil only for lenten dishes. They still use mainly vinegar to sour their dishes, while Rumanians like sour bran. The Hungarians frequently add roasted or fried food to a dish, while the Rumanians use semi-raw salad-like garnishings. Cornmeal is a good example to further illustrate these differences. Rumanians prepare cornmeal with milk or curd, or with oil and salted or smoked fish, while Hungarians fry a little onion or fry the cornmeal itself.

Now, compared to Hungarian cuisine, what makes Transylvanian (and Sekler) cuisine special? Several things, such as the use of herbs and spices (wild thyme, ginger and saffron) in larger quantities and more imaginative ways, with more fidelity to tradition; the particular cult of scones, leavened and other kinds of baked pastries (at the expense of pastas); the frequency of fruit soups and fruit

Home tent-oven (Désháza, Szilágyság region)

sauces; and finally an obvious influence of the other Transylvanian ethnic cuisines and far eastern, especially Chinese, cooking. Particularly conspicuous is the prodigious use of certain local vegetables such as eggplant and corn, since they are not used in traditional Hungarian cooking. Finally, the method of mass food preparation left a smaller imprint on the Transylvanian Hungarian cuisine than on the cooking of the Great Plain of Hungary – especially Budapest.

In the Transylvanian cuisine the word spicy does not mean hot and burning but something completely different – although it is true that in Old Transylvania, as in the aristocratic Hungarian kitchens, the chefs of the rich competed in the use of various more expensive oriental or colonial spices. In general, the Transylvanian cuisine is fond of pepper and sweet paprika, but only in moderation, while the Rumanians, on the other hand, use a great deal of hot spices and paprika. Those who are curious to know what spicy Transylvanian food is really like should taste lamb soup with tarragon. Another dish, 'slushy' cabbage in the Transylvanian manner, for instance, features dill and savoury, but not paprika. Caraway seed flavours not only their liqueur, but even the simplest soup, and especially roast chops. Similarly aniseed is not only an additive to spirits but is also used in various scones and buns. And many additional herbs may be added to marinades for ham, bacon or game: coriander, marjoram, juniper berries and wild thyme, to mention only a few. These spices do not burn the mouth; if they did, people would not taste the flavour. When a dish still tastes a little too hot, Transylvanians eat a bit of horseradish, which has a sharpness that does not bite in the mouth or throat.

Strangers to this food are astonished at the variety of fruit soups – cherry, gooseberry, red currant, apricot, apple or plum – which can be sweet, slightly sour or flavoured with smoked meat. The skill and art needed to prepare any good sour fruit soup is appreciated by most people on first tasting it. Since Transylvania is a fruit growing country, there are thousands of methods of preserving and drying fruit there; dried fruit is used for soups, sauces and teas. In addition to herb teas, cranberry, myrtle berry (from both black and red berries) and rose hip teas are common. Fruit vinegars, primarily made from wild apples and pears, are used more often than wine vinegar. In the past, at least three types of vinegar had to be offered on a table: wine, apple, sour cherry, rose, or other vinegars, one of which was customarily seasoned with tarragon or thyme. Today most of the apple vinegar used is commercially made. Several varieties of mustard also had to be served: common mustard and the so-called Hungarian mustard cooked with grape juice, minced quince, and mustard flour. Even today no decent pork feast is complete without a choice of mustards.

Transylvanian cuisine uses a large amount of preserved smoked meats in its dishes, and there are unique varied preparations of beans, vegetables and other produce. The spring soup, called *fuszulyka* soup, contains green beans, lettuce and fresh hops, while the *zakotas* soup contains pork, lettuce, tarragon, parsley, onion, savoury, sour cream, and eggs. There are other similar soups with names just as mysterious. The always resourceful poor prepared various purées from what was available: for example a type of jelly cooked from blanched oatmeal, eaten with milk or plum juice. There was hardly a plant, herb, tree, or flower that did not have a special role in Transylvanian cuisine. It was as if the Transylvanians followed the ancient Sumerian proverb: 'Do not pull up anything; it may one day bear fruit'.

While quoting the past, it should be noted that the milk loaf, doughnuts, buns, and the famous biscuits of Torda are remnants of ancient sacrificial treats brought to Transylvania, probably by the Khazar Jews. Sacrificial biscuits – actually a honey bread – made of wheat, rye and honey, baked in

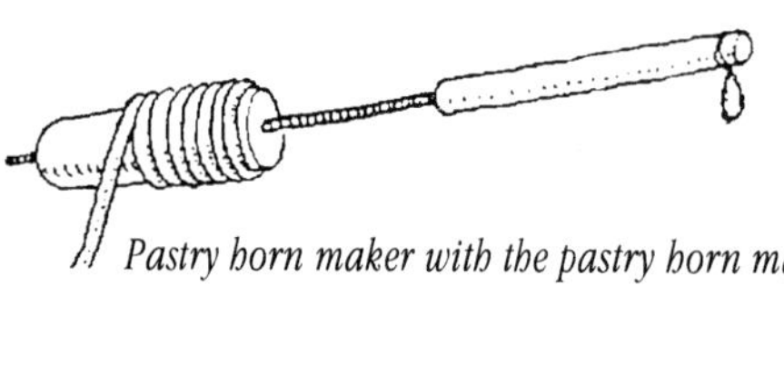

Pastry horn maker with the pastry horn material shown as it is rolled (Sztána, Kalotaszeg region)

the ancient river region of Persia and in Egypt, recall Abraham's pilgrimage to Melchizedek. There he sacrificed bread, as did the Jews to the father-in-law of Moses six centuries later, and to Christ two thousand years later.

The most ancient terms of the Hungarian cuisine can be traced to the first written relics of civilisation. István Szócs finds the Hungarian word *sül* (bake) in early Sumerian and Egyptian texts, where other etymons of basic words were also discovered. *Sül* is still used in connection with scrambled eggs or meat fried in bread crumbs.

Of the characteristic dishes the most important is stuffed cabbage with pork; it is widely eaten at Christmas, at Easter, at Whitsuntide, and at other feast days both in villages and in towns. Various kinds of *tokány* and *paprikás* are also feast dishes as well as the pastry horn. This latter is a true Transylvanian speciality, not authentically produced in other parts of the world. The genuine pastry horn is made of finger-thick, feather-light leavened dough; made with egg yolks, it is rolled round a wooden cylinder, brushed with melted butter and sugar, sprinkled with chopped nuts, and baked to perfection over charcoal embers.

The so-called *flekken* is a characteristic roast that is very popular also in the Saxon and Rumanian cuisines. The roast lamb, or roast pork, is really tasty only when prepared over hot charcoal, and the lamb (or pork) *flekken* – medallions cut from the leg – are authentic only when the outside is reddish brown and crisp and the inside milky white and soft.

III. THE ETHNOGRAPHER

The survival of traditions and the variety of regional colours are the common and remarkable characteristics of the Hungarian regions and village groups of Transylvania. There are two reasons for this variety: the varied hills of the region and the coexistence of inhabitants who have different languages. This is why Hungarian ethnographers have been studying Transylvania with particular interest for about 125 years. Great personalities like László Kőváry, Balázs Orbán, János Kriza, István Győrffy, Károly Viski or, the two giants, Béla Bartók and Zoltán Kodály, have dealt in their works partly or wholly with Transylvania. The names of Lajos Kelemen, Attila T.Szabó, László Debreczeni and Géza Vámszer are worth mentioning from the period between the two world wars.

The ethnographic activity of Károly Kós jr., who lives in Kolozsvár, began during World War II. He was born in Sztána of Kalotaszeg in 1919. His father was a famous architect and writer (e.g. Kós, 1934). In 1944 Kós jr. gained a doctoral degree in ethnography at the University of Kolozsvár. He was working then as a research fellow of the museum and the Academy. His main research topic was Transylvanian Hungarian folk culture, and he published a number of works from 1947. His activity is internationally outstanding – well known and respected.

Concerning food, one of his favourite topics was studying traces of the collection of edible plants.

Traces of ancient collection of edible plants can be found primarily in connection with children's delicacies and among the descriptions of dearth-foods of old times. Some time ago beech nuts *(tátorján – Crambe tataria)*, hemlock root (*Conium maculatum*), hazelnuts *(martilapu – Tussilago farfara)*, a great variety of mushrooms, thorn-apple (*Crataegus monogyna*) and sloe (*Prunus spinosa*) had great importance for eating. There are many plants that are collected even now for making jam, such as raspberry, wood strawberry, hips, cornel (*Cornus mas*), *makracseresznye (Prunus silvestris)*, cranberries (*Vaccinium myrtillus vs. vitis-idaea*), and elder, while wild apples and wild pears are collected for making vinegar and *pálinka* (Hungarian brandy), as well as the honey-rich flowers of acacia (*Robina pseudoacacia*) and elder eaten fried with eggs (Kós, 1985).

Several forms of trapping wild bees were practised in Transylvania, while home beekeeping was an important activity. The traditional forms of fishing and hunting were also known. Kós has dealt with the former Transylvanian fairs as regional events in several of his works. What he has written about food at the fair at Páncélcseh, a village in central Transylvania, is of particular interest (Kós, 1976).

The Fair at Páncélcseh

The inhabitants of about 160 villages of the region bordered by the rivers Szamos and Almás obtained the majority of their necessities at the nearby village markets even in the last century. Páncélcseh was located in the centre of the region and was the most important of the markets. It had a cattle market and a fair famous throughout the area and as big as a town, where the inhabitants of 60 to 100 villages could purchase a wide variety of industrial products with the income from the agricultural produce that they sold. The cattle market was based on buffalo husbandry that was successful on the poor grazing land of the area. The basis of the fair was provided by both local handicraftsmen who were familiar with the needs of the area and the growing of vegetables, as well as the local carters. Near the end of the century five shops, three pubs, a timber yard and two big mills were built with the object of both serving and refreshing the fair. The two big national fairs at Páncélcseh were held in accordance with the traditions of such fairs on traditionally important days: one on the 23rd and 24th June, at the beginning of summer, and the other on the 8th and 9th of September, on the birthday of the Blessed Virgin Mary. On the first day of these two day big fairs there was a cattle market, and a general fair on the second. In 1870 the village also got the right to hold a market on Tuesdays.

Selling on Canvas

Various kinds of food, greens, earthenware vessels, pots and other folk products were sold from the bare earth or from canvas spread on the ground in the middle of the market around the cross that had been erected to commemorate the emancipation of the serfs in 1848.

Those peasants who owned more than one pig, even after the pig killing that had begun on Saint Andrew's Day (30 November), brought a lot of *orjaszalonna* [spare rib bacon], *félszalonna* [side bacon], and pots of lard to the Tuesday markets. Beside the village smoked bacon, *sósszalonna* [salted bacon], was available from the Armenian dealers. People from the villages of Hagymás and Völcs brought *ruca* [duck], and *liba* [goose] to the market. *Juhtúró* [sheep's milk cheese], and *sajt* [cheese], were brought from May by the shepherds in the area. Sometimes at the time of the great fast, Rumanian herrings from Szamos were brought in barrels by merchants from Dés.

Poppy and walnuts could be bought at the fair before the great feasts, and in one of the nearby streets sometimes four or five carts from Diósad were standing with big wine barrels selling wine to both sellers and buyers. People from Diósad also frequently brought *pálinka* [Hungarian brandy]. *Alma* [apple] were brought in carts by people from Kide, but many also came from Kalocsa and Szilvás as well. Fruits were measured by the *véka* [bushel], and the *kupa* [a kind of cup]. Onion growers from Páncélcseh bought plums for making jam in exchange for onions; usually four or five strings of onions for a bushel of plums. Big quantities of *paradicsom* [tomatoes], paprika and *uborka* [cucumber, for preserving] were brought to the big autumn fair, while *pityóka* [potatoes], *káposzta* [cabbage], *karalábé* [kohlrabi], *répa* [carrots], *celler* [celery],

Cheese press

petrezselyem [parsley], *cékla* [beetroot], *paszternák* [parsnip], *retek* [radish], *tök* [vegetable marrow] and a lot of *hagyma* [onions] were brought to the weekly markets in October and November. The main buyers of the vegetables were the middle classes of the village. The garden women of Páncélcseh always sold paprika powder milled in coffee grinders. They also brought various vegetable seeds measured in cups or thimbles.

The most spectacular product of their folk industry was earthenware vessels. Only the potters from neighbouring Köblös came to the weekly markets on Tuesdays, but at the two big fairs there were potters from Tihó, Désháza, Zilah and Torda. The *főzőfazék* [glazed cooking pot], *tál* [big plate], *csupor* [a kind of mug], and a pot lid were regular products of the potters from Köblös. At the big autumn fairs there were lots of big pots for cabbage and jam, *uborkáskanta* [a special pot for cucumber], pálinka jugs and jam strainers, while at the big summer fair there were *röstöllő* [lunch holders], pots with handles, *zörgőkorsó* [jugs with a fixed strainer], and *kanta* [another kind of pot]. Simpler plates for everyday use and more ornamental ones for hanging on the wall were also produced. The potters from Tihó also made red unglazed pottery with white stripes for various kitchen uses. People made these pots waterproof and long lasting by melting down fat in them before the first use.

Fair Delicacies

Tents offering tasty cooked meats and *pogácsa* [biscuits] could not be missed at the fair of Páncélcseh. Since the pubs in the village only served alcohol, these tents acted as restaurants, snack bars and confectionery shops. The tents selling *pogácsa* were set up on the busiest spot, facing the cattle market, but those selling meat were in the streets near the swing where the young people gathered. Four to six people from Páncélcseh and Torda made special peppered roasts fried in much hot fat called *kofapecsenye* [roughly: market-woman style roast]. There were women who sold the roasts in a special type of fresh loaf cut in half with the roast in the middle. People ate them sitting on the ramparts. Other women from Páncélcseh and Szamosújvár sold *hütyü*, a kind of sausage made from chitterlings, and *hurka*, stuffed with spicy rice, blood, lungs, and minced meat.

However most people coming to the fair brought their own food, so they were looking for some kind of sweetmeat. For example honey in the comb was brought in big pots by the country women and sold in cubes on cabbage leaves. There was also a traditional market delicacy called *mézespogácsa* [honey biscuit]. Even in the thirties (this century) one could see 15 to 20 tents selling *pogácsa*. Four or five people from Torda brought large quantities of big finger shaped *pogácsa* split open on the top. This kind was eaten on the spot, or married couples bought them for each other as *vásárfia*, fairing, a kind of present from the fair. In the tents selling *pogácsa*, *mézespálinka*

Wooden matrix for the decoration of mézespogácsa

[Hungarian brandy with honey], was available which attracted the young people very much.

Károly Kós made a lot of masterly drawings on the spot and when researching in museums; all the illustrations in the present study have been selected from these drawings (Kós, 1994).

IV. THE WRITER

The most outstanding Transylvanian writer, and indeed one of the most significant in all Hungarian literature, is Áron Tamási. He was born, one of the many children of a székely (Sekler) peasant family, in 1897 in Farkaslaka. After finishing his studies at the Trade Academy in Kolozsvár, between 1923 and 1926 he lived in the United States. In 1944 he moved from Transylvania to Budapest, where he lived until his death in 1966.

Áron Tamási created a modern, high level, original and very characteristic literature based on the Sekler folk tale and ballad world as well as on the Sekler people's everyday life (Czigány, 1984). His writings show some resemblance to the works of the French writer Giono. One of his critics called the rich collection of his short stories the 'Hungarian Thousand and One Nights'. Among his novels the most outstanding and most popular is his Abel trilogy, especially the first part *Ábel a rengetegben* (Abel Alone), 1932. The boy Abel, who is the model of the Sekler folk, is able to overcome robbers and the police by his own physical and mental skill, and by humour. Besides, in spite of his young age he is able to feed himself without problems.

The reader can learn more about the food of the people who live in the mountains from his autobiographical novel about his childhood entitled *Bölcső és Bagoly* (The Cradle and the Owl) that was first published in 1953. Among the many interesting details it is worth mentioning the lines about beech nut oil, which are also of value as a historical source.

> We collected the beech-mast from the ground, because the tree is so thoughtful that it offers it to ones hand when ripe. We brought home only ten to twenty cups of them each year because in our village nobody used the oil or hardly put it into the food except on Good Friday. But on that day everybody ate cabbage with oil and the so called *mácsik* which was a kind of pasta with oil. Well, the beechnuts were prepared for Good Friday; they were taken to the mill where the miller pressed them until the savoury and fragrant oil was obtained.

Rigorous order and devotion surrounded eating and everything connected with it, not only in old Transylvanian villages but also in the small towns. The living conditions of poor people was another factor that contributed to the appreciation of food and reverence for eating. The child Áron Tamási goes to the field to work with his father for the first time. It is impossible to read these memorable lines without emotion.

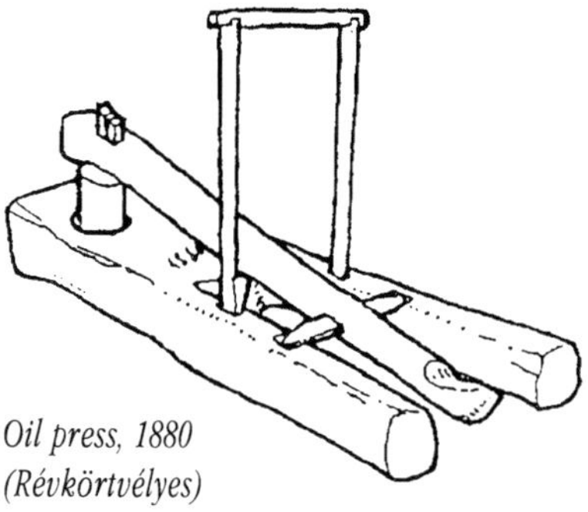

Oil press, 1880 (Révkörtvélyes)

> Soon after the noonday bell, the girl, my sister Anna, arrived. She brought a pot of bean soup in a holder that was still steaming when she took it out and took off its lid.
> Anna was a very practised housekeeper in spite of her young age; she laid a table cloth and two plates for us on the fragrant ground; then she sliced bread for us and took two rounded fried doughnuts from her satchel, one for my father and the other for the two of us. When my father looked at her inquiringly about this wedding-like

ceremony, she answered with a laugh:

'My mother told me that she sent all this in honour of the smaller man who was going to work for the first time today.'

Well, this was a great thing and my father told her:

'So, pour out the beans!'

Anna poured out the soup into our plates which created a cloudlike smell under our noses. The soup was rich with both soft bean pods and big pied beans and also *tövös* which is a sweet radish-like plant that I had never seen before [it is parsnip] but that provides a particularly good sweet flavorous taste to the bean soup.

This was the celebration of my becoming a worker in the fields.

Of course usually the *tokány* was meant to be food for a feast; Áron Tamási refers in several places in his book to those happy Sunday mornings when the air became rich with the smell of the chicken *tokány* freshly made by his mother. Later, when he returned as a famous writer from Kolozsvár to his home village and then from Budapest, now across the new frontier, chicken *tokány* was never missing from the table. On these occasions he always stayed in his other sister Ágnes's house; she was also a very good housekeeper. The author of the present paper, being a student at that time, was lucky enough to be on brotherly terms with Áron Tamási who encouraged him to go to the famous subalpine village. Thus he met Tamási's brother and sisters and had the pleasure of enjoying Aunt Ágnes's kind hospitality. He was also able to spend time, sometimes weeks, in Tamási's favourite room during the years after his death.

Once Aunt Ágnes told me when peeling onions that her brother Áron had been very fond of large red onions because of their good sweet taste, so it was not by chance that she used this type of onion when she made *tokány* for him. Even now I seem to remember the quick movements of Aunt Ágnes as she makes *tokány*, the precious cast iron pot and also the way she stirs the *puliszka* and then, when it is ready, how she skilfully cuts it with a thread on a wooden board. And of course the flavours of that time are still with me.

The various kinds of *tokány* are well known as typical Hungarian food, but the cookery books only describe it as made of beef or sometimes of pork. This is one of the reasons why I give the following recipe, but it is also to commemorate this great writer.

Summer kitchen (Impér, Székelyföld region)

Chicken *Tokány* (*Csirketokány*) à la Áron Tamási

1 kg chicken
170 g smoked bacon
200 g large red onion, finely chopped
2 cloves of garlic, finely chopped
60 g fresh and very ripe tomato, not peeled, chopped
3 sprigs fresh tarragon, finely chopped
salt and freshly ground black pepper to taste
100 ml dry white wine

Clean the chicken, cut it into large pieces and take out only the large bones. Wash thoroughly and cut into finger-sized pieces. Cut the bacon into tiny cubes, fry in a pan on moderate heat. Add the onion and saute over medium heat till limp. Add the chicken including giblets and liver, the tomato, garlic and tarragon as well as pepper and salt. Stir adding the wine gradually. Simmer covered until the chicken is tender.

Serve hot with *puliszka*.

Cornmeal Porridge (*Puliszka*)

Bring half a litre of water to a rapid boil and slowly sprinkle in 200 ml of coarse cornmeal, stirring all the time. Keep stirring and cook over low heat for about 6 minutes. Add 1 tsp salt; adjust salt if necessary.

The hot *puliszka* should be poured out onto a wooden board. One then has to wait for a while for it to cool and harden; then it can easily be cut into cubes with a thread. These cubes should be served warm with the *tokány*.

Puliszka was only the food of poor people. Áron Tamási had to eat it very frequently in his childhood, therefore later in his life he avoided it. As he told me, the only exception was when he ate tokány since this can only be eaten with *puliszka*. As he pointed out, with chicken *tokány* even *puliszka* gets a special flavour...

The third novel of Tamási that I shall mention is a sort of historical chronicle entitled *Hazai tükör* (Domestic Mirror). This was also first published in 1953 and describes the changes in Transylvania between the years of 1832 and 1853. At the centre of the novel are the events in Transylvania during the Hungarian revolution and war of independence of 1848 and 1849.

There is a description of an ox roast on the occasion of the wedding of Domokos Zeyk and Baroness Júlia Kemény. Three ten *akó* and two five *akó* barrels (an *akó* is an old measure of capacity, roughly 55 litres) waited for the aristocratic guests in the cellar of the big manor house in Malomfalva. The barrels were full of 'the famous wine of Bucsumás with a flavour and bouquet such that if a mouse smelled a drop of it, it would look for the cat until death.' Let us see what preceded the wine drinking!

The Roasting of an Ox in Transylvania

A master was brought from somewhere who was known throughout the region to be skilled in roasting an ox. This master had two forked poles driven into the ground and made a big carved rod that could be laid into the forks of the poles that stood opposite each other. The skinned ox was pulled onto the rod. Its guts had been properly cleaned out, but the splendid horns on its head and its hooves were left on. After this the master fixed the ox to the rod of the spit using long spikes driven through its backbone and some through its sides too. The ox was then salted inside and out and strewn with pepper; its horns and hooves were wrapped in wet cloths. The master had put a fat capon into the stomach of a fat sheep and the sheep was then put into the stomach of the ox. Handles to turn the spit were attached and a fire was lit under the ox on both sides. A strong lad stood at each handle to turn the ox slowly like turning a grindstone while the master basted the huge mass of beef with scientific skill so that every one who tasted it would never forget its flavour.

There were two kinds of basting liquid prepared in two huge ceramic kettles: one was dripping topped up with salted water and the other a rich mixture of flavours with pepper, *aszú* wine, tarragon, marjoram, sage, and thyme as well as onion and wild apple. From time to time the master took out the capon and smelled it to judge the progress of the ox's roasting.

Well, the ox had been long roasting and when the lads stopped turning, the master began to skilfully carve the delicious smelling ox. The hot roast was put on huge boards that were taken to the wedding guests. There were more than a hundred people present. The roasted ox, being the crown of all dishes, was traditionally served last; as the saying goes: 'put it on the head of appetite'. One might think therefore that people would pick at it instead of really eating the wonderful roast, but it was not so. A lot of wine was already under their belts; the ladies were nearly screaming with delight, while the gentlemen were groaning with pleasure as they attacked the meat.'

The writer used a handwritten book from the 16th century Transylvanian princely court as a source for this scene. It is, as far as we know, the first Hungarian cookery book; it was first published in 1893 under the title of *Szakács Tudomány*. The author was a Transylvanian master cook. There are nearly 900 dishes listed in the book that, considering their variety and methods of preparation, are on a level with the contemporary dishes at the French, Italian and Spanish princely courts. However this very valuable cookery book does not mention the 'flavour preparation', the basting liquids reported by Tamási, so one can assume that there were also other sources, unknown to us, used by the writer.

The author of this study is not the only one who can remember unforgettable suppers eaten with Áron Tamási in the sixties. In the Sipos Halászkert in Old Buda, Tamási ordered a dry Kadarka wine appropriate not only to the Fisherman's Broth with paprika (*Halászlé*) but also matching its red colour; and in the Kis Royal in Buda the spices, savory and tarragon, reminding him of his Transylvanian native land, were brought for him without his asking. Áron Tamási knew all the restaurants with the best kitchens in Budapest at that time, but most frequently he went to the Kis Royal close to his home. The head waiter saluted him like a prince, always arranging employees to line up as he entered the restaurant. This great and honest mark of respect could be explained by the writer's reputation, but also by his big tips.

V. TOP PERSONALITIES OF HUNGARIAN TRANSYLVANIAN GASTRONOMY

The outstanding gastronomic expert and writer Turós writes that the Transylvanian cuisine is 'an original and wonderful piece among the values of the universal Hungarian cuisine'. So it is quite understandable that no cookery book representing our national cuisine lacks Transylvanian recipes. Frequently the names of the dishes (like Transylvanian, Sekler, from Hargita, etc.) refer to the places of their origin. In all of the most valuable Hungarian cookery books published during recent decades – such as those by Károly Gundel, János Rákóczi, Emil and Lukács Turós and József Venesz, – there is a great number of Transylvanian specialities. Besides these classical works however, there are less known cookery books that represent the characteristic 'colours' of the Transylvanian cuisine with emphasis and expertise. One of the best is an excellent cookery book by the outstanding folksong artist Erzsébet Török.

It is necessary to speak of four gastronomers, originally from Hungary, who have become famous in western countries. We stress their importance not only because they are world famous, but also because they all have a true feeling for the unique values of Transylvanian cuisine and have contributed at a very high level to its becoming public property. It may be that the things that are important, characteristic and specially valuable can be observed and seen and picked out from a great distance. Not only can the unity of the Hungarian cuisine be better evaluated from afar but in that way also its place in the world can be defined more realistically. Although none of them were born in Transylvania – only Louis Szathmáry's family originated from there – they have all had close connections with Transylvania, though in different ways..

George Lang's (born 1924; lives in New York and in Budapest) famous work, *Cuisine of Hungary*, is not only one of the best Hungarian cookery books in the world, but it was a starting point, a sort of inspiration at the beginning of a new age of cookery books that contain also historical, social and cultural backgrounds, i.e. they are not cut off from their environment. 'Every country's cookery should have a book like this' wrote Jane Grigson. Lang shows the gastronomic profiles of the Hungarian regions. He differentiates five regions, one of them Transylvania which is shown in a modern way with valuable new data.

Lang proposes a special Transylvanian menu after the recipes: Fresh Dill Soup, *Heránytokány* as in Marosszék, Transylvanian Bandit's Meat with Cornmeal Dumplings, Cabbage Salad, Liptó Cheese Spread with Green Peppers, Varga Strudel-Cake.

Louis Szathmáry (born 1919; lives in Chicago) established without doubt the greatest private collection of gastronomic books and documents in the world among which there are about 400 works dealing only with Transylvania. At the beginning of the forties he lived in Transylvania for years and this period had a great impact on his life. He has written a series of outstanding cookery books and his literary and publicising activity – this latter concerns mostly Transylvania – is also of great importance. He published in particular excellent and characteristic Transylvanian recipes in his cookery book of 1975, for instance Beef soup, *Mitite, Székely Tokány*.

Egon Ronay (lives in Berkshire and London) is a widely known personality of gastronomy about whom Kovi wrote the following in 1985. 'Some years ago in New York City I had the good fortune of meeting the notable gastronomer Egon Ronay, author of the best-selling English restaurant and hotel guide. (Mr. Ronay is of Hungarian origin, and one of his father's famous restaurants in Budapest was the only one with Transylvanian cooking. Each day the chef would contribute exquisite homeland specialities to the menu.) In a recent interview, Ronay elaborated on his theories, based on years of study and experience. He stated that in the history of food, there are essentially three outstanding cuisines: the French, which is the foundation of Western European and American cuisines; the Chinese, with its unbelievable variety, richness of flavour and colour and three thousand years of tradition; and the Transylvanian. His listeners seemed surprised, since most of them had never heard of Transylvania except as the home of Dracula.'

There are detailed, good recipes published in the first part of the Egon Ronay Cookery Series about famous Transylvanian dishes: Choucroute, Slushy Cabbage, Stuffed Cabbage; interesting cultural material is also included where, among other things, is written as follows: Transylvania 'a stunningly varied, sumptuous cooking resulted, most herb conscious and blissfully ignorant of dietary reticence, a gastronomic bridge between East and West.'

Paul Kovi (born 1924, lives in New York) has written a monograph-like book on *Transylvanian Cuisine* that is outstanding and unique even now on this subject. Kovi had been educated at the University of Kolozsvár and he returned to Transylvania later as well. He researched his recipes not unlike the way Bartók and Kodály collected their marvellous folk music. Kovi went from village to village, kitchen to kitchen and heart to heart to find the nearly lost art of the original Transylvanian cooking and flavours. By the time he began to organise his final work, he had gathered over 20,000 recipes. From these he selected more than 300 from the cuisines of all the peoples of Transylvania.

In addition he made interesting statements in his studies, for example, about the connection between Transylvanian and Chinese gastronomy. 'For example, ginger, one of the most important Chinese spices, was equally popular in Transylvania. To my knowledge, it is only these two cuisines that combine cabbage, pork and freshwater lobster or crayfish. In both places this combination was served in egg pastry rolls... In my opinion, the short, very hot paprika-pepper, popular both in China and Transylvania, is of Chinese and not of Mexican origin unlike most other peppers of Europe. My theory is based on the assumption that during medieval times and well into the 16th century, the continental China/Europe trade route must have had its end station in Transylvania...'

****

Emil Turós, who was also brought up with Transylvanian cuisine, writes that he has found a real joy in everyone, cooks and housewives, connected with it. 'This spirit, this heart is the greatest value of Transylvanian Hungarian cuisine... You need not worry about a cuisine's future when so much care is taken in preparing a trout that it will be remembered by everyone who has eaten it,'

Egon Ronay states after nearly half a century (1989): 'Transylvanian cuisine is magical. It is tragic it should be part of an endangered culture.' The spirit and heart of the old cooking are still alive though perhaps less than in the past, and so, we must believe – on the evidence of the great personalities mentioned in this study – in another 1,000 year future for this great cuisine.

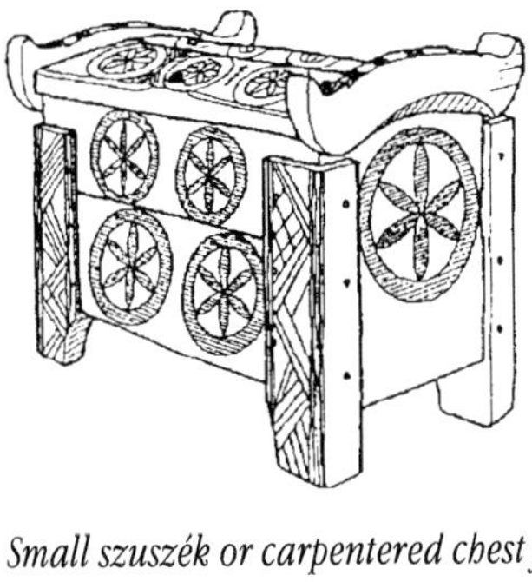

Small szuszék or carpentered chest for storing salt, measuring 50 x 21 x 36 cm (Magyarókereke, Kalotaszeg)

BIBLIOGRAPHY

Bartók, Béla and Zoltán Kodály. *Transylvanian Hungarians, Folksongs*. Popular Literary Society, Budapest, 1921. (Reprinted ÁKV, Budapest, 1987).

Czigány, Lóránt. *The Oxford History of Hungarian Literature*. Clarendon Press, 1984.

Gundel, Károly. *Gundel's Hungarian Cookbook*. Corvina, Budapest, 1994. (first pub. in Hungarian, Budapest, 1956)

Kós, Károly. *Erdély*, Kolozsvár, 1934. Tr. as *Transylvania, an outline of its cultural history*. Szépirodalmi, Budapest, 1989.

Kós, Dr. Károly jr. *Tájak, falvak, hagyományok* (Regions, Villages, Traditions). Kriterion, Bucharest, 1976.

Kós, Dr. Károly jr. *Mihez kezdjünk a természetben* (What to do in the Environment?). Mezőgazdasági, Budapest, 1985.

Kós, Dr. Károly jr. *Néprajzi Képeskönyv Erdélyből* (Ethnographic Picture Book from Transylvania). Tárogató, Budapest, 1994.

Kovi, Paul. *Transylvanian Cuisine*. Crown, New York, 1985. (Originally Kövi, Pál. *Erdélyi lakoma*, Bucharest, 1980).

Köpeczi, Béla and Gábor Barta, eds. *History of Transylvania*. Akadémiai, Budapest, 1994.

Lang, George. *The Cuisine of Hungary*. Wings Books, New York, 1994. (First pub. New York, 1971).

Rákóczi, János. *Konyhaművészet* (Art of Cookery). Minerva, Budapest, 1964.

Ronay, Egon. *The Unforgettable Dishes of my Life*. Gollancz, London, 1989.

'Szakács Tudomány, az erdélyi fejedelem udvari szakácskönyve a 16. századból' (Science of Cookery, court cookbook of the Prince of Transylvania from the 16th century). In *Régi magyar szakácskönyvek* (Old Hungarian Cookery Books). Athenaeum, Budapest, 1893.

Szathmáry, Louis. *The Chef's New Secret Cookbook*. Regnery, Chicago, 1975.

Tamási, Áron. *Bölcső és Bagoly* (The Cradle and the Owl). Szépirodalmi, Budapest, 1953.

Tamási, Áron. *Hazai tükör* (Domestic Mirror). Ifjúsági, Budapest, 1953.

Tamási, Áron. *Ábel a rengetegben*. Erdélyi Szépmíves Céh, Kolozsvár, 1932. Tr. by M. Kuttna as *Abel Alone*, Corvina, Budapest, 1966.

Török, Erzsébet. *Mit főzzünk?* (What to Cook?). Minerva, Budapest, 1968.

Turós, Emil. 'Gondolatok az erdélyi konyháról' (Thoughts on Transylvanian Cuisine) in *Magyar Szakács* (Hungarian Cook), XVIII:7, 1943, 37-39.

Pottery ware for cooking cabbage; vapour is flowing through the canal of its ear into the pot placed beside it (Désháza, Szilágyság region)

Carolina Weltzin – Cook or Other?

Renée Valeri

Preparing and consuming food is a very personal experience as well as it being significant in the social situation. To what extent are the relationships between the pots and the plate and the person constants over time? Do women cook differently from men? Or is it only a matter of doing it in a different situation? Is the difference only in the hours and the space, and – maybe – the audience? And did the same conflicts as today arise a couple of centuries back in the life of women, trying to reconcile the demands of household chores and of a career?

Trying to cull evidence from historical sources about something as ephemeral as cooking and taste can be a frustrating experience. Without the main evidence, the food itself, it is hard to judge what the relative skills of the performers were. In Sweden, a great deal of the social life has traditionally taken place in the private sphere – the sphere of women. One could of course speculate that this has given less opportunity for the public display of the cooking skills of those involved. It might also have had some effect on the proportions between men and women in the profession of cooks and/or cookbook writers.

In the Swedish cookbooks printed before 1850, 16 have men as authors[1] and 21 women (as for the 12 remaining, we do not know). Among these women, I have chosen to focus on Carolina Weltzin, (1754–1812), a woman who, unlike most other female cookbook authors, is mentioned in one of the Swedish biographical dictionaries. However, of the twelve lines consecrated to her, only two concern her activities other than being the daughter of a controversial clergyman, the sister of a medical councillor, the wife of an assessor and the mother of a prominent doctor.

The only thing we learn about her own identity is that she was 'a busy writer and translator of literature, and of some works of history and economy.' Ironically, none of these[2] has survived, whereas her cookbooks were re-edited several times. Indeed, being a professional cook or author of cookbooks seemed only exceptionally to have been deemed worthy of mentioning in any of the several compilations of prominent Swedish men and women in existence.

Still, from the perspective of today, her contributions to the history of cookery in Sweden turned out to be far more important than her other publications. With an honesty rather unusual in the field, she would in her prefaces admit to the foreign origin of her material, and even refer to publications by other women. She also shows a sensitivity to the social background of her presumptive readers, and a concern for their means an obvious factor determining whether they would try the recipes or not, but one rarely touched upon by other authors.

It is actually one of the great paradoxes in the history of cooking, that although women are traditionally dealt the role of cooks, whether gifted for it or not, whether interested in it or not, men have been the chefs and interpreters of cooking. Did the women not know what they were doing? Or did they just not talk about it? In spite of the impression some gourmets might make, the competence of cooking is of course inseparable from the skill of tasting and combining and balancing, in short, of having a developed taste. This is however a competence that is both in the head and in the hand. What is in the hand, and in the palate, is indeed difficult to transcribe into words. It differs from many art forms in the sense that the result is not only ephemeral but that the recipient's ability to appreciate it is linked to his/her cultural conditioning. It is a performance that involves several senses, and that which is most involved, the taste, is very much subject to a mixture of personal idiosyncrasies, memories and even physical factors.

And it's a skill which is hard to describe. Good cookbooks are brief and to the point and produce the proper result. Others produce situations similar to the one described by a colleague of mine who had asked a neighbour at his summer house for help with cutting down a tree and started to discuss how to go about it. Finally, the neighbour interrupted him: Do you want to cut down the tree or should we talk it down?

But there are women who can certainly both talk about food and make it: Elizabeth David, M.F.K. Fisher and many others in our time. So did they, earlier on, just not have an audience for their thoughts about food?

The analysis of food by the eaters, the gastrosophie of Brillat-Savarin, and of his Swedish counterpart, Hagdahl[3], had yet to come at the time of Carolina Weltzin. During the eighteenth century, cookbooks were still handbooks, lists of recipes, instructions on how to cook and how to do the household tasks. Women authors were at the forefront of telling the others how to use new products: Susanne Egerin[4] gave the first recipe for how to make coffee and chocolate in 1733. Less fanciful but more systematic and very complete, Cajsa Warg's *Hjelpreda*[5] was re-edited several times and even translated into German. Much more exciting however, but strangely unknown, is the almost contemporary cookbook of Johan Winberg.[6] It reveals a passionate cook just as burning with pedagogic zeal as Cajsa Warg – and without her weakness for nutmeg, the pervasiveness of which makes many of her recipes less palatable to a twentieth century taste.

At the end of the eighteenth century, it is obvious that the situation of those less lucky in society had given rise to some philanthropic movements even in Sweden. Pamphlets (in translation) were published on *soupe dauphinoise* and Rumford Soup. It is at this time that two women, Anna Maria Rückerschöld and a little later Carolina Weltzin, started publishing cookbooks at their own expense – cookbooks of a new character.

The first one, Anna Maria Rückerschöld, wrote four, giving in the first one[7] some potato recipes 'because of the unusual economic profit that this blessed plant gives the household.' In 1796, she even received a medal from the Patriotic Society for her book *Poor man's pantry and kitchen*,[8] a book of household advice for the poor.

The scant biographic information available tells us she was the daughter of an ennobled justice of appeal, and married to an accountant named Dahl. Generous with advice to young women, her *Household Catechism*,[9] explaining to 'Young Girls their right Mission in the World' is a vivid illustration of the creation of the Angel of the House – a figure being increasingly perceived as a threat to the integrity of late twentieth-century women, but who was identified and attacked already by Virginia Woolf. To Mrs Rückerschöld, however, there is no ambiguity: woman must make good the man's loss of paradise since she was the cause of Adam's and all humankind's perdition and misery. Created for his use and help, her main goal must be to become a good housewife. Therefore, train the little girls in all household chores, and the scourge of ignorant servants can be remedied by the knowledgeable housewife, capable of guiding them in their tasks through her own experience. Obviously, Mrs Rückerschöld is a cook and a housewife.

More nuanced in her teachings, Carolina Weltzin can take credit not only for the first complete potato cookbook in Sweden[10] (1802) but three larger general cookbooks.[11]

But was she a cook? Indeed, can we assume that all the cookbook authors of the past – women and men – were cooks themselves? Or were they compilers, translators, even entrepreneurs feeding a need for cookbooks brought about by changes in society? And why does it seem that female authors of these handbooks are more common in Sweden than for instance in France, where only lately the 'cuisine de femme' has gained recognition?

The scant information on Mrs Weltzin's life does not provide many clues. She became a widow in 1787, at the age of 33, but she did not start publishing until fifteen years later.[12] One can suspect that it is not unusual for women – widows, divorcees, spinsters – to turn their skills to the benefit of the general public. In this she reminds us of a German woman, 200 years earlier, Anna Weckerin. Married to the doctor of the city of Colmar, as a widow she published – encouraged by her daughter and son-in-law according to the preface – a considerable cookbook in 1598[13]. It is inspired by the very modern opinion that a proper diet is the best preventive medicine[14] – without, however the humoral theories that permeate the dietetic treatises published in various European countries in the early seventeenth century.

If the Weckerin book is a woman talking to other women, it would be tempting then to say that the French cookbooks that start appearing during the following century are by men talking to other men (or chefs to chefs). The Scandinavian tradition is different: not only the first one, a compilation of Danish recipes by an anonymous author[15] is addressed by him(?) to Danish women. Even direct translations of French works, like La Varenne and Pierre de Lune, when they are published in Stockholm – by men – towards the end of the seventeenth century, claim to be intended for ladies, for women cooks. Also the handbook[16] by Ditlev Maius, chef of queen Christina, has the form of a dialogue between two women, one experienced and one ignorant.

But these exist alongside handwritten books of recipes owned by women, filled with desserts and preparations based on fruits, drinks etc

It seems that women's cookbooks reflect the basic dilemma of the cook: cooking for feeding others and cooking for pleasure. A cook must appease hunger, making a nice meal for the eaters (family or guests) within the limits of what is economically, culturally and socially acceptable food.

The changing handwriting, and sometimes languages, in the early Swedish handwritten cookbooks testify to a lot of recipe swapping – as if they were like scrapbooks or maps of one's social networks. Today many women's (and men's?) collections of recipe clippings and cookbooks tell similar stories of what one would like to cook – and sometimes of course does cook. But it is also armchair travelling, dream consumption, the experiences of another world or another life, the pursuit of pleasure in fantasy form – or maybe in an allowable form of luxury.

In Sweden this found (until quite recently) one very palpable expression in the cakes and cookies served with coffee (a parallel to the tea parties in England) where in spite of an ethic of restraint and democracy, women could give in to their wishes of producing luxury goods without jeopardizing the family economy. And in a time where the social networks were more lively than today, get good exercise in honing these skills.

Earlier, the frequency of recipes of desserts, of puddings and purées found in women's cookbooks also indicates a deeper difference between the Germanic or northern world of taste and that reflected in cookbooks influenced from France.

Examining the works of a particular cook raises many questions, only few of which can be answered through the historical sources available in Sweden. Why are we so interested in the cooks that we actually make a symposium on them? By the wish to identify with them? Because they are the painters, composers or performers of the art of cooking? What can we achieve other than small biographies on persons that we know only by, at most, the echoes of them, whereas the true magic disappeared with them? Even watching a cook perform means little as long as we don't get to taste the result and compare it with our other experiences.

Is there a difference between male and female cooks, and which one(s) in that case? Were the cookbook writers of the past necessarily cooks? Why were there no female chefs in the past? Is there an opposition or even antagonism between the everyday cooking delegated to women, and the cooking done by men? How were the two connected? Or did the same conflicts as today arise a couple of centuries back in the life of a woman trying to reconcile the demands of her household chores and her career? Could the competence of being a good cook also turn into a threat, a way of not getting credit for one's skills, and at the same time being taken for granted, something that could be turned against women as a backlash, a trap made for us to keep us in our proper place – but with our agreement? These are questions asked by many women, daughters and wives today, questions with no easy answers. Who wants to give up being a good cook?

In a way, Carolina Weltzin is a sister to many contemporary women in her juggling of her different roles – cook, author and mother. At the same time, her cookbooks show an effort to adapt to different circumstances: new products, common and more refined recipes, international and local cooking. In other words, a rather modern woman...

REFERENCES

[1] Two of these are published under a female pseudonym, two do not give the author's name.

[2] In spite of alluring titles, such as 'Robert, or the Man such as he should be' (and...' as he should not be'), 'Reading for Pleasure and as a Pastime', etc.

[3] *Kok-konsten som vetenskap och konst* (Cookery as science and art), Stockholm 1879.

[4] *En nödig och nyttig hus-hålds- och kok-bok...* (A necessary and useful household andcookbook...), Stockholm 1733.

[5] *Hjelpreda i Hushållningen För Unga Fruentimber* (Guide in Housekeeping for Young Women), Stockholm 1755.

[6] *Kok-Bok, Hwilken lärer grunden till Kokeriet...* (CookBook which teaches the elements of Cookery...), Stockholm 1761.

[7] *En liten hushålls-bok...* (A small household book...), Stockholm 1785.

[8] *Fattig mans visthus och kök...* Stockholm 1796.

[9] *Försök till en liten hushålls-cateches...*, Stockholm 1800.

[10] *Anwisning till Potäters mångfaldiga begagnande* (Directions for diverse uses of potatoes),Stockholm 1802, reprinted 1806 and 1819. It is not bound, is printed on bad paper and seems meant for the use of readers of modest means. It is, according to the preface, a compilation mainly from foreign sources, but the addenda on the simpler uses of potatoes are 'to a large extent based on own experiments'.

[11] *Ny kokbok. Eller Anwisning till en myckenhet nu brukliga mat-Räters Tillredande:...* (New Cookbook. Or Direction for the preparation of many now common dishes), Stockholm 1804; *Anvisning till tarfvelig matredning. ...* (Direction for frugal cookery), Stockholm 1805; and *Daglig helpreda i köket: eller anwisning till en tarflig matredning för hvarje dag i året* (Daily helper in the kitchen: or direction for frugal cookery for each day of the year), Stockholm 1808, a 'translation with changes'.

[12] At that time her son was grown up and moved away from home; he studied from 1793 in Lund, then in Uppsala, finishing in Stockholm and Åbo. Her publishing career coincides with his getting his doctor's degree and leaving for the East Indies as a surgeon. Maybe there is an antagonism between the role of mother and a publishing career: 'CW — cook or mother?'

[13] *Ein Köstlich new Kochbuch von allehand Speisen...* (A precious new cookbook for all manners of food...), Amberg 1598.

[14] The approach being not only: 'How good is the food? How healthy is it?' but: 'There is a way to health through good food'.

[15] *Koge Bog: Indholdendis et hundrede fornødene stycker...* (Cook Book: Containing one hundred useful items...), Copenhagen 1616.

[16] *Stockholmisch Kock-Gesprächs Vortrab...* Stockholm 1644.

Mrs. A. B. Marshall
Ice-creammonger Extraordinary

Robin Weir

Agnes Marshall was a formidable woman in every aspect of her life and career at a time when it would have been difficult for her to pursue a career of the type that she did. A woman of seemingly boundless energy, she was at the forefront of technology, science and marketing. She was in a league superior to Mrs. Beeton, but was the unfortunate victim of circumstances that have robbed her of the acclaim that she rightly deserves.

In the world of ices and ice-cream Agnes B. Marshall should be credited with four major contributions:

1. Writing two of the most important books ever written on ices that popularised them in Britain among the upper and middle classes in the late 19th century.

2. Selling a unique ice and ice-cream making machine - she may well have invented it. (Unfortunately all the Marshall archives were destroyed in a fire at Cassell's, the owners of Ward Lock and Co., in 1955.)

3. Being the first person in the world known to record putting ice-cream or sorbet in a cone or cornet.

4. Being the first person, in 1901, to suggest the making of ice-cream using liquified gas. This was only a short time after the process of liquifying gas had been discovered.

Her entrepreneurial approach to business had her selling a unique design of ice-cream machine and early refrigerators, known as Ice Caves, as well as all sorts of equipment including bombe and ice-cream moulds, foods, flavourings and colourings. She also ran courses in the making of all manner of ices as well as general cookery at her cookery school in Mortimer Street in London. There were frequent references made to ices in the weekly magazine she started, *The Table*.

Books on Ices

Prior to 1900 there were very few books written exclusively on ices or ice-cream:

M. Emy, *L'Art de Bien Faire les Glaces d'Offices*, Paris, 1768.
Fillipo Baldini, *De' Sorbetti*, Naples, 1775.
Thomas Masters, *The Ice Book*, 1844.
Agnes B. Marshall, *The Book of Ices*, London, 1885.
Agnes B. Marshall, *Fancy Ices*, London, 1894.

Her books made ices available to a very large audience and this was helped by the considerable increase in availability of farmed ice, mainly from Norway. They are well written and accurate and the recipes work well.

Her contribution to the development and popularisation of ices was considerable: her books were sold in large quantities in Britain and America as well as in the colonies. Sales of *The Book of Ices* were in excess of 24,000 copies and *Fancy Ices* over 5,000 copies.

Ice-cream Machines

The traditional ice-cream machine, which was invented by Nancy Johnson in 1843, is in the shape of a wooden bucket in which a tinned container, connected to the cranking handle, revolves around a stationary paddle. Contrary to popular belief, she *did* patent it and a patent for the Nancy Johnson machine dated July 29th 1843 has just been discovered in the United States by Ed Marks. This pre-dates Thomas Masters' (1844) machine.

This shape was commercialised by a large number of companies and is still being manufactured in the United States by White Mountain Inc.

The surround to the container is filled with ice and salt to freeze the ice-cream in the container. The frozen ice-cream is continually scraped from the wall of the container as it revolves, by the paddle.

I have searched for over ten years for a Mrs. Marshall Ice-cream machine and in the last three years have been fortunate enough to find four in existence; one in an English Heritage house and the other three I have been able to buy and have restored. In fact I found two in one week: one in England and one in Lancaster, Pennsylvania. I will demonstrate at least one of them during my delivery of this paper.

The unique feature about Mrs. Marshall's machines was that they were wide and shallow. The larger they were, the wider they were. For the range of sizes and prices see the advertisement below. One pound sterling in 1900 is equal to £34.05 today. The special feature of the machines was that the salt and ice were mainly under the pan and not up the sides as in the Nancy Johnson type.

She also maintained that the ices and sorbets could be made in three minutes in her machines. The normal time for a tall machine was about 20 minutes.

The growth of home manufacture of ices was made possible by the availability of machines and the development of ice farming in both America and Norway and the importation of ice into London by Carlo Gatti[1] and the Wenham Lake Company Ltd.

The Ice-cream Cone or Cornet

It seems that Mrs. Marshall can also be credited with the origin of the ice-cream cone. This is a theory that we aired in our book *Ices*[2]. No one has so far challenged this or been able to find an earlier reference to the use of wafer, almond or biscuit cones being used for serving ice-cream.

The first mention of cornets is in Mrs. Marshall's *Cookery Book*: Cornets with Cream - *Cornets à la Crème*.

> These cornets can also be filled with any cream or water ice, or set custard or fruits, and served for a dinner, luncheon or supper dish.[3]

Although not mentioned in *The Book of Ices*, cornets are mentioned in a number of places in *Fancy Ices*, 1894.

Margaret Cornets[4]

These cornets are made with:

> half a pound of ground almonds, 4oz castor sugar and 4oz of fine flour and two whole eggs, a saltspoon full of vanilla essence and one tablespoon full of orange flower water.

The cornets are then filled with half ginger ice-water and half apple ice-cream.

Christine Cornets[5]

For the cones or cornets, she uses the same recipe as for the Margaret Cornets, which are then decorated with royal icing and dipped in chopped pistachio nuts.

Ice for Christina Cornets

Take half a pint of vanilla custard (*Book of Ices* p26), add a quarter of a pint of stiffly-whipped cream, and mix with it two ounces of any nice dried fruits, such as greengage, apricot, dried ginger, cherries &c., cut into very tiny dice shapes, as much ground cinnamon that will cover a three penny-piece, the same quantity of ground ginger, and a tablespoonful of Marshall's Maraschino syrup; mix well together, freeze dry, and use.

Making Ice-cream with Liquified Gas

In *The Table*, 24th August 1901, Mrs. Marshall writes:

> Liquid air will do wonderful things, but as a table adjunct its powers are astonishing, and persons scientifically inclined may perhaps like to amuse and instruct their friends as well as feed them when they invite them to the house. By the aid of liquid oxygen, for example each guest at a dinner party may make his or her ice cream at the table by simply stirring with a spoon the ingredients of ice cream to which a few drops of liquid air has been added by the servant; one drop in a glass will more successfully freeze champagne than two or three lumps of ice, and and in very hot weather butter may be kept in better condition on the table and make milk free from any suspicion of sourness by adding a drop of liquid air to an outer recepticle into which a jug or butter dish is placed. Liquid air will, in short, do all that ice does in a hundredth part of the time. At picnics it would be invaluable, and surely ought to be kept freely on hand in hospitals.[6]

Mrs. Marshall was also frequently outspoken and was a ceaseless campaigner for improvements in the quality of food hygiene, for example, January 26th 1895 in her column 'Across the Table':

While the Society of Public Analysts are about it, it is to be hoped they will agitate against the vile concoctions sold as ice-creams in the public streets. Dr Klein's awful revelations to the Islington Vestry concerning a number of random samples recently analysed by him ought assuredly to excite attention in influential quarters. It is high time the sale of such poisonous filth were stopped, for disease among the lower classes must be spread alarmingly by these means, and upon the health of the masses that of the classes necessarily depends to a large extent. Every vendor of refreshments, whether itinerant or otherwise, should be licensed, and placed under constant inspection. By this means alone can the pure and wholesome ingredients and sanitary utensils for the preparation of comestibles be assured.

In her column on 'Ice and Ices', 3rd August 1901, having extolled the virtues of 'The Great Gunter', she rails against the itinerant Italian vendors at the other end of the social ladder selling ice-cream with their 'ha'penny licks' and 'Okey-Pokey':

Hokey-pokey, however, had this advantage over its rival eaten from a glass — namely, that it could be carried away and consumed at leisure. Besides being variously flavoured, hokey-pokey was dreadfully sweet, dreadfully cold, and hard as a brick. Swede turnip, converted into pulp, was known to have formed its base in lieu of more expensive supplies from the cow. Nevertheless, such adulteration is harmless compared to the awful foreign substances, including enormous numbers of sewage bacteria even, that have been found to permeate Italian ice-cream, which is often prepared amidst the most loathsome conditions. For 20 years the Medical Press has agitated that in order to put a stop to this horrible state of affairs, ice-creammongers should be licensed, and manufacture regulated in the same way as the milk traffic. This measure is now enforced by the sanitary committees of certain towns, and where London is concerned the County Council are reported to be taking the matter up.

Mrs. Marshall deserves a special place in the history of ices and ice-cream for her unique contributions to the development of one of the most popular foods in Britain.[7] The ices and ice-cream business in Britain should top one billion pounds sterling for the first time in 1995 - if the good weather continues.

The London Canal Museum at 12/13 New Wharf Road, Kings Cross, London N1 9RT, (open daily 10.00 to 16.30) is housed in the building built by Carlo Gatti in the 1850s to store ice. The ice, imported from Norway, was unloaded at Limehouse and carried along the Regent's Canal to Battlebridge Basin by barge and then unloaded and stored. The two vast interconnecting underground pits each 34 feet in diameter and 40 feet deep are still visible and are currently being excavated. Gatti's delivery carts were kept on the ground floor of the building and the horses on the first floor. [8]Ice was shipped from Norway; the type of ship they used carried (from March to October only, the fiords being iced up the rest of the year) approximately 400 tons of ice per trip. [9]Ice was delivered around London seven days a week. An iceman's cart held about two tons and he made three trips each day. Right up to the second world war an iceman was paid only three pounds per week and three pounds ten shillings if he worked on Sundays. In 1995 value this is equivalent to £77 and £90 respectively. This was their basic pay; anything they made above that they kept.

Mrs. Marshall's Books

Marshall, Agnes Bertha. *The Book of Ices*, 1885, Marshall's School of Cookery, London.

—, *Fancy Ices*, 1894, Simkin, Marshall, Hamilton, Kent & Co., London.

—, *Mrs. A.B.Marshall's Cookery Book*, 1888, Marshall's School of Cookery, London.

—, *Mrs. A.B.Marshall's Larger Cookery Book*, 1891, Simkin, Marshall, Kent & Co., London.

Acknowledgements

I would like to thank the following for helping to make this paper possible: Dr. and Mrs. Peter Barham for coming to Oxford to demonstrate making Ice-cream using liquid nitrogen; John Deith for finding the quotation on page xxx from Mrs. Marshall's magazine *The Table*, 24 August 1901 and for general help and information on Mrs. Marshall. Ed Marks for discovering the new information on the Nancy Johnson patent. Janet Clarke for finding the Mrs. Marshall bottle and Alan Robinson of the North West Museums Service for discovering the largest of the Marshall ice-cream machines. Tess and Mike McKirdy for the loan of the Marshall's Catalogue of Moulds and Special Kitchen Equipment (24 pages). Gwenda Hill for the loan of the Marshall's 'Bills of Fare', cookery school programme, June 1890. Charles Haworth and his company, H & J E Buckley Ltd. (Coopers) for remaking the wooden buckets for the three machines. Christopher Fagg of Cassells for information on the destruction of the Mrs. Marshall archives in a fire at their offices in London in 1995. The Bank of England for the figures on the current and past value of the pound.

REFERENCES

[1] Kinross, Felicity. *Coffee and Ices*, 1991, The Canal Museum, London
[2] Liddell, Caroline and Robin Weir. *Ices*, 1993, Hodder & Stoughton, London.
[3] 1888 edition p 329, later editions p 402.
[4] *Fancy Ices*.
[5] *Fancy Ices*.
[6] During the Symposium at lunch on the Saturday Dr. Peter Barham from Bristol University Physics Department, demonstrated the technique of making ice-cream almost instantly using liquid nitrogen. Symposiasts were able to taste the excellent result.
[7] It is curious that Elizabeth David in her book *Harvest of the Cold Months* (Michael Joseph 1994, p63 and caption to plate 9) dismisses Mrs. Marshall in four lines, particularly as her mother, before she was married, had been a pupil at Mrs. Marshall's Cookery School.
[8] Kinross.
[9] Kinross.

BY ROYAL LETTERS PATENT.
MARSHALL'S PATENT FREEZER.

HIGHEST AWARD: INTERNATIONAL INVENTIONS EXHIBITION.

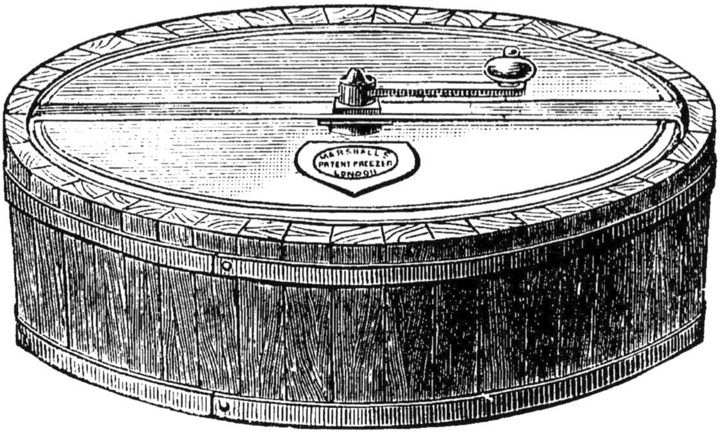

COMPLETE VIEW.

IS PRAISED BY ALL WHO KNOW IT
FOR

CHEAPNESS in first cost.   CLEANLINESS in working.
ECONOMY in use.   SIMPLICITY in construction.
RAPIDITY in Freezing.

No Packing necessary.   No Spatula necessary.

Smooth and Delicious Ice produced in three minutes.

SIZES—No. 1, to freeze any quantity up to 1 quart, **£1. 5s.**; No. 2, for 2 quarts, **£1. 15s.**; No. 3, for 4 quarts, **£3**; No. 4, for 6 quarts, **£4**. Reputed measure only. Larger sizes to order.

VERTICAL SECTION.

Showing the fan inside, which remains still while the pan revolves and scrapes up the film of ice as it forms on the bottom of the pan.
The ice and salt is also shown *under* the pan; there is no need to pack any round the sides.

BY ROYAL LETTERS PATENT.
MARSHALL'S PATENT ICE CAVE.

HIGHEST AWARD: INTERNATIONAL INVENTIONS EXHIBITION.

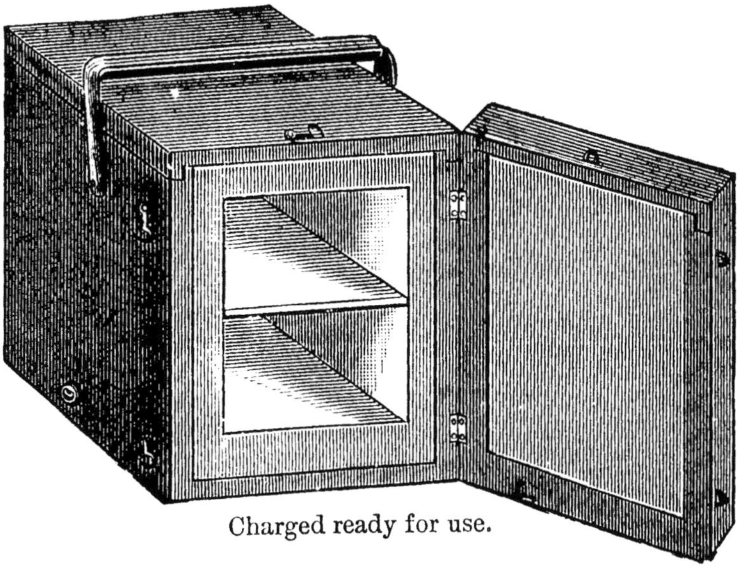

Charged ready for use.

Antonin Carême: The Good, the Bad, and the Useful

Barbara Ketcham Wheaton

Marie Antonin Carême is the most famous of nineteenth-century French cooks. His students and their successors studied his writings, or at least paid lip-service to him well into the twentieth century. I have seen copies of his books covered with annotations by long-gone cooks. Gastronomes and food writers have praised him as one of the great geniuses of haute cuisine. His grandiloquent claim that there are five branches of the fine arts, and the greatest of these is confectionery is notorious.

If you have read any of his books, you know that he is conceited, that his recipes are written in a tangled prose, that his *pièces montées* are, to our modern eyes, an extravagant waste of ingredients, and his menus are elaborate, pretentious, and heavy. I would like to suggest that to understand Carême's life and contribution we have to suspend judgment for a little while.

Much of what we know about him comes from his own writings. He was a self-promoter, whose resumé seems to have been in a constant state of upward revision. It might be noted here that this makes it difficult to describe what his job-title was at any given moment. I have tried to make my descriptions appropriately evasive in this paper. Only Alexis Soyer among nineteenth-century French chefs approached his ability to attract attention, or to make claims of expertise and even genius. But in fact, Carême really did rise from humble origins to the top of his profession. He really did work for some of the most prominent individuals of his day, and he did enjoy direct contact with these often unapproachable people. Embedded within his disorganized prose are the insights of an impassioned perfectionist. He really is worthy of notice.

He was born into an impoverished workman's family in a shed in a builder's workplace on the rue du Bac in Paris on the 8th of June, 1783. Depending on which source you believe, he was one of fifteen or twenty-five children. When he was ten years old his father took him to the Barrière du Maine at the edge of Paris, and told the boy to go forth into the world to make his own life, because his family could not support him. Carême tells us that he was taken in by the proprietor of a cheap tavern nearby, where he learned the first elements of his métier. It has been suggested that in fact he entered upon some sort of modest apprenticeship.[1] At critical moments in his life he was able to engage the interest and support of those in a position to help him. We do not know the moment at which, against all odds, he learned to read and write. In about 1798, at the age of eighteen he began three years of work for Bailly, one of the best pastrycooks in Paris, on the rue Vivienne. Talleyrand was but one of Bailly's distinguished clients. There Carême rose to a position of responsibility. Bailly allowed him to take two afternoons each week to visit the nearby old royal library (now, and for a little while longer, the Bibliothèque Nationale), where he studied architectural prints in the Cabinet des Estampes and read cookbooks from other countries and from past times. At the end of three years he was ready to move on, first to another pastrycook, whom he describes only as the successor to M. Gendron, and then opening his own shop on the rue de la Paix in 1803, which continued to operate for a decade. All through the nineteenth century one can see the luxury trades in France being democratized. Luxury goods and activities which had been almost exclusively the prerogatives of the court and the very rich became available to anyone who could pay for them. Excellent ingredients could be bought in the markets and shops; beautifully prepared food could be bought in restaurants. As the century goes on the same thing happens with travel, clothing, and reading matter. But with the single exception of this shop, about which he has little to say, Carême held aloof from this more commercial sphere, restricting his services to the more exclusive world of power and great wealth. After his youthful work in a cheap tavern, neither he nor his great students, Jules Gouffé and Félix Urbain Dubois ever cooked in a restaurant.

It is not surprising, then, that at the same time as he opened his shop he set out on what was to become an intermittent but spectacular career as a specialist pastrycook at the great imperial, social and governmental banquets. He called these his *grands extraordinaires*. They were triply useful to him: they must have paid well; he gained the experience of working with established masters of the craft, of whom he speaks again and again in his writings, and finally, they were excellent advertising. Despite his participation in the *extraordinaires*, Carême was often very critical of how they were organized and executed. He devotes a chapter in the second volume of the *Pâtissier royal parisien* to a critique, often quite harsh, of these events.

For the rest of his life he cycled between working on these events, writing, and working for longer periods of time with a single employer, and trips abroad to serve monarchs and diplomats.

In the ten years beginning in 1804 Carême began to earn his great reputation as the organizer and executor of remarkable meals. Established in his career, he married Henriette Sophie Mahy de Chitenay on 18 October, 1808. From 1804 to 1814 he was directing the kitchens of Talleyrand, that most supple and epicurean of political and social survivors. At the same time he organized special events. Among these were festivities at the marriage of Jérôme Bonaparte, Napoleon's brother, to Catherine of Wurtemberg (1807), the marriage of Napoleon himself to Marie-Louise of Austria (1810), and for the birth of their child, the King of Rome (1811), as well as other events at the Tuileries, the Foreign Office, and the Hôtel de Ville. Carême never let patriotism interfere with his own career interests. For example, after the defeat of Napoleon, the English and Russians occupied Paris. Alexander I, the Tsar of Russia, accompanying his army, engaged Carême's services during his stay at the Elysée-Napoléon palace (1814), and again for several weeks the following year. The great public eating event of 1815 was the banquet Carême organized for the Allies near Châlons in Champagne. It presented immense logistical problems, most of which were overcome.

In the same year he published his first two books: *Le Pâtissier royal parisien,* an illustrated two-volume compendium of recipes for all the preparations that an accomplished pastry cook would need to know, with extensive general observations about the composition and execution of the most elaborate menus, and *Le Pâtissier pittoresque,* which contains more than a hundred engravings of designs for pièces montées, with more or less sketchy instructions for executing them.

There followed a period of brief, high-profile engagements and frenetic travel. By this time Alexander I was trying to get him to go to Russia, but July of 1816 saw him in England, directing the kitchens of the Prince Regent, first at Carlton House in London, and subsequently at the Royal Pavilion in Brighton. Homesickness drew him, briefly, back to France. (I wonder if his family ever saw him.) He directed the Tsar's kitchens at the Congress of Aix-la-Chapelle in 1818, and Lord Stewart's when the latter was the ambassador in Vienna, returning to London with him. Soon he was in Paris again, and then finally agreed to go to St. Petersburg. To his annoyance, the Tsar was making a 40-day visit to Archangel, and Carême found Russian kitchen politics and cost-controls not to his liking, so he returned to Paris again, enduring a harrowing ocean voyage. The next year or two were spent with Princess Bagration, until her health failed (!). Conveniently, Lord Stewart needed his services again, first in Austria and then in London, for the coronation of George IV. Perhaps it is just as well that Carême did not work on the coronation banquet itself, which seems to have been one of the great organizational snafus in all gastronomic history.[2] The noblemen serving the royal table discovered that there were no serving implements. The meal was served in such congested circumstances that the ladies seated at table could not move away from underneath the candles, which, in the oppressive heat, dripped onto the food, clothing, and people's faces, smearing the ladies' make-up. At the end of the meal guests in full court dress and spectators alike pillaged the food left on the table and stole the plate. Carême must have been glad not to have been involved, though it must be noted that the maître d'hôtel, chef de cuisine, and officier de bouche all seem to have been French.[3]

In 1821 he produced his *Projets d'architecture dédiés à Alexandre Ier* and *Projets d'architecture pour l'embellissement de Paris*, both of which attempted to use the insights gained from making *pièces montées* to advance the cause of planning the monumental city, based on his studies in the Cabinet des Estampes. His next publication was the *Maître d'hôtel* (1822.) Offers of employment in France and abroad continued to come in, but he resisted all calls to leave France, contenting himself with writing, and with cooking for his *grands extraordinaires*.

In 1823 he was engaged by James de Rothschild, the head of the French branch of the great banking house, to direct his kitchens. De Rothschild, and his wife, Betty, lived in princely style in Paris and at their château at Boulogne, just downstream from Paris. While in their service Carême published *Le Cuisinier parisien* (1828). The Rothschild dinners were famous; the most influential, aristocratic, and creative members of Paris society dined there. Lady Morgan (born Sydney Owenson) describes a luncheon she enjoyed in July of 1829. Both she and Carême were sufficiently impressed by the experience to produce written accounts of it.[4] Lady Morgan drove out to the estate towards the end of a sweltering day. The meal was served *en ambigu* (the whole meal set out at once on the table) as the sun went down, in a pavilion surrounded by orange trees and fountains. The company included James and Betty de Rothschild, Rossini, and other celebrities and members of high society. The silver and porcelain were brilliant. 'All the details of the service proclaimed the science of the fine things of life, an exquisite simplicity.' The dessert course ornamented the center of the table, and the entrées were placed around it. It was the variety and proportion that proclaimed Carême's special skills; there were no 'English spices' or 'black sauces'; instead, the flavors were delicate; the perfume of truffles made one think it was January; the vegetables had their natural colors, and the mayonnaise seemed to have been mixed in snow. The meal concluded with a *plombière* (a pastry cream, usually flavored with a fruit liqueur, and enriched with fresh or preserved fruits, served chilled) with its cool sweetness and the flavor of its fruit.[5] She goes on to discuss the meal as she would a theatrical performance or a concert: 'I firmly avow that it had required less genius to compose some plays than to execute this fine and handsome dinner.' She was overcome with delight to find that Carême had inscribed her name on a column on one of the *pièces montées* considering it a greater distinction even than seeing her by-line in *Blackwood's* or the *Quarterly Review*. After coffee, she met with Carême in the garden, and they indulged in a little mutual admiration. He included an epistle to her in the first volume of *L'Art de la cuisine française*. Her praise had confirmed his status, not only as a cook, but as a man of letters: 'She spoke to me of my writings; I spoke to her of hers.'[6]

It was, in a way, his swan-song. Carême was worn out by a life that began in deprivation and ended with decades of hard work in carbon-monoxide laden kitchens and the stress of organizing the *extraordinaires* and other high-visibility meals (and contending with outsized egos?). He retired from Baron de Rothschild's service, to finish writing his books. Unfortunately, he died on 12 January, 1833, with only three volumes of his final work completed, the extensively illustrated *L'art de la cuisine française au XIXe siècle*. It was — in two final volumes by his student, Pluméry. He was survived by a daughter, Marie, and a generation of grateful followers.

At this year's Symposium we are thinking about individuals who have influenced food for better or worse. How does Carême measure up? What did his career do for himself, for his employers, colleagues, students, and later readers? What was his long-term influence on the course of haute cuisine?

He rose from obscurity and abject poverty to international fame and a measure of prosperity. He did so by working in a field that had no intrinsic prestige, and which offered no guarantee of financial reward. There is no question that through talent, hard work, imagination and an ability to get along with people and get things done, he earned himself a life that was full of satisfaction for himself despite all his talk of suffering.

The decades of his working life saw intense social and political instability, revolution, war, and the rapid making and unmaking of fortunes. In this world, along with the pleasures of the table that Carême supplied to his employers was the certainty that his expensive and demanding services could help to certify their position at the pinnacle of society. In his writings he managed to link himself with the opulent cooking of the ancien régime, and with the generation of cooks which preceded him. It was a society that to some extent forged artificial links with the ancien régime to legitimize itself; Carême's appropriation of the culinary traditions of that age (even while he criticized old-fashioned methods and flavor combinations) suited their needs very neatly.

In the society of his peers he considered himself supreme, and his grateful students and their students in turn continued to spread this point of view.

Most of us think first of his *pièces montées* when we think of his work.[7] These ornamental structures, made of pastry and confectionery, were his pride and joy. His designs for them are meticulously drawn, although I can report from my own experience that the elevations of his structures in the *Pâtissier pittoresque* do not always match their accompanying floor plans. When one compares the plates in the works on architecture and travel to which he refers with his own designs, one finds that he has played some very strange games indeed with proportion and scale. Typically, he appropriates from monumental structures one or more ornamental features, cramming them together without any intervening plain areas. The designs he produced for the embellishment of St. Petersburg reveal a similar lack of proportion, bordering on the grotesque. The eclecticism that was to characterize nineteenth-century art and architecture was exactly to his taste. It seems not to have mattered to him at all if one used a 'Turkish cabaña' or a 'Babylonian ruin', a 'Chinese temple' or an 'English belvedere'. It must be said, however, that there is a playfulness to them which can be quite charming. Later *pièces montées*, such as Gouffé's, were to be heavier and darker in color, but Carême very specifically calls for light, bright colors, used in restrained quantities. I have tried coloring them according to his instructions, and have ended up with images that have much in common with other products of nineteenth-century design, such as the Royal Pavilion at Brighton, which was under construction while he was working there, and smaller buildings in France, some made for pleasure, and others for use.

His recipes can be confusing to read. They were usually written in paragraph form, and while quantities are usually given, they sometimes wander into discursiveness somewhere in the middle. He digresses to discuss useful details of execution. For example, he writes about making mayonnaise that for dependable results one should make it in the *garde-manger* or some other cold place, and to make it as quickly as possible; when it is finished and firm one should add a few drops of water to whiten it.[8] At other times he exhorts ambitious young chefs to follow his example and the examples of his predecessors; the great Laguipierre who died during the retreat from Moscow was one of his heroes.

It need hardly be said that his recipes are complicated, expensive, and time-consuming to execute. In 1985 the Culinary Historians of Boston cooked a meal using them—our Carême Bicentennial Bash (a year late). We were rather disappointed to find that there was not a great diversity of flavor, because so many dishes relied on the same combinations of basic mixture, that the laborious preparation time destroyed the possibility of freshness, and, not surprisingly, that one cannot compose a complicated presentation and serve it hot.

In reading Carême's aphorisms in *L'Art de la cuisine française* one feels as if one were hearing thoughts going on inside the writer's head. Often he is instructing his employer on the need for giving his chef de cuisine a completely free hand with the budget and meal arrangements: 'The rich man [a common beginning to his aphorisms] inspired by the genius of gastronomy is the god Comus personified; his knowledge embellishes banquets.'[9]

Sometimes one hears echoes of angry confrontation: 'It is a very depressing situation for a famous chef to serve only a man who is not sensual and who interferes and judges. I repeat, it is the worst of conditions for a culinary artist.'[10]

'Cooks are not always appreciated nowadays in France; it is only the love of science which sustains them in their work.'[11]

'A man born to wealth can be identified by his good table manners, and by the gift which he makes to the servant who waits on him.'[12]

And sometimes one hears the advice given to the aspiring student at the master's side. He talks about behavior: 'The servant who gives himself over to drink loses both the good will of the great and the respect of his equals.'[13]

And about career strategies: A cook, he tells us, should change employers whenever his sense of self-interest tells him he should, because his employer will be quick to dismiss the cooks whose skills do not please him.[14]

And about domestic politics: 'The cook's position is always envied by the staff in a household who have learned nothing.'[15]

He knew the difficulties of the work. 'The cook too often spends his working life in kitchens below ground level, where artificial light and the fire weaken his eyesight; and then the dampness of the walls and the drafts of air give him rheumatism and make his life painful. If the kitchens are on ground level the cooking is healthier, but he always sees the same four walls covered with copper pots, whose reflection makes him lose his sight; add to this the stress he suffers from demanding and difficult work; and then the poisonous gas from the charcoal braziers, which he breathes every moment of the day. This is the life of the cook.'[16]

His attitude towards his employers and other gastronomes seems to have been one of enthusiastic servility, well tinged with self-interest. He was well repaid. He became a society pet. The Tsar gave him a diamond ring, Metternich a gold snuffbox. I believe that it was a real advantage to him that he lacked a sense of proportion, because his exaggerated self-importance carried him farther than modesty would have done, and because it helped to fuel the ambitions of generations of chefs, in France and abroad. What would the Tsar have been without him, or Talleyrand, or James de Rothschild?

He got his wish: the myth he created as the story of his life, has become the official one. One reads, in the *Larousse Biographical Dictionary,* this entry: 'Carême, Marie Antoine (1784-1833) French chef de cuisine and author. He wrote *La Cuisine Française,* etc. As Talleyrand's cook, he played an important part at the Congress of Vienna.'[17]

REFERENCES

[1] This biographical summary is based on Georges Bernier, *Antonin Carême, 1783-1833: La sensibilité gourmand en Europe,* Paris: Le Pré aux Clercs; Colette Gilles-Mouton, 'Biographie d'Antonin Carême', in Délégation à l'Action Artistique de la Ville de Paris, *L 'Art de la cuisine française au XIXe siècle: Antonin Carême,* Paris: Mairie du IIIe arrondissement, Orangerie de Bagatelle, 1984, 26-28; and L. Rodil, *Antonin Carême de Paris,* Marseille: Laffitte, 1980.

[2] Robert Huish, *An Authentic History of the Coronation of His Majesty, King George the Fourth.* London, 1821, 248-278.

[3] Huish, ibid.

[4] Lady Morgan, 'Un diner chez m. Le comte de Ségur et chez Madame de Rothschild au château de Boulogne', *Les Classiques de la table,* edited by Frédéric Fayot, Paris, 1843, 509-513.

[5] Antonin Carême, *Le Pâtissier royal parisien,* Paris, 1815, 2:142-144.

[6] Carême, *Souvenirs,* 463.

[7] See also Ann Grieve, 'Les avatars de l'architecture des Lumières chez Marie-Antonin Carême: le pâtissier architecte

(1783-1833)'; *Papilles* 8 (April 1995): 37-50; Alice Wooledge Salmon, 'Enduring Fantasies', *Petits Propos Culinaires* 8 (June 1981): 49-59.
[8]Carême, *Le Pâtissier royal parisien*, Paris, 1815, 2: 10.
[9]Carême, *L'Art de la cuisine française,* Paris, 1833 2: iv.
[10]Ibid., vii.
[11]Ibid., xvii.
[12]Ibid., xvii-xiv.
[13]Ibid., xxiv.
[14]Ibid., xx.
[15]Ibid., xxii.
[16]Ibid., xx-xxi.
[17]*Larousse Biographical Dictionary.* Edited by Magnus Magnusson and Rosemary Goring, 5th ed. Cambridge, New York: Larousse, 1990, 260.

The Cooks (and Others) at Erddig

Margaret Willes

When I learnt that the subject for this year's symposium was to be cooks, I was delighted as I have always wanted to investigate exactly who produced the food in an English country house in succeeding generations. My rapture was somewhat modified when the theme was developed into cooks that influenced what we eat, for the examples I had chosen manifestly did not change the course of culinary history. But revolutionary cooks are rare beings – sometimes they are not cooks at all, sometimes they didn't change the course of history, history brought it upon them (the neolithic man or woman who discovered the delights of roast pork, for instance). My cooks are the stuff of which the *evolution* of cooking is made, so here I am still.

Of all the historic houses with which I work, Erddig holds a very special place. You could say that it was the house that changed the National Trust's history. Unlike the great treasure houses of Petworth or Kedleston, it was acquired by the Trust in 1973, not for its architectural importance, or even its contents, although it has some outstandingly fine furniture, but because of the servants. The Yorkes, who lived at Erddig for over two hundred and fifty years, had a close relationship with the men and women who looked after them. They were also great hoarders, so that the collection of accounts, diaries, inventories, portraits and photographs that came with the house enabled the Trust to build up a fascinating picture of domestic life over the centuries. I recommend anyone not familiar with Erddig to read *The Servant's Hall* by Merlin Waterson.

Because of this unusual combination of survivals, I felt that it would be possible to build up a picture of the cooks, and accordingly dived into the Erddig archives. My search was rather like a detective novel – full of suspense, surprises and disappointments, but no gore. I hope the result will build up a picture of how a country house of a moderate size fed itself in the eighteenth and nineteenth centuries.

Erddig lies just outside Wrexham: when it was built it lay in the county of Denbighshire, now it resides in Clwyd. It was begun in the 1680s by Joshua Edisbury, High Sheriff of Denbighshire, but the costs of building, combined with unfortunate financial speculation, brought him to bankruptcy, and the estate was bought up in 1716 by one of his creditors, John Meller, a wealthy London lawyer. Why he should choose to acquire a country house in the remote border region of England and Wales is a mystery, for Meller was very much a sophisticated metropolitan man, as will be seen in the style of his household. He proceeded to extend Erddig, filling it with the finest furniture and furnishings of the period. As by this time he was in his mid-fifties, much of the work was supervised by his nephew, Simon Yorke.

When Meller died in 1733, Erdigg passed to Simon and remained in the Yorke family for nearly two and a half centuries. The eldest sons were invariably called Simon or Philip, so they are distinguished by numbering. By the time Philip III offered his house and estate to the National Trust in 1973, Erddig was in trouble, the house having suffered over half a century of decay, made worse by undermining from coal workings. A programme of restoration took place, and now the house, estate buildings and gardens are all returned to their former glory. But visitors enter not through the front door, but through the estate, stable and laundry yards. For it is the household life at Erddig which makes it so fascinating.

John Meller's household divided its time between his London house in fashionable Bloomsbury Square and Erddig. As he never married, the household was run by his sister, referred to in accounts as Madam Mellor. This could have been either Aliza Roberts or Elizabeth Mynne.

A list of Meller's servants, drawn up by Simon Yorke at Michaelmas 1725, gives an idea of the size of the household and the comparative status of the servants. Fourteen people are listed. The housekeeper heads the list with an annual wage of £10, followed by his aunt's maid, £6, John Jones the butler, £10, the coachman, £8, the laundrymaid, £4 and other maids, £3 and £2 10s. But conspicuously the highest paid servant was the cook, at an annual wage of £21. Meller's earlier accounts had suggested a much lower wage – Betty the cook and brewer receiving 10s in the spring accounts, on a par with the gardener, whose annual wage was £10. The years 1725 and 1726 are the only time in Erddig's history that the cook is paid much more than the other staff, leading me to wonder whether Meller splashed out and hired himself a male cook – even a French chef, ousting poor Betty and retiring her to the brewhouse.

The kind of food consumed at Erddig in the early 1730s is substantial but plain, so any French cook may have been short-lived. On Tuesday 13 October 1730, dinner was as follows (I have laid it out in the way it was written).

A Fry'd Soal

stewed apples   sallet   goose roasted

Ribs of Beef Roasted

Boiled beef for ye [Servants'?] Hall

A recipe book dated 1685 survives at Erddig. At the front of the book are various notes about transactions in London including 'For Mr Thomas Mynne at his home in Red Lion Court in Watling Street'. John Meller's sister Elizabeth was married to Thomas Mynne, so I attribute the book to her. In the 1680s she would have been in her thirties, with one known living child, Frances.

The recipes begin with sauces for various birds, proceed through frying chicken and drying neats' tongues, to making spiced cakes, rice pudding and puff paste. Many of the culinary recipes are for the still room – preserving salads, pickling flowers (Appendix I) and candying roots.

Did Elizabeth run her brother's household, or did she give her recipe book to her sister Aliza? The one small detail we know is that she was fond of venison. An undated letter from Aliza invites her and Frances to dine on venison at John Meller's house. A recipe for roast venison is included in the recipe book (Appendix I), and this favoured dish may well have come from the Myddeltons' deer park at Chirk Castle, a close neighbour to Erddig.

The extent of the kitchen and service quarters at Erddig are vividly recorded in the 1726 inventory: a pantry and boiling room within the bakehouse, brewhouse, cheese room, dairy and scullery, kitchen, butler's room, housekeeper's room, wet larder, beer cellar and still room. The kitchen was well equipped with a multitude of utensils, including mechanical spits. The housekeeper's room also suggests an abundant and sophisticated household, with Chinese and Japanese porcelain echoing the fine lacquered furniture that filled John Meller's state rooms. Recorded in the stillroom is a small pan for Elizabeth Mynne's gastronomic delight, venison.

With the passing of Erddig to Simon I York in 1733, Erddig became a family home, run by his wife Dorothy. Simon's pocket book for the 1750s and 60s gives the names of his servants and their wages. In 1750 the cook was Margaret Hughes, employed initially at £6 per annum, rising to £7 the following year. Cooks come and go in the next few years – all women, and mostly with Welsh names. Their wages rise to £9 in 1759, but the promotion of kitchen maid Jane Roberts to head cook in July 1762 increased her wage only from £2 10s to £6 – perhaps because she was inexperienced and would need more help from Mrs Yorke. There is no reference to a housekeeper at this period, though this doesn't mean there wasn't one – as a senior servant paid by the Yorkes' agent, John Caesar.

Two recipe books survive from this period. The first, begun in 1765, contains a remarkably rich assortment of recipes (Appendix II). The compiler has carefully recorded the provenance of particular recipes, donors and places. Several Norfolk place names make me suspect that this book may not have originated in Erddig, but came into the family with one of the Yorke brides. Nevertheless, it does give an idea of the kind of dishes favoured by moderately wealthy households of this period. Several dishes are Indian, including this one to make Indian pickle:

> Take Vinegar one Gallon Garlick one pound Ginger one pound Turmeric, mustard seed, long pepper and salt of each 4 oz's, the Garlick must be peel'd and salted three days, then washed and salted again, and let stand three Days longer, then washed and dried in the Sun, the Ginger must be put into Salt water 12 hours, then scraped and cut into thin slices and set by till the rest of the ingredients are ready, the mustard seed bruised, the Turmeric powdered and the long pepper whole. Whatever is put into it that is above the size of a walnutt must be cut in slices, salted and dried in the sun.

Mrs Grigson – an ancestor maybe? – provides a recipe for stewing carp. Marble of Calves Head is an old recipe, recorded as from Mrs Watts, Dereham, 1702, while a whole series of recipes are taken from Mrs Raffald's very newly printed book, *The Experienced English Housekeeper*, published in 1769.

The other book, providing, in the main, medical recipes, makes references to Mrs Yorke, which places it more firmly at Erddig. It provides one vivid example of how household tips might be disseminated: a recipe for the purge is credited as provided by Mrs Lawrence on the stage coach from Bristol, 1739.

A letter from Dorothy Yorke to her son Philip, dated 30 November 1765, refers to a housekeeping problem. The agent, John Caesar, had been negotiating board wages for the Erddig servants. He proposed 2s 6d for women, 3s for men. The servants counter-proposed 3s for women, 4s for men, which Dorothy urged Caesar to accept, noting 'whilst I keep house, I shall not pinch my servants'. Philip clearly took this message to heart when he took over the running of Erddig in 1767, and the relationship between master and servant became a close one. Perhaps his most extraordinary innovation was to commission in the 1790s a series of portraits of his servants from a local artist, John Walters of Denbigh, and to add to them *Crude Ditties*, verses celebrating their lives and characters.

All the portraits, with one exception, are of male servants, so sadly we don't have an image of either the head cook or the housekeeper. The one female chosen for posterity is Jane Ebbrell, housemaid, or as Philip calls her, 'spider-brusher to the Master'. Her expression is particularly grumpy – possibly she felt affronted at being singled out for portraiture. It may be delicacy towards the female sex which prevented Philip from commissioning further portraits, but political correctness as we know it did not affect his decision. The particularly effective portrait of Edward Prince, head carpenter, depicted with the tools of his trade, and with Erddig in the background, is accompanied by a statement that he had had four wives 'And if the present don't survive/Hopes to rebuild them up, to five'. What Mrs Prince mark IV thought of this, history luckily doesn't record.

Although the cook is not represented, we do have portraits of her kitchen man and her butcher from Wrexham. The former is Jack Nicholas:

> ...in the Kitchen corner stuck,
> He pluck'd the fowl, and drew the duck,
> Or with the basket on his knees,
> Was sheller-general to the peas.

Aged 71 when his portrait was painted, Jack was kept at Erddig out of charity rather than usefulness, receiving 8d a day.

Thomas Jones, the Wrexham butcher, is portrayed outside his Wrexham shop, 'in his figure, not emaciate, is rather somewhat calefaciate.'

These portraits were hung in the new servants' hall provided by Philip Yorke. In the 1770s, on the advice of the architect James Wyatt, he re-designed the domestic offices in the basement area, with the New Kitchen and scullery as a separate building to reduce the hazard of fire, the larders, laundry and bakehouses, the rooms for the housekeeper, butler and agent, and the servants' hall where the staff below stairs took their meals and their leisure. All these rooms survive in this arrangement, though the kitchen was reunited with the house in the nineteenth century.

In the 1790s and early 1800s, the housekeeper's room was the demesne of first Molly Salusbury, later of Sarah Lloyd. Their household accounts show the kind of food luxuries that could not be supplied by the extensive kitchen gardens and the estate at Erddig, and thus had to be bought from Wrexham and Chester. They also show how the housekeeper was the linchpin of the house, for amongst the foods purchased are accounts for paying casual workers, tuning of harpsichords, sweeping of chimneys, while letters from Philip Yorke when he was away from Erddig are full of instructions and messages to be passed on to the cook. The accounts for 7 April 1798 read:

A leg of veal and head	7s 11d
A quarter of lamb's head	6s 4d
Cakes	2s 8d
Muffins	2s 0d
Washerwoman	2s 2d
poor	6d
oringsis [oranges]	2s 6d

Philip died in 1804 and Erddig passed to his eldest son, Simon II. His accounts give some idea of the comparative status of the various servants in the early nineteenth century: in 1813 John Caesar, the agent responsible for the whole estate, received an annual salary of £60; the housekeeper, Mrs Davies was paid £31 10 0s; the cook, Margaret Humpreys received £21; her kitchen maid, Elizabeth Hussey, £6. Oddly, two years later, the cook, Francis Stocker/Hocker was down to 12 guineas a year, rising to 14 guineas in 1817 – is this again because she was less experienced, and therefore required close supervision and help from the housekeeper and Mrs Yorke?

An inventory was carried out at Erddig in 1835, following the death of Simon II. Like its predecessor, made a hundred years earlier, it reveals well-equipped service rooms, including plenty of utensils for the production of ices and iced puddings so favoured by the Georgians. It also reveals that the inside servants were accommodated in the attics of the house: the cook enjoyed a tent bedstead with a feather bed, a chest of drawers, two chairs, a table and a washstand with glass, but no carpet – this luxury was provided only for the housekeeper's bedroom.

Following the tradition set by his father, Simon II had commissioned in the years before his death a series of portraits of servants employed at Erddig. These are all men servants, working on the estate. But images of the cook, the housekeeper and the housemaids begin to appear with the arrival of photography. A daguerreotype of 1852 shows Mary Webster, housekeeper and former cook, with a verse added some years later by Philip II:

> Upon the portly frame we look
> Of one who was our former cook
> ...She knew and pandered to our taste
> Allowed no want and yet no waste.

From this time on, the roles of housekeeper and cook were combined. This was made possible by the fact that the household at Erddig, unlike many Victorian establishments, was not huge: Simon II had only four surviving children, his son Simon III, also had four, while Philip II, who inherited in 1894, contracted a disastrous first marriage and his two sons, Simon IV and Philip III, were born in the first years of the twentieth century. A pocket book dating from 1866 gives details of the number of servants allowed meals in the house. On 9 June 1866, this consisted of 3 men, 8 females, and John Roberts the stableman could come in for his supper.

Two handwritten recipe books have survived from this period: the first was begun in 1839 by Victoria Cust, then aged 15, who was to marry Simon Yorke III; the second is begun by her, but then moves into another hand, probably that of her daughter-in-law, Louisa, who married Philip II in 1902. Neither of these recipe books are as extensive or complete as the 1765 book mentioned earlier. By the time Victoria arrived at Erddig, the cook was probably able to read and therefore used either recipes from her own written records or from a printed and published book.

Harriet Rogers, who succeeded Mary Webster as cook and housekeeper, took her recipe books with her when she left Erddig to act as ladies' maid to Simon III's sisters. The books, together with letters and other papers, are still in the possession of her family, enabling a remarkably full picture to be built up. Harriet came from one of the dynasties that served the Yorkes over the generations. Her father was Thomas Rogers, the estate carpenter, whose portrait commissioned by Simon II in the 1830s shows him at his workbench. His daughter was educated by Victoria Yorke, and her first surviving letter dating from 1844 shows a considerably better hand than those displayed by the Yorke children.

Harriet started life in the servants' hall at Erddig as children's nurse, then lady's maid, before taking over as cook/housekeeper. She took her recipes from three main sources. First she kept her own handwritten book, with such delights as Oyster and Anchovy Omelette, Exhibition Lunch Biscuits, and the favourite pudding of Sir Watkin Williams Wynn of Wynnstay, a near neighbour and, like the Yorkes, a byword for benevolence towards staff and tenants. This kindly baronet favoured a rich steamed pudding of candied peel, beef suet, apricot jam, milk and brandy, served with an equally rich sauce of sherry wine, apricot syrup and butter. In addition, Harriet had that domestic mainstay, Mrs Beeton's *Book of Household Management*, in the 1869 edition. Her third source, presumably for more exotic concoctions, was Charles Elme Francatelli's *Cook's Guide*, 1862.

Although the Erddig household was not huge by the standards of the time, combining cook and housekeeper must have been an arduous role, which may explain why Harriet chose to move on after twenty years. One person who found the dual role more than enough was Mrs Harrison. In a letter dated 9 December 1897, a domestic drama is unfolded. The butler, John Jones, addresses himself to the Yorke agent, W.C. Hughes, because Philip II, who inherited Erddig in 1894, spent most of his time out of the country, seeking solace from his disastrous marriage in travel abroad. Mrs Harrison had been dismissed following unpleasantness over some pheasants, and Jones had been given notice too. His letter reveals that the cook, under stress through lack of kitchen maids, had recourse to the beer from his pantry. Asking to be taken back, he ends with this heartfelt sentiment: 'I could do very well with a good sensible woman, which I am sure the house should be one of the happiest in the land. But as it is one of the most miserable all through one person'.

This lamentable, and untypical, state of affairs was rectified with the arrival of Philip's second wife, Louisa, in 1902. She has left not only her recipe books, but also detailed plans of dinners and parties at Erddig in the first years of this century. On 17 August 1908, for instance, there were sixteen at dinner, which consisted of 'clear soup', 'fish soufflé', 'chicken in aspic', 'saddle of mutton', 'grouse', 'Venetian cream', 'pudding a l'aube' (?), 'luxette a l'oeuf', 'tomato piramids' and 'desert'. The dining-room table was decorated with pink carnations, white sweet peas and smilax. After dinner, amusements consisted of playing bridge and going to visit the attic storey, where a fire had earlier broken out in one of the servant's bedrooms. (Appendix III).

The last cook-housekeeper to preside over anything like a full complement of staff was Miss Brown, who arrived in 1907 and left in 1914, at the outbreak of the First World War which was to prove such a watershed in the life of the English country house. Life was never to be the same again.

What does emerge from the records is that there were three key players in the preparation of food at Erddig: the cook, the housekeeper and the mistress of the house. Apart from one brief period in the 1720s, when John Meller apparently paid his cook considerably more than the other servants in the household, the cook's status was a modest one, on a par with the coachman, below the agent, the housekeeper and the butler. The cooks appear also to have been always women. It is doubtful, until the 1840s when the housekeeper's role was combined with that of cook, that she could read and write. Cooks were thus dependent either on word of mouth instruction initially from their mother and training up as a kitchen maid, or – once they had become head cook – from the mistress of the house and the housekeeper.

Revealingly, Dorothy Yorke says in one of her letters, dated 12 April 1769, 'Margaret still assists me as cook', before going on to wonder at cooks receiving annual wages of £25, as opposed to the 10 guineas which was the norm at Erddig. 'Assists' makes me suspect that Dorothy, and the Mrs Yorkes who succeeded her, were much more responsible for the cooking than I had originally thought. The ideas for recipes culled from friends, neighbours, and the lady in the stage coach, were as important, if not far more important an influence on the cooking at Erddig than any printed cookery book by an author who might claim to have changed the course of culinary history. I should not really be surprised by this, for my own mother owned no printed cookery book by a professional cook – with the predictable exception of Mrs Beeton – but instead took her inspiration from her handwritten recipes built up gradually over the years.

Sources and acknowledgements

The Erddig papers are in the Clwyd Record Office at Hawarden. I am grateful to the Assistant County Archivist for help with my research. I would also like to thank Beryl Jones for her help with information on Harriet Rogers.

Appendix I: Culinary and Medical Recipe Book, c. 1685 *(D/E1203)*

To pickle Broom Buds

Take your broom buds before they be yellow (...) Make a brine of vinegar and salt which you must do by shaking it together till it be melted. Then put in your broom buds and keep them stirred once a day till they sink in the vinegar to keep them close.

For Preserving of Salad (Solete)

Take any of the flowers aforesaid [broom, cucumber, samphire, purslane] after they have been picked clean from the stalk and the white cut clean away and washed and dried. Take a galipot and first strew a little sugar in the bottom, they lay a layer of flowers in the bottom, then cover them with sugar and so done till you have filled the pot. Press them down with your hand and [put] the sharpest vinegar you can get to them.

To Rost Venison

After you have washed your venison clear from the blood, stick it with cloves on the outside and lard it with muton larde or porke larde, but mutton is the best. Then spit it and rost it by a socking [slow] fire. Take vinegar, brad crums and the gravy which comes from the venison and boyle them in a dishe, then season it with sugare, cinamon, ginger and salt, and serve the venison upon the sauce.

(Reproduced and adapted for modern use in *The Art of Dining: history of Cooking & Eating* by Sara Paston-Williams, published in 1993 by the National Trust; and in *A National Trust Book of Historical Recipes* compiled by Paston-Williams, 1995).

Appendix II: Culinary Recipe Book (D/E 2551a)

To Stew Carp. Mrs Grigson. 63

Take a Carp & knock him on the Head, then prick his Tail, save all his Blood, then Scale him & lay him in a large Stew pan, with a Bundle of Sweet herbs, an onion, whole pepper & as much water and Vinegar as will cover him, with some mace. So let them Stew together 'till they are Enough then Dish them up, having prepared the sauce as Follows. Take some red wine, 2 or 3, anchovies some mace & whole pepper, Lemon peel, an Onion some Horse Radish a little Vinegar, let all these Stew together a little while, having put in the Blood of the Carp then strain the Liquor from the Herbs, put in some Butter Roll'd in flour, giving it a boil, Then put into your Dish, with Sliced Lemon, & the Spawn of the Fish Fry'd.

To Make Anchovy Ketchup.

Take a pint of Red Wine, put in 20 Anchovys 2 Onions Stuck full of Cloves 2 or 3 blades of Mace boil it ½ away it will Keep many Years.

Marble of Calveshead.

Mrs Watts, Dereham 1782

Boil the Head with the tongue, 'till you can take the meat clear from the bone, cut it into pieces about an Inch thick, season them to your taste with pepper, salt & mace put it into a China bason, tie it down close with a Cloth, let it boil two hours, than take the cloth off & lay a Trencher upon the top, with a Weight upon it, then let it stand till the next day, then take it out of the bason & put in two or three Spoonfuls of strong Jelly, the put the meat in again — When you want to take it out for use, dip the bason in warm water — Half a Head will fill a pint bason, which takes an hour to boil — —

To preserve Damosins. _mrs Harvey_

Take three pounds of powder Sugar, to ½ a peck of Damosins, put a layer of Sugar to a layer of Fruit, tye them down with a Bladder in a large pot & infuse them in a Kettle of Water — let them stand 'till the Sugar is Dissolv'd — than take them out & put them in smaller pots — than put on a Brandyed paper over them — & than run some mutton Fat over them ——

Receipts from Mrs Raffelds, printed Book

To Make an Almond pudding.

Boil the peels of 2 Lemons very tender, beat ½ a pound of Almonds in rose Water very fine, and a pound of sugar finely pounded & Sifted, melt ½ a pound of Butter, & let it stand 'till Cold, beat the Yolks of 8 Eggs, & the Whites of 4, Mix them & beat them altogether, & Bake it in a puff paste

Appendix III: Dinner Book

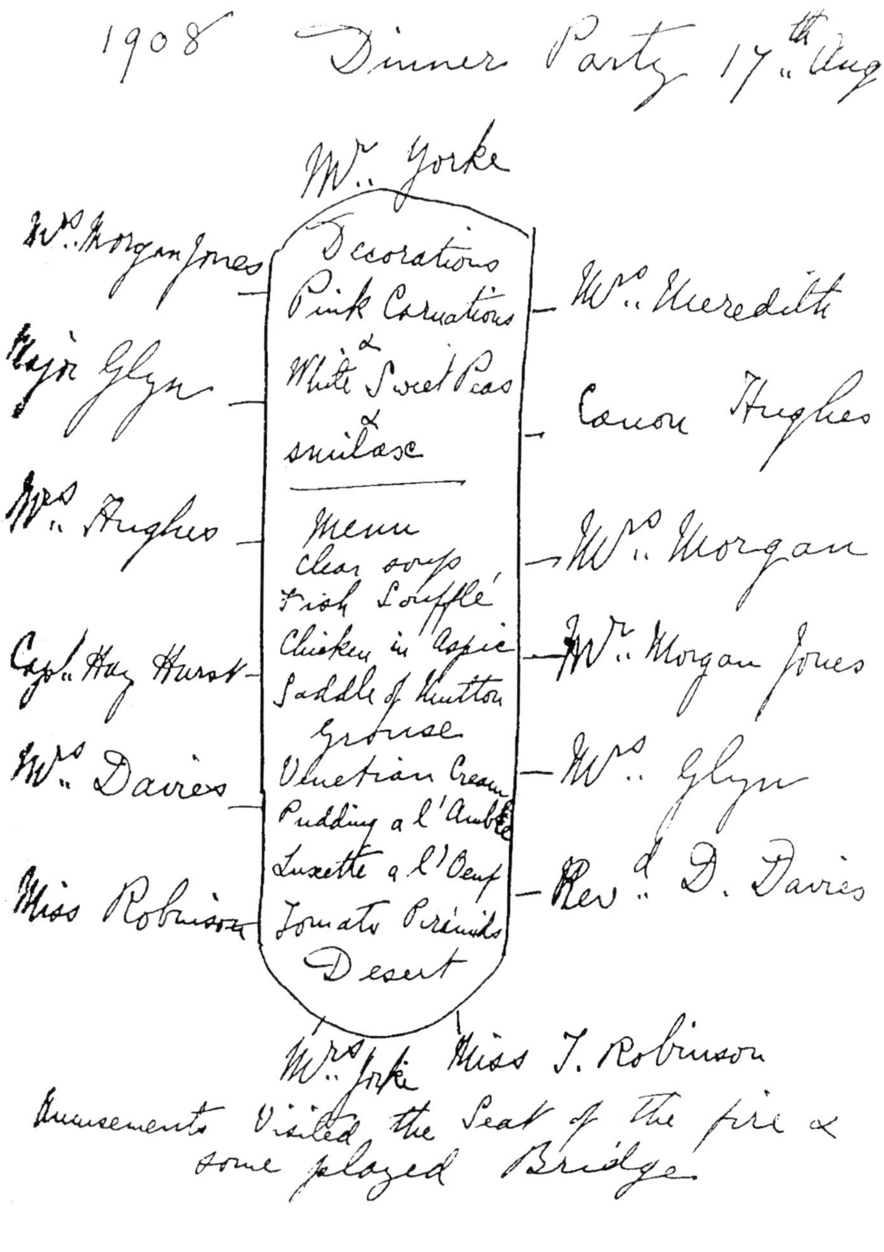

1908   Dinner Party 17th Aug

Mr Yorke

Mrs Morgan Jones —   Decorations   — Mrs Meredith
               Pink Carnations
Major Glyn —   & White Sweet Peas   — Canon Hughes
               & smilase
Mrs Hughes —   Menu   — Mr Morgan
               Clear soup
               Fish Soufflé
Capt Hay Hurst —   Chicken in Aspic   — Mr Morgan Jones
               Saddle of Mutton
               Grouse
Mrs Davies —   Venetian Cream   — Mrs Glyn
               Pudding a l'Ambre
               Luxette a l'Oeuf
Miss Robinson —   Tomato Prinuds   — Revd D. Davies
               Desert

Mrs Yorke   Miss J. Robinson

Amusements visited the seat of the fire & some played Bridge.

Dorothy Hartley (1893-1985)

Mary Wondrausch

Dorothy Hartley, writer on food and the countryside was born on 17th October, 1893 at the Grammar School Skipton, Yorkshire, the youngest child of the Rev. Edward Hartley (1849-1923) and his wife Amy (1853-1932) formerly Eddy. Dorothy Hartley's father was headmaster of the Grammar School and her mother came from Froncysyllte, nr. Llangollen in Wales where the family owned properties and stone quarries.

Dorothy Hartley was educated at The Convent in Skipton then Loughborough High School and Nottingham Art School.

During the First World War she worked in a munitions factory.

In 1919 she attended Regent Street Polytechnic in London where she was a prize pupil and the skills she developed there are visible in her many books, eleven in total. Although she attended art school rather than university, she was a 'natural writer' as her books and journalistic career prove.

In 1920 she taught at the Nottingham School of Art and Design and in 1924 she became General Assistant to the Art Department of Regent Street Polytechnic.

Between 1925 and 1931 Batsford published her 'Life and Work of the People of England' in six volumes, in conjunction with M. Elliot and in 1930 Knopf published the 'Old Book', a medieval compilation.

Dorothy Hartley travelled to Africa in the 1930s journeying by car from Cairo to the Congo – the resulting photographs were exhibited in the Imperial Institute. During this period she advised John Grierson on documentary film.

In 1931 *Thomas Tusser (1557)* edited with notes by Dorothy Hartley and illustrated from early illuminated manuscripts, was published by County Life.

Between 1932 and 1936 Miss Hartley travelled by bicycle and in her car 'Rabbit' around the British Isles with pen, pencil and camera, writing weekly articles for the Daily Sketch on rural folk and their trades.

In 1935 Batsford published *The Countryman's England*, illustrated with invigorating photographs beautifully taken with her beloved Brownie camera. Dorothy Hartley developed and processed most of these negatives herself.

Intrigued by her studies of early manuscripts in the British Museum Library, in particular Geraldus Cambrensis, she set out in the 1930s on a journey through Ireland based on this prelate's survey of its peoples and land, written during the reign of Henry II in 1164. Her resulting book *Holiday in Ireland* was published by Drummond in 1938.

In 1939 she wrote a paper for the League of Nations – *For those who work on the land*, and in the same year she started planning her famous book 'Food in England'.

In the early 1950s she was teaching Domestic Economy, writing scripts for the B.B.C. and appearing on television. In 1954 her book *Food in England* (published by MacDonald) proved a treasure of information on the gathering, storing and cooking of food from the 12th to the 20th century. The clarity and detail of both the text and illustrations make it particularly accessible to a wider public.

Dorothy Hartley gave a series of public lectures at University College London on Food History and was a special examiner on this subject. She also lectured at Goldsmiths College and that same year was presented with the highest award for women journalists.

She illustrated a book for the Ministry of Agriculture and Fisheries, performed on television with Philip Harben (1953) and advised on the Archer wireless programmes. In between these professional activities she juggled with the maintenance of her house in Froncysyllte and its six cottages occupied by a constant stream of tenants and visitors.

Water in England (published by MacDonald in 1964) is a remarkable book, full of valuable information on holy springs, well digging, leather jugs, spa hotels, electric baths, etc.

Much of her thought and writing was engorged with minute details of the relationship between an object and its function – the scythe to the height of the wheat cut – the exact width of a linen sheet to the linen press. Her knowledge of early agricultural life led ultimately to a monumental photographic bequest to the Reading Museum of English Rural Life and her letters to the Keeper. Her visits to this Centre from its conception to her death in 1985 were always a source of pleasure to her.

Living as she did alone in in a remote place, coming from a generation that used a pen rather than the telephone – letters became her principal contact with a wider world. She died peacefully in her bed at the age of 92 in 1985 at Fron House, Froncysllte, near Llangollen, Wales where she had spent so many creative years.

Dorothy Hartley's book *Food in England* was the first modern publication, both scholarly and eminently readable, recording the history and folklore of English food. The illustrations (by the author) were clear and instructive – the book is as full of magic and potions as any medieval herbal and has become a classic in its time; the focus for all those who write about English Food.

Dorothy Hartley's Publications

Henslow, Thomas Geoffrey Wall. *Early Poems*. Illustrations by D.Hartley. The Gentlewoman, London, 1917.

Hartley, Dorothy Rosaman and Margaret Mary Victoria Elliot. *Life and Work of the People of England. A pictorial record from contemporary sources*. 6 vol. B.T.Batsford, London, 1925-31.

Braun, Adolphe Armand. *Figures, Faces and Folds. A practical reference book on woman's form and dress and its application in past and present art...* With sections on drapery and anatomy by D. Hartley. B.T.Batsford, London, 1929.

Elliot, Margaret Mary Victoria and Dorothy R. Hartley. *How Medieval Folk Lived*. A.Wheaton & Co. Exeter, 1930.

Hartley, Dorothy Rosaman. *The Old Book. A medieval anthology*. Ed. and illuminated by D. Hartley. A.A.Knopf, London, 1930.

—, *Mediæval Costume and Life*. B.T.Batsford, London, 1931.

—, ed. *Thomas Tusser... his Good Points of Husbandry*. Country Life, London 1931.

—, *Here's England*. Rich & Cowan, London, 1934.

—, *The Countryman's England*. B.T.Batsford, London, 1935.

—, *Holiday in Ireland*. Lindsay Drummond, London, 1938.

—, *Made in England*. Written and illustrated by D.Hartley. Methuen, London, 1939.

—, *Food in England*. Macdonald, London, 1954.

—, *Water in England*. Macdonald, London, 1964.

1995 Symposiasts

Dr. Michael Abdalla, ul. Szydlowska 53/10, 60-656 Poznan, POLAND
Dr. Joan P. Alcock, 24 Queensthorpe Road, Sydenham, London SE26 4PH
Mrs. Anne Andrews, 243 Whetstone Lane, Aldridge, Walsall WS9 0HH
Josephine Bacon, 82 Stonebridge Road, London N15 5PA
Mrs. Priscilla Bain, 7 The Norton, Tenby, Dyfed, SA70 8AA
Mrs. Anne Bamborough, 18 Winchester Road, Oxford OX2 6NA
Dr. Peter Barham, H.H.Wills Physics Lab., Tyndall Avenue, Bristol BS8 1TL
Ann Barr, 36 Linton House, 11 Holland Park Avenue, London W11 3RL
Rosemary Barron, 12 Centenary Way, Cheddar, Somerset BS27 3DG
Dr. Sven-Erik Bergh, Postfach 78, CH-6314 Unteraegeri (Zug), SWITZERLAND
Michelle Berriedale-Johnson, 5 Lawn Road, London NW3 2XS
Maggie Black, 167 Putney Bridge Road, London SW15 2NZ
Dr. A. Blake, Director for Food Sci. & Tech., Firmenich SA, 1 route des Jeunes, CH 1211 Geneva 8, SWITZERLAND
Fritz Blank, Deux Cheminées, 1221 Locust Street, Philadelphia, PA 19107, USA
Lynne Bradshaw, Lychwood House, Caldy, Wirral L48 1LP
Peter C.D.Brears, 4 Woodbine Terrace, Headingley, Leeds LS6 4AF
Marilyn Bright, 11 Sion Hill Avenue, Dublin 6W, IRELAND
Margaret Brooker, 77 Dresden Road, London N19 3BG
Lynda Brown, Church House, Skirmett, nr. Henley-on-Thames, Oxfordshire RG9 6TD
Deirdre Bryan-Brown, Rose Cottage, 14 Henley Road, Shillingford, Wallingford, Oxfordshire OX10 7EH
Charles Campion, 286 Ombersley Road, Worcester WR3 7HD
Kathleen Cardlin, c/o Dorothy Max, 251 West 89 Street, New York, NY 10024, USA
Ruth Carroll, Pembroke College, Oxford OX1 1DW
Mollie Chadsey, 19 Finlay House, Phyllis Court Drive, Henley on Thames RG9 2H
Heather Chadwick, 8 New Buildings, Well Street, Exeter EX4 6JD
Lisa Chaney, 40 Southfield Road, Oxford OX4 1NZ
Robert Chenciner, High Onsett, The Flat, nr. Bewcastle, Cumbria
Mark Cherniavsky & Anne Willan, Chateau de Fey, Villecien, 89300 Joigny, FRANCE
Janet Clarke, 3 Woodside Cottages, Freshford, Bath BA3 6EJ
Dr. Helen Clifford , 37 Woodstock Road, Witney, Oxon OX8 6EB
Claire Clifton, Winchelsea Cottage, High Street, Winchelsea, East Sussex TN36 4EA
Professor Michael Coe, 376 Saint Ronan Street, Newhaven, CT 06511, USA
Katarzyna Cwiertka, Van der Palmstraat 100, 3022 VZ Rotterdam, THE NETHERLANDS
Andrew Dalby, 5 Primrose Way, Linton, Cambridge CB1 6UD
Alan & Jane Davidson, 45 Lamont Road, London SW10 0HU
Caroline Davidson, 5 Queen Anne's Gardens, London W4 1TU
Silvija Davidson & David Natt, 83 Park Hall Road, West Dulwich, London SE21 8ES
Alun & Gilli Davies, Glebe Farm, St. Andrews Major, South Glamorgon CF6 4HD
Joy Davies & Gareth Spencer Jones, 501 Cinnamon Wharf, 24 Shad Thames, London SE1 2YJ
Andrea Dearden-Esty, Shamrock Quay, Southampton SO1 1QL
John Deith, 31 Hurlands Close, Farnham GU9 9JF
Mrs. Carol Dery, Department of Classics, University of Wales, Lampeter, Dyfed SA48 7ED
Christopher Driver, 6 Church Road, London N6 4QT
Christine Dyce, 11 Kirklee Terrace, Glasgow G12 0TH
Sarah Edington, 26 Maze Road, Kew, Richmond TW9 3DE
J.Audrey Ellison, 135 Stevenage Road, Fulham, London SW6 6PB
Michael Erben, School of Education, The University, Southampton SO9 5NH
Sarah Jane Evans & Rachel Evans, Crescent Wood Cottage, 6 Crescent Wood Road, London SE26 6RU
James Fallon, 128 Penn Green Road, Landenberg, PA 19350-9106, USA
Clare Ferguson, 5 Colville Terrace, London W11 2BE
Professor Doreen G. Fernandez, 3 First Street, Acacia Lane, Mandaluyong, Metro Manila 1501, PHILIPPINES

Ove Fossâ, Parkveien 11, N-4300 Sandnes, NORWAY
Dr. Robert Frey, 194 Sutherland Avenue, London W9 1RX
Susan Friedland, Harper & Row, Publishers Inc., 10 East 53rd Street, New York, NY 10022, USA
Elizabeth Gabay, 20 Grange Road, London N6 4AP
Monsieur Henri Gault, 12 avenue de la Grande Armée, 75017 Paris, FRANCE
Anne & Patrick Gibbins, The Lodge, 56a Nightingale Lane, London SW12 8NY
Richard Grant, 13 Hemdean Hill, Caversham, Reading, RG4 7SB
Barbara Haber, Radcliffe College, 10 Garden Street, Cambridge, MA 02138, USA
Shelley Handler, 1560 Green Street #4, San Francisco, CA 94123, USA
Vicky Hayward, Hortaleza 102, Atico Uno, 28004 Madrid, SPAIN
Jane A.D. Hedges, Fulscot Manor, Didcot, Oxfordshire OX11 9AA
Anissa Helou, 67 Littlebury Road, London SW4 6DW
Professor Constance Hieatt, 304 River Road, Deep River, CT 06217, USA
Gwenda V. Hill, Blaysworth Manor, Colmworth, Bedford, MK44 2LD
Victoria F. Hingley, 92 Portland Street, Norwich NR2 3LF
Miss S.C.Holland, Castle Veterinary Surgery, 1 Tilehurst Road, Reading RG1 7TW
Geraldene Holt, Clyst William Barton, Plymtree, Cullompton, Devon EX15 2LG
Prof. Richard F. Hosking, 9-4-703 Hakushima kukenko, Naka ku, Hiroshima 730, JAPAN
Rosalind Irwin, 2 Villa Place, Sowerby, Thirsk, North Yorkshire YO7 1LT
Abed Jaber, 20 Reighton Road, London E5 8SG
Tom Jaine, Allaleigh House, Blackawton, Totnes, Devon TQ9 7DL
Eve Jochnowitz, 21 East 10th Street #2a, New York, NY 10003, USA
Dr. Brigid Keane, c/o Portnoy q. v.
Professor D.T.Kelly, Hallstrom Institute of Cardiology, University of Sydney, Royal Prince Alfred Hospital,
    Camperdown, N.S.W., 2050, AUSTRALIA
Mary Wallace Kelsey, Department of Nutrition & Food Management, Oregon State University, Milam Hall 108,
    Corvallis OR 97330-5103, USA
Aglaia Kremezi, 33 Robertou Galli, 11 742 Athens, GREECE
Barbara Kuck, Curator, Johnson & Wales University, Culinary Archives and Museum, 315 Harborside Boulevard,
    Providence, RI 02905, USA
Marion Kumar, c/o Anne Gibbins, The Lodge, 56a Nightingale Lane, Londom SW12 8NY
Giana & Nicholas Kurti, 38 Blandford Avenue, Oxford OX2 8DZ
Mark Lake, Packman Grey & Lake, Unit A, London Stone Business Estate, Broughton Street, London SW8 3QR
Janet Laurence, The Grooms, East Lydford, Somerton, Somerset TA11 7HD
Margaret Leibenstein, 47 Larchwood Drive, Cambridge, MA 02138-4638, USA
Jane Levi, 26 Hurst Street, Herne Hill, London SE24 8EG
Mrs. Audrey Levy, 60 Gloucester Road, Kingston-upon-Thames, Surrey KT1 3RB
Dr. Paul Levy, P.O.Box 35, Witney, Oxon OX8 8BF
Pat Llewellyn, 48c Kentish Town Road, London NW1 9PU
Rocìo Lûpez de Diego, Avenida Pablo Iglesias 15, 28003 Madrid, SPAIN
Elisabeth Luard, Quinish Garden, Dervaig, Isle of Mull, Argyll PA75 6QL
Jenny Macarthur, 13 Wavell Road, Maidenhead, Berkshire, SL6 5AB
Jeremy MacClancy, Institute of Social Anthropology, 51 Banbury Road, Oxford OX2 6PE
Bettina Mann, Grosse Kurfuestenstrasse 52, 33615 Bielefeld, GERMANY
Professor & Mrs. G. Mars, 53 Nassington Road, London NW3 2TY
Sarah Martin, The Manor House, The Green South, Warborough, Oxfordshire OX9 8DN
Laura Mason, 4 Saint John Street, York YO3 7QT
Dorothy Max & Kathleen Cardlin, 251 West 89th Street, NYC NY 10024, USA
Carolyn McCrum, 57 Oakthorpe Road, Oxford OX2 7BD
Mike & Tessa McKirdy, Cooks Books, 34 Marine Drive, Rottingdean, Sussex BN2 7HQ
Richard C. Mieli, 4 Longfellow Place #1703, Boston, MA 02114, USA
Janny de Moor, Ulco de Vriesweg 29, 8084 AR 't Harde, THE NETHERLANDS
Dr. H. & Mrs. F.Morrow Brown, Highfield House, Highfield Gardens, Derby DE3 1HT
Dawn & Douglas Nelson, Passe Renard, Averon-Bergelle, 32290 Aignan, FRANCE

LIST OF SYMPOSIASTS

Ingar Nilsson, Filippavagen 6B, 222 41 Lund, SWEDEN
Jill Norman, 1 Rosslyn Hill, London NW3 5UL
Rupert Parker, 151 Wilberforce Road, London N4 2SX
Dorothea A. Pelham, 6 Portland Road, Oxford OX2 7EY
Robert W. Pemberton, USDA-ARS, 3205 College Avenue, Fort Lauderdale, Florida 33314, USA
Edite Vieira Phillips, 503a, Garden Flat, Liverpool Road, London N7 8NS
Olive Portnoy, Oaktrees, Woodman Lane, Sewardstonebury, London E4 7QR
Professor Jo Marie Powers, University of Guelph, Hotel & Food Administration, Guelph, Ontario, N1G 2W1, CANAD
Kathryn Preece, 62 Co-operation Road, Fishponds, Bristol
Thane Prince, 25A Lonsdale Square, London N1 1EW
Daniel Quirici, 8 Montpelier Square, London SW7
Iris Raven, Catscradle, Newchurch West, Chepstow, Gwent NP6 6DA
Gillian Riley, 11 Kersley Road, London N16 0NP
Alicia Rios, Avenida General Peron 19 - 8JC, 28020 Madrid, SPAIN
Cherry Ripe, 1 Tivoli Street, Paddington 2021, NSW, AUSTRALIA
Joe Roberts, 31 Brock Street, Bath BA1 2LN
Ms. Jane Root, Wall to Wall Television Ltd., 8/9 Spring Place, London NW5 3ER
Brenda S. Rose, 626 London Road, Davenham, Northwich, Cheshire CW9 8LG
Alison Ryley, 14 Howard Drive, Huntingdon, NY 11743 3033, USA
Helen Saberi, 75 Haldon Road, London SW18 1QF
Barbara Santich, 13 King Street, Brighton, 5048 SA, AUSTRALIA
Alan Saunders, The Food Programme, ABC, GPO Box 9994, Sydney, NSW 2001, AUSTRALIA
Liz & Gerd Seeber, 10 The Plantation, London SE3 0AB
Maria José Sevilla, Foods from Spain, Institute for Foreign Trade (ICEX-UK), Spanish Embassy Commercial Office, 66 Chiltern Street, London W1M 1PR
Regina Sexton and Shane Lehane, The Yellow House, Vicarstown, Co. Cork, IRELAND
Roy Shipperbottom, 9 Southgate, Heaton Chapel, Stockport, SK4 4QL
Ralph & Kate Shirley, 39 Uttoxeter Road, The Studio, Foston, Derby DE6 5PX
Birgit Siesby, I H Mundtsvej 4B, DK-2830 Virum, DENMARK
Helen J. Simpson, Burton Court, Eardisland, nr. Leominster, Herefordshire HR6 9DS
Raymond Sokolov, 34 Barrow Street, New York, NY 10014-3735, USA
Colin Spencer, 194 Dalling Road, London W6 0ER
Rosemary Stark, 6 Chamberlain Street, London NW1 8XB
Jeffrey L. Steingarten, 29 West 17th Street, New York, NY 10011, USA
Dr. Layinka M. Swinburne, 16 Foxhill Crescent, Leeds LS16 5PD
Dr. Louis & Mrs. Sadako Szathmary, 630 West Webster Avenue, Chicago, IL 60614, USA
Anne Tait, Ridgeway Cottage, Glanvilles Wootton, Sherborne, Dorset DT9 5QF
Dr. Gabor Tasnadi, H-1113 Budapest, Vill·nyi ˙t 60, HUNGARY
Martha Brooks Taylor, 101 Westcott Street, Apt. 1906, Houston, TX 77007-7033, USA
Malcolm Thick, 2 Brookside, Harwell, Oxon OX11 0HG
Professor C. & Mrs. Rita Tyler, 22 Belle Avenue, Reading, Berks, RG6 2BL
Dr. Renee Valeri, Lunds Universitet, Etnologiska inst. med Folklivsarkivet, Finngatan 8, S-223 62 Lund, SWEDEN
Kim van Gestel-Maclean, Oude Amersfoortseweg 12, 1213 AD Hilversum, NETHERLANDS
Harlan Walker, 294 Hagley Road, Birmingham B17 8DJ
Robin Weir, 104 Iffley Road, London W6 0PF
Barbara K. Wheaton, 268 Elm Street, Concord, MA 01742-2247, USA
Dr. John M. Wilkins, Department of Classics & Ancient History, University of Exeter, Queen's Building, The Queen's Drive, Exeter EX4 4QH
Margaret Willes, 17 Appleby Road, London E8 3ET
Linda Williams, 1 Reed Mansions, Cambridge Road, Wanstead, London E11 2PX
Nancy Winters, 21 Montpelier Street, London SW7
Mary Wondrausch, The Pottery, Brickfields, Compton, Guildford, Surrey GU3 1HZ
Dr. Theodore Zeldin, Tumbledown House, Cumnor, Oxford OX2 9QE
Sami Zubaida, 2 Avenue House, Belsize Park Gardens, London NW3 4LA